The Wilson Chronology of Human Rights

Other Titles in the Wilson Chronology Series

Other Titles from H. W. Wilson

The Wilson Chronology of Human Rights

Edited by David Levinson

A Berkshire Reference Work

The H.W. Wilson Company
New York ♦ Dublin
2003

Library of Congress Cataloging-in-Publication Data

The Wilson chronology of human rights / edited by David Levinson.
     p. cm
    "A Berkshire Reference Work"
    Includes bibliographical references and index.
    ISBN 0-8242-0972-9
    1. Human rights—History—Chronology. I. Levinson, David, 1947– II. H.W.
Wilson Company.

JC571 .W4725 2003
323'.02'02—dc21

                                                    2002193399

Printed in the United States of America

The H. W. Wilson Company
950 University Avenue
Bronx, NY 10452

www.hwwilson.com

Contents

Preface

The notion that all human beings have certain rights, simply by virtue of being human, appears very early in history. A variety of ancient and medieval texts, from Buddhist scriptures to the Magna Carta, undertake to define the precise rights (and the corresponding obligations) of individuals, family members, occupational groups, and social classes, and to ensure that these rights are understood and respected by all. What we now call "human rights" are dealt with explicitly in such 18th-century political documents as the American Declaration of Independence and the U.S. Consititution, and in the French Declaration of the Rights of Man; the continuing evolution of these concepts is reflected in numerous 20th-century regional and international declarations, conventions, resolutions, and laws. Since the end of World War II, human rights have become a matter for worldwide concern, an element in international relations, and the subject of international law. Many organizations and governments now routinely gather information and issue reports on human rights around the world.

Human rights became a central issue in the postwar world for several reasons. The war itself included such horrors as genocide by the Nazis against Jews, gypsies, gays, and the handicapped, and large-scale violations, on both sides, of civilian and prisoner rights; these crimes, when they became known, aroused widespread revulsion. Subsequently, as colonial empires disintegrated, indigenous peoples and ethnic minorities claimed rights they had previously been denied. In the United States the civil rights campaign carried out by African Americans inspired other groups—Native Americans, women, gays, the disabled—to protest other forms of injustice. In some respects, today's worldwide interest in human rights reflects the spread of Western values, particularly the emphasis on individualism and the promise of liberty and justice, as well as a determination never to repeat the atrocities of the past. That such atrocities can still occur became evident in the 1990s in Rwanda and in the former Yugoslavia.

It needs to be emphasized that the worldwide interest in human rights is not without its controversies and conflicts. Three are most significant. The first is a question of interpretation—does the concept of human rights as set forth in the Universal Declaration and subsequent documents apply only to individuals or also to entire groups, such as religious groups, ethnic minorities, or indigenous peoples? Human rights advocates argue that rights should be extended to entire groups, as a mechanism for offering broader protection. But many national governments prefer to define rights as individual rights only, so as to limit human rights cases to adjudication within their own borders.

The second controversy concerns "affirmative action" programs, like those for African Americans in the United States and for Untouchables in India. The issue is whether individuals and groups who were subjected to discrimination in the past should be afforded special, compensatory rights in the present. Some believe this is only fair and the only way to reverse the ill effects of discrimination. Others believe such differential treatment, no matter how well intentioned, is itself a form of discrimination, either against individual members of the compensated group, who may not wish to be so identified, or against members of other groups that are not eligible for special treatment.

The third controversy concerns the cross-cultural relevance of current conceptions of human rights. To some in the non-Western world, the current definitions and laws are seen as reflecting Western individualistic values and ignoring non-Western values, which may place the needs of the group above those of the individual. This is especially an issue for nations that rely (formally or informally) on Islamic law, which places the Muslim community in the forefront. Some experts see this "Western bias" as an impediment to the adoption and enforcement of human rights protections in all nations.

The purpose of this volume is to provide a chronological history of human rights. While the United States receives the most detailed coverage, much information is provided about other regions and nations and about international developments. The earliest entry is for c. 3000 b.c.e., with chronology running through 2002.

Human rights are defined broadly and the chronology is divided into nine chapters:

1. Human Rights—General
2. Civil Rights
3. Religious Rights
4. Women's Rights
5. Indigenous Rights
6. Children's Rights
7. Gay Rights
8. Disabled Rights
9. Refugee Rights

Each chapter provides coverage of events, trends, people, publications, laws, court cases, government action and inaction, organizations, inventions, discoveries, and ideas bearing on human rights. Chapter 1 also provides extracts from key documents. Particularly for the post-1945 period, much attention is given to international developments.

Numerous sources were consulted to compile this chronology. These include governmental, organizational, and individual Web sites; books, periodicals, newsletters; newspapers; and human rights documents and reports. Readers are directed to the bibliography for a list of major sources and works that can provide additional information on human rights.

Compiling this chronology was a group effort, and the following individuals merit acknowledgment and thanks for their contributions: Mickey Friedman, Robert Ridinger, Ben Manning, Marcy Ross, and Ann Farkas. At H. W. Wilson, Lynn Messina, Gray Young, Jennifer Peloso, Norris Smith, and Sandra Watson.

David Levinson
February 2003

CHAPTER ONE

HUMAN RIGHTS—GENERAL

c. 1200 B.C.E.	God gives Moses the Ten Commandments, which Moses delivers to the Hebrews; the Commandments form the basis for moral codes and rules of civil behavior in the Western world. Human rights are first mentioned in the Bible in Genesis 1:27 (New English Bible): "So God created man in his own image, in the image of God created he him; male and female created he them." Other mentions of human rights in Judaism, including political rights, positive rights, and obligations, appear in the books of Exodus, Leviticus, Deuteronomy, and Proverbs.
c. 500–300 B.C.E.	The moral precepts of Buddhism are set down in northern India by Siddhārtha Gautama, the Buddha and the founder of Buddhism. The Buddha teaches that humans can overcome the suffering inherent in life by practicing moral and physical purification.
449 B.C.E.	The Twelve Tables set forth in ancient Rome establish rules for fair trials—including the use of evidence and restrictions on bribery—and benefit the plebeian class of citizens.
c. 400 B.C.E.	The Greek philosopher Plato, in his *Republic*, sets forth his ideas of absolute justice, common good, and universal standards of conduct. According to Plato, the just state is one in which each class carries out its proper duties; class is determined by the level of education a person attains, and the political rulers in this ideal state are philosopher-kings.
c. 390–305 B.C.E.	The Chinese Confucian philosopher Mencius (Meng-tzu) discusses human rights and states: "The individual is of infinite value, institutions and conventions come next, and the person of the ruler is of least significance." Mencius believes that humans are innately good and that goodness is a keystone of life.
384–322 B.C.E.	The Greek philosopher Aristotle writes about equality and justice and political and legal rights, in works such as the *Nicomachean Ethics* and *Politics*; for Aristotle, moral virtue is a mean between two extremes, while intellectual virtue is not, and only adult, well-educated men can attain excellence. Other Greek thinkers concerned with human rights are the fifth-century B.C.E. playwright Sophocles and the Stoic philosophers.
52 B.C.E.	The Roman politician and scholar Marcus Tullius Cicero writes the *Laws*, in which he argues for natural law and universal human rights: "a citizen of the whole universe, as it were a single

city."

55–135 C.E.   The Greek philosopher Epictetus of Hierapolis in Asia Minor, known from the *Discourses* published by his student Arrian after Epictetus's death, argues for an ethical system based on tolerance of others. Because humans are powerless, they must desist from worldly deeds and accept that only God is perfect.

413–426   In *The City of God*, the Christian theologian Saint Augustine of Hippo sets forth a model for world peace and order and condemns war, although he allows that some wars may be "just."

c. 632   In Islam, human rights are mentioned in the Qur'an, fully compiled in the eighth century. Sura 6:15 instructs: "Take not life which God hath made sacred except by way of justice and law." The Qur'an also discusses political and legal rights, human dignity, and entitlements.

1066   William the Conqueror, duke of Normandy before his invasion and conquest of Britain, recognizes the rule of law and in his Coronation Charter of 1066 vows to rule justly, make laws, and control violence.

1215   The Magna Carta is granted by King John of England to nobles and church officials who demand an end to what they view as abuses of power. This "English Great Charter" of liberties is proposed as a solution, in place of resorting to violence, the common means of resolving disputes; it becomes a symbol of revolt against oppression; in England, the Petition of Right (1628) and Habeas Corpus Act (1679) are based on the Magna Carta, which is revised and reissued in 1216, 1217, and 1225.

Preamble

John, by the grace of God, king of England, lord of Ireland, duke of Normandy and Aquitaine, and count of Anjou, to the archbishop, bishops, abbots, earls, barons, justiciaries, foresters, sheriffs, stewards, servants, and to all his bailiffs and liege subjects, greetings. Know that, having regard to God and for the salvation of our soul, and those of all our ancestors and heirs, and unto the honor of God and the advancement of his holy Church and for the rectifying of our realm, we have granted as underwritten by advice of our venerable fathers, Stephen, archbishop of Canterbury, primate of all England and cardinal of the holy Roman Church, Henry, archbishop of Dublin, William of London, Peter of Winchester, Jocelyn of Bath and Glastonbury, Hugh of Lincoln, Walter of Worcester, William of Coventry, Benedict of Rochester, bishops; of Master Pandulf, subdeacon and member of the household of our lord the Pope, of brother Aymeric (master of the Knights of the Temple in England), and of the illustrious men William Marshal, earl of Pembroke, William, earl of Salisbury, William, earl of Warenne, William, earl of Arundel, Alan of Galloway (constable of Scotland), Waren Fitz Gerold, Peter Fitz Herbert, Hubert De Burgh (seneschal of Poitou), Hugh de Neville, Matthew Fitz Herbert, Thomas Basset, Alan Basset, Philip d'Aubigny, Robert of Roppesley, John Marshal, John Fitz Hugh, and others, our liegemen.

1265–1273 In his *Summa Theologica*, the Christian theologian Saint Thomas Aquinas distinguishes between natural and divine rights and argues that natural rights underlie justice, peace, and unity. He also distinguishes between just wars (those in self-defense, with the goal of a peaceful termination or waged for the common good) and unjust wars (those for plunder or power or those waged cruelly).

1579 The *Vindiciae Contra Tyrannos* (Defense of liberty against tyrants) is written by exiled French Huguenots (Protestants). The document stresses freedom from state authority and the importance of individual conscience and freedom of expression.

1583–1645 The Dutch jurist Hugo Grotius sets forth the first known statement of the doctrine of humanitarian intervention in his *De Jure Belli ac Pacis* (On the rights of war and peace). Grotius argues that nations have the right to intervene in the internal affairs of other nations when citizens of those nations are being severely mistreated.

1601 The Poor Laws enacted in England create institutions to care for sick, aged, and mentally ill people. The laws and the poorhouses they create are later criticized by social reformers, who see them as contributing to these problems rather than alleviating them, as well as denying full rights to the poor, ill, and insane.

1628 In the Petition of Right, the English Parliament asks King Charles I to limit illegal activity by government officials regarding taxation, billeting of soldiers in private homes, imprisonment without cause, and declaration of martial law. Although the king resists the changes, government action does bring change leading to constitutional reform.

1632–1704 The English philosopher John Locke advocates individual rights; he sets forth the idea that certain rights are self-evident and classifies the rights of "life, liberty, and property." Locke's ideas influence American statesmen such as Thomas Jefferson, although Jefferson does not consider the right to property as basic and substitutes the right to happiness in its place.

1689 The Bill of Rights enacted in England is based on the Declaration of Rights enacted earlier in the year. Although the Bill covers a wide range of legal and political rights, it actually has little impact on the authority of the monarch, because Parliament's power to select the monarch and its authority over the national treasury already limit the power of the king.

An Act for declaring the rights and liberties of the subject and settling the succession of the crown.

WHEREAS THE LORDS SPIRITUAL AND TEMPORAL, AND COMMONS, ASSEMBLED AT WESTMINSTER, LAWFULLY, FULLY, AND

FREELY REPRESENTING ALL THE ESTATES OF THE PEOPLE OF THIS REALM, DID UPON THE THIRTEENTH DAY OF FEBRUARY, IN 1689, PRESENT UNTO THEIR MAJESTIES THEN CALLED AND KNOWN BY THE NAMES AND STYLE OF WILLIAM AND MARY, PRINCE AND PRINCESS OF ORANGE, BEING PRESENT IN THEIR PROPER PERSONS, A CERTAIN DECLARATION IN WRITING, MADE BY THE SAID LORDS AND COMMONS, IN THE WORDS FOLLOWING: Whereas the late King James the Second, by the assistance of divers evil counselors, judges, and ministers employed by him, did endeavour to subvert and extirpate the protestant religion, and the laws and liberties of this kingdom.

By assuming and exercising a power of dispensing with and suspending of laws, and the execution of laws, without consent of parliament.

By committing and prosecuting divers worthy prelates, for humbly petitioning to be excused concurring to the said assumed power.

By issuing and causing to be executed a commission under the great seal for erecting a court called, The court of commissioners for ecclesiastical causes.

By levying money for and to the use of the crown, by pretence of prerogative, for other time, and in other manner, than the same was granted by parliament.

By raising and keeping a standing army within this kingdom in time of peace, without consent of parliament, and quartering soldiers contrary to law.

By causing several good subjects, being protestants, to be disarmed, at the same time when papists were both armed and employed, contrary to law.

By violating the freedom of election of members to serve in parliament.

By prosecutions in the court of King's bench, for matters and causes cognizable only in parliament; and by divers other arbitrary and illegal courses.

And whereas of late years, partial, corrupt, and unqualified persons have been returned and served on juries in trials and particularly divers jurors in trials for high treason, which were not freeholders.

And excessive bail hath been required of persons committed in criminal cases, to elude the benefit of the laws made for the liberty of the subject.

And excessive fines have been imposed; and illegal and cruel punishments inflicted.

And several grants and promises made of fines and forfeitures, before any conviction or judgment against the persons, upon whom the same were to be levied.

All of which are utterly and directly contrary to the known laws and statutes, and freedom of this realm. . . .

1724–1804 In Königsberg, Germany, the philosopher Immanuel Kant supports the creation of a federation of nations to sustain human rights and argues that such a federation could end human rights abuses. His ideas are believed to have partly inspired the League of Nations, created in Europe in the aftermath of the First World War.

1737–1809 The political philosopher Thomas Paine (who emigrates from Britain to America in 1774) argues that government has a responsibility to support its citizens and in *The Rights of Man* (1791–1792) strongly advocates that governments take action to end and prevent poverty and to provide for fair taxation and universal education. In his pamphlet *Common Sense* (1776), Paine contends that the American colonies must declare independence from England, thereby aiding the cause of the Revolution.

1776 Virginia becomes the first colony (and later state) in the United States to guarantee human rights when it issues a Declaration of Rights, which influences the Bill of Rights (the first 10 amendments of the U.S. Constitution) and state constitutions.

1776 The Declaration of Independence, written in Philadelphia, Pennsylvania, by Thomas Jefferson during the Continental Congress, is the first national declaration of independence to mention human rights explicitly; it is adopted by representatives of 12 colonies, New York delegates not receiving permission to adopt it until a few days later; it is then signed by 53 members of the Congress and later by 3 members who were absent. The Declaration states: "We hold these truths to be self-evident, that all men are created equal, that they are endowed by their Creator with certain unalienable Rights, that among these are Life, Liberty, and the pursuit of Happiness. That to secure these rights, Governments are instituted among Men, deriving their just powers from the consent of the governed."

1789 The Declaration of the Rights of Man and of the Citizen is enacted in Paris, France, by the National Assembly. An influential document in the human rights movement, it lists the rights to which all men are entitled, such as participation in the making of laws, equitable taxation, freedom of religion, and equality of all before the law; the Declaration implicitly negates the divine right of kings, which had been the foundation of the French monarchy.

1791 Constitutional protection of human rights in the United States is enacted through the Bill of Rights, the first 10 amendments to the Constitution, which are adopted by Congress and include freedom of speech; the right to bear arms; freedom from unreasonable searches; the right not to be tried twice for the same crime and not to be deprived of life, liberty, or property without due process; the right to a speedy trial and trial by jury; among others. The rights apply only to the federal government, not the state governments, and are later defined through a series of Supreme Court cases. The Bill of Rights serves as a model for rights clauses in many other national constitutions.

The Bill of Rights

Amendments 1–10 of the Constitution

Amendment I—Congress shall make no law respecting an establishment of religion, or prohibiting the free exercise thereof; or abridging the freedom of speech, or of the press; or the right of the people peaceably to assemble, and to petition the government for a redress of grievances.

Amendment II—A well regulated militia, being necessary to the security of a free state, the right of the people to keep and bear arms, shall not be infringed.

Amendment III—No soldier shall, in time of peace be quartered in any house, without the consent of the owner, nor in time of war, but in a manner to be prescribed by law.

Amendment IV—The right of the people to be secure in their persons, houses, papers, and effects, against unreasonable searches and seizures, shall not be violated, and no warrants shall issue, but upon probable cause, supported by oath or affirmation, and particularly describing the place to be searched, and the persons or things to be seized.

Amendment V—No person shall be held to answer for a capital, or otherwise infamous crime, unless on a presentment or indictment of a grand jury, except in cases arising in the land or naval forces, or in the militia, when in actual service in time of war or public danger; nor shall any person be subject for the same offense to be twice put in jeopardy of life or limb; nor shall be compelled in any criminal case to be a witness against himself, nor be deprived of life, liberty, or property, without due process of law; nor shall private property be taken for public use, without just compensation.

Amendment VI—In all criminal prosecutions, the accused shall enjoy the right to a speedy and public trial, by an impartial jury of the state and district wherein the crime shall have been committed, which district shall have been previously ascertained by law, and to be informed of the nature and cause of the accusation; to be confronted with the witnesses against him; to have compulsory process for obtaining witnesses in his favor, and to have the assistance of counsel for his defense.

Amendment VII—In suits at common law, where the value in controversy shall exceed twenty dollars, the right of trial by jury shall be preserved, and no fact tried by a jury, shall be otherwise reexamined in any court of the United States, than according to the rules of the common law.

Amendment VIII—Excessive bail shall not be required, nor excessive fines imposed, nor cruel and unusual punishments inflicted.

Amendment IX—The enumeration in the Constitution, of certain rights, shall not be construed to deny or disparage others retained by the people.

Amendment X—The powers not delegated to the United States by the Constitution, nor prohibited by it to the states, are reserved to the states respectively, or to the people.

1889–1890

The International Conference of American States is held in Washington, D.C. Future conferences deal with such matters as extradition of criminals; codification of international law; copyrights, patents, and trademarks; and status of aliens and diplomatic personnel. The conference is held largely as a result of the efforts of the U.S. secretary of state, James G. Blaine, a leading Republican politician and diplomat.

1891

The papal encyclical *Rerum Novarum* (Of new things), issued by Pope Leo XIII, is the first Roman Catholic document dealing with the rights of the wealthy and the poor and calling for a consideration of the conditions of working people. It sets forth a framework for defining the rights of rich and poor, capitalists and laborers, and advocates labor unions and just wages.

1917

The Mexican Constitution is enacted and is the first national constitution to pay special attention to the rights of the poor. The Constitution recognizes the long pattern of exploitation of Mexican workers by foreign firms and nations and among its provisions are:

(Article 5.1) No person can be prevented from engaging in the profession, industrial or commercial pursuit or occupation of his choice.

(Article 27) The Nation shall at all times have the right to impose on private property such limitations as the public interest may demand, as well as the right to regulate the utilization of natural resources . . . in order to conserve them to ensure a more equitable distribution of public wealth.

1919

The International Labour Organization (ILO), founded after World War I by the action of the Treaty of Versailles, is the first multilateral organization established to deal with human rights, specifically workers' rights. The ILO Constitution is written by the Labor Commission, composed of representatives from nine nations and chaired by Samuel Gompers, head of the American Federation of Labor (AFL). Two 19th-century industrialists, Robert Owen of Wales and Daniel Legrand of France, had recognized the need for such an organization; the ILO is the only major entity created by the Treaty of Versailles to survive into the 21st century.

Preamble to the ILO Constitution

Whereas universal and lasting peace can be established only if it is based upon social justice;

And whereas conditions of labour exist involving such injustice, hardship, and privation to large numbers of people as to produce unrest so great that the peace and harmony of the world are imperilled; and an improvement of those conditions is urgently required; as, for example, by the regulation of the hours of work including the establishment of a maximum working day and week, the regulation of the labour supply, the prevention of unemployment, the provision of an adequate living wage, the protection of the worker against sickness, disease, and injury arising out of his employment, the protection of children, young persons, and women, provision for old age and injury, protection of the interests of workers when employed in countries other than their own, recognition of the principle of equal remuneration for work of equal value, recognition of the principle of freedom of association, the organization of vocational and technical education and other measures;

Whereas also the failure of any nation to adopt humane conditions of labour is an obstacle in the way of other nations which desire to improve the conditions in their own countries;

The High Contracting Parties, moved by sentiments of justice and humanity as well as by the desire to secure the permanent peace of the world, and with a view to attaining the objectives set forth in this Preamble, agree to the following Constitution of the International Labour Organization. . . .

1936   The Constitution of the Soviet Union deals extensively with human rights; lists civil, political, economic, and social rights; and also enumerates citizens' duties to the state. Citizens are granted the right to work and the right to education, and women are given equal rights with men in all spheres of life, although the Constitution is more honored in the breach than in the observance. Some examples of these constitutionally protected rights and duties are:

(Article 12) In the USSR work is the duty of every able-bodied citizen, according to the principle: "He who does not work, neither shall he eat." In the USSR the principle of socialism is realized: "From each according to his ability, to each according to his work."

(Article 118) Citizens of the USSR have the right to work—the right to guaranteed employment and payment for their work in accordance with its quantity and quality. . . .

(Article 121) Citizens of the USSR have the right to education. . . .

(Article 122) Women in the USSR are afforded equal rights with men in all spheres of economic, state, cultural, social, and political life. . . .

(Article 127) The citizens of the USSR are guaranteed inviolability of the person. No person may be placed under arrest except by decision of a court or with the sanction of a State Attorney.

1939   The first worldwide violation of many human rights begins with the start of World War II. During the war, which ends in 1945 and involves nations on all continents, the world experiences six years of human rights violations and immense amounts of resources spent on creating destructive weapons. Human rights violations during the war and the desire to control such matters in the future play a major role in the growth of the human rights movement in the postwar years.

1941   In his State of the Union message to Congress on January 6, President Franklin D. Roosevelt outlines four essential freedoms that his government hopes to see established throughout the world: freedom of speech and expression, freedom of religion, freedom from want, and freedom from fear.

1941   The Atlantic Charter declaration of the British prime minister Winston Churchill and the U.S. president Franklin D. Roosevelt, the first British-American agreement dealing with human rights, addresses a variety of international human rights issues such as the requirement that nations respect people's right to choose their own forms of government; that, after the destruction of "Nazi tyranny," nations should seek a peace under which all nations can live safely without fear or want; and that to encourage a general sense of security through renunciation of force, potential aggressors should be disarmed. The Atlantic Charter is incorporated into the Declaration of the United Nations in 1942.

The President of the United States of America and the Prime Minister, Mr. Churchill, representing His Majesty's Government in the United Kingdom, being met together, deem it right to make known certain common principles in the national policies of their respective countries on which they base their hopes for a better future for the world.

First, their countries seek no aggrandizement, territorial or other;

Second, they desire to see no territorial changes that do not accord with the freely expressed wishes of the peoples concerned;

Third, they respect the right of all peoples to choose the form of government under which they will live; and they wish to see sovereign rights and self government restored to those who have been forcibly deprived of them;

Fourth, they will endeavor, with due respect for their existing obligations, to further the enjoyment by all States, great or small, victor or vanquished, of access, on equal terms, to the trade and to the raw materials of the world which are needed for their economic prosperity;

Fifth, they desire to bring about the fullest collaboration between all nations in the economic field with the object of securing, for all, improved labor standards, economic advancement, and social security;

Sixth, after the final destruction of the Nazi tyranny, they hope to see established a peace which will afford to all nations the means of dwelling in safety within their own boundaries, and which will afford assurance that all the men in all lands may live out their lives in freedom from fear and want;

Seventh, such a peace should enable all men to traverse the high seas and oceans without hindrance;

Eighth, they believe that all of the nations of the world, for realistic as well as spiritual reasons must come to the abandonment of the use of force. Since no future peace can be maintained if land, sea, or air armaments continue to be employed by nations which threaten, or may threaten, aggression outside of their frontiers, they believe, pending the establishment of a wider and permanent system of general security, that the disarmament of such nations is essential. They will likewise aid and encourage all other practicable measures which will lighten for peace-loving peoples the crushing burden of armaments.

Franklin D. Roosevelt

Winston S. Churchill

1946   The United Nations Commission on Human Rights is established as the first such commission. Authorized by Article 48 of the United Nations Charter, it is charged with investigating and reporting on human rights violations around the world and commissioning studies of human rights situations and issues.

1946   The Church World Service is founded by the World Council of Churches as an ecumenical Christian humanitarian assistance agency to provide various forms of assistance for economic development and to aid victims of natural disasters and refugees.

1948   The General Assembly of the United Nations adopts the Universal Declaration of Human Rights, and for the next twenty years the Commission on Human Rights uses the Declaration as a basis for setting standards and creating a body of human rights law. The International Covenant on Civil and Political Rights and the International Covenant on Economic, Social, and Cultural Rights are adopted by the General Assembly in 1966; the Universal Declaration and the two Covenants are commonly referred to together as the International Bill of Human Rights.

The Preamble to the Universal Declaration reads as follows:

Preamble

Whereas recognition of the inherent dignity and of the equal and inalienable rights of all members of the human family is the foundation of freedom, justice, and peace in the world,

Whereas disregard and contempt for human rights have resulted in barbarous acts which have outraged the conscience of mankind, and the advent of a world in which human beings shall enjoy freedom of speech and belief and freedom from fear and want has been proclaimed as the highest aspiration of the common people,

Whereas it is essential, if man is not to be compelled to have recourse, as a last resort, to rebellion against tyranny and oppression, that human rights should be protected by the rule of law,

Whereas it is essential to promote the development of friendly relations between nations,

Whereas the peoples of the United Nations have in the Charter reaffirmed their faith in fundamental human rights, in the dignity and worth of the human person and in the equal rights of men and women and have determined to promote social progress and better standards of life in larger freedom,

Whereas Member States have pledged themselves to achieve, in co-operation with the United Nations, the promotion of universal respect for and observance of human rights and fundamental freedoms,

Whereas a common understanding of these rights and freedoms is of the greatest importance for the full realization of this pledge,

Now, therefore,

THE GENERAL ASSEMBLY

Proclaims this Universal Declaration of Human Rights as a common standard of achievement for all peoples and all nations, to the end that every individual and every organ of society, keeping this Declaration constantly in mind, shall strive by teaching and education to promote respect for these rights and freedoms and by progressive measures, national and international, to secure their universal and effective recognition and observance, both among the peoples of Member States themselves and among the peoples of territories under their jurisdiction.

1948   The American Declaration of the Rights and Duties of Man is adopted by the Ninth International Congress of American States in Bogotá, Colombia. The Declaration enumerates a long list of legal, political, religious, intellectual, property, labor, economic, and cultural rights, but it is not considered part of the Charter of the Organization of American States and therefore is not legally binding on member nations.

American Declaration of the Rights and Duties of Man

Preamble

All men are born free and equal, in dignity and in rights, and, being endowed by nature with reason and conscience, they should conduct themselves as brothers one to another.

The fulfillment of duty by each individual is a prerequisite to the rights of all. Rights and duties are interrelated in every social and political activity of man. While rights exalt individual liberty, duties express the dignity of that liberty.

Duties of a juridical nature presuppose others of a moral nature which support them in principle and constitute their basis.

Inasmuch as spiritual development is the supreme end of human existence and the highest expression thereof, it is the duty of man to serve that end with all his strength and resources.

Since culture is the highest social and historical expression of that spiritual development, it is the duty of man to preserve, practice, and foster culture by every means within his power.

And, since moral conduct constitutes the noblest flowering of culture, it is the duty of every man always to hold it in high respect.

1949

The Council of Europe is established as the first European organization for human rights by Belgium, Denmark, France, Ireland, Italy, Luxembourg, Netherlands, Norway, Sweden, and the United Kingdom and later is expanded to include 32 European nations. The Council is set up to protect human rights and promote European unity; it also establishes a number of special bodies and expert committees such as the European Committee on Crime Problems, European Commission of Human Rights, and European Court of Human Rights.

1950

The Nuremberg Principles, adopted by the International Law Commission of the United Nations and the United Nations General Assembly, establish the authority of nations to punish violators of human rights and eliminate the often-used defense that a person acting under orders of a superior is not responsible for human rights violations he or she carries out. The first among several new international conventions addressing war crimes after World War II, the Nuremberg Principles are, ironically, officially announced in London on the day the United States drops the second atomic bomb on Nagasaki, Japan.

Principles of the Nuremberg Tribunal, 1950

Principle I—Any person who commits an act which constitutes a crime under international law is responsible therefore and liable to punishment.

Principle II—The fact that internal law does not impose a penalty for an act which constitutes a crime under international law does not relieve the person who committed the act from responsibility under international law.

Principle III—The fact that a person who committed an act which constitutes a crime under international law acted as Head of State or responsible Government official does not relieve him from responsibility under international law.

Principle IV—The fact that a person acted pursuant to order of his Government or of a superior does not relieve him from responsibility under international law, provided a moral choice was in fact possible to him.

Principle V—Any person charged with a crime under international law has the right to a fair trial on the facts and law.

Principle VI—The crimes hereinafter set out are punishable as crimes under international law:

a. Crimes against peace:

  i. Planning, preparation, initiation, or waging of a war of aggression or a war in violation of international treaties, agreements, or assurances;

  ii. Participation in a common plan or conspiracy for the accomplishment of any of the acts mentioned under (i).

b. War crimes: Violations of the laws or customs of war which include, but are not limited to, murder, ill treatment, or deportation to slave-labor or for any other purpose of civilian population of or in occupied territory, murder or ill treatment of prisoners of war, of persons on the seas, killing of hostages, plunder of public or private property, wanton destruction of cities, towns, or villages, or devastation not justified by military necessity.

c. Crimes against humanity: Murder, extermination, enslavement, deportation, and other inhuman acts done against any civilian population, or persecutions on political, racial, or religious grounds, when such acts are done or such persecutions are carried on in execution of or in connection with any crime against peace or any war crime.

Principle VII—Complicity in the commission of a crime against peace, a war crime, or a crime against humanity as set forth in Principle VI is a crime under international law.

1964   The Cairo Declaration on Human Rights, set forth by nonaligned nations, outlines a strategy for achieving peace around the world and addresses many human rights issues, including those of special importance in the non-Western world, such as self-determination, apartheid, racial discrimination, and colonialism.

1969   The American Convention on Human Rights is signed at the Inter-American Specialized Conference on Human Rights at San José, Costa Rica. The preamble affirms the intention of the American states to support liberty and justice, stating:

The American states signatory to the present Convention,

Reaffirming their intention to consolidate in this hemisphere, within the framework of democratic institutions, a system of personal liberty and social justice based on respect for the essential rights of man;

Recognizing that the essential rights of man are not derived from one's being a national of a certain state, but are based upon attributes of the human personality, and that they therefore justify international protection in the form of a convention reinforcing or complementing the protection provided by the domestic law of the American states;

Considering that these principles have been set forth in the Charter of the Organization of American States, in the American Declaration of the Rights and Duties of Man, and in the Universal Declaration of Human Rights, and that they have been reaffirmed and refined in other international instruments, worldwide as well as regional in scope;

Reiterating that, in accordance with the Universal Declaration of Human Rights, the ideal of free men enjoying freedom from fear and want can be achieved only if conditions are created whereby everyone may enjoy his economic, social, and cultural rights, as well as his civil and political rights; and

Considering that the Third Special Inter-American Conference (Buenos Aires, 1967) approved the incorporation into the Charter of the Organization itself of broader standards with respect to economic, social, and educational rights and resolved that an inter-American convention on human rights should determine the structure, competence, and procedure of the organs responsible for these matters,

Have agreed upon the following . . .

1979   The Action Internationale Contre la Faim (International Action against famine) is founded in France as the first international organization specifically to combat famine. Through regional offices elsewhere in Europe and in Africa, the organization raises money to support projects that prevent famine or lessen the effects of existing famines, mainly in sub-Saharan Africa.

1980   The Andean Commission of Jurists is founded in Bogotá, Colombia, as the first international human rights organization in the Andean region. The Commission is composed of judges from Bolivia, Chile, Colombia, Ecuador, Peru, and Venezuela, who develop programs and guidelines for the participating nations.

1981   The African Charter on Human and People's Rights is adopted by the leaders of the nations that form the Organization of African Unity and is formally ratified by the African nations in 1986. Unlike many other human rights documents, this one explicitly recognizes both the rights of individuals and the rights of groups; rights of groups are especially important in Africa, where ethnic and religious groups compete for power in the postcolonial era.

African [Banjul] Charter on Human and Peoples' Rights

Preamble

The African States members of the Organization of African Unity, parties to the present convention entitled "African Charter on Human and Peoples' Rights,"

Recalling Decision 115 (XVI) of the Assembly of Heads of State and Government at its Sixteenth Ordinary Session held in Monrovia, Liberia, from 17 to 20 July 1979 on the preparation of a "preliminary draft on an African Charter on Human and Peoples' Rights providing inter alia for the establishment of bodies to promote and protect human and peoples' rights";

Considering the Charter of the Organization of African Unity, which stipulates that "freedom, equality, justice, and dignity are essential objectives for the achievement of the legitimate aspirations of the African peoples";

Reaffirming the pledge they solemnly made in Article 2 of the said Charter to eradicate all forms of colonialism from Africa, to coordinate and intensify their cooperation and efforts to achieve a better life for the peoples of Africa, and to promote international cooperation having due regard to the Charter of the United Nations and the Universal Declaration of Human Rights;

Taking into consideration the virtues of their historical tradition and the values of African civilization which should inspire and characterize their reflection on the concept of human and peoples' rights;

Recognizing on the one hand, that fundamental human rights stem from the attributes of human beings which justifies their national and international protection and on the other hand, that the reality and respect of peoples' rights should necessarily guarantee human rights;

Considering that the enjoyment of rights and freedoms also implies the performance of duties on the part of everyone;

Convinced that it is henceforth essential to pay a particular attention to the right to development and that civil and political rights cannot be dissociated from economic, social, and cultural rights in their conception as well as universality and that the satisfaction of economic, social, and cultural rights is a guarantee for the enjoyment of civil and political rights;

Conscious of their duty to achieve the total liberation of Africa, the peoples of which are still struggling for their dignity and genuine independence, and undertaking to eliminate colonialism, neo-colonialism, apartheid, Zionism, and to dismantle aggressive foreign military bases and all forms of discrimination, particularly those based on race, ethnic group, color, sex, language, religion, or political opinions;

Reaffirming their adherence to the principles of human and peoples' rights and freedoms contained in the declarations, conventions, and other instrument adopted by the Organization of African Unity, the Movement of Non-Aligned Countries, and the United Nations;

Firmly convinced of their duty to promote and protect human and peoples' rights and freedoms taking into account the importance traditionally attached to these rights and freedoms in Africa;

Have agreed as follows . . .

1981   America's Watch is founded to monitor human rights in the Americas. It is affiliated with Human Rights Watch and focuses on Latin America, especially on human rights in nations with totalitarian regimes supported by the United States.

1985   Asia Watch is founded to monitor human rights in Asian nations and to issue reports on the human rights situation in Asia.

1985   Soviet leader Mikhail Gorbachev initiates the policies of *glasnost* (openness) and *perestroika* (economic and political restructuring) and, as a result, Communism would collapses in the Soviet Union and Eastern Europe, Germany would be reunified, and Yugoslavia would disintegrate. *Glasnost* allows the media more freedom of expression, opens up the political process to non-Communists, restores some degree of religious freedom, and eases movement in nations and across national boundaries; it also indirectly leads to repression of some minority religions, ethnic- and religious-based conflicts, and a reduced role for women in Russian society.

1986   Physicians for Human Rights is founded as the first physicians' organization for human rights and begins operation in 1987 in Somerville, Massachusetts. It is founded as an association of health professionals who use medical science to investigate and prevent human rights violations around the world.

1987   The African Commission on Human and People's Rights, the first African human rights organization, begins operation following the ratification of the African Charter on Human and People's Rights in 1986. The commission's task is to enforce the provisions of the 1986 charter, including establishing procedures for handling complaints about human rights violations and assisting

African nations to establish human rights policies and programs.

1990   The United Nations General Assembly passes a resolution dealing with the definition of human rights. Traditionally, human rights were defined as negative rights (freedom from some government action) or positive rights (entitlement to government protection or intervention); recent discussions identify a third category of rights—solidarity rights—which have yet to be clearly defined, although the United Nations has endorsed building solidarity among human beings.

1993   The United Nations issues the Vienna Declaration and Programme of Action, calling for global action on human rights, at the World Conference on Human Rights held in Vienna. The declaration emphasizes United Nations control of human rights efforts; an end to discrimination against women, children, and minorities; development of plans by member nations to combat human rights problems; improved reporting of human rights violations; and education.

1993   The United Nations Office of the High Commissioner for Human Rights is created by the United Nations General Assembly, after the World Conference on Human Rights—held in Vienna, under the auspices of the United Nations—calls for its creation. It becomes the coordinating office for human rights activities, centralizing all other organs and agencies under the newly proposed reforms of the United Nations.

1994   The international human rights hot line is established by the United Nations Commission on Human Rights. Open 24 hours a day, the hot line can be reached by phone or fax from around the world so that people can quickly report human rights violations.

1995   The Human Rights International Film Festival is hosted by Human Rights Watch. The festival is organized to help people understand human rights issues through film.

1995   The People's Decade for Human Rights Education, the first decade for human rights education, begins in 1995 and runs until 2005. It is initiated by the United Nations for the purpose of compiling, updating, and distributing information about human rights.

1999   Amnesty International condemns the killing, by Revolutionary Armed Forces of Colombia (FARC) guerrillas who had supposedly acted independently of the FARC organization, of three U.S. indigenous rights activists working in Colombia as part of a campaign to support the U'wa indigenous community; their blindfolded and tied-up bodies were dumped over the border in Venezuela. The FARC leadership takes responsibility for the murders and announces that it will try the commander responsible, though Amnesty International fears that such a trial will be quick and will end in a death sentence.

2001   Human Rights Watch announces that almost half of the 1.2 million U.S. antipersonnel land mines supposedly necessary for the defense of South Korea are stored in depots in the United States.

The United States had refused to sign the 1997 Land Mine Treaty, stating that land mines were needed in the event of an attack by North Korea, but only 5 percent of the land mines are immediately available to U.S. troops in South Korea.

2001   The second federal prisoner to be executed since 1963, Juan Raul Garza is put to death by the U.S. government at the new federal death row in Terre Haute, Indiana, the first person executed in the federal lethal-injection chamber; Garza had been sentenced to death in 1993 under the 1988 federal drug kingpin statute (allowing the death penalty for murders resulting from large-scale drug dealing) for murders committed in the operation of a drug ring in Brownsville, Texas. The first instance since 1976 of the use of unsolved offenses in a foreign country as a factor in the punishment phase of a trial, Garza's case is considered "antithetical to the most basic and fundamental judicial guarantees" by the Inter-American Commission on Human Rights, because evidence of Garza's alleged involvement in unsolved crimes for which he had never been charged was introduced at his sentencing; the Commission called Garza's death sentence arbitrary and capricious and stated that his execution would be a "deliberate . . . violation" of U.S. obligations under international law.

2001   The United States threatens Egypt with sanctions because of the imprisonment of the human rights activist Saad Eddin Ibrahim, a sociology professor who has dual U.S.-Egyptian citizenship. Ibrahim had pleaded not guilty to charges of accepting foreign funds without government approval to make a film (never shown) damaging to Egypt but was sentenced to seven years in prison.

2002   In northern Chile near Peru, the military detonates three types of antipersonnel land mines buried during the regime of the dictator Augusto Pinochet to protect Chile's borders. Under a 1997 treaty signed in Ottawa, Chile must get rid of all its buried land mines, some 120,000, in 10 years; the detonation is also a signal of amity to Peru and Bolivia, with whom Chile has experienced strained relations.

2002   After the African governments nominate Libya to chair the United Nations Commission on Human Rights for 2003, Human Rights Watch states that Libya should not chair the commission. "Countries with dreadful human rights records should never be in charge of chairing the Commission," declares the Global Advocacy director of Human Rights Watch.

2002   The U.S. think tank the Council on Foreign Relations reports that countries around the world still view the United States as arrogant and hypocritical in the area of human rights and that the United States has done nothing to ameliorate this view.

2002   Amnesty International reports that the execution of the Mexican national Javier Suarez Medina in Texas this year constitutes a human rights violation on the part of the United States, as Javier Suarez was never informed of his right under the Vienna Convention on Consular Relations to contact his consulate. The

U.S. Department of State merely sends Mexico its regrets for the treaty violation and asks the Texas Board of Pardons and Paroles to pay attention to the violation when considering Javier Suarez's petition for clemency; in view of the record of Texas in granting clemency, such a request is meaningless.

2002   Stating that world opinion will pressure the United States to change its stance, British ministers meeting at the World Summit on Sustainable Development in Johannesburg, South Africa, predict that U.S. president George W. Bush will support the 1997 Kyoto Protocol calling for industrialized nations to cut carbon dioxide emissions.

2002   In Bhopal, India, a court rules that Warren Anderson, the former chairman of the U.S.-based corporation Union Carbide, must face homicide charges for the 1984 Bhopal gas disaster and orders the Indian Central Bureau of Investigation (CBI), which had applied to reduce the charges to negligence, to proceed with the case. If Anderson is extradited to India for trial and is found guilty, he could be sentenced for up to 20 years; 3,000 people were killed by the gas leak and half a million injured.

2002   Michael Melchior, deputy foreign minister of Israel, sides with Great Britain's chief rabbi Jonathan Sacks in criticizing those on the Israeli right who ignore the moral dilemmas of the Israeli-Palestinian conflict. Describing the situation as a "deep Jewish ethical crisis," Melchior warns of tragic consequences for Israel if the Palestinian situation is not remedied.

CHAPTER TWO

CIVIL RIGHTS

c. 3000 B.C.E. Evidence of slavery appears in southern Mesopotamia (modern Iraq), where the Sumerians use slaves to plant and harvest crops and to construct the canals for the irrigation systems bringing water to the crops. The Sumerian word for slave means "person from a foreign land," an indication that slaves are captives seized in battle rather than local inhabitants.

c. 2184–1785 B.C.E. In Egypt during the Middle Kingdom, the Papyrus Brooklyn 35.1448 mentions 27 adults referred to as *hem-nesu* and *hemet* ("king's slave" and "female slave," respectively); "king's slave" may refer to a criminal. There is also a record of a camp where the families of runaway slaves are imprisoned.

1766–1045 B.C.E. In China, slavery exists during the Shang dynasty. By the time of the Han dynasty (206 B.C.E.–220 C.E.), about 5 percent of the population are estimated to be slaves.

c. 1750 B.C.E. The law code established by King Hammurabi of Babylon (modern southern Iraq) includes laws referring to slaves. For example, if a man acknowledges his children by a female slave along with the children of his first wife, the slave's children share in the man's estate, with the oldest son of the first wife receiving an extra share; if he does not acknowledge the slave's children, they do not share in his estate, but their mother and they themselves are set free.

c. 1750 B.C.E. The law code of King Hammurabi of Babylon mentions capital punishment for several crimes. If an upper-class man strikes the pregnant daughter of another upper-class man and she has a miscarriage and dies, the miscreant's daughter is put to death; if a house collapses and kills the owner, an upper-class man, the builder of the house is put to death.

1100–1070 B.C.E. The Adoption Papyrus, written during the reign of the pharaoh Ramses XI, mentions a woman, unable to conceive, who adopts the children of the union between her husband and a slave, thus conferring freedom on them.

712–404 B.C.E. Contracts for the sales of slaves are preserved in Egypt. The name of the slave owner is tattooed onto the palm of the slave's right hand.

c. 635 B.C.E. Led by Aristomenes, the Messenians, the inhabitants of a fertile area in Greece who had been defeated by the Spartans during the First Messenian War (735 B.C.E.), rebel against the Spartan policy of taking half of all that the Messenians produce and reducing them to semislavery. Victorious for a few years, Aristomenes is betrayed by an ally and captured by the Spartans but escapes and wages war for more than 11 years before finally being killed.

594 B.C.E.   Solon, a Greek statesman and reformer, bans the enslavement of free Athenians for debt. Following Solon's reforms, wealthy Athenians replace their slaves with slaves purchased from northern Africa and western Asia to provide the necessary labor, especially in the silver mines in Laurium, a seaport southeast of Athens.

c. 538–331 B.C.E.   Slaves in the Persian Empire are eunuchs, men castrated before puberty to ensure that they do not become sexually involved with the women of the Persian monarch's harem and thus remain loyal to the ruler. Eunuchs are used to guard the private sanctums of rulers in many other cultures, including Rome and China.

490s–300 B.C.E.   One-third of the population of Greece are estimated to be slaves. Many slaves are freed after Philip II, king of Macedonia, defeats the Greeks at the battle of Chaeronea in 338 B.C.E.

c. 480–460 B.C.E.   The law code of Gortyn, an ancient site in southern Crete, is thought to reflect early Greek law; it distinguishes among the rights of rulers, free people without political rights, agricultural serfs, and indebted slaves. Penalties for crimes reflect class status, and more evidence is necessary to convict a master than a slave; masters have parental rights over the children of their serfs and slaves, though serfs can marry and even, if there are no relatives, inherit from their masters.

450 B.C.E.   The Twelve Tables of Rome, the Roman law codes, are formulated by 10 magistrates called decemvirs, and the tablets are placed in the Forum in Rome. Compiled because the common people had complained that the unwritten laws as interpreted by patrician judges did not protect them, the Twelve Tables institute equal laws for all; several crimes call for the death penalty, including disseminating libels or insulting songs and arson.

399 B.C.E.   In Athens, Greece, Socrates commits suicide by drinking hemlock, a poison. He had been sentenced to death for ignoring the Greek gods and for corrupting the morals of the young, and, though his friends plan for his escape, he chooses to die for his beliefs rather than flee.

c. 350 B.C.E.   The Greek philosopher Aristotle, in his *Politics*, considers slavery a natural, necessary reality of the state and believes that slaves are inferior to free people. According to Aristotle, the master provides intellect and foresight; the slave, labor; the master should be guided in his treatment of slaves by his clear need for them to follow his rule.

c. 340s B.C.E.   Isocrates, an Athenian orator with conservative views, argues against Sparta's freeing Messene, the capital city of Messenia. In his *Archidamus*, Isocrates warns against conceding to demands that the Spartans free Messene as the price of peace; arguing as a Messenian, he decries the possibility that Sparta's former slaves would rule over him.

c. 326–313 B.C.E.   In Rome, a law abolishing debt bondage and imprisonment of people for private debts is passed, revising the early Roman laws, the Twelve Tables. The revised law abolishes the previous law that had punished default of debts with slavery and that had included the concept of *nexum*, whereby a debtor voluntarily enters into a contract enslaving himself until the debt is satisfied.

263–146 B.C.E.   During the Punic Wars between Rome and Carthage, when the Romans capture some experienced Carthaginian agricultural workers, they make them slaves to work in the fields growing fruit, grain, olives, and grapes. The Romans capture great numbers of slaves and expand their plantations; they also increase their trading partners throughout and beyond the Mediterranean.

c. 200 B.C.E.   Cato, a Roman politician and orator, publishes *De agri cultura* (On agriculture), in which he provides insight into the practice of slavery in Rome and offers practical advice to slave owners. Cato suggests that when slaves complain of illness, they be fed less; that if it rains, they work inside; and that on holidays they work on building public roads.

c. 135 B.C.E.   Tiberius Gracchus, a Roman military leader and politician, issues the *Lex agraria* (agrarian law) in Rome, to deal with the increasing numbers of farmers who have lost their lands to the burgeoning estates and have fled to the cities and poverty. The *Lex agraria* requires that public lands be taken from the large and wealthy landowners and redistributed to soldiers who have completed their army service; the Roman Senate opposes Tiberius's support of the common people, and months later Tiberius is killed in a riot.

106–43 B.C.E.   The Roman orator Cicero writes several essays about life in the late Roman republic, declaring that even slaves should be treated justly. He tells of the death of his own slave: "It has moved me more than, it seems, the death of a slave should."

c. 100 B.C.E.   In the *Manu Smriti* (laws of Manu—Sanskrit for "man"), the ancient laws of India, there is evidence of slavery. The Hindu epic the *Mahabharata* mentions that these laws were written by the first Manu, or Brahma (ultimate ground of being); they support the caste system, with the Brahman caste supreme, and specify the proper observance of rituals.

c. 73 B.C.E.   Made a praetor by the Roman Senate, the powerful financier Marcus Licinius Crassus pursues the rebelling slaves led by Spartacus, a Roman slave, and defeats them in brutal combat. After crushing the rebellion, Crassus has thousands of the defeated slaves crucified along the Appian Way in Rome.

c. 90 C.E.   Epictetus, a Greek Stoic philosopher teaching in Rome, believes that in spite of human laws that might validate slavery, natural laws make all men brothers; it is human nature to act kindly toward others, and those who act otherwise suffer. Epictetus also believes that the slave who frees him- or herself from attachment to external things fares far better than the apparently free master who is bound to material wealth, laziness, and tyranny.

c. 115   After defeating Dacia (modern Romania) and making it a province of the Roman Empire, the emperor Trajan has a column erected in Rome to celebrate the victory. Decorated with sculptures, the column includes scenes of slaves.

591   Pope Gregory I, called Gregory the Great, issues his *Liber pastoralis curae* (Book of pastoral care), stating his thoughts on slavery: Even though masters and slaves might be created equal, nevertheless slaves are required to obey their masters and to understand their lower status. Slavery, he acknowledges, results from human laws, not from the laws of nature; in his private life, Gregory allows two of his own slaves to purchase their freedom.

c. 726   The *Ecloga*, an amalgam of laws clarifying the Roman laws that the Roman emperor Justinian had codified in the sixth century, is promulgated by the Byzantine emperor Leo III. The *Ecloga* addresses the issue of slavery, clarifies the means by which a master can free a slave, and stipulates who can own slaves; Justinian's code and the *Ecloga* form the basis of European civil law.

c. 850   The slave trade from East Africa begins, and Muslim farms and households of the Persian Gulf region use African slaves. East African slaves are said to have worked at extracting salt and clearing land in Mesopotamia (modern Iraq), but they revolt, discouraging the use of African slaves there.

870   After Vikings seize many inhabitants of the town of Alt Clut (modern Dumbarton) in Scotland, they take them to be sold in Dublin, Ireland, the site of a major slave market. There is thought to have been widespread enslavement throughout the Celtic areas of the British Isles from the fifth century onward.

c. 1000   The law of King Hywel Dda, who rules Wales in Great Britain, sets out some legal relationships of slavery and reveals the many-leveled structure that characterizes it. For example, the highest level of female slave is defined much like a servant, *gwinyddol*, and is not required to perform outdoor agricultural labor; a female slave made pregnant by a free man must be replaced by another woman for as long as she cannot perform her duties, and if she dies in labor the owner must be financially compensated.

1086   Compiled at the order of William I (William the Conqueror), king of England, the Domesday Book is a survey of the royal estates and tenants and an account of the workers. Approximately 10 percent of the population recorded are slaves, and in some counties the figure is as high as 20 percent.

1351   During the rule of King Edward III of England, the Statute of Treason is enacted. Many offenses are punishable by death, including counterfeiting coins, violating the king's companion and certain women of the royal family, and plotting the death of the king, queen, or royal heir.

1381   The leader of the Peasants' Revolt in England, Wat Tyler, protests before King Richard II about the imposition of a poll tax as well as economic hardships burdening the peasantry. He is beheaded; John Ball, another participant, is put to death in front of the king.

1415   Prince Henry of Portugal sends 240 ships to conquer the vital port of Ceuta on Morocco's coast opposite Gibraltar. Both a strategic base for defending the Straits of Gibraltar and the doorway to the riches of Africa's trade in gold and slaves, Ceuta becomes the port the Portuguese use to transport slaves to Portugal and to market slaves within Africa; before long, the Portuguese begin to use slave labor on their sugar plantations on the islands of Madeira and Cape Verde in the Atlantic Ocean.

1426   In Great Britain, Parliament enacts the *peine forte et dure* (penalty of duration) law, which calls for the torture of a condemned man. Large stones are piled on his chest; he is fed bad bread on the first day of torture, then bad water, and "so shall he continue until he die."

1434   Pope Eugene IV issues *Creator Omnium* (Creator of all) from concern that the existence of slavery on the Canary Islands endangers the conversion of slaves. The *Creator Omnium* declares that anyone transporting and selling converted slaves from the islands will be excommunicated, but this applies only to converted slaves and does not threaten the policy of enslaving unconverted prisoners captured in war.

1435   Pope Eugene IV issues the papal bull *Romanus Pontifex* (Roman pope), modifying a previous edict banning the capture of slaves in the Canary Islands. After King Duarte of Portugal intervenes, the Pope revises his position and grants the Portuguese the right to capture the remaining unconverted natives in the Canaries.

1442   Pope Eugene IV issues *Illius Qui* (Those who), at the request of Prince Henry of Portugal, who asks the pope to confer the status of a crusade on Henry's military raids along the coast of West Africa and his subsequent enslavement of the captives. The papal bull grants forgiveness of sins to every man who participates in the campaigns.

1444   The Portuguese claim the Île de Gorée, an island off the coast of Senegal in Africa, where they establish a shipping center and transit point for trading in freshwater, fuel, and slaves. Subsequently controlled by the Dutch, British, and French, Gorée has 118 slave houses; slaves come from Nigeria, Senegal, and Mali; in four centuries almost 20 million slaves are brought here, and around 6 million die here.

1462   Pope Pius II, corresponding with the political leader of the Canary Islands, denounces the slave trade as a crime and the Christians who enslave the African peoples as criminals.

1479   The Treaty of Alcaçobas-Trujillo, negotiated between Spain and Portugal, ends a war fought over Queen Isabella's seizure of the throne of Castile in northern Spain and sets boundaries for each nation's territory and sphere of influence. The treaty has the effect of guaranteeing Portugal's control of mainland Africa, the Azores, Madeira, and the Cape Verde Islands, thus preserving Portugal's control of the growing trade in African slaves.

1492   Beginning with Columbus's arrival in the New World, indigenous people are captured, used as slaves, and trained to serve as interpreters. When the Indians rebel against the first European settlement Isabela (now northern Dominican Republic) in 1495, many are transported to Spain to be sold as slaves.

1497–1528   The taking of Indian slaves soon becomes commonplace in the New World; the English (John Cabot in 1497), the Portuguese (Gaspar Côrte-Real in 1500), the French (Giovanni da Verrazano, Italian but in French service, in 1524), and the Spanish (Hernando de Soto and Francisco Vásquez in the 1540s) all take Indian slaves in the New World. Native Americans in turn take Europeans as slaves, including Álvar Núñez Cabeza de Vaca, Spanish explorer, captured in Florida in 1528 and held for a time.

1500s   The *asiento*, a contract between the Spanish government and an entrepreneur—a plantation owner, for example—is introduced in the Spanish slave trade. A contractor orders a number of slaves, with their prices established in the *asiento*, from Spanish officials who gather the slaves and transport them; these officials receive a salary from the money gained from the *asiento*; abolished in 1789, the *asiento* system is thought to have governed the transfer of at least 900,000 slaves to the Americas.

1500–1550s   The American Indian population throughout the areas of New Spain drops from 25 million to approximately 16 million, as a result of disease, the horrors of slavery, and the abuses of the *encomienda* system, whereby a landowner leases Indians to work as slaves on his plantation, agreeing to convert them to Christianity.

1502   Spain brings African slaves to work on the sugar plantations of the Caribbean islands. Based on the *Siete Partidas* (Seven protectors), laws created between 1263 and 1265, the legalization of slavery in Spain provides legal justification for the enslavement of many millions of slaves taken from Africa; the laws allow slaves to marry, inherit property, and buy their freedom, but slave life in the Spanish colonies is cruel and harsh.

c. 1512   A slave trade between the Kongo kingdom (around the Congo River in Africa) and Portugal begins when the king, Nzinga Mbemba, later baptized and called Alfonso I, grants a gift of 320 slaves to the Portuguese representative of King Manuel I. As trade grows to between 5,000 and 10,000 slaves a year, Mbemba loses control of it; in 1526, he warns the Portuguese monarch John III of the brutality of the slave traders and the illegal seizure of his subjects, but his warning has no effect.

1513   The Laws of Burgos is established by a royal committee of legal experts and theologians, convened in Burgos, Spain, to resolve a dispute between the *encomenderos*, the Spanish conquistadors in the New World who hold slaves under the *encomienda* lease system, and the Dominican friars who believe that the Taino people of Hispaniola (modern Haiti) must be treated like the other vassals of the Spanish crown if they are to be converted to Christianity. The committee decides that while the Taino deserve decent treatment, they must still be subject to the control of their *encomenderos*; because the laws are difficult to enforce, abuse is widespread, and the laws do not protect Indian slaves captured during war or Indians who had refused Spanish dominion or *rescate* ("rescue") from their pagan existence.

1514   Bartolomé de Las Casas, a Spanish priest and historian, is an early critic of the Spanish treatment of Indians in the New World; Las Casas presses King Charles I of Spain to prohibit slavery and to enforce more humanely the *encomienda* system, whereby Spaniards use Indian labor in return for giving them religious instruction and protection.

1531   In England, the Parliament passes an act legalizing death by boiling.

1534   An executioner for the city of London is appointed in England. After four years of hanging others, he is convicted of theft and hanged.

1537   Pope Paul III, in *Veritas Ipsa* (Very truth), denounces the enslavement of Indians.

1539   A Roman Catholic Church synod of Hispaniola (modern Haiti), in *Sinodos Diocesanos* (Diocesan synod), decrees that slaves from Guinea in West Africa should be baptized before they are delivered to their owners.

1540–1541   The Spanish explorers of the New World Hernando de Soto and Francisco Vásquez de Coronado record their observations of the enslavement of Native Americans by other tribes. De Soto observes captured Indians, and Coronado travels to the pueblo of Cicúye in North America and encounters two slaves from the Wichita and Pawnee tribes.

1555   The first ghetto, isolating Jews behind a walled-off region of a city, is established in Rome, Italy. The idea spreads to many other cities in Europe; Jews are locked in the ghetto at night and must often wear a distinctive badge on their clothing when they leave the ghetto during the day.

1569   During the reign of Queen Elizabeth I, the Cartwright decision maintains that "England was too pure an air for slaves to breathe in." Slavery has not existed in England since the end of the Middle Ages.

1575   André Thevet, a French Franciscan friar and geographer, publishes *Cosmographie Universelle* (Universal cosmography), in which he encourages the view that black Africans are "stupid, bestial, and blinded by folly"; Thevet had visited the New World very briefly, exploring only in the vicinity of modern Rio de Janeiro. Thevet claims to have been the first to transplant *Nicotiana tabacum*, the tobacco plant, from Brazil to France, but others dispute this; he asserts that smoking clears the head, and he practices what he preaches.

1581   The Dutch abandon their allegiance to the Spanish, who had ruled over the Netherlands, in the Act of Abjuration. The act declares that "God did not create the subjects for the benefit of the Prince, . . . but the Prince for the benefit of the subjects."

1588   Slavery is abolished in Lithuania.

1600s   The New Haven Colony passes a strict set of laws regulating behavior on the Sabbath. Called "blue laws" for the color of the paper on which they are printed, they prohibit drunkenness, ornate dress, the breaking of the Sabbath, and violations of rules of family discipline. Blue laws prohibiting the sale of alcohol on Sunday will persist in many parts of the United States into the 21st century.

1617   John Rolfe, an English colonist in the Virginia Colony, experiments with cross-breeding the bitter strains of tobacco native to Virginia with tobacco from the West Indies. Like sugarcane, which does not grow in the colder climates of North America, tobacco is a labor-intensive crop that spurs the slave trade; Virginia tobacco farmers purchase African and West Indian slaves to increase their profits.

1619   African slaves are imported into Jamestown in the Virginia Colony when it is reported that a Dutch man-of-war sells to the "cape merchant" of the Virginia Company: "twenty and odd negars."

c. 1620   Indentured servitude is introduced into the Virginia Colony when servants in Great Britain sell themselves for a period of three to seven years to a master in return for passage to America and "freedom dues" of goods and possibly land on completion of their servitude. Unlike their counterparts in the English system, masters in America can sell their indentured servants, and treatment is often far harsher in America; nevertheless, 60 percent of those emigrating from Britain are estimated to be indentured servants until the growing slave trade lessens the demand for white workers.

1620s   In South Carolina, the development of rice farming spurs the slave trade, and soon Africans from what is now Ghana, who are experienced in growing rice, become prized slaves.

1621   The Dutch West India Company is founded and granted a government monopoly for trading in the Americas, the islands of the Atlantic, and Africa below the Tropic of Cancer. The Dutch begin to fight the Portuguese and Spanish for control of their African colonies, largely to gain access to the gold and slave market.

1621–1738   The Dutch West India Company transports and sells more than

270,000 slaves in the Americas; the slaves are chained below deck in hot and crowded quarters, and mortality rates aboard Dutch ships average about 16 percent. In 1738, the company loses its monopoly, and other Dutch companies assume its share of the slave trade.

1623   Gypsy women are executed by drowning in Edinburgh, Scotland.

1623   Anthony, son of Isabel and William, is the first African-American to be baptized in the American colonies, when he becomes a member of the Anglican Church in Jamestown, Virginia.

1624   The first-known African-American child born in the American colonies is William Tucker, born in Jamestown, Virginia.

1625   Huigh de Groot (Latin: Hugo Grotius), a Dutch scholar, politician, and lawyer, publishes *De Jure Belli ac Pacis* (Of the law of war and peace), a book on international law. Grotius has ambivalent views of slavery, defining it as lifelong servitude in return for the necessities of life, and on the other hand as contrary to nature.

1626   The Dutch West India Company brings 11 slaves to New Amsterdam, present-day New York City. By 1644, 40 percent of the people living in the New Netherland Colony are African slaves.

1627   The first French colonists arrive on the Caribbean island of Saint Kitts, and African slaves are imported two years later. By 1780, approximately 40,000 slaves a year are imported to the French-controlled islands in the Caribbean.

1630   British authorities in the Massachusetts Bay Colony execute by hanging one of the Pilgrims who had sailed over on the *Mayflower*.

1631   The British construct a fort and trading center at Kormantine on the west coast of Africa; it becomes the main port for Britain's trade in gold and slaves. In 1665, the British lose the fort to the Dutch, who rename it Fort Amsterdam and take over the trade in gold and slaves, along with the significant profits.

1639   Pope Urban VII criticizes the enslavement of Indians in Brazil, Rio de la Plata (between Uruguay and Argentina), and Paraguay, when he communicates with the Apostolic Chamber of Portugal.

1640   Richard Fetherston, chaplain to Catherine of Aragon, the first wife of the English king Henry VIII, is hanged for contesting the king's right to marry the wife of his dead brother.

1641   The first American colony to recognize slavery as legal is the Massachusetts Bay Colony, as part of its law code, the Body of Liberties. The code states that slaves must be captives taken in wars and strangers who sell themselves into bondage; these slaves are to have "all the liberties and Christian usages which the law of God established in Israel."

1641   The Massachusetts Bay Colony issues Capital Lawes, which invoke the death penalty for many crimes, including witchcraft, blasphemy, and worship of a god other than the biblical God.

1642	The Virginia Colony passes a law punishing whites for harboring fugitive slaves. The law stipulates a fine of 20 pounds of tobacco for every night the violator provides refuge for a runaway slave; slaves captured after a second attempt at escape are to be branded.
1643	The New England colonies agree among themselves to convict runaway slaves. The only evidence necessary to convict a slave of illegally fleeing his master is certification of the deed by a magistrate.
1648	Great Britain exports Irish political prisoners to its Caribbean colonies. Between 1648 and 1655, 12,000 captured Irish "undesirables" are sold into indentured servitude.
1652	Fort Carolusburg, named for the Swedish monarch Charles X, is constructed on the Cape Coast (West Africa, modern Ghana) by the Swedish Africa Company, to serve as a center for Sweden's slave trade. Later changing hands from the Swedes to the Danes and the local chief to the Dutch, the fort finally becomes a British port, which in the 18th century sends around 17,000 slaves yearly to the Americas; it remains British until the late 19th century.
1652	Sir John Hawkins, an English naval commander, illegally ships about 300 slaves from Sierra Leone in West Africa to Hispaniola (modern Haiti) in the Spanish West Indies. The voyage is so profitable that his next trip is supported by English nobles, and Queen Elizabeth offers Hawkins a warship for his 1654 voyage; ultimately, the British transport 5.5 million slaves across the Atlantic.
1660	Slave codes are established in the Virginia Colony that recognize the legal status of slavery and decide that a black child's status is determined by the race of the mother. With whites increasingly fearful of the possible power of the slaves, the codes prohibit slaves from leaving their masters' plantations to gather together without permission, bear arms, or testify against whites in court; disobedience is punished by branding, whipping, and maiming.
1661	Emanuel and Dorothy Pieterson petition the Dutch colonial administration of New Netherland (present-day New York State) to name Anthony van Angola "a free Negro." The Pietersons, free blacks, had adopted Anthony as a child following the death of his mother.
1662	A statute issued in the Virginia Colony, On the Nativity Conditions of Slavery, declares that children born in Virginia are slave or free depending on the condition of the mother and that any Christian fornicating with a black man or woman shall pay "double the fines imposed by the former act."
1664	The Maryland Colony passes a law forbidding the marriage of English colonists to black men, to prevent free English women from marrying black slaves. All imported Africans are considered slaves, and women marrying slaves are to be considered slaves as long as their slave husbands live.

1664	The French king Louis XIV, aided by his adviser Cardinal Armand Richelieu, transfers possession of the Caribbean islands from their private owners and places them under the auspices of the Compagnie des Indes Occidentales, the French West Indies Company, to increase the wealth of his kingdom. The king controls the right to trade in the colonies and can prevent the transfer of precious commodities to the islands.
1670	The Virginia Colony denies the right to vote to freed slaves and indentured servants. The law establishes that all non-Christians imported "by shipping" to the colony are slaves for life; those slaves who travel to Virginia by land must serve as slaves until the age of 30 years if they are children and, if they are adults, they must serve for 12 years.
1670s	France imports slaves to its Caribbean islands to promote the growth of sugar-plantation economies, after the indigenous peoples die from disease and enslavement. French slave ships carry more than a million slaves to the Antilles, and as many as 150,000 more are thought to have died en route.
1672	The Virginia Colony passes a law establishing a bounty for the capture and death of escaped rebellious slaves. These slaves, known as maroons, establish communities in remote mountains, forests, and swamps in the southern colonies.
1672	The Danish are estimated to have transported about 100,000 slaves from eastern Africa to the West Indies from 1660 to 1806. In 1671, the Danish West Indian Company had received permission from the crown to create a colony in the West Indies, and about 100 European settlers arrived in Saint Thomas; a hundred slaves are imported.
1675	In the Virginia Colony, Phillip Corven, a black servant of Anny Beazley, petitions the colonial administration to be discharged from servitude. Having been promised in Beazley's will that he would gain his freedom, three barrels of corn, and a suit of clothing after serving her cousin Humphrey Stafford for eight years, Corven instead is sold to another owner after some years with Stafford and is not given his freedom.
1679	In England, Parliament passes the Habeas Corpus Act, which guarantees that citizens cannot be detained or imprisoned arbitrarily.
1682	Two friars, Francisco José de Jaca and Epifanio de Morains, are arrested for preaching against slavery in churches in Cuba; acquitted in Spain the next year, they are prohibited from returning to Cuba. Their declarations that African slavery is immoral, that slaves must be freed, that it is just to free them, and that slave owners who refuse to free their slaves cannot receive pardon from the church are endorsed three years later by authorities of the Roman Catholic Church in Cuba.
1682	A resolution passed in Virginia states that "all Negroes" are considered slaves.

1685   The French king Louis XIV promulgates the Code Noir (Black code) to regulate the slaves in the French Caribbean islands. According to the code, slaves are considered property and cannot congregate or carry weapons; runaway slaves can be shot or have their ears cut off. Slaves must be baptized and receive training in Catholicism; the laws also allow for intermarriage.

1688   The Society of Friends (Quakers) in Germantown, Pennsylvania, protests slavery, declaring it a violation of Christian teaching and the rights of man.

1690   In his *Two Treatises on Government*, the English philosopher John Locke writes of the "natural rights" of man, who comes into the world in a "state of perfect equality," with "a title to perfect freedom and . . . enjoyment of all the rights and privileges of the law of nature equally with any other man." He has the power "not only to preserve his property—that is his life, liberty, and estate—against the injuries and attempts of other men, but to judge . . . the breaches of that law in others."

1692   Nineteen townspeople in Salem, Massachusetts, are executed for witchcraft. Sarah Bishop, Sarah Good, and Rebecca Nurse are among those hanged. Giles Corey has stones pressed on him until he dies.

1697   A policy is established in New York City requiring the separate burials of slaves. In 1712, the African Burial Ground in Manhattan is mentioned; 10,000 to 20,000 slaves are estimated to have been buried in the six-acre site between 1712 and 1798.

1700   The first slave ship to leave Liverpool, England, is *The Blessing*. By 1730, as many as 15 ships leave Liverpool to pick up slaves in West Africa, and the numbers increase to 50 a year by the 1750s, as many as 100 in the 1770s, and almost 130 in the 1790s. It is estimated that in the 18th century 75 percent of European slave ships depart from Liverpool, transporting 1.5 million slaves.

1700s   The *capitães do mato* or *capitães do campo* (bush captains), professional slave catchers responsible for capturing runaway slaves in Brazil, often attack and destroy villages formed by escaped slaves in remote areas of the country. The *capitães* are paid a bounty in gold for each slave returned and are even rewarded for slaves killed while resisting capture; in this case, the *capitães* must deliver the slaves' heads.

1700s   The Ashanti, a group of people in present-day southern Ghana, take control of parts of West Africa and stop the export of slaves from areas under their control. The Ashanti do not ban slavery, however, for they have a complex slave system of their own.

1701   The Society for the Propagation of the Gospel in Foreign Parts is established in Great Britain by the Church of England to convert slaves to Christianity. While providing some education, both secular and religious, the church maintains strict segregation and relegates blacks to separate slave galleries and even separate buildings; a majority of black Christians in the American colonies are Anglican because their owners are.

1704	Elias Nau, a French immigrant living in New York City, founds the Catechism School, the first school in New York to accept slaves.
1705	Virginia enacts a slave code, collecting and revising various laws passed in preceding years about slaves and setting forth regulations determining how slaves must act and the penalties for breaking these regulations. Slaves are punished for owning guns and running away; whites may be punished for having sexual relations with blacks or for aiding runaway slaves. Similar slave statutes are enacted in South Carolina, Maryland, and North Carolina.
1712	In Maiden Lane in New York City, 27 armed slaves set fire to the outhouse of a white man and fire on those who come to douse the fire. Nine whites are killed, and the state militia is called out; 21 blacks are executed, and 6 commit suicide. Slave legislation is toughened, and the death penalty required for willful burning of property and conspiracy to murder.
1717	Danish colonists from Saint Thomas in the West Indies colonize the island of Saint John and establish plantation agriculture there.
1718	In Great Britain, Parliament passes the Transportation Act, providing that convict labor be transported to the British plantations in the Caribbean and to the American colonies.
1730	During the Maroon War between runaway slaves in Jamaica and the British colonial authorities, Cudjo, the son of a prince of the Akan, a people of the Kormantine of West Africa; his brothers Johnny, Quacu, and Accompong; and his sister Nanny lead almost 5,000 armed slaves who successfully fight the British using guerrilla war tactics. In 1739, they sign an agreement with the colonial authorities giving them control of the land they occupy, although they agree to return any future runaway slaves to the British.
1732	King George II grants a charter to the British colony of Georgia, which is to be directed by Georgia trustees and settled by a combination of unemployed Britons and Protestants. Slavery is prohibited because the trustees are convinced slaves would threaten social stability, but within several years colonists are working for the right to employ slave labor.
1733	Brutal conditions are imposed on the slaves by the Danish colonists who came to the island of Saint John in the West Indies after overfarming on Saint Thomas forced them to move. One hundred and fifty slaves organize and destroy around 25 percent of the island's slave-based plantations.
1736	During the Choson dynasty in Korea, King Yongjo orders a 50 percent reduction in the amount of tribute paid by slaves. An increase in the landless poor and improvements in agriculture resulting in increased harvests with fewer laborers reduce the need for slaves; in 1775, King Yongjo exempts female slaves from paying tribute.

1737	When the Dutch slave ship *Leusden* goes down off the coast of Suriname (formerly Netherlands Guiana) in South America, some 702 slaves are believed to have drowned.
1738	A majority of white colonists in Savannah, in the Georgia colony, petition for slavery, while others, primarily German-born colonists and Highland Scots, weigh in for maintaining a ban on slavery. Mainly pro-slavery colonists move from Georgia to South Carolina; the Savannah trustees abandon their policy of no slavery and in 1752 withdraw the colony's charter rights.
1739	After a slave named Cato gathers a band of slaves near Stono in South Carolina, the group kills two warehouse guards and seizes guns and ammunition, marching south, they hope, to Florida. Along the way, they kill 25 to 30 whites, but armed whites retaliate, and more than 30 blacks are killed.
1740	A slave code passed in South Carolina prohibits slaves from raising livestock. The law provides for the seizure and forfeiture of any animals owned by slaves and punishes slaves who claim they had been illegally placed in bondage, with large financial penalties for making "false appeals."
1740	South Carolina passes a law forbidding the education of slaves.
1741	In letters to the king of Portugal and the bishop of Brazil, Pope Benedict XIV calls for freeing the Indian slaves of these two countries.
1741	The czarina Elizabeth Petrovna, daughter of Peter the Great, becomes empress of Russia and abolishes capital punishment.
1741	Some 50 slaves attempt to set fire to a fort in New York City. Two of the slaves who confess to the crime are burned alive before an angry mob; shortly afterward, 29 other blacks are executed, as well as two white men and two white women.
1754	John Woolman's *Considerations on the Keeping of Negroes* is published in Philadelphia, Pennsylvania. A Quaker, Woolman had witnessed slavery on the plantations of Virginia and North Carolina and urges his readers to reaffirm human equality; copies of the essay are distributed at the annual meetings of Quakers in Philadelphia and London, helping to spur the Quaker abolitionist movement.
1754	Georgia becomes an English crown colony and adopts the pro-slave laws of South Carolina. In two decades, the number of slaves increases from 600 to 15,000, about 50 percent of the total population.
1758	The first black college graduate in the Western Hemisphere is Frances William, born in Jamaica, who graduates from Cambridge University in Great Britain.
1762	The first African-American physician in the United States is James Derham, a slave who was born in Philadelphia, Pennsylvania. Derham trains as an assistant to his master, a doctor, and after purchasing his freedom becomes a doctor to blacks and

whites in Philadelphia.

| 1762 | After being convicted of killing his son, Jean Calas is executed in France. Soon after, prompted by the publication of the *Traité sur la tolérance* (Treatise on toleration) in 1763 by the French writer Voltaire, authorities acknowledge that the son had committed suicide, and the family is compensated for the miscarriage of justice. |

1762   In *Du contrat social* (On the social contract), Jean-Jacques Rousseau, the French philosopher, writes: "Man is born free but everywhere he is in chains." In the same year, Rousseau publishes *Émile*, in which he states that women, being inferior, cannot claim the same rights as men.

1763   The French writer Voltaire publishes his *Traité sur la tolérance* (Treatise on toleration), writing that natural law requires religious freedom. Nevertheless, he is not free of the bigotry of his time, declaring that blacks are naturally the slaves of others and that they have "a few more ideas than animals"; Voltaire also has shares in the slave-trading Compagnie des Indes.

1764   The Italian jurist and economist Cesare Beccaria publishes *Dei Deletti e Delle Pene* (On crimes and punishments), an early and influential study of criminal punishment. Beccaria advocates abolishing capital punishment and torture and other cruel punishments of prisoners.

1765   A member of the House of Burgesses in Virginia, the orator Patrick Henry opposes the British-imposed Stamp Act, declaring, "Caesar had his Brutus; Charles the First, his Cromwell; and George the Third—may profit by their example."

1770   The abbé Guillaume-Thomas-François de Raynal, a French historian, publishes *Histoire philosophique et politique des établissements et du commerce des Européens dans les deux Indes* (Philosophical and political history of European businesses and commerce in the two Indies) with the French encyclopedist Denis Diderot. The French Parliament orders the book burned because the authors criticize the clergy and the Europeans' treatment of the Indians in the Indies.

1770   Crispus Attucks, an American hero who was probably African-American and perhaps a runaway slave, is one of three Americans killed by British fire during the Boston Massacre.

1772   William Murray, earl of Mansfield and British lord chief justice, rules that a fugitive slave walking on British soil is free. He decides that James Somersett, a runaway slave from Virginia and now in Great Britain, cannot be reclaimed by his owner.

1773   In a letter to Robert Pleasants about slavery, the American orator Patrick Henry writes that it is amazing to find slavery in a country "above all others, fond of liberty."

1773   The slaves of Boston and elsewhere in Massachusetts petition the governor, asking him to consider their condition. Although some slaves may be vicious, many others are not and are willing to assume the duties of citizens rather than struggle under the miserable state of slavery.

1775   George Washington, general of the American forces, announces that blacks may not enlist in the army, following a decision by the Continental Congress, even though two African-American soldiers, Peter Salem and Salem Poor, were commended for their service at the recent Battle of Bunker Hill in Boston. Salem had killed Major John Pitcairn, the British commander, and both Poor and Salem received commendations from the Massachusetts court.

1775   John Murray, earl of Dunmore and British governor of Virginia, promises freedom to slaves who join the British army. About 100,000 slaves are thought to have run away during the course of the Revolutionary War; by year's end, Washington announces that his army now accepts free blacks.

1776   The Revolutionary patriot George Mason writes the Virginia Bill of Rights, which declares that "all men are by nature equally free and independent and have certain inherent rights."

1776   Writing to her husband, the statesman John Adams, Abigail Adams declares that women will rebel if they have no voice or representation in the laws of the United States.

1776   The Declaration of Independence, written by Thomas Jefferson and issued in Philadelphia, Pennsylvania, states: "We hold these truths to be self-evident, that all men are created equal, that they are endowed by their Creator with certain unalienable rights, that among these are life, liberty, and the pursuit of happiness. That to secure these rights, governments are instituted among men, deriving their just powers from the consent of the governed."

1776   Lemuel Haynes publishes the essay *Liberty Further Extended*, describing the need to extend freedom to African-Americans and declaring that the Declaration of Independence must be expanded to cover blacks; Haynes, abandoned by his African father and Scottish mother, had earned his freedom working as an indentured servant on a Massachusetts farm; when free, he at once joined the Revolutionary cause, fighting heroically for America. After the war, he would return to Massachusetts, study Latin and Greek, and become a preacher, serving in churches with white as well as black members; he would receive an honorary degree from Middlebury College in Vermont in 1804.

1776   David Hartley, a member of Parliament in Great Britain, declares slavery to be "contrary to the laws of God and the rights of man."

1777   The Constitution of Vermont is the first constitution in the United States to ban slavery.

1779   The U.S. Congress recommends that Georgia and South Carolina create battalions of American slaves to fight the British; since 1776, the South Carolinian John Laurens has been urging that

Congress promise emancipation to blacks in return for military service, and he is charged with building political support for the idea in his state. While the army supports the idea, slave owners oppose any plan freeing the slaves, and the measure is voted down in both states.

1779 The slaves of Stratford and Fairfield in Connecticut petition the general assembly, declaring their abject state and their desire for freedom. Knowing that they cannot attain it themselves and unwilling to use violent means, they ask that the assembly grant them relief from slavery.

1779 After Jeremiah Leaming, a resident of Connecticut, joins the British troops in Norwalk, Pomp, his slave, escapes and is held by the state of Connecticut as part of his master's forfeited estate. Pomp petitions the general assembly for his freedom, noting that he is well able to support himself and his family but cannot do so unless the state consents.

1780 Seven African-Americans in Dartmouth, Massachusetts, petition the state house of representatives for relief from taxation, on the grounds that, being slaves, they do not enjoy the profits of their labor or the rights of inheritance and have nevertheless served in battle during the war.

1783 Two British Quakers, John Lloyd and William Dillwyn, publish the treatise *The Case of Our Fellow Creatures, the Oppressed Africans, Recommended to the Serious Consideration of the Legislature of Great Britain, by the People Called Quakers*, arguing against the slave trade. The authors implore the British people to imagine themselves as slaves and to denounce slavery's destruction of the family; 10,000 copies are printed and distributed to King George and all members of Parliament, members of the clergy, justices, and headmasters of schools.

1783 The state court of Massachusetts, in *Commonwealth v. Jennison*, reaffirms the antislavery provision of the state's law. After Quaco Walker, a slave falsely claimed by Nathaniel Jennison, flees to the farm of his former master's brother, Jennison travels there, beats Walker, and brings him back as his slave; Chief Justice Cushing rules that Jennison had violated the state's Declaration of Right and is guilty of assaulting a free man.

1783 The Quaker-led Committee on the Slave Trade, established in Great Britain, organizes a petition campaign to Parliament to demand that the slave trade be declared illegal.

1787 Quobna Ottobah Cugoano, a slave, writes an antislavery pamphlet, *Thoughts and Sentiments on the Evil and Wicked Traffic of the Slavery and Commerce of the Human Species, Humbly Submitted to the Inhabitants of Great Britain*; Cugoano had been captured in the village of Ajumakoon in Ghana in Africa, transported to Grenada, then taken to England by his owner, Alexander Campbell, and baptized as John Stuart. In his pamphlet, he argues against current justifications for slavery and reminds his readers of the immorality of slavery and of slaves' rights to resist.

1787   The U.S. Continental Congress passes an ordinance prohibiting slavery or involuntary servitude, except as punishment for a crime, in the Northwest Territory (area around the Great Lakes and between the Ohio and Mississippi Rivers).

1787   The U.S. Constitution is adopted, sanctioning the "three-fifths compromise," the fact that Southern states may count slaves as three-fifths of a person when determining their population and thus their representation in the federal House of Representatives.

1787   The Society for Effecting the Abolition of the Slave Trade is founded in Great Britain. Following the lead of the American abolitionist movement, the British begin to lobby in Parliament and mount a large educational campaign to rally public support for an end to slavery.

1787   The Philadelphia Society for Alleviating the Miseries of Public Persons is organized in Philadelphia, Pennsylvania, with the aim of abolishing capital punishment and working for prison reform.

1787   The Free African Society, an organization of free blacks in America, is established by Richard Allen and Absalom Jones, both of whom were born into slavery; Allen, a Methodist, converted his owner, Stokley Sturgis, a farmer who later agreed to accept $2,000 for Allen's freedom. The society advocates the end of slavery and the establishment of equal relations between blacks and whites; Allen later founds the African Methodist Episcopal Church.

1787   Free blacks, led by Prince Hall, petition the Massachusetts House of Representatives for the right to equal education. Born in Barbados in 1748, Hall came to Massachusetts as a teenager, served as a soldier in the Revolutionary War, became a Methodist minister, and founded the Negro Masonic Order.

1788   The Société des Amis des Noirs (Society of Friends of Black People) is founded in France by Jacques-Pierre Brisot de Warville. This upper-class group works with the Estates-General in Paris to pass legislation condemning slavery, but powerful colonial interests oppose their efforts.

1788   Free blacks in Massachusetts petition against the kidnapping and sale of free blacks into slavery. Organized by Prince Hall, also the sponsor of a petition asking for slaves to have the right to education, the appeal protests the capture of three free blacks of Massachusetts, their transport by boat to Martinique, and their sale.

1788   Abdual-Rahahman Ibrahima, a prince of the Fulani, a Nigerian people, is captured in Guinea, West Africa, after a battle with a rival commander over control of the slave trade; arriving in Natchez on the Mississippi River, he is sold as a slave and encounters a white man he had saved in his home town of Timbo. After a journalist tells Ibrahima's story, he is freed and returns to Guinea.

1789   *The Interesting Narrative of the Life of Olaudah Equiano, or Gustavus Vassa, the African; Written by Himself* recounts the story of the author's kidnapping in Nigeria, his journey to the West Indies, and his life of slavery that takes him to Virginia, London, Georgia, the Mediterranean, and the Arctic under different masters. Having purchased his freedom, Equiano begins to write against slavery; his life story goes through nine printings in England in five years and is translated and published in the Netherlands, Germany, Russia, and the United States.

1789   Henri Grégoire, abbé and French revolutionary, publishes his *Mémoire en faveur des gens de couleur* (Memoir on behalf of colored people), arguing for extending the right to vote in France to mulattos and free blacks. Grégoire, the bishop of Blois, is a member of the Credentials Committee of the National Assembly; he advocates for the rights of Africans and Jews during the French Revolution and denounces slavery.

1790   In Great Britain, Parliament passes an act outlawing the burning of people at the stake. Stating that burning is cruel and inhuman, the act substitutes hanging in its place.

1790   The U.S. Congress passes an act stating that murder, forgery, robbery, and rape are punishable by death.

1790   A French colonial law delegates to colonial assemblies the right to determine who can vote; citizenship and the right to vote are granted to men over the age of 25 years who own property and pay taxes; however, by not specifically requiring the colonial assemblies to grant the vote to free men of color, the law allows the assemblies to continue to exclude them. Jacques Vincent Ogé, a native leader of the Société des Amis (Society of Friends), along with Jean-Baptiste Chavanne, organizes the free blacks of Saint Domingue (Santo Domingo, part of the island of Hispaniola) to resist and seizes the island town of Grande-Rivière; routed by French colonial troops, they are captured, tried, and executed.

1791   The French National Assembly responds to the revolt in Saint Domingue on Hispaniola (modern Haiti) by ruling that all men who are born to free parents and who are financially qualified are considered full citizens; when colonial whites refuse to enforce the decree, armed conflict breaks out. Creole slave leaders from dozens of plantations revolt against the French slave owners, and within a month 40,000 slaves are involved in the rebellion.

1791   The First Amendment of the U.S. Constitution, guaranteeing the exercise of major civil rights, is adopted. The amendment states: "Congress shall make no law respecting an establishment of religion, or prohibiting the free exercise thereof, or abridging the freedom of speech, or of the press; or the right of the people peaceably to assemble, and to petition the government for a redress of grievances."

1791   The Fourth Amendment to the U.S. Constitution, establishing safeguards against unreasonable searches, is adopted. The amendment states: "The right of the people to be secure in their persons, houses, papers, and effects, against unreasonable searches and seizures, shall not be violated, and no warrants shall issue, but upon probable cause, supported by oath or affirmation, and particularly describing the place to be searched, and the persons or things to be seized."

1791   The Fifth Amendment to the U.S. Constitution, setting up safeguards against self-incrimination and double jeopardy and guaranteeing due process, is adopted. The amendment states: "No person shall be held to answer for a capital, or otherwise infamous crime, unless on a presentment or indictment of a grand jury, except in cases arising in the land or naval forces, . . . when in actual service in time of war or public danger; nor shall any person be subject for the same offence to be twice put in jeopardy of life or limb; nor shall be compelled in any criminal case to be a witness against himself, nor be deprived of life, liberty, or property, without due process of law; nor shall private property be taken for public use, without just compensation."

1791   The Sixth Amendment to the U.S. Constitution, establishing the right to a jury trial and the right to confront witnesses and to have counsel, is adopted. The amendment states: "In all criminal prosecutions, the accused shall enjoy the right to a speedy and public trial, by an impartial jury of the state and district wherein the crime shall have been committed, . . . and to be informed of the nature and cause of the accusation; to be confronted with the witnesses against him; to have compulsory process for obtaining witnesses in his favor, and to have the assistance of counsel for his defence."

1791   The Seventh Amendment to the U.S. Constitution, establishing the right to a jury trial in common lawsuits, is adopted. The amendment reads: "In suits at common law, where the value in controversy shall exceed twenty dollars, the right of trial by jury shall be preserved, and no fact tried by a jury, shall be otherwise reexamined in any court of the United States, than according to the rules of the common law."

1791   The Eighth Amendment to the U.S. Constitution, establishing guarantees against unreasonable bail and unduly cruel punishment, is adopted. The amendment reads: "Excessive bail shall not be required, nor excessive fines imposed, nor cruel and unusual punishments inflicted."

1791   The Ninth Amendment to the U.S. Constitution, establishing that adoption of the Bill of Rights (the first 10 amendments) does not deny other, nonenumerated rights, is adopted. The amendment states: "The enumeration in the Constitution, of certain rights, shall not be construed to deny or disparage others retained by the people."

1791   Free blacks in South Carolina petition the state senate, protesting the prohibition against African-Americans testifying in court and instituting legal action. The petitioners state that, although they do not ask to be placed on an equal footing with white people, they do ask for the right to redress wrongs against them, a right now denied them by the prohibition.

1792   The French government approves the guillotine (a beheading machine promoted as producing a quick and painless death by Joseph-Ignace Guillotin, a physician and advocate of capital punishment) for executions. Between 1793 and August 1794, more than 2,500 people are sent to their death at the guillotine as enemies of the French Revolution, including Antoine Barnave, president of the Constituent Assembly; Georges-Jacques Danton, a radical who had voted to execute the king; Robespierre, the revolutionary who had sent Danton to his death; Antoine-Laurent Lavoisier, the chemist who among other accomplishments had discovered oxygen; and King Louis XVI and Queen Marie Antoinette.

1792   Benjamin Banneker, a black astronomer and mathematician, writes Thomas Jefferson, then U.S. secretary of state. Banneker asks how Jefferson can have written the words of the Declaration of Independence while allowing the continuation of slavery; he accuses the Founding Fathers of being guilty of the very act they detest in others.

1792   The London Revolution Society writes to the American Society of Friends of the Constitution, asking them to end slavery in the United States.

1792   Denmark rules that it will abolish slavery after 1803.

1793   The Upper Canadian Abolition Act provides that former fugitive slaves who enter Canadian territory are free. In 1819, slave owners prevail on the U.S. secretary of state to negotiate with Canada to reverse this policy, but Canada rebuffs them, and diplomatic entreaties to British authorities to end this free haven for slaves continue to be fruitless for decades to come.

1793   The U.S. Congress passes the Fugitive Slave Act, which makes it a crime to aid and harbor a fugitive slave or to hinder his or her arrest.

1793   Eli Whitney, an American inventor, invents the cotton gin, which separates the cotton seeds from the fiber; because of its use, cotton production increases dramatically in the American South, and the need and rationale for slavery expand with rising profits. By 1840, the United States produces 60 percent of the world's cotton; by 1860, cotton plantations produce a billion pounds of cotton.

1793   Although slaves are not allowed to post letters in the U.S. postal system and are prohibited by law from being taught how to read and write, some manage to circumvent the laws. A letter from a slave called Secret Keeper Richard to another slave, Secret Keeper Norfolk, is discovered in Yorktown, Virginia; it describes preparations for an armed uprising.

1793   A free black writes a letter to the governor of South Carolina, informing him about a planned slave revolt and advising him to be on his guard.

1793　African-Americans of South Carolina petition the state senate to relieve them of the poll tax that had been instituted on all blacks, in addition to the taxes they must pay on their property and trade.

1793　The French commissioner of Saint Domingue (modern Haiti), Léger Félicité Sonthonax, issues a decree freeing all loyal slaves who join the French forces. The decree responds to the growing revolutionary ferment among the slaves and the war between France and the forces of Spain and Great Britain.

1793　After the execution of King Louis XVI of France during the French Revolution, Spain and Great Britain go to war with France; the Spanish colonial authorities of Santo Domingo, the colony neighboring Saint Domingue, make alliances with two of the leaders of the rebellion there, Jean-François and Jorge Biassou, who soon control a large portion of northern Saint Domingue.

1794　In Paris, the National Convention of France decides to abolish slavery. Soon afterward, Napoleon reinstitutes slavery in the French colonies, though he cannot defeat the revolutionary movement among slaves in Saint Domingue (modern Haiti).

1794　The Revolutionary Convention in Paris affirms the abolition of slavery, and Toussaint Louverture, a former slave born on the Bréda sugar plantation and an emerging leader of the rebellion, shifts allegiance to the French and begins fighting against the forces opposed to the French Revolution, including his former allies.

1795　The plantation owners on the Dutch-controlled island of Curaçao in the Antilles, West Indies, force their slaves to work on Sundays and unfairly punish them all for the offense of a single slave. Influenced by the rebellion in Saint Domingue, the slaves rebel, but in a month the Dutch employ superior force, offer a general pardon for everyone involved except the leaders, and give freedom to any slaves who capture the leaders. The leaders of the revolt are tortured and hanged.

1795　Slaves and free blacks on the island of Granada in the West Indies resist the increasingly tyrannical administration of the British who had taken control of the island from the French; the British refuse free French-speaking blacks the right to vote and hold office. Led by Julien Fédon, a free black planter, approximately 7,000 free and enslaved blacks rebel, but the British defeat the rebels, summarily executing prisoners and sending others into exile. Much of the island's economy is destroyed during the rebellion.

1795　The French and Spanish sign the peace treaty of Bayle, settling the conflict over Saint Domingue and leaving the rebel leader Toussaint Louverture in control of a large army of slaves. From 1796 to 1801, he wrests increasing autonomy from the French-educated Creole elite and French authorities, occupies the Spanish Santo Domingo, and thus rules the entire island.

1797   The African-American Masonic Lodge is organized in Philadelphia, Pennsylvania, by James Forten Jr., a sail maker and abolitionist; Absalom Jones of the African Episcopal Church; and Richard Allen of the African Methodist Episcopal Church.

1797   Four former slaves from North Carolina, now living free in Philadelphia, Pennsylvania, petition the U.S. Congress to overturn North Carolina's slave laws, which had been passed to counter the efforts of those who freed their slaves, and which allowed once freed slaves to be recaptured. The petitioners had to leave North Carolina and escape pursuit after their masters had freed them, but Congress does not accept their petition.

1798   The Alien and Sedition Acts passed by the U.S. Congress and signed by President John Adams give the president the power to expel any noncitizen posing a threat to the country and to muzzle the freedom of the press. The acts are opposed by Thomas Jefferson, then vice president, and James Madison and expire in 1801, during Jefferson's presidency.

1798   The U.S. Congress passes the Naturalization Act, increasing the number of years an immigrant must live in the United States before applying for citizenship from 5 to 14.

1799   New York State passes a law beginning a gradual freeing of slaves.

1799   The Society for Missions in Africa and the East of the Church of England is founded in Great Britain to create missions in Africa and India in the hope that conversion, religious instruction, education, and self-improvement will end the slave trade. With an evangelical mission, the society believes that religious-based British civilization will bring progress to the Africans.

1800   Gabriel Prosser, son of an African-born mother and a slave of Thomas Prosser, a Virginia planter, plans to seize the arsenal in Richmond, Virginia, and lead a slave army to revolt and create an independent black state in Virginia; the slaves assemble on the outskirts of Richmond, but Governor James Monroe orders the militia to retaliate. Gabriel and about 34 confederates are arrested, tried, and hanged.

1800   Free blacks in Philadelphia, Pennsylvania—including Absalom Jones, a former slave and the first minister of Saint Thomas's African Episcopal Church in Philadelphia—petition the U.S. Congress to abolish slavery and the 1793 Fugitive Slave Act. Jones asks Representative Robert Wain of Pennsylvania to introduce the petition, which dies in a House committee, where it is stated that the petition has "a tendency to create disquiet and jealousy."

1801   The royal family of Korea decides to free the slaves working on its farms.

1802   Denmark rules slavery illegal.

1802   Arthur, a slave owned by William Farrar of Henrico County, Virginia, calls on American slaves to rebel and join him in an armed uprising. A few months later, an anonymous letter arrives at the home of a Mr. Mathews of Norfolk, Virginia, warning him of the coming rebellion.

1802   Napoleon Bonaparte's rise to power in France and his desire to use Saint Domingue as the center for his foreign-policy designs bring large numbers of French troops to the island, although he is unable to reinstate plantation slavery. Captured by French forces, Toussaint Louverture is arrested and sent to France, where he dies in jail in 1803 at Fort Joux.

1803   With years of military experience behind them, combined with a yellow-fever epidemic that strikes the French armies, the former slaves of Saint Domingue rout the French, and, in 1804, Haiti proclaims its independence.

1804   The so-called Black Laws passed in Ohio restrict the civil rights of free blacks.

1806   President Thomas Jefferson sends a message to the U.S. Congress, asking it to "withdraw the citizens of the United States from all further participation in those violations of human rights which have been so long continued on the unoffending inhabitants of Africa, and which the morality, the reputation, and the best interests of our country, have long been eager to proscribe."

1807   The General Abolition Bill passed in Great Britain makes it illegal for British subjects to trade in slaves and calls for fines of 100 pounds for each slave purchased, transported, or sold by a British subject. British ships used for transportation of slaves can be confiscated, and insurance companies indemnifying slave ships or property used for the slave trade can be fined.

1807   The African Institution is founded in Great Britain with the aim of encouraging the enforcement of existing legislation against the slave trade, convincing other nations to enact similar legislation, establishing non-slave-trading opportunities with African nations, promoting written versions of African languages, and bringing better medical care to Africa. A moderate group, it is founded by members, including Zachary Macauley, the former governor of Sierra Leone in Africa, and the bishops of London, Bath, and Wells; James Stephen of the institution creates a registry of slaves, documenting the names, dates, and family members of each slave and recording tales of ill-treatment.

1808   The U.S. Congress passes a law prohibiting the importation of African slaves and setting a fine of $800 for buying an illegally imported slave and a fine of $20,000 for transporting slaves in a slave vessel. The law is never adequately enforced.

1808   The Reverend Peter Williams of the New York African Church writes praising the law against the slave trade.

1808   An essay on the origin of slavery is published by the Sons of Africa in Boston, Massachusetts.

1808	After the enactment of the 1807 British General Abolition Bill, the British Navy establishes the antislavery squadron, also known as the African or preventive squadron, and Great Britain sends ships to interdict the maritime slave trade and to enforce the rule barring British subjects from participating in slavery. The ships concentrate on the 2,000 miles of the West African coast, and by 1838 as many as 36 ships are involved; because of the enormous territory patrolled, the squadron encounters fewer than 15 percent of the slave ships at sea between 1811 and 1867 and liberates only about 160,000 slaves of the almost 3 million transported from Africa.
1810	Henry Burch, a free black man, petitions the general assembly of Virginia, requesting permission for his two sons, slaves he had purchased, to continue residing in the state. The petition is sent in response to a 1806 Virginia law mandating that all slaves who had purchased their freedom leave the state unless the legislature grants permission to stay.
1811	In Louisiana, slaves belonging to the plantation owner Manual Andry rebel, kill him, and wound his son; then, continuing their onslaught, they move south along the river toward New Orleans, led, it is believed, by Charles Deslonded, another slave of Andry. Whites retaliate by dispatching militias and federal troops, commanded by Major Homer Virgil Milton; almost 300 well-armed troops meet between 150 and 500 slaves armed only with knives used to cut sugarcane and massacre them; 21 slaves are found guilty by Saint Charles Parish judge Pierre Bauchet St. Martin and sentenced to death.
1813	Argentina decides to abolish slavery gradually.
1813	At the African Methodist Episcopal Church in New York City, George Lawrence makes a speech denying black inferiority: "the noble mind of a Newton could find room, and to spare, within the tenement of many an injured African."
1813	The British Society for Missions in Africa and the East changes its name to the Church Missionary Society and soon after centers its operation in Freetown, now the capital of Sierra Leone and the best harbor in West Africa, where many slaves captured by British antislavery–squadron vessels are brought. The society operates schools and missions for the captured slaves and sometimes even purchases slaves to be educated and converted.
1814	Pope Pius VII writes a letter to the king of France, denouncing the support of the slave trade by any members of the Roman Catholic Church.
1814	The Netherlands rules that slavery is illegal.
1816	A law is enacted in Georgia prohibiting anyone from enticing a slave to run away. Any free black who entices a slave to flee from his or her master would serve a year in jail and face sale as a slave for life.
1816	The American Colonization Society is established in the United

States by people who believe that American slaves cannot adequately participate with other Americans in a democratic society and urge them to return to Africa; many prominent white Americans, including Francis Scott Key and Andrew Jackson, endorse the society, which receives financial support from the U.S. Congress and several state legislatures. African-Americans generally oppose the initiative, and even slaves given the opportunity of colonization in Africa refuse to go; Richard Allen, pastor of the African Methodist Episcopal Church, and James Forten Sr. and Absalom Jones of the African Episcopal Church, all of Philadelphia, Pennsylvania, organize active opposition to the society.

1817   A group of free black men in Richmond, Virginia, responds to the campaign of the American Colonization Society to export blacks back to Africa. The men agree that it would ultimately benefit blacks to be colonized but state that they prefer living in their country of birth rather than being exiled to a foreign land; they ask Congress to grant them some territory in the West for this purpose.

1817   A meeting of African-Americans in Philadelphia, Pennsylvania, chaired by James Forten, responds to the campaign of the American Colonization Society to export blacks back to Africa. The group strongly disapproves of the society's suggestion and feels itself entitled to enjoy the benefits of America; the men also condemn the implied stigma cast on black people by the notion that they must be returned to Africa.

1817   Great Britain and Spain negotiate a treaty to abolish trading in slaves.

1818   General Andrew Jackson defeats a combined force of blacks and Native Americans at the battle of Suwannee in Florida, ending what Jackson describes as a "savage and negro war."

1818   The preamble of the Constitution of the Pennsylvania Augustine Society for the Education of People of Colour is issued; the Society was organized by some of Philadelphia's most active free African-Americans.

1818   Abraham Camp, a free black man, writes to the American Colonization Society, volunteering to participate in the campaign of exporting blacks back to Africa. Camp states that he, his family, and friends love America, but, as they do not share in its liberties, they prefer to leave.

1819   International courts of mixed commission are established to try cases involving slave ships seized in apparent violation of treaties between Great Britain, nations of Europe, and the Americas. Each case is heard by a commissioner of the same country as the slave-ship owner and a commissioner from the country that had seized the vessel; if the case ends in conviction, the slaves are freed and the ship sold at auction, with the moneys split between the two countries.

1819   The Congress of Angostura, held in Venezuela, meets to establish the preliminary laws for the new republic of Colombia, created after Simon Bolívar, a South American revolutionary and states-man, leads inhabitants of northern South America to victory in the battle of Boyacá (in modern Colombia), winning independence from Spain. The 140,000 slaves in the area play a critical role on the plantations and in the mines and serve as soldiers for both sides; Bolívar argues for the immediate abolition of slavery, but the congress endorses a more gradual approach, giving slaves who served in the war against the Spanish colonial forces their freedom; new slaves cannot be introduced, and the remaining slaves gain freedom dover time.

1819–1871	International courts of mixed commission are held in Sierra Leone, Rio de Janeiro, Havana, Suriname, Luanda, the Cape Verde Islands, New York, and Cape Town.
1820	The *Mayflower of Liberia* sets sail from New York City for the West African country of Sierra Leone, with 86 blacks aboard.
1820	The U.S. Congress passes the Missouri Compromise, whereby slavery is prohibited north of latitude 36°30' and permitted to the south. Maine thereby becomes a free state and Missouri a slave state.
1820	The home of John Read, a free black living in Kennet Township, Pennsylvania, is invaded by two white men: Griffith, a slave owner, and his associate Shipley. Asserting that he is a free man, Read attacks the invaders and kills them; he is acquitted of killing Griffith, but is convicted of manslaughter of Shipley and sentenced to nine years in prison.
1821	The *Alligator*, a ship of the U.S. Navy, departs America for West Africa, to interdict slave vessels, enforce the American ban on the slave trade, and transport a delegation from the American Colonization Society to Africa in search of land to purchase so that American slaves might be returned to the African continent. Dr. Eli Ayres of the society purchases land in exchange for muskets, knives, hats, and shoes and names it Liberia; the *Alligator* successfully seizes slave vessels, including a Portuguese vessel, the *Mariano*, which sinks in 1822 in the Florida Keys after action against pirates from Cuba.
1821	The *Moral Advocate*, a magazine devoted to the abolition of capital punishment, is published by Elisha Bates, a Quaker, in Mount Pleasant, Ohio.
1821	Supported by the American Colonization Society, the republic of Liberia is established in West Africa as the future home for American blacks whom the society hopes to repatriate. Monrovia, named for the U.S. president James Monroe, is the capital.
1822	Rolla, a slave of Governor Bennett of South Carolina, makes a statement about the Vesey slave revolt before he, along with 36 other blacks, is hanged. The rebellion is planned by Denmark Vesey, a slave, who is believed to have enlisted thousands of slaves within 80 miles of Charleston, South Carolina; several informers betray the revolt, and 137 blacks and 4 whites are arrested.

1822	Great Britain negotiates a treaty with Zanzibar in East Africa, halting the slave trade.
1822	In the American Colonization Society's colony of Liberia, it is estimated that by 1899 more than 15,000 former slaves have been resettled. In the years before 1842, more than 40 percent of the slaves are estimated to die in the first six months of their resettlement; the society maintains political control of the territory until 1847, when Liberia gains its independence.
1823	The Society for Mitigating and Gradually Abolishing Slavery throughout the British Dominions (also known as the Anti-Slavery Society) is established in Great Britain to help enact measures ensuring better treatment for slaves, while continuing efforts to ban slavery. The society hopes to attract the support of moderate people who advocate humane treatment even if they do not fight for the abolishment of slavery.
1823	U.S. president James Monroe formulates the Monroe Doctrine, asserting the preeminence of U.S. power and interests in the Americas: "The American continents, by the free and independent condition which they have assumed and maintained, are henceforth not to be considered as subjects for further colonization by any European powers. . . . We . . . declare that we should consider any attempt on their part to extend their system to any portion of this hemisphere as dangerous to our peace and safety."
1823	A law abolishing slavery is passed in Mexico, although Mexico is party to a settlement allowing slaves in Texas.
1824	One year after the Central American Federation of Costa Rica, El Salvador, Guatemala, Honduras, and Nicaragua separates from Mexico, slavery is abolished there. At this time, there are relatively few slaves in the territory, and many slave owners disregard the new law.
1826	After Levi and Catherine Coffin move from the slave state of North Carolina to Indiana, they allow runaway slaves to stay in their home, feed and encourage them, and take them to other sympathetic abolitionists farther north. The Coffins help about a hundred people a year to make the trip on the Underground Railroad safely to the North and Canada; they also help establish a school for local black children and journey to Canada to help provide better living conditions for former slaves.
1827	Slaves living in New York State are freed.
1827	The first African-American newspaper published in the United States is *Freedom's Journal*. Published by Samuel Cornish and John B. Russwurm in New York City, the paper aims to present a true picture of the black condition.
1827	The U.S. newspaper *Freedom's Journal* publishes an account of the lynching of a black man near Tuscaloosa, Alabama. After a planter seized a black man whom he accused of theft and began to beat him, the black stabbed the planter, who died; a mob of 70 or 80 white men, presided over by the justice of the peace, con-

demns the black; they tie him to a tree and burn him to death.

1827   The U.S. newspaper *Freedom's Journal* publishes a letter from a black woman declaring the importance of education for women and stating that mothers should make sure that their daughters are educated in more than housekeeping.

1828   The Cherokee Republic in the state of Georgia is organized, with a constitution modeled on the U.S. Constitution. The Cherokee constitution includes laws regulating enslavement of blacks, such as instituting punishment of Cherokee slave owners for marrying their slaves, buying goods from them, or selling them liquor; slaves cannot vote or hold political office and are considered as property, being bought and sold to settle debts.

1829   David Walker, a dealer in old clothes in Boston, Massachusetts, who had been born to a free mother in North Carolina, becomes active in the Boston Colored Association and publishes a militant antislavery pamphlet entitled *Walker's Appeal, in Four Articles: Together with a Preamble, to the Coloured Citizens of the World, but in Particular, and Very Expressly, to Those of the United States of America, Written in Boston, State of Massachusetts, September 28, 1829.*

1829   The president of Mexico, Vincente Guerrero, of mixed Indian and European descent, a hero of Mexican independence and advocate of poor people, declares the slaves free and commits himself to a program of financial compensation to slave owners. Fiercely opposed by the Americans in the Texas section, he exempts that area but is overthrown and executed shortly thereafter.

1829   In Cincinnati, Ohio, whites attack black residents, forcing 1,200 African-Americans to flee to Canada for safety.

1830   A *firman,* or decree, emancipating Christian slaves who had maintained their religious beliefs is issued in the Ottoman Empire.

1830   An annual national convention of African-Americans first occurs at the Bethel Church in Philadelphia, Pennsylvania. The convention elects the Right Reverend Richard Allen as president and states that it has met to consider the possibility of establishing a homeland in Upper Canada, to escape the recently enacted laws subjecting free black people to restrictions on their residence.

1830   The American abolitionist William Lloyd Garrison, coeditor of the Baltimore, Maryland, newspaper *Genius of Universal Emancipation*, is imprisoned after a slave trader brings a suit for libel.

1831   The American abolitionist William Lloyd Garrison publishes the newspaper the *Liberator*, demanding the immediate dismantling of slavery. Arthur Tappan, a wealthy supporter of abolition, provides funding for the *Liberator*, and the paper is published until 1865.

1831   Nat Turner, leader of a slave revolt in Virginia, is hanged; during the rebellion, 60 whites and more than 100 blacks were killed; 13 slaves and 3 free black men are captured, tried, and executed by hanging. While imprisoned, Turner writes his autobiography, describing his singularity as a child and his God-given mission to free slaves.

1831 On the island of Jamaica, Samuel Sharpe, a slave from Montego Bay, and other slaves born on Jamaica, lead a rebellion that erupts after slaves are prohibited from worshiping in churches of their choice. The British send two companies of troops to Montego Bay to repel the thousands of slaves; 300 are executed by hanging following their conviction, and plantation owners burn Baptist and Methodist churches in retaliation for the rebellion.

1832 Thomas Roderick Dew publishes the *Review of the Debate in Virginia Legislature of 1831 and 1832*, responding to the debate in the Virginia House of Delegates over the issue of abolishing slavery after Nat Turner's rebellion; Dew argues that the costs of deporting slaves would be prohibitive and that most slaves would never adjust to conditions in Africa. Emancipation would never work, he claims, because white Virginians would be unwilling to absorb black slaves into the social and economic fabric; Dew insists that slavery works well for slaves and foresees a gradual replacement of slave labor in Virginia by free white immigrants, while slavery would be confined to the deeper Southern states.

1833 The U.S. Supreme Court rules in *Barron v. Baltimore* that the Bill of Rights is held to apply only to actions by the federal, not the state, government. This principle is eroded through a series of court decisions beginning in the 1920s with First, Fourth, Fifth, Sixth, and Eighth Amendment rights extended to state action.

1833 Prudence Crandall's boarding school for girls in Canterbury, Connecticut, is the first school in the state to accept black students, when Crandall decides to accept Sarah Harris. The school orders Crandall to dismiss Harris or the white students would be dismissed; Crandall refuses and begins a school for black girls instead, but state legislators pass legislation making it difficult for out-of-state black children to attend Connecticut's schools. Crandall is arrested, convicted by the Connecticut Supreme Court, and imprisoned, but later freed on appeal on a technicality. Townspeople harass her, and a mob attacks the school, until Crandall is forced to close the school.

1833 The Reverend Nathaniel Paul of London, England, writes to Judge Andrew T. Judson, criticizing his conviction of Prudence Crandall. Paul writes that he is lecturing on slavery in the United States and will use the Crandall affair in his talks.

1833 Rhode Island is the first state in the United States to ban public executions, ordering them all to be held in private.

1833 In Great Britain, Parliament passes the Emancipation Act, which makes it illegal for British subjects to trade in slaves throughout the empire. Abolitionist pressure combined with rising public concern about, and knowledge of, recent slave uprisings in British Guiana, Jamaica, and Barbados lead to the Act, which allows a transitional period of five years before the end of slavery.

1833   A statute allowing for the extradition of fugitive criminals from foreign countries is passed in Canada, and U.S. slaveholders institute suits demanding recovery of fugitive slaves, based on the fact that their slaves had stolen property from them by running away. A Canadian court rules that Solomon Mosely had committed theft when he stole his owner's horse, took it to Buffalo, New York, sold it, and kept the money when he crossed into Canada; ordered to be extradited, Mosely escapes.

1833   William Lloyd Garrison, the publisher of the *Liberator*, an anti-slavery journal, founds the American Anti-Slavery Society; by 1839 the society has grown to 200,000 members. Critical of the prejudice that he thinks characterizes the American Colonization Society's attempts to send slaves back to Africa, Garrison advocates the immediate end of slavery with compensation to slave owners.

1833   The Philadelphia Negro Library is founded in Philadelphia, Pennsylvania, by a group of black residents, with the intention of cultivating literary pursuits in young people.

1834   Although the British Emancipation Act threatens the economic interests of British colonists, who try to subvert and ignore it, more than 775,000 slaves have been freed from plantations in the British colonies.

1834   South Carolina passes a law prohibiting the education of black children, slave or free.

1834   The first U.S. patent granted to an African-American is to Henry Blair, for a seed planter.

1835   U.S. president Andrew Jackson tries to prohibit the sending of abolitionist literature through the U.S. mail to Southern states.

1835   North Carolina passes a law prohibiting whites from teaching free blacks.

1836   Angelina Grimké, daughter of a slaveholder in Charleston, South Carolina, publishes *An Appeal to the Christian Women of the South*, in which she tries to convince other women that slavery violates Christian teachings and human and natural law. Reaction in the South is hostile; postmasters seize and intercept copies of the pamphlet.

1836   Sarah Moore Grimké, the older sister of Angelina Grimké, publishes *An Epistle to the Clergy of the Southern States*, arguing that the rights of slaves and of women are equally important and that abolition and women's emancipation are moral imperatives. In 1839, the two sisters and Sarah's brother-in-law Theodore Weld edit the study *American Slavery As It Is*.

1836   A letter published in the *New York Sun* by David Ruggles describes the kidnapping of a free black man. George Jones is falsely charged with assault and battery, and, when he goes before the court to answer the charge, the judge takes the word of some men present in the court who claim that Jones is a runaway slave.

1836   White settlers break away from Mexico to declare the independent republic of Texas, whose constitution states that all inhabitants living in the territory at the time of independence would be granted citizenship unless they had been disloyal. White settlers then begin a campaign to expel Mexicans from their land and force them back to Mexican territory.

1837   Elijah P. Lovejoy, a newspaper editor and publisher and a dedicated abolitionist, is shot and killed by an angry mob in Alton, Illinois, where he had moved to publish the *Alton Observer*. In 1833, he had been forced to leave Saint Louis, after publishing in the *Saint Louis Observer*, a Presbyterian weekly that advocated pacifism and an end to slavery, a strong criticism of the public burning of a mulatto sailor for the death of a white police deputy and of the judge's lenient treatment of those who were guilty of the killing of the sailor.

1837   Canada passes legislation allowing blacks to vote.

1837   At a mass meeting in Philadelphia, Pennsylvania, African-Americans protest the decision of the Pennsylvania Constitutional Convention denying them the right to vote. An appeal endorsed at the meeting states that the Pennsylvania Constitution gives every freeman over the age of 21 the right to vote, without reference to color or caste.

1837   The Reverend Theodore S. Wright gives a speech in Utica, New York, about prejudice in the abolitionist movement, at the convention of the New York State Anti-Slavery Society. Wright urges people to discuss openly the evils of slavery and the rights of blacks to equal treatment until slavery is abolished.

1838   Thomas Van Renselaer of Boston, Massachusetts, describes his treatment as a free black man on a steamboat bound for Providence, Rhode Island. Although he had bought a ticket for a berth at $3.50 above the regular fare, a man forces him to leave the cabin and stay on deck, and the captain of the steamboat does not intervene.

1838   Angelina Grimké publishes a philosophical treatise on women's rights entitled *Letters on the Equality of the Sexes and the Condition of Women*, analyzing the conditions of women in the United States and around the world. She writes about legal discrimination, the lack of educational and employment opportunities, and the subjugation of wives by their husbands and argues for new biblical interpretations supporting the equal rights of women as moral beings.

1839   Because bringing slaves into Cuba is no longer permitted, the slave traders on the Portuguese slave vessel the *Tecora* claim their slaves are Cuban, and they are put aboard the Spanish slaver *Amistad* for the trip from Havana to Princípe, Cuba. The slaves had been illegally brought to Havana on the Tecora from the island of Lomboko in West Africa; during that voyage, more than half the human cargo of men, women, and children died.

1839   Off the coast of Cuba, the *Amistad* is seized by 53 black men who had been sold into slavery in Africa; in the mutiny, the rebels kill the captain and cook. The U.S. Coast Guard captures the *Amistad*, which is brought to New York City. U.S. president Martin Van Buren decides to return the ship and the mutineers to Cuba.

1839   Several members of the Homes Missionary Society, together with the Western Evangelical Missionary Society and the Committee for West Indian Missions, organize the American Missionary Association to provide support for the captured Africans who had seized control of the Spanish slave ship *Amistad*. Largely white, the association nevertheless has African-Americans actively participating and voting; all the members are ministers or lay participants of integrated church congregations.

1839   The Liberty Party is founded as an antislavery political party in Warsaw, New York, by Samuel R. Ward and Henry Garnet and others breaking away from the more radical American Anti-Slavery Society. Garnet, a clergyman, had been born a slave in Maryland and works for abolition among blacks.

1839   The U.S. Department of State refuses to issue a passport to a black man, on the grounds that African-Americans are not citizens.

1839   The Danish islands of Saint Thomas, Saint John, and Saint Croix in the West Indies introduce free, compulsory, universal education for all, including slaves. This is prompted in part by continuing efforts of the Lutheran Church, which began providing education for slaves in 1790.

1840   Some members of the American Anti-Slavery Society challenge William Lloyd Garrison's fervent views that the U.S. Constitution is pro-slavery and that the Union itself might have to be dissolved over the critical issue of slavery. They leave to form the more moderate Foreign and American Anti-Slavery Society.

1840   British authorities in the Bahamas, acting to enforce Great Britain's 1833 ban on slavery, seize 38 slaves from the U.S. ship the *Hermosa* when it comes aground near Abaco (in the Bahamas) on a trip from Virginia to New Orleans, Louisiana. Despite protests from the ship's owners and the U.S. consul, a court in Nassau, the Bahamas, frees the slaves.

1840   A report from the World Anti-Slavery Conference in London reveals that the female delegation is excluded from the meeting. Charles Remond also addresses the racial prejudice rampant in the Northern states of America, where blacks are segregated in churches, stagecoaches, and steamboats.

1840   Massachusetts repeals the law forbidding the marriage of whites with blacks, mulattos, or Native Americans.

1841   South Carolina passes a law forbidding black and white mill workers to look out the same window.

1841	A regulation in Atlanta, Georgia, requires black witnesses in court, when swearing an oath before testifying, to use a different Bible than that used by white witnesses.
1841	Solomon Northup, a kidnapped African-American, publishes *Twelve Years a Slave*, describing the auction in New Orleans, Louisiana, at which he is sold as a slave. The slaves are given new clothing and told to move smartly and precisely "while customers would feel of our hands and arms and bodies, turn us about, ask us what we could do, make us open our mouths and show our teeth, precisely as a jockey examines a horse."
1841	Slaves aboard the ship *Creole* revolt during a voyage from Hampton, Virginia, to New Orleans, Louisiana. Taking control of the ship, the slaves sail to the Bahamas, where they are granted asylum.
1841	The Spanish government claims the slaves on the *Amistad* and urges their return as Spanish property. The former president John Quincy Adams agrees to defend the slaves before the U.S. Supreme Court, which rules that the slaves are innocent of the charges and that according to international law the men are free; they are sent back to Africa.
1842	Great Britain negotiates a treaty with Mexico, in which the two countries agree to abolish trading in slaves.
1842	The U.S. Supreme Court, in *Prigg v. Pennsylvania*, overturns a Pennsylvania statute forbidding the kidnapping of fugitive slaves. After Edward Prigg had been convicted under a Pennsylvania statute that made it a felony to carry away any blacks for the purpose of detaining them as a slave, the Supreme Court overturns the conviction and affirms that the authority to regulate policy about fugitive slaves properly resides with Congress, not with the states.
1844	A mass meeting of blacks in Boston, Massachusetts, issues a resolution protesting school segregation and charging that segregated public schools violate the state constitution. The protesters demand that the school committee allow black families to send their children "to the schools established in the respective district" in which they live, but their requests are denied.
1845	Solomon Northup, a kidnapped black, describes the working conditions on a cotton plantation in Bayou Huff Power in Louisiana, where he is taken after being sold at auction. Working from first light to moonlight, those new at picking cotton are beaten on their first day and made to work as fast as possible to set the standard they must attain on following days; if pickers fall below their quotas, they are beaten; on average, slaves must produce about 200 pounds each day.
1845	The American abolitionist Frederick Douglass, himself a slave who had escaped to the North, publishes an autobiography of his experiences as a slave—*Narrative of the Life of Frederick Douglass, an American Slave*—describing the soul-crushing experiences of a field worker. Lecturing in Great Britain and Ireland,

Douglass accumulates the funds to buy his freedom, becomes the editor of an abolitionist newspaper, and at the outbreak of the Civil War helps to recruit black soldiers.

1845   The first African-American lawyer admitted to the bar in the United States is Macon B. Allen, in Worcester, Massachusetts.

1846   Using the concept of Manifest Destiny as justification, the United States invades Mexico and at the Treaty of Hidalgo ending the Mexican War is granted half the territory of Mexico, including Texas, California, and much of New Mexico, Arizona, and parts of Colorado, Utah, and Nevada. Mexican residents of this territory are granted one year's time to choose either Mexican or U.S. citizenship; 75,000 opt to become U.S. citizens.

1846   In a letter to the abolitionist Henry Wright, Frederick Douglass replies to Wright's suggestion that, if Douglass purchases his freedom from his owner, he is tacitly recognizing the principle that one man can own another. Douglass replies that he paid off his purchaser not because the man had a right to own him but because Douglass wanted him to give up his legal claim on him so that Douglass and his family could live in peace.

1847   Michigan becomes the first state to abolish capital punishment for all offenses except treason.

1847   The first African-American to graduate from a U.S. school of medicine is David John Peck, who graduates from the Rush Medical College in Philadelphia, Pennsylvania.

1847   In *Jones v. Van Zandt*, the U.S. Supreme Court affirms the imposition of a $500 fine for concealing and harboring a fugitive slave. In 1842, Van Zandt, a citizen of Ohio, had participated in the attempt to aid and conceal slaves fleeing from Warton Jones, a slaveholder of Kentucky, a violation of sections of the state act that impose a fine for harboring fugitive slaves.

1848   Slavery is abolished in the Danish West Indies islands of Saint Thomas, Saint John, and Saint Croix, after the slaves reject an offer by King Christian VIII of Denmark to free all children born to slaves on his birthday and to postpone full emancipation until 1859. After almost 8,000 slaves gather to demand complete freedom, the governor decrees emancipation; some plantation owners resist, and there are riots, but slavery is abolished.

1848   France rules it illegal to trade in slaves throughout its colonies. The French colonists, however, employ a strategy of creating protectorates not subject to French law and installing what they claim are tribal governments, with chiefs dependent on the slave trade.

1848   Postmasters in Virginia are required to notify police about any abolitionist literature in the mails; the police seize and burn this literature.

1849   Harriet Tubman escapes from slavery in Maryland and travels to Philadelphia, Pennsylvania, using the position of the North Star as her guide. Tubman returns to Virginia and Maryland on more than 20 occasions to lead some 300 slaves to freedom, stopping at Underground Railroad safe houses along the way.

1850   The U.S. Fugitive Slave Act is passed as part of Senator Henry Clay's Compromise. The law gives slave owners the right to pursue and capture their runaway slaves in states that had prohibited slavery and calls for the punishment of those who help in the escape of slaves; federal marshals give rewards to those who participate in the capture of runaway slaves.

1850   The U.S. Foreign Miners Tax Law requires a tax to be paid by anyone not a citizen.

1850   The American League of Colored Laborers, established in New York, is the first African-American labor union in the United States. Samuel Ward is elected president; the union's mandate is to train skilled crafts workers and to support and create black-owned businesses.

1851   In *To Our Old Masters*, Henry Bibb, an ex-slave from the United States, writes a series of letters detailing life for slaves and fugitive slaves. Residing in Ontario, Canada, Bibb writes that, though slavery has always existed, slaves have never accepted their condition; Bibb tells slave owners that the civilized world hates them.

1851   In Brazil, the Parliament passes legislation prohibiting the slave trade, yet from 1865 to 1870, when Brazil is allied with Argentina and Uruguay against Paraguay, the army purchases slaves to fight. Surviving slaves are awarded their freedom.

1851   Virginia passes a law requiring that freed slaves leave the state within one year of their freedom or be enslaved again.

1851   In Pennsylvania, U.S. marshals along with Edward Gorsuch and his relatives arrive in Christiana, a Quaker village, to recover two slaves, Joshua Hammond and Nelson Ford, who fled two years earlier and are hiding at the home of a black farmer, William Parker; when Parker's wife alerts their neighbors, many, black and white, gather to prevent the seizure of Hammond and Ford. Gorsuch refuses to retreat, and in the ensuing melee Gorsuch is killed and three of his group wounded. President Millard Fillmore sends U.S. Marines along with a contingent of police from Philadelphia to Christiana; 40 blacks and 6 whites are arrested, but Hammond, Ford, Parker, and two others flee to Canada and successfully resist extradition.

1852   Harriet Beecher Stowe publishes *Uncle Tom's Cabin*, bringing abolition into the public arena. More than 300,000 copies of the novel are sold in its first year of publication.

1852   Martin R. Delany, born to a slave father and free mother, writes *The Condition, Elevation, Emigration, and Destiny of the Colored People of the United States, Politically Considered*, partially in response to the U.S. Fugitive Slave Act; Delany points out that racism is at the heart of slavery and that the proper response is self-determination and emigration to found an African-American state. Delany later writes a novel, *Blake; or, The Huts of America*, and serves as a major leading African-American troops during the Civil War.

1852   The California Supreme Court rules in *People v. Tanner* that the death penalty is constitutional for the crime of grand larceny, and Tanner is hanged.

1852   Wells Brown, an African-American, publishes the novel *Clotel, A Tale of the Southern States*, in the United States.

1853–1855   Joseph-Arthur de Gobineau, a French diplomat and philosopher, publishes his *Essai sur l'inégalité des races humaines* (Essay on the inequality of the human races), in which he expounds his theory of Aryan, or white, racial superiority. His anti-Semitic writings influence the German composer Richard Wagner and Adolf Hitler as well as eugenicists in Europe and the United States; the U.S. immigration legislation of 1921 and 1924, limiting immigration from eastern and southern Europe, owes something to his now completely discredited notions.

1854   The 15-year legal battle over the *Hermosa*, the slave ship seized by British authorities, is finally brought before a commission of claims, with representatives from the British and U.S. governments. Because the representatives cannot agree on a mutual solution, the case is decided in 1855 by an umpire, Joshua Bates, a London banker, who rules that the ship's owner is due compensation of $16,000.

1854   Venezuela decides to abolish slavery gradually.

1854   The U.S. Congress passes the Kansas-Nebraska Act, repealing the Missouri Compromise of 1820, and removing the prohibitions against slavery north of the 36°30' latitude in the Louisiana territory. Crafted by Senator Stephen Douglas of Illinois, the Kansas-Nebraska Act declares that the citizens of the territories of Kansas and Nebraska have the right to determine whether to permit slavery in their territories; pro slavers from Missouri quickly move into Kansas, and the political parties splinter along pro- and antislavery lines. At that time, there are approximately 4 million slaves in the U.S. South, worth about $3 billion to the plantation economy.

1854   Thomas Wentworth Higginson, a minister, tries without success to free the fugitive slave Anthony Burns in Boston, Massachusetts, when Burns's master turns down an offer of $1,200 raised by Boston abolitionists. Higginson becomes involved in the Massachusetts Kansas Committee, actively supporting the free-state settlers and helping to secure guns and ammunition; he helps raise money for John Brown's 1859 raid on Harpers Ferry and comes to Brown's defense after he is captured.

1854   Margaret Douglass, a white seamstress who runs a school for African-American children in violation of Virginia law prohibiting the education of slaves or freed blacks, is arrested and spends a month in jail.

1854	The first African-American college in the United States is Ashmun Institute (Lincoln University), established in Oxford, Pennsylvania.
1855	Massachusetts passes a law abolishing school segregation.
1855	A law passed in the state of Massachusetts forbids state officials to aid federal officials in capturing fugitive slaves.
1855	Berea College, in Berea, Kentucky, is established by the American Missionary Association and accepts its first black student in 1866. The association helps to found other integrated schools and colleges, including Fisk University in Memphis, Tennessee; Atlanta University in Atlanta, Georgia; LeMoyne, now LeMoyne-Owen College, in Memphis; Hampton Normal and Agricultural Institute, now Hampton University, in Hampton, Virginia; and Tougaloo College in Tougaloo, Mississippi. The association works not only for an end to slavery but also for the abolishment of class privilege, greed, and hatred; for better conditions for Chinese and Japanese immigrants; and for the rights of Native Americans and of poor whites in Appalachia.
1855	John Mercer Langston becomes the first African-American to win election to office in the United States when he is elected to serve as the clerk of Brownhelm Township in Ohio.
1856	Virginia establishes an inspection system to ensure that every boat leaving its ports is checked to prevent fugitive slaves from escaping by sea. Runaway slave hunters are offered financial compensation, including a mileage allowance for travel. By 1860, 15 whites and free blacks are serving prison sentences for encouraging or participating in the escape of slaves.
1857	In *Scott v. Sandford*, known as the Dred Scott case, the U.S. Supreme Court rules that slaves are not citizens of the United States. Dred Scott argues that since his master, Dr. John Emerson, had moved him from St. Louis, Missouri, into territories where Congress had prohibited slavery, he is now a free man, but Chief Justice Roger B. Taney writes that not only are freed slaves not citizens but they are considered as property; this judgment officially renders the Missouri Compromise unconstitutional: Congress cannot prohibit slavery in certain territories.
1857	Laws passed in Maine and New Hampshire grant freedom and citizenship to African-Americans, in defiance of federal fugitive-slave laws.
1857	A *firman*, or decree, abolishing slavery throughout the Ottoman Empire is issued, except for the territory of the Arabian peninsula. The excluded territory includes Mecca and Medina, areas where slave merchants exercise significant power.
1859	The U.S. Supreme Court, in *Ableman v. Booth*, decides that state courts cannot overrule federal laws and decisions supporting slavery. After Sherman Booth and John Rycraft are convicted by a federal court for aiding a fugitive slave, they appeal to the Wisconsin State Supreme Court, which orders their release and

rules that the U.S. Fugitive Slave Act of 1850 is unconstitutional. The U.S. Supreme Court denies the ruling and the ability of state courts to overturn federal courts, declaring that it "would subvert the very foundation of this Government" and reaffirming that the Fugitive Slave Act of 1850 is "in all its provisions fully authorized by the Constitution."

1859	Hoping that militant action will spark a nationwide revolt of slaves, the abolitionist John Brown attacks the U.S. arsenal at Harpers Ferry, Virginia, with 22 whites, free blacks, and former slaves. Federal troops and the local militia surround the armory and kill 10 of Brown's men; John Brown is hanged in Virginia.
1860	Arkansas passes a law prohibiting the employment of free blacks on boats in state waters.
1860	The first African-American baseball team to tour the United States is the Brooklyn Excelsiors.
1860	The social reformer Jane Addams establishes the first settlement house for poor people in the United States, when she founds Hull House in Chicago, Illinois. Hull House becomes a center of social reform and plays a leading role in advocating new rights for workers, poor people, children, and women. In 1931, Addams is awarded the Nobel Prize for Peace for her work in the international peace movement.
1861	Great Britain annexes Lagos in southwest Nigeria and rules that the slave trade is illegal there.
1861	Representatives of South Carolina, Florida, Georgia, Alabama, Louisiana, and Mississippi meet and decide to secede from the United States over the protection of domestic slavery and to form the Confederate States of America. Soon after, Texas, Virginia, Tennessee, Arkansas, and North Carolina join the Confederacy, and Jefferson B. Davis, a planter, politician, and military officer, is elected president.
1861	The Georgia Code, the common law of the state of Georgia, classifies residents into five categories: citizens of Georgia, residents who are not citizens, aliens, slaves, and free people of color; all people of color are slaves or must prove that they are not slaves. Slaves are a form of property, with no rights; they cannot purchase their freedom without an act of the legislature, and masters cannot free their slaves in their wills.
1861	The U.S. Congress passes the Confiscation Act, providing for the confiscation of any property used, with knowledge and consent by an owner, in the act of aiding or abetting an insurrection against the United States. Directed against the Southern states, the law includes slaves as property to be legally seized, and slaves so seized are freed, often with no place to go.
1861	Private William H. Johnson is shot by a firing squad for desertion from the Union Army during the Civil War.
1861	The U.S. secretary of the navy decides to authorize the enlistment of blacks in the navy. On the same day, General John C.

	Frémont announces military emancipation in Missouri, but President Abraham Lincoln countermands the decision.
1861	Czar Alexander II of Russia issues a decree freeing house serfs from their lords.
1861	The first African-American to hold a U.S. federal civilian post is William C. Neil, who is appointed a postal clerk in Boston, Massachusetts.
1862	The first African-American woman in the United States to earn an M.A. degree is Mary Jane Patterson, at Oberlin College.
1862	Captain Nathaniel Gordon becomes the first ship captain hanged in New York City for violating the ban on the slave trade.
1862	U.S. president Abraham Lincoln recommends a voluntary colonization program for free blacks in Liberia or Haiti. The next month, the U.S. Congress passes a joint resolution in support of gradual emancipation; the Senate passes a bill emancipating the slaves of the District of Columbia, providing slave owners $300 a head compensation and allocating $100,000 for Lincoln's colonization plans.
1862	General David Hunter orders the emancipation of slaves in South Carolina, Georgia, and Florida, but President Abraham Lincoln countermands the proclamation.
1862	Robert Smalls, a former slave and crew member in the Confederate Navy, sails the Confederate ship the *Planter* from Charleston, South Carolina, and surrenders it to the United States. Smalls later serves five terms in the U.S. House of Representatives.
1862	The U.S. Congress authorizes the recruitment of black soldiers into the Union Army. While white soldiers receive $13 a month and $3.50 clothing allowance, black soldiers are paid $7 a month, with $3.00 for clothing; 38,000 blacks of the 186,000 who serve in the army die during the Civil War.
1862	At a mass meeting of African-Americans on Long Island, New York, a resolution is issued criticizing President Abraham Lincoln's plan for African colonization. The people state that they are not different from other Americans, that they consider America their country and feel a closeness to the land and the white inhabitants, and that they want to stay in the United States and enjoy the benefits constitutionally extended to white citizens.
1862	The First South Carolina Volunteers, an all-black regiment in the Union Army, is established during the Civil War. Thomas Wentworth Higginson, the Boston minister and abolitionist, is named colonel, and the recruits are freed slaves.
1862	The U.S. Homestead Act passed in the U.S. Congress allows people to settle on and claim "vacant" land, in actuality land often owned by Mexicans.
1863	U.S. president Abraham Lincoln issues the Emancipation Proclamation, declaring that all slaves residing in the Confederate

states that are fighting the Union are free; the proclamation does not apply to the approximately 800,000 slaves living in Missouri, Delaware, Maryland, and Kentucky, the border states, and it is more symbolic than legal, the abolition of slavery requiring the passage of an amendment to the U.S. Constitution. Lincoln had previously recommended a plan of gradual emancipation tied to financial compensation to slave owners, and he seems far more concerned with the strategic necessity of crippling the slave economy of the Confederacy than with any deep sense of the immorality of racism or slavery.

1863   The American Freedmen's Inquiry Commission is established by the U.S. Congress to determine how best to make the transition from slavery and how to integrate former slaves into American society. Inviting testimony from former slaves and slave owners, the commission acknowledges that slavery has shattered family life and cohesion, and it advocates programs to assist slaves, such as the Port Royal Experiment initiated in South Carolina.

1863   Fanny Kemble's *Journal of a Residence on a Georgian Plantation in 1838–1839* is published in England; Frances Anne Kemble, a famous beauty and member of a celebrated British family of actors, had married Pierce Butler of Philadelphia, Pennsylvania, unaware that he owns a 2,000-acre Georgia rice plantation where they will live. Kemble's narrative highlights the inhumane treatment of Butler's many slaves, the filthy slave quarters, the sick children, and the dehumanization of the slave overseers. Kemble divorced Butler in 1848 and returned to the stage.

1863   A race riot occurs in New York City when poor whites protest the Civil War Draft Law, which allows wealthy whites to pay $300 for an exemption from service. Poor whites, mainly working-class German and Irish immigrants, turn their rage on blacks, who are not forced to serve in the Army and who, the rioters suspect, might take their jobs. About 1,000 people die, nearly all black; similar riots happen at the same time in Boston, Massachusetts, and Troy, New York.

1863   Convinced that the U.S. Constitution must be amended, Elizabeth Cady Stanton and Susan B. Anthony organize the Women's Loyal National League, the first suffrage organization in the United States to oppose slavery. The league collects the signatures of 400,000 Americans who advocate the end of slavery; Stanton had initiated the women's suffrage movement in 1848, while Anthony, who also advocates women's suffrage, is one of the first to argue for African-American suffrage.

1864   The U.S. Congress passes legislation mandating equal wages for black and white soldiers.

1864   Capital punishment is abolished in Romania.

1864   Sergeant William Walker of the Third South Carolina Regiment, a black soldier, is court-martialed for protesting the discriminatory conditions of military service for blacks and is shot.

1864   The first African-American woman to graduate from a U.S. medical school is Rebecca Lee Crumpler, who receives a medical decree from New England Female Medical College.

1864   The Geneva Convention on victims of war is signed, committing the signatory governments to care for any wounded during a war, regardless of nationality; the Convention is later revised to protect victims of warfare at sea (1907), prisoners of war (1929), and civilians in time of war (1949). The Geneva Convention is the first multilateral agreement of the Red Cross, which was established to care for victims of war but later aided in the general prevention and relief of human suffering. The "Red Cross" is the name used in countries under Christian sponsorship, whereas "Red Crescent" (adopted in 1906 at the insistence of the Ottoman Empire) is the name used in Muslim countries.

1865   After the Civil War, the Southern states pass laws maintaining white supremacy; in South Carolina, for instance, African-Americans entering the state are required to post a $1,000 bond to guarantee their good behavior. Another regulation allows employers to whip their black employees, and other states pass thinly veiled regulations against "vagrancy" and mandate curfews.

1865   J. T. Shutten publishes the first African-American newspaper in the American South: the *Colored American*, in Augusta, Georgia.

1865   The American Freedman's Aid Commission is established as a coalition committee of freedman-aid societies in Boston, New York, Chicago, Cincinnati, and Philadelphia; it is organized to deal with the social and economic obstacles faced by the large numbers of newly freed slaves after the Civil War. The commission works closely with the new federal agency, the Freedman's Bureau, to increase educational opportunities for African-Americans. Abolitionists like Frederick Douglass, who had been born a slave, criticize it for encouraging blacks to rely on the generosity of whites, while other interest groups pressure the commission to include as recipients of its aid program Southern whites sympathetic to the Union, and evangelicals push it to add religious instruction to its curriculum. It disbands in 1869.

1865   The Ku Klux Klan is established in Pulaski, Tennessee, by six former officers of the Confederate Army, to harass the Republican governments newly in office and their leaders in the Southern states and to maintain the power of whites over blacks in the South. Wearing white robes and masks, Klan members terrorize opponents and burn crosses, eventually becoming an illegal organization.

1865   The 13th Amendment to the U.S. Constitution, abolishing slavery, is adopted. The amendment reads in part: "Neither slavery nor involuntary servitude, except as a punishment for crime whereof the party shall have been duly convicted, shall exist within the United States, or any place subject to their jurisdiction."

1865   The states of Connecticut, Wisconsin, and Minnesota deny African-Americans the right to vote.

1865   The first African-American to gain the rank of major in the U.S. Army is Martin R. Delany. Delany has many skills: he is a writer, has graduated from Howard University Medical School, and serves in the U.S. Army Medical Corps.

1865   The first African-American attorney to practice before the U.S. Supreme Court is John Rock.

1866   Fisk University, a university for African-Americans, is established in Nashville, Tennessee.

1866   The first African-Americans to serve in a legislative assembly are Charles Mitchell and Edward Walker, elected to the Massachusetts House of Representatives.

1866   A race riot occurs in Memphis, Tennessee, when whites target black veterans. Forty-eight people are killed, and several black women are raped.

1866   During a race riot in New Orleans, Louisiana, 35 people are killed, and more than 100 are injured, when police help to spark violence against blacks.

1867   Capital punishment is abolished in Portugal.

1867   Atlanta University in Atlanta, Georgia, is founded as an undergraduate college. Atlanta University becomes the first all-black graduate school in the United States when it receives its charter for graduate education in 1929.

1867   The state of Iowa and the Dakota Territory decide to grant African-Americans the right to vote.

1867   The first African-American to graduate from Harvard University School of Dentistry is Robert Tanner Freeman.

1868   The U.S. National Association of Baseball decides to exclude teams with black players. The association declares that if blacks are admitted, disagreements will arise among the clubs.

1868   The 14th Amendment to the U.S. Constitution, elaborating on equal protection and due process, is adopted. The amendment states, "All persons born or naturalized in the United States, and subject to the jurisdiction thereof, are citizens of the United States and of the state wherein they reside. No state shall make or enforce any law which shall abridge the privileges or immunities of citizens of the United States; nor shall any state deprive any person of life, liberty, or property, without due process of law; nor deny to any person within its jurisdiction the equal protection of the laws."

1868   The first African-American elected a lieutenant governor of a state is Oscar Dunn, a captain in the Union Army and a former slave, who is elected to that office in Louisiana.

1868   The U.S. Congress votes to override a presidential veto of a bill extending to African-Americans the right to vote in the District of Columbia. President Andrew Johnson had vetoed the legislation.

1869   The first African-American to be appointed to serve in the U.S. Diplomatic Corps is Ebenezer Don Carlos Bassett, who becomes the minister to Haiti.

1870   The first African-American elected to the U.S. Senate is Hiram R. Revel, who is elected to that office from Mississippi.

1870   The first African-American to graduate with honors from Harvard University is Richard Greener, who becomes a lawyer in South Carolina and then in 1879 dean of the Howard University Law School.

1870   Jonathan Jasper Wright is appointed associate justice of the South Carolina Supreme Court and becomes the highest-ranking African-American judicial officer in the United States. Whites constantly try to have him removed.

1870   The Netherlands abolishes capital punishment.

1870   The first two African-Americans elected to the U.S. House of Representatives are Joseph Rainey of South Carolina and Jefferson Long of Georgia.

1870   The 15th Amendment to the U.S. Constitution, declaring that rights cannot be denied on racial grounds, is adopted. The amendment states in part, "The right of citizens of the United States to vote shall not be denied or abridged by the United States or by any state on account of race, color, or previous condition of servitude." Though the amendment has the effect of limiting the rights of states to infringe on the rights of African-Americans, soon after its passage former leaders of the Confederate states begin a campaign of poll taxes and literacy tests designed to thwart African-Americans from registering to vote.

1871   The *Lei do ventre livre* (Law of free birth), passed by the Parliament in Brazil, grants freedom to children born of slaves; owners of Brazilian coffee plantations oppose the legislation. Under the law, the masters of the mothers are responsible for providing care until the children are 8 years old and for that care are granted cash reimbursements from a national fund as compensation or the right to the child's labor until he or she is 21; the law requires a national slave registry and provides national funds to purchase freedom for some slaves.

1872   The first African-American to serve as governor of a state is Pinckney Benton Stewart Pinchback, who is appointed temporary governor of Louisiana.

1872   The first African-American to attend the U.S. Naval Academy at Annapolis, Maryland, is James Henry Conyers.

1872   The first African-American woman to practice as a physician is Rebecca Cole, who practices in New York City.

1873   The first African-American to serve as a municipal judge is M. W. Gibbs, elected in Little Rock, Arkansas.

1873	The first African-American woman believed to be formally certified as a physician is Susan McKinney.
1873	The U.S. Senate refuses to seat an African-American, Pinckney Benton Stewart Pinchback, who had been elected to the U.S. Senate from Louisiana; Senate debaters raise questions about the election process in Louisiana, but many believe Pinchback's race is at issue. Appointed temporary governor of Louisiana in 1872, Pinchback had previously won election to the U.S. House of Representatives.
1873	Under pressure from Great Britain, Zanzibar, a region in East Africa, bans the use of public slave markets with the signing of the Kirk-Barghash Treaty.
1874	The Gold Coast in East Africa ends the slave trade.
1874	Frances Stewart, a grandmother, is hanged in London, England, for killing her grandchild.
1876	The U.S. Civil Rights Bill, prohibiting racial discrimination in public accommodations and setting fines for failing to carry out the law, is enacted.
1876	The first African-American to be awarded a Ph.D. degree in the United States is the physicist Edward A. Bouchet, of Yale University.
1876	The first African-American medical school in the United States is the Meharry Medical College, established in Nashville, Tennessee.
1877	In *Ex parte Jackson*, the U.S. Supreme Court rules that sealed packages and letters in the U.S. mail are secure against unreasonable search and seizure. A man indicted for knowingly and unlawfully depositing in the mail a circular enclosed in an envelope concerning a lottery offering prizes is tried, convicted, fined $100, and sentenced to jail until the fine is paid; Justice Stephen Johnson Field writes that sealed packages and letters sent with letter postage in the U.S. mail and not meant to be opened for inspection are as free from unreasonable searches and seizures under the Fourth Amendment as if they were still in the senders' homes.
1878	A peace treaty between the Spanish and Cubans, the Peace of Zanjón, recognizes that slaves who fought with the Cubans for independence would gain their freedom.
1879	The U.S. Supreme Court decides, in *Strauder v. West Virginia*, that a West Virginia law denying blacks the right to serve as jurors violates the 14th Amendment. A defendant asks to have his case removed from state court to the U.S. Circuit Court because, as a black man and former slave and because blacks cannot serve on a jury, he believes that he would not receive the same benefits under the laws of West Virginia as would white citizens; Justice William Strong writes that the West Virginia statute disagrees with the 14th Amendment and is discriminatory.

1879	The first African-American woman to gain a degree in nursing is Mary E. Mattoney, who graduates from the New England Hospital for Women and Children in Boston, Massachusetts.
1881	The first state to require segregation in railroad cars is Tennessee. Other states follow suit.
1883	The U.S. Supreme Court rules that the Civil Rights Act of 1875 is unconstitutional, in relation to several cases brought in appeal of $500 fines for a variety of violations of the Civil Rights Acts, including a conductor of a railroad company who denies a black woman the right to ride in the white ladies' car; innkeepers who deny a black person accommodations; and a theater owner who denies admission to a black patron. Justice Joseph Bradley states that the 14th Amendment does not give Congress the power to pass legislation such as the Civil Rights Acts (which declare that all people are entitled to equal accommodations and privileges, without referring to adverse state legislation) and that redress must be sought either in the laws of the states or in such corrective legislation as Congress may adopt.
1883	France rules that any slave entering French territory is freed.
1883	The Abolitionist Confederacy of Brazil is founded by José do Patrocíno, owner of the Brazilian newspaper *Gazeta da Tarde* (Evening gazette), and the organization soon organizes marches and distributes its manifesto. Brazil, which by 1600 provided most of Europe with more than 55 million pounds of sugar each year, had been one of the largest and richest slave-owning societies in the Western Hemisphere; not only do slaves carry out the difficult work of planting, cutting, and processing sugarcane, but from 1702, the discovery of rich gold deposits increases the need for slave labor in the country.
1884	The first African-American to become a major-league baseball player is Moses Fleetwood Walker, who plays in the American Association for Toledo, Ohio.
1884	The May Day movement begins in the United States when the Federation of Organized Trades and Labor Unions passes a motion calling for an eight-hour workday. The movement is based primarily in Chicago, Illinois, and is organized by the anarchist group the International Working People's Association.
1885	The first African-American baseball team is the Cuban Giants of New York City. The Giants are all waiters at a hotel on Long Island, New York, and the team is established by Frank Thompson.
1885	The first African-American elected to the supreme court of South Carolina is Jonathan Jasper Wright.
1885	The Sexagenarian Law passed by the Parliament in Brazil gives freedom to elderly slaves.
1886	The Colored Farmers' Alliance is established in the United States to help improve the life of African-American farmers. By 1890, the alliance has a membership of 1 million.

1886   The U.S. Supreme Court decides, in *Boyd v. United States*, that the demand to produce papers, and the use of that evidence against defendants, is unconstitutional. In a case involving the seizure and forfeiture of 35 cases of plate glass from the Port of New York and the prosecution of the defendants for violations of an 1874 Act, the defendants are ordered to produce the invoice of the cases; they comply under protest and are convicted; Justice Joseph Bradley writes that the notice to produce the invoice is unconstitutional and violates the Fourth Amendment.

1886   The Georgia State Supreme Court rules to sustain the will of a slave owner's bequest of half a million dollars to a black woman. The deceased man's white relatives unsuccessfully argue that a white man does not have the right to leave property to his illegitimate black children.

1886   During a strike at the McCormick Reaper Works Factory in Chicago, Illinois, on May 3, police open fire on the demonstrators, killing four and wounding many others.

1886   In connection with the strike at the McCormick Reaper Works Factory in Chicago, Illinois, a labor rally in support of the eight-hour workday is held in Haymarket Square on May 4. It ends in violence, as a bomb explodes, killing one police officer and wounding 70 others. Eight anarchists—only one of whom is actually known to have attended the rally—are convicted of conspiracy to commit murder, although the origin of the bomb is never discovered and no evidence is found connecting the defendants with the bomb. Four of them are hanged on November 11, 1887, one commits suicide in prison, and the remaining three are pardoned in 1893.

1888   Slavery is ended in Brazil.

1889–1890   At the Brussels Conference held in Brussels, Belgium, the United States, the Ottoman Empire, Denmark, Sweden, Russia, Austria, Holland, Great Britain, Germany, France, Portugal, Italy, Spain, Zanzibar, Persia, and the Congo meet to negotiate a treaty banning the African slave trade. The General Act for the Repression of the African Slave Trade distinguishes between domestic slavery and other forms of exploitation of human labor and also justifies increased European action on the African continent under the guise of bringing Christianity to backward people and ending the slave trade.

1890   William Francis Kennedy becomes the first person to be executed by electrocution, in New York.

1890   The constitutional convention of Mississippi establishes literacy and "understanding" tests and a poll tax for prospective voters, used to discourage potential black voters from registering.

1890   One of the first African-American millionaires in the United States is Thomy Gafon, a moneylender and real estate speculator in Louisiana.

1890   The first black boxer to win a world title is George Dixon of Halifax, Nova Scotia, who defeats Nunc Wallace in London, England.

1892   A football match between two black college teams is played in the United States, when the Biddle College team defeats Livingstone College, 4 to 0.

1892   The U.S. Congress passes an act that reduces the number of capital offenses from 17 to 3: treason, rape, and murder.

1895   The court of the Choson dynasty in Korea abolishes slavery.

1896   In *Plessy v. Ferguson*, the U.S. Supreme Court rules that separate but equal accommodations based on race do not violate the Constitution. When a man of mixed race purchases a first-class railway ticket and refuses to move to the colored section of the train, he is arrested and charged with violating a statute providing separate but equal accommodations for white and black passengers; Justice Henry B. Brown denies the claim that the law violates the 13th and 14th Amendments and states that a statute distinguishing between races merely on the basis of color does not destroy the legal equality of the races.

1896   *The Suppression of the African Slave Trade to the United States of America, 1538–1870*, by the educator and writer W. E. B. Du Bois, is published in the United States by the Harvard Historical Studies. Du Bois uses the records of West African slave ports and other primary sources to demonstrate that even while the United States is claiming to halt the Atlantic slave trade, as many as 250,000 slaves are imported between 1808 and 1862.

1896   In *Rosen v. United States*, the U.S. Supreme Court affirms the conviction of a man who sent an obscene 12-page paper through the mail. Justice John Marshall Harlan writes that even though the defendant claims that he did not regard the paper as obscene, he has committed an offense by mailing the paper.

1897   In Zanzibar in East Africa, a ruling outlaws the legal status of "slave." In 1909, the institution of slavery is abolished.

1898   As a result of an amendment to the constitution of Louisiana, which includes a grandfather clause to voting statutes, black voters are disenfranchised. The 130,000 black voters of 1896 are reduced to 5,000 black voters in 1900.

1900   W. E. B. Du Bois, the American educator, addresses an international Conference of African and New World intellectuals in London, England. He declares race *the* problem of the 20th century.

1900   Booker T. Washington, the American educator who had been born a slave in Virginia, establishes the National Negro Business League in Boston, Massachusetts, as an association of African-American businesspeople.

1901   Ending its policy of not accepting minority members, the American Federation of Labor allows the affiliation of the Federación Libre de los Trabajadores (Workers Labor Federation).

1902   *Off Bloomingdale Asylum*, shot in Paris, France, is the first film to use black actors.

1903	A ruling in French West Africa abolishes the rights of masters over slaves.
1903	In *Giles v. Harris*, the U.S. Supreme Court rules that it cannot undo a case of discrimination in voter registration. Although 5,000 black citizens of Montgomery County, Alabama, had been denied the right to enroll to vote under statutes of the Alabama Constitution, Justice Oliver Wendell Holmes writes that the Court cannot correct a political wrong; such an act is in the hands of the state or the federal legislative branch.
1903	The first African-American woman to become a bank president is Maggie Lena Walker, who establishes the Saint Luke Penny Thrift Savings Bank in Richmond, Virginia.
1905	In France, a ruling outlawing any transaction in humans is issued. By 1906, slaves in French colonies begin leaving their masters, and it is believed that between 1906 and 1913 almost a million slaves leave their slave owners.
1905	Germany rules that any slave in East Africa born after 1890 is free. Only 10 percent of slaves, unsure of their status, leave immediately, though within the next decade, most slaves leave their slave owners.
1906	Spurred on by press reports that white women had been attacked by black men, a race riot erupts in Atlanta, Georgia; rioters kill 12 people, including several well-respected African-Americans. Many blacks decide to leave Atlanta, and following the riot interracial groups, organized by the Atlantic Civic League, meet to discuss how to improve communication between the races and how to improve living conditions for blacks.
1906	After African-American soldiers respond to racial taunting, a race riot breaks out in Brownsville, Texas, and three whites are killed. Despite protests from the black community, President Theodore Roosevelt orders that the soldiers receive dishonorable discharges from the Army; three years of advocacy by Senator Joseph Foraker of Ohio finally results in a court of inquiry and reenlistment of some of those involved.
1907	Kansas abolishes capital punishment.
1907	The first African-American to receive a Rhodes scholarship to study at Oxford University is Alain Locke, who publishes *Race Contacts and Interracial Relations* in 1916. In 1918, Locke is awarded a Ph.D. from Harvard University, and in 1924 he publishes *The New Negro*.
1908	The U.S. Supreme Court, in *Berea College v. Kentucky*, upholds segregation in a private institution. Although Kentucky has a law prohibiting biracial education, Berea College allows it and is indicted by a grand jury in Madison County, Kentucky; Justice David Josiah Brewer writes that Berea College has whatever right to teach that the state gives it, but no natural right to teach anyone.
1908	Alpha Kappa Alpha, an African-American fraternity, is estab-

lished at Howard University in Nashville, Tennessee.

1908   The first African-American heavyweight boxing champion is Jack Johnson, who defeats Tommy Burns.

1909   The National Association for the Advancement of Colored People (NAACP) is established in New York City by a coalition of black leaders and white progressives, including the educator and psychologist John Dewey, the social reformer Jane Addams, and Helen Frances Garrison Villard, wife of the financier and journalist Henry Villard. The formation of the NAACP is spurred in part by a 1908 race riot in Springfield, Illinois, near Abraham Lincoln's birthplace; until Martin Luther King Jr.'s Southern Christian Leadership Conference is founded in 1957, the NAACP is the primary advocate for the rights of black people in the United States.

1910   The National Urban League, established in New York City, helps Southern blacks who migrate to the North to make the transition to life in the Northern United States.

1910   Portugal abolishes slavery, following intense public discussions of the transfer of slaves from Angola (former Portuguese West Africa) to work on the cocoa plantations of São Tomé and Principe, an island west of the African mainland.

1910   An imperial edict is issued in China abolishing slavery, with a prefaced historical overview explaining when the practice of slavery was introduced into China and how it became established.

1910   *The Crisis*, the newsletter of the National Association for the Advancement of Colored People (NAACP), is first published, with W. E. B. Du Bois as editor.

1914   In *Weeks v. United States*, the U.S. Supreme Court decides that seizure of private papers violates the Constitution. Justice William Rufus Day writes that the Court cannot sanction using unlawful seizures and forced confessions to convict a person.

1914   The Universal Negro Improvement Association, established by the nationalist Marcus Garvey in Jamaica, advocates civil rights for blacks, economic self-sufficiency, racial pride, and a return to a black-governed state in Africa. In 1916, Garvey establishes a chapter in New York.

1915   *The Birth of a Nation*, an epic film by D. W. Griffith, romanticizes the post–Civil War Klan and its tactics. The film is wildly popular; the NAACP and other groups protest its showing in vain.

1915   Using the previous Klan as a model, a new organization, the Invisible Empire, Knights of the Ku Klux Klan, arises in Georgia; becoming active in many parts of the country after World War I, the Klan now opposes not only blacks but anyone who is not a white Protestant. Associating itself with a Nazi-financed organization, the German-American Bund, it holds a rally in 1940; it disbands in 1944 because it cannot pay back taxes owed to the government, and in 1947 Georgia revokes the Klan char-

ter. The Klan revives, however, during the civil rights movement
and is involved in bombings and racial violence; gaining members after passage of the 1964 Civil Rights Act, the Klan survives, with its leaders seeking and winning public office.

1915 The U.S. Supreme Court, in *Guinn v. United States*, rules that
grandfather clauses that states had been using to deny voting
rights to African-Americans are outlawed.

1915 For the first time in modern warfare, Germany uses poison gas
during World War I, on the western front not far from Ypres
(Ieper) in Belgium. German soldiers line up gas cylinders and
release them to break through the French and Canadian lines;
without protection from the deadly gases, which had never been
encountered before, those who cannot escape suffer an agonizing
death or permanent disability. After this initial use, all sides
begin using poisonous gas.

1915 U.S. president Woodrow Wilson signs the La Follette Seamen's
Act, giving sailors the full rights of free men, including living
wages and humane treatment while aboard ship.

1916 The Association for the Study of Negro Life and History is
founded by the historian Carter G. Woodson to ensure that African-American life is realistically portrayed. Born the son of
former slaves, Woodson receives a Ph.D. from Harvard University and edits the *Journal of Negro History*.

1917 The American Friends Service Committee, created by American
Quakers, provides positive alternatives to military service in
World War I, educates people about conscientious objection to
war, and fights for civil and human rights.

1917 More than 40 African-Americans are killed when rioters in East
Saint Louis, Illinois, respond to the employment of black workers
in a factory. Martial law is declared.

1917 In Houston, Texas, white civilians fight with black soldiers; 2
blacks and 17 whites are killed. Thirteen blacks are executed for
participating in the fight.

1917 The U.S. Supreme Court, in *Buchanan v. Warley*, rules that a
Louisville ordinance had prevented a black man from purchasing
property and building a house on a predominantly white block.
Justice William Rufus Day writes that the ordinance was
designed to promote public peace by preventing racial conflicts,
but police power cannot justify the passage of a law that violates
the Constitution.

1917 The first African-American man to be a pilot is Eugene Bullard,
who flies as a member of the Lafayette Flying Corps of the
French Army deployed on the western front during World War I.

1917 Thousands of African-Americans participate in a silent march in
New York City to protest against lynchings, such as the public
burning of Jesse Washington, a 17-year-old youth who was mentally handicapped. Washington, convicted of rape and murder,
was forcibly taken from the courtroom by a mob of almost 15,000

whites in Waco, Texas.

1917   The U.S. Congress passes the Selective Service Act, requiring resident Mexicans who are not citizens of the United States to register with local draft boards even though they are not eligible to be drafted.

1917   The 24th Colored Infantry Regiment in Houston, Texas, is disarmed, and soon after members are victimized and beaten by local police. When members of the regiment learn that a lynch mob is headed for them, they arm themselves and confront the mob; 2 blacks and 17 whites are killed, including 5 policemen. Ninety-nine soldiers are sent to prison, for terms of several years to life, and 13 are hanged.

1918   The first African-American to earn a license as a shipmaster is Hugh N. Mulzac, who must find work as a steward and cook rather than as master of a ship. Not until 1942 does he become shipmaster of a Liberty ship transporting troops into combat during World War II.

1919   In *Schenck v. United States*, the U.S. Supreme Court rules that protection of free speech does not include creating a "clear and present danger." Justice Oliver Wendell Holmes states that many things that would be permissible to say in peacetime can so hinder the war effort that they are not protected by the Constitution in time of war: "The most stringent protection of free speech would not protect a man in falsely shouting fire in a theatre and causing a panic."

1919   Austria abolishes capital punishment.

1919   The first African-American to play professional football in the United States is Fritz Pollard, who plays for the Akron Indians. In 1916, he had been the first black to play in the collegiate Rose Bowl, when he played for Brown University.

1919   The U.S. filmmaker Oscar Micheaux makes a motion picture, *Within Our Gates*, on the subject of lynching.

1919   W. E. B. Du Bois, the African-American educator, helps to organize the Pan-African Congress, held in Paris, France, with representatives from around the world. The congress adopts proposals asking that natives of Africa and people of African descent be given land and natural resources, that natives not be exploited in the granting of concessions for natural resources, that profits from extraction of natural resources be taxed for the benefit of natives, and that slavery, corporal punishment, and forced labor be abolished.

1919   In the towns of Hoopspur and Ratio, Arkansas, two separate incidents of black-white violence escalate into a large-scale conflict, with whites coming from all over the state and from Mississippi and Tennessee to fight in Arkansas; the official death toll is 25 blacks and 5 whites killed, but more than 100 blacks are thought to have been murdered. Blacks are arrested and brought to trial before an all-white jury, with court-assigned lawyers who call no witnesses on their behalf and do not request a change of venue; by the time the trials are over, 15 blacks have been sentenced to death and 80 sent to prison for terms of 1 to 20 years.

1919   In Louisiana, a mob organized by the white supremacy group the Loyalty League attacks Sol Dakus, a black man who is organizing workers to protest mistreatment by a Louisiana lumber company; white workers defend him from the mob, and four of them are shot and killed. Thirteen police officers are arrested for the murders, but a grand jury refuses to indict them.

1919   The African Blood Brotherhood, a radical American labor organization, is established to bring about cooperation between black and white workers, to gain entry for blacks into unions, to organize cooperatives to help raise living standards, and to acquaint the white world with the lynchings and other inhumanities that blacks suffer.

1920   In *Silverthorne Lumber Co. v. United States*, the U.S. Supreme Court rules that seizure of company documents without a warrant while the suspects are in custody violates the Constitution. The defendants were arrested at home and detained in custody at the same time that representatives of the Department of Justice and U.S. marshals went without authority to the company office, searched all the books and documents, and seized them. Justice Oliver Wendell Holmes writes that, although the documents were returned, the prosecution made use of copies to bring a new indictment, and that neither the documents nor the information it wrongly gained can be used against the defendants.

1920   A national convention of Marcus Garvey's Universal Negro Improvement Association, held in Madison Square Garden in New York City, is attended by 25,000 people from across the United States, who hear Garvey advocate black nationalism and a return to Africa.

1920   The American Civil Liberties Union (ACLU) is founded to advocate, educate, and litigate issues concerning the Bill of Rights, such as the freedom of speech, press, assembly, and religion. The ACLU pursues court cases to ensure that Americans are not denied due process of law.

1920   The 19th Amendment to the U.S. Constitution, guaranteeing women the right to vote, is adopted. The amendment states: "The right of citizens of the United States to vote shall not be denied or abridged by the United States or by any state on account of sex. Congress shall have power to enforce this article by appropriate legislation."

1921   International PEN (Poets, Playwrights, Essayists, Editors, and Novelists) is an authors' rights organization established to protect and promote freedom of thought, speech, and expression and a free press throughout the world.

1921   Sweden abolishes capital punishment.

1921   The U.S. Supreme Court, in *Gouled v. United States*, decides that the surreptitious removal of a document during a friendly visit and the use of it as evidence violates the Constitution. In this case, which involves a conspiracy to defraud the government, Justice John H. Clarke writes that the Fourth Amendment, which prohibits unreasonable searches and seizures, makes it illegal for a government officer to search secretly a person's private papers.

1921   A petition signed by 50,000 Americans, both black and white, is presented to President Warren Harding by James W. Johnson, secretary of the National Association for the Advancement of Colored People, on behalf of imprisoned members of the 24th Colored Infantry Regiment in Houston, Texas. The petition asks for clemency and pardon for the soldiers on the grounds of their military records, the evidence of local animosity and violence against blacks, and the extremely harsh punishments already handed out to the soldiers, 13 of whom had been hanged summarily and without the right of appeal.

1921   When the United States decides to limit the number of immigrants allowed to enter the country, Congress passes the Immigration Restriction Act, in which quotas for each country are set at 3 percent of immigrants from that country then living in the United States as of 1910. President Warren Harding, a conservative, signs the act into law; most Asians had already been prohibited entry with earlier legislation.

1921   The first African-American woman pilot is Bessie Coleman, who receives her license in France, where she had to travel for pilot training. Because of racial bias, Coleman cannot receive training in the United States; she is granted a license by the Fédération Aeronautique Internationale.

1923   In *Moore v. Dempsey*, the U.S. Supreme Court deliberates on the lack of a fair trial in a riot case in Phillips County, Arkansas, in 1919. The Federal District Court judge in Arkansas had previously ruled in favor of the state's claim that even if the defendants had been unfairly convicted they no longer had a remedy at law, but the Supreme Court challenges that ruling and sends the case back to the judge to hear the facts, with Justice Oliver Wendell Holmes stating that the judge must examine the facts, which, if true, make the trial invalid.

1923   The first African-American basketball team in the United States is the New York Renaissance.

1924   The League of Nations reluctantly creates the Temporary Slavery Commission under pressure from the British Anti-Slavery and Aborigines Protection Society, to investigate contemporary slave trading in Ethiopia. Charged with investigating all forms of slavery, the Commission looks into debt-bondage, forced labor, the sale of women as brides, children sold into domestic servitude, and the plight of women sold as concubines; despite the commission's limited power, its work prompts the drafting of the Slavery Convention of 1926.

1924   In *Hester v. United States*, the U.S. Supreme Court decides that
                the testimony of officers who while trespassing observe a defen-
                dant hand illegal whiskey to another is admissible. The case
                involves revenue officers who, while concealed, observe the
                defendant hand someone a quart bottle of illicitly distilled whis-
                key; Justice Oliver Wendell Holmes writes that there is no legal
                basis for claiming that the revenue officers' testimony is illegal.

1924   Arguing against capital punishment in a 12-hour summation,
                the renowned lawyer Clarence Darrow succeeds in obtaining life
                sentences for Richard Loeb and Nathan Leopold Jr., the Chicago,
                Illinois, college students who had senselessly killed a schoolboy,
                Bobby Franks. Darrow is a staunch opponent of capital punish-
                ment, and none of his clients, some 50 of whom had been charged
                with murder, is ever sentenced to death; Darrow defends John
                Scopes at the so-called monkey trial in 1925.

1924   Affected by eugenicists' specious analyses of intelligence that
                characterize people of "Nordic" (western European) stock as
                superior, the U.S. Immigration Restriction Act limits annual
                immigration from each nation to 2 percent of that nationality
                residing in the United States as recorded in the 1890 census,
                before the great influx of immigrants from eastern and southern
                Europe, thus effectively increasing immigrants from "Nordic"
                Europe and limiting those from regions that eugenicists have
                labeled inferior. As a result, during the 1930s, when refugees
                from eastern Europe try to emigrate to the United States, the
                quotas prevent their entry even when the western European quo-
                tas are not filled; thousands who are denied entry to the United
                States die in Nazi prison camps.

1925   The Brotherhood of Sleeping Car Porters, a black labor union, is
                organized by A. Philip Randolph. The union not only advocates
                for its members but becomes a strong force for social and political
                reform in the United States.

1925   The Protocol for the Prohibition of the Use in War of Asphyxiat-
                ing, Poisonous, or Other Gases or of Bacteriological Methods of
                Warfare is adopted in reaction to the use of poison gas in World
                War I. More than 140 nations, including all major nations, are
                parties to the protocol.

1925   In *Gitlow v. People*, the U.S. Supreme Court supports a New
                York law prohibiting the advocacy of, or teaching about, the over-
                throw of the government. Convicted for criminal advocacy, Ben-
                jamin Gitlow, an avowed socialist, appeals on the ground that
                the exercise of free speech is punishable only when speech
                results in a likelihood of substantive evil, but Justice Edward
                Terry Sanford states that freedom of speech does not extend to
                speech that tries to overthrow the government.

1925   The U.S. Supreme Court decides that seizure, without a warrant,
                of evidence from an automobile does not violate the search-and-
                seizure provisions of the Fourth Amendment. In *Carroll v.
                United States*, which deals with whiskey being transported ille-
                gally into the country by automobile, Chief Justice William

	Howard Taft writes that the Fourth Amendment protects against unreasonable searches, not all searches.
1925	In *Agnello v. United States*, the U.S. Supreme Court rules that the seizure of narcotics in a defendant's house several blocks away from his place of arrest and without a warrant violates the Fourth and Fifth Amendments. Justice Pierce Butler states that officers may search without a warrant the place where a person is arrested, but this right does not extend to other places.
1926	The League of Nations passes the Slavery Convention, which declares that participating nations oppose slavery.
1926	The first African-American woman attorney to practice before the U.S. Supreme Court is Violette Anderson.
1927	In Great Britain, the British Labour Party's *Manifesto on Capital Punishment* is issued. Twenty-seven political leaders advocate the abolition of the death penalty.
1927	The U.S. Supreme Court affirms a California law prohibiting organizing, or membership in, an organization advocating, "criminal syndicalism" (acts that aim for industrial or political change). In *Whitney v. California*, the defendant had been convicted based on her organizing, and membership in, the Communist Labor Party, which is ruled to violate the California Criminal Syndication Act of 1919; Justice Edward Terry Sanford writes that the California Act meets the requirement of due process in that it explicitly informs people what actions render them liable for penalties.
1927	In *United States v. Lee*, the U.S. Supreme Court decides that the seizure of a boat more than 12 miles from land in the course of an arrest is legal. The case involves the Coast Guard seizure of a motorboat in waters known as Rum Row; Justice Louis Brandeis states that the law gives the Coast Guard the authority to search and seize American vessels on the high seas when there is probable cause.
1927	In *Nixon v. Herndon*, the U.S. Supreme Court rules that a Texas law prohibiting African-Americans from voting in a Democratic Party primary violates the 14th Amendment.
1928	Sierra Leone in West Africa bans slavery.
1928	In *Olmstead v. United States*, the U.S. Supreme Court rules that wiretapping telephone calls does not amount to search or seizure under the Fourth Amendment. In a case involving information about a conspiracy to import liquor unlawfully, much of the evidence central to the prosecution is obtained by wiretapping; Chief Justice William Howard Taft writes that the Fourth Amendment does not pertain to that procedure.
1929	Albon Holsey creates the Colored Merchants Association in New York City and begins a campaign to have black merchants establish stores from which blacks will buy.
1929	The League of United Latin American Citizens is created in

Texas to fight for increased opportunities for Mexican-Americans.

1929   The Board of Education in New York City decides that the word *negro* will be spelled with a capital *N*. In 1930, the *New York Times* introduces the same policy.

1930   The National Association for the Advancement of Colored People (NAACP) begins a campaign against the confirmation of John Parker to the U.S. Supreme Court. Parker, who had stated that he opposes blacks voting, is defeated because of the NAACP's work.

1930s   Father Charles E. Coughlin, Roman Catholic priest and pastor of the Shrine of the Little Flower in Royal Oak, Michigan, gives weekly radio broadcasts attacking Jews, communism, Wall Street, and President Roosevelt's New Deal administration. The broadcasts attract a wide and loyal audience, but in 1942 the Church orders Coughlin to stop broadcasting; in the same year, Coughlin's magazine, *Social Justice*, which expresses the same ideas as his broadcasts, is banned from the U.S. mail for violating the Espionage Act of 1917.

1931   In *Aldridge v. United States*, the U.S. Supreme Court rules that in death-penalty cases prospective jurors can be questioned about racial prejudice.

1931   The first African-American to receive a master's degree in nursing in the United States is Estele Massey Osborne, who graduates from Columbia University Teachers College in New York City.

1931   The U.S. Supreme Court reverses a California conviction for displaying a red flag in a public place, in *Stromberg v. California*. The appellant, a member of the Young Communist League, had been convicted under a section of the California penal code forbidding the use of a red flag, but Justice Charles Evans Hughes states that, as one of the section's provisions violates the guarantee of liberty in the 14th Amendment, and as the section is worded so vaguely, it is unclear whether the appellant was convicted under that or another clause.

1931   The trial in Scottsboro, Alabama, becomes a national and then international cause when civil rights organizations and liberal and radical whites like the lawyer Clarence Darrow join blacks in denouncing the frame-up and unfair conviction of the defendants, nine young black men—the "Scottsboro Boys"—who, largely on the basis of the testimony of the two supposed victims, are said to have raped two white women. Although one woman soon recants her testimony, eight of the defendants are sentenced to death, and the ninth, a 13-year-old, is given life imprisonment. Appeals drag on for six years, and the Supreme Court twice declares mistrials; five indictments are dropped, and four defendants receive long prison sentences, but by 1946 all but one are paroled.

1931   When the Chicago chapter of National Urban League in Saint

Louis, Missouri, begins a boycott of stores whose clientele is black but whose workers are almost entirely white, the Jobs for Negroes movement begins in this city. Organizations in cities like Chicago, New York, and Pittsburgh begin similar efforts with such slogans as "Don't Buy Where You Can't Work."

1933   Albert Forsythe and Charles Anderson are the first two African-American civilian pilots to complete a transcontinental aircraft flight.

1934   The U.S. Congress defeats antilynching legislation; President Franklin D. Roosevelt had not supported the bill.

1935   The first African-American woman to serve as a public school principal in New York City is Gertrude Eise Ayer, who takes over P.S. 24 on Madison Avenue and 128th Street in Manhattan.

1935   The term *affirmative action* appears in the U.S. Wagner Act, which requires employers to take affirmative action to end discrimination against workers because they are union members.

1936   Nigeria bans slavery.

1937   During Japan's invasion of China, large numbers of Chinese women are raped by Japanese soldiers.

1937   The first African-American federal judge is William H. Hastie, who serves on the District Court of the American Virgin Islands in the West Indies.

1938   In *Missouri ex rel. Gaines v. Canada*, the U.S. Supreme Court rules that educational facilities for blacks must be equal to, even if separate from, those of whites. A black man claims that he is denied admission to the State University of Missouri School of Law because of race; Chief Justice Charles Evans Hughes writes that Missouri has not established any educational institutions for blacks wishing to study law, which constitutes a denial of equal privilege, so that the individual is entitled to be admitted to the law school of the state university and was wrongfully excluded.

1938   The United States Fair Labor Standards Act (FLSA) establishes a minimum wage of 25 cents an hour and requires that workers be paid one and a half times their regular rate of pay after 40 hours of work in a workweek.

1939   The first African-American woman to serve as a judge in the United States is Jane Matilda Bolin, who is appointed by New York City mayor Fiorello La Guardia to the Court of Domestic Relations.

1939   France decides to end public executions after the public killing of Eugene Weidmann creates enormous negative publicity. Guillotined outside the Palais de justice in Versailles, France, Weidmann had been convicted for murdering six people; a large crowd watches his execution, and photographs of the occasion appear in the French press.

1939   The Daughters of the American Revolution (DAR) refuse to allow the famed African-American soprano Marian Anderson to sing in Constitution Hall in Washington, D.C., prompting the First Lady, Eleanor Roosevelt, to resign from the DAR. The secretary of the interior provides the use of the Lincoln Memorial, and 75,000 Americans come to hear Anderson perform.

1939   The U.S. Supreme Court decides, in *Hague v. Committee for Industrial Organization*, that people have a right to assemble peacefully to discuss public questions. Jersey City, New Jersey, officials had arrested members of the Committee for Industrial Organization for distributing leaflets and had refused them the right to meet publicly to discuss labor issues; Justice Owen Roberts writes that the right to assemble in public must not be abridged under the guise of regulation.

1939   The Legal Defense and Educational Fund of the National Association for the Advancement of Colored People is organized to wage an all-out battle in the U.S. court system to end racial discrimination.

1939–1945   During World War II, the Japanese military enslaves between 100,000 and 200,000 women to provide sexual services for the troops. Called *jugun ianfu* (comfort women), they are often Korean and are referred to officially as military supplies; those who attempt escape are often beaten and sometimes killed.

1939–1945   During World War II, Germany and Japan ignore the provisions of the Geneva Convention of 1906 and 1929 in their treatment of Allied prisoners. The Geneva Convention sets forth international rules for the humane treatment of prisoners, such as not compelling them to give any information beyond name, rank, and serial number; giving prisoners adequate food, clothing, and shelter; delivering mail and parcels to them; and not treating them like criminals.

1940   The U.S. Supreme Court decides, in *Cantwell v. United States*, that a state law requiring an official to issue permits for religious solicitation violates the defendants' 1st and 14th Amendment rights. The case involved three Jehovah's Witnesses arrested in New Haven, Connecticut, for soliciting donations in violation of a state law; Justice Owen Roberts states that the Connecticut statute deprives the appellants of their liberty without due process of law.

1940   Benjamin O. Davis Sr. is the first African-American to gain the rank of brigadier general in the U.S. Army.

1940   The first U.S. postage stamp honoring an African-American is the Booker T. Washington 10-cent stamp issued as one of the Famous Americans series.

1940   The first African-American to win an Academy Award is Hattie McDaniel, who wins an Oscar for best supporting actress for her role as Mammy in *Gone with the Wind*.

1941   President Franklin D. Roosevelt signs an executive order requiring special measures to counter discrimination in the employment of workers in the defense industries and government.

1941   The 99th Pursuit Squadron, the Tuskegee Airmen, is an African-American squadron in the U.S. Army Air Force, commanded by Colonel Benjamin O. Davis Sr. Approximately 600 black pilots are trained and fly during World War II.

1942   The first African-American commissioned an officer in the U.S. Naval Reserve is Bernard Robinson, a medical student at Harvard University.

1942   General George DeWitt issues a proclamation leading to the forced removal of Americans of Japanese ancestry from the West Coast of the United States. Because the Pacific Coast is considered subject to attack or invasion as well as acts of espionage and sabotage, certain areas are designated as military areas, such as the southern part of Arizona and the entire coastal region of the three Pacific Coast states, including the city of Seattle, Washington, and certain persons are excluded from them.

1942   Formed to manage Americans detained by the government, the War Relocation Authority is created. President Franklin D. Roosevelt authorizes the director of the authority to create and effectuate programs for the removal, relocation, maintenance, and supervision of Japanese Americans.

1942   The U.S. Congress passes an act making it a crime to enter, remain in, or commit an act in restricted military areas.

1942   According to a proclamation issued by U.S. general George DeWitt, all alien Japanese, Germans, and Italians and all people of Japanese ancestry living in certain designated military areas and zones must observe a curfew between 8 P.M. and 6 A.M. The military commander also issues a series of Civilian Expulsion Orders directing that all persons of Japanese ancestry, both alien and nonalien, be excluded from designated portions of military areas, including their places of residence, and requiring a member of each family and each individual living alone to report to a designated civil-control station for orderly evacuation and resettlement.

1942   In *Goldman v. United States*, the U.S. Supreme Court decides that the use of a listening device placed against a wall to overhear a conversation does not violate the Fourth Amendment. In a case involving defendants indicted for conspiracy to violate the Bankruptcy Act, where such a listening device was used, Justice Owen Roberts writes that listening to the defendant in the next room talk into a telephone receiver is not interception of a wire communication and therefore not a violation of the Fourth Amendment.

1942   The U.S. Supreme Court reverses an Oklahoma decision to sterilize a defendant twice convicted of crimes amounting to felonies involving moral turpitude, in *Skinner v. State of Oklahoma ex rel. Williamson*. Sterilization proceedings had been instituted against a man twice convicted for robbery; Justice William O. Douglas writes that the Oklahoma act violates the defendant's

14th Amendment rights.

1942   Five months after the Japanese bomb Pearl Harbor, President Franklin Roosevelt signs an executive order allowing the removal and detention of all persons of Japanese ancestry from the West Coast of the United States because of "military necessity." Of the 110,000 people detained, 71,986 are U.S. citizens, and nearly 15,000 are women between the ages of 15 and 30 years; the evacuation order is rescinded in January 1945.

1942   Helmuth Günther Hübener, age 17 years, is beheaded in Nazi Germany for listening to foreign radio broadcasts.

1943   The first Liberty Ship (warship built during World War II) named for an African-American is the *George Washington Carver*, named after the American botanist and launched from New Jersey to carry troops and supplies.

1943   The first African-American admitted to the U.S. National Institute of Arts and Letters is W. E. B. Du Bois, head of the Sociology Department at Atlanta University in Atlanta, Georgia.

1943   In *Kiyoshi Hirabayashi v. United States*, the U.S. Supreme Court upholds the conviction of an American citizen of Japanese ancestry for violating a military curfew and failing to report to a civil-control center to register. Although the defendant asserted that his indictment should be dismissed on the grounds that he is an American citizen and has no connection to Japan, Chief Justice Harlan Fiske Stone writes that whatever we may think of the loyalty of Japanese Americans, Congress and the executive branch have grounds for thinking that some of them constitute a danger to national security.

1943   The Congress of Racial Equality (CORE) is established as a national organization working for civil rights in the United States.

1944   In *Korematsu v. United States*, the U.S. Supreme Court upholds the legality of expelling persons of Japanese ancestry from areas on the West Coast during World War II. In the case of a Japanese American arrested for not evacuating his home, Justice Hugo L. Black writes that it is within the war power of Congress and the executive branch to exclude persons of Japanese ancestry from military areas.

1944   The United Negro College Fund is created to increase and coordinate fund-raising efforts for black colleges and universities in the United States, which are beset by financial problems.

1944   The first African-American to be accredited as a White House news correspondent is Harry McAlpin, a reporter with the Atlanta *Daily World*.

1945   The first African-American nurse commissioned in the U.S. Naval Reserve Corps is Phyllis Mae Daley.

1945   The New York State Fair Employment Practices Commission is established to investigate and deal with discrimination in the workplace.

1945   In Gary, Indiana, a thousand white students leave school to boycott integrated classes.

1945   The U.S. soldier Private Eddie Slovik is executed by a firing
squad for desertion during World War II.

1945   The U.S. Supreme Court rules that the use of a confession allegedly made by a suspect held incommunicado and not allowed to
see a lawyer violates his constitutional rights. In *Malinski v. People of State of New York*, a man charged along with two others in
the murder of a police officer during a robbery is held incommunicado by the police; Justice William O. Douglas declares that
the man's confession was coerced by force and fear and cannot be
allowed to stand.

1945   After World War II, the former French premier Pierre Laval is
executed by firing squad for collaborating with the Nazis. Laval
had been the effective head of state of the Vichy government in
France, a regime existing under German authority.

1946   The International Labour Organization issues the Declaration of
the Convention Concerning Forced or Compulsory Labour, stating that each party to the Convention must take steps to suppress forced labor.

1946   The British traitor William Joyce, son of Irish immigrants, had
joined pro-Fascist groups in England before going to Germany in
1939. Taking a job with Joseph Goebbels's propaganda ministry
in Berlin, he made pro-Nazi radio broadcasts to Great Britain
under the name of Lord Haw Haw, urging the British to surrender. Convicted of treason by the British, he is hanged.

1946   The U.S. Supreme Court decides that people living in a company-
owned town do not forfeit their 1st- and 14th-Amendment rights.
In *Marsh v. Alabama*, a Jehovah's Witness is convicted for distributing religious literature on the streets of Chickasaw, Alabama, a town owned by the Gulf Shipbuilding Corporation;
Justice Hugo L. Black declares that the managers of the town
"cannot curtail the liberty of press and religion of these people
consistently with the purposes of the Constitutional guarantees,"
and that an Alabama statute enforcing such action violates the
1st and 14th Amendments.

1946   In *Morgan v. Virginia*, the U.S. Supreme Court rules to prohibit
racial segregation in interstate bus travel. A black woman was
arrested and fined for refusing to move to the back of a bus, on
the basis of a Virginia law; Justice Stanley Forman Reed writes
that the Virginia statute interferes with commerce, in the sense
of a balance between local police power and the need for national
uniformity in the regulations for interstate travel. Despite the
Court's ruling, segregated bus travel is still practiced in the
southern states.

1946   In response to a series of racial disturbances in both northern
and southern cities, U.S. president Harry S. Truman creates the

National Committee on Civil Rights in the United States to investigate racial divisions and make recommendations for improving relationships between the races. When the committee delivers its report, *To Secure These Rights*, in 1947, it advocates an end to racial bigotry and urges adoption of a program designed to eliminate racial segregation.

1946   The United Nations Centre for Human Rights, founded in Geneva, Switzerland, establishes the Commission on Human Rights. The commission studies and promotes human rights policies throughout the world and as part of its mandate creates the Subcommittee on the Prevention of Discrimination and Protection of Minorities and the Working Group on Enforced or Involuntary Disappearances.

1947   The first African-American baseball player in the U.S. major leagues in the 20th century is Jackie Robinson, who plays for the Brooklyn Dodgers in Brooklyn, New York. An extraordinary baseball player, Robinson would become the first African-American to be elected to the Baseball Hall of Fame.

1947   The first African-American journalist granted press credentials to cover the U.S. Senate and House of Representatives is Louis Lautier, the Washington, D.C., bureau chief of the Negro Newspaper Publishers Association. Opposed originally by the Standing Committee of Newspaper Correspondents, he gains admission after the Senate Rules Committee intercedes.

1947   The first African-American commissioned an officer in the U.S. Navy is John Lee, who serves on the USS *Kearsage*.

1947   Capital punishment is abolished in the Soviet Union.

1947   The Congress of Racial Equality (CORE) begins the Journey of Compliance to test compliance with the U.S. Supreme Court decision in *Morgan v. Virginia* banning racial segregation in interstate bus travel; a group of young white and black men begin riding buses; when they are arrested in North Carolina, the whites are sentenced to 30 days on a chain gang, and the blacks to 90 days. CORE also organizes Freedom Rides in the Deep South; one bus in Birmingham, Alabama, is fire-bombed, and a white mob beats up the passengers.

1948   The first African-American commissioned as an officer in the U.S. Marine Corps is John Earl Rudder.

1948   In *Shelley v. Kraemer*, the U.S. Supreme Court rules that courts may not enforce restrictive covenants on housing. When a black couple purchases a home whose previous owner had signed an agreement restricting the house from blacks, other homeowners file suit, and the Missouri Supreme Court rules to evict the black couple; Chief Justice Fred M. Vinson states that by granting such restrictive covenants, states restrict the equal protection of the law, and therefore the courts' actions cannot stand.

1948   At the Democratic Party National Convention, conservative Southern delegates walk out to protest civil rights positions favored by the party. The conservatives organize the Dixiecrat Party.

1948   The Universal Declaration of Human Rights is adopted by the United Nations General Assembly. The declaration proclaims that all people are free and equal and are entitled to all the freedoms set forth in the declaration without consideration of race, color, sex, religion, social status, or national origin; it also supports the abolition of slavery and the banning of torture and other cruel punishment.

1948   The United Nations General Assembly adopts the Convention on the Prevention and Punishment of the Crime of Genocide. The convention declares genocide a crime under international law.

1948   The former Japanese prime minister Hideki Tojo is hanged for crimes against humanity committed during World War II. Tojo resigned his post in 1944 because of shame at the Japanese reverses in the Pacific.

1948   U.S. president Harry S. Truman issues an executive order ending racial segregation in the armed forces.

1948   The International Labour Organization issues the Convention Concerning Freedom of Association and Protection of the Right to Organize, stating that workers and employers can join organizations of their own choosing. Each party to the convention agrees to promote the necessary undertakings so that employees and employers can exercise their right to organize.

1948   Apartheid is established as the official policy of the government of South Africa. An Afrikaans term for "separation," apartheid mandates a political, social, and economic division based on color; in pursuit of that division, the government passes the 1950 Population Registration Act, which develops a classification system for South Africans based on their race, and the 1950 Group Areas Act, which creates separate residential areas for blacks and whites.

1948   The World Policy Institute is founded in New York to influence U.S. foreign policy in regard to human rights and the right of all people to self-determination.

1949   The International Labour Organization issues the Convention Concerning the Application of the Principles of the Right to Organize and to Bargain Collectively, stating that workers must be protected against antiunion discrimination and cannot be fired for union activities.

1949   The first African-American pilot in the U.S. Naval Reserve is Leroy Brown, who is killed in action in Korea in 1950.

1949   The first African-American to graduate from the U.S. Naval Academy at Annapolis, Maryland, is Wesley A. Brown.

1949   The first African-American baseball player to win the National League's Most Valuable Player award is Jackie Robinson of the Brooklyn Dodgers; Robinson was the first black player signed to a major-league baseball team in the 20th century, and in 1962 he would become the first black player inducted into the National Baseball Hall of Fame. Roy Campanella, Robinson's teammate, a black catcher, wins the award in 1951, 1953, and 1955 and becomes the second black player elected to the Baseball Hall of Fame.

1949   In *Wolf v. People of the State of Colorado*, the U.S. Supreme Court rules that evidence that would be excluded under due-process considerations in a federal trial can be used in a state trial. Justice Felix Frankfurter states that the 14th Amendment does not forbid the use of evidence obtained by an unreasonable search and seizure in a prosecution in a state court.

1950   The Leadership Conference on Civil Rights, a coalition of national organizations promoting civil rights in the United States, is formed in Washington, D.C. The conference studies and evaluates the enforcement records of federal agencies on civil rights legislation.

1950   South Africa establishes the South African Immorality Act, forbidding any sexual activity between white Africans and colored Africans. The act is an integral part of the South African government's policy of apartheid, the institutional separation of the races, and white dominance of blacks.

1950   The Soviet Union reinstitutes capital punishment for crimes of treason, terrorism, and espionage.

1950   The United Nations issues the Convention for the Suppression of the Traffic in Persons and of the Exploitation of the Prostitution of Others, stating that prostitution and its accompanying traffic in people are dangerous to individuals and communities. Parties to the convention must punish those in any way involved with prostitution.

1950   The European Convention on Human Rights is adopted, stating that everyone's right to life must be protected by law, and cruel punishments and torture must be outlawed. The convention also declares that everyone has a right to a fair and public hearing by an impartial court and a right to freedom of expression and public assembly.

1950   The first African-American woman to win a Pulitzer Prize for poetry is Gwendolyn Brooks, for *Annie Allen*.

1950   The first African-American to receive the Nobel Prize for Peace is Ralph Bunche, the U.S. diplomat and scholar.

1950   The first African-American to become a professional hockey player is Arthur Dorrington, playing for the Atlantic City Sea Gulls.

1950   The first African-American to win a Tony Award is Juanita Hall, for her supporting role as Bloody Mary in the Broadway musical *South Pacific*.

1950   The U.S. Supreme Court, in *McLaurin v. Oklahoma*, rules that once an educational institution admits a black student, distinctions in treatment cannot be based on race.

1950   The European Convention on Human Rights declares its commitment to the right to unionize.

1950–1953   During the Korean War, North Korea uses brainwashing, a form of psychological warfare, with much success to indoctrinate prisoners with Communist propaganda, the first time that this technique is known to have been used as a tactic in warfare.

1951   The U.S. Supreme Court affirms the conviction of members of the Communist Party for conspiring to overthrow the U.S. government by force and violence. In *Dennis v. United States*, the petitioners were convicted for organizing the Communist Party and for advocating the overthrow of the government; Justice Fred M. Vinson states that the petitioners claim that the law under which they were convicted stifles free expression, free speech, and a free press, but the group was convicted because it does not merely discuss, it advocates, overthrowing the government.

1951   Illinois governor Adlai Stevenson mobilizes the National Guard to suppress a race riot in Cicero, Illinois, when 3,000 whites violently protest the efforts of a black family to move into a previously all-white neighborhood.

1951   With the bombing of Harry T. Moore, the leader of the National Association for the Advancement of Colored People, in Mims, Florida, a campaign is under way to assassinate local leaders of the U.S. civil rights movement. During the next 12 months, there are 40 such bombings throughout the South.

1951   The U.S. Congress passes the Mexican Farm Labor Supply Program and the Mexican Farm Labor Agreement, ensuring a supply of cheap labor of an estimated 350,000 Mexican farm workers for U.S. agriculture.

1952   The U.S. Congress passes the Immigration and Nationality Act, also known as the McCarran-Walter Act, setting restrictive limits on immigration except from the Western Hemisphere. Even from there, prospective immigrants are screened to exclude homosexuals and Communists.

1952   In *Adler v. Board of Education of the City of New York*, the U.S. Supreme Court affirms the rights of the New York City Board of Education to deny employment to members of the Communist Party. Justice Sherman Minton writes that those who advocate overthrowing the government of the United States have the right to assemble, speak, and think as they wish, but they have no right to work for the state on their own terms; if they wish to work only on their own terms, they must go elsewhere.

1953   The Municipal Appeals Court in Washington, D.C., outlaws segregation in local restaurants, after a campaign to integrate restaurants led by Mary Church Terrell, a 90-year-old advocate of desegregation. Terrell, from a prominent black family, was born during the Civil War and lived to play a major part in ending segregation in public facilities in Washington, D.C.; she was a proponent of women's suffrage and one of the founders of the National Association for the Advancement of Colored People.

1953   Lavrenty Beria, as head of the Commissariat for Internal Affairs (NKVD) in the Soviet Union, was responsible for purges, imprisonments, and tortures under Joseph Stalin, general secretary of the Central Committee of the Communist Party. When Stalin dies and Georgy Malenkov comes to power, Beria is executed, partly because he had hoped to succeed Stalin and was a threat to the new government.

1953   The first African-American awarded the U.S. National Book Award is Ralph Ellison, for his novel *The Invisible Man*.

1953   The U.S. Supreme Court affirms the decision of Washington, D.C., courts that restaurants cannot refuse to serve blacks. In *District of Columbia v. John R. Thompson Co., Inc.*, the Court rules that, based on an 1873 law making it a criminal act for owners of public eating establishments to refuse to serve patrons solely because of race or color, well-behaved black people must be served.

1953   African-Americans in Baton Rouge, Louisiana, begin a bus boycott to protest racial discrimination.

1953   In Chicago, Illinois, some 1,000 police officers are called in to break up riots protesting against integrated housing in the city.

1953   A Convention to Suppress the Slave Trade and Slavery is issued by nations around the world to revise the international commitment of the Brussels Conference to end the slave trade. The parties to the convention agree to prevent and suppress the slave trade and to end all forms of slavery and forced labor.

1953   The United Nations Convention on the Political Rights of Women declares its intent to implement the principle of equality of rights for women and men in the United Nations Charter. The convention states that women have the right to vote and to hold political office on the same terms as men.

1954   The first African-American appointed a permanent delegate to the United Nations is Charles H. Mahoney.

1954   The National Negro Network is the first black radio network to begin broadcasting in the United States. The first program, *The Story of Ruby Valentine*, stars Tony Award–winner Juanita Hall and is sponsored by Phillip Morris and Pet Milk.

1954   The U.S. Supreme Court acknowledges the exclusion of Hispanic Americans as jurors in Texas. In *Hernandez v. Texas*, a man convicted for murder had offered motions to quash his indictment, alleging that persons of Mexican descent are systematically excluded from jury service, and that that exclusion deprives him of equal protection under the 14th Amendment, but the Court denies the motions. Chief Justice Earl Warren writes that no person with a Mexican or Latin American name has served on a jury in the Texas county for the past 25 years, evidence of discrimination, as are segregated schools, toilets, restaurants, and other facilities in the county.

1954   In *Brown v. Board of Education of Topeka*, the U.S. Supreme Court decides that segregation of children in public schools on the basis of race deprives them of equal protection under the law. Black children in the states of Kansas, South Carolina, Virginia, and Delaware brought cases to obtain admission to public schools that admitted only white children but were denied admission by courts that affirmed the decision of *Plessy v. Ferguson* that separate but equal facilities are constitutional. Chief Justice Earl Warren writes that segregation by race deprives minority children of equal opportunities for education, and the effect is greater when the segregation is legally established: "In the field of public education, the doctrine of 'separate but equal' has no place."

1954   After the U.S. Supreme Court decision in *Brown v. Board of Education of Topeka, Kansas*, large-scale integration occurs in the public school systems of Baltimore, Maryland, and Washington, D.C.

1954–1958   Operation Wetback, a program to deport illegal Mexican immigrants, is established in the United States. Almost 4 million Mexicans are deported, most without deportation hearings; many legal Mexican Americans are caught up in this campaign, sometimes being arrested and detained without reason.

1955   The first African-American singer to perform in a solo role with the Metropolitan Opera in New York City is the contralto Marian Anderson, who sings the role of Ulrica in Guiseppi Verdi's *Un Ballo in Maschera* (A masked ball). Anderson had studied in the United States and Europe; a concert tour of Europe in the 1930s had won her international recognition. She is appointed an alternate U.S. delegate to the United Nations in 1958 and is awarded the Presidential Medal of Freedom in 1963 and a Congressional Gold Medal in 1978.

1955   The U.S. Supreme Court rules that public school desegregation must be implemented with "all deliberate speed."

1955   Fourteen-year-old Emmett Till, a black youth visiting from Chicago, Illinois, is lynched in Money, Mississippi, for allegedly making advances toward a white woman.

1955   The U.S. Interstate Commerce Commission prohibits segregation on public vehicles used in interstate commerce.

1955   Ushering in the civil rights movement in the United States, Rosa Parks, a seamstress, refuses the bus driver's order to give up her seat on the bus in Montgomery, Alabama, and is arrested for violating the city's laws on segregation. During a bus boycott throughout Montgomery sparked by her arrest, local whites use violence, civil suits, and harassment in an unsuccessful attempt to frighten civil rights leaders and protesters; Martin Luther King Jr., one of the boycott organizers, emerges as a national leader. The next year, King's Montgomery home would be bombed, but the U.S. Supreme Court would rule against the segregation of public buses.

1955   The AFL-CIO Department of Civil Rights is established in 1955 in Washington, D.C., to work for equal opportunity and to implement state and federal legislation and internal union programs in regard to expanded employment opportunities for minorities.

1955   The American Buddhist Association is created in Chicago, Illinois, to educate Americans about Buddhism and to encourage the understanding of Buddhist principles and culture.

1955   Austria bans the National Socialist (Nazi) Party; Nazis are prohibited from assembling, broadcasting, or publishing Nazi propaganda. Austrians are also barred from making public statements that attempt to excuse or justify Nazi actions before and during World War II.

1956   Nat King Cole, born in Montgomery, Alabama, is attacked in Birmingham, Alabama. The attack on Cole, a popular African-American singer who is respected internationally, reveals the growing fury of Southern white resistance to desegregation.

1956   The United Nations Supplementary Convention on the Abolition of Slavery, the Slave Trade, and Institutions and Practices Similar to Slavery is issued to intensify the elimination of the slave trade and practices relating to slavery, debt labor, forced marriage, and selling babies.

1956   The first African-American to attend the University of Alabama is Autherine Lucy, who is admitted under court order. She is suspended a few days later, following anti-integration riots by white students, and about three weeks after that she is expelled for making "false . . . outrageous" statements about University of Alabama officials.

1956   Anti-black riots occur throughout the southern United States as school integration begins, particularly in cities and towns in Texas, Tennessee, and Kentucky.

1957   U.S. president Dwight D. Eisenhower deploys federal troops to enforce the desegregation of public schools in Little Rock, Arkansas, in the face of resistance by Governor Orval Faubus, who had called out the National Guard. The federal troops ensure the admission of black children, who must pass a screaming white mob on their way into the high school.

1957   In *Roth v. United States*, the U.S. Supreme Court sustains a conviction for mailing obscene material. Justice William J. Brennan writes that the question in the case is whether the federal obscenity statute violates the 1st, 9th, and 10th Amendments; the justices hold that obscenity is not protected by the Constitution.

1957   The International Labour Organization issues the Convention concerning the Abolition of Forced Labour, which states that parties to the convention agree to suppress and not use forced labor for any reason, including political coercion, punishment, economic development, or discrimination.

1957   The American tennis champion Althea Gibson becomes the first African-American to win the All-England Championships at Wimbledon in England.

1957   The civil rights reformer and clergyman Martin Luther King Jr. founds the Southern Christian Leadership Conference (SCLC) in New Orleans, Louisiana, with headquarters in Atlanta, Georgia, to fight for racial equality, using nonviolent tactics. In the mid-1960s, King's approach is challenged by more radical black groups like the Black Power movement, but King shifts his focus to the northern United States; his efforts to gain civil rights for blacks through nonviolence bring him the Nobel Prize for peace in 1964.

1957   Martin Luther King Jr. speaks at a demonstration at the Lincoln Memorial in Washington, D.C., in support of voting-rights reform for African-Americans. The public protest is attended by 15,000 demonstrators.

1957   The black residents of Tuskegee, Alabama, boycott white merchants in the city to protest the Alabama State Legislature's redrawing of voting districts to prevent blacks from using their political power. The legislature's gerrymandering makes black districts smaller.

1957   The Congressional Hispanic Caucus is founded in Washington, D.C., to promote the participation of Hispanics in all levels of government.

1958   The former Hungarian premier Imre Nagy, secretly tried in Budapest in 1957, is found guilty and executed for his role in the Hungarian Revolution of 1956. A national hero, Nagy had promised free elections and Soviet withdrawal from Hungary at the outset of the Revolution; he had also asked Western powers for aid in rebuffing the Soviet occupiers, but Russian forces quashed the Hungarian attempt at freedom.

1958   The Arab Lawyers Union, founded in Cairo, Egypt, is an organization of lawyers from many Arab nations in the Middle East and North Africa. The union seeks to promote human rights and legal representation in the region.

1958   The U.S. Supreme Court rules that, when officers break into a home without notice of authority and purpose, an arrest is unlawful, and evidence seized inadmissible. In *Miller v. United States*, Justice William J. Brennan writes that, although breaking down a door to arrest someone for a felony may be lawful in some cases, it is unlawful when the officer first fails to state his authority and purpose for entering.

1958   The first African-American writer to win the New York Drama Critics' Circle Award for Best American Play is Lorraine Hansberry for *A Raisin in the Sun*. The play is the first by a black woman to be produced on Broadway.

1958   The first African-American woman employed as an airline stewardess is Ruth Carol Taylor, who flies for Mohawk Airlines.

1959 The first African-American hired to coach an integrated professional basketball team in the United States is John McLendon, who leads the Cleveland Pipers in the National Industrial Basketball League.

1960 Integration of the public schools in New Orleans, Louisiana, encounters resistance and violence, after U.S. District Court judge J. Skelley Wright prohibits implementation of the state's anti-integration laws and the school board approves plans to admit five black children to two all-white schools. Before the schools can open, the state legislature votes to seize control of New Orleans schools, fires its school superintendent, and orders the schools not to open. Judge Wright then issues a court order prohibiting state interference in the city's school system. White parents launch a boycott as four black children come to school.

1960 Four students from North Carolina Agricultural and Technical State University in Greensboro, North Carolina, refuse to give up their seats at a lunch counter that serves only whites; they begin a new phase of the civil rights movement by practicing nonviolent protest and enduring harassment and violence without fighting back. Within a few weeks, students are sitting in at segregated lunch counters throughout the South, and pickets and protesters throughout the country begin targeting Woolworth's, a national chain that practices segregation in the South.

1960 Nine students who participate in sit-ins in Montgomery, Alabama, are expelled from Alabama State University by the state board of education, and 1,000 demonstrators are met by state and local police as they march to the capitol building.

1960 In Sharpeville, South Africa, members of the South African police and army kill demonstrators protesting the pass laws, which require black South Africans to carry documents governing their ability to move in restricted white areas.

1960 The U.S. Supreme Court, in *Shelton v. Tucker*, reverses the dismissal of an Arkansas teacher for refusing to list organizations he is connected with. According to Arkansas law, anyone employed as a teacher, superintendent, or principal in a public school must submit an affidavit listing all organizations to which he or she belongs and has belonged during the past five years, and, as a member of the National Association for the Advancement of Colored People, the defendant is dismissed; Justice Potter Stewart finds that the state law interferes with personal freedom.

1960 The home of Z. Alexander Looby, a black councilman and an attorney for student civil rights demonstrators, is bombed in Nashville, Tennessee; though Looby and his family escape unharmed, several homes are damaged and several interns are injured at the nearby Meharry Medical Center. Led by the Reverend C. T. Vivian, 2,000 people march on Nashville's city hall to protest the bombing and the police's failure to confront racial violence.

1960   Martin Luther King Jr., along with other protesters, is arrested at a sit-in in a department store in Atlanta, Georgia. After a judge in Decatur, Georgia, revokes King's parole on a minor traffic charge and sentences King to four months in a Georgia maximum-security prison, John F. Kennedy, running for president of the United States, and his brother Robert help to secure King's release.

1960   The Student Nonviolent Coordinating Committee (SNCC) is formed in Raleigh, North Carolina, by college students involved in the civil rights sit-ins in the South. SNCC's leaders, including Robert Moses, John Lewis, Charlie Cobb, Bernice Reagan, Stokely Carmichael, and H. Rap Brown, promote aggressive attacks on segregation, in contrast to the nonviolent strategies of Martin Luther King's Southern Christian Leadership Conference and the Urban League.

1960   U.S. president Dwight D. Eisenhower signs the U.S. Voting Rights Act, passed to strengthen the Voting Rights Act of 1957. The new act authorizes the federal courts to appoint voting referees empowered to register black voters in areas where, because of racial discrimination, they had been denied the right to vote; referees are to be appointed if court action by the Justice Department under the Civil Rights Act of 1957 proves that local registrars had unjustly disqualified people on racial grounds.

1961   U.S. vice president Lyndon B. Johnson creates the President's Committee on Equal Employment Opportunity to ensure greater opportunity in the workplace for minorities. The committee requires that government contractors not discriminate against applicants or employees; employers must take affirmative action to make sure that minority applicants are hired.

1961   The British lawyer Peter Benenson founds Amnesty International, to work for the release of prisoners of conscience, including political prisoners who have not employed violence. The organization also acts to end torture, to guarantee fair trials, and to end capital punishment; it is awarded the Nobel Prize for peace in 1977.

1961   In *Silverman v. United States*, the U.S. Supreme Court rules that unauthorized physical penetration of a person's premises for eavesdropping violates the Fourth Amendment. To help arrest a man for gambling offenses, District of Columbia police use a "spike mike" installed in a vacant adjacent house so as to make contact with the heating duct of the suspect's house; Justice Potter Stewart writes that eavesdropping with such an intrusive device is "beyond the pale of even those decisions in which a closely divided Court has held that eavesdropping accomplished by other electronic means did not amount to an invasion of Fourth Amendment rights."

1961   The U.S. Supreme Court decides that refusing to serve an African-American in a leased restaurant in a building built with public funds for public purposes violates the 14th Amendment. In *Burton v. Wilmington Parking Authority*, the Supreme Court of Delaware holds that the appellant is not entitled to relief because the restaurant's action is not state action within the meaning of the 14th Amendment; Justice Tom C. Clark writes that when a state leases public property the 14th Amendment must be complied with by the lessee.

1961   Sponsored by the Congress of Racial Equality (CORE), a group of interracial bus riders travels through the South, testing compliance with the ruling of the Interstate Commerce Commission that interstate travelers cannot be discriminated against. The Freedom Riders are subjected to angry crowds, harassment, and sometimes vicious beatings.

1961   In *Scales v. United States*, the U.S. Supreme Court decides that the 1950 Internal Security Act does not violate constitutional rights of political expression and association. The defendant, who had been convicted on the membership clause of the act, which makes it a felony to be a knowing member of any organization advocating the overthrow of the U.S. government by force or violence, claims that the act violates the due-process clause of the Fifth Amendment; Justice John Marshall Harlan writes that one who is an active rank-and-file member of the Communist Party, a criminal organization, is no more immune from prosecution than is the Party member who actually carries out a criminal act.

1961   In *Mapp v. Ohio*, the U.S. Supreme Court rules that evidence obtained by searches and seizures in violation of the Constitution is inadmissible in criminal trials in state courts, thereby overthrowing its decision in *Wolf v. Colorado*. In the case of an Ohio woman convicted for possession of lewd and lascivious books seized by police from her home without a warrant, Justice Tom C. Clark writes that the right to privacy in the Fourth Amendment is enforceable against the states and that the right to be secure against state officers' invasions of privacy is constitutional in origin.

1962   The first African-American hired as a network television news correspondent is Mal Goode.

1962   U.S. Supreme Court Justice Hugo L. Black orders James Meredith to be admitted to the University of Mississippi in Oxford, Mississippi, and rioters, spurred in part by Governor Ross Barnett's fierce opposition to integration, greet Meredith and U.S. marshals. The federalizing of the National Guard in Mississippi is necessary to regain order in the city; James Meredith eventually graduates in 1963.

1962   When Southern University in Baton Rouge, Louisiana, expels sit-in demonstrators, students respond with large-scale protests. University administrators, pressured by state officials anxious to end the sit-in movement, close the school for 10 days in an attempt to end the protests.

1962   Black churches in Sasser, Georgia, regularly used for civil rights meetings, are bombed.

1962   U.S. president John F. Kennedy signs a prohibition against racial discrimination in federally funded housing. Targeted primarily at housing projects and apartments, it has little impact on homes not in commercial neighborhoods; the prohibition attempts to deal with violations through voluntary compliance and then administrative or court action if necessary.

1962   Cesar Chavez, from a family of migrant farmworkers, creates the United Farm Workers Organizing Committee in California to fight for the rights of low-income farmworkers. The organization launches a successful strike and boycott of nonunion grape growers in 1965, which results in a union contract in 1970; in 1966, it affiliates with the AFL-CIO and is called the United Farm Workers of America.

1963   Two black students are admitted to the University of Alabama, despite Governor George Wallace's threat to block their admission. President John F. Kennedy orders the federalization and deployment of National Guard troops to ensure that the students are enrolled and appears on national television that evening to urge the end of racial discrimination.

1963   In *Bantam Books, Inc. v. Sullivan*, the U.S. Supreme Court decides that Rhode Island's informal system of censorship violates the 14th Amendment. The Rhode Island Legislature created the Rhode Island Commission to Encourage Morality in Youth, with powers to notify distributors and police about readings considered unsuitable for youth; Justice William J. Brennan writes that the 14th Amendment requires states to regulate obscenity in ways that do not curtail constitutionally protected expression, but states that the commission's acts are unconstitutional.

1963   Martin Luther King Jr. helps to organize large-scale nonviolent protests against segregation in Birmingham, Alabama; these are met with extraordinary police violence; the Birmingham police commissioner Eugene "Bull" Connor uses dogs and fire hoses against the peaceful demonstrators and fills the city jails. Demonstrations continue until an agreement is signed calling for gradual desegregation of public accommodations; immediately thereafter, homes and businesses of civil rights leaders are bombed, and riots break out.

1963   In an interracial march on Washington, D.C., 250,000 people come to press for federal action to guarantee equal rights for all. Martin Luther King Jr. delivers his famous address: "I have a dream that one day . . . the sons of former slaves and the sons of former slaveholders will be able to sit down together at the table of brotherhood. . . . When we let freedom ring, we will be able to speed up that day when all God's children . . . will . . . join hands and sing . . . Free at last! Free at last! Thank God almighty, we are free at last."

1963   A bombing of the 16th Street Baptist Church, a black church, in

Birmingham, Alabama, results in the death of four young girls.

1964   The U.S. Civil Rights Act outlawing racial discrimination in employment and education is passed by the Congress. Title VII of the act creates the Equal Employment Opportunity Commission and allows for affirmative action to counter discrimination in the workplace. Chapter 21 of Title 42, prohibits discrimination in places of public accommodation. The act gives all persons full access to any place of public accommodation, without discrimination or segregation on any grounds, and forbids states to deny a citizen's right to vote on the basis of race or color.

1964   The U.S. Supreme Court decides, in the landmark case of *New York Times Co. v. Sullivan*, that factual error, factual content, or both, defamatory of official reputation, are insufficient to award damages for false statements unless "actual malice" is alleged and proved. In a case brought by L. B. Sullivan, commissioner of Public Affairs of Montgomery, Alabama, against four black clergymen and the *New York Times*, Sullivan objected, among other things, to the newspaper's statement that student demonstrators fighting for rights guaranteed by the Constitution and Bill of Rights are met by a "wave of terror," including such acts as bombing the house of Martin Luther King Jr.; Justice William J. Brennan writes that, though some of the statements are not strictly accurate (for instance, King's house has indeed been bombed twice, but the bombings occurred before Sullivan took office), anyone claiming to be defamed by the account must show malice or go without remedy. The decision marks the end of southern politicians' attempts to use libel law to keep the hard facts of discrimination out of the media.

1964   Malcolm X withdraws from the U.S. Black Muslim movement, the Nation of Islam, led by Elijah Muhammad, after visiting Africa, discovering another view of Islam, and deciding to seek accommodation with whites. Malcolm X's father had been a supporter of Marcus Garvey and the movement to create an African homeland.

1964   Racial violence erupts in cities across the United States; in New York City, a riot occurs after a black teenager is shot by white policemen, and other riots break out in cities including Jersey City, Chicago, and Philadelphia. The National Guard is called out, buildings burned, and many are injured.

1964   During Freedom Summer, The Student Nonviolent Coordinating Committee (SNCC) brings black and white college students from all over the country to help register black voters in the South, where they are often met with hostility and violence. After the bodies of three young civil rights workers—James B. Chaney, Andrew Goodman, and Michael Schwerner—are discovered in shallow graves near Philadelphia, Mississippi, two dozen whites, including local law-enforcement officials, are charged with complicity in their murders.

1964   The U.S. Supreme Court rules that the Civil Rights Act does not violate the Constitution's commerce clause, in *Heart of Atlanta*

Motel, Inc. v. United States. The owner of a motel in Atlanta, Georgia, which restricts service to white people only, claims that in passing the Civil Rights Act Congress has exceeded its power to regulate commerce under Article I of the Constitution and the Fifth Amendment by denying him the right to choose his guests; Justice Tom C. Clark writes that the purpose of the act is to vindicate the "deprivation of personal dignity" accompanying denials of equal access, which is within the power of Congress.

1964   Martin Luther King Jr. is awarded the Nobel Prize for Peace for his civil rights work.

1964   The A. Philip Randolph Educational Fund is established in New York City to defend human and civil rights and to work to eliminate racial prejudice and discrimination.

1964   The 24th Amendment to the U.S. Constitution, prohibiting the abridgment or denial of the right to vote because of a failure to pay a poll or any other tax, is adopted. Its passage ends attempts by several Southern states to use a poll tax to limit the participation of poor black voters.

1964   The federal government forces 19 elementary schools in the state of Mississippi to accept 57 black students.

1965   U.S. president Lyndon B. Johnson signs an executive order calling for affirmative action in employment and requiring suppliers and firms that contract to do government work to take affirmative action to ensure that minority applicants are employed. The executive order, as implemented by the Labor Department's revised order, requires contractors to set goals and timetables for employing minority workers.

1965   Martin Luther King Jr. and others attempt to register black voters in Selma, Alabama, the county seat of Dallas County, but his effort to register at a previously segregated hotel is met with violence, and blacks attempting to register to vote are arrested. A federal district court issues an order prohibiting interference with those attempting to register, but 1,700 protesters, including King, are arrested, and one demonstrator, Jimmie Jackson, is beaten to death by state troopers. As demonstrators attempt to cross the Edmund Pettus Bridge in Selma, they are attacked by troopers with clubs, whips, tear gas, and cattle prods; a white minister, James Reeb, a participant in the movement, is killed by three white men.

1965   A federal judge orders Alabama state officials not to interfere with a planned 50-mile protest march from Selma, Alabama, to the state capital in Montgomery; as many as 50,000 demonstrators from across the country join the march, during which a white marcher from Michigan is murdered on a Alabama highway.

1965   In *Cox v. Louisiana,* the U.S. Supreme Court reverses the conviction of a civil rights leader for obstructing public passages and disturbing the peace during a demonstration in Baton Rouge, Louisiana. When the Reverend B. Elton Cox leads a demonstration of 2,000 to protest the arrest of 23 students for picketing stores with segregated lunch counters in Baton Rouge, the city police and the sheriff's office ask him to disband; when he refuses and the marchers continue to the courthouse, police intervene and try to break up the demonstration with tear gas. Cox is arrested and convicted; Justice Arthur Goldberg writes that the record does not support the contention of a breach of the peace, and that the Louisiana law under which Cox has been convicted is unconstitutionally restrictive.

1965   While making a speech in New York City, Malcolm X is assassinated, apparently by members of the Black Muslim movement. *The Autobiography of Malcolm X* is published after his death.

1965   U.S. president Lyndon B. Johnson makes a speech in support of racial integration at Howard University in Washington, D.C., invoking the slogan of the civil rights movement: "We shall overcome."

1965   Daniel Patrick Moynihan, the American scholar who serves in the government under Presidents John F. Kennedy and Lyndon Johnson, publishes *The Negro Family*, which argues that contemporary black poverty and its concomitant social problems stem from the breakup of the African-American slave family and the continuing history of the absence of strong black fathers in the family. Based in part on Stanley Elkins's book *Slavery: A Problem in American Institutional and Intellectual Life* (1959), Moynihan's work helps to shape President Lyndon Johnson's Great Society social programs and prompts vigorous debates and challenges by social historians and civil rights activists, who protest that slave families forged their own deep bonds and that males had a strong presence in slave families.

1965   The Murder Act passed by Parliament in Great Britain proposes the abolition of capital punishment within five years.

1965   Vermont, New York, West Virginia, Iowa, and Oregon abolish capital punishment.

1965   In the Watts section of Los Angeles, California, the poorest part of the city, violence breaks out after an incident between black residents and the police. Homes are burned, and the National Guard is mobilized; 34 people die, 3,500 are arrested, and about $225 million in property damage occurs.

1965   *Maquiladora* programs (assembly plants constructed by U.S. and multinational companies using cheap Mexican labor and foreign-made parts) are established in Mexican border towns as part of the response to the ending of the *bracero* program (importing Mexican agricultural workers to the United States for seasonal labor) in 1964.

1965   The U.S. Immigration and Nationality Act is revised to abolish the system of quotas by national origin for immigrants.

1966   The first African-American hired as a baseball umpire in the major leagues in the United States is Emmett Ashford, who had worked his way up from the Southwestern International League in 1952 to become umpire-in-chief of the Pacific Coast League in 1965.

1966   The first African-American woman to serve as a U.S. federal judge is Constance Baker Motley, in New York City.

1966   The first African-American hired to coach a major-league sports team in the United States is Bill Russell, who takes over the Boston Celtics, the basketball team that he led to many championships as a player.

1966   The United Nations International Convention on the Elimination of All Forms of Racial Discrimination declares that parties to the convention must guarantee economic and educational rights. They must also guarantee the right to join unions, the right to housing and public health, and the right to educational opportunities, and they must work to eliminate all forms of discrimination.

1966   The first African-American appointed by a U.S. president to a cabinet position is Robert C. Weaver, who becomes head of the Department of Housing and Urban Development.

1966   In *South Carolina v. Katzenbach*, the U.S. Supreme Court affirms the constitutionality of the 1965 Civil Rights Act. South Carolina had filed a complaint seeking an injunction of enforcement of the act after it had been passed; Chief Justice Earl Warren writes that South Carolina's injunction is denied: "[T]he heart of the act is a complex scheme of stringent remedies aimed at areas where voting discrimination has been most flagrant."

1966   The United Nations International Convention on the Elimination of All Forms of Racial Discrimination is issued, to eradicate racial discrimination and government policies based on racial superiority in some parts of the world. Parties to the convention must work to oppose and eradicate apartheid, theories of racial superiority, and segregation.

1966   The U.S. Supreme Court decides that a park willed in trust to the city of Macon, Georgia, for whites only is subject to equal-protection requirements. *Evans v. Newton* concerns land that the city of Macon decides not to manage on a segregated basis, and in an ensuing suit the Supreme Court of Georgia affirms that the donor had the right to give his property to a limited class; Justice William O. Douglas states that the public nature of the park requires that it be treated as a public institution under the 14th Amendment, no matter who now owns it.

1966   In Botswana, South Africa, an amendment to the the country's new constitution grants citizenship to children of Botswanian women and non-Botswanian men. The old law was considered discriminatory to women, although women in Botswana remain under their husbands' control in financial matters such as securing a bank loan.

1966   In *Miranda v. Arizona*, the U.S. Supreme Court requires that defendants must be given full and effective warning of their rights at the onset of interrogation by police or a prosecuting attorney. Chief Justice Earl Warren declares that, to ensure that people are given their rights under the Fifth Amendment, they must be warned that they have a right to remain silent, that any statement they make can be used against them, and that they have a right to a lawyer; they may waive these rights, but must also be allowed to stop talking whenever they wish.

1966   The Declaration of the International Covenant on Civil and Political Rights is issued, stating that everyone has the right of self-determination, that everyone has the right to life and the right not to be subjected to torture, slavery, or forced labor. Everyone should be treated the same before the courts and should be given a fair public trial; everyone charged with a crime should be presumed innocent until proved guilty.

1966   The U.S. Freedom of Information Act (FOIA) is signed into law, to take effect July 4, 1967. Intended to foster transparency in government, the act allows individuals access to most of the internal records of federal agencies, including the FBI. Amendments passed in 1996 extend the access to electronic files.

1967   The U.S. Supreme Court decides, in *Keyishian v. Board of Regents*, that New York statutes disqualifying teachers if they are members of subversive organizations are unconstitutional. After faculty members of the State University of New York at Buffalo had refused to sign a certificate declaring they were not Communists and were dismissed, a three-judge federal court rules against them; Justice William J. Brennan states that the statutes are too broad and sweeping and violate First Amendment rights.

1967   In *Loving v. Virginia*, the U.S. Supreme Court rules that a Virginia law prohibiting interracial marriages violates the 14th Amendment. Chief Justice Earl Warren states that laws restricting the rights of citizens because of race are not constitutional.

1967   The U.S. Supreme Court rules that New York's law permitting eavesdropping violates the constitutional protections of the 4th and 14th Amendments. In *Berger v. New York*, Justice Tom C. Clark writes that a warrant can be issued only for probable cause and must describe the place to be searched and things to be seized; New York's law allows a trespass of home or office by general warrant and thus violates the 4th Amendment.

1967   In *Katz v. United States*, the U.S. Supreme Court decides that governmental electronic eavesdropping at a telephone booth violates the Fourth Amendment. Justice Potter Stewart writes that the government argues that its agents (in this case, an agent who had tapped a phone booth) should not be subject to Fourth Amendment requirements, because no physical penetration of the phone booth occurred, but the Fourth Amendment covers not only tangible items but also oral recordings.

1967   The first African-American appointed to the U.S. Supreme Court is Thurgood Marshall.

1968   The U.S. Supreme Court, in *Green v. County School Board of New Kent County*, rules that a freedom-of-choice plan does not necessarily abolish school desegregation. The school system of New Kent County in rural Virginia had two schools, one white and one black; to continue receiving federal aid, the school system adopts a freedom-of-choice plan for desegregating the schools, in which students may choose which school they attend each year. Justice Brennan states that the school system in New Kent County remains a dual one, because no white students choose the black school; in effect, the school board has delegated to parents and children the responsibility for desegregation that *Brown* places on school boards.

1968   The U.S. Supreme Court reverses the dismissal of a teacher for criticizing an Illinois board of education's allocation of school funds and its policies about informing local taxpayers, in *Pickering v. Board of Education*. Justice Thurgood Marshall writes that the free-speech clause of the First Amendment is so important that a state cannot authorize damages by a public official for criticism directed at him or her unless the criticism is shown to be false or made with reckless disregard for truth.

1968   South Carolina police fire at students from South Carolina State College at Orangeburg after protests at a segregated bowling alley; three students die. The protests had resulted in suspensions for some of the students involved and the mobilization of the National Guard; attempts to hold police officers accountable for the deaths fail.

1968   The National Advisory Commission on Civil Disorders in the United States, also known as the Kerner Commission, issues a report. Appointed by President Lyndon B. Johnson in the wake of the racial violence of 1967, the commission declares that "white racism" is the main cause of the violence and that the country is moving toward two communities, separate and unequal.

1968   The first African-American to win the U.S. Open Men's Singles Tennis Championship in New York City is Arthur Ashe. As a professional player, Ashe wins the World Court and Wimbledon championships in 1975 and the Australian Open Doubles Championship in 1977, before retiring.

1968   La Raza Unida is formed in Texas to give Spanish-Americans a greater say in the political, social, and economic life of their communities. In 1971, La Raza Unida Party wins a city election in Crystal City, Texas.

1968   Martin Luther King Jr. is assassinated in Memphis, Tennessee, where he is leading demonstrations in support of garbage workers on strike; King was most recently speaking out on the connection between racial injustice at home and the unjust war in Vietnam and was in the midst of organizing the Poor Peoples Campaign, calling for a broad coalition of poor and unrepresented Americans to occupy the streets and monuments of Washington, D.C. James Earl Ray is convicted of the murder, but many, including members of the King family, believe his claim that he was framed. Racial violence and looting spread through American cities following King's assassination.

1968   The Reverend Ralph Abernathy, the new president of the Southern Christian Leadership Conference, continues Martin Luther King Jr.'s planned Poor Peoples Campaign and the construction of Resurrection City, a campsite in the heart of the nation's capital. Poor whites, blacks, Mexican Americans, and Native Americans gather to protest poverty and the lack of economic opportunity for minorities.

1968   In the Glenville section of Cleveland, Ohio, race riots result in eight blacks and three white police officers being killed and damages of $1.5 million.

1968   Jim Gregory wins his struggle to become the first white player on the all-black football team the Tigers of Grambling State University in Louisiana. His story inspires the book *My Little Brother Is Coming Tomorrow* (1971) by Bruce Bahrenburg, as well as a made-for-TV movie called *Grambling's White Tiger* (1981) starring Olympic gold-medal decathlete Bruce Jenner as Gregory.

1969   Los P.A.D.R.E.S. (The fathers) is created in Los Angeles, California, largely by Hispanic Catholic priests, to help poor people achieve progressive social change. P.A.D.R.E.S. stands for Padres Asociados para Derechos Religiosos, Educativos, y Sociales (Fathers associated for religious, educational, and social rights).

1969   ASPIRA Association, Inc., is founded in Washington, D.C., as a grassroots organization providing educational assistance and leadership development to Hispanics. ASPIRA has an educational-counseling program for high school and college students.

1969   The U.S. Supreme Court affirms, in *Gaston County v. United States*, that North Carolina's literacy test denies or abridges the right to vote on account of race or color. Justice John Marshall Harlan writes that the 1965 Voting Rights Act prohibits literacy tests such as that for which North Carolina is suing; if the black population of North Carolina is poorly educated, it is because the state systematically segregates education, forces blacks to attend poor schools, and pays black teachers less than white ones.

1969   The first African-American to direct a symphony orchestra in the United States is Henry Lewis, who leads the New Jersey Symphony.

1969   In *Stanley v. Georgia*, the U.S. Supreme Court reverses a man's conviction for possession of obscene material. The case involves the conviction of a man for possession of films ruled to be obscene, found during a search of his home for materials concerning his alleged bookmaking activities; Justice Thurgood Marshall writes that the state obscenity statute violates the First Amendment insofar as it punishes the private possession of obscene matter; the right to receive even material of no social worth is protected by the Constitution.

1969	The American Convention on Human Rights, known as the Pact of San José, Costa Rica, is signed. Parties to the convention agree to ensure that people can enjoy their rights and freedoms without discrimination for any reason; the convention establishes a Commission on Human Rights to promote respect for human rights and an Inter-American Court of Human Rights.
1969	Two Black Panther Party leaders, Mark Clark and Fred Hampton, are shot and killed in Chicago, Illinois, and four others are wounded, as police fire 200 rounds into Hampton's apartment on a tip that he is stockpiling weapons. Police claim someone in the apartment had fired a shotgun, but Panther leaders claim that all the shooting is done by the police; no one is ever brought to trial.
1969	In Great Britain, both houses of Parliament amend the Murder Act to abolish capital punishment.
1969	The U.S. Department of Labor announces that its Philadelphia Plan for minority hiring is legal under the executive order mandating equal-employment clauses in federal contracts. The guidelines specify that no contractor who does not meet the standards will lose a federal contract if he or she makes a "good faith effort" to recruit minority workers.
1969	Harvard University announces the creation of an Afro-American Studies program, after a faculty committee reports that studying blacks in America is a "legitimate and urgent academic endeavor."
1969	The first African-American–owned company to become publicly traded is the Parks Sausage Company, traded on the National Association of Securities Dealers Automated Quotation (NASDAQ).
1969	The first African-American proposed for a seat on the New York Stock Exchange is Joseph L. Searles III, who becomes a trader and partner with Newburger, Loeb & Co.
1969	In *Alexander v. Holmes*, the U.S. Supreme Court rules that school segregation must end at once. Chief Justice Warren Burger does not support the Nixon administration's appeal to delay the desegregation of Mississippi schools and writes that to continue operating segregated schools is now no longer constitutionally possible.
1969	The U.S. Court of Appeals for the Fifth Circuit in New Orleans, Louisiana, directs school districts in Mississippi to file plans for desegregating its schools within a week.
1970	The governor of Mississippi, John Bell Williams, announces that while the state accepts the courts' ruling on desegregation, Mississippi will create a private school system for white children. Governor Williams announces his support for income-tax credits of up to $500 a year for people who donate to educational institutions.

1970   Federal marshals supervise the enrollment of black children in Mississippi's all-white schools. Many white parents picket and boycott the integrated schools. In the town of Woodville, the boycott is so successful that only 2 white children come to the district school with 1,400 black children; in Yazoo City, business leaders urge compliance with the desegregation order, and 1,500 white students come to class.

1970   Robert Finch, U.S. secretary of Health, Education, and Welfare, expresses concern about using tax-exempt status for the new segregated private school system in the South. Finch asks the Treasury Department's Internal Revenue Service to rethink its present policy and states that about 400 private schools for whites had opened since the passage of the 1964 Civil Rights Act.

1970   The Federal District Court in Washington, D.C., orders the Internal Revenue Service to stop granting tax-exempt status to segregated schools in Mississippi. While the order does not affect the private all-white schools already granted tax-exempt privileges, it stops action on the schools pending or about to file, unless they can demonstrate that they would admit black students.

1970   A federal district court judge, Manuel Real, orders the Pasadena, California, school district to ensure that no school in its district has a majority of nonwhite students. Judge Real's decision includes provisions for teaching assignments, hirings and promotions, and new school construction.

1970   Defying the deadline set by the U.S. Supreme Court, 20 school districts of the 40 under court orders in Mississippi, Georgia, and Alabama refuse to comply by desegregating their schools. Some schools close, and other school systems cooperate with white boycotts; the Burke County system in Georgia declares a freedom-of-choice plan, even though the courts had ruled against its validity.

1970   Two hundred white men and women smash the windows of a bus with baseball bats and ax handles, injuring 39 black children whom the bus is carrying to a newly integrated school in Lamar, South Carolina. State police clear the mob with tear gas.

1970   The U.S. District Court upholds the constitutionality of the Department of Labor's Philadelphia Plan for minority hiring. Judge Charles R. Weiner in Philadelphia, Pennsylvania, rules against the request for an injunction by the Contractor's Association of Eastern Pennsylvania, stating that the employment program does not violate the Civil Rights Act of 1964, because it "does not require the contractor to hire a definite percentage of a minority group," only to make a "good faith" effort.

1970   Two black college students die during protests at Jackson State College in Jackson, Mississippi.

1970   The U.S. Justice Department files a suit against the United States Steel Corporation and the United Steelworkers of America for violating the Civil Rights Act of 1964. The Justice Department also names the AFL-CIO and 12 union locals in its action, which charges that the parties practice racial discrimination in their employment policies at U.S. Steel plants in the Birmingham, Alabama, area.

1970
The first African-American to win the Mr. America bodybuilding title is Chris Dickerson.

1970
J. Edgar Hoover, director of the U.S. Federal Bureau of Investigation, claims that black militant civil rights groups are "encouraged . . . from without"; Hoover encourages the view that civil rights organizations are infiltrated and sometimes controlled by Communist agents. He launches a campaign of wiretapping and discrediting influential leaders of the movement, after his 1969 yearly report had claimed that there had been more than a hundred attacks on members of the police by black extremist groups.

1970
In a report to the Joint Chiefs of Staff on racial tensions in the U.S. military, General William C. Westmoreland states that black soldiers have lost faith in the army, and that the race problem in the army reflects the country's race problem. The report reveals that the number of black junior officers is decreasing even though the numbers of black noncommissioned officers of lower rank are increasing; even though one of every eight soldiers is black, one-fourth of all punishments without trials are meted out to blacks.

1970
The U.S. Supreme Court upholds the decision of the Georgia Supreme Court to return the property of the previously restricted Bacon Park in Macon, Georgia, to the heirs of the donor. Justice Hugo L. Black rules that the state courts had properly interpreted state law concerning the effect of a Georgia will, and that their ruling that the park's trust should be terminated violates no constitutionally protected rights.

1970
The National Association for the Advancement of Colored People (NAACP) opposes the nomination to the Supreme Court of Judge G. Harrold Carswell of Florida and urges the Senate to reject him because of his pro-segregation views. Bishop Spottswood, chairman of the NAACP, reminds senators that 125 organizations opposed Carswell's nomination to the Fifth Circuit of the U.S. Court of Appeals in 1969; the Senate votes to reject Carswell.

1970
Bishop Spottswood, chairman of the National Association for the Advancement of Colored People (NAACP), accuses the administration of President Richard M. Nixon of following a calculated policy of working against blacks. Addressing the NAACP's annual convention in Cincinnati, Ohio, Spottswood highlights Nixon's nomination of G. Harold Carswell to the Supreme Court, the memo by Nixon's domestic adviser Daniel Patrick Moynihan proposing that the issue of race can benefit from benign neglect, and the administration's unwillingness to pursue aggressively school desegregation.

1970
After four nights of rioting in which 43 people are shot, a curfew is declared for Asbury Park, New Jersey. Mayor Joseph Mattice agrees to consider demands for better housing, jobs, and police

action against the drug trade, and the curfew is lifted.

1970
New Bedford, Massachusetts, endures four nights of rioting, and African-Americans and Puerto Ricans riot in Hartford, Connecticut.

1970
The U.S. Court of Appeals in Philadelphia, Pennsylvania, orders the Department of Housing and Urban Development (HUD) to promote fair housing when evaluating applications for federal support for housing projects. HUD is told to hold public hearings, or find out by other means, to evaluate whether a housing project will maintain or worsen segregated housing patterns; bound by the Civil Rights Acts of 1964 and 1968, HUD must determine whether urban renewal and minority housing needs outweigh the disadvantages of increasing racial concentration.

1970
Black army officers petition the U.S. secretary of the army, requesting an inquiry into racial bias in army housing policy in West Germany. Seven officers, including Captain Curtis R. Smothers, a military judge, charge discrimination and claim that an open court of inquiry is necessary to determine the facts and find solutions to the army's noncompliance with regulations.

1970
The Comisión Femenil Mexicana Nacional, Inc. (National Commission of Mexican Women), is established in Los Angeles, California, to work for the rights of Hispanic women. The Comisión runs the Chicana Service Center, where it offers employment training; the Centro de Niño, with a bilingual child-development program; and Casa Victoria, a group home for teens.

1971
The Federal Labor Panel decides that Bethlehem Steel Corporation's seniority system discriminates against black workers. Bethlehem, the second biggest producer of steel in the United States, disputes the panel's unanimous decision but nonetheless establishes new quotas in hiring, training, and promotion of black workers.

1971
The U.S. Supreme Court affirms that district courts have broad powers to remedy school segregation, in *Swann v. Charlotte-Mecklenburg Board of Education.* Justice Warren Burger's decision supports the Federal District Court's goal of eliminating all state-imposed segregation from public schools.

1971
The first African-American to become an admiral in the U.S. Navy is Samuel L. Gravely Jr.

1971
The U.S. Supreme Court decides, in *Griggs v. Duke Power Co.,* that the use of an intelligence test or the requirement of a high school diploma not significantly related to job performance violates the Civil Rights Act of 1964. The Duke Power Company required that employees have a high school diploma or pass an intelligence test to hold certain jobs or be promoted, but black employees claim that this violates Title VII of the Civil Rights Act. Chief Justice Warren Burger writes that the company discriminates in its employment practices in assigning blacks to low-level jobs, making promotions difficult for them, and requiring tests or diplomas that have no connection to the job.

1971   The Carnegie Commission on Higher Education issues a report urging a tripling of federal aid to black colleges. The report, *From Isolation to Mainstream: Problems of the Colleges Founded for Negroes*, calls for financial support from corporations, states, and foundations to increase enrollment from 150,000 to 300,000 students.

1971   The U.S. Supreme Court rules that North Carolina's Anti-Busing Law is invalid and prevents implementation of constitutional desegregation plans, in *North Carolina State Board of Education v. Swann*. Chief Justice Warren Burger writes that a state-imposed restriction on a school system works to obstruct the establishment of a unitary school system, and it must give way.

1971   The U.S. Department of Health, Education, and Welfare (HEW) decides to implement crosstown busing to desegregate schools in Austin, Texas. Responding to the Supreme Court's ruling in *Swann v. Charlotte-Mecklenburg Board of Education*, HEW decides that busing is necessary in Austin, but District Court judge Jack Roberts rules against HEW and accepts the school board's plan for a series of learning centers in the arts, avocations, and sciences, which would be available to all elementary students; if necessary, all students could be bused to those centers. Some black junior high students are assigned to schools not completely black.

1971   The U.S. Bureaus of Labor Statistics and the U.S. Bureau of the Census issue a report that states that blacks are far behind whites in economic prosperity. The report, *The Social and Economic Status of Negroes in the United States, 1970*, reveals that 28.9 percent of black families are headed by women, as opposed to 9 percent of white families; while blacks had increased their median income by about 50 percent during the 1960s, they still earn about 60 percent of whites' salaries. About 50 percent of black-occupied housing in rural areas is considered substandard, as opposed to 8 percent of white housing in rural areas.

1971   U.S. president Richard M. Nixon issues a directive about the Department of Health, Education, and Welfare (HEW) plan for busing in Austin, Texas. President Nixon counters HEW's plan for crosstown busing and orders HEW secretary Elliot Richardson to provide aid for attempts by school districts to keep busing at the minimum legal requirement; the Nixon administration makes it clear that officials could lose their jobs if they unduly advocate busing as the solution to desegregation of schools.

1971   The U.S. Commission on Civil Rights charges that the air force is busing children of military personnel in Texas to perpetuate racial segregation. The commission claims that rather than have children from the Laughlin Air Force Base attend the nearby schools of San Felipe, the air force is busing students farther away to the predominantly white schools of Del Rio, and that the Nixon administration's decision to use busing at a minimum undermines efforts to integrate school systems.

1971   Documents stolen from the Media, Pennsylvania, office of the

Federal Bureau of Investigation (FBI) and released to the public reveal FBI director J. Edgar Hoover's comments about campus disorders involving blacks and threatening the country's stability. The reports show that college organizations and conventions of black students are monitored by the FBI.

1971 The U.S. Supreme Court decides, in *New York Times Co. v. United States*, that the government cannot legally restrain the publication of classified Vietnam War papers, known as the Pentagon Papers, by the *New York Times* and the *Washington Post*. Justices Hugo L. Black and William O. Douglas write that the First Amendment protects the freedom of the press, and newspapers should be praised for publishing the Pentagon Papers, rather than being condemned.

1971 The Illinois Supreme Court issues indictments against Illinois prosecutors for obstructing justice in cases against police officers who had raided the Black Panthers, after Illinois Criminal Court judge Joseph Power refuses to act on the judgment of a grand jury and sits on the indictments. The chief prosecutor of Chicago and the police superintendent of the city are 2 of 14 law-enforcement officers charged with conspiring to obstruct justice by trying to suppress or thwart the prosecutions of eight police officers involved in the shooting deaths of Mark Clark and Fred Hampton, Black Panther leaders, in 1969.

1971 New York State troopers storm the prison at Attica, New York, to end a prison strike. Forty-three people are killed during the violence; many of the prisoners killed are black, and nine prison guards held as hostages die.

1971 The first official interracial marriage in North Carolina takes place when a black man marries a white woman in Durham County.

1971 The United Nations Declaration on the Rights of Mentally Retarded Persons states that mentally retarded persons have the same rights as other human beings; they are entitled to the proper care and therapy to help them develop their potential, and if possible they should remain with their families; they have the right to economic security and the right to engage in meaningful work to the greatest extent possible; they must not be exploited or mistreated, and if they must be institutionalized, they should be protected against abuse.

1971 Las Hermanas–United States of America (The Sisters–USA) is created in San Antonio, Texas. The members, mostly Roman Catholic nuns, are organized in 12 regional chapters to engage Hispanic women in the Church and to advocate for the needs of Hispanics.

1972 The U.S. Supreme Court decides that a state can grant a liquor license to a private club that practices racial discrimination. After K. Leroy Irvis, the black majority leader of the Pennsylvania House of Representatives, had been refused service in a restaurant of the Harrisburg Loyal Order of the Moose, Justice

William Rehnquist declares that the fact that the state has the power to issue liquor licenses does not "sufficiently implicate the state in the discriminatory guest policies" of private clubs.

1972   In *Furman v. Georgia*, the U.S. Supreme Court rules that imposition of the death penalty constitutes cruel and unusual punishment. In the case of a black man and convicted murderer sentenced to death pursuant to Georgia law, Justice William O. Douglas writes that the death-penalty law is discriminatory because its application displays discriminatory patterns, being applied more to minorities than to the general population.

1972   The National Education Association reports that 30,000 black teachers have lost their jobs in the southern United States during the last two decades, with the greatest drops in Delaware, Missouri, and Kentucky.

1972   The U.S. Army reverses the dishonorable discharges of black soldiers involved in the 1906 Brownsville, Texas, race riot; President Theodore Roosevelt discharged the soldiers even though they were responding to racial taunting by whites. In 1973, the army awards $25,000 to the lone survivor of the incident.

1972   Receiving time off for good behavior, Jimmy Aldredge, Jimmie Snowden, and Horace Doyle Barnette are released from federal prison two years after being sentenced to a three-year term for conspiracy in the deaths of three civil rights workers in Mississippi. The three had been convicted on conspiracy charges for the 1964 murders of James Chaney, Andrew Goodman, and Mickey Schwerner, participants in the 1964 Freedom Summer actions in Neshoba County, Mississippi.

1972   The National Black Feminist Organization is founded in New York City. One of the leaders, Eleanor Holmes Norton of the New York City Human Rights Commission, stresses that black women need not sacrifice their needs to black men; the group emphasizes that black liberation must include liberation for black women.

1972   The National Conference of Puerto Rican Women is established in Washington, D.C., to promote the participation of Puerto Rican women in the social, political, and economic life of the United States.

1972   The Afro-Asian Center is founded in Saugerties, New York, to promote communication among social-studies teachers throughout the United States, Africa, and Asia and to facilitate cultural understanding.

1972   U.S. president Richard M. Nixon signs an education bill that delays all court-ordered school busing for desegregation of schools until all court appeals have been concluded or until 1974. The legislation prohibits federal funds for busing unless the community requests those funds and only in instances where there is no danger to the "health, safety, or education" of the students; federal officials cannot encourage or require busing unless it is "constitutionally required."

1972	The black parents of Oklahoma City, Oklahoma, ask for federal protection of their children on school buses after racial violence. The parents make their request to the school board, the U.S. attorney, and U.S. marshals.
1972	Two black students are killed during a protest at Southern University in Baton Rouge, Louisiana. Police first deny that their officers had fired on the students, then suggest the firing was accidental.
1973	The International Labour Organization's Convention Concerning Minimum Age for Admission to Employment declares that states that are party to the convention must pursue the abolition of child labor and must raise the age of admission to work to one consistent with the best interests of the child. The minimum age must be not less than the age the child completes compulsory education and in no case under 15 years; this age applies to most work except for family holdings that do not employ hired workers.
1973	The U.S. Supreme Court, in *Espinoza v. Farah Manufacturing Co.*, rules that the national-origin provisions of the Civil Rights Act do not include alien residents. After a citizen of Mexico and legal alien resident is denied employment as a seamstress in San Antonio, Texas, because of long-standing policies against hiring aliens, the woman sues, claiming a violation of the 1964 Civil Rights Act. Justice Thurgood Marshall writes that for federal employment, the Congress presumes that national-origin discrimination does not affect the requirement of citizenship for employment, even though various executive orders have prohibited discrimination based on national origin.
1973	The Alberta Human Rights Commission of Canada is established in Alberta, to ensure compliance with the Canadian Individual's Rights Protection Act. The commission is charged with public education and with investigating charges of discrimination based on race, national origin, color, religion, physical disability, and age.
1973	In *White v. Regester*, the U.S. Supreme Court affirms the disestablishment of reapportioned multimember election districts by a district court in Texas because of racial discrimination. The Texas redistricting plan had divided the 150-member house among 79 single-member and 11 multimember districts; Justice Byron White writes that the district court had rightly invalidated some of the redistricting and notes that Texas makes political access difficult not only for blacks but also for Mexican-Americans.
1973	Arthur Ashe participates in and wins a tennis tournament in South Africa despite its policy of apartheid against those classified as "nonwhite." He is the first tennis player of his race to be permitted to compete in South Africa, and he uses the opportunity to promote racial equality in that country.
1974	The U.S. Department of Health, Education, and Welfare (HEW)

reports that, 20 years after *Brown v. Board of Education*, schools in Topeka, Kansas, are still segregated. The report shows that a large number of schools have disproportionate numbers of minority students, that a policy of transfers slows desegregation, and that facilities at the predominantly black elementary and junior high schools are inferior to those at white schools; HEW orders the Board of Education of Topeka to submit plans to remedy the situation.

1974   A study of public school children in Pittsburgh, Pennsylvania, funded by the Department of Health, Education, and Welfare (HEW), finds that nonwhites score lower on intelligence tests because of environmental factors, not genetic differences. The study concludes that differences in test results between different racial groups are "exclusively a matter of environment"; this report contrasts with the often discussed theories of the physicist William Shockley, who claims that poor and socially disadvantaged blacks are victims of heredity and genetics, not environment.

1974   The U.S. Supreme Court, in *Lau v. Nichols*, rules that the failure of San Francisco, California, schools to provide language instruction to non-English-speaking students of Chinese ancestry violates the Civil Rights Act of 1964. The federal district court had denied relief in this case, and the Court of Appeals affirmed that decision; Justice William O. Douglas writes that the school district in the suit receives federal funding and therefore is subject to the Civil Rights Act section on discrimination on grounds of race, color, or national origin.

1974   The U.S. Department of Labor, the Equal Employment Opportunity Commission, and the steel industry negotiate an agreement ending job discrimination against minorities and women in the steel industry. The agreement calls for nine steel companies to award $30 million in back pay to black and Hispanic victims of job bias and to launch a five-year plan to end discrimination in the workplace.

1974   The civil rights director of the Department of Health, Education, and Welfare, Peter Holmes, reports that in 1964 there were almost no black students attending white schools in the 11 Southern states; by 1968, 18.4 percent of black students were in majority-white schools; by 1970 it was 39.1 percent; and by 1972 up to 44 percent. The figures for black students attending all-black schools went from 68 percent in 1968 to 14.1 percent in 1970 and 9.2 percent in 1972. Nevertheless, Holmes expects to see an increase in segregation in Northern school systems.

1974   The U.S. district court judge W. Arthur Garrity Jr. rules that the Boston, Massachusetts, school system is "unconstitutionally segregated." Judge Garrity orders a desegregation plan forbidding school enrollments of more than 50 percent minority students, and the city begins a busing program, which sparks violent protests and boycotts among whites in South Boston, Dorchester, and Hyde Park.

1974	The U.S. Catholic Conference announces its opposition to capital punishment.
1974	The 1970 United Nations Economic and Social Council resolution requests the General Assembly to consider drafting the Declaration for the Protection of Women and Children in Emergency and Armed Conflict, which is issued four years later. The declaration covers the issues put forward by the Basic Principles for the Protection of Civilian Populations in Armed Conflict, which is also adopted this year, but with specific regard to the effects of these violations on women and children.
1974	After Bahrain becomes an independent nation with the end of British rule in 1971, the emir moves to restrict the rights granted citizens under the 1973 constitution. The State Security Act limits political demonstrations, weakens due process in the prosecution of antigovernment activity, and prohibits labor strikes that may cause harm to the nation.
1975	The U.S. Commission on Civil Rights issues a report urging President Gerald R. Ford to enforce school desegregation effectively. The report states that the government cannot turn back because of resistance in Boston or elsewhere and charges that government agencies had failed to enforce existing legislation to guarantee equal educational opportunities for minorities and women.
1975	In Washington, D.C., the U.S. District Court judge John H. Pratt rules that the Department of Health, Education, and Welfare must enforce school-desegregation laws in 125 school districts. Judge Pratt's ruling, in response to a 1971 suit by the National Association for the Advancement of Colored People Legal Defense Fund, affects school districts in 16 states with voluntary desegregation plans; Pratt states that not responding to the order would trigger an end to federal funds for those school districts.
1975	The first African-American golfer to participate in the Masters Tournament in Augusta, Georgia, is Lee Elder.
1975	The first African-American woman physician to be commissioned in the U.S. Navy's medical corps is Dr. Donna P. Davis.
1975	The first African-American four-star general in the United States is Daniel James.
1975	The first African-American to manage a major-league baseball team in the United States is Frank Robinson, who takes over the Cleveland Indians.
1975	The first African-American–owned and –operated television station in the United States is WGPR-TV in Detroit, Michigan.
1975	Joann Little, a 20-year-old black woman, pleads self-defense for murdering a white prison guard, Clarence Alligood, who, she alleges, attempted to rape her while she was held in the Beaufort County jail for breaking and entering. Also filing suit against Alligood's estate, she requests the Federal District Court to protect female inmates from sexual abuse by male personnel who

supervise them; an interracial jury acquits her.

1975   James B. Adams, associate director of the Federal Bureau of Investigation (FBI), testifies before the U.S. Senate Intelligence Committee that the FBI spied on Martin Luther King Jr. throughout the 1960s to determine whether he and the civil rights movement were under the influence of Communists. Although the FBI found no evidence of Communist influence, it had used 16 electronic bugs and eight wiretappings and sent anonymous letters and recordings to King's wife.

1975   The United Nations Declaration on the Rights of Disabled Persons states that disabled persons must not be discriminated against and must be given all the medical services and counseling that will help them integrate fully into society.

1975   The Asian American Legal Defense and Education Fund is founded in New York City to provide bilingual legal defense and counseling for Asian Americans who cannot afford these services. The fund also litigates cases involving immigration, employment, housing, voting-rights issues, and violence against Asian Americans.

1975   The Fund for Free Expression is organized to promote civil liberties for writers and to support the ability of writers and journalists to work without censorship. The organization is a precursor to Human Rights Watch.

1975   The emir of Bahrain suspends the 1973 constitution, enacted after British rule ended in 1971. At the same time, the democratically elected legislature is dissolved, and the nation has been ruled as an absolute monarchy ever since.

1975   The Asociación Nacional Pro Personas Mayores (National association of Hispanic older people) is formed in Los Angeles, California, to advocate for older Hispanic people. It offers a national employment-assistance program and operates the National Hispanic Research Center.

1976   Two thousand people protesting court-ordered desegregation fight the Boston police near South Boston High School in Massachusetts. More than 40 police officers are injured.

1976   The United Nations International Covenant on Economic, Social, and Cultural Rights guarantees the right to work. States party to the covenant must protect the right of everyone to work, to earn a fair salary with equal pay for equal work, to work in healthful conditions, to be promoted on the basis of seniority and capability, to enjoy periods of leisure and paid holidays, to join freely operating trade unions, and to strike when necessary. Children must be protected from exploitation and unhealthy work conditions and must not be allowed to work if they are below a minimum age. The covenant also guarantees the right to education that fully develops the individual and enables everyone to live in a democratic society. States that are parties to the covenant must achieve a system of free compulsory primary education available to all and free secondary and higher education.

1976   Residents of the slums of Soweto Township in South Africa rebel against their living conditions and the attempts of white South African police to relocate them to white-created "homelands."

1976   The National Urban League issues *The State of Black America*, which reports that many gains that blacks had made during the last decade were eroded in 1975. The report notes a decline in middle-income black families, from one-fourth to one-fifth of all black families; black family income is 58 percent of white family income, down from 61 percent a few years earlier; black unemployment is at 14.1 percent.

1976   Some 1,500 students in Pensacola, Florida, riot over plans to change the name of the school team from Rebels to Raiders, because black students objected to the name and the use of the Confederate flag at sporting events. Four whites are injured by gunfire, and soon after, crosses are burned on the lawns of members of the school board, a bullet is fired at the home of a black board member, and two homes are burned.

1976   Herbert Gutman publishes *The Black Family in Slavery and Freedom*, prompted in part by Daniel Patrick Moynihan's 1965 report. Having studied plantation records, Gutman argues that many children born into slavery were given their fathers' names and, despite the violence of slavery and deliberate attempts to strip away African-American family identity, many families did create stable relationships.

1976   The U.S. Supreme Court rules that private schools cannot exclude minority students. In a case involving black children who are refused admission to private schools in Virginia, Justice Potter Stewart states that parents have a First Amendment right to send their children to schools that support the notion that racial segregation is desirable, but the schools themselves are not protected by the First Amendment for excluding racial minorities.

1976   The U.S. Supreme Court decides that victims of reverse discrimination (discrimination against whites or males) may sue in federal court. White employers of a company claim they had been fired for the same offense as that committed by a black employee who was not fired; the Court rules that the Civil Rights Act of 1964 is not limited to discrimination against a particular race.

1976   The Equal Rights Congress is founded in Los Angeles, California, as a coalition of national minority organizations concerned about all forms of discrimination, including those based on race, color, religion, sex, and economic status.

1977   The Committee Against Anti-Asian Violence is formed in New York City to oppose violence directed against Asian Americans. The committee hosts forums and discussions about discrimination and racial violence.

1977   The International Association against Torture is established in Italy to work toward ending the use of torture around the world, especially in Latin America and the Caribbean. It monitors human rights abuses, hosts conferences, organizes fact-finding delegations, and issues reports.

1977   After the U.S. Supreme Court decision in *Furman v. United States* (ruling that the death penalty is cruel and unusual punishment), Gary Gilmore is executed by firing squad in Utah. Gilmore was convicted of murdering two people.

1977   The U.S. Department of Health, Education, and Welfare cuts funding to the public schools of Chicago, Illinois, because the schools violate civil rights laws, including having an inadequate bilingual program and too many black teachers in schools with a large black student body.

1977   The first African-American appointed secretary of the U.S. Army is Clifford Alexander Jr.

1977   The first African-American appointed general manager of a professional basketball team in the National Basketball Association is Wayne Embry, who takes over the Milwaukee Bucks.

1977   In Washington, D.C., U.S. District Court judge John Pratt rules that the Department of Health, Education, and Welfare violated civil rights laws by failing to order "adequate racial desegregation" in six Southern states. Judge Pratt orders desegregation plans for institutions of higher education in North Carolina, Arkansas, Oklahoma, Florida, Georgia, and Virginia "to balance the proportion of black and white students in schools that receive federal aid."

1977   The first African-American woman to serve in a U.S. presidential cabinet is Patricia Roberts Harris, who takes over the Department of Housing and Urban Development.

1977   The U.S. Supreme Court decides, in *Milliken v. Bradley*, that a district court can order compensatory or remedial programs for schoolchildren who have been subjected to segregation. The case involved the efforts of the Detroit school board to correct official acts of racial discrimination that it, and the state of Michigan, had committed.

1977   Governor Mills Goodwin of Virginia announces that his state will not accept the "federal racial quotas" of the Department of Health, Education, and Welfare (HEW) for school desegregation. The announcement comes a day after HEW's court-imposed deadline for receiving racial-desegregation plans from Southern states.

1977   The U.S. Supreme Court affirms, in *Fullilove v. Klutznick*, the minority business enterprise (MBE) provision of the 1977 Public Works Employment Act. The MBE provision requires that, without an administrative waiver, at least 10 percent of federal funds granted for local public-works projects must be used by the state or local grantee to procure services or supplies from businesses owned by minority groups "who are Negroes, Spanish-speaking, Orientals, Indians, Eskimos, and Aleuts." Chief Justice Warren Burger writes that when a Congressional program comes under review by the Court, it should be upheld if there is reasonable assurance that the program is constitutional.

1978   Human Rights Watch is created as Helsinki Watch, to monitor the compliance of Soviet-bloc countries with the human rights provisions of the Helsinki Accord. In 1988, the various Watch committees established to monitor civil rights violations around the world would be joined into Human Rights Watch, based in New York City with offices in London, Moscow, Hong Kong, Los Angeles, Brussels, and Washington, D.C., to publicize human rights abuses such as torture, disappearances, censorship, and unfair imprisonment.

1978   The Commission for the Defense of Human Rights in Central America monitors human rights activities in Central America, providing education and legal assistance.

1978   The Lawyers Committee for Human Rights is established with headquarters in New York City and offices in Oakland, California, and Washington, D.C., to advocate for the rights of victims of human rights abuses. Its International Human Rights Program monitors abuse throughout the world.

1978   A study issued by the Southern Poverty Law Center in Montgomery, Alabama, surveys Florida, Georgia, and Texas and finds that 45 percent of death-row inmates are blacks who killed whites, 50 percent are whites who killed whites, and only 5 percent are blacks who killed blacks; no whites who killed blacks were on death row. According to Morris Dees, director of the Southern Poverty Law Center, the study reveals that blacks represent a larger proportion of death-row inmates than they do the general population.

1978   The publication of documents from the Federal Bureau of Investigation (FBI) reveals that the FBI gave information about the Freedom Riders to a known member of the Ku Klux Klan (KKK). Obtained in a suit against the FBI by Walter Bergman, who was partially paralyzed after the bus he was riding on was attacked by the Klan in Anniston, Alabama, in 1961, the documents, published in the *Detroit Free Press*, show that the FBI knew that Sergeant Thomas Cook of the Birmingham, Alabama, police was passing FBI information about the buses to KKK leadership and that the Birmingham police agreed to arrive at the bus terminals 15 or 20 minutes late to give the Klan enough time to attack the civil rights riders.

1978   The U.S. Supreme Court rules that the federal government is not required to pay for court-ordered school busing. Kentucky governor Julian Carroll had tried to secure federal funding to offset the costs of school-desegregation busing programs in Louisville and Jefferson County and had unsuccessfully challenged federal laws prohibiting federal funding of busing.

1978   In *Regents of the University of California v. Bakke*, the U.S. Supreme Court rules that the University of California cannot take race into account when making admissions decisions. The University of California at Davis medical school had offered a special admissions process to encourage the application and acceptance of minority candidates; applicants in the regular admissions process had to have maintained a 2.5 undergraduate grade-point average, but this was not the case for minority applicants. After Allan Bakke, a white male, is denied admission in both 1973 and 1974, even though, he claims, he is more qualified than some of the minority applicants who were accepted, he sues, claiming that he was excluded on the basis of race; Justice Lewis Powell declares that the medical school's admission program for minorities is undeniably a "classification based on race and ethnic background."

1979   The first African-American woman to become a longshoreman is Audrey Neal, who takes a job at the Bayonne Military Ocean Terminal in Bayonne, New Jersey.

1979   The U.S. Supreme Court, in *United Steelworkers of America, AFL-CIO-CLC v. Weber*, rules that a voluntary affirmative-action plan by private parties to end racial segregation does not violate Title VII of the Civil Rights Act. A white production worker sued, claiming that the affirmative-action plan negotiated as part of the collective-bargaining agreement signed by the steelworkers and Kaiser Aluminum Chemical Corporation violated his rights because he was discriminated against because of his race; Justice William J. Brennan writes that Title VII does not forbid voluntary plans for genuine affirmative action by employers and unions.

1979   The Action Internationale Contre La Faim (International action against famine) is founded in France specifically to combat famine. Through regional offices elsewhere in Europe and in Africa, the organization raises money to support projects preventing famine or lessening the effects of existing famines, mainly in sub-Saharan Africa.

1979   The International Federation for Human Rights (Helsinki Watch) is founded in Vienna, Austria, to publicize human rights abuses in Eastern Europe, the Soviet Union, Turkey, and Afghanistan.

1980   The American Buddhist Movement is organized in New York to unify Buddhist groups and organizations in the United States and to encourage the study of the relationship between the Buddhist and American cultures.

1980   In *Vitek v. Jones*, the U.S. Supreme Court decides that the involuntary transfer of a prisoner to a mental hospital without adequate notice or opportunity for a hearing violates the due-process clause of the 14th Amendment. A man serving time for robbery in a Nebraska prison was transferred to a penitentiary hospital and placed in solitary confinement, where he set his mattress on fire and burned himself severely; after treatment, he was sent to the security section of a state mental hospital; Justice Byron White writes that a convicted felon is subject to the same rights enjoyed by ordinary people concerning confinement to a mental hospital.

1980   Violence erupts in Miami, Florida, after the acquittal in a Tampa, Florida, court of four white deputy sheriffs in the beating death of a black insurance executive; 15 people die during the rioting. The trial, which was moved from Miami to give the defendants a fair trial, involved charges that, after the police officers had beaten the man to death, they attempted to make it look as though he had died in a motorcycle accident; the Tampa jury was composed only of white men. After the verdict, black organizations ask that the prosecutor, State Attorney Janet Reno, be fired.

1980   The U.S. Refugee Act, passed by Congress, broadens the definition of a refugee from one who flees a Communist country to encompass other situations. The revision allows thousands of refugees from other countries to apply for U.S. citizenship.

1981   The United Nations International Convention on the Elimination of All Forms of Discrimination against Women states that discrimination against women makes it difficult for them to participate on equal terms with men in social, political, and economic life. Changes in men's roles, as well as those of women, are necessary to give women equal opportunity, and parties to the convention are urged to take every means, including legislative, to ensure the full development of women.

1981   Americas Watch is established to monitor free-speech and human rights issues in Central and South America and the Caribbean region. In 1988, it would become part of the newly formed Human Rights Watch headquartered in New York City.

1981   Capital punishment is abolished in France, where the last execution had taken place in 1977.

1982   The U.S. Supreme Court rules, in *United States v. Ross*, that police officers with probable cause to believe that contraband is concealed in an automobile they have stopped may conduct a warrantless search. Justice John Paul Stevens states that if probable cause dictates stopping a vehicle, it also dictates a complete search of the vehicle and its contents.

1982   Charles Brooks is executed by lethal injection in Texas.

1982   The Institute for the Study of Genocide is established at John Jay College in New York City to promote the study of genocide's causes and how to prevent it.

1983   The U.S. Supreme Court decides, in *United States v. Knotts*, that the use of a hidden beeper placed by police to enable them to follow a vehicle does not violate the Fourth Amendment. With the consent of the chemical company, a narcotics agent placed a beeper inside a five-gallon container of chloroform purchased by a man suspected of using the chemical to manufacture illicit drugs, and they eventually traced the beeper signal and the container to a residence, where the agents found a narcotics laboratory; Justice William Rehnquist writes that somebody driving in an automobile on a public thoroughfare has no reasonable expectation of privacy, and the use of the beeper to help trace the car does not alter this situation.

1983   U.S. president Ronald Reagan vetoes a bill allocating $20 million for the school-desegregation program in Chicago, Illinois. The veto stymies a desegregation plan ordered by U.S. district court judge Milton I. Shadur, who at the same time orders the freeze of additional federal funding for education; President Reagan, in announcing his veto, declares that "the better course is to seek swift reversal of the district court's order."

1983   The first African-American woman to win the Miss America contest is Vanessa Williams, who is forced to give up the title after nude photographs of her are published.

1983   The Human Rights Research Association is founded in Canada to promote human rights activities in Africa, publish information, and develop a library.

1983   The U.S. District Court in Kalamazoo, Michigan, rules that there is a preponderance of evidence that the Federal Bureau of Investigation (FBI) knew that the Ku Klux Klan (KKK) planned to attack the Freedom Riders. Eighty-four-year-old Walter Bergman's suit claims that the FBI knew that it was giving its intelligence about the Freedom Riders to police officers linked to the KKK, which then attacked Bergman at the Anniston, Alabama, bus station during a 1961 Freedom Ride; Bergman was confined to a wheelchair as a result of the attacks. Alabama police deliberately delayed protecting the Freedom Riders.

1983   The state senate of Louisiana votes unanimously to repeal the state's racial-classification laws, according to which a person is considered black if he or she is 1/32 black.

1983   U.S. president Ronald Reagan signs legislation designating the third Monday in January as Martin Luther King Jr. Day, to honor the slain civil rights leader.

1983   The U.S. Supreme Court, in *Whisenhunt v Spradlin*, rules that the suspension of an Amarillo, Texas, policeman and policewoman for dating and spending nights together violates their due-process and privacy rights. Justice William J. Brennan writes that there is no evidence that the laws of Amarillo forbid private, off-duty, lawful sexual relations, and the policy reasons for disciplining the pair had never before been stated by the police department, the city, or the state.

1984   Judge Enslen of the U.S. District Court in Kalamazoo, Michigan, awards Walter Bergman $50,000 in damages, in Bergman's suit against the Federal Bureau of Investigation (FBI). Bergman claims that the FBI knew that it was giving its intelligence about the Freedom Riders to police officers linked to the Ku Klux Klan, who were responsible for beating Bergman so severely that he remained unable to walk for the rest of his life.

1984   The U.S. Supreme Court decides, in *Firefighters Local Union No. 1784 v. Stotts*, that remedies to correct racial discrimination cannot encroach on bona fide seniority systems. The case involves two black members of the Memphis, Tennessee, Fire Department who filed suit claiming that department and city officials discriminated in hiring and promotion decisions. Justice White writes that Title VII protects bona fide seniority systems; furthermore, as there is no evidence that the black employees protected from layoff were discriminated against, and there was no award of seniority to them, it cannot be argued that voluntary actions encroaching on seniority systems are permitted.

1984   The U.S. Supreme Court overturns a decision by the U.S. Court of Appeals for the Third Circuit and rules that federal laws prohibiting racial or sexual discrimination by institutions extend only to the affected unit, not the institution as a whole. Justices Lewis Powell and Sandra Day O'Connor declare that civil rights laws cover only the programs receiving federal aid, not the entire institution, and that this case is an example of "overzealousness" on the part of the federal government.

1984   The United Nations International Convention against Torture and Other Cruel, Inhuman, or Degrading Treatment or Punishment states that each party to the convention must institute every possible measure to prevent torture for any reason; a state of war does not justify torture, nor does an order from a superior. States may not return a person to a country in which that person can be expected to undergo torture.

1985   Asia Watch is founded to monitor human rights violations in Asia. It publishes information and helps to organize international support for human rights activities and activists. In 1988, it becomes part of the newly formed Human Rights Watch, headquartered in New York City.

1985   The first African-American to go into space is Guion S. Bluford Jr., aboard the U.S. space shuttle *Challenger*.

1985   The first African-American to pilot a space mission is Frederick D. Gregory, at the controls of the *Challenger/Spacelab 3*.

1985   The U.S. General Accounting Office (GAO) agrees to pay $3.5 million in back pay to 300 black employees denied promotion because of racial discrimination. The Equal Employment Opportunity Commission declares that the GAO used two separate promotion systems, which produced racial discrimination; as part of the settlement, 32 black evaluators receive immediate promotion, and the GAO reforms its selection programs to increase the percentage of minorities in upper-level positions.

1985   Ryan White, a 14-year-old hemophiliac who contracted AIDS from tainted blood-clotting products, is forbidden to attend public school in Kokomo, Indiana. His family ultimately wins a court battle to overturn the ban, and White resumes his schooling in the nearby town of Cicero.

1986   The U.S. Immigration Reform and Control Act establishes a program to provide legal status to aliens residing in the country before January 1, 1982. Under this program, a significant number of Hispanics without documents register for citizenship.

1986　　In *Batson v Kentucky*, the U.S. Supreme Court rules that a defendant can demonstrate purposeful discrimination in a prosecutor's preemptory challenges. In a case involving a black man indicted for burglary in Kentucky, the prosecutor used his peremptory challenges to remove the remaining blacks from the jury pool after the judge had excused certain jurors, and an all-white jury was picked; the defendant's lawyer moved to discharge the jury, claiming the prosecutor's removal of blacks violated the defendant's rights under the Sixth and 14th Amendments, but the judge denied the motion. The Supreme Court of Kentucky affirmed the judgment, but Justice Lewis Powell writes that a defendant has the right to be tried by a jury whose members are not picked by discriminatory means.

1986　　The U.S. Congress passes an act opposing apartheid and imposing economic sanctions on South Africa. A section of the legislation stipulates that the sanctions will be removed only when political prisoners are released; the act is the result of long-standing political organizing by groups like Trans-Africa and supporters of Nelson Mandela, the imprisoned charismatic leader of the African National Congress.

1986　　Physicians for Human Rights is established to discourage the use of torture and human rights abuses, to provide medical aid to victims, and to advocate for imprisoned health professionals.

1987　　U.S. Supreme Court justice Thurgood Marshall, during a television interview, states that President Ronald Reagan ranks at the bottom of the list of U.S. presidents "in protecting and advancing civil rights." Marshall, the only black member of the Supreme Court, declares that whoever calls the shots determines whether there is integration or discrimination, and that in this regard Reagan did not do his job.

1987　　In *McClesky v. Kemp*, the U.S. Supreme Court rules that a study showing disparity in imposing the death sentence in Georgia based on the race of the murder victim is not grounds to overturn a sentence. A black man convicted of armed robbery and the murder of a white police officer in Georgia claimed that the Georgia capital-sentencing process is administered in a racially discriminatory manner and offered a statistical study demonstrating that conclusion; Justice Lewis Powell writes that a defendant alleging an equal-protection violation must prove that discrimination is purposeful, and that to apply an inference drawn from a statistical study is not comparable to a specific instance of a person committing murder and paying the penalty.

1987　　Klaus Barbie ("the Butcher of Lyon"), head of the Gestapo in Lyon, France, between 1942 and 1944, is tried in France for crimes against humanity; the list of Barbie's crime is so lengthy that the entire first day of the trial is necessary to enumerate them all. Barbie had personally tortured those he interrogated and was responsible for thousands of deaths of those suspected of being Jews or members of the Resistance. Seized by U.S. authorities after World War II, Barbie was recruited for counterintelligence and moved with his family from Germany to Bolivia to live under the name Klaus Altmann; he was tracked down and extradited in 1972, and the U.S. government later officially apologized to France.

1987 Minority students on the campus of the University of Massachusetts rally to demonstrate against racism following the occupation of New Africa House and racial violence against Puerto Rican students. An agreement between school administrators and minority students calls for action against those who commit racial violence and increased school programs promoting multicultural awareness.

1987 The U.S. Supreme Court rules, in *United States v. Paradise*, that a temporary one-for-one program of promoting blacks does not violate equal-protection guarantees. The case involves the efforts of the National Association for the Advancement of Colored People and black members of Alabama's state police to bring about fair hiring and advancement policies. Justice William J. Brennan writes that the pervasive discriminatory behavior of the Alabama state police creates the need for relief, and the one-for-one requirement lasts only until the police produce a program that does not discriminate against blacks.

1988 A poll by the *Atlanta Constitution* shows that 75 percent of those polled in Alabama favor flying the Confederate flag over the state capitol in Montgomery. The previous year, the Alabama branch of the National Association for the Advancement of Colored People had begun a campaign to remove the flag, to them a symbol of support for slavery and resistance to integration; Governor Hunt of Alabama announces the flag will fly until a majority of Alabamans decide to remove it.

1988 U.S. president Ronald Reagan vetoes legislation overturning the 1984 Supreme Court ruling in *Grove City College*, limiting an institution's need to prohibit discrimination based on race, age, sex, or handicap to the offending program receiving federal funds, not the entire institution. The House of Representatives voted 315 to 98 and the Senate 75 to 14 to counteract the Court's decision; President Reagan claims that the legislation, entitled the Civil Rights Restoration Act, offers unwarranted federal intervention in corporations and "institutions with religious affiliations."

1988 The U.S. Congress overrides the presidential veto of the Civil Rights Restoration Act by a vote of 73 to 24 in the Senate and 292 to 133 in the House of Representatives. The act provides exemptions for small businesses, churches, welfare recipients, and farmers receiving price-support aid, but extends civil rights coverage to entire institutions.

1988 A study by Douglas Massey and Nancy Denton in the *American Journal of Sociology*, titled "Suburbanization and Segregation in U.S. Metropolitan Areas," reveals that major barriers to blacks in integrated housing in the U.S. suburbs still exist.

1988 The American Council of Education issues a report, "One-Third of a Nation," showing that the United States is "moving backward" on full participation by minorities. Published in the *Chronicle of Higher Education*, the report states that in most measures of individual and social well-being there are gaps, some of which are widening, between the majority of people and minorities; in 1986, 31.1 percent of blacks and 27.3 percent of Hispanics live below the poverty limit. The council urges colleges and universities to increase minority enrollment, to develop a multicultural atmosphere that supports minority students and encourages them to succeed, and to encourage the hiring of minority teachers.

1988 The U.S. Federal Bureau of Investigation (FBI) begins an affirmative-action program to hire more minority workers. FBI director William Sessions introduces the program because 311 Hispanic FBI agents filed a class-action suit alleging discrimination in promotions and assignments of agents, and a black agent filed racial-harassment claims against white colleagues; in an FBI workforce of 9,507, there are 417 blacks and 439 Hispanic agents.

1988 The U.S. Navy issues a report on an internal study that reveals "widespread but subtle bias against black and Hispanic sailors." The study shows that blacks and Hispanics are granted promotion less quickly than whites and that the navy fails to recruit in minority areas, to encourage attitudes of racial equality in training recruits, and to allow minorities equal access to technical areas of specialization.

1988 The first Hispanic appointed to serve as U.S. secretary of education is Dr. Lauro F. Cavazos, appointed by President Reagan.

1988 The first political party founded to promote democracy in Myanmar (Burma) is the National League for Democracy (NLD), founded by the political activist Daw Aung San Suu Kyi to combat the authoritarian military government that had seized power in 1962. NLD is repressed by the government in 1989, and many leaders are imprisoned; although the NLD is victorious in the 1990 elections, the government ignores the results. In 1991, Daw Aung San Suu Kyi is awarded the Nobel Prize for peace.

1989 The U.S. Supreme Court, in *City of Richmond v. J. A. Coson Co.*, rules that a Richmond, Virginia, program to set aside 30 percent of the total value of construction projects to companies with at least 50 percent minority ownership is unconstitutional. The provision was enacted because only 0.6 percent of city contracts, worth $25 million, had gone to minority companies, even though the city was 60 percent black; Justice Sandra Day O'Connor writes that the quota is "an unlawful form of reverse discrimination"; quotas that are not connected with any injury suffered by anyone are not covered by the equal-protection clause of the 14th Amendment.

1989 The first African-American to head a major U.S. professional-sports league is Bill White, who becomes the head of baseball's

National League. White was an all-star first baseman during his playing days and a broadcaster for the New York Yankees.

1989   The U.S. Supreme Court rules that employees have the burden of disproving their employers' assertion that they enforce neutral racial practices, in *Wards Cove Packing Company, Inc., v. Frank Atonio et al.* The case involved the claim of Alaskan natives, Filipinos, and Asians that they were the victims of racial discrimination by their employers at a salmon cannery. The Supreme Court overturns the decision of the U.S. Court of Appeals for the Ninth Circuit that the minority workers proved their case, and Justice Byron White writes that when minorities claim that, statistical evidence shows they are victims of discrimination, employers need only show that there is a legitimate reason. Absence of minority workers in skilled positions is not evidence of bias in cases where it reflects a lack of qualified minority applicants.

1989   The U.S. Supreme Court, in *Personnel Board of Jefferson County, Alabama, et al., v. Robert K. Wilks et al.*, rules that white firefighters adversely affected by a court-ordered affirmative-action plan may file suit alleging discrimination. After Birmingham, Alabama, set up an affirmative-action program, the Court of Appeals denied an injunction to white firefighters challenging the plan; when another group of white firefighters filed suit, the court of appeals allowed them to sue, stating that they were not party to the first decree. Justice William Rehnquist agrees with the court of appeals decision that the agreement between one group of employees and their employer cannot settle the conflicting claims of another group.

1989   The U.S. Supreme Court decides that an old civil rights law may no longer be the basis for claiming racial harassment in the workplace, in *Patterson v. McLean Credit Union*. A black woman who worked as a teller in North Carolina and claimed that her supervisor did not promote her and harassed her because of her race sued, citing an old law; Justice Anthony Kennedy states that the old law may not be cited as a basis for racial-harassment suits in the workplace as it covers only racial discrimination in making and enforcing private contracts.

1989   U.S. Supreme Court justice Thurgood Marshall makes a speech criticizing recent Supreme Court decisions against affirmative action. Addressing federal judges, Marshall declares that the latest Court decisions put at risk the civil rights of all citizens; he sees the recent decisions as a deliberate limiting of civil rights.

1989   The first African-American to be elected mayor of the city of New York is David Dinkins, elected by a little more than 40,000 votes over Rudolph Giuliani.

1989   The first African-American to be elected governor of the state of Virginia is Douglas Wilder, elected by a margin of only 7,000 votes out of 1.7 million cast.

1989   The first African-American to serve as chairman of the Joint Chiefs of Staff is General Colin L. Powell, who is also chief military adviser to President George H. W. Bush.

1989   In a television interview on *60 Minutes*, former President Ronald Reagan claims that civil rights leaders exaggerate the racism in America and that they try thereby to keep themselves in the spotlight. He complains that his accomplishments in the field of civil rights have been minimized.

1989   White teenagers mistake Yusuf Hawkins, a black teenager, for another young black man believed to be dating a white girl in the predominantly white Bensonhurst neighborhood of Brooklyn, New York, and shoot him to death. His death spurs large-scale protests against racism in the city; only one of the five whites accused of his murder is convicted.

1989   Civil rights leaders like Benjamin Hooks of the National Association for the Advancement of Colored People, U.S. congressmen Ronald Dellums and John Lewis, Atlanta mayor Andrew Young, and the Reverend Jesse Jackson urge the Reverend Ralph Abernathy to reconsider what he has written in his memoir *And the Walls Came Tumbling Down* about Martin Luther King Jr.'s relationships with women; they suggest that he say instead that he made distortions and errors. Abernathy, once the head of King's organization, claims that King was with two women on the night of his assassination; two civil rights workers, Abjuda Abi Naantaanbuu, one of the two women Abernathy named, and Bernard Lee, claim to have been present at the time Abernathy mentioned and state that Abernathy was drunk and had fallen asleep.

1989   The names of 40 civil rights workers are inscribed on a black granite monument erected by the Southern Poverty Law Center, designed by Maya Lin (sculptor of the Vietnam Veterans Memorial in Washington, D.C.), and dedicated in Montgomery, Alabama, to commemorate those who died in the civil rights struggle. The names include Medgar Evers and Martin Luther King Jr., and a quotation of Dr. King reads: "We will not be satisfied until justice rolls down like waters, and righteousness like a mighty stream."

1989   Ronald H. Brown becomes the first African-American to serve as chairman of a major American political party when he is elected chairman of the Democratic Party.

1990   The Korean Council for the Women Drafted for Military Sexual Slavery by Japan is founded in Seoul, Korea, with the help of Korean Church Women United as a coalition of 36 women's organizations. The council works for recognition of the crimes committed by the Japanese against Korean "comfort women" (called *jugun ianfu* by the Japanese), who had been sold into slavery to serve the sexual needs of Japanese soldiers before and during World War II; many were killed or forced to commit suicide when the war ended.

1990   Nelson Mandela, the leader of the African National Congress (ANC), a multiracial organization opposed to apartheid, is released from prison after having been jailed for 27 years. The South African premier F. W. de Klerk agrees to his release after years of an international campaign.

1990 In *Smith v. Ohio*, the U.S. Supreme Court decides that a warrantless search providing the evidence for the probable cause of an arrest is unconstitutional. The Court rules that, though the Fourth Amendment may allow a brief detention of property, it forbids the search of that property unless it is accompanied by a warrant issued for probable cause.

1990 Television executive Ron Townsend becomes the first African-American member of the Augusta National Golf Club in Georgia. Augusta changes its whites-only policy after witnessing the uproar caused by the scheduling of the Professional Golfers' Association (PGA) Championship at the Shoal Creek Country Club in Birmingham, Alabama, another club that discriminates against African-Americans.

1990 In Selma, Alabama, black students stage a sit-in to protest the firing of the city's first black school superintendent, Norward Roussell. The 6-to-5 white majority on the school board fired Roussell despite the opposition of blacks in the city, but 70 percent of the students in Selma's schools are black. The sit-in forces the school board to compromise and allow Roussell to finish out his contract.

1990 The first Hispanic to serve as U.S. surgeon general is Antonia C. Novello, appointed by President George H. W. Bush.

1990 The United Nations International Convention on the Protection of the Rights of All Migrant Workers and Members of Their Families states that parties to the convention must protect migrant workers and their families, not force them to perform slave labor, and not make them undergo cruel or unusual treatment or punishment.

1991 The videotaped beating of Rodney King by white police officers in Los Angeles, California, is widely broadcast.

1991 The U.S. Supreme Court rules that criminal defendants may object to race-based exclusion of jurors, in *Powers v. Ohio*. After a white man indicted for murder in Ohio objected to the prosecutor's using his peremptory challenges to eliminate black jurors, the judge overruled his objections, and the impaneled jury convicted Powers; Justice Anthony Kennedy writes that the equal-protection clause prohibits a prosecutor from using peremptory challenges to exclude otherwise qualified persons from a jury solely for reason of race.

1991 The establishment of the National African-American Museum as part of the Smithsonian Institution in Washington, D.C., is announced. The museum will house and exhibit black art and images from black history.

1991 The U.S. District Court for the Northern District of California, in *KQED, Inc. v. Daniel B. Vasquez, Warden of San Quentin Prison*, bans the recording of executions.

1991   The National Civil Rights Museum is dedicated at the former Lorraine Motel, the site of Martin Luther King Jr.'s assassination in Memphis, Tennessee.

1991   The presidential election in Benin, West Africa, is the first free multiparty election since Benin achieved independence from France in 1960. Before the election, the government led a public-relations campaign to guarantee a free and open election and to encourage people to vote; the former dictator Mathieu Kerekou is elected president and forms a government through a coalition of political parties.

1991   The U.S. Congress passes the Civil Rights Act, partly as a response to the Supreme Court's 1989 ruling in *Patterson v. McLean Credit Union*, in which the Supreme Court held that a provision of the Civil Rights Act of 1964, prohibiting racial discrimination in the making and enforcing of contracts, does not apply to conduct occurring after the formation of a contract. The 1991 legislation changes the 1964 act by adding the following sections: "(b) For purposes of this section, the term 'make and enforce contracts' includes the making, performance, modification, and termination of contracts, and the enjoyment of all benefits, privileges, terms, and conditions of the contractual relationship. (c) The rights protected by this section are protected against impairment by nongovernmental discrimination and impairment under color of State law."

1992   Rioting breaks out in Los Angeles, California, after the announcement that the white officers accused in the Rodney King beating had been acquitted; the trial was shifted to suburban Simi Valley. Looting and violence greet the announcement, and 12 people die; National Guard troops are deployed, and President George Bush sends 1,500 Marines and 3,000 members of the U.S. Army. Many stores looted and destroyed are owned by members of the Korean community.

1992   The U.S. Supreme Court decides that a criminal defendant's lawyer may not use peremptory jury challenges in a racially discriminatory manner, in *Georgia v. McCullum*. In a case involving a grand-jury indictment in Georgia charging the white respondents with beating and assaulting two blacks, the prosecutor claimed that race was a factor in the attack and made a motion requiring the respondents to articulate a racially neutral explanation for their peremptory challenges, a motion denied by the trial judge; Justice Harry Blackmun writes that if a court allows jurors to be excluded because of bias, whether by the state or the defense, it is unconstitutional.

1992   The U.S. Supreme Court rules that a statute prohibiting display of a symbol that arouses anger in others on the basis of race, religion, or gender violates the First Amendment. In *R. A. V. v. City of St. Paul*, teenagers allegedly burned a homemade cross on the lawn of a black family and were charged with violating the Saint Paul, Minnesota, Bias-Motivated Crime Ordinance; Justice Antonin Scalia states that the First Amendment does not allow the city of Saint Paul to "impose special prohibition on those speakers who express views on disfavored subjects"; even though burning a cross is contemptible, the city has other means of dealing with it.

1992   A U.S. Federal Reserve regional-bank study issued in Boston, Massachusetts, reveals that blacks and Hispanics have higher rejection rates for mortgages than do whites. With similar criteria in their applications, whites are rejected at a rate of 11 percent, compared with 17 percent for minorities.

1992   Free elections are held in Angola in Southwest Africa for president and the legislature. However, the outbreak of civil war between rival political factions prevents a runoff between the candidates for president, and the current president, dos Santos, remains in office; the war also prevents open elections for local offices scheduled in this year.

1992   In an effort to guarantee free elections in the Bahamas, an island chain southeast of Florida, indelible ink is used to mark people who have voted, thereby removing the possibility of the same person voting more than once, a major form of election fraud in previous elections.

1992   Workers are given the right to form labor unions in Armenia and are granted the right to strike. Labor laws also guarantee the rights of women workers, although men dominate the labor force.

1992   The U.S. Supreme Court rules, in *Freeman v. Pitts*, that a district court need not retain control over every aspect of a school-desegregation plan. The case involves a court-ordered desegregation decree in action beginning in 1969 for the DeKalb County School system, a suburban area of Atlanta, Georgia. Justice Anthony Kennedy writes that the district court has a right to withdraw supervision where it is no longer needed. Regarding residential segregation and the resultant effect on school segregation, Kennedy also states that the district court had heard evidence showing that racially stable neighborhoods are unlikely to emerge, not because of state action but because of private choices, a fact that does not have constitutional implications and is difficult to address through judicial actions.

1992   The U.S. Supreme Court rules, in *United States v. Fordice*, that policies that have segregative effects without educational justification violate the equal-protection clause of the 14th Amendment. The case involves the claim that Mississippi maintained a segregated higher education system. Justice Byron White states that a state must eradicate policies that foster segregation or it is acting in violation of the Constitution and that unnecessary duplication of courses in white and black colleges is a continuation of separate but equal policies.

1992   The first African-American woman elected to the U.S. Senate is Carol Moseley Braun of Illinois. She loses a bid for reelection in 1998.

1993   The World Conference on Human Rights issues the Vienna Declaration and Programme of Action, stating that nations must remove the obstacles preventing every person from enjoying full human rights and must prevent human rights abuses. The conference declares its commitment to promoting human rights and freedoms, which are universal in nature.

1993   The U.S. Supreme Court, in *St. Mary's Honor Center et al. v. Hicks*, rules that although an employer's explanation for employee dismissal is not believable, it does not entitle a plaintiff to judgment. The case involves a claim by a black correctional officer at a halfway house operated by the Missouri Department of Corrections that his dismissal by his new superiors violated Title VII of the 1964 Civil Rights Act. Justice Antonin Scalia, writing for the Supreme Court, states that rejection of the defendant's reasons for firing an employee does not automatically mean that a judgment can be awarded to the plaintiff; the burden of proof is always on the plaintiff to show that discrimination was the reason for the firing.

1993   The first African-American woman appointed to serve as U.S. surgeon general is Dr. Jocelyn Elders, appointed by President Bill Clinton.

1993   In a civil suit brought against two of the police officers in the Rodney King beating, Lawrence Powell is convicted of using unreasonable force and violating King's rights, and Stacy Koon is convicted of letting Powell's actions occur.

1993   U.S. president Bill Clinton withdraws the nomination of Lani Guinier, his candidate for head of the Civil Rights Division of the Justice Department. The nomination of Guinier, a black law professor, becomes controversial when congressmen attack her views on voting rights.

1993   The American Anti-Slavery Group is founded in Washington, D.C., by Mohamed Nacir Athie, a Mauritanian diplomat living in exile; Charles Jacobs of the United States; and David Chand from southern Sudan, in response to the contemporary slave trade in Sudan and Mauritania and to bring attention to the plight of African slaves in Arab countries. In 1996, the U.S. House Committee on International Relations holds hearings on the matter, and the *Baltimore Sun* newspaper writes a series detailing the trade in African children by Arab traders in Sudan.

1994   A group of international experts on environmental protection and human rights, presided over by Fatma Zohra Ksentini, special rapporteur on Human Rights and the Environment for the United Nations Sub-Commission on Prevention of Discrimination and Protection of Minorities, issues the Draft Declaration of Principles on Human Rights and the Environment. It states that all people have the right to a secure, healthy environment, andthat this right is interdependent with civil, economic, political, and social human rights.

1994   The U.S. Supreme Court decides, in *Rivers v. Roadway Express,*

Inc., that the 1991 Civil Rights Act does not apply to cases brought before its passage. The case involves two petitioners, who refused when told by a supervisor to attend disciplinary hearings, filed a successful grievance, again refused to attend disciplinary hearings, and were fired. Justice John Paul Stevens writes that Congress did not include in the revised act any statement that indicates the revisions are meant to be retroactive.

1994   A study of slavery in Mauritania, West Africa, undertaken by Human Rights Watch, describes the discriminatory policies that the government of Mauritania employs against blacks, such as slavery and forced Arabization. The study is quoted during hearings held by the U.S. Congress in 1996.

1994   The U.S. Federal Death Penalty Act is passed by Congress and signed by President Bill Clinton. The act, part of the 1994 Federal Crime Control Act, mandates the death penalty for 60 additional offenses.

1994   The United Nations Security Council passes a resolution on genocide in Rwanda in central Africa, expressing the United Nations' concern at the genocide occurring in Rwanda. The resolution also states that the United Nations is establishing a tribunal to bring to justice those responsible for the violations of international law taking place in that country.

1995   The death penalty is reinstated in New York State after the election of George Pataki as governor.

1995   South Africa abolishes capital punishment.

1995   The U.S. Supreme Court reverses a Court of Appeals decision in support of race-based subcontractor compensation, in *Adarand Constructors v. Pena*. The case involves a suit contesting the award of a contract stating that the company would be compensated for subcontracting some of its work to small minority-controlled business; the company that submitted the lowest bid to construct guardrails as part of a highway-construction project in Colorado sued, claiming that awarding the contract to another company violated the equal-protection clause of the Fifth Amendment. The Supreme Court vacates the judgment of the court of appeals, which had rejected the suit; Justice Sandra Day O'Connor writes that the case is remanded for further proceedings; the Court uses three propositions when evaluating racial classifications: the evidence for racial criteria must be obvious, the standard of review under the equal-protection clause does not depend on the race of those benefited or burdened by a classification, and equal-protection analysis under the Fifth Amendment area is the same as under the 14th.

1995   Spain abolishes capital punishment for military offenses, the last crimes for which capital punishment was used in the country.

1996   The United Nations Security Council issues a resolution on ethnic violence in the Abkhaz Republic, an autonomous republic in the country of Georgia. The resolution condemns the ethnic killings and stresses the need for settling the dispute, including the political status of the Abkhaz Republic, for respecting the sovereignty of Georgia, and for ensuring that refugees can return to their homes.

1996   The United Nations Security Council issues a resolution about establishing peacekeeping forces to ensure that Eastern Slavonia, Baranja, and Western Sirmium remain part of the republic of Croatia, to safeguard the mutual recognition of the successor states of the former Yugoslavia, and to de-mine the region.

1996   Gaspar Biro, the human rights monitor for the United Nations, testifies before the Committee on International Relations of the U.S. Congress about the large-scale slave trade in African women and children in Sudan. The slaves are captured by armed Arab militias, and many are forcibly converted to Islam and given Arabic names.

1996   Kevin Vigilante, a physician member of the Freedom House Puebla Program on Religious Freedom, testifies before the Committee on International Relations of the U.S. Congress that on the program's visit to the Sudan the members encountered people being sold as slaves for $15. Vigilante declares that slavery is increasing and that the government sponsors abductions of children.

1996   The U.S. Supreme Court, in *United States v. Armstrong*, rules that a defendant claiming to be singled out for prosecution on the basis of race must make a threshold showing that the government has not prosecuted similar suspects of other races.

1996   Free elections are held in Bangladesh for the Parliament, for the most part free of violations that had marred previous elections, such as attacks on and harassment of voters, bombings and burnings of headquarters of political opponents, and vote rigging.

1997   The United Nations Security Council issues a resolution about holding free and fair elections in Liberia. The resolution reiterates that Liberia must take responsibility for achieving peace. It also expresses the United Nations' concern at the delay in carrying out elections.

1997   The first independent broadcast media in Benin, West Africa, begin operating. As with the print media, these radio and television stations are free to criticize the government and political parties and often do so, making them a powerful force in national politics.

1997   The legislation mandating the U.S. Commission on Civil Rights to safeguard equal protection of the laws is revised. The responsibilities of the commission now include studying and collecting information about legal developments constituting discrimination and appraising federal laws and policies with respect to discrimination.

1997   The Council of Europe's Convention on Human Rights and Biomedicine, held in Oviedo, Spain, states that parties to the convention must protect all people in connection with the use of biology and medicine. Human interests must prevail over those of science; everyone shall have equal access to health care; research in the area of health must be carried out according to professional standards.

1997 The United Nations Committee on the Elimination of Discrimination against Women issues recommendations, declaring that no society has as yet given women full and equal participation. Political decision making must be shared by both men and women and must take in account the equal welfare of both.

1997 The United Nations Security Council issues a resolution about Eastern Slavonia, Baranja, and Western Sirmium of the republic of Croatia, reiterating the need for Croatia to respect the human rights of all people, regardless of ethnic origin. Croatia has full responsibility for safeguarding the civil rights of all residents, and refugees have the right to return to their homes to live in safety.

1997 The legislation mandating the U.S. Commission on Civil Rights is revised to safeguard the right to vote. The revisions include statements that allegations of citizens deprived of their right to vote shall be investigated.

1998 In *Campbell v. Louisiana*, the U.S. Supreme Court rules that a white criminal defendant has the right to raise equal-protection objections to discrimination against black grand jurors. In the case of a white man indicted for second-degree murder by a grand jury in Louisiana, the defendant presented evidence that no black person had ever served as a grand-juror foreperson during the last 16 years and attempted to quash the indictment on the grounds that his grand jury was constituted in violation of the equal-protection provisions in the fair-cross-section requirements of the 6th and 14th Amendments; Justice Anthony Kennedy writes that the defendant has the right to raise an equal-protection challenge to the jury selection.

1998 The United Nations Security Council issues a resolution on conditions in Sierra Leone in West Africa, declaring its concern at the suffering caused by rebel attacks. The resolution condemns the resistance of remnants of the ousted government and demands that they surrender.

1998 The United Nations Security Council issues a resolution on the ethnic conflict in Afghanistan, stating its concerns at the Taliban's escalation of conflict and the concomitant suffering it has caused. It reiterates its concern about the continuing discrimination against women and the other human rights violations, and it urges the secretary-general to continue trying to send a mission to investigate the numerous violations of international law in the country.

1998 The U.S. Department of Justice revises the equal-opportunity policy so that it states that the department seeks to eliminate discrimination and to ensure equal employment, and that no one is subject to retaliation for opposing this policy or participating in judicial proceedings relating to it.

1998   The U.S. Department of Education revises its nondiscrimination policy about programs receiving federal assistance through the department. The revisions state that nobody shall be excluded from any program receiving federal assistance from the department.

1998   The U.S. Supreme Court, in *Oncale v. Sundowners Offshore Services, Inc., et al.*, rules that same-sex sexual harassment in the workplace is actionable under Title VII. Justice Antonin Scalia writes that, according to Title VII of the 1964 Civil Rights Act, it is unlawful for an employer to discriminate against anyone on the basis of race, color, religion, sex, or national origin, and that the statutes have no basis for allowing same-sex harassment.

1999   The United Nations Declaration on the Right and Responsibility of Individuals, Groups, and Organs of Society to Promote and Protect Universally Recognized Human Rights and Fundamental Freedoms is issued. The declaration states that all persons have the right to strive for the realization of human rights and that every country has a responsibility to take the necessary steps to promote human rights for all persons.

1999   An international appeal to protest the compilation of a database of "Gypsy-type" and "Roma/Sinti" people by the government of Bavaria, a state in Germany, is led by Simon Wiesenthal of the Jewish Documentation Center and Vanessa Redgrave of International Artists against Racism. A long list of actors, film directors, and human rights activists speaks out against the German state's registration of Gypsies, their names, addresses, and car licenses as a violation of the International Convention on the Protection of Minorities; the appeal declares that the terms used to justify these actions are those used in Nazi propaganda to justify the German racial policy of the time.

1999   At the Conference of Arab Human Rights Activists, held in Casablanca, Morocco, 100 representatives from more than 15 Arab nations meet behind closed doors to discuss human rights abuses. The conference is convened by Bahey El-Din Hassan, director of the Cairo Institute for Human Rights Studies; members of several delegations cancel because of pressure from their national governments and concern for their safety.

1999   The U.S. Supreme Court rules that schools are liable for damages for failing to stop severe and pervasive sexual harassment, in *Davis v. Monroe County Board of Education*. Teachers and administrators failed to address complaints made by the mother of an African-American girl who had been persistently harassed over a five-month period by a male classmate in the fifth-grade class at Hubbard Elementary in Forsyth, Georgia; Justice Sandra Day O'Connor writes that funding recipients are liable for damages where they are deliberately "indifferent to sexual harassment" that is so severe and pervasive that the victim is denied equal access to education.

1999   Revolutionary Armed Forces of Colombia (FARC) guerrillas, supposedly acting independently of the FARC organization, murder three U.S. indigenous-rights activists working in Colombia as part of a campaign to support the U'wa indigenous community; their blindfolded and tied-up bodies are dumped over the border in Venezuela. The FARC leadership takes responsibility for the murders and announces that it will try the commander responsible, though Amnesty International fears that such a trial will be quick and will end in a death sentence.

2000   During registration for voters in the coming general elections in Zanzibar, an island that is part of Tanzania, East Africa, groups from the ruling party object when opposition-party members appear to register; in conflicts between the two, the police decide in favor of the ruling party. Many people entitled to vote are not registered, and the ruling party brings in a large number of Tanzanian mainlanders who are not entitled to vote in Zanzibar and allows them to vote.

2001   The Immigration and Naturalization Service (INS) and the Federal Bureau of Prisons deny Human Rights Watch access to detention centers holding people arrested in relation to the September 11 terrorist attacks investigation. INS also states that it will not release information about a Pakistani citizen who died in INS custody unless Human Rights Watch can produce a document signed by the man and stating his permission for the release of information.

2002   The International Helsinki Federation for Human Rights (IHF) expresses its concern about the Russian journalists and researchers working with foreign organizations whom the Russian Security Services recently charged with espionage and high treason for disseminating nonclassified information about nuclear waste and other topics relating to human health and safety. The IHF finds violations of due process and denials of the right to a fair trial, bail refused, accused persons imprisoned for lengthy periods, and trials delayed for years.

2002   Although denied by the Japanese government for decades, Koji Iwata, presiding judge of the Tokyo district court, acknowledges that the Japanese Imperial Army had flouted the Geneva and Hague Conventions by spreading plague, typhoid, and other forms of biological warfare, killing thousands of Chinese civilians in Manchuria during the Japanese invasion of China in 1940–42. At the conclusion of the five-year court case filed by 180 mostly Chinese plaintiffs, however, the court rejects the claims for compensation, stating that reparations had been covered by international peace treaties; Japanese veterans of the Manchurian campaign confessed in court to cultivating anthrax, typhoid, and cholera, dropping infected fleas over villages, and vivisecting prisoners of war.

2002   Forty-five groups meeting in Athens, Greece, for the General Assembly of the Euro-Mediterranean Human Rights Network express concern about violations of the universal international standard for the rights of foreigners who arrive in Greece seeking asylum or come as migrants and are taken into custody. Greece does not ensure that interpreters are present, often does not inform foreigners of their rights, limits access to lawyers, and sentences them to prison or deports them after a trial that lasts only a few minutes.

2002   A U.S. federal court orders the Justice Department to identify all suspects held since the September 11 attacks, most of whom have yet to be charged. Many of those detained have only minor immigration violations.

2002   The judge of the Sixth Circuit Court of Appeals in Cincinnati, Ohio, orders the U.S. government to open to the public the deportation hearings for foreign nationals detained after the September 11 attacks; in a condemnation of the Bush administration's civil rights policy, the court states that a government "operating in the shadow of secrecy stands in complete opposition to the society envisioned by the framers of our Constitution."

2002   The U.S. Justice Department announces that two former drug informants for the Dallas, Texas, Police Department have pleaded guilty in U.S. District Court in the Northern District of Texas to conspiring to violate the civil rights of numerous Dallas citizens. The defendants packaged counterfeit drugs, planted them on innocent people, and then received cash payments from the Dallas police for turning in the victims; many of the people who were falsely accused spent months in jail.

2002   Assistant Attorney General Ralph Boyd Jr. and U.S. Attorney for the Western District of New York Michael Battle announce an indictment against six people involved in a scheme to hold Mexican migrant workers at camps near Buffalo, New York. The defendants had recruited undocumented Mexican boys and men in Arizona and transported them to crowded camps to perform agricultural work; they had used guards to terrorize the migrant workers, making them work in conditions of forced labor.

2002   The U.S. Justice Department announces that three former employees of Wackenhut Corrections Corporation were found guilty of civil rights conspiracy charges. The defendants, guards in the Lea County Corrections Facility in Hobbs, New Mexico, had beaten an inmate, kicking him many times in the head, and then lied and falsified reports to justify the use of force.

2002   Six members of the Montana Front Working Class Skinheads are sentenced to prison terms after they are convicted on federal civil rights charges, according to the U.S. Justice Department. The defendants interfered with the rights of minorities to use public parks and had attacked an African-American and two Hispanics in a park in Billings, Montana; the members of the skinhead group chased the victims, threatened them with clubs, chains, and metal bars, and yelled racial slurs.

2002   A civic forum sponsored by the Russian government represents the first time that a Russian president agrees to meet with leaders of civic groups protesting Russia's human and civil rights violations, but a spokesperson for the protesters states that President Vladimir Putin merely spoke to the leaders about his interest in dialogues with civil rights leaders and then left the room. The civic leaders ask the West to increase the pressure on Russia to improve its civil rights record.

2002   The U.S. Supreme Court rules, in *United States v. Drayton, Christopher, et al.*, that the Fourth Amendment does not necessitate police officers who are conducting a routine drug search to advise bus passengers of their right not to cooperate and their right to refuse to agree to being searched.

2002   In *Ring v. Arizona*, the U.S. Supreme Court rules that a jury, not a judge, must find "aggravating factors" when those factors cause the judge to impose a death penalty rather than a lesser sentence.

2002   Three U.S. Supreme Court judges, Justices Stevens, Ginsburg, and Breyer, state that the Court should consider abolishing the death penalty for killers who commit crimes as minors, in the case of a Texas inmate, Toronto Patterson, scheduled to die for a killing committed when he was 17. The three cannot convince the other justices, and Patterson is executed.

2002   The 15 foreign ministers of the European Union, meeting in Helsingoer, Denmark, may be willing to compromise on U.S. demands that Americans be exempted from prosecution by the International Court on War Crimes. Italy and Great Britain have already agreed to sign a bilateral agreement with the United States.

2002   In the aftermath of the September 11, 2001, terrorist attack on the World Trade Center and the Pentagon, the federal government enacts new laws, policies, and procedures designed to catch and punish those responsible and to prevent future terrorist attacks. Some of these relating to the detention of prisoners, legal representation, and alleged invasions of privacy are criticized by civil liberties groups.

2002   At the 100th birthday and retirement party for U.S. Senator Strom Thurmond (Republican from South Carolina), Senate Majority Leader Trent Lott (Republican from Mississippi) says that the United States would have been better off if Thurmond, who ran on a segregationist ticket against Harry S. Truman, had been elected president in 1948. The statement creates a scandal that leads to Lott's stepping down as majority leader and the appointment of Senator Bill Frist of Tennessee to the post.

CHAPTER THREE

RELIGIOUS RIGHTS

2000 B.C.E.   In a hieroglyphic text on wooden coffins from El-Bersheh in Egypt, the creator god describes his good deeds that made creation possible: "I made every man like his fellow. I did not command that they do evil, [but] it was their hearts which violated what I had said."

330 B.C.E.   The first Hindu law codes, the *Dharmsutras* (Sanskrit: righteousness threads), explain and support the caste system, in which a person is born into a specific occupational group and must marry in that group and retain the same group status for his or her life. These rules are eventually turned into verse, called *Dharmashastras* (righteousness science), in modern times also used to refer to the entire corpus of ancient Indian laws.

240 B.C.E.   Buddhism is established as the state religion of Ceylon (modern Sri Lanka) when King Asoka of India sends his son Mahendra, a Buddhist monk, to convert King Tissa and others in that country.

206 B.C.E.   Confucianism emerges as the state ideology of China during the Han dynasty, when many distinctive features of Chinese society are created. Confucianism provides practical rules guiding the relationships between the powerful but good ruler and his obedient, humble subjects, and the mastery of Confucian literature becomes the basis for a civil-service examination system that survives until the early 20th century.

185–145 B.C.E.   In India, King Pushyamitra, a devout Brahman (highest Hindu caste), persecutes the devotees of the religions of Jainism and Buddhism, who are forced to move from east-central India (modern Bihar state) to west-central India (modern Gujarat state). Pushyamitra, a general in the army of the Maurya dynasty, rose to power by murdering the last Maurya king; the usurper intended Brahmanism to replace the Buddhism of the Maurya kings.

180–157 B.C.E.   Influenced by his wife the empress Dou, the emperor Wendi, of the Han dynasty in China, is the first Chinese ruler to embrace Taoism. Dou, a believer in Taoism, a religion concerned with achieving long life and good luck, has her son, the future emperor Jingdi, study Taoist literature, and father and son become Taoists.

139 B.C.E.   Fearing that astrologers will cause slaves to revolt, Roman rulers repress astrology and expel its practitioners from Rome and

Roman Italy. Nevertheless, court astrologers probably continue to practice their arts.

12 B.C.E. Political power and religious authority in the Roman Empire are merged when the emperor Augustus becomes head of the state religion with the title Pontifex Maximus (supreme priest). Divus Agustus (divine Augustus), as he would be called after his death in 14 C.E., is honored with altars and temples dedicated to him in the western regions of the empire.

11 C.E. Emperor Augustus bans astrology in the Roman Empire, and subsequent rulers maintain the ban for a hundred years. The ban, however, generally applies only to astrologers who serve the common people, while court astrologers, who rely on Greek systems of astrology, often continue to serve the emperors.

c. 28 Fooled by his wife Herodias and daughter Salome, Herod Antipas, son of Herod I and ruler of Judea, orders John the Baptist, a Jewish prophet who had criticized his policies, to be beheaded. Later, however, Herod would avoid crucifying Jesus, sending him instead to the Roman overlord of Judea, Pontius Pilate, for judgment.

c. 30 Jesus is crucified as an enemy of the Roman state. Claims by his adherents that he is resurrected and appears among them mark the beginning of the Christian religion.

c. 35 The Greek word *Christianos* (Christian) is one of several terms used to refer to followers of Jesus of Nazareth in Antioch, Syria, and other Greek-speaking areas and later in Rome. The word *Christos* is the Greek translation of the Hebrew word *mashiah*, for *messiah* (anointed), a designation that the early Christians applied to Jesus.

c. 35 Stephen, known as the protomartyr, is condemned by the Sanhedrin (supreme religious and political council of Jews in Jerusalem) for blaspheming Jewish law. A deacon of the early Christian community, which at that time was made up of Jews, Stephen is executed by stoning for preaching that Jesus is the messiah, the prophesied deliverer of the Jews, who will come again as predicted in the Bible (Isa. 7–12). Saul of Tarsus, later Saint Paul, approves of and is present at the stoning (Acts 12).

45 Beheaded by Herod Agrippa I, last king of Judea, James (later Saint James the Great) is the first of the Twelve Apostles to be executed and martyred. The brother of Saint John the Evangelist, James becomes the patron saint of pilgrims and laborers and later the patron saint of Spain, where his cult develops in the ninth century at the church of Santiago de Compostela, based on the belief that his body had miraculously been transported there.

49 A council of Jewish Christian leaders meeting in Jerusalem discusses how closely the new religion must adhere to Judaism.

52 According to Syrian Christian tradition, the Christian presence in India dates from the time that Thomas (later Saint Thomas), one of Jesus' disciples, travels to southwestern India and converts several Hindus to Christianity.

59	The emperor Mingdi recognizes Confucius as the patron of scholars in China. Every school is ordered to organize a solemn banquet to honor venerated figures and to instill reverence and propriety among people rather than to propitiate spirits.
64	The emperor Nero begins to persecute Christians in Rome, at a time that the new sect is a tiny minority amid the pagan Roman population.
64–70	When the Jews of Jerusalem revolt against the emperor Nero and their Roman overlords, Roman armies, led by the future emperor Vespasian and his son Titus, crush the rebels of Judea, destroying the Temple, carrying off its sacred paraphernalia to Rome, and disrupting the early Christian Church in Jerusalem. Henceforth Jerusalem is no longer an important center of Christianity, and Jews are dispersed to east and west.
c. 65	By order of the emperor Nero, Paul is executed in Rome. After founding churches throughout western Asia and in Rome, Paul was arrested in Jerusalem and imprisoned in Caesaraea in Palestine before being sent to Rome.
70–77	Taoism is repressed in China when Liu Ying, a half-brother of the emperor Mingdi, is exiled on charges of fomenting a Taoist conspiracy. Liu Ying eventually commits suicide, and thousands of people are accused, tried, and executed on charges of using magic for subversive purposes.
c. 70–156	After Polycarp, bishop of Smyrna (modern Izmir in Turkey), is burned at the stake at the instigation of an anti-Christian mob, the institution of martyrdom is established in Christianity. The account of Saint Polycarp's execution, one of the earliest in Church history, introduces some basics of martyrdom: it follows the same pattern as the suffering of Christ, involves the collection of relics by followers (the cult), and requires specific forms of prayer by their followers.
75	King Gogidubnus of Britain shows his allegiance to Rome by building temples to honor the Roman gods Minerva and Neptune, though few people worship the Roman deities.
78–123	Buddhism spreads in central Asia during the reign of King Kaniska of the Kushan dynasty, who rules over the northern Indian subcontinent. A Buddhist convert, Kaniska assumes the Buddhist title *Devaputra* (son of divine being) and is said to have convened a Buddhist council in Jalandhara, Kashmir.
c. 79	In India, the Jain religion splits into two sects: the Digambaras (sky-clad, i.e., naked) and the Svetambaras (white-clad, i.e., wearing white clothing). The more liberal Svetambara monks admit women to their ranks and declare them capable of attaining *nirvana* (extinction of being); the strict Digambara monks reject women and believe in absolute poverty to the extent that they refuse to own or wear clothing.
90	Buddhist monks establish a monastery at China's imperial capi-

tal of Luoyang.

100   The Samaritans appear as a sect in and around the Roman city of Neapolis (now Nablus on the West Bank; formerly Samaria, capital of Israel); the region north of Judea came to be known as Samaria after the Assyrians conquered the kingdom of Israel in the eighth century B.C.E., and the population practiced a form of Judaism, with a Samaritan Pentateuch, supposedly an old text of the first five books of the Bible. A few Samaritans still practice their religion today, living around Mount Gerizim outside Nablus, said to be the site of their temple.

c. 100   Jews arrive in India to establish a community on the southwestern coast.

100–300   Jewish communities emerge in Spain, although Jews settled here centuries earlier.

c. 110   Gaius Plinus Caecilius (Pliny the Younger), governor of the Roman province of Bithynia in northwest Asia Minor, begins following Christian teachings and abandons the worship of pagan Roman gods.

132–135   During the reign of the emperor Hadrian, another Jewish revolt in Jerusalem prompts a final Roman onslaught; the Romans destroy the city and rebuild it as a Roman city dedicated to the worship of Jupiter. Jews are forbidden to live in the city, or even to enter the gates, on pain of death, and they begin to be persecuted throughout the Roman Empire.

135   Valentinus, an influential Gnostic poet and teacher from Alexandria, Egypt, settles in Rome and seeks a role in the Christian Church. Because his Gnostic views on Christianity depart from orthodox Christian beliefs (Gnosticism, one of many sects in early Christianity, emphasizes knowledge of spiritual truth), the Church refuses to make him bishop of Rome; afterward, he abandons the Roman Church and attracts followers who found a number of Gnostic sects that survive into the early third century.

138–212   After Hadrian's death, more-moderate Roman emperors gradually relax the restrictions on Jews and Judaism in the Roman Empire.

c.150   Heresy becomes an important concept in Christian doctrine as Church leaders seek to control religious diversity among followers.

160–175   A synod (Greek *synodos*: assembly) of Christian bishops from different communities takes place in Asia Minor, and the synod becomes an important means of creating unity among the dispersed Christian communities in Asia, Europe, and Africa.

165–166   Laozi, the founder of Taoism, is deified in China, represented as a deity who lives in the heavens and presides over the universe and who from time to time appears on earth to advise the emperors.

185   Montanism, a millenarian movement in Christianity, appears in

Asia Minor when Montanus, a schismatic Christian, prophesies the approaching end of the world and the arrival of heaven on earth. The movement spreads to Rome and North Africa; it is condemned as heresy by the Christian Church in 200 but remnants linger on for centuries.

193–211 The Roman emperor Septimius Severus begins an era of systematic persecution of Christians in the Roman Empire by requiring governors of Roman territory to persecute Christians because they are more loyal to their god than to the emperor. Temporarily halted in 222–35 during the rule of Alexander Severus when Jesus receives a place in the Roman pantheon, the persecution resumes in 235 under the emperor Maximinus and continues until 244, when Philip the Arabian stops it.

200s The Inner Shrine of Ise, the most important shrine of Shintoism (the primary Japanese religion), is founded in Japan as the center of the Yamato clan's worship of its divine ancestors and of the sun goddess Amaterasu Omikami, the mythical ancestor of the imperial family. The shrine is not opened to the public until the late 15th century.

200s–300s The kingdom of Funan on the southern coast of Cambodia enjoys much maritime trade with India, and Hindu influence in Cambodia is evident in brick and stone temples to the Hindu gods Siva and Vishnu.

212 Jews, like all other free men in the empire, are granted Roman citizenship.

227 During the Sasanid dynasty in Persia, Zoroastrianism becomes the state religion. Based on the Avesta, the ancient Persian sacred text, the religion has an organized priesthood, with a high priest second in power only to the king; Sasanid rulers persecute followers of other religions including Judaism, Christianity, Manichaeanism, Hinduism, and Buddhism.

249–251 In a period of especially harsh persecution, the Roman emperor Decius forces Christians to abandon Christianity or die. Many Christians abandon their religion, but many others are tortured and die.

255 Plotinus, who developed Neoplatonic philosophy, argues against astrology and influences the Christians in Rome to reject it.

261 The emperor Gallienus issues an edict of toleration for Christians in the Roman Empire and restores their property that had been seized.

c. 273 Gregory the Illuminator, a missionary to Asia Minor, leads a mass conversion of pagans to Christianity and later becomes the patron saint of the Armenian Church.

277 At the urging of the Zoroastrian high priest Kartir, the Sasanid king Bahram I executes Manes (Mani), the founder of Manichaeanism, in Persia. Thereafter, the Manichaean religion, which blended elements of Christianity and Zoroastrianism, is repressed.

288	In China, the Taoist scholar Wang Fu levels a harsh attack on Buddhism, claiming that it is merely a coarsened form of Taoism.
c. 300	King Trdat of Armenia converts to Christianity through the influence of Gregory the Illuminator, and Armenia becomes a Christian land. Armenia is thus the oldest uninterruptedly Christian country in the world.
303–312	The reign of the Roman emperor Diocletian marks the last period of major Christian persecution in the Roman Empire; churches are destroyed, books burned, Christians forbidden to assemble, and church officials and then commoners tortured and killed. The persecution is partly motivated by invaders threatening from the East; the resulting disruption of life is blamed on the Christians.
305	Saint Alban becomes the first Christian martyr in Britain, when, during the general persecution of Christians throughout the Roman Empire, he refuses, in the face of torture and eventual execution, to renounce Christianity. The city and cathedral of Saint Alban's are named in his memory.
312	As the first Roman emperor to accept Christianity, Constantine, according to popular belief, has a prophetic dream before his victory over the rival Roman emperor Maxentius at the Battle of Milvian Bridge, which makes him sole emperor of the western half of the empire. In the dream, Constantine sees a cross with the words *In hoc signo vinces* (In this sign you shall conquer).
313	The Edict of Milan, issued by the Roman emperors Constantine (of the West) and Licinius (of the East), grants Christians religious freedom throughout the empire.
315	After the acceptance of Christianity in the Roman Empire, the emperor Constantine issues edicts repressing Jewish communities in Roman lands.
325	Constantine convenes the (First) Council of Nicaea (in modern Turkey) to end the conflicts about doctrine, practice, and authority in the Christian Church, particularly the disputes over Arianism, the doctrine that Christ is not equal in divinity to God. Attended by bishops, most of whom represent churches in Asia and Egypt, the council rejects Arianism, using the word *homoousion* (Greek: of like substance) to define the relationship between God and Christ, or Father and Son; it declares that God has three aspects—Father, Son, and Holy Spirit; it establishes the worship of Mary as the Mother of God; and it gives the sees (seats of bishops) of Rome, Alexandria, and Antioch authority over other sees in their regions.
c. 350	Chinese scholars synthesize the doctrines of Confucianism, Taoism, and Buddhism.
350	The Roman emperor Constantius, the son of Constantine, orders pagan temples closed and sacrifices banned; paganism survives only in large cities such as Rome and Alexandria.
357	All forms of astrology—court, popular, and scientific—as well as

magicians and diviners are banned in the Roman Empire. Greek astrology nevertheless continues to be practiced in private.

361–363 The last period of Christian repression in the Roman Empire occurs during the reign of the emperor Julian, who was raised a Christian but admires the old Roman paganism. His efforts to restrict Christianity and promote paganism fail, and after his death in 363 Christianity is again the official religion of the empire.

364 The Council of Laodicea in Syria condemns astrology as a form of paganism and superstition. Nevertheless, only astrology as practiced by uneducated astrologers is banned, while "scientific" astrology based on the Greek system continues.

375 King Sosurium, the 17th ruler of the Koguryo Kingdom of Korea, establishes Buddhism as the spiritual foundation of the state and makes Confucius's teachings its legal basis.

380 Christianity reaches its greatest influence in the Roman Empire when the emperor Theodosius I bans paganism, declares Christianity the official religion of the empire, and affords special privileges to the clergy.

380 Priscillian, the bishop of Avila in Spain, is excommunicated for espousing Gnosticism, a religious philosophy that stresses the attainment of esoteric spiritual knowledge as the way to attain freedom from the evils of the flesh. He is executed in 386, but his cult survives into the following century.

381 The (First) Council of Constantinople continues the attempt to unify Church doctrine, practice, and authority; decisions reached at Nicaea in 325 are ratified; the teachings of Apollinarius, bishop of Laodicea in Syria, which question the human nature of Christ, are condemned; and an expanded version of the Nicene Creed, first formulated at the Council of Nicaea, is introduced. The bishop of Constantinople is made the second-highest official in the Christian Church, after the bishop of Rome; this decision makes Constantinople the effective center of Christianity in the East and the patriarch of Constantinople, later called the ecumenical patriarch, the leader of Orthodox Christianity.

384 Buddhism is repressed in Korea when Buddhist doctrines are rejected by the state and adherents persecuted.

386 The state of Northern Wei in China adopts a sinicization policy chiefly Confucian in character. Confucian values dominate the central bureaucracy, recruitment of officials, and even local governance.

390 As a demonstration of the power of the Christian Church, Emperor Theodosius I is rebuked by the bishop of Rome for massacring citizens of Thessalonica (now Thessaloníki) in Greece and does penance outside the door of the cathedral in Milan.

402 Taoists in China commit mass suicide when the Taoist priest Sun En fails in a rebellion against the government and, after his defeat, drowns himself.

403	The Byzantine empress Eudoxia and the patriarch of Alexandria depose John (later Saint John Chrysostom, "golden-mouthed") as archbishop of Constantinople because of his eloquent preaching against the wealthy and powerful; popular with the ordinary public, he is reinstated in 404, again banished, and dies in exile in Armenia. He would become one of the fathers of the Eastern Orthodox Church.
410	In Britain, the mass conversion of Celtic peoples (the indigenous British population) to Christianity begins after the Romans withdraw from Britain.
411	The Visigoths (Germanic invaders of Europe) conquer Spain and grant the Jews living there religious freedom, until 484.
416	Augustine of Hippo, one of the fathers of the Roman Catholic Church, condemns astrology in his work *De civitate Dei* (The city of God). Saint Augustine sees astrology as inconsistent with the beliefs of Christianity, and other Christian writers of the period also equate astrology with paganism and heresy.
418	In the western Roman Empire, Jews are prohibited from holding public office. In the same year, Jews on the island of Minorca in the Mediterranean Sea are forced to convert to Christianity; many die or flee.
429–431	The Vandals (Germanic invaders) attack North Africa, destroy churches and Christian religious objects in the city of Hippo, and loot the city.
442	The Taoist Kou Qianzhi initiates the emperor of the Northern Wei in China, Tai Wudi, into Taoism, thus confirming his imperial virtue. The ceremony formally elevates Taoism to a state religion in China, and in 446 the emperor proscribes Buddhism, the first time Buddhism is banned in a Chinese state.
451	At the Council of Chalcedon in modern Turkey, Catholic bishops, trying to resolve the disputes between the sees of Alexandria and Antioch and those of the western bishops, set forth the Creed of Chalcedon, which states the doctrine of the two natures of Christ—divine and human—in one person in two forms. Eastern churches that reject the two-natures doctrine, the so-called Monophysites, include the Coptic Church in Egypt, the Armenian Church, and the Nestorians (a Persian Christian sect that believes that the divine and human natures of Jesus are separate).
452	When the Northern Wei emperor Tai Wudi, a strong supporter of Taoism, is assassinated, Buddhism is restored in China.
455	The Vandals, adherents of the Arian form of early Christianity, in which Jesus is of a different nature from God the Father, loot Rome and persecute Catholics. Under Pope Leo I, the city is rebuilt and the Church restored.
482	After the Vandals conquer North Africa, they ban Catholicism there, because of a dispute about the nature of Christ, by prohibiting Catholics from assembling, taking over the churches, and

ending the authority of the bishops. The schism is repaired, but remains one in a continuing series of tensions between the Eastern and Western Churches.

492–496
Pope Gelasius I in Rome sets forth a model of church-state relations in which the church has spiritual authority and responsibility for moving the people toward eternal salvation while the state is responsible for caring for the people and maintaining the polity.

496
Clovis, king of the Franks (Germanic invaders who move into much of Europe), and 3,000 of his soldiers convert to Christianity following a victory over his German rivals. The Franks become supporters of the Roman form of Christianity and are partly responsible for the domination of Roman Catholicism in Europe.

603
To legitimize its political power, the ruling family of Japan introduces the legend that the imperial line originated from the sun goddess Amaterasu at a time corresponding to 660 B.C.E., a date that would be six centuries too early. In the legend, the sun goddess sends her grandson Ninigi no Mikoto to rule over Japan and presents him with the imperial regalia—sword (courage), mirror (purity), and sacred jewel (benevolence)—used at the accession ceremony of each new emperor. Jimmu, the mythical first emperor, is a great-grandson of Ninigi. The early dating is reinforced by an imperial edict of 1881.

604
Prince Shokotu of Japan issues the Seventeen-Article Constitution, centralizing and codifying the bureaucratic structure of the government and officially retitling the emperor as Tenno, or heavenly sovereign. The imperial court begins to follow an elaborate calendar of rites derived from Buddhism, Taoism, and Shinto.

612
After the Visigoth conquerors in Spain convert to Christianity, they give the Jews a choice of converting or leaving the country.

618
Gaozu, the first emperor of the Tang dynasty in China, is assured by the 10th patriarch of Shangqing (supreme purity) Taoism, Wang Yuanzhi, that he has received the mandate of heaven, thus confirming his legitimacy. Shangqing Taoism uses meditation and other mystical devices recorded in early Tao manuscripts, which had been collected and edited by Tao Hongjing, the ninth patriarch, around 485.

619
Muhammad, the founder of Islam, is threatened with harm by political enemies in Mecca after the death of his uncle, Abu Talib, who provided political protection.

c. 620
Tirujnanasambandhar, a Hindu holy man, converts the formerly Jain king of the Pandya dynasty in Madura in southern India to Hinduism. Jain tradition claims that the king then impales 8,000 Jains.

622
Muhammad and his followers, who emigrate from Mecca to Medina, establish the first Muslim state in Arabia. For Muslims, this emigration marks the first year of the Muslim, or hegira

(emigration), calendar.

624   The Muslim state emerges as a political force in Arabia when, at the Battle of Badr, near Medina in Arabia, the Muslims win their first significant victory over the rival Meccans. In the Qur'an, the Battle of Badr is viewed as Allah's endorsement of Islam.

624–629   China's court astrologer Fu Yi, a non-Buddhist, attacks Buddhism as a foreign intrusion and urges the emperor Gaozu to suppress it and force Buddhist priests and nuns to return to lay life. Three months later, after the emperor is removed in a palace coup, the anti-Buddhism measures are withdrawn, but in 629, the new emperor Taizong orders execution as the penalty for illegal ordination of Buddhist monks.

628   In Constantinople, the emperor Herculis orders all Jews living in the Byzantine Empire to convert to Christianity.

630   Muhammad and his Muslim armies enter Mecca, clear the central shrine of idols and shrines, convert the Meccans to Islam, and join with them to defeat the rival city of Taif in Arabia. The Muslim state now emerges as the most powerful force in Arabia, with the shrine of Mecca its holy center.

631   The Year of Deputations, in Muslim tradition, comes when most Bedouins, nomadic tribes of the desert, send delegates to Medina to accept Islam as their religion.

c. 633   Oswald, king of Northumbria in Britain, chooses to convert to Christianity. Monks from the monastery on the island of Iona in the Inner Hebrides assist in the conversion, which is supported as well by his brother Oswin, after Oswald's death in 642.

637   An imperial edict during the Tang dynasty in China gives Taoist clergy preference over Buddhist clergy. A second edict attacks Buddhism as a foreign religion and claims that it lacks the profundity of native Taoism.

637   The Muslims conquer Mesopotamia (modern Iraq), and Islam becomes the state religion.

638   The Muslims conquer Palestine and permit Jews to return to the city. Establishing the concept of the "people of the Book," the Muslims allow Jews and Christians in lands under Muslim control to practice their religions, although they are subjected to special taxes and periodic repressions, massacres, and exiles during the next centuries. Another category of unbelievers, such as Buddhists, are forced to convert to Islam.

638   The Council of Toledo, in Toledo, Spain, orders all Jews in Spain either to convert to Christianity or to leave. Many convert, although the Jewish community survives in Spain.

639–642   After the Muslims wrest Egypt from the Byzantine Empire, they give Coptic Christians (members of the Monophysite Christian Church) in Egypt the choice of converting to Islam or paying additional taxes as non-Muslims.

651   After conquering Khorasan (in present-day northeastern Iran),

the Muslims force Zoroastrians to convert to Islam or flee. Some Zoroastrians migrate along the Silk Road to China, where they establish communities that last into the 10th century.

663–664

At the Synod of Whitby in Britain, the king of Northumbria decides that the bishop of Rome, rather than Celtic Christian bishops in Britain, is the ultimate arbitrator of religious matters. Church leaders also decide to ban the practice of Celtic religion and to replace it with Christianity.

c. 680

Wilfrid, a Christian missionary in Britain and later bishop of York, successfully converts many Saxons in Sussex to Christianity. Britain is now almost entirely Christian.

680

Husayn, grandson of Muhammad and son of Ali, the fourth caliph, revolts against the reigning caliph and is assassinated. He becomes a martyr for the Shia Muslims, one of two main branches of Islam, who believe that Muslims should be ruled by descendants of Ali.

689

The Visigothic rulers of Spain classify Jews as slaves, as part of a general pattern of religious repression.

691

During the Tang dynasty in China, the empress Wu establishes Buddhism as the state religion and forces Confucianism and Taoism into secondary roles.

700s

Because of a growing revival of interest in the philosophy of Confucius, a civil-service examination based on Confucian precepts becomes a requirement for all candidates for government positions in China.

702

In Japan, the emperor Mommu institutes the Taiho Civil Code, which consolidates earlier reforms, regulates the activities of Shinto priests, and spells out the details of the court ritual, the cult of all Shinto divinities (not just the national gods but also the worship of clan and communal deities), and the procedures of such practices as the great offering, the propitiation of spirits, divination, and augury. The code remains in effect until 757.

711–716

The Moors (Muslims from North Africa, part native Berbers, part Arab invaders) conquer much of Spain and grant Jews religious freedom.

717

During the Muslim Umayyad dynasty in western Asia, the Code of Umar (Omar) II, caliph of Baghdad, introduces restrictions against Jews: they cannot hold public office or build or repair synagogues and must wear a yellow patch on their clothes. Nevertheless, the Muslim rulers of Baghdad ignore these restrictions, and the Jews enjoy much freedom.

717–720

Umar (Omar) II, caliph of Baghdad, develops a new system of taxation that taxes all Muslims at the same rates regardless of their ethnic identity but requires non-Muslims to pay additional taxes.

741

The emperor Shomu of Japan mandates a provincial Buddhist temple system with a monastery and a convent for each province, where prayers and readings to protect the realm are to be conducted.

741   Emperor Xuanzong of China orders the establishment of Taoist schools, with official examinations on Taoist texts; prominent Taoists assume important roles at court. Xuanzong also promotes efforts to harmonize the Three Teachings—Confucianism, Buddhism, Taoism.

742–798   Khri Song, probably the first true Buddhist king of Tibet, arranges debates between Indian and Chinese Buddhists and then between Indian Buddhists and practitioners of the local Bon religion. Ultimately, the king favors the Indian or Tantric Buddhists.

744   At the Council of Leptines (near Ath in modern Belgium), the Roman Catholic Church decides to eradicate paganism in Europe.

751   A combined Arab Muslim, Tibetan, and Turkic army fights the Chinese at the Talus River in central Asia. When the Chinese lose, the Muslims gain control of central Asia and continue the conversion of the inhabitants to Islam, which began earlier in the century.

754   In an alliance forged between the Franks and the Catholic Church in Rome, the Franks cede control of Italy to the Church; in return, the pope grants the Franks the title Patricians of the Romans. The Papal States in Italy survive until 1870, when Italy is unified as a nation.

c. 760–860   The Shailedra dynasty in Java adopts Hinduism as the state religion.

785   The Irish Catholic Synod of Calcuth in Northumberland (northern England, on the Scottish border) bans tattooing because of its associations with the native Celtic religion.

787   After the (Second) Council of Nicaea (the seventh and, according to Eastern Orthodox Christianity, last ecumenical council), the schism between the Churches of Rome and Constantinople widens. The council supports the veneration of images of Christ and saints, a practice rejected by the Byzantine Church.

788   A Confucian-based civil-service examination system is established in Korea to select public officials of the southern Korean kingdom of Silla. Like that of the Chinese, the system is based on knowledge of the Confucian classics.

789   In southern India, the Hindu ruler Sankara orders 789 loads of the sacred books of the Jains placed on boats and sunk. Some texts are preserved in Nepal and in southern India, and after Sankara's death Jains recover copies of all their books and reproduce them.

800   In an effort to formalize the split between the Church in Rome and the Church in Constantinople, Pope Leo III crowns Charlemagne, ruler of the Franks and Lombards (Germanic invaders of

Europe), emperor of Rome.

802–1432 During the kingdom of Angkor, the Khmer (Cambodian) people are politically unified; the temple complexes, mostly Hindu but also some Buddhist, play a central role in this unification. The temples own slaves and vast estates, and wealthy Khmer often enrich the temples to ensure prosperity in the next life.

816 Louis the Pious succeeds his father, Charlemagne, as Holy Roman Emperor when he is crowned by Pope Stephen IV at Reims, France. The pope emphasizes that the emperor's authority flows from the Church in Rome.

823 Rome becomes the site of coronations of the Holy Roman Emperors, with the crowning there of Lothar by Pope Paschal I.

829 The Catholic Synod of Paris rules that witchcraft is punishable by death.

840–846 During the reign of the emperor Wuzong in China, his chief minister, Li Deyu, supervises the suppression and even destruction of Buddhist, Taoist, Nestorian, Zoroastrian, and Manichaean temples and monasteries. Christians are persecuted as well, although the small Jewish and Muslim communities are less troubled. When a new emperor comes to the throne, the persecutions are ended, but some curbs remain on Buddhist temple building and ordination and little confiscated property is restored.

850–859 The Mozarabs (Christians in Muslim Spain) in Cordova launch a series of revolts to protest against pressures to assimilate into Muslim society.

858–879 The schism between the Churches of Constantinople and Rome is widened when the Byzantine emperor Michael III removes Ignatius as the patriarch of Constantinople and replaces him with Photius. In Rome, Pope Nicholas I objects; Photius is deposed and then restored, but friendly relations are restored for the moment by a council in Constantinople, with authority still shared by the two churches.

875 During the Tang dynasty inChina, the ruler orders the celebration of Taoist ritual to end a drought and an epidemic. The emperor himself confers the purple robe, a mark of great distinction, on the Taoist master Du Guangting, who becomes an influential imperial adviser.

878 The Byzantine emperor Basil I orders the Jews in the empire to convert to Christianity.

910 The Benedictine monastery in Cluny, France, is founded by William I, duke of Aquitaine. The monks are allowed to elect their abbot, or leader, without interference from the state, and as a result the monastery is free from the ties to secular authority that confuse the division of state and church elsewhere in Europe.

918–943 In Korea, King T'aejo (Wang Kon) issues 10 injunctions to serve as the basis of future government; these include the importance of national defense, Buddhism, unity among the aristocratic clans, and strength of local government.

924–939 Aethelstan, Anglo-Saxon king of Britain, enacts laws making witchcraft punishable by death.

927 In Japan, the *Engishiki* (Procedures of the Engi era), a 50-volume legal compilation, covers the duties of the priesthood, the ritual calendar, ancient ritualistic prayers, and a register of deities. As the most comprehensive document of Shinto (native Japanese religious) rituals in classic form, the *Engishiki* becomes a sacred text of the Shinto religion.

931 Pope John XI authorizes Odo (later Saint Odo), abbot of Cluny monastery in France, to reform the monasteries of France and Italy. Odo is also said to have introduced a form of musical notation using letters.

945 When the Shia Muslim Buyid dynasty of Persia takes control of Baghdad's Islamic empire, it increases taxes on Jews, Christians, and Sunni Muslims and restricts their role in Persian society.

957 Sviatoslav I, grand duke of Kiev in Russia, reverses the policy of his mother, Olga, who was baptized a Christian by the patriarch of the Orthodox Church in Constantinople, and maintains the worship of pagan deities.

961 During the Song dynasty in China, debates among exponents of the Three Teachings of Confucianism, Buddhism, and Taoism are prohibited, and the activities of Buddhists and Taoists are limited.

963 The Holy Roman Emperor and king of Germany, Otto the Great, charges Pope John XII with treason and removes him from office, appointing in his place Pope Leo VII. The new pope, a layman, must take a pledge of allegiance to the emperor, a requirement that would remain in place for about 100 years.

988 Prince Vladimir, the grand duke of Kiev in Russia, converts to Orthodox Christianity, and Russian Orthodoxy begins to develop its own liturgy and status as an independent church. Indigenous religions are repressed over the next several centuries.

991–1031 Al-Qadir, caliph of the Muslim Abbasid dynasty centered in Baghdad, assumes a religious role as defender of Sunni beliefs against the claims of the Shia Muslims.

996–1021 Al-Hakim, caliph of the Muslim Fatimid dynasty in Egypt, represses Christianity and Judaism in that country and supports Shia missionaries who pronounce him a god.

997–1038 During the reign of Saint Stephen, whose father, Geisa, brought Christianity to Hungary, the country becomes Roman Catholic. The population is converted, archbishoprics and bishoprics are established, and the Benedictines are given special status, although paganism is not entirely abolished.

c. 1000 The Hindu rulers of India grant the Jews of Cochin, a region in southwest India, civil and political rights.

1009–1225
Confucianism is accepted in Vietnam as the basis for the civil-service examinations used to recruit the educated classes into the government; it also becomes the official state ideology.

1033
During the Song dynasty in China, Taoists are forbidden to build new temples.

1035
About 6,000 Jews are killed in a period of political unrest in Muslim Fez, Morocco.

1044
Jews and Muslims are expelled from Constantinople after being blamed for riots occurring there.

1050–1150
Many clergy in western Europe unite under the bishop of Rome and declare their union a separate political body, not under the rule of any secular leader.

1054
The schism between the Eastern and Western Churches becomes permanent after centuries of dispute over papal authority and church doctrine. Pope Leo IX and Orthodox Patriarch Michael Cerularius excommunicate each other, and the two Churches go their separate ways.

1059–1061
With the papacy of Nicholas I, the Holy Roman Emperor no longer selects the new pope and other Church officials as had been the policy for the last hundred years. Nicholas is elected under a new system of papal elections by a council of cardinals.

1066
Although Christians had been missionaries in Scandinavia since the ninth century, most of the populace is pagan, and they begin to persecute Christians.

1069
King Malcolm Canmore of Scotland bans the Celtic religion from being practiced and replaces it with Christianity.

1070
Vijayabahu I of Rohana in Ceylon (modern Sri Lanka) expels Hindu invaders from southern India, who had reigned for 75 years over this region of Ceylon. The king rebuilds Buddhist temples destroyed by the Hindu occupiers.

1070
William the Conqueror, the Norman who had invaded and conquered England at the Battle of Hastings in 1066, invites Jews to the British Isles to serve as finance officials.

1071
The Oghuz Turks, Muslims who had come from central Asia and founded the Seljuk dynasty in present-day Iran and Iraq, move into Anatolia under their sultan, Alp Arslan, and defeat the Byzantines at the Battle of Manzikert, capturing the Byzantine emperor Romanos I. The Turks then seize Jerusalem, causing the Jewish community there to disperse and motivating Pope Urban II to call for the First Crusade, to free the Holy Land from infidels.

1073–1085
Pope Gregory VII, in an attempt to increase his political power and place himself at the center of religious power, declares that secular rulers have no jurisdiction over the Catholic Church and that only the pope may appoint bishops, convene Church councils

to determine doctrine, and establish monasteries.

1075
Pope Gregory VII issues the papal edict *Dictatus papae* (Dictate of the pope), arguing that papal authority comes from God, who is the sole judge of the pope's actions. The pope's edict opposes the actions of Holy Roman Emperor Henry IV, who chooses his own archbishop of Milan and publicly ridicules the pope; in response, the pope excommunicates Henry and his supporters and removes him as Holy Roman Emperor.

1077
The excommunicated and deposed Holy Roman Emperor Henry IV seeks and receives absolution from the pope, but is prevented from resuming his rule by political rivals and is excommunicated again when he refuses to let the pope decide the matter. Nonetheless, Henry defeats his rivals, regains the emperorship, and marches on Rome, forcing the pope to flee; although the pope is restored to power by political supporters, Rome is burned in the fighting, and the pope dies in exile.

1081
In Japan, some 1,000 Buddhist monks from Enryakuji on Mount Hiei, sacred to Japanese Buddhism, move on the capital at Heian-kyo (modern Kyoto). About 200 of the monks are armed; this and subsequent protests—in 1107, 1113, 1139, 1169, and 1177—are spurred by Buddhist sectional rivalries, opposition to court appointments, and government weakness in the face of growing domestic disorder.

1087
During the Heian era in Japan, *insei* (cloister government—rule by former emperors who retired to become Buddhist monks) begins after Emperor Shirakawa abdicates. While reigning emperors head the traditional court and bureaucracy, former emperors (usually emperors' fathers or grandfathers) assert control through their own retinues and administrations located in a Buddhist monastery; the *insei* system lasts intermittently in some form until 1840.

1091
The Christian rulers of Castile in central and north-central Spain, an area that remained free of Moorish rule, restrict Jewish civil and political rights.

1095
Pope Urban II initiates the First Crusade by calling together knights at Clermont in France and in an emotional message asking them to liberate Jerusalem from Muslim rule. He is responding to a request from the Byzantine emperor Alexius I Comnenus for assistance in repelling the Seljuk Turks.

1096
During the First Crusade, crusaders attack Jewish communities in the Rhine Valley in Europe. They kill Jews or force them to convert to Christianity; to avoid conversion, many Jews would commit suicide.

1096
Hungarian forces refuse to participate in the crusaders' attacks on Jewish communities, and crusader attacks on Jews subsequently lessen.

1098
The crusaders lay siege to the Muslim-ruled city of Antioch in Syria and take it after four months.

1099	The crusaders capture Jerusalem, looting the city and killing or driving off many Jewish and Muslim inhabitants, although the Jewish community survives. The Latin Kingdom of Jerusalem is established with Godfrey of Bouillon, duke of Lower Lorraine in France, as ruler and with a papal representative in residence.
1100	The Byzantine emperor Alexius I Comnenus moves to repress the Bogomil sect (a Bulgarian Christian sect claiming that God has two sons, one good and one evil) as an enemy of Orthodox Christianity. Bogomil texts are burned, adherents imprisoned, and the sect's leader Basil executed, but the repression is unsuccessful and the sect remains active.
1100s	Catholic theologians decide that a couple need only declare verbal consent, without a priest or witness, to have a legal marriage.
1115	Rulers of Christian Spain grant both Jews and Muslims limited freedoms, to control frictions that have arisen between the two.
1130	During the Jurchen Jin dynasty in China, the emperor strictly controls religion by regulating religious life—for instance, by ordering that monks may not be ordained without government authorization.
1144	In Norwich, England, claims of blood libel against Jews surface; Jews are said to use the blood of Christians to prepare the matzos for the Passover ritual. Although known to be false, the charge would be leveled against Jewish communities in Europe repeatedly over the centuries.
1148	The Roman Catholic Church condemns the Albigensians in France as heretics; they are condemned again in 1184 and 1215. The Albigensians believe that matter is evil and that Jesus is a spirit who was never born.
1153	The last Buddhist king of the Maldive Islands in the Indian Ocean converts to Sunni Islam and founds a sultanate. Many Buddhist sites are destroyed in the early years of Islamic rule, and Buddhism gradually dies out in the Maldives.
1164	In the *Constitutions of Clarendon*, King Henry II of Britain seeks to regain control over the Catholic Church and to limit papal authority. Included in the *Constitutions* are such points as the king's power to settle controversies arising from church patronage and the king's right to grant the bestowal of churches.
1165	The Jews of Yemen on the southern Arabian peninsula are forced to convert to Islam by Shia Muslims.
1175	The Waldenses emerge as a Roman Catholic sect in Lyon, France. Followers of Peter Waldo, who gave up his life as a wealthy merchant to become a wandering preacher, the Waldenses stress spirituality and criticize materialistic Church practices, which leads to their persecution beginning in 1179.
1176	Jews are made serfs in Spain and become the property of the rulers.
1176–1177	At the Battle of Legnano in Italy, the forces of the Lombard

League in Italy, who are allied with the Roman Catholic Church in Rome, defeat the forces of Holy Roman Emperor Frederick I Barbarossa, who has deposed the pope and attempted to conquer the Lombard states. The defeat and the Treaty of Venice in 1177 give the pope new power over political rulers.

1179   The Third Lateran Council of the Roman Catholic Church refuses to recognize the French Waldenses as a sect of Catholicism. The council also requires that Jews live in communities or neighborhoods separate from Christians.

1182   With the spread of anti-Jewish sentiment in Europe, Jews are expelled from France and later from other European countries.

1184   At the Council of Verona in Italy, Pope Lucius III bans the Waldenses, a sect in France, from Roman Catholicism because of their unauthorized preaching. The Waldenses respond by organizing a separate religion centered in Provence in southern France; in the 16th century, they become Calvinists.

1187–1195   Under the Brahmanic legal system of King Nissankamalla of Ceylon (modern Sri Lanka), the ruler must be a Buddhist.

1190   Bowing to Buddhist pressure, the emperor of the Jin dynasty in China formally proscribes the Quanzhen school of Taoism, which teaches that life is in the hands of people, not of gods, and that people can attain long life through hard work. The ban has little or no effect, and Quanzhen Taoism gains an even wider following.

1197   When Muslims sack the great Buddhist university of Nalanda, and in 1203 the University of Vikramasila, in India, Buddhism begins to disappear in India, and most Buddhist monks from northern India disperse to Tibet, Nepal, and southern India. Buddhism had been on the decline in India for several centuries, partly because of its gradual assimilation into Hinduism but also because of the growth of popular *bhakti* (devotional) sects, which make the Buddhist monastic institutions appear isolated and extravagent, and because of the decline of the royal patronage on which monastic Buddhism depends.

1198–1216   During the papacy of Innocent III, the Roman Catholic Church has extensive control over the political rulers of Europe and can remove and select them as it chooses.

1200   At the request of Buddhists, who want to suppress the Pure Land Buddhist movement (emphasizing devotion to the Buddha of Light rather than meditation) in Japan, the Kamakura shogunate (military rulership) orders the expulsion of all Pure Land priests.

1200s   The popes of this time use their power to make the Church in Rome a wealthy institution. By the century's end, papal involvement in politics, finances, and the law begins to erode the public trust in the spiritual authority of the Catholic Church's hierarchy.

1200s   The chronicle *Flores historiarum* (Flowers of history), ascribed to various English Benedictines at St. Alban's Cathedral, including John de Cella, Roger of Wendover, and Matthew Paris, includes the tale of the Wandering Jew. The Jew is forced to wander throughout the earth as punishment for having ignored Jesus on his way to the Crucifixion; Jesus condemns him to live until the Second Coming (when Jesus returns to judge humanity at the end of time), and this story, often given an anti-Semitic slant, is widely repeated for centuries, with the Wandering Jew reported in many cities and many lands, and inspires works of literature and art.

1204   Buddhists unsuccessfully petition the imperial court in Japan to ban the teachings of the Amida Buddhist movement concerning the exclusive invocation of the sacred name of Amida Buddha, because they fear that his doctrines undermine their own power. *Amida* is the Japanese name for the Buddha of Infinite Light, the central figure in Pure Land Buddhism.

1208–1229   After the Albigensians, a Christian sect that opposes Roman Catholicism, murder the papal representative Peter of Castelnau, the Church initiates a war to destroy the sect.

1209   The first crusade to destroy the Waldenses (Christian sect in southern France) is launched by Pope Innocent III. Although 80 members of the sect are burned in 1211, the crusade fails, and the Waldenses survive in Germany, Spain, and northern Italy.

1210   A council of Roman Catholic bishops in Paris rules that Aristotle may not be taught at the University of Paris. The decision is approved by the pope in 1215 but is not fully enforced.

1215   Pope Innocent III calls the Fourth Lateran Council, which places restrictions on Jews, including the requirement that they wear distinctive clothing, special hats, or badges of colored circles or six-pointed stars on their cloaks to identify them as Jews. The council also prohibits Christians from doing business with Jews.

1222   A British deacon who converts to Judaism to marry a Jewish woman is hanged.

1231   With his constitution *Excommunicamus* (We excommunicate), Pope Gregory IX institutes the Inquisitio Haereticae Pravitatis (Inquisition of heretical evil) and the office of inquisitor, who answers only to the pope; inquisitors are primarily Franciscans or Dominicans, who are supposedly learned and free of ambition. The pope creates the Inquisition to counter any similar action by Holy Roman Emperor Frederick II; most inquisitorial activities are at first confined to Germany and Aragon, though in effect they extend to all Europe.

1231   The Christian rulers of northern Spain begin to retake southern Spain, starting with the conquest of Cordoba in 1236 and of Seville in 1248 by Ferdinand III of Léon and Castile, marking the decline of Muslim rule.

1232   In Japan, the regent Hojo Yasutoki and a council of advisers issue the Joei Formulary Laws, the first written laws describing the correct conduct of the shoguns (military rulers) in administering justice and establishing new land-tenure systems. Land-tenure regulations continue to afford special privileges to Shinto-shrine and Buddhist-temple landholdings.

1233	The Statute of Jewry Laws in Britain places limits on Jewish business activity and commands their loyalty to the king.
1236	The Holy Roman Emperor Frederick II extends to the entire Holy Roman Empire the doctrine that Jews are serfs and the property of their rulers.
1237	The emerging nomadic Mongol Empire, already occupying a large part of North China, institutes a civil-service examination system and claims to be a Confucian state.
1240	Rabbi Yehiel of Paris defends Judaism against charges made by Pope Gregory IX in 1236.
1243	In Germany, Jews are accused of desecrating the host (eucharistic bread or wafer).
c. 1250	As a result of the translations of astrological texts from Greek and Arabic into Latin in the preceding centuries, some leading European scholars such as Roger Bacon, Albertus Magnus, and Thomas Aquinas accept the validity of astrological predictions, although many leaders of the Church criticize astrology as anti-Christian.
1257–1258	The conflict between Taoists and Buddhists in China escalates into warfare, and temples and monasteries are destroyed.
1258	Kublai Khan, Mongol ruler and founder of the Mongol dynasty in China, convenes a conference of Buddhists, Taoists, and Confucian mediators to debate issues of religious disagreement in China. Siding with the Buddhists, he judges them to have won the debate and orders Taoist works burned and confiscated property to be returned to Buddhist owners.
1261	Nichiren, founder of the Nichiren Buddhist sect in Japan, is exiled now and again in 1271 to remote regions of Japan, eventually spending the final years of his life with a few followers on the slopes of Mount Fuji, predicting the downfall of a degenerate Japan. Nichiren preaches that the essence of Buddhism lies in the Lotus sutra and that all men are manifestations of Buddha.
1264	Jews fleeing from Germany settle in Poland and are valued for their technical and intellectual skills.
1265	*Las siete partidas* (Seven-part code), written in Castilian Spanish, is compiled by order of King Alfonso X of Castile, though the laws do not go into effect until 1348; they are enforced throughout Spain and in Spanish possessions throughout the world. The laws show hostility toward the Jews, but at the same time protect the religion and property of the Jews and the Moors (Muslims from North Africa who earlier conquered southern Spain).
1271	When Kublai Khan establishes the Yuan dynasty in China, he restores traditional Confucian court rituals, promotes transla-

tion of the Confucian classics into Mongolian, and makes overtures to Buddhist and Taoist religious groups. He also supports the small Muslim communities, composed mainly of Arab, Persian, and central Asian Muslims who settled in China as merchants and traders centuries earlier.

1274–1308   In Korea, King Ch'ungyol, who favors neo-Confucian ideas, establishes a national academy to foster the study of these ideas and seeks to imbue the ethics of Confucius with a spiritual justification. This policy ends a previous pattern of cooperation between Buddhism and Confucianism, and the two hereafter conflict.

1281   Kublai Khan condemns all Taoist works in China except the *Tao de Jing*, ordering them burned and the printing blocks smashed. He also forbids Taoists to sell charms and forces some monks to convert to Buddhism.

1285–1303   King Philip the Fair of France invades the Vatican because of a conflict over the power of the state versus that of the Roman Catholic Church. The French almost capture Pope Boniface VIII, who dies a month later, leaving the Church severely weakened and in a period of decline and weak leadership.

1290   King Edward I of England expels the Jews after confiscating their property.

1293   After harsh restrictions are placed on the Jewish community in Naples, Italy, all the residents convert to Christianity, flee, or are killed. The Jewish community in Naples is eradicated.

1294   During the Yuan dynasty in China, Chengzong, a grandson of Kublai Khan, issues an edict calling for the veneration of Confucius.

1295   The Mongol rulers of Persia declare Islam the official religion, order all Buddhist buildings to be destroyed, and exile all Buddhist monks.

1295   During the reign of Indravarmnan III of Cambodia, Theravada Buddhism, a conservative form of Buddhism, becomes the dominant religion and remains so until the 15th century.

1306   Almost 100,000 Jews are expelled from France. Although they are allowed to return in 1315, few do so, and they are expelled again in 1322.

1311–1320   In the Mongol Yuan dynasty, during the rule of the emperor Buyantu, the interpretation and commentaries of the neo-Confucian school are made obligatory in China.

1336   The independent Muslim states emerging in India include Bengal (1336–1576), Kashmir (1346–1589), Gujarat (1407–1572), Jaunpur (1394–1479), Malwa (1401–1531), and Deccan (1347–1601), each ruled separately from the Hindu Delhi sultanates. These new states seek Hindu converts to Islam but also desire an accommodation with the Hindu majority and respect local or regional customs.

1336	The state of Vijayanagar is the first Hindu state in India to tolerate all religions. Located in southern India, the Hindu Vijayanagar rulers support indigenous cultural traditions, involve Jains in many activities, and patronize learning, literature, art, music, and architecture; the state endures until 1565.
1339	The Northern and Southern Courts period in Japan is an era of political disruption and strife when the emperor has no real power; the old ideologies of the divine descent of the imperial line, the unique superiority of Japan, and the power of Shinto re-emerge.
1348	During the Black Death, bubonic and pneumonic plagues that decimate Europe until 1351, 25 to 33 percent of the population dies, and the Jews in some communities, particularly in Germany, are blamed; the German Jews flee to Poland to evade persecution. The isolation of Jews from the Christian community and their religious rituals that stress cleanliness may account for the fact that a lower percentage of the Jewish population perishes in the plague.
1348	Yaji, the Hausa chief of Kano in West Africa, appoints Muslim teachers to positions in his government. Like other rulers in West African states and chiefdoms, he turns to Islam to legitimize his rule and to unify his community; his chiefdom lasts until 1385.
1350	The Augsburg Bible, a German translation of the Old Testament, is issued, and between 1389 and 1400 the New Testament is published in German as the Wenzel Bible. Church authorities oppose the use of vernacular bibles, and they are banned by the German emperor in 1369 and by the pope in 1375.
1367	Jews are expelled from Hungary.
1368–1644	During the Ming dynasty in China, the civil-service examination is formalized into three steps: the *hsiu-ts'ai* (cultivated talent), held at the local prefecture level; the *chu-jen* (recommended man), given at the prefecture capital; and the *chin-shih* (advanced scholar), held at Peking (Beijing). The testing matter is limited to the Nine Classics of Confucianism.
1377	John Wycliffe, an English theologian who has criticized the extravagances and corruption of the Roman Catholic Church and advocated new ideas including predestination, the supremacy of the New Testament as the basis of religious authority, and the translation of the Bible into vernacular languages, is condemned as a heretic for questioning the authority of the pope. His teachings and writings greatly contribute to the Protestant Reformation.
c. 1387–1400	In Geoffrey Chaucer's *Canterbury Tales*, "The Prioress's Tale" revives charges of blood libel against the Jews.
1389	At the Battle of Kosovo in today's southern Yugoslavia, the Ottoman Turks led by Sultan Murad I defeat the Serbs; Serbia is crushed, and this area of eastern Europe comes under Muslim

control. The Serbs nevertheless believe that the land will eventually be restored to their control, a belief that plays a role in the conflict between the Serbs and the Albanians living in the Kosovo region of Yugoslavia at the dawn of the 21st century.

1391 In Castile and Aragon in Spain, Jews are attacked, mainly by poor people and the working classes in the cities; the weak Spanish rulers are unable to protect the Jewish communities. Tens of thousands of Jews are forced to convert to Christianity; some do so willingly, but others only from necessity. These converted Jews are labeled *conversos* (converted Jews), *marranos* (literally, swine), New Christians, or crypto-Jews; many continue to practice Judaism in secret, while others genuinely adopt Catholicism and enrich Spanish culture in many areas.

1392 During the Yi dynasty in Korea, the country is transformed into a Confucian society, which lasts until 1910. The early rulers of the dynasty are neo-Confucians who seek to create a new social and political order based on a moral vision reflecting Confucian values, rituals, and ethics; they suppress Buddhism and confiscate all lands held by Buddhist temples.

1394 King Charles VI of France expels the Jews.

1399 In England, the death penalty is instituted as punishment for heresy, in reaction to the ideas of the theologian John Wycliffe and the reform movement initiated by him.

1406–1428 After the Chinese invade and conquer Vietnam, they require that Chinese culture be instituted there, and Chinese Confucianism takes hold alongside the dominating Buddhism.

1412 A major migration of Jews from Spain to North Africa and western Asia begins when Jews are ordered confined to Jewish quarters in Spain.

1414 Sigismund, king of Germany, convenes the Council of Constance, held at Konstanz, Germany, with the pope's approval, to crush the Hussite movement, a Bohemian religious and national movement led by reformer John Hus. Sigismund at first promises to protect Hus, who has been influenced by John Wycliffe's ideas, but the king and the council condemn him as a heretic when he refuses to recant his views before the council, and in 1415 Hus is burned at the stake; the Hussite revolt persists for another 20 years, despite Sigismund's persecutions.

1415 The Council of Constance reviews the beliefs of John Wycliffe, who died in 1384, and orders that his body be dug up and burned to halt the dissension caused by his heretical views. The order is carried out in 1428.

1421–1454 Jews are expelled from Germany and Austria and are forced to emigrate farther into eastern Europe.

1431 Jeanne d'Arc (Joan of Arc) is burned at the stake in Rouen, France, after being convicted of heresy and sorcery. While leading an army against British invaders in the course of the Hundred Years War, she is captured, sold to the British, and ultimately condemned by French churchmen; after her death, she is proclaimed innocent in 1456 and canonized in 1920.

1438 The Muslim rulers of Morocco establish a *mellah* (quarter) for the Jews in the city of Fez.

1440–1469 After the Aztecs defeat the Tepanecs in 1427 and become the rulers of the valley of Mexico, the Aztec grand vizier Tlacaelel, brother of the ruler Montezuma I, orders all written records of rival groups destroyed and has an Aztec mythology created, with the Aztecs portrayed as the chosen people of the sun god Huitzilopochtli. In this new Aztec mythology, the Aztecs are required to take prisoners and sacrifice them to the gods, and, when Tlacaelel dedicates a new temple to the sun god in the capital city of Tenochtitlán (today Mexico City), 20,000 victims are sacrificed.

c. 1450 In *Fortalitium fidei*, Alfonso de Espina, Franciscan theologian and archbishop of Thermopolis, attacks the *conversos* (converted Jews of Spain) for continuing to practice Judaism in private or for remaining Jews at heart and condemns them as a threat to Spanish society. The book urges the expulsion of Jews and harsh treatment of all converts; these ideas reflect the views of many Church leaders in Spain who doubt the faith of the *conversos* and other converts in Spain.

1450–1519 During the Wars of the Flowers between the Aztecs and neighboring peoples in Mexico, the Aztecs capture prisoners to be sacrificed to the Aztec gods. In the Aztec religion, offerings of human and animal blood are vital for the continuation of life, and many captives are needed to satisfy the gods.

1455 In Korea, Sejo usurps the throne of the boy-king Tanjong and is criticized by many Confucian scholars, who see this as an unforgivable violation of Confucian principles. Their complaints are met by bloody purges.

1463 All of Orthodox Christian eastern Europe falls under Muslim control, except for Russia.

1471 The pope gives considerable freedom to the Jews in central and northern Italy, in view of their financial support in the form of taxes paid to the Church.

1478 Pope Sixtus IV establishes the Inquisition as a tribunal for investigating and punishing heretics. Its work focuses mainly on identifying Jewish and Muslim (forced) converts to Christianity who are believed to continue to practice their religions in secret. By 1640, 16 permanent tribunals had been established.

1478 With the permission of Pope Sixtus IV, King Ferdinand V and Queen Isabella I of Spain establish an inquisition to investigate *marranos* (Spanish: swine) and *conversos* (converted Jews) in Aragon and Castile, and many are burned at the stake in public executions. The motivations for the inquisition are both religious and political, as the monarchs seek the support of wealthy urban merchants who see the Jews as economic competitors. After 1502, Muslims are investigated, and in the 1520s Protestants become victims; although directed by the Catholic Church in Spain, the Spanish Inquisition is more a political tool than a religious instrument.

1484   Pope Innocent VIII issues the papal bull *Summis desiderantes* (Desiring with supreme ardor), condemning the spread of witchcraft in Germany and initiating two centuries of oppression and the execution of women as sorcerers and witches across Europe. One year later, in the Italian city of Como, 41 women are burned to death, and it is estimated that 300,000 women are put to death as witches during the next 200 years.

c. 1486   In the wake of his bull condemning the spread of witchcraft in Germany, Pope Innocent VIII authorizes two Dominican scholars, Heinrich Krämer and Johann Sprenger, the latter an inquisitor in the Tirol region of Austria, to eradicate the unholy practices. The two men publish *Malleus maleficarum* (Witches' hammer), describing the vile nature and acts of witches and the legal procedures for trying them; translated into many languages, the *Malleus* becomes one of the most popular and widely read books in Europe.

1492   The Spanish crown expels all Jews from Spain. Many emigrate to European Turkey, where they find refuge under the Muslim attitude of tolerance; by the 16th century, Constantinople has the largest population of Jews in Europe. Jews expelled from Britain, France, Germany, and Switzerland at the same time settle in Poland and Russia.

1493–1528   In the Songhai Empire in West Africa, Islam becomes the state religion during the reign of Askiya Muhammad Ture. Muslim religious teachers are afforded much status, and ties are established with Muslims in Mecca, but, aside from the ruling classes and the traders, most other people continue to practice indigenous religions.

1495   Jews are expelled from Lithuania, though the order is rescinded in 1503.

1497   Under pressure from Spain, Portugal expels its Jewish population.

1498   After being convicted of heresy in 1495 and having been excommunicated, the Dominican monk Girolamo Savonarola is hanged and then burned at the stake in Florence, Italy. Savonarola sought to implement a series of major religious reforms in an attempt to restore the Dominican order to its original spiritual purpose and purity, and his fiery protests against the sinfulness and luxury of the wealthy and powerful inspired huge followings, which brought him acclaim but also threatened the authority of the Church.

1498   In Korea, Prince Yonsan initiates the *muo sahwa*, or purge, in which many neo-Confucian intellectuals considered disloyal are executed or exiled.

1499–1500   The Muslims of Granada, Spain, rebel when forced to convert by

Francisco Jimenez de Cisneros, Queen Isabella's confessor; after the Spanish put down the rebellion in 1502, the Muslims are given the choice to convert or leave. Many choose conversion, but the lack of resources for educating them in Catholicism means that the *Moriscos* (Spanish Muslims who become baptized Christians) continue to dress and speak like Muslims, secretly practice Islam, and live isolated from the Christian community.

c. 1500   In Moscow, the political center of Russia at this time, a dispute develops among leaders of the Russian Orthodox Church: one group, the Possessors, argues that the Church should own much property and should be closely aligned with the Russian grand duke, whereas the other group, the Non-Possessors, prefers the Church to own little property and be free of state control. The Possessors are victorious, and some Non-Possessors are condemned as heretics.

1500–1650   Europe is swept by a witchcraft craze, when both Catholics and Protestants consider witchcraft a dangerous activity and seek to repress it. Before this time, witchcraft was generally viewed as an activity without any major harmful effects.

1501–1648   Jews in Poland and Lithuania enjoy considerable economic freedom, the population increases tenfold, and the region becomes the center of Jewish cultural life in eastern Europe.

1506   The German philosopher and Protestant reformer Johannes Reuchlin writes *De rudimentis hebraicis* (Rudiments of Hebrew), one of the first Hebrew-language textbooks. Reuchlin argues that a literal understanding of biblical passages is required to understand broader theological issues and that thus it is necessary to study Hebrew, but this view is contrary to the position of the established Church, and he is convicted of heresy.

1509   Desiderius Erasmus, the Dutch scholar, writes *Encomium moriae* (The praise of folly), in which he criticizes hypocrisy in the Roman Catholic Church. Erasmus at first accepts the Protestant Reformation but later rejects it and urges reform in the Roman Catholic Church.

1511   Antonio de Montesino, a Spanish Dominican missionary, suggests that the Indians of the New World are human and have souls, and he denounces the Spanish treatment of the Indians. In 1512, he argues his position so strenuously before the king of Spain that the king is moved to improve Spanish conduct toward the Indians.

1512   The Laws of Burgos, capital of Old Castile in Spain, force colonists in the New World to end their harsh treatment of Indians, although the Indians must swear allegiance to the Catholic Church. The laws also require that the Indians be read the *Requerimiento* (Request), which sets forth the Christian story of creation.

1515   The Dominican monk Bartolomé de Las Casas, who owns land and Indian slaves on Española (Hispaniola, or Haiti), begins to document the mistreatment of Indians as he gathers information for his *Historia de las Indias* (History of the Indies).

1516 King Francis I of France and Pope Leo X, son of Lorenzo de' Medici, enter into a concordat giving the king the authority to appoint bishops and abbots in France.

1517 A Jewish ghetto is established in Venice, Italy, and, in 1555, another in Rome. Jews are allowed to leave the ghettos to conduct business but otherwise must live there; in towns too small to support a ghetto, distinct Jewish quarters or streets develop.

1517 Bartolomé de Las Casas, the Dominican monk and Spanish settler on Hispaniola, travels to Spain and asks King Charles I to halt the mistreatment of the Indians in the Spanish New World. Despite his sympathy for the Indians, until late in his life Las Casas supports the African slave trade.

1517 Martin Luther, an Augustinian monk and university professor, posts his *Ninety-five Theses* on the door of the Wittenberg Cathedral in Germany, marking the formal start of the Protestant Reformation. Calling for a formal discussion in the Roman Catholic Church of the statements or propositions he poses in his theses, which describe the moral and spiritual corruption of the clergy, the abuses of church authority, and the sale of indulgences (remission of sins), Luther finds no response from the Church except for condemnation by the pope.

1519 Chungjong, ruler of Korea, responds to the demands of the meritorious elite and purges Confucians.

1519–1521 Indian religions in Mexico are systematically devastated when the Spanish led by Hernán Cortés move across Mexico from Veracruz to Tenochtitlán, destroying all symbols of Indian religions and replacing them with crosses.

1520 Pope Leo X issues the papal bull *Exserge Domine* (Arise, O Lord), in which he condemns 41 of Martin Luther's ideas as heresy; he does not excommunicate Luther but forbids him to perform the duties of a Catholic priest. Luther burns the bull and a copy of the Church's canon law.

1521 Holy Roman Emperor Charles V summons the Diet of Worms in Germany; the Diet issues the Edict of Worms condemning Martin Luther as a heretic and banishing him from the city of Worms. The edict is not enforced.

1521 Pope Leo X issues the papal bull *Honestis* (To people of honor), in response to the actions of several towns that refuse to burn suspected witches. The bull declares that any official who refuses to execute witches will be excommunicated.

1522–1566 During the Ming dynasty in China, the emperor Shizong abolishes many religious offices, limits imperial spending on temples and rituals, and begins to persecute Buddhists. He then becomes interested in Taoist promises of health and long life and supports Taoist scholars and practitioners.

1524 The first Spanish Catholic missionaries arrive in Mexico and attempt to convert the Indians.

1524–1525 During the Peasants' War in Germany, rural peasants revolt against the nobility over land and farming rights. Many peasants are adherents of Lutheranism as an alternative to the Catholicism of the nobility, but Martin Luther does not support the revolt, which is suppressed by the nobles.

1526 Zahir-ud-Din Muhammad, known as Babur, captures Delhi in India, suppresses Afghan and Hindu resistance, and establishes the Mughal Empire in south Asia. A descendant of Genghis Khan, Babur is a Mongol who ruled an area in today's Afghanistan before becoming emperor of India; his dynasty maintains a policy of tolerance toward Hindus.

1526 The Tyndale Bible, an English translation of the New Testament made by William Tyndale, is printed in Germany and distributed in Britain, where it is condemned by Church authorities and by the lord chancellor, Thomas More. In 1535, Tyndale is captured, imprisoned, tried, and convicted of heresy in Brussels; he is strangled and then burned at the stake.

1526 Efforts begin to convert the Saami (Lapps) of northern Scandinavia to Christianity when King Gustavus Vasa of Sweden sends missionaries to the north. The mission is short-lived and ineffective.

1526 The Muslims of Valencia and Aragon in Spain are forced to convert, and Islam is officially prohibited in the country.

1527 Phothisarat, ruler of Lan Xang, one of the kingdoms of Laos, encourages the practice of Buddhism and issues a decree banning sacrifices to local spirits.

1527 King Henry VIII of England, wishing to divorce his wife, Catherine of Aragon (who has failed to produce a male heir to the throne), and to marry Anne Boleyn, is refused a divorce by the Church. The king views this as Church interference in the affairs of state, because producing a royal heir is a political, not a religious, matter.

1527 The Swiss Brethren, an Anabaptist movement in Switzerland at odds with the Swiss Reformation movement, issue the Brotherly Union declaration, later known as the Schleitheim Articles, which define the basic beliefs of the Anabaptist movement, including separation of church and state and rejection of oath taking. The Anabaptists also believe that only adults can participate in church rituals as members of the church.

1529 At the Diet of Worms in Germany, five German territories and 14 cities protest the opposition of the Roman Catholic Church to Lutheran ideas developing in northern Germany. The word *protest* is used in the edict that is issued, and the term *Protestant* comes from this event and usage.

1530 At the Diet of Augsburg in Germany, Holy Roman Emperor Charles V rejects the Augsburg Confession, the basic creeds and doctrine of Lutheranism. Meant as an act of conciliation toward the Church, the confession is criticized by some Protestant reformers as too mild in its calls for reforms.

1532   The French Protestant reformer William Farel leads a movement expelling the bishop, occupying churches and the city cathedral, and destroying religious texts in Geneva, Switzerland. He also replaces the Roman Catholic Mass with services based on the Protestant Bible.

1534   The Church of England is established when the British Parliament passes the Act of Supremacy at the direction of King Henry VIII. Establishing that the English monarch is the supreme head of the Church of England, the act ends papal religious authority in Britain.

1534–1535   An Anabaptist faction overthrows the civil and church government in Münster, Germany, in an attempt to create an ideal Christian community. Lutherans and Roman Catholics join forces to drive off the Anabaptists.

1535   Thomas More (later a saint), lord chancellor of England, is beheaded for refusing to support Henry VIII in his conflict with the Roman Catholic Church. At his execution, More proclaims that he is "the king's good servant, but God's first."

1535   In Texcoco, Mexico, the Spanish gather and destroy all pictorial records of Indian life, including much information about the Aztec religion.

1535–1540   Eradicating the Roman Catholic Church in Britain, King Henry VIII closes monasteries, executes officials who remain loyal to the Church, and confiscates Church property.

1536   An inquisition is established in Portugal to identify and punish *conversos* (converted Jews), who are believed to practice Judaism in secret.

1536   In the First Helvetic Confession, Protestant reformers attempt to make Protestantism the religion of Switzerland. The confession stresses the Protestant ministry and the role of the state in promoting religion and emphasizes the precedence of the Bible, not dogma, as the authority for church and worshipers.

1537   Pope Paul III declares that the Indians in the Americas are worthy of conversion to Christianity.

1540   Robert Barnes, a British reformer and prior of the Augustine monastery in Cambridge, who preaches Lutheranism, is burned at the stake in Britain.

1540   The Mennonites, a Protestant sect derived from the Anabaptists, flee from the Netherlands to avoid religious persecution and move to northern Germany and the Vistula River delta region, which is under Polish control.

1540   Four witches are burned in Wittenberg, Germany.

1542   Witchcraft in Britain is made a felony punishable by death.

1542	Pope Paul III establishes the Congregation of the Inquisition, or Roman Inquisition and Holy Office, to address the spread of Protestantism. Unlike the earlier inquisitions that were concerned with witchcraft, heresy, and other "false beliefs" that could cause public disturbances, this inquisition deals with intellectual infringements of orthodox belief that might surface in writings.
1542	Spanish colonial legislation, the *Leyes nuevas* (New laws), provides protection for the Indians in the New World; the *Leyes* draw on the work of the Dominican Bartolomé de Las Casas, who argued against the evils of exploiting the Indians. Though the *Leyes* are often not enforced, no other European colonial powers even offer the indigenous inhabitants similar legal protection.
1543	The publication of Martin Luther's *About the Jews and Their Lies* marks the emergence of modern anti-Semitism in Europe.
1550	King Charles V of Spain suspends Spanish exploration of the Americas and calls a meeting of leading theologians at the Council of 14 in Valladolid, Spain, to address the questions of whether American Indians are equal or inferior to Europeans and whether the Spanish should use force to eradicate native religions and replace them with Christianity. All participants agree that the Indians must be converted to Christianity.
1550–1600	In Korea, the teaching of Confucianism is encouraged in village schools, private academies, and institutions of learning throughout the country.
1553–1558	Roman Catholicism is temporarily reestablished in Britain when Mary Tudor, half-sister of Elizabeth, becomes queen. A supporter of Roman Catholicism, she severely represses the Church of England; hundreds of Protestants are burned at the stake, Protestant leaders are imprisoned or exiled, Catholic priests are restored, and Catholic doctrine and worship reintroduced.
1554	At a council of the Russian Orthodox Church in Moscow, the Non-Possessors, who advocate separation of church and state, are condemned.
1554–1592	The Hutterites, an Anabaptist sect in Moravia and Slovakia, attract followers from neighboring Germany and Austria and establish numerous communities based on the communal ownership of property. The Hutterites refer to these years of growth and expansion and peace as the Good Period and the Golden Period.
1555	In Mexico, the Roman Catholic Church restricts accession to the priesthood and membership in religious orders to European men, which eliminates the opportunity for American Indian men converted to Catholicism to become priests.
1555	Pope Paul IV issues a papal bull requiring Jews in Europe to live in ghettos and to have only minimal contact with Christians.
1555	The Peace of Augsburg, signed in Augsburg, Germany, by both Roman Catholics and Lutherans, marks the formal acceptance of

Protestantism in Germany. It gives Protestant princes the right to own Protestant church property and sets forth the principle of *cuius regio, eius religio*: the religion of the ruler becomes the religion of his state. Following a series of Protestant-Catholic wars in the 1530s and 1540s, territorialism was tried in the Holy Roman Empire.

1557   Queen Mary of England orders the body of Martin Bucer dug up and burned. Bucer, a German Dominican, had left the order and adopted Protestantism in 1521; he was aiding the Reformation in England when he died in 1551.

1559   John Knox, an ordained Roman Catholic priest who converted to Protestantism and is a follower of the French reformer John Calvin, supports a Protestant revolt against the Roman Catholic regent of Scotland, Mary of Guise, the mother of Mary queen of Scots. With the help of Queen Elizabeth and after the regent's death, the Protestants gain control of the Scottish government.

1559   In an attempt to limit the influence and spread of Protestantism, Pope Paul IV and the Council of Trent publish the *Index of Forbidden Books*. The *Index* includes three-fourths of the available books in Europe, such as the works of the Dutch philosopher Erasmus and all non-Latin Bibles.

1559   Queen Elizabeth I of England introduces the Oath of Supremacy, which requires those who hold political office to acknowledge the monarch as the "supreme governor" of the Church of England. This is unacceptable to Catholics.

1559   German rulers try to repress Protestantism and to revitalize Roman Catholicism. These efforts continue throughout the century until by 1600 the spread of Protestantism in Germany has been controlled.

1560   The *Confession of Faith*, written largely by the Protestant reformer John Knox, is adopted by the Scottish Parliament and remains the creed of Scotland for 200 years.

1560   A Spanish-style inquisition is established in the Portuguese colony of Goa off the coast of India.

1560   The information that the Franciscan priest Bernardino de Sagahun has gathered since 1529 about the Indians in the valley of Mexico and their culture before the Spanish conquest in 1521 is repressed by the Spanish king and the Church hierarchy. De Sagahun organized the material into a series of volumes called *A General History of the Things of New Spain*, which Spanish authorities see as hostile to Spain and to Roman Catholicism because the information documents, from the Indian point of view, the effects of Spanish colonization.

1562–1598   Roman Catholics and Huguenots (Protestants) in France are embroiled in intermittent conflicts, and the Catholics persecute the French Huguenots in an effort to eradicate them.

1563   The British law governing witchcraft and spiritualism is expanded to make all activities that involve the use of evil spirits punishable by death.

1563	In Germany, Johann Weyer writes *De praestigiis daemonum* (Of the deceptions of demons), a criticism of the witch-hunting craze in Europe, which he thinks mistakenly focuses on punishing demented old women rather than catching genuine criminals. The book has little effect on the social tensions created by the European obsession with witches or on the zeal with which witches are sought out.
1565	Calvinist nobles in the Netherlands revolt against their Spanish Catholic overlord, King Philip II of Spain. Precipitated by the king's treatment of the Netherlands as a Spanish province, such as his refusal to ban the Spanish Inquisition there, the revolt is marked by pillaging of Catholic churches; when the revolt is put down in 1567, the Netherlands is in a state of anarchy.
1565	During the reign of Pope Pius IV, the *Index of Forbidden Books* is revised to make it less extreme.
1566	Philip II of Spain forbids the *Moriscos* (Muslims who converted to Christianity) in Granada to use the Arabic language or to wear Muslim clothing. In 1569, the *Moriscos* revolt and are forced to leave Granada and move to areas of northern Spain.
1566	After a trial of witches in Britain, a woman accused of witchcraft is hanged.
1569	Jews in Poland are granted broad economic and civil rights.
1569–1572	The Polyglot Bible is published by a group of scholars working in Antwerp (in today's Belgium, on the Dutch border). Parallel translations of the biblical text in Latin, Greek, Syriac, and Aramaic, along with a lengthy commentary, are meant to facilitate an accurate reading of the Hebrew Bible and to help reconstruct the Aramaic that would have been the original language of the New Testament.
c. 1570	Roman Catholic Jesuit missionaries founding a mission to the Powhatan and Piscataway Indians in Maryland are killed by the Indians, who resist Spanish settlement.
1570	A Spanish-style inquisition is established in Peru.
1570s	The Japanese emperor Nobunaga leads a campaign attempting to limit the political and military power of the Buddhist True Pure Land sect, which emphasizes devotion to the Buddha of Infinite Light, who can grant the devotee rebirth in an eternal paradise, the Pure Land. The campaign lasts for 10 years and includes the destruction of temples and the execution of thousands of monks and sect leaders.
1570–1602	During the rule of Idris B. Ali, of the Kanuri state centered in Bornu in West Africa, Islam becomes the state religion. Islamic law becomes state law, mosques are built, and the capital city becomes a center of Islam in West Africa.
1572	A Spanish-style inquisition is established in Mexico.

1572	During the Saint Bartholomew's Day Massacre in Paris, France, thousands of Huguenots (French Protestants) are killed even though Catholics have promised to protect them. Fighting spreads across France and lasts for six weeks.
1573	After the death of King Sigismund II of Poland, the nobility approves the *Pax dissidentium* (Peace of the dissenters), which grants equal rights to Protestants and Roman Catholics in the country. The decision is vehemently opposed by the Polish Catholic Church, but it becomes law in Poland.
1573	Spain issues the Comprehensive Orders for New Discoveries, which prohibit the use of military force to convert Indians in the Americas to Catholicism. As the exploration of North America is in its early stages, this means that missionaries will become the primary agents for subjugation of the Indians of Spanish North America.
1574	Murad III, sultan of the Ottoman Empire, enforces earlier laws requiring Jews to wear unique clothing and also banning the repair or construction of synagogues.
1574	In central Asia, Jews are forced to convert to Islam. Many convert, but many also continue to practice Judaism in secret.
1576	Pope Gregory XIII, in his papal bull *Nuper ad nos* (Recently to us), rules that *mestizos* (people of mixed European and American Indian blood) can become priests, especially in light of the absence of priests in the Americas who speak American Indian languages. However, the order is ignored, and no *mestizos* or Indians become priests until 1794.
1576	Holy Roman Emperor Rudolf ends the toleration of Protestants in Bohemia (in modern-day Hungary).
1577	*A General History of the Things of New Spain*, compiled and written in the valley of Mexico by the Spanish Franciscan Bernardino de Sagahun from 1529 on, is the earliest and fullest description of Indian life in the Americas, but Inquisition officials cite it as a work of heresy, and Sagahun is excommunicated. He sends one Spanish-language copy of the 12-volume work to Spain, but somehow it finds its way to Florence, Italy; after its discovery in 1985, it becomes known as the Florentine Codex.
1578	The Mongol prince Altan Khan, who is Buddhist, bestows the honorific title of Dalai Lama (priest with oceanlike wisdom) on Sonam Gyatso, the abbot of Drepung Monastery in Tibet.
1578	In Austria, King Rudolf and his successor, King Ferdinand, repress Protestantism, and Roman Catholicism reasserts itself. By 1628, nearly all Austrians are Roman Catholic.
c. 1580	Obera, a Guarani Indian in Paraguay, proclaims that he is the messiah and calls on his followers to reject Christianity, revolt against Spanish rule, and follow his new religion, which combines elements of Indian religions and Christianity. The movement is suppressed and ends with many Indians being massacred.

1580	The Council of Four Lands, which begins to emerge in Poland, becomes a self-governing organization for Jewish communities in what are later parts of Poland, Russia, and Lithuania.
1582	During the Mughal dynasty in India, the Muslim emperor Akbar, who is remarkably tolerant of India's many religions, promulgates a new syncretistic religion, *Din-i Ilahi* (divine faith), after seven years of talks with Hindus, Jains, Parsis (Zoroastrians settled in India), Buddhists, and Jesuits, at his religious assembly, *Ibadat Khanah* (house of worship). Orthodox Muslims oppose this heresy, which attracts few adherents and ends with the end of Akbar's reign in 1605.
1583	Two followers of Robert Browne, an English Separatist, are executed for distributing Browne's treatises, written in 1581. The Brownists, who believe in the complete independence of individual church congregations from state control, are predecessors of the Congregationalists.
1585	The Spanish repress the playing of an Indian ball game in Mexico to eradicate native religious beliefs and practices and to aid in the conversion of the Indians to Catholicism.
1587	Emperor Hideyoshi, who recently unified Japan after 500 years of decentralized rule, orders all foreigners, primarily Roman Catholics, to be expelled. The order is not enforced, but it establishes a new antiforeigner policy followed by Hideyoshi's successors.
1587–1632	King Sigismund III of Poland represses Protestantism with the help of the Jesuits, and Roman Catholicism becomes the national religion of Poland. For his actions, Sigismund III becomes known as the King of the Jesuits.
1588–1629	The ruling Safavid dynasty in Persia persecutes rival Muslim Sufi (Muslim mystic) orders.
1590	Large numbers of Jewish *conversos* (converts to Christianity) move from Portugal and Brazil to the northern Netherlands, which is now independent of Spain. Although the *conversos* seek religious freedom, they continue to practice Judaism in secret.
1598	King Henry IV of France issues the Edict of Nantes, which ends more than 30 years of religious civil war in France between the Catholic majority and a sizable minority of French Protestants known as the Huguenots. The edict grants religious freedom to the Huguenots in return for their allegiance to the French crown and proclaims the following rights for French Protestants: freedom of religious belief, the right of private worship wherever they live, the right to conduct public worship in a number of specific towns and castles, the right to hold public office, and the right to control a number of walled towns and castles for their protection.
1598 on	The Spanish conquest and colonization of southwestern North America, which began in 1590, focuses on destroying the native religions, persecuting Indian religious leaders, and forcibly con-

verting Indians to Christianity. Many Indian tribes maintain their religions in secret.

c. 1600   A large number of Jews flee from Russia and Poland, where they have been subject to repressions such as forced conversion to Eastern Orthodoxy, and settle in Czechoslovakia. Relaxed economic and civil restrictions resulting from rapid economic growth and expansion here also attract Jews.

1604   Practicing magic is classified as a capital crime in Britain.

1606   Guru Arjun, the fifth Sikh guru (holy man, leader of Sikhs), becomes the first Sikh martyr when he is killed by the Muslim Mughal emperor Jahangir. The Sikh religion is monotheistic and does not accept the caste system prevalent in India.

1606   King James I of England, formerly King James VI of Scotland, sets forth the Oath of Allegiance, making allegiance to the throne paramount for all subjects. The oath is endorsed by leaders of the Church of England but causes difficulty for other Protestants and for Roman Catholics, who feel that it conflicts with their primary allegiance to God.

1606   During the guruship of Guru Hargobind, the sixth Sikh guru, the role of the guru expands as he becomes both the religious and secular leader of the Sikh community in India. Sikhs now often come into conflict with the Muslim Mughal rulers of northern India.

1607   Some Puritans in Britain, having failed to convince the Church of England to reform its practices in accord with Puritan beliefs, move to the Netherlands, where they are allowed to worship as they please.

1607   John Smyth, founder of the Baptist Church in Britain in 1606, flees with his followers to the Netherlands to escape prosecution for the Baptists' failure to worship in their Anglican parish churches.

1609   King Philip III of Spain expels around 300,000 Christianized *Moriscos* (converted Muslims) from Spain. They settle in Muslim communities in North Africa, where they contribute to the revitalization of Islamic culture in the region.

1609   The new Holy Roman Emperor Matthias reinstigates a policy of tolerance toward Protestants in Bohemia (part of modern Hungary).

1614–1630   The Edo period in Japan, 250 years of peace and prosperity under the Tokugawa shoguns (military rulers), also ushers in persecution of Roman Catholics. Spanish, Italian, and Portuguese priests and Japanese who have converted in the last 50 years are killed, forced to flee, or forced to reject Christianity. Westerners are excluded from society, and social order and stability based on Confucian principles of rigid class stratification and strict morality are imposed, affecting nearly all areas of everyday activity.

1620	The Roman Catholic Church in Mexico declares that the use of peyote by American Indians, even for ritual purposes, is the work of the devil and prohibits Christians from using it.
1620	Some 1,000 Puritans set sail from Britain to America, where they found the first Puritan colony in the Americas, Plymouth Plantation in Massachusetts Bay Colony, as a Christian theocracy in which Puritan principles guide community life and the state and church support each other. During the next few decades, tens of thousands of other Puritans follow and establish colonies in New England, Long Island, and the Caribbean islands.
1622	After a war between the Turks and the Hapsburg rulers, the Hutterites are expelled from Moravia and flee to Slovakia, where they decline in numbers due to the ravages of the Thirty Years War.
1632	Because Catholics have been persecuted in the other British colonies in the Americas, Cecilius Calvert, the second lord Baltimore, a Roman Catholic, grants freedom of religion to all Christians in Maryland.
1633	The astronomer, mathematician, and physicist Galileo Galilei is condemned by the Catholic Inquisition in Italy for publishing the fact that the solar system is heliocentric (Copernican system) and that the planets do not revolve around Earth; he is forced to renounce his belief. In 1983, the Catholic Church acknowledges that Galileo was treated unfairly, and in 1992 it officially accepts Galileo's ideas as correct.
1633	The Zuni Indians of New Mexico revolt against Spanish rule and kill two Spanish Catholic missionaries.
1636	Providence Plantations colony of Rhode Island is established by Roger Williams after he fled from the Massachusetts Bay Colony, where he was threatened with deportation to Britain. A critic of the religious restrictions imposed in Massachusetts, Williams advocates religious freedom.
1637	Anne Hutchinson is banished from the Massachusetts Bay Colony for expressing her personal theological opinions during prayer meetings she conducts each week at her home. A follower of the minister John Cotton, Hutchinson proclaims that good works are not sufficient indicators of a person's salvation, and that everyone may come to know God through direct personal revelation. On August 30 her teachings are pronounced heretical, and she is banished on November 17. In March 1638 she is officially excommunicated after refusing to recant her opinions.
1638	The Puritans establish the first Indian reservation for the Quinnipiac Indians in New Haven, Connecticut. One condition of settlement on the reservation is that the Indians reject their religion and accept Christianity.
1639–1640	The Bishop's Wars between England and Scotland arise from the attempt of King Charles I of England to impose Anglican religious practices on the Scottish Church.

1642–1648	Civil war in England opposes the forces of King Charles I (Cavaliers) and those of Parliament (Roundheads, from their short haircuts), which try to limit the king's power and support Puritan reforms to the Anglican Church. The king favors the established Church of England and resists reforms, but the Roundheads triumph for a time, and the king is beheaded in 1649.
1643–1647	The Westminster Assembly in Britain meets to end religious conflicts and to weaken the authority of the Church of England. Dominated by Presbyterians from Scotland and members of other Reformed churches in Europe, the assembly produces a series of creeds that become the basis of Presbyterianism, though the Presbyterians lose influence after 1648 when those who favor religious toleration come to power.
1644	The Puritans of the Massachusetts Bay Colony deny membership in the colony to all Baptists who have been convicted of religious crimes in Britain. Because there are numerous laws repressing British Baptists, the Puritans' denial of membership to Baptists convicted of religious crimes effectively shuts them out of the colony.
1647	The first Unitarian (believer that God has only one person) to be persecuted in Britain, the theologian John Biddle, writes *Twelve Questions*, which questions the doctrine of the Trinity. Biddle spends nearly half his life in prison as punishment for expressing his religious beliefs.
1647	George Fox, founder of the Society of Friends, or Quakers, and his followers are imprisoned for disseminating the belief that divine inspiration is a higher source of religious experience than religious authority or dogma.
1647	Under the leadership of Sivaji, who accepts all religious beliefs, Hindus revolt against Muslim rule in India and establish the Hindu state of Maratha, thereby weakening the Mughal dynasty.
1647–1648	The Baptists enjoy a short period of religious freedom, which ends when Parliament issues the Ordinance for Punishing Blasphemies and Heresies.
1648	The treaties of the Peace of Westphalia, which ends the Thirty Years War in Europe, establish the primacy of state over church. In the peace negotiations, held in Westphalia in Germany, Spain and the Holy Roman Empire finally agree with France and Sweden that the states of the empire are to be independent, thus making the Holy Roman Empire ineffective and creating the map of modern Europe.
1649	The Catholic-controlled Assembly of Maryland passes the Act Concerning Religion, which grants religious freedom to all Christians in Maryland.
1652	The Baptist minister John Clarke of Rhode Island, in his *Ill News from New England*, argues for a policy of religious toleration in the British colonies in America.

1654	Peter Stuyvesant, governor of the Dutch colony of New Netherland, opposes the settlement of Jews who arrive in the capital city of New Amsterdam from Brazil, but he is overruled by the Dutch West India Company. While the Jews have much economic freedom, restrictions on civil rights and religious freedom remain in place.
1655	Puritan forces in Maryland defeat the pro-Catholic government, ending religious freedom in Maryland and initiating persecution of Roman Catholics.
1656	Oliver Cromwell, lord protector of the short-lived Commonwealth of England in the wake of the civil war, grants religious rights to Jews when he allows them to resettle in Britain.
1657	Quakers settle in Rhode Island, and despite calls for their persecution by Puritans, they are allowed to live peacefully. In New Amsterdam, however, Quakers who settle there are persecuted by the local authorities until the Dutch West India Company orders the Quakers to be left alone.
1658	Nikon, the Russian Orthodox patriarch of Moscow, declares his supremacy to the czar. The czar, however, rejects this view and forces Nikon to resign.
1658–1707	The Muslim Mughal emperor 'Alamgīr (Aurangzeb) of India reverses the long-held policy of religious toleration and tries to force the Hindus to adopt Islam. This leads to Hindu resistance and revolts, and by the end of his reign the Mughal Empire begins to decline.
1659	Puritans in the Massachusetts Bay Colony hang four Quakers.
1660s	After Quakers become active in the government of Rhode Island, a new law is passed making conscientious objection to military service legal in the colony.
1661	The Cart and Whip Law enacted in the Massachusetts Bay Colony allows the arrest of Quakers, their transport by cart to Rhode Island, and their being whipped in each village along the way.
1661–1665	In Britain, the Clarendon Code, passed during the ministry of Edward Hyde, first earl of Clarendon, bans from municipal and church positions those who do not take the sacraments at a parish church; makes worship by Nonconformists (non-Anglican Protestants such as Baptists and Quakers) illegal if more than four outsiders are present; and bans Nonconformist ministers from living or visiting within five miles of any place they minister. Some of the restrictions are lightened in 1689, but others remain in effect until the 19th century; even then, Nonconformists cannot serve in Parliament or attend universities.
1662	The Church of England is restored to religious primacy in Britain through the Act of Uniformity.
1663	Under a royal charter granted by King Charles II, the Rhode Island and Providence Plantations are established as an inde-

pendent entity with the governor and other officials elected by the settlers rather than appointed by the king. The charter also grants religious freedom, which has always been a characteristic of Rhode Island; Jews, Quakers, and other sects persecuted elsewhere in America find refuge here.

1664   Britain takes control of New Amsterdam and the colony of New Netherland from the Dutch and permits religious freedom in New York. In Britain, however, the Conventicle Act, meant to curtail the religious activities of Quakers and Baptists, makes it a crime punishable by imprisonment or deportation to worship in any church other than the Church of England.

1665   The Jews of New York are given religious freedom and civil rights by the British.

1665   Japan's shogunate issues the *Shosha negi kannushi hatto* law code, which places Shinto shrines and priests under the control of the Yoshida lineage, the powerful warrior family of the shogunate.

1666–1667   The Russian Orthodox Church condemns the Raskolniks (dissenters, the Old Believers sect) and declares them schismatics for rejecting church reforms approved by the patriarch of Moscow and for insisting on maintaining traditional church rituals.

1667   In the colony of Virginia, a law is passed stipulating that conversion to Christianity does not entitle an African slave to freedom. Other colonies pass similar laws in subsequent years, always with the intent of maintaining slavery.

1671–1711   Swiss Mennonites (a Protestant sect derived from Anabaptists) emigrate from Switzerland to Alsace, a region in France, and the Palatinate, a region now part of Germany, to escape persecution.

1673–1677   A Muslim *jihad*, or holy war, erupts in Mauritania in West Africa, when the native Berbers seek a return to traditional Islam and accuse their Arab rulers of being lax in their devotion to Islam. The Arabs suppress the revolt and come to dominate the region.

1675   When he refuses to convert to Islam, the Sikh guru Tegh Bahadur is executed by the Muslim Mughal ruler of India, 'Alamgīr (Aurangzeb).

1675   After the Quakers lose political power and when the colony becomes involved in King Philip's War (named after an Indian chief) with the Indians, the right of conscientious objection is discontinued in Rhode Island.

1675–1677   The Rogerenes in Connecticut suffer persecution for their beliefs. Founded by the religious leader John Rogers, the Rogerenes believe in separation of church and state, baptism for believers only, no Sabbath worship, and a literal interpretation of the Bible. In 1818, the Connecticut Constitution mandates separation of church and state, and the Rogerenes disappear.

1676   Jews are expelled from Yemen and their property destroyed. In

1680, they are allowed to return.

1680   After Pueblo Indian religious leaders are arrested and whipped, the Indians revolt against Spanish rule, kill a dozen priests, and drive the Spanish from the Southwest back into Mexico. The revolt is led by Popé, a Taos Indian religious leader who has been punished by the Spanish.

1682   William Penn, a Quaker who has received a grant of land from King Charles II to settle a debt owed to Penn's father, founds the new English colony of Pennsylvania (named Penn's Woods in honor of Penn's father) and names its first city Philadelphia, city of brotherly love. Penn's Frame of Government for the colony and the constitution and laws that follow establish freedom of thought and religious freedom, although only those who believe in God and Christ are allowed to hold public office; Penn also establishes an elected assembly that may have been a model for the writers of the Constitution.

1682   A new charter establishes religious freedom in the Massachusetts Bay Colony and effectively ends the persecution of Quakers, Baptists, and others by the Puritans.

1683   In Japan, the shogunate issues a series of laws banning expensive clothing and regulating food, house size, and scale of entertainments. According to Confucian principles, consumption is to be proportional to status.

1685   France enacts the *Code Noir* (Black code), requiring that all slaves in French colonies in the Caribbean be baptized and instructed in Roman Catholicism.

1685   The Edict of Nantes is revoked, and the Huguenots flee from France to other European countries and North America.

1685   John Locke's *Letter on Toleration* is written. It is first published in Latin, anonymously in 1689, and translated into English in the same year by William Popple. In the *Letter* Locke advocates limited religious toleration on the grounds that a government cannot compel conscientious religious belief.

1685   The last person executed for treason on religious grounds in Britain is a woman Baptist. Her crime is harboring rebels who fought against the king during the civil war.

1689   The repeal of the Conventicle Act passed in 1664 ends religious restrictions on Nonconformists such as Baptists and Quakers in Britain. Other laws, such as those requiring Quakers to pay extra taxes and banning Puritans and Quakers from Parliament and the universities, remain in effect until the 19th century.

1692   Emperor K'ang-Hsi of China issues an edict allowing Jesuit, Dominican, and Franciscan missionaries to operate freely.

1692   After the European witch craze has died down, it reemerges in Salem in the Massachusetts Bay Colony. During the witch trials, 19 women are executed as witches.

1692–1696   The Spanish reconquer the southwest region of North America after having been driven south into Mexico by the Pueblo revolt of 1680. The Spanish harshly repress the Pueblo Indian religion.

1701   In Britain, Parliament passes the Act of Settlement, which requires the monarch to be a member of the Church of England and to maintain the Church's status as the official church of the nation.

1701   William Penn, a Quaker and the founder of Pennsylvania, issues the Charter of Privileges, granting freedom of worship to all who believe in God and restricting the right to hold public office to Christians.

1705   The British enact laws repressing Catholicism in the American colonies. Roman Catholics are denied the right to vote or hold office in Pennsylvania, and religious freedom is not restored until the American Revolution.

1706   Doña Béatrice, founder of the first African Christian movement to resist Catholicism, is executed by the Portuguese in Africa. After her death, the movement grows into major resistance to Portuguese rule.

1706   The British monarch pressures Pennsylvania to deprive Jews, Roman Catholics, and Unitarians in Pennsylvania of religious freedom.

1708   Religious freedom is granted in Connecticut, although everyone must continue to support the Puritan Church.

1710   During the reign of Peter I (known as Peter the Great) in Russia, major efforts begin to convert the Muslim Tatar (Turkic-speaking) population to Russian Orthodoxy. Muslims are baptized, children sent to Russian schools, and Russian Orthodox churches built in Tatar villages. The policy ends in 1764 as it disrupts life in some settlements vital to Russian trade.

1724   In China, Emperor Yung-cheng orders Roman Catholic missionaries to be deported to Macao (peninsula on the coast of southeast China), although some are allowed to remain in Peking (Beijing). The action is motivated partly by the rejection by Pope Clement XI of the Jesuit position accommodating Chinese cultural traditions such as ancestor rites, and by the end of the century the Roman Catholic presence in China has almost completely vanished.

1727   In Connecticut, Quakers, Baptists, and Anglicans (members of the Church of England) are exempted from making payments to the Puritan Church.

1728   The Shinto priest Kada Azumamaro petitions the shogunate in Japan to establish a *kokugaku* (school of national learning), after he becomes convinced that only a revival of the true way of the *kami* (native spirits) will protect the country.

1731   Quakers are freed from having to pay support to the Puritan Church in Massachusetts. The same exemption is granted a few years later to Baptists and Anglicans (members of the Church of

England).

1732	All Christians except Roman Catholics are granted religious freedom in the state of Georgia.
1733–1760s	In Slovakia, a region in Eastern Europe that is part of the Austro-Hungarian Empire ruled by the Roman Catholic Hapsburgs, the Hutterites (a Protestant sect derived from the Anabaptists) are singled out for severe persecution. Their churches are closed, books are confiscated, and they are forced to baptize their children as Catholics.
1734	In Germany, dissident Protestant sects that disagree with both the Lutherans and the Roman Catholics, such as the Salzburgers and Schwenkfelders, are so harassed that they leave Germany and settle in America.
1736	The witchcraft laws are repealed in Britain, though such activities are still illegal. New laws state that witchcraft does not actually exist and that people who claim to be witches do not really have supernatural powers, are not agents of the devil, and cannot harm others.
1747	Appearing in Bohemia (part of modern Hungary), the Abrahamites claim to be neither Christians nor Jews. Persecuted for their beliefs, they disappear after 1781.
1749	Benjamin Franklin, in his *Proposals Relating to the Education of Youth in Philadelphia*, suggests the establishment of a "publick religion" based on Protestant Christianity for the states in America.
1750	Frederick II (called Frederick the Great), elector of Brandenburg (a region that includes modern western Poland and Prussia, a state in north-central Germany), grants rights to the Jews in Prussia.
1753	In Britain, Parliament passes the so-called Jew Bill, granting newly arrived Jewish immigrants the same rights as those enjoyed by Jews already living there. Public opposition is so fierce that the bill is repealed the same year.
1764	The Russian czar confiscates lands belonging to the Russian Orthodox Church, part of a continuing effort to limit the Church's role. The government also confiscates the Church's serfs and reduces the level of state financial support.
1769	Establishing a series of missions along the coast of California, the Spanish begin to colonize the west coast of America and to bring the Indians under Spanish control. The missions garrison troops, convert Indians to Catholicism, and become agricultural centers, using the Indians as slave labor; they effectively destroy the Indian cultures of the region, despite frequent Indian revolts. The first mission is founded by the Jesuit Father Juniperro Serra at San Diego, and others are founded in the following decades as far north as San Francisco.
1770–1859	The Hutterites living in eastern Europe move to Russia to avoid

persecution by their Muslim Ottoman rulers.

1771	Jews are given permission to settle in Sweden.
1772	The Council of Lima, held in Lima, Peru, ends the practice of not allowing American Indians and *mestizos* (those of mixed European and American Indian blood) to become Roman Catholic priests.
1772–1773	Ann Lee, the founder of the Shakerism (communally living ascetic Protestant) sect in America, is arrested and imprisoned in Manchester, England, for disturbing the Sabbath by participating in the Quaking Shaker services.
1773	Ending the Russian efforts to convert Muslim Tatars to Russian Orthodoxy, Catherine the Great institutes a new policy that allows the revitalization of Muslim culture through the building of schools and mosques and the formation of Muslim organizations.
1773	The Negro Baptist Church is established in Savannah, Georgia, when Andrew Bryan and George Leile, former slaves, begin preaching without congregations. The Church is opposed by plantation owners, and George Leile is forced to move to Haiti.
1775	The Kamia Indians in southern California destroy the Spanish Catholic mission at San Diego, in the first revolt against the Spanish mission system in California. Several more revolts follow in other regions of California, but none is successful in ending Spanish control and destruction of Indian cultures.
1776	In its Declaration of Rights written by George Mason, a member of the Virginia Legislature, Virginia gives Baptists, Presbyterians, and other denominations religious freedom but allows the Anglican Church to remain the state church.
1776–1780	After the American Revolution, the 19 state constitutions drafted during this period all contain explicit statements protecting religious freedom. However, in most states these provisions are thought of as protecting the religious freedom of Christians.
1777	The Virginia Statute for Religious Freedom, drafted by Thomas Jefferson, declares that the exercise of religion is a natural and inalienable right bestowed by God and outside the authority of legislatures or courts.
1777	During the American Revolution, most states pass acts requiring people to take an oath of allegiance and promising to take up arms to defend the country. When Quakers, Mennonites (sect derived from Anabaptists), and Amish (strict Mennonite sect) refuse to take the oath for religious reasons and refuse to fight in accord with their belief in pacifism, some are jailed and some are threatened with the loss of land and property, but most remain loyal to their religious beliefs.
1781	Emperor Joseph II of Austria (which includes part of modern Hungary) issues an edict granting religious freedom to Protestants. The Roman Catholic Church remains the national church,

but Calvinists, Lutherans, and others are now allowed to build small chapels and run schools.

1781   Emperor Joseph II of Austria (which includes part of modern Hungary) issues his Edict of Tolerance, which seeks to involve Jews more in economic activities.

1782   The last known legal execution of a witch in Europe takes place in Switzerland.

1786   Lemuel Hayes becomes the first African-American minister to pastor a white congregation. Hayes, a minuteman (member of a group of armed men prepared at a moment's notice to fight the British) in the Revolution, serving under Paul Revere and in 1775 helping to repel the British from Concord Bridge in Massachusetts, was licensed to preach by the Congregational Church of Connecticut in 1780, the first black minister certified by a mostly white denomination.

1787   In the Caucasus, a *jihad*, or holy war, is led by Muslim Sufis (mystics) seeking a return to traditional Islam, the adoption of Islamic law, and an end to Russian rule. The revolt is defeated but creates lasting hostility between Muslims in the region and Russians.

1787   After a group of black Christians are forced to sit in segregated seating at the Saint George Methodist Episcopal Church of Philadelphia, Pennsylvania, Richard Allen, Absalom Jones, Dorus Ginnings, and William White walk out rather than submit. In 1794, Allen, a former slave who purchased his freedom for $2,000, founds the Mother Bethel African Methodist Episcopal Church in Philadelphia; a separate African Methodist Church is founded in New York City in 1798.

1787   The Northwest Ordinance extends freedom of worship from the original American states to the Northwest Territory.

1788   The ruler of the Hausa states (now northern Nigeria in Africa) exempts the large Muslim population from payment of taxes and gives them the right to wear Muslim dress and greater freedom to seek converts.

1788   Russia grants a special charter of privileges to the Mennonites (derived from the Anabaptists), allowing them religious freedom and exemption from military service.

1789   The French National Assembly adopts the Declaration of the Rights of Man as a preamble to the republic's new constitution. The document sets forth, among other rights, freedom of religion and expression, and it serves as a model for later declarations of human rights.

1790   A new ruler revokes the grant of special privileges to the Muslim community in the Hausa states in Africa, given two years earlier.

1790–1791   During the French Revolution, officials of the Roman Catholic Church in France are required to sign an oath of compliance with the new constitution, but the Church objects that the requirement places clergy in the position of having to choose between loyalty to the state or to the Church. Pope Pius VI condemns the oath and forbids clergy to sign, leading to a split in the French Catholic community between the constitutionalists, who sign the oath, and the nonconstitutionalists, who refuse to sign.

1791   The Bill of Rights, making up the first 10 amendments of the U.S. Constitution, is ratified when the Virginia Legislature passes it, thus fulfilling the constitutional requirement that 75 percent of the (13 original) states must pass a constitutional amendment for it to become law.

1792–1794   During the Reign of Terror in France, those Roman Catholic priests who refuse to sign a loyalty oath are exiled or forced into hiding, and some are sentenced to death. Many churches are closed, and even the use of the Gregorian calendar is discouraged.

1795   The Reign of Terror ends in France; Catholicism revives, churches closed during the last three years reopen, and clergy come out of hiding or exile. Nonetheless, the role of the Church is reduced in favor of civil institutions in marriage, education, and other matters previously largely controlled by the Roman Catholic Church.

1797   Jews in the Netherlands are granted civil rights.

c. 1800   Islam is established as the state religion of the kingdom of the Mossi, a diverse people living in present-day Burkina Faso in West Africa, when the ruler becomes Muslim.

1801   In France, a new concordat governing state-church relations and negotiated by Napoleon, the first consul, and Pope Pius VII replaces the previous one of 1516. The state retains control of the Church as it continues to have the right to appoint bishops; Church property taken during the French Revolution is not returned, and the clergy are now supported by the state. This agreement lasts until 1905.

1804   In the Hausa states (modern northern Nigeria), Muslims, led by the religious scholar Uthman don Fodio, refuse to leave the region and are attacked by the forces of the state of Gobir, one of the Hausa states. The Muslims launch a *jihad*, or holy war, against Gobir and other Hausa states, which ends in 1808 with a Muslim victory and the states united under Muslim rule.

1804   Czar Alexander I of Russia issues a constitution of the Jews, which places economic and civil restrictions on them, requires them to live only in specified areas, and allows them to attend public schools as a means to convert them to Orthodoxy.

1805   After gaining independence from France a year earlier, Haiti creates a constitutional separation of church and state and guarantees religious freedom. These constitutional provisions weaken the influence of the Roman Catholic Church, which refuses to recognize the new government.

1805   Muhammad Ali, governor of Egypt for the Ottoman Empire, creates a dynasty free of Ottoman control that lasts until 1952 and achieves and retains power partly by creating a strong central government and military and by weakening the power of Muslim leaders.

1806   According to decrees governing the role and status of Jews in France, issued by Napoleon, the Jews are given religious freedom, but they may not settle in northeast France, and Jewish economic activity is limited. Thirteen regional Jewish councils, called consistories, are given responsibility for administering Jewish communities and integrating Jews into French national life.

1809   After the British displace the Muslim Mughal dynasty as rulers of northern India, they negotiate the Treaty of Amritsar (city in Punjab) with the Sikh leader Ranjit Singh, giving the Sikhs control of the southern Punjab region. With British support, Singh displaces other local Sikh leaders and expands the territory under his control. In 1846, the Treaty of Lahore (capital of Punjab) gives the Sikhs explicit control of the region.

1812   The pale of settlement is established in Russia as a region of 25 provinces (including parts of modern western Russia, Belarus, Poland, Lithuania, and Ukraine) where Jews must live. Jews cannot travel outside the pale without official permission and are restricted to certain occupations; most are farmers.

1812   In Britain, Parliament repeals the Conventicle Act of 1664 and the Five Mile Act of 1665, which placed restrictions on Nonconformists, and thereby affords them more religious freedom.

1816   The Pennsylvania Supreme Court rules in favor of the independence of the Mother Bethel African Methodist Episcopal Church in Philadelphia, and it remains free from white control.

1816   A Muslim *jihad*, or holy war, led by Seku Amadu, a Fula (one of the Fulani, pastoral people of northern Nigeria), deposes the non-Muslim Bambara rulers (native Africans of the upper Niger River) and creates the Muslim state of Masina, with its capital at Hamdallahi. The state extends from Tombouctou (Timbuktu), a town in Mali, to the Volta River and lasts until 1862.

1817   Led by the Muslim teacher Ma Ba, a *jihad*, or holy war, in the Senegambia region of West Africa fails in the attempt to create a Muslim state. Nevertheless, the jihad does result in the conversion of the Wolof people, the major ethnic group in modern Senegal, to Islam.

1817   Fleeing persecution, the Pietists, a German sect emphasizing Bible reading and individual spiritual experience, emigrate from Germany to America, where they establish a communal society at Zoar, Ohio. The community enjoys some economic success but dissolves in 1898.

1818   The restrictions on Jewish economic activities and settlement in northeastern France, enacted in 1806, are removed.

1818   Connecticut ceases funding the Congregational Church (Protestants emphasizing independence of individual churches), which is thus disestablished (i.e., no longer the official church); Congregational churches in New Hampshire and Massachusetts are disestablished in 1819 and 1833, respectively. Churches must now raise their own funds; many voluntary associations are founded to support church activities.

1819　　The U.S. Congress authorizes funds to Christian mission groups to establish schools for American Indians and otherwise to provide programs to "civilize" them.

1819–1825　　The czar of Russia orders that a Russian translation of the Bible, based on the original Hebrew and Greek texts, be destroyed. The Russian liturgy is written in Old Church Slavonic, in an alphabet based on Greek, brought by two Greek monks to the Slavs; when Russia converted to Orthodox Christianity in 988, the liturgy, written in this alphabet, translated Greek ideas into what was then vernacular Russian but is not the vernacular in the 19th century.

1820s　　In the wake of large emigrations from Ireland and Germany, which increase the numbers of Roman Catholics in the United States, a wave of anti-Catholicism spreads across the country in the 1830s. Reflecting concerns among Protestant ministers about papal criticisms of Protestantism, anti-Catholicism results in anti-Catholic publications, anti-Catholic associations, and attempts to limit Catholic influence in American society.

1821　　After independence from Spain, Peru establishes Roman Catholicism as the state religion and bans all other religions. Although the ban is relaxed, Roman Catholicism remains closely linked to the state in Peru.

1826　　Mahmud II, sultan of the Ottoman Empire, institutes major military, governmental, and religious reforms to cope with threats posed by Russians, Greeks, and Egyptians. In these reforms, the power of Muslim scholars is limited, and much mosque land is placed under government control.

1826–1846　　The Spanish missions in California are removed from the control of the Roman Catholic Church. Although the Spanish government attempts to establish Indian settlements on the land, American settlers quickly take the land from the Indians.

1828　　The British Parliament repeals the Test Act (1673) and Corporation Act (1661), which had imposed legal restraints on the religious freedom of Nonconforming churches in England.

1829　　The British impose a ban on the custom of suttee (Sanskrit *sati*: devoted woman) whereby a widow throws herself on her husband's funeral pyre, sometimes by choice but other times because relatives force her to kill herself. The practice persists despite the ban, even in rare cases to the present.

1830–1840　　Norikiyo, the head of Kyoto's Kami Kamo shrine, travels to Edo (modern Tokyo) to found the new sect of Uden (Raven tradition) Shinto. This sect is strongly opposed by the Japanese government, and Norikiyo is exiled in 1847.

1831	Canada grants full political rights to Jews.
1832	The czar places the Lutheran Church in Russia under the control of a governmental commission and terminates the independent status of the Lutheran churches in Estonia and Latvia.
1832–1847	The Muslim Berber religious and political leader Abd al-Qadir leads a *jihad*, or holy war, against French rule in northern Algeria. Drawing support from the Sufi Qadiriya order, which concerns itself with humanitarian and economic activities, the Muslims establish a state and control two-thirds of Algeria by 1839, but in 1844 they and their Moroccan allies are defeated by the French at the Battle of Isly, and in 1847 Abd al-Qadir is deported to France and then exiled to Damascus in Syria.
1833–1838	When Mormons attempt to establish a settlement in Missouri, they fail because of hostility from local residents. The Mormons had also been the target of violence by non-Mormons in Ohio before fleeing to Missouri, and they are persecuted and their leaders imprisoned in Illinois in 1838 and 1839.
1834	The Inquisition ends in Spain.
1834	The Ursuline convent and school in Charlestown, Massachusetts, is burned by a mob motivated by anti-Catholic sentiments.
1838	The British Parliament passes laws removing the requirements that members of Protestant churches register the births of children with the Anglican Church and have their marriages blessed by the Church.
1839	The Noble Rescript of Gülhane grants religious equality to non-Muslims in the Ottoman Empire. The declaration is aimed primarily at Christians, whose support the sultan seeks in reforming Ottoman society.
1842	Laws limiting religious freedom are repealed in Norway, and religious freedom is established in 1845.
1843	In an effort to end the conflict between the Maronite Christians (followers of Eastern Orthodoxy but also submitting to the Roman pope) and the Druze (Islamic sect) minority in Lebanon, the Ottoman sultan creates a Maronite state in the north and a Druze one in the south, with a national council representing both groups. The arrangement leads to 15 years of peace but ends with war between the Maronites and a short-lived Druze-Muslim coalition in 1859 and 1860.
1843	John Bright, a Quaker textile manufacturer, is elected to the British Parliament.
1844	Anti-Catholic riots breaking out outside Philadelphia, Pennsylvania, involve Nativists, whose agenda is partly anti-Catholic, and Catholics. The violence leaves 13 people dead.
1844	Joseph Smith, the founder of the Mormon Church, is killed along with his brother, while awaiting trial in Illinois. Brigham Young,

an early follower of Joseph Smith, becomes the new leader of the Mormon Church.

1844   A constitutional ban on religious conversion in Greece prohibits activities designed to convert people from Greek Orthodoxy. The ban is reinforced and then extended to cover all religions in subsequent constitutions of 1952 and 1975.

1844   The British Anti-State-Church Society, later the Liberation Society, is founded with the aim of ending the status of the Church of England as the national church.

1846   In search of freedom, the Mormons migrate from Illinois, where the church continues to experience hostility from non-Mormons, with Mormon buildings burned, Mormons attacked, and political support for their cause diminishing. They begin their migration westward, eventually settling in Utah.

1847   The first Jew elected to the House of Commons in Britain is Lionel Rothschild, head of the London banking house, but he is not allowed to be seated until 1858. His son, the first Baron Rothschild, is the first Jew to sit in the House of Lords, in 1885.

1848   Seeing the Babi sect of Shia Islam as a political threat, Shah Nasr-ed-Din of Persia orders persecution of the sect, founded by Ali Muhammad, a Persian religious leader who calls himself Bab, or gateway to spiritual truth. After two years of revolt, many Babi are killed, and the Bab himself is executed in 1850. Babism survives in Persia, and in 1853 Mirza Hoseyn Ali Nuri (called Baha Allah), a follower of Bab, breaks away from Islam to found a new faith, Baha'i, which teaches the spiritual unity of humanity.

1848   Jews in Denmark are granted civil rights.

1848   Waldenses (Christian sect that adopted Calvinist principles) in Italy are granted religious freedom.

1849   The Japanese emperor declares the practice of worshiping, and conducting pilgrimages to, Mount Fuji illegal and thus represses the Shinto-based Fuji societies.

1852   Kabaka Mutesa of the Buganda kingdom of East Africa adopts Islam as a unifying force to replace the existing indigenous religions.

1852   The British Parliament passes a law setting aside space in cemeteries for the burial of members of Protestant denominations other than the Church of England, but not until 1880 are clergy from those denominations allowed to officiate at funerals in the cemeteries.

1853   The First Chinese Temple is erected in San Francisco's Chinatown, and by 1900 there are 400 such shrines on the West Coast. These syncretistic temples enshrine popular folk deities, which include elements from Buddhism, Taoism, and Confucianism.

1854   Non-Anglican Protestants are first admitted to Oxford University in Britain to study for the B.A. degree, with Cambridge University following suit in 1856.

1855   Jew's College in London is founded as a seminary to train Orthodox Jewish rabbis and teachers for work in Great Britain and the
United States.

1855   American Congregational missionaries establish a mission in
Brazil to attempt to convert Roman Catholics in Latin America.
In 1856, a similar mission is established by Presbyterians in
Colombia.

1856   The Hamaiouni Line law, enacted in Egypt during the period of
Ottoman rule, effectively prohibits Christian denominations
from building new churches and from rehabilitating old ones.
The law controls the spread of the Coptic Christian Church (a
Monophysite church) in Egypt and remains in effect today.

1856   The Illustrious Rescript Edict is imposed in Turkey by the British, French, and Austrians through the negotiations ending the
Crimean War. The edict, which gives new rights to non-Muslims
and weakens the power of Muslims and Christian religious leaders, is intended to move Turkey toward secularization.

1856   In Yunnan Province in southern China, Muslims revolt against
the weak Qing dynasty and establish a Muslim state, which lasts
until 1873.

1857   When Muslims and Hindus serving in the British Indian Army
in Bengal, India, are given new cartridges that they believe to be
greased with the fat from pigs and cows, which is offensive to
both Hindu and Muslim beliefs, they mutiny, beginning the
Sepoy Rebellion against British rule (a Sepoy is an Indian soldier
in the British army). The British repress the revolt and place
more blame on the Muslims than on the Hindus, although both
are involved; some 60 British missionaries are killed, mainly in
the north of India.

1857   After contacts with, and loss of territory to, Russia and England
earlier in the century, Persia moves toward westernization and
modernization with economic, administrative, and military
reforms that are often instituted with British and Russian assistance.

1857   The Mormon War, a short-lived series of skirmishes, property
burnings, and relocations by Mormons, results in the stationing
of troops near Salt Lake City, Utah. The war follows a period of
religious revitalization by the Mormons, combined with ongoing
political conflict between Mormons and non-Mormons.

1857   The separatist Nederduitse Gereformeerde Kerk (Dutch
Reformed Church) in South Africa rules that racial segregation is
permissible in the church.

1859   Charles Darwin publishes *On the Origin of Species by Means of
Natural Selection*, setting forth his theory of biological evolution.
Darwin's *The Descent of Man* follows in 1871. Both works call
into question the accuracy of the Judeo-Christian version of Genesis.

1860	Roman Catholicism is reestablished as the official religion of Haiti. Most of its adherents belong to the urban elite, while voodoo, based on African religions and ancestor worship, continues to draw most of its practitioners from the rural population.
1860	The first professorship established in the United States for the study of science and religion is the Perkins Professorship of Natural Science in Connection with Revelation, offered at the Columbia Theological Seminary in Columbia, South Carolina.
1862	The Morrill Anti-Bigamy Act passed by the U.S. Congress prohibits polygynous (more than one wife) marriage and is seen by Mormons as a form of religious repression; Mormon society is disrupted as Mormons flee federal and state agents. The act is strengthened by the Edmunds Act of 1882 and the Edmunds-Tucker Act of 1887.
1863	Olympia Brown is the first U.S. woman to be ordained as a minister of a regular denomination when she becomes a minister of the Universalist Church in the United States.
1863	Henry McNeal Turner becomes the first African-American chaplain in the U.S. Army.
1864	In the *Syllabus of Errors*, Pope Pius IX condemns both religious freedom and the separation of church and state.
1865	Jews in Sweden are granted civil rights.
1865	The Philosophical Society of Great Britain (the Victoria Institute) is founded to combat the evolutionary theory of Charles Darwin.
1866	The Belton Women's Commonwealth (also called the Sanctificationists) is organized by Martha McWhirter in Belton, Texas, to practice celibacy, seek a perfect Christian life, and become financially independent from spouses. In the 1880s, the group has about 50 women members, as well as 4 men, and several flourishing businesses, including three farms and a hotel; selling the hotel and retiring from their various business activities in 1899, they relocate to Washington, D.C., and dissolve in the 1930s when the last member dies.
1867	The American Protective Association, founded in Iowa, is an anti-Catholic organization that gains followers and political strength in the 1880s and 1890s, in response to economic problems and anti-immigrant sentiments, then declines and disbands in 1911.
1867	Jews are granted civil rights in the Austro-Hungarian Empire.
1868	When Japanese nationalists overthrow the Tokugawa Shogunate and restore imperial rule, the government decrees the separation of Shinto and Buddhism and effectively establishes Shintoism as the state religion.
1869	At a preliminary meeting of the Metaphysical Society at Cambridge University in England, Thomas H. Huxley, the British biologist and defender of Darwin's theory of evolution is said to

invent the term *agnostic*, to refer to a person who neither believes nor disbelieves in God. In the 1870s, he apparently uses the term in conversation to suggest the proper skeptical attitude for scientific investigation and to distinguish between those who doubt and atheists, who deny the existence of God.

1869   Religious freedom is granted to Christians in Finland who are not Lutherans.

1870   In Italy, ghettos are abolished,and Jews are granted some civil rights, after nearly 100 years of having rights expanded and then taken away.

1870   The U.S. Congress ends military control of Indian-agent posts on Indian reservations and gives the positions to Christian missionaries, who are also put in charge of Indian schools and training programs.

1870–1871   After more than 30 years of resistance to French rule, Muslim farmers in Algeria revolt, precipitated by the French government's failure to provide adequate aid during a serious drought. The French repress the revolt, seize much of the farmers' land, and restrict the practice of Islam.

1870–1884   During the Great Promulgation Campaign to create a state religion in Japan, the government begins to stress the Great Teaching to foster public reverence and obedience toward the emperor, the *kami* (native spirits), and the nation. The campaign is carried out by a corps of national evangelists, both Shinto and Buddhist priests, along with entertainers, actors, storytellers, ministers of new religions, and ideologues of National Learning.

1871   During the *kulturkampf* (culture war) in the German Empire, newly unified after the Franco-Prussian War, the Prussian-dominated government, led by Bismarck, the first chancellor, persecutes Roman Catholics, seeking to create undivided loyalties to Germany. The persecutions lessen after 1886.

1871   Jews are admitted to universities in Great Britain. Major universities also admit students of all Protestant denominations to almost all academic programs, although non-Anglicans are still not permitted to hold teaching positions.

1871   Jews are granted full civil rights in Germany.

1873   The Woman's Temperance Crusade, founded in New York State and Ohio, works to end the consumption of alcoholic beverages through education programs in schools and restrictions on the importation and sale of liquor. The members use prayer and the singing of hymns to influence owners of taverns to close their businesses.

1874   Affecting the rights of Muslims in Algeria, the French *Code de l'indigénat* (Code of natives) defines many Islamic practices as treason and makes Muslims accused of these crimes subject to imprisonment and loss of land.

1874   Civil rights are granted to Jews in Switzerland.

1874	The Public Worship Regulation Act passed in Great Britain seeks to control the adoption of Roman Catholic practices in the Church of England.
1874	Christians in Iceland who are not Lutherans are granted religious freedom.
1874–1879	Seeking religious freedom and open farmland, the Hutterites (sect derived from Anabaptists) emigrate from Russia to the United States, where they establish communities in South Dakota.
1875	Dayananda Sarasvati, a Hindu Brahman and wandering mendicant from Gujarat state in India, founds the Arya Samaj Hundu (Noble Society) reform movement, promoting Hinduism as a monotheistic religion and seeking to convert untouchables to Hinduism. The movement is anti-Muslim and anti-Christian.
1876	Jews are granted civil rights in the Ottoman Empire, at a time when the empire is weakened and on the verge of collapse.
1876	In *The Freethinker's Guide* by the British atheist Charles Bradlaugh, atheism is defined as not positing no God but as being without the idea of God.
1876–1908	The Japanese government officially recognizes 13 Shinto sects that are seen as autonomous religious groups.
1879	The German writer and politician William Marr, in the title of his *League of Anti-Semites*, introduces the term *anti-Semite*. Although technically referring to speakers of Semitic languages, including Arabs who speak Arabic, the term has since been used refer only to to hatred of Jews.
1881	Claiming that the ban is meant to protect Indians, who inflict wounds on themselves during the ceremony, the U.S. government prohibits the Sun Dance, a popular ceremony performed by American Plains Indian tribes to revive the glories of ancient Indian culture. The ceremony, which requires group dancing, fasting, and vision quests, is held annually in the spring or early summer at the start of hunting season, and the government fears that Indian leaders might use the large Indian gatherings to organize a revolt against government control; Indians continue to practice the cult in secret.
1881	After the Russian czar Alexander II is assassinated when a member of a radical group throws a bomb in his carriage, massive *pogroms* (organized massacres) are carried out against Jews. Hundreds of Jewish communities are attacked, Jewish property is destroyed, and Jews are beaten and killed. These *pogroms* and the enactment of restrictive laws governing Jews increase their desire to immigrate to America or elsewhere.
1881–1903	Jewish settlers from Russia and Romania make *aliyah* (Hebrew: going up—i.e., to permanent settlement in the Holy Land) to establish small farming communities in Palestine.
1882	Fearing that British reforms and modernization are eroding the

influence of Hinduism, Hindus establish cattle-protection societ-ies in India to stress traditional Hindu beliefs and practices, including the prohibition on eating beef.

1882   Zoroastrians in Persia are granted civil rights when the Muslim Qajar dynasty ends the practice of heavily taxing the Zoroastrian religious minority. Zoroastrians gain new freedoms and thereby improve their economic status in Persian society.

1882   The Koten kokyusho (Institute for the study of Japanese docu-ments) is established in Tokyo, Japan, to serve as the sole educa-tion center for Shinto priests and to gather and study materials concerning the *kokutai*, or distinctive Japanese national entity. This institute reflects the *Kokugaku* (Japanese learning) school of thought, which stresses the study of Japanese works rather than Chinese or Buddhist writings and the return to a purely Japanese society purged of foreign elements.

1882   The Society for Psychical Science is founded in Great Britain to conduct and report on scientific studies of spiritual phenomena, including the possibility that dead people can make their pres-ence known through a sensitive medium or psychic.

1883   The Muslim intellectual and journalist Ismail Gasprinskii begins to publish *Terjuman* (Translation), a Russian-Turkish bilingual paper representing Muslim interests in the Crimea in southern Russia. He advocates Muslimism and Turkism (union of all Mus-lims and of all Turkic peoples) and introduces new ways of teach-ing Arabic.

1884   The Canadian Indian Act bans Native American religious cere-monies, such as the Sun Dance and the potlatch (feast at which the host's wealth is lavishly distributed to the guests) among the Indian tribes of far western Canada. The government fears that these ceremonies, which bring together large numbers of Indi-ans, might be used by Indian leaders to revolt; in 1985, the act is amended to bring it into line with the Canadian Charter of Rights and Freedoms by removing discrimination, restoring sta-tus and membership rights, and increasing Indians' control over their own affairs.

1885   The Indian National Congress political party, founded in India, represents the emerging Hindu middle class. It does not attract Muslims, who are concerned about Hindu agitation for self-rule and Hindu dominance.

1887   The Muslim Education Conference, a Muslim-dominated politi-cal party, is founded in India as a Muslim response to the Hindu-dominated Indian National Congress.

1887   The U.S. Congress passes the Edmunds-Tucker Act, upheld by the Supreme Court in 1890, which dissolves the Mormon Church to end polygynous marriage. In the wake of the act, the govern-ment seizes Mormon property, restricts Mormons' individual civil rights, and assumes the management of Mormon organiza-tions. The church continues to resist ending polygyny but, facing financial ruin, in 1890 adopts the manifesto issued by the president of the Mormons, Wilford Woodruff, in which he states that Mormons will follow the law and ban polygyny.

1888 The Muslims in Indonesia revolt in an attempt to end Dutch rule and to create a Muslim state, but the Dutch put down the revolt.

1890 The president of the Society of Latter-day Saints (Mormons), Wilford Woodruff, issues the manifesto stating that, as Congress has outlawed polygyny, the Mormons will abide by the law and officially reject polygynous marriage.

1890 At Wounded Knee in South Dakota, U.S. soldiers kill more than 300 Indians, including many women and children, to put an end to the Ghost Dance cult. The last major engagement of the Indian wars in the West and the last major massacre of Indians, Wounded Knee destroys the cult, which was a movement to restore the glory of ancient Indian culture.

1890 Jews are granted full civil and political rights in Great Britain.

1894–1906 The Dreyfus affair in France signals the emergence of anti-Semitism as a public issue, when the Jewish army officer Alfred Dreyfus is accused of passing military secrets to the Germans and is court-martialed and imprisoned on Devil's Island, a French penal colony off the coast of French Guiana. Believing him innocent, his defenders charge his accusers with anti-Semitism, and the ensuing public debate helps to bring him to trial again in 1899. Dreyfus is retried, convicted again, but pardoned, and in 1906 the verdict is reversed; evidence from German records found in 1930 proves his innocence.

1895 Jews are granted full economic and religious rights in Hungary.

1896 Theodor Herzl, a Hungarian who is considered the founder of Zionism, writes *Der Judenstaat* (The Jewish state), advocating the establishment of a Jewish state in Palestine.

1900 The Urdu Defense Association is formed by young Muslims in India, who urge a more confrontational approach in dealing with the British colonial government. Members of the association reject the conciliatory attitude advocated by many leaders of the Muslim community in India.

1900 The International Council of Unitarian and Other Liberal Religious Thinkers and Workers is founded in Great Britain to promote religious tolerance and cooperation and to develop social welfare programs around the world. In 1961 the name is changed to the International Association for Religious Freedom.

1900 The British government places restrictions on modern-day Druids, who claim to revive ancient Celtic religious practices and believe that Stonehenge in southern Britain was an ancient Druid ceremonial site. By prohibiting worship at Stonehenge, the government intends to protect the stones and the site itself, which are being damaged by the worshipers.

1900–1908 The Public Peace and Order Police Law is enacted in Japan to grant the police wide powers over religious bodies. The law allows surveillance of religious activities and establishment of a strict system of bureaucratic control over religious bodies; it also prohibits Shinto and other religious leaders from joining political parties.

1901–1902   In Malawi in southeast Africa (then the Central British Africa Protectorate), John Chilembwe, a religious leader ordained a minister in the black Baptist Church in the United States, founds the Providence Industrial Mission. The organization develops a successful education system and becomes the locus of resistance to British colonial rule; killed while leading a revolt in 1915, Chilembwe becomes a national hero.

1902   The American geologist George McCready Price, in his *Outlines of Modern Christianity and Modern Science*, argues that the world was created recently in accord with the story in Genesis but that a worldwide environmental catastrophe altered the geological record to make it appear that evolution had taken place.

1903   Fearing the political influence of Muslim leaders over the largely Muslim population, the French colonial government in Senegal, West Africa, restricts the activities of Muslims. Schools are required to use the French language; restrictions are placed on Muslim religious teachers; French becomes the language of the legal system; and Arabic-language publications are banned.

1903–1911   Laws are enacted in Egypt to limit the influence of Muslim leaders. The laws restrict the role of Muslim scholars and local Muslim teachers, control Sufi (mystic Islam) activities, and place the education system under the state—the culmination of a 100-year effort to bring the Muslim community under government control.

1904–1905   The Maji-Maji revolt against German rule in Tanzania, East Africa, a religious millenarian movement, is led by Ngwale Kinjikitile, known to his followers as Bokero. Bokero preaches that the performance of religious rituals will force the Germans to leave; the Germans repress the revolt, executing Bokero and killing thousands of his followers.

1905   In Russia, the Decree on Religious Toleration supersedes earlier legislation and gives all residents of the Russian Empire the right to freely choose any religion.

1905   Amid attempts at political modernization, state civil-service examinations based on Confucian texts are abolished in China.

1905   Muslims from various Muslim areas of Russia, such as Ukraine, the city of Kazan in central Russia, and Azerbaijan in Transcaucasla, meet secretly to form the Russian General Muslim Party, a political party representing Muslim interests.

1905   To control sectarian conflicts, the British government in India divides Bengal, a region in northwest India, into Hindu and Muslim provinces. In 1911, the British government reverses the partition.

1905   The Dutch government places Muslim education in Indonesia under government control in an attempt to control Muslim religious and political movements.

1905
As a deliberate plan after the failed 1905 revolution in Russia, the Russian government incites anti-Semitism to distract people from social problems; one propaganda tool is the document called *The Protocols of the Elders of Zion*. Published in Russia, the book describes a Jewish plan to take control of the world but is actually a forgery written in Paris for the Russian government.

1905
The Laws of Separation enacted in France terminate the privileged status of the Roman Catholic Church in that country and end the practice of distinguishing between recognized and non-recognized religions, although some religions continue to be granted recognized status in a few departments (districts). The Catholic Church in Rome objects to the laws in a 1906 encyclical of Pope Pius X, *Vehementer Nos* (On the French Law of Separation).

1906
During a constitutional crisis in Persia, Islam is constitutionally established as the state religion to resolve a conflict between the secular and Islamic communities.

1906
The All-India Muslim League is a political party founded in India to represent Muslim interests. It remains the political voice of Muslim interests in India for the next 50 years.

1906
Designed to limit the immigration of Russian Jews to Great Britain, the Aliens Bill passed by the British Parliament in 1905 is enacted. At the time, Jews are being persecuted in Russia, and many seek to emigrate elsewhere.

1906
The Religionists' Concord Association is established in Japan by leaders of Shinto, Buddhism, and Christianity. In 1912, representatives of these three religions vow to support the emperor and to work together to promote national morality.

1907
The Ministry of Home Affairs in Japan begins to bring local shrines under centralized control, and their festivals are transformed into the rites of state Shinto.

1908
After Sikhs begin moving from India to western Canada and California to seek work in the expanding economy there, the Canadian government restricts settlement by Sikhs. In 1913, California also restricts settlement, and Sikh immigration is effectively curtailed until the 1950s.

1908
The *Budi Utomo* (Bold Endeavor) organization, a Hindu-Buddhist revival movement, is founded in Indonesia by non-Muslim Javanese. In 1917, it breaks with the Dutch government and seeks cultural and political autonomy for the nation.

1909
Responding to requests from Muslim leaders for separate elections for Muslim communities, the British colonial government in India allows such elections on a limited basis. The decision angers Hindu leaders and increases strains between Muslims and Hindus.

1909
The Society of Helpers is founded by Muslims in India to bring

together Muslims in Persia, Afghanistan, and Turkey to assist Indian Muslims in expelling the British from India.

1909　　　The Arand Marriage Act, enacted in India to create a new Sikh marriage rite, ends the use of the Hindu rite by Sikhs and further separates Sikhism from Hinduism.

1910　　　The Pormalin, a revitalization movement among the indigenous Batak people of Sumatra in Indonesia, is formed in reaction to Dutch colonialism and Christian missionary efforts. The movement involves spirit possession, worship of traditional priest-kings, and some Christian practices; it flourishes for about 10 years.

1910　　　After Japan annexes Korea, the Japanese occupation government institutes the oppressive cultural policy of compelling Shinto worship, to make all Koreans loyal subjects of Japan.

1911　　　Sikhs from India immigrate to Great Britain and form a Sikh community, but British resistance to Sikh settlement stifles the development of other communities until after 1945.

1911　　　In Japan, all schools must have their students attend ceremonies at Shinto shrines, a requirement that Japanese Christians criticize as impinging on their religious freedom.

1911–1912　The Sarekat Islam party, a Muslim nationalist political party, is founded in Indonesia. It is renamed the Partai Sarekat Islam in 1923 and the Partai Sarekat Islam Indonesia in 1929.

1912　　　The government of Saint Vincent Island in the Caribbean bans the Shaker sect, an indigenous movement based on elements of Christianity, African religions, and local customs. The ban is lifted in 1965.

1912　　　The Japanese government convenes the Three Religions Conference, with representatives of Shintoism, Buddhism, and Christianity. Christianity is designated as one of the three religions in place of Confucianism, reflecting both the decline of Confucianism and the spread of Christianity since the 1880s.

1912　　　Claiming that peyote is addictive and that it causes physical and mental harm to users, the U.S. government, religious organizations, and other groups strongly criticize the use of peyote by American Indians in their religious rituals.

1912　　　In Great Britain, the Salvation Army is granted the right of public assembly. Since its founding in 1865, members of the group have often been insulted and assaulted when they meet in public.

1912–1916　The Contestado Revolt in Brazil, involving peasants and rural laborers, is led by José Maria II, who claims to be a brother of Joao Maria, a 19th-century messiah figure. The revolt is put down by government forces who kill Maria and about 3,000 of his followers.

1913　　　The Anti-Defamation League of the B'nai B'rith is founded in the United States to combat anti-Semitism.

1914	The Peyote Society, or Union Church Society, and the First Born Church of Christ are founded as American Indian religious organizations centered on the ritual use of peyote.
1915	The first Jew to be lynched in the United States is Leo Frank, manager and part-owner of a pencil factory in Atlanta, Georgia, who in 1913 was accused, tried, and convicted of murdering 14-year-old Mary Phagan, an employee of the factory. Though the evidence against Frank is weak, popular opinion, stirred up by populist writer and politician Tom Watson, results in a death sentence. In 1915, the governor of Georgia reduces the sentence to life imprisonment, and later in the year a mob takes Frank from jail and lynches him. Evidence produced years later shows that Frank was innocent, and in 1986 Georgia formally pardons him.
1915	The British government establishes a religious council in British Malaya to manage Islam there. It collects religious taxes and becomes a major institution for religious reform and a source of political stability.
1915	During the German military advance on Russia in the First World War, the Russian government formally abolishes the pale of settlement as a place where Jews are required to live.
1916	The Lucknow Pact, entered into by the leaders of the Indian National Congress and the All-India Muslim League in India, seeks to end British rule, gain dominion status for India, expand voting rights, and elect 80 percent of legislative councillors, rather than have them appointed by the British. The leaders agree that the Muslim minority must have separate electorates and more seats in the legislature than actually required according to their percentage of the population.
1916	Quakers in Great Britain refuse to serve in the military during the World War I. Many are imprisoned after the government institutes conscription to maintain a military force.
1916–1917	When Russia begins drafting Muslims for service in World War I, the Muslim community is offended because up to now it has been exempt from service in the Russian army and also because Muslim participation is confined to noncombat duty. The Muslims launch a *jihad*, or holy war, that spreads across central Asia but is interrupted by the Russian Revolution in 1917.
1917	In Indonesia, the Sarekat Islam political party calls for a renewal of Islam and for fundamental political and economic reforms by the Dutch government.
1917	The Balfour Declaration, a letter prepared in 1916 by Arthur James Balfour, foreign secretary in the cabinet of Prime Minister David Lloyd George, and issued in 1917, states that the British government supports Zionism and the creation of a Jewish state in Palestine. The British intent is to gain the support of Jews and of neutral countries for the Allies in the World War I and later to establish British oversight in the strategically located area of Palestine.

1917	In Ukraine, a major persecution of Mennonites continues for three years. Mennonites are persecuted first by the German forces controlling the region during World War I and then from 1918 through 1920 because of the anarchy caused by the Russian Revolution.
1917	The first constitution created in Russia after the revolution gives all citizens religious freedom.
1917	After independence from Spain, Mexico enacts a constitution with many provisions seeking to limit the power of the Roman Catholic Church, which has played a significant role in Mexico ever since the country was colonized by Spain in the 16th century.
1917	The first Muslim government in central Asia is formed in Russian Turkestan (roughly present-day Turkmenistan, Uzbekistan, Kyrgyzstan, Tajikistan, and Kazakhstan) during the Russian Revolution. The Bolsheviks, however, renege on their promise of freedom and in 1918 invade Turkestan, removing the Muslim government and placing the region under Bolshevik military control. The region is later incorporated into the Soviet Union.
1917–1920	Muslims in Kazakhstan, the Caucasus, and Azerbaijan also seek to create independent nations following the Russian Revolution and the fall of the Russian Empire. Although these nationalist aspirations are at first supported by Bolshevik leaders, they are ultimately rejected, and all three regions are later incorporated into the Soviet Union, which is formed in 1922.
1918	The Native American Church, a pan-tribal American Indian religion, is officially established and incorporated in Oklahoma, drawing adherents from many tribes living in the region, including the Comanche, Kiowa, Apache, Cheyenne, and Oto. At the time, several states have enacted laws banning peyote use, and the U.S. Congress is considering a similar law.
1918	In the United States, Mennonites, Amish, and Quakers, whose religious beliefs include pacifism, are required to provide two years of alternative service as conscientious objectors in lieu of military service. The requirement remains in place until conscription ends in 1976.
1918	During World War I, the Hutterites (an Anabaptist sect) in South Dakota refuse to serve in the military, and some move from South Dakota to Manitoba and Alberta, Canada, to avoid persecution and to establish settlements.
1918	The new constitution of the German Weimar Republic creates a separation of church and state and guarantees religious freedom. However, the government continues to collect taxes to be distributed to the churches, and religion continues to be taught in the schools.
1918	In Russia, the Bolshevik government issues the decree of January 23 depriving all religious bodies of legal standing and the right to own property or engage in educational activity. Over the

next 20 years, tens of thousands of clergy are executed and more than 90 percent of all houses of worship are closed or destroyed.

1918–1919 Joseph Franklin Rutherford, leader of the Jehovah's Witnesses, and seven other leaders of the religion are convicted of violating the U.S. Espionage Act for refusing to support the United States in World War I because, in accord with Witness beliefs, they remain neutral. They are released in 1919 on bail, their convictions are reversed on appeal, and the government drops the case.

1919 Seeking to make Algeria part of France, the French government grants limited voting rights to Muslims in Algeria who are educated or who serve in the military. Although the Algerians are French subjects, the only Muslims eligible to become French citizens are those who renounce Islam, and the Muslim population is severely restricted in the right to travel and gather in public.

1919 The Central Sikh League is established in India to represent Sikhs, mainly in their dealings with the British.

1919 With 80 percent of the members of the state legislatures voting in favor, the ratification of the 18th Amendment to the U.S. Constitution takes effect. The amendment, prohibiting the manufacture, sale, and transport of alcoholic beverages, is viewed as a major victory by fundamentalist Christians who were active in seeking its ratification, but Prohibition is far from strictly enforced.

1919–1924 The Khilafat movement, a pan-Islamic movement in India, is formed in an attempt to influence the post–World War I peace process and especially to ensure that the Ottoman sultan remains the leader of the Islamic world. The movement fails to achieve its goals when the sultanate is abolished, but it subsequently plays a role in anti-British politics in northern India when it is aligned with the Hindus.

1920 Jewish settlers organize the Haganah, a military organization, in Palestine, where Arabs outnumber Jews by more than two to one.

1920 Jews in Palestine establish the position of chief rabbi, who has ultimate authority over religious and family matters. The post is actually filled by two rabbis, one for the Ashkenazic (eastern European) and one for the Sephardic (western European) Jewish communities, both of which are represented among the Jews living in Palestine.

1920 The Meiji Shrine in Tokyo is completed after five years of largely volunteer construction by youth groups and by Shinto and Buddhist religious groups. Dedicated to the worship of the deified emperor Meiji, who died in 1912, and of the empress, the Meiji Shrine promotes emperor worship and brings Shinto into new prominence.

1920 An English translation of *The Protocols of the Elders of Zion* begins to appear in the *Dearborn Independent*, a weekly journal published by Henry Ford in Dearborn, Michigan. The *Times* of

London exposes the work as a forgery in 1921, and after public protests Ford discontinues publishing anti-Semitic literature.

1920	The Shiromani Gurdwara Parbandhak Committee is formed in India to take charge of managing the temples, a role that affords it much political power in the Sikh community in the Punjab region of northern India.
1920–1922	The Muslim Basmachi Revolt, a national guerrilla uprising, erupts in the Uzbek region of central Asia in response to Bolshevik control of Muslim Turkestan and is initially successful, with Muslims taking parts of the countryside and threatening major cities such as Bukhara. The newly formed Soviet Union helps to quell the revolt by returning confiscated land to Muslim communities, affording Muslim law some authority, and supplying food to the region.
1920s	For the first time non-Anglican Protestants are appointed to professorships in theology at Oxford and Cambridge Universities in Great Britain, as the influence of the Anglican Church weakens. However, such positions are still barred to Roman Catholics and agnostics or atheists.
1921	The Church of Jesus Christ on Earth through the Prophet Simon Kimbangu is founded in the Belgian Congo by Simon Kimbangu, an oil worker and former Baptist ministerial student. The church, promising an end to Belgian rule, combines Christian and African beliefs; Kimbangu is imprisoned for 30 years and dies in prison, but after independence in 1960 the church becomes the largest African church in central Africa.
1921	The Peyote Church of Christ in Nebraska is founded by American Indians as a religious group centered on peyote use.
1921	In Japan, the headquarters of Omotokyo, a new religious sect, are raided by the Kyoto police, and its leaders are accused of lèse-majesté (a crime against the sovereign) because its founder's tomb resembles that of the emperor.
1922	The Soviet government removes Muslim political leaders from power in the Muslim central Asian republics and replaces them with Muslims or non-Muslims loyal to the Soviet government in Moscow. The policy is extended to other Muslim regions of the Soviet Union, and by 1938 all Muslim leaders who were in power in 1920 have been replaced.
1922	The Balfour Declaration is made part of the League of Nations mandate for Palestine, in which Britain is temporary overseer of the Jews and Arabs in Palestine. Ultimately, the independent state of Israel is born here in 1948, against the protests of Palestinians and others.
1922	A quota on the number of Jewish students admitted to Harvard College in Cambridge, Massachusetts, is established, and quotas become a common practice at elite colleges in the United States.
1922	The Muslim-Hindu National Unionist Party is founded in the Punjab region of northern India to represent the interests of

farmers.

1923   Kemal Ataturk, a Turkish statesman, establishes the Republic of
            Turkey as a secular state, abolishes the caliphate in 1924, and
            brings to an end Islam's dominance as a state religion in 1928.
            The new government secularizes education, bans Islamic dress,
            closes religious schools, places religion under government admin-
            istration, and replaces Islamic law with civil laws.

1923   T. T. Martin, a Baptist minister, publishes *Hell and the High
            Schools*, a book that argues against teaching the theory of evolu-
            tion in the United States.

1923   A law prohibiting the teaching of the theory of evolution in public
            schools is passed in the state of Oklahoma. Similar laws are later
            passed in Florida, Tennessee, and Mississippi.

1923–1927   Mennonites emigrate from Russia to Canada, with some 18,000
            Mennonites arriving in Canada. The existing Mennonite commu-
            nities in the western plains provinces of Canada assist the emi-
            gration.

1924   Representatives of Hindu, Muslim, Parsi (Zoroastrian), Sikh,
            and Christian communities in India convene a congress at Delhi.
            They agree to form local committees to prevent religious con-
            flicts, but militant Hindus and Muslims continue to agitate for
            independence and to clash with each other.

1924   The Soviet Union initiates a policy designed to eliminate religion
            as a significant part of life, with the intent of creating a secular
            nation in which all citizens are loyal to the state. Although Rus-
            sian Orthodoxy is perhaps less subject to restrictions than other
            religions, new laws enacted over the next six years forbid reli-
            gious organizations from both existing and owning property. The
            new laws end religious education, allow for the arrest and
            imprisonment of religious leaders, and close churches, mosques,
            synagogues, and temples.

1924   British runner Eric Liddell refuses to compete in his best event,
            the 100-yard dash, at the Olympic Games in Paris, France,
            because the qualifying heats are to be run on a Sunday. A devout
            Presbyterian, Liddell instead runs the 400-yard dash and wins
            the gold medal, setting a world record and attributing his victory
            to God.

1925   The Baha'i religion is classified as non-Muslim in Egypt, which
            leads to discrimination against members of the sect.

1925   The Sikh Gurdwaras Act, passed by the British colonial govern-
            ment in India, places Sikh temples under Sikh management and
            officially recognizes Sikhism as a distinct religion.

1925   The new constitution in Chile establishes religious freedom, but
            the Roman Catholic Church remains politically active and influ-
            ential and is perceived as enjoying special privileges not avail-
            able to other religions or denominations.

1925   At the Scopes trial in Dayton, Tennessee, the defendant, John

Thomas Scopes, a biology teacher accused by Tennessee of teaching evolution rather than the biblical account of creation required by the state's newly enacted Butler Act (1921), is found guilty and fined $100. In the trial's circus atmosphere that is reported worldwide (and gains the proceedings the name of the Monkey Trial), the respected statesman William Jennings Bryan is the prosecutor against the eloquent Clarence Darrow, who argues for the defense that the Butler Act is unconstitutional while admitting that Scopes indeed had broken the law. The guilty verdict is set aside by the appeals court, and the Butler Act is repealed in 1967; the trial embarrasses Protestant fundamentalists and causes the movement to lose support in the United States.

1926   After receiving Lebanon as a mandate from the League of Nations in 1920, France creates Grand Liban (Great Lebanon) as a dependent republic in an attempt to quell the constant religious and political controversies in the region. The president is required to be a Maronite Christian (member of a Uniate church, with Orthodox liturgy but subject to the pope), the prime minister a Sunni Muslim, and the president of the national assembly a Shia Muslim; Grand Liban becomes the independent state of Lebanon in 1943.

1926   The Soviet Union bans the use of Arabic and requires the Latin alphabet to be used to write all Turkic languages spoken in the republics. As many Muslims in central Asia speak Turkic languages and use the Arabic Qur'an, the policy restricts contacts with the outside Muslim world and makes it more difficult to practice Islam in the Soviet Union.

1926   Authorities in Germany begin arresting Jehovah's Witnesses and confiscating their religious texts; similar actions are taken by the United States, Romania, Hungary, Italy, and many other nations into the 1930s. Government authorities are concerned about Witnesses' claims that Jehovah began to rule the world in 1914 and also about their refusal to salute the national flag; in many cases, the Witnesses win relief in court cases.

1928   The Muslim teacher Hasan al-Banna founds the Muslim Brotherhood, a Muslim reform movement, in Egypt, seeking to end British rule, remove Western influences from Egyptian society, and revive a form of fundamental Islam based on the Qur'an. The brotherhood draws a large following in Egypt until it is repressed by the government in 1954.

1928   The Peace Preservation Law is used in Japan as a tool for the ongoing investigation and oppression of "heretical" new religions. Regarded officially as little more than superstition, such so-called pseudo-religions are declared *jakyo* (evil religions) and are prosecuted in 1926, 1928, and 1938.

1928   The Baha'i religion is repressed in the Soviet Union.

1928   In a popular vote in Oklahoma on the question of teaching the theory of evolution in public schools, voters by a two-to-one margin vote to ban the teaching of evolution.

1929 The Lateran Concordat and Treaty, which creates the Vatican as an independent city-state under the rule of the pope and a commission of cardinals, resolves the conflict between the Roman Catholic Church in Rome and the nation of Italy. The concordat gives the Vatican the 109 acres on which it stands as well as 160 acres outside it, gives Roman Catholicism special status in Italy, and requires that it be taught in the schools.

1929 In accord with new economic and social policies in the Soviet Union, Mennonite communities are dissolved, and some 6,000 Mennonites flee to Germany and then to Canada and South America. About 8,000 Mennonites are killed or imprisoned.

1929 An amendment to the constitution of the Soviet Union removes the right of the people to hear religious teachings while continuing to allow them to hear antireligious propaganda. The government is also given new and broad rights to control religion and religious behavior.

1930 In the Soviet Union, the government puts severe controls on the establishment of *waqfs*, income-producing properties given as charity to the Muslim community, which are important sources of income for mosques and religious schools.

1930 Sir Muhammed Iqbal, a Muslim poet and philosopher and president of the Muslim League in India, argues for the creation of a Muslim state in northwest India, separate from Hindu India. Hindu leaders want a single state, but Muslims, concerned about discrimination as a religious minority, demand a separate Muslim nation, which later becomes the nation of Pakistan.

1930s The Maum Muda Muslim movement, a pan-Islamic movement in British Malaya, is aligned with pan-Islamic movements in other countries and is opposed to British rule. It is repressed by both the government and traditional Muslim leaders.

1931 A new constitution in Afghanistan is created in general accord with Islamic law. The new constitution reverses policies enacted in 1923 designed to make Afghanistan a secular nation.

1931 Muslims in Ethiopia are constitutionally granted full rights. Because Muslims are a minority in the Christian nation and live mainly in the east, however, the government continues to enforce policies that attempt to limit the influence of Islam and end the threat of Muslim separatism.

1932 The kingdom of Saudi Arabia is created as an Islamic state from the provinces of Hejaz (site of Medina and Mecca) and Nejd (center of Wahhabi Islam) by Abdul Aziz Ibn Sa'ud, whose family has ruled Arabia since 1780. By reviving the puritanical fundamentalist Wahhabi form of Islam, Ibn Sa'ud gives his kingdom great influence in the Arab world; he forges treaties with neighboring countries and helps found the Arab League in 1946.

1932 The Japanese Ministry of Education rules that the Yasukuni Shrine in Tokyo, dedicated to the spirits of soldiers who died in battle for Japan, is a nonreligious institution that aims to instill patriotism and loyalty, so that Japanese of all religions must participate in Shinto ritual.

1932 The Evolution Protest Movement founded in Great Britain plays a major role in resisting the teaching of biological evolution and in the criticism that evolution is a theory, not an established fact.

1932 The Soviet government introduces internal passports, which register a person's place of residence and nationality, a category that covers religion as well (e.g., Jewish nationality). Changes in residence must be registered on the passports, and the documents are necessary to work, get married, be admitted to an educational institution, and travel.

1933 The National Socialist Party (Nazi Party) under the leadership of Adolf Hitler comes to power in Germany and revokes the 1919 constitution, thereby ending freedom of religion.

1933 Nazi Germany passes a law banning Jews from government employment, although Jews in positions considered vital to the government are not immediately dismissed. In the same year, Jewish books are burned, boycotts are initiated against Jewish businesses, and prominent Jews are forced to resign their positions and leave Germany.

1934 The Jewish Autonomous Oblast (region) or Birobidzhan in Siberia is established in the Soviet Union as a place for Jews to settle. Most of the inhabitants are non-Jewish.

1934 The Pastors' Emergency League is formed in Germany by leaders of many Lutheran, Reformed, and other churches in reaction to government efforts to bring religion under state control.

1935 The Nuremberg Laws promulgated at the annual meeting of the National Socialist Party in Nuremberg, Germany, prohibit Jews from voting, restrict them from public employment, prohibit them from marrying non-Jews, and deprive them of citizenship.

1936 Uzbekistan, Kazakhstan, Azerbaijan, Turkmenistan, Tajikistan, Kyrgyzstan, eight smaller autonomous republics, and four even smaller autonomous provinces are formed in the Soviet Union when the government completes its reorganization of the Muslim peoples.

1937 Pope Pius XI issues the encyclical *Mit Brenender Sorge* (With burning sorrow), condemning Nazism and criticizing Nazi assaults on the freedom of the Roman Catholic Church. The Nazi government responds by increasing its repression of Catholicism.

1937 The new constitution of Ireland guarantees religious freedom, although it acknowledges that Roman Catholicism occupies a special position as the religion of the majority of the people. This clause is removed by referendum in 1972.

1937 South Africa prohibits Jewish immigration, in response to Jews fleeing from Germany.

1937 The British Peel Commission recommends that Palestine be divided into Jewish and Arab states, in an effort to deal with the continuing conflict. The recommendation is accepted by the Jews and rejected by the Arabs.

1937
The *Kokutai no hongi* (Fundamentals of the national entity) issued by the ministry of education in Japan rejects "false doctrines of individualism" and views the emperor as "a deity incarnate who rules our country in unison with the august will of the Imperial Ancestors." The treatise is used as a school text to disseminate imperial nationalist propaganda.

1937–1945
During the rule of the dictator Getúlio Dornelles Vargas in Brazil, African-based religions are repressed as possible sources of resistance to the government.

1938
Chinese Communists, headquartered in Shaanxi Province in northern China, initiate a policy of accommodation toward Muslims by guaranteeing them religious freedom and granting them full rights.

1938
On *Kristallnacht* (Crystal night, in reference to glass from broken shop windows), the Nazis provoke anti-Jewish riots in Germany. About 200 synagogues are burned, Jewish businesses are looted, and many Jews are arrested.

1939
The American Baptist Bill of Rights issued by the Southern, Northern, and National Baptists calls for separation of church and state.

1939
After four years of persecution by the government, Buddhism is almost eradicated in Mongolia. About 2,000 Buddhist monks and abbots are executed.

1939
The Religious Organizations Law in Japan grants the state the power to regulate all religions and to mobilize religion for the war effort, suppress dissent, and strengthen the Shinto position.

1940
The Kentucky legislature passes a law banning the use of reptiles in religious services. The law is aimed at some Pentecostal Christians who practice snake handling and is in response to reports of injuries and deaths resulting from snakebites; in subsequent years, many other states in the South and Midwest pass similar laws.

1940
The Navajo tribal council bans the use of peyote in Indian religious ritual. Peyote was a sacrament of the Native American Church, one of a number of religions with adherents among the Navajo.

1940
The Church of Christ in Japan is formed as a government-controlled Christian church as a means of controlling Christians in the country. Following World War II, the church reorganizes and is free of government control.

1940
The U.S. Supreme Court in *Minersville School District v. Gobitis* overturns lower-court decisions and rules that school systems can require children of Jehovah's Witnesses to salute the flag of the United States. The decision leads to verbal and physical

assaults on Witnesses who continue to refuse to instruct their children to salute the flag, but the Court reverses its decision in 1943 when it rules that the government cannot force individuals to salute the flag or to engage in other similar behavior.

1940

In *Jones v. City of Opelika*, the U.S. Supreme Court rules that the government can place a license tax on the distribution of religious material. This decision is reversed in 1943, in the Court's *Murdock v. Commonwealth of Pennsylvania*.

1941

The term *final solution* is first used in Nazi Germany when Hermann Göring, Hitler's second-in-command, sends a directive to Reinhard Heydrich, the chief of the Security Main Office, ordering him to organize a final solution to the Jewish problem in Europe. Jews must wear yellow stars on armbands or badges; emigration of Jews from German-occupied territories is banned; and tens of thousands of Jews are sent to ghettos in Poland. By the time Nazi Germany falls, 6 million Jews have been murdered in the death camps.

1941–1945

The restrictions on Muslims in the Soviet Union, dated to 1928, are relaxed to win Muslim support during World War II. Islam is formally recognized as an official religion; Muslims are permitted to form administrative organizations; a seminary is founded in Tashkent in central Asia; and the closing of mosques slows.

1942

At the Wannsee Conference in Berlin, Germany (held on the Wannsee, a large lake in the Grunewald Forest in Berlin), the decision to execute the "final solution"—the extermination of all the Jews in Europe—is discussed with leaders of German government ministries. The Germans begin to build extermination camps, in addition to concentration camps; mass extermination of Jews in death camps begins in Germany, Poland, and Ukraine; and some 2.7 million Jews are killed in 1942.

1943

In *West Virginia State Board of Education v. Barnette* the United States Supreme Court upholds the right of Jehovah's Witnesses not to salute the flag on religious grounds.

1943

Joseph Stalin, brutal dictator of the Soviet Union, orders the liquidation of Kalmykia on the northwest shore of the Caspian Sea because of supposed collaboration between the Kalymks and the Nazi German invaders. The Kalmyk people, nomadic Buddhists descended from western Mongols who long ago migrated westward to settle in Russia, are deported to Siberia and central Asia; one-third die en route. Those who survive return in 1957, and the Kalmyk Autonomous Soviet Socialist Republic is reestablished in 1958.

1943

In the *Algerian Manifesto*, Algerian Muslim political leaders criticize French rule and demand an Algerian constitution and full political and legal rights for Muslims. The *Manifesto* is rejected by the French government in 1944.

1943

Raphael Lemkin, a Polish Jewish legal scholar who fled to the United States, uses the term *genocide* to describe the German efforts to eradicate all Jews. The term subsequently becomes a generic label for all efforts by one ethnic or religious group to eradicate another.

1943   The Soviet Union abolishes the Ukrainian Catholic Church and turns its property over to the Russian Orthodox Church. In 1989 the Soviet government restores the Ukrainian Catholic Church.

1944   The Soviet Union deports Muslims living in European Russia, including such groups as the Mtskhetians in Georgia and the Crimean Tatars, to Asiatic Russia, claiming that they are supporters of Nazi Germany.

1944   The Umma Party is formed in Sudan by members of the Muslim Mahdist (followers of a Muslim leader with messianic pretensions) movement that was suppressed by the British and Egyptian rulers beginning in 1899 but has retained influence in rural areas.

1945   In *Giroud v. United States*, the U.S. Supreme Court rules that the promise to bear arms was not intended by Congress when making the law and that citizenship should not be denied because of an applicant's religious convictions.

1945   General Douglas MacArthur, commander of the Allied Occupation Forces in Japan, issues a law abolishing Shinto as the state religion and calls for the abolition of the ideology asserting that the emperor and the Japanese people and islands are superior to the rest of the world. Shinto education is removed from public schools; textbooks treating Shinto mythology as history are rewritten; and compulsory shrine visits by students cease. Specifically forbidden are the "use in official writings of the terms 'Greater East Asia War' (*Dai Toa Senso*), 'The Whole World under One Roof' (*Hakko Ichi-u*), and all other terms whose connotation in Japanese is inextricably connected with State Shinto, militarism, and ultranationalism."

1945   The Religious Corporations Ordinance guarantees religious freedom in post–World War II Japan. The law also safeguards the religious freedom and property rights of religious organizations on the basis of the separation of church and state, but many abuse the ordinance by registering as religious organizations to avoid taxes, causing the ordinance to be replaced in 1951 by the Religious Juridical Persons Law.

1945   The government of Indonesia creates a national ideology called Pancasila (Five principles), which forms the philosophical basis of the country and is an attempt to create a nation that includes people from hundreds of ethnic groups and religions; the government resists creating an Islamic nation (although the majority of Indonesians are Muslims) and instead develops the new ideology, which stresses national unity, justice, and inclusiveness. Nonetheless, the new constitution adopts many Islamic legal principles as national law, and other religions seen as threatening Islam are often repressed in later years.

1946   The new constitution in Japan clearly separates religion and the state, a departure from the 1889 constitution and government policy, which often linked the government and Shinto. However, the 1946 separation principle is interpreted liberally by the government and courts, and the government supports and participates in various religious activities such as the erection of Shinto shrines.

1946 In violation of its constitution, the Soviet Union secretly enacts policies designed to ban religious activity by many religious minorities, including Eastern Rite Catholics (Uniates), Pentecostal Christians, Jehovah's Witnesses, Russian Old Believers, and nonmainstream branches of Russian Orthodoxy.

1947 Great Britain oversees the partition of India into the two self-governing dominions of India and Pakistan; the plan is approved by the Muslim League and by the All-India Congress, and a mass movement ensues of Hindus, Muslims, and Sikhs who find themselves on the wrong side of the new international boundaries. As many as 20 million people eventually relocate, and up to 3 million of these are killed in fighting and massacres on both sides of the new border, especially in the Punjab.

1948 The government of Communist Romania closes the churches of the Eastern Rite Catholic Church in Romania (a Uniate Church of the Eastern rite but under the pope's authority) and gives much of its property to the Eastern Orthodox Church. The government is opposed to the Uniate Church because of its ties to the West and to the Vatican.

1949 Pope Pius XII orders that Catholic Communists be excommunicated, in an effort to stem the power of Communism in Europe and especially in Italy.

1949 The new constitution of West Germany guarantees religious freedom but also gives the government authority to grant nonstatus religions status as religions.

1949 The Communist government of Albania ends the guarantee of religious freedom and requires all religious leaders to sign a pledge of loyalty to the state.

1949 The new constitution of Costa Rica establishes Roman Catholicism as the state religion but grants religious freedom to other religions and denominations.

1949 The Communist government of Hungary places religious organizations and religious activity under governmental control, with the opportunity for worship severely curtailed.

1950 The Sioux Indians convene a dance along the lines of the traditional Sun Dance ceremonies that was banned by the U.S. government in 1904.

1951 Several million Indians, most of them Hindu untouchables (lowest Hindu caste), begin converting to Buddhism as a means of increasing their social standing. Buddhism, which began in India almost 2,500 years earlier, had virtually disappeared there before this time.

1951	The Canadian government ends restrictions on Native American religious practices, which were imposed in 1884.
1951	The Fraudulent Mediums Act enacted by the British Parliament contains a provision that witchcraft causes no harm, and the act's passage allows the Wicca movement to go public. The movement is eclectic in its beliefs and draws on Celtic and other European pagan beliefs and practices as well as freemasonry.
1952	Poland's new constitution establishes freedom of religion in this Communist country.
1953	The Chinese Catholic Patriotic Association is formed as the central organization for all Roman Catholics, Catholic churches, and Catholic organizations in China. The government considers the association to have more authority than the Vatican, and priests must follow association policies.
1954	Santa Lucia Island, an independent nation in the Windward Isles of the West Indies, bans the Obeah religion, a traditional form of sorcery used to ward off or cure the effects of evil forces. Many people ignore the ban and continue to practice obeah in private.
1954	In an effort to limit the political influence of Islam, the Egyptian government bans the Muslim Brotherhood, which was founded in 1928. The movement goes into hiding until it reemerges in 1967; the government campaign to bring Islam under state control lasts into the 1970s and also includes seizing land owned by Muslim communities, placing Muslim leaders under government administration, weakening the role of Islamic law, and modernizing the education system.
1954	The Three-Self Patriotic Movement is organized by the Communist government of China to place all Protestant denominations under centralized control. With adherence to government policy considered most important, differences among the denominations are minimized.
1954	The U.S. Congress adds the phrase "under God" to the Pledge of Allegiance, which is commonly recited at public events and in schools.
1955	The U.S. Congress adds the phrase "In God We Trust" to currency.
1956	In an effort to gain political control of Tibet, China acts to weaken the influence of Tibetan Buddhist leaders and Tibetan Buddhism in general by arresting and killing lamas (monks) and nuns and destroying temples and monasteries.
1956	Pakistan's new constitution establishes Islam as the state religion, with all laws to be reviewed by a board of Muslim scholars.
1956	The Orthodox rabbinate in Israel prohibits the practice of Reform Judaism.
1956	The Soviet Union allows a Jewish school to operate legally and also allows the first Jewish prayer books to be published in the

country since 1917.

1956	The first Sikh, and the first American of South Asian ancestry, to be elected to the U.S. Congress is Dalip Singh Saund of California, who represents the Berkeley district.
1956	After Morocco becomes independent of France and Spain, Islam is established as the state religion. Other religions are not banned but are subject to various restrictions, including restrictions against the right to seek converts.
1956	China begins to suppress religious expression, with religious leaders arrested, churches, temples, and mosques destroyed, shrines damaged, and books confiscated. The Communist government views religion as an impediment to economic and political development.
1957	François (Papa Doc) Duvalier, president of Haiti, accepts voodoo, Haitian beliefs based on African practices, as a religion, with the view that it can diminish the power of the Roman Catholic Church.
1957	The Southern Christian Leadership Conference (SCLC), an African-American religious organization formed to fight for civil rights in the United States, is founded by Martin Luther King Jr., Ralph Abernathy, Andrew Young, Jesse Jackson, and other black leaders representing Baptist churches and other organizations. The SCLC leads the civil rights movement in the United States, with King using nonviolent civil disobedience such as boycotts as a means for change, rather than the legal actions of the National Association for the Advancement of Colored People, hitherto the main black organization working for civil rights.
1957	China allows the founding of the Constitutional Catholic Church, the first Catholic Church to be organized in Communist China. Created with government permission, the church is under government control and is not recognized by the Vatican.
1957	In the Union of Malaya (formerly British Malaya, present-day Malaysia), Islam is established as the state religion following independence from Britain. At the same time, religious freedom is guaranteed in the new constitution.
1957	China ends its policies of accommodation to Muslims in response to Muslim calls for more autonomy and to complaints about the government. The government relocates Han Chinese to Muslim regions, closes mosques and schools, ends local political autonomy, and in 1958 closes the Chinese Islamic Association that was founded in 1953.
1957	The All-Muslim Nation Union Muslim political party is founded as the first Islamic political party in Tanganyika (later Tanzania).
1957	Native American sacred sites used by the Umatilla, Nez Percé, Yakima, and other Indians in the state of Washington are destroyed when the area is flooded after construction of the Dalles Dam on the Columbia River in Oregon.

1958   The tax-exempt status of the Church of Scientology in the United States is revoked by the Internal Revenue Service because of concerns about methods the church uses to attract and retain members and about whether the church is a profit-making business or a religion.

1959   Efforts to repress the Santeria (combining African Yoruba and Roman Catholic practices and beliefs) religion in the United States begin shortly after Cuban immigrants bring the religion to the United States. Although the religion is practiced in private by only a minority of Cubans (the majority are Roman Catholics), it comes to the attention of animal-rights advocates, the media, and government agencies in New York and Florida who are concerned about animal sacrifice in Santeria rituals.

1959   Fleeing to India to escape the Chinese repression of religion and culture in Tibet and in the wake of an unsuccessful rebellion against the Chinese, Tenzin Gyatso, the 14th Dalai Lama, leader of the Buddhist community in Tibet, establishes the government-in-exile of Tibet at Dharmsala, India, 35 miles from the Tibetan border. Accusing the Chinese of genocide, he is eventually joined by some 100,000 followers who are granted political asylum in India.

1959   Shortly after ascending to the papacy, Pope John XXIII revises the Good Friday Mass to make it less offensive to Jews by doing away with the phrase *pro perfidis Judaeis* (the invocation to pray "for the faithless Jews"). Instead, he asks Christians simply to pray for the Jews.

1960   A Rastafarian (member of a Jamaican cult preaching the eventual return of blacks to Africa and using marijuana in its ritual) leader, Claudius Henry, his wife, and 12 followers are arrested in Jamaica and accused of treason against the British Crown. Henry and two followers are convicted and sentenced to 10 years in prison, and his son and three other Rastifarians are killed in a gunfight with British troops.

1960   The Church of Jesus Christ on Earth through the Prophet Simon Kimbangu (Christian sect founded by Kimbangu, who preached freedom from Belgian rule) becomes the national religion of Zaire (former Belgian Congo) in Africa, when the country becomes independent of Belgium. Though the Belgians repressed the religion and imprisoned Kimbangu for 30 years until his death, the church grew to some 3 million members and was the first independent African church to join the World Council of Churches.

1960   John F. Kennedy is the first Roman Catholic to be elected president of the United States.

1960   Islam becomes the state religion of Mauritania when the West African country becomes independent of French rule.

1960   Some rabbis in Israel express doubts about whether the Bene Israel (Jews from Bombay, India) are actually Jews and thus whether they should be allowed to live in Israel under the Law of Return (passed by the Knesset in 1950, the law gives every Jew the right to emigrate to Israel). The Bene Israel protest from 1962 through 1964, and the Israel rabbinate finally accepts them as Jews.

1960–1964   The Soviet Union conducts a campaign to eliminate religion from Soviet life. The campaign fails, but many religious buildings are seized by the government, religious leaders arrested and imprisoned, worship services disrupted, some religions such as Seventh-day Adventists denied representative bodies, and all religions except Baptists prevented from convening national conventions.

1961   Burma (present-day Myanmar) makes Buddhism the state religion and initiates the policy that "whatever is Burmese is Buddhist and whatever is Buddhist is Burmese." The policy creates friction with ethnic minorities of Muslims, Christians, and followers of traditional religions.

1961   After the 1959 Cuban Revolution and the establishment of a Communist government, Fidel Castro, Cuba's leader, sees the Roman Catholic Church as a supporter of the overthrown dictatorship of Fulgencio Batista; Church schools are taken over by the government, and priests are either forced to leave Cuba or to go into hiding. The Catholic hierarchy, which was close to the former rulers, no longer enjoys influence in Cuba.

1961   Karl Adolf Eichmann, who designed Nazi Germany's program to exterminate Jews, is tried and convicted in Israel for crimes against humanity and the Jewish people; he is convicted and sentenced to death. Israel's actions in kidnapping Eichmann from Argentina in 1960 and trying him for crimes committed in another country are criticized by some as violations of international law.

1961   The World Council of Churches condemns anti-Semitism and declares that the Jews are not to be blamed for the crucifixion of Jesus.

1962   The U.S. Supreme Court in *Engel v. Vitale* rules that prayer in public schools violates the establishment (of religion) clause of the First Amendment to the U.S. Constitution.

1962   Baha'i organizations, the Divine Life Society, and other small religions and organizations are repressed in Indonesia on the grounds that they are a threat to national unity. The Baha'i religion is completely banned in 1972.

1963   Pope John XXIII issues *Pacem in Terris*. It is the first official Catholic document to recognize a right to religious freedom.

1963   In *Abingdon School District v. Schempp*, a case brought by the atheist Madalyn Murray, the U.S. Supreme Court rules that mandatory prayer and Bible recitations in public schools are unconstitutional on the grounds that actions by the government to promote or limit religious expression are unconstitutional. The Court also rules that the government may neither take a hostile view of religion nor promote it.

| 1964 | The new constitution of Afghanistan establishes Islam as the state religion and allows Islamic law to be used when no secular law exists to decide an issue. |

1964   The new constitution of Afghanistan establishes Islam as the state religion and allows Islamic law to be used when no secular law exists to decide an issue.

1964   The U.S. Civil Rights Act bans religious discrimination in housing and employment. Subsequent amendments require employers to make reasonable efforts to accommodate the religious beliefs and practices of their employees.

1964   In Israel, a law provides for protection of and full access to Jewish, Christian, and Muslim religious places. Nonetheless, Christians and Muslims continue to feel that the law is not enforced equally and complain that less attention is afforded their sites than Jewish ones.

1965   *Dignitatis Humanae* (The Declaration on Religious Freedom) is passed by the Second Vatican Council and signed by the pope. It holds that all human persons possess the right to religious freedom and that this right must be protected as a civil right by the state.

1965   The Second Vatican Council of the Roman Catholic Church declares that Jews are not responsible for the crucifixion of Jesus.

1965   U.S. tax law is revised to accommodate the religious beliefs of the Amish, a strict Mennonite sect that immigrated to America in the 18th and 19th centuries. The federal government excuses the self-employed Amish from paying the tax for Social Security, which they see as a questioning of God's ability to care for them; even Amish who work outside the community and are entitled to Social Security payments do not accept them. The revision ends years of conflict, with the government at times seizing Amish property for nonpayment of taxes.

1965   The Church of Scientology is banned in Australia, but the Australian High Court lifts the ban in 1983, and the group's tax-exempt status is restored in 1984.

1965   The U.S. Supreme Court rules in the case of *United States v. Seeger* that conscientious objectors need not be members of a pacifist religious group such as the Quakers or Hutterites because religion is a personal matter, and that conscientious-objector status can be given for nonreligious reasons. Similar cases involving conscientious objectors to military service include *Welsh v. United States* (1970) and *Gillette v. United States* (1971).

1965   Los Angeles Dodgers pitcher Sandy Koufax, called "the Great Jewish Hope" by Dodgers owner Walter O'Malley, refuses to pitch the first game of the World Series because it falls on Yom Kippur, the holiest day in the Jewish calendar. The highly controversial decision makes Koufax a hero to the American Jewish community, while others criticize him for putting his personal beliefs ahead of the team's interests. Don Drysdale pitches in Koufax's stead, and the Dodgers lose the game 8–2, although they win the Series four games to three.

1966 At the Second Vatican Council, Pope Paul VI abolishes the *Index of Forbidden Books*, first published by the Roman Catholic Church in 1559.

1966 During the Cultural Revolution in China, religion in general is harshly repressed, with much of the repression aimed at the Muslim Hui (now living in northwest China, descendants of Muslims who traveled to China in the 7th–14th centuries and married Chinese women) and other Muslim peoples, because Islam is the major minority religion in China. Mosques are closed, copies of the Qur'an confiscated, and religious teachers intimidated; the repression lessens in 1970.

1966 India creates the state of Punjab in northern India. Sikhs form the majority of the population in the state, with Hindu and Muslim minorities.

1966–1967 Continuing its campaign to repress religion, Communist Albania closes religious institutions, arrests clergy, and confiscates religious property. The program effectively ends the practice of any religion in Albania so that the country is an atheistic state.

1966–1969 During the Cultural Revolution in China, 6,000 Tibetan monasteries and temples are demolished, their artwork and libraries destroyed, and monks dispersed; religious activity is banned in Tibet, as is traditional Tibetan dress. Taoism and Islam are also repressed at this time, and more than a million Tibetans are thought to have been killed.

1967 After Israel defeats Egypt in the Six-Day War, the Muslim Brotherhood, which was banned in 1954, reemerges as a political force and advocates a return to traditional Islam and the end of Western influence.

1967 The Dewan Da'wah Islamiyah, a Muslim missionary organization, is founded in Indonesia by the Muslim Muhammadiya organization to strengthen Islam in the nation and to control the efforts of Christian missionaries.

1967 The Navajo Tribal Council lifts its ban on peyote use for Navajo Indian members of the Native American Church.

1968 The Partai Muslimin Indonesia, a Muslim political party, is allowed to organize in Indonesia after 20 years of generally successful repression of Muslim political parties and movements. More radical Muslim reformers are, however, barred from leadership roles.

1968 The Unification Church (full name: The Holy Spirit Association for the Unification of World Christianity), founded in 1954 by Sun Myung Moon, is officially recognized as a religious organization in Great Britain.

1969 The Moro National Liberation Front is founded as a political organization by Muslims on the island of Mindanao in the Philippines. The goal of the organization is to free Muslims from rule by the central Filipino government.

1969	The Israelite Mission of the New Covenant is recognized as an official religion in Peru. The religion, which combines Christianity and ancient Inca beliefs, has a large following among poor people.
1969	In Japan, the Yasukuni Shrine Bill, presented to the Diet (Japan's legislative body) by the conservative Liberal Democratic Party, seeks to change the shrine's status to that of a special non-religious foundation and to place the shrine under the jurisdiction of the prime minister. The numerous opponents of this move, fearing that government administration of Yasukuni would constitute a restoration of state Shinto and would open the door to a revival of Japanese militarism, collect 3,277,405 signatures of those who oppose the bill; although presented repeatedly during the next decades, it is defeated each time.
1969	The Inter-American Convention on Human Rights, guaranteeing religious freedom in the Americas, is adopted by representatives of nations in the Americas at a special conference on human rights in Costa Rica. It becomes law in 1978 when ratified by 11 nations.
1969	The California Board of Education, seeking to establish principles and a curriculum for the teaching of science, considers creationism (explaining evolution as God's creation) as a public-education issue. The new policy does not allow for the teaching of creation science but reduces evolution to an unproved theory.
1970	According to the new constitution of Iraq, Islam is established as the state religion, although *shari'a* (Islamic law) does not become the civil law, and religious freedom is granted to other religions. However, many of these other groups, including Jews, Christians, and Shia Muslims, are subject to persecution.
1970	Blue Lake and the surrounding land in New Mexico is returned to the Taos Indians. The Taos consider the lake a sacred pilgrimage site; in the 1880s, the government had seized it as part of Carson National Forest.
1970	*Biology: A Search for Order in Complexity*, a high school biology text prepared by the Creation Research Society and published in the United States, uses creationism to explain the origin of the universe and of evolution. The book sells moderately well in its first year, but then goes out of print after being banned in Indiana.
1970	After Fiji becomes independent of Great Britain, conflict develops between the native Fijians and the Asian Indians (Hindus, Muslims, Sikhs), who form the majority of the population. Seeking to take political control of the nation, the native Fijians attack Hindu temples and Muslim mosques, compelling some Indians to leave and thereby making the Fijians the majority population.
1970s	The Bharatiya Janata Party emerges in India as a supporter of Indian nationalism and of India as a Hindu nation.

1970s	In Algeria, fundamentalist Muslims promote their agenda of creating an Islamic society by attacking women who do not wear veils, destroying businesses that sell alcoholic beverages, and disrupting the teachings of religious teachers with whom they disagree.
1970s	Various organizations emerge in the United States and Europe for the purpose of identifying new cults and sects, providing the public with information about them, and assisting people who are concerned about the well-being of relatives or friends who had joined cults. Some in the movement use deprogramming as a technique to end a recruit's adherence. These organizations are referred to as the anticult movement.
1970s	The social scientist Robert Bellah, in his books *Beyond Belief* (1970) and *Broken Covenant* (1975), discusses the concept of civil religion in the United States. He views civil religion as a set of beliefs, not necessarily religious in origin or expression, that unify the American people in the absence of overarching religious beliefs shared by all.
1972	The United States returns Mount Adams in the state of Washington to the Yakima Indians. The Yakima consider the mountain sacred; it was designated part of Gifford Pinchot National Forest some 70 years earlier.
1972	Bangladesh, independent only since 1971, introduces a new constitution, which bans political activity by religious groups, in an effort to control the influence of Muslim fundamentalists.
1972	In *Wisconsin v. Yoder*, the U.S. Supreme Court rules to exempt Amish children from public school attendance by deciding that they need not attend high school. The decision is a victory for the Amish, who want to raise their children in Amish communities and see attendance at high schools outside the community as a threat to their cultural survival.
1972	After Idi Amin seizes the presidency of Uganda in East Africa in a military coup, he expels all Asian Indians including Sikhs, Hindus, and Muslims and confiscates their property; some return to India, leaving all or much of their property and possessions behind, while others move to Canada and the United States. Asians are not forced to leave other East African nations such as Kenya, although many do so in the 1970s due to discrimination.
1972	The National Academy of Sciences and the American Association for the Advancement of Science issue statements objecting to the teaching of religious beliefs as science and to the teaching of creationism as an alternative to biological evolution.
1973	Islam becomes the state religion of Pakistan. Although Muslims account for 97 percent of the population, since Pakistan became a nation in 1947 there has been debate about the role of Islam in Pakistani society.
1973	After the end of the whites-only immigration policy in Australia, peoples from Asia and Hindus and Muslims from India as well as

Muslims and Buddhists from Southeast Asia settle in Australia.

1973 In *Roe v. Wade*, the U.S. Supreme Court rules that laws restricting abortion during the first six months of pregnancy are unconstitutional. Although the decision does not directly address religion, many Roman Catholics and fundamentalist Protestants view the ruling as an injustice to the unborn.

1973–1974 China attacks Confucius and Confucian thought as reactionary. Disgraced officials such as the former defense minister Lin Biao are stigmatized as "the Confuciuses of contemporary China."

1974 The government of Dominica, an island in the West Indies, bans the Dreads of Dominica in the Caribbean, an offshoot of Jamaican Rastafarianism.

1974 The National Assembly legalizes abortion in France, despite the opposition of the Roman Catholic Church.

1974 The South African separatist Nederduitse Gereformeerde Kerk (Dutch Reformed Church) issues *Human Relations and the South African Scene in the Light of Scripture*, a justification of the policy of apartheid (racial segregation) practiced in South Africa.

1974 The Citizens Freedom Foundation is founded in the United States as a central organization to coordinate the anticult activities of the many small, local anticult organizations that have emerged. In 1985, its name changes to the Cult Awareness Network; it remains active until 1995 when it declares bankruptcy following a lawsuit by Pentecostal Christians.

1974–1985 Falashas (Ethiopians who practice a variety of Judaism) are airlifted from Sudan, where they have fled from Ethiopia, to Israel.

1975 In a case brought by Evangelical Christians, who practice snake handling and who want to test the constitutionality of a state law that bans handling snakes and drinking poison for religious purposes, the Tennessee Supreme Court upholds the state law. In 1976, the U.S. Supreme Court refuses to hear the case on appeal.

1975 In Somalia, the government that came to power through a military coup in 1966 moves to end the influence of Islam and to create a national state based on socialism. As nearly all Somalis are Muslims, the effort to control Islam is only partially successful.

1975 Mu'ammar al-Gadhafi, leader of Libya, issues his *Green Book*, which promulgates his belief that a return to the basics of Islam as set forth in the Qur'an should be the basis of the Libyan state.

1975 The United Nations General Assembly passes Resolution 3379, equating Zionism with racism. In 1989, the General Assembly revokes the resolution by a vote of 111 to 25 with 13 abstentions.

1975 *The Guidelines and Suggestions for Relations with Judaism*, issued by the Roman Catholic Church, acknowledges that Judaism is a living, evolving religion and asks Catholics to combat anti-Semitism.

1975 The Supreme Constitutional Court in Egypt rules that only

Islam, Christianity, and Judaism are protected by the Egyptian constitution. This ruling subjects adherents of other religions such as Baha'i to discrimination and repression.

1975   After the end of the Vietnam War, when the Vietnamese Communist government unifies the North and South, all expressions of religion (primarily Buddhism and Roman Catholicism) are repressed. Religion is seen as a hindrance to the national socialist ideology.

1975–1978   A former physics professor, William L. Pierce, publishes *The Turner Diaries* (although the listed author is Andrew MacDonald). The book sets forth two major ideas of the Christian Identity movement—resistance to the U.S. government and creation of an Aryan (white Protestant) nation.

1975–1979   Seizing control of Cambodia, the Communist Khmer Rouge, led by Pol Pot, persecutes Cambodians of all religions; Buddhists are singled out, with many of their monasteries destroyed, and some 60,000 Buddhist monks are driven out of Cambodia or killed. In 1979, Vietnam invades Cambodia and drives Pol Pot and his Khmer Rouge into hiding.

1975–1990   A bitter, long-lasting civil war in Lebanon is fought over, among other issues, the Muslim desire for greater representation in the government, which by a 1943 agreement is controlled by Christians. The war involves many factions, including Christians, Muslims, Druze (Muslims), Palestinians, Israelites, and Syrians; it is concluded by the Taif agreement, which gives more power to the Muslim majority.

1976   The Uruguayan priest J. L. Segundo writes *Theology of Liberation*, a book providing a model for applying Christian theology to problems of social inequality in Latin America.

1976   After the death of Mao Zedong in China, the impact of foreign capitalism leads to a weakening of ideological Marxism and a reemphasis on the classic Confucian values of discipline, thrift, and task orientation, which harmonize well with the capitalist sensibility.

1976   Muslims are again allowed to pray in mosques and practice Islam in China, but, in the western regions where there are large numbers of Muslims, they are given only limited political power.

1976   After being accused of being agents of the secret police, the Jehovah's Witnesses are expelled from Mozambique in Southeast Africa and flee to neighboring Malawi. In the same year, Jehovah's Witnesses are also banned in Indonesia as a threat to national unity.

1976   The Motor-Cycle Crash Helmets (Religious Exemption) Act passed in Great Britain exempts Sikhs, who wear a turban required by religious belief, from the requirement of wearing safety helmets on motorcycles. The law is later used as a basis for exempting Sikhs from wearing other types of special headgear such as construction helmets.

1976	Conflict breaks out in East Timor (formerly Portuguese Timor) when the East Timorese seek independence following the end of Portuguese rule, while Indonesia seeks to incorporate the region as a province. Most East Timorese are Roman Catholics, whereas the Indonesians are mainly Muslims; the Roman Catholic Church supports independence. The conflict is resolved in 1999 when the East Timorese vote for independence.
1976	China ends opposition to Confucianism.
1976–1990s	Buddhists in Bangladesh resist Muslim control. Tribal peoples in the southeastern Chittagong Hill Tracts region of Bangladesh, mostly Buddhists of Tibetan descent, begin a guerrilla campaign against government resettlement of Bengali Muslims in the hill region; the military and Muslim settlers are targeted, and 3,500 people are killed.
1977	President Anwar el-Sādāt of Egypt becomes the first Arab leader to visit Israel. Sadat addresses the Knesset (Israeli parliament), and his visit is seen as an early and important step in the resulting peace treaty between Egypt and Israel.
1977	The Soviet Union allows prayer books from the United States to be shipped to Jewish congregations in Russia for the first time since 1917.
1977	Poland recognizes the Mormon Church.
1977	The Japanese Supreme Court overturns a 1971 decision by the High Court in the city of Nagoya banning the use of public funds for Shinto rites. The Supreme Court argues that the rites are secular and hence the use of the funds is constitutional; thus the ruling encourages the restoration of state Shinto.
1977	The U.S. Alliance for the Preservation of Religious Liberty is established by the Church of Scientology, the Unification Church, and the Children of God to protect their freedom. All three groups are being criticized and at times investigated and charged by the government with being profit-making entities and not really religions.
1977	The Supreme Court of India rules that the right to propagate religion awarded by the constitution does not give a person the right to convert others to one's own religion. The decision is a victory for Hindus who oppose conversion efforts by members of other religions among the Hindu majority in India.
1977	General Muhammad Zia ul-Haq, after seizing power in Pakistan, establishes a new policy limiting non-Muslim participation in government, making Islamic law the national law and requiring that schools teach Islam and that the media support Islam.
1977	After the Cultural Revolution ends in China, the government embarks on a new policy of allowing religious worship so long as it does not interfere with the goals of the government, although the state still controls religious organizations. People now can worship openly; among the religions benefiting from this new tolerance are Taoism, Islam, Christianity, and Buddhism.

1978	The American Indian Religious Freedom Act passed by the U.S. Congress guarantees Eskimos, Aleuts, American Indians, and native Hawaiians the right to practice their indigenous religions. However, in 1988 the Supreme Court rules that the act is essentially a statement of government policy and thereby renders much of the act unenforceable.
1978	The fundamentalist minister Jerry Falwell establishes the Moral Majority as a political movement promoting Christian values as the basis for American society. In 1989, Falwell dissolves the movement when financial contributions decline and its influence on the political process seems to be waning.
1978	Scientology founder L. Ron Hubbard and two members of the Church of Scientology are sentenced to prison in absentia and fined for fraud in France. In 1985, the Church of Scientology's tax-exempt status is removed in the United States on the grounds that it is a profit-making organization.
1978	On National Foundation Day in Japan, Asahikawa City on Hokkaido Island holds a formal tribute to the imperial state, with the participation of the prefectural governor, the mayor, and the Self-Defense Force company, who together, accompanied by military music, proceed to the local nation-protecting Shinto shrine.
1978	The new constitution of Sri Lanka (formerly Ceylon) provides for state support for Buddhism as well as freedom of expression of other religions, which include Hinduism, Christianity, and Islam.
1978	The constitution of Spain bans the establishment of a state religion and establishes freedom of religion.
1979	Pope John Paul II visits Poland and provides symbolic support for Solidarnosc (Solidarity), a trade union led by Lech Walesa, which opposes Communist rule. The pope visits twice more, providing moral support for the movement, which in 1989 topples the Communist regime.
1979	The Australian Aboriginal (indigenous inhabitant) minister Djiniyini Gondarra leads a religious revival among members of the Aboriginal Christian Uniting Church in Australia. The revival focuses on combining Christian and Aboriginal beliefs and practices, creating Aboriginal unity, and bringing justice and freedom to Aboriginal peoples in Australia.
1979	After Shah Reza Pahlevi goes into exile from Iran, Ayatollah Ruhollah Khomeini proclaims Iran an Islamic republic, which brings a return to strict observance of Muslim beliefs and practices. In 1980, the new constitution establishes the Islamic Republic of Iran with Islam the state religion and *shari'a* (Islamic law) the law of the land. Although some religious freedom is afforded to Jews, Christians, and Zoroastrians, these groups along with Baha'is and Sunni Muslims are persecuted.
1979	Islamic militants in Saudi Arabia oppose government-modernization policies and ties to the West and seize the Grand Mosque

in Mecca, with some 160 people killed.

1979   The Archaeological Resources Protection Act passed by the U.S. Congress prevents looting of archaeological sites on Indian and government land, including many Indian burial grounds, sacred sites, religious objects, and remains of ceremonial buildings.

1979   The Religious Roundtable, founded in the United States, is organized to train fundamentalist Christians to become more involved in politics. It ceases to function after 1980.

1979   The new constitution of Nigeria in West Africa prohibits the establishment of a state religion and guarantees religious freedom, but does not eliminate competition and conflict between Christians and Muslims.

1979   The government of Peru ends preferential treatment and patronage of the Roman Catholic Church, and in the next year the Roman Catholic Church in Peru becomes an independent entity.

1980   Oscar Arenulfo Romero, archbishop of San Salvador, capital of El Salvador in Central America, is assassinated while saying Mass; several dozen mourners are killed and hundreds injured in an attack days later. Dozens of Roman Catholic clergy who are seen by the government as supporting the Sandinista rebels (who are seizing control in Nicaragua) are murdered in El Salvador during this period of civil unrest.

1980   In the Soviet Union, Religious dissidents from the Baptist, Pentecostal, and Russian Orthodox churches are arrested or exiled to prevent the government from being embarrassed by protests staged during the Olympic Games, which are being held in Moscow.

1980   China establishes the China Christian Council to control the distribution of the Bible.

1980   As part of the new tolerance toward religion in China, the Potala Palace in Lhasa, Tibet, the home of the Dalai Lama, who remains in exile in India, is reopened, and Buddhists are again allowed to conduct pilgrimages to shrines and sites in Tibet.

1980   *Creation / Evolution*, a scientific journal founded to refute the scientific credibility of creation science or creationism, begins publication in the United States.

1980   The U.S. Supreme Court in *Stone v. Graham* rules that it is a violation of the First Amendment to the Constitution for the Ten Commandments to be posted in public classrooms.

1981   The African Charter on Human and People's Rights is adopted and in 1986 is put in force after ratification by member nations of the Organization of African Unity. The charter calls for religious freedom throughout Africa.

1981   In *Widmar v. Vincent*, the U.S. Supreme Court for the first time clearly sets forth the equal-treatment principle, whereby religious organizations may use public facilities on the same terms as nonreligious organizations.

1981	The General Assembly of the United Nations adopts the Declaration on the Elimination of All Forms of Intolerance and of Discrimination Based on Religion or Belief.
1981	The Universal Islamic Declaration of Human Rights is adopted by Islamic nations. The declaration is similar to the United Nations declaration of 1948 but is based on Islamic law as found in the Qur'an and *shari'a*.
1981–1983	Vietnam establishes state-controlled religious organizations for Buddhism, Catholicism, Protestantism, and other religions.
1982	Acting in violation of U.S. immigration law, more than 200 U.S. churches, Protestant and Catholic, help Salvadorans escape the conflict in their country and provide them shelter. In 1985, the government places on trial 12 individuals, including a nun, two priests, and two ministers involved in the movement; 8 of the accused are convicted in the trial in Arizona.
1982	U.S. president Ronald Reagan supports an amendment to the Constitution calling for prayer in public schools. Such prayer was ruled unconstitutional by the Supreme Court in 1963.
1982	A new constitution in Turkey provides for religious freedom and prohibits criticism of any religion. These measures relax the general prohibition on religion that began in 1924 when the government began to create a secular state.
1982	Under attack from individuals, organizations, and government agencies in Britain and the United States, Sun Myung Moon, founder of the Unification Church, is convicted of income-tax evasion and serves 13 months in prison. Critics charge that followers are brainwashed, followers do not identify themselves as belonging to the church when collecting money, and that too much money is invested in business enterprises; the government action is criticized by leaders of other religions and denominations who view it as an assault on the freedom of religion.
1982	In China, the Central Committee of the Chinese Communist Party issues a new policy on religion. It allows for the restoration of churches, temples, and other religious buildings but also makes clear that religion must be kept separate from politics, education, and marriage and family life.
1983	In Ireland, voters support a constitutional referendum to make abortion illegal. The ban is supported by Roman Catholics but criticized by Protestants and Jews.
1983	China relaxes its controls on the practice of Islam and begins distributing copies of the Qur'an. In the same year, the Institute of Islamic Theology is allowed to reopen in Beijing.
1983	Morocco confines the practice of the Baha'i religion to private worship.
1983	In Great Britain, the Sikhs are designated as an ethnic group and therefore are entitled to protection under the Race Relations Act. The classification determines that the Sikhs share a unique

history and an independent status that make them more than a religion.

1983   Bob Jones University, a fundamentalist Christian university in Greenville, South Carolina, loses its tax-exempt status as a religious organization, the first institution of higher learning in the United States to do so. A U.S. Supreme Court ruling in *Bob Jones v. United States* views the university's policy of prohibiting dating between white and African-American students as discriminatory and therefore revokes its tax-exempt status.

1983   In *Marsh v. Chambers* the U.S. Supreme Court rules that it is constitutional for legislative bodies to retain and pay chaplains.

1984   Desmond Tutu, the Anglican archbishop of Cape Town, South Africa, becomes the first Anglican minister to win the Nobel Prize for Peace, awarded in recognition of his opposition to apartheid.

1984   In an effort to quash the Sikh separatist militancy, India imposes direct rule in the Punjab, and the Indian army attacks militants at the Golden Temple in Amritsar in the Punjab, desecrating the sacred Sikh site; in retaliation, the Sikh bodyguards of Prime Minister Indira Gandhi assassinate her, setting off widespread Hindu-Sikh riots in the Punjab and in Delhi, with almost 3,000 Sikhs killed in revenge for the assassination. The fighting initiates a decade of violence involving Sikh separatists and the Indian army.

1984   The Equal Access Act passed by the U.S. Congress allows students to hold prayer groups in public schools and public colleges and universities; critics view the law as a violation of the constitutional principle of separation of church and state. In 1990 in *Board of Education of the Westside Community Schools v. Mergens*, the U.S. Supreme Court upholds the constitutionality of the Equal Access Act.

1984   The Malaysian Consultative Council of Buddhism, Christianity, Hinduism, and Sikhism is founded in Malaysia to address discrimination against non-Muslims.

1984   The new constitution of Norway establishes the Evangelical Lutheran religion as the state religion, but provides freedom of religion for other religions and state support for established religious organizations.

1985   In an attempt to appease Muslim fundamentalists, Egypt revises family law to make it more compatible with Islamic law. The government repeals laws governing divorce and child custody that were at odds with *shari'a* (Islamic law).

1985   A court in Denmark rules that the Church of Scientology is a profit-making entity and must pay taxes. In the following year, leaders of the European and African offices of the church, located in Copenhagen, are expelled from Denmark.

1985   Japan's Prime Minister Nakasone Yasuhiro and his cabinet lead the government's first official postwar tribute at the Yasukuni

Shinto Shrine in Tokyo on the anniversary of Japan's surrender in World War II. This raises a storm of protest from Japan's former colonies in Asia, who see Yasukuni as a symbol of Japan's aggression, militarism, and glorification of war; shocked by the international outcry, led by China, Nakasone suspends all future official tributes, as does the succeeding government.

1985   The U.S. Supreme Court rules, in *Wallace v. Jaffree*, that an Alabama law requiring a one-minute period of silence in all public schools "for meditation or voluntary prayer" is unconstitutional. The Court decides that the law violates the First Amendment because it hampers the individual's right to choose either any religious faith or none at all.

1985   The Human Rights Act prohibiting religious discrimination is passed in Canada.

1985   A law permitting the sale of contraceptives is enacted in Ireland. The sale of contraceptives has been banned or controlled since 1935 in accord with the wishes of the majority Roman Catholic population.

1986   The new constitution of Greece establishes the Eastern Orthodox Church of Greece as the country's "prevailing" religion (about 98 percent of Greeks are Greek Orthodox), with limited religious freedom granted to other religions. The constitution, however, weakens the ties between church and state.

1986   As part of Mikhail Gorbachev's new policy of *glasnost* (openness) in the Soviet Union, some restrictions on worship and the organization of religion are ended.

1987   The U.S. Supreme Court, in *Edwards v. Aguillard*, rules that requiring the teaching of creationism alongside evolution in schools is a form of religious advocacy and therefore unconstitutional under the First Amendment. The decision is a setback for advocates of creationism and creation science.

1987   The new constitution of the Philippines creates an absolute separation of church and state and grants religious freedom for all, including the freedom to have no beliefs at all.

1988   The constitution of Bangladesh is amended to make Islam the state religion. Opposition parties protest the decision, and a general strike paralyzes Dhaka, the capital.

1988   In the United States, the Williamsburg Charter is published as a celebration and reaffirmation of the First Amendment religious liberty clauses of the U.S. Constitution.

1988   The Oregon Supreme Court rules that the use of peyote, a mildly hallucinogenic drug, by members of the Native American Church is a religious activity protected by the First Amendment to the U.S. Constitution.

1988   A new constitution in Brazil creates a separation between church and state, reflecting the reality that the Roman Catholic Church is no longer dominant in national life. Many Brazilians now adhere to numerous Protestant denominations, African-Brazilian religions, and other beliefs.

1988   In Great Britain, the Education Reform Act requires that religious education in public schools reflect the Christian nature of British society and that prayers be Christian ones.

1989   Tenzin Gyatso, the Dalai Lama, the highest-ranking official in Tibetan Buddhism, is awarded the Nobel Prize for Peace, in recognition of his leadership of the nonviolent protest against Communist Chinese control of Tibet and repression of Buddhism. Despite his decades-long campaign condemning the Chinese occupation of Tibet, and despite gaining great respect, as well as a large following of Westerners, for his sanctity, his mission receives little support from the world's governments.

1989   After the overthrow of Communism in Romania, the new government ends the ban on the Uniate Church (Eastern Orthodox in liturgy but subject to the dictates of the pope) dating to 1948. However, local discrimination against church members continues in some places, and the issue of the return of confiscated church property that had been given to the Eastern Orthodox Church remains unresolved.

1989   Ayatollah Ruhollah Khomeini, the ruler of Iran, issues a *fatwa* (legal ruling) calling for the death of Salman Rushdie, an Indian Muslim and author of the novel *The Satanic Verses*, which was published in Great Britain; many Muslims considered passages of the book blasphemous to Islam. Rushdie goes into hiding; the ruling is lifted by the Iranian government in 1998.

1989   In post-Communist Bulgaria, the government attempts to control the Turkish Muslim minority of about 1 million people and to assimilate them into the Eastern Orthodox population by banning various Muslim practices and attempting to force Turks to take Bulgarian names.

1989   Restrictions on Jehovah's Witnesses in eastern Europe and Africa are lifted.

1989   After a successful coup by Islamic fundamentalists in Sudan, the country establishes *shari'a* (Islamic law) as the law of the nation and begins persecuting non-Muslims, including Roman Catholics and Coptic Christians (Christianity developed in Egypt).

1989   The so-called *hijab* case in France concerning three Muslim girls, who were expelled from public school for wearing a veil in accord with Islamic practice, leads to administrative and judicial rulings that in 1994 result in local school authorities being given the power to determine whether religious symbols can be worn in school.

1989–1990   The new democratic government of Hungary eases restrictions on religion that were in place under the Communist government since 1949.

1990   The U.S. Supreme Court decides, in *Employment Division v. Smith*, that the free-exercise clause of the First Amendment to the Constitution does not provide protection from religion-neutral application of criminal law. The case involves an Indian in Oregon who was fired from his job for using peyote for religious purposes and was then denied unemployment compensation; the ruling reinforces a similar ruling in 1988 and allows local law-enforcement officers to prosecute members of the Native American Church for using peyote.

1990	After the departure of the Vietnamese occupiers of Cambodia, Premier Hun Sen declares Buddhism the state religion. In the same year, there is a revival of Buddhism, which was repressed by Communist rulers, in Laos and Mongolia.
1990	With the end of Communist rule in Eastern Europe and the easing of restrictions on religion, the Vatican establishes ties with Czechoslovakia, Romania, and Hungary and begins discussions with the Russian Orthodox Church over control of religious property in Russia.
1990	During the Gulf War, Saudi Arabia alters its traditional policy and permits the stationing of troops from the United States and other nations on its soil but requires them to moderate their dress and public behavior so as not to insult Saudi morality. Senior Saudi religious scholars criticize the move.
1990	The Front Islamique du Salut (FIS, or Islamic Salvation Front), the first Islamic political party to win major election victories in modern Algeria, is victorious in local and parliamentary elections. However the existing government refuses to leave office, as it objects to the FIS's agenda of creating an Islamic state.
1990	The Renaissance Party is founded by Muslims to help revive Islam in the former Soviet republics. One of many such parties that emerge after the collapse of the Soviet Union, the party includes members from the central Asian republics, the Caucasus, Russia, and Siberia.
1990	The Gayssot Law prohibits the publication of literature denying the Holocaust, the first such law passed in France.
1990	The U.S. Native American Grave Protection and Repatriation Act protects Indian burial grounds and graves and requires that all organizations supported by federal funding inventory American Indian materials in their collections and return Indian skeletal material and artifacts of cultural significance to the appropriate tribes.
1990	Egypt bans the practice of the Baha'i religion and confiscates all Baha'i assets. Baha'i is seen by many Muslims as an insult to Islam.
1990	The Law on Freedom of Conscience adopted in the Russian Federation provides for religious freedom and ends the restrictions on religion instituted during the Communist era in the Soviet Union.
1991	Melayu Islam Beraja (Malay Islamic Monarchy), the government-supported religious ideology in Brunei, a sultanate in

Southeast Asia, results in the strengthening of traditional Islamic values.

1991   Oregon is the first state in the United States to legalize the religious use of peyote by American Indians.

1991   The Places of Worship Act enacted in India protects shrines, churches, mosques, and temples that were places of worship when India achieved independence in 1947. The act is meant to diffuse conflict between Hindus and Muslims over thousands of Muslim mosques that Hindus claim were built centuries ago on sites previously occupied by Hindu temples.

1991   Cuba eases restrictions on religious worship that it had instituted as part of a policy of atheism in 1961. Under the new policy, nonatheists are allowed to join the Communist Party.

1992   The High Court of Ireland, in the so-called X case, rules that a mother may travel to another country to have an abortion if there is a grave threat to her life. The decision weakens the ban on abortion and causes much controversy among the majority–Roman Catholic population.

1992   Cuba begins to tolerate the open expression of religion among adherents of the two major religions—Roman Catholicism and Santeria (incorporate elements of African Yoruba deities and Roman Catholic ritual)—as well as among Baptists, Presbyterians, and the small community of Jews. Nonetheless, religious organizations and activities are monitored and controlled by the government.

1992   The 1917 constitution of Mexico is revised and new laws enacted to remove some earlier restrictions on religion that were aimed at the Roman Catholic Church. The new laws give religious organizations legal standing, allow religious schools, and make it possible for religious organizations to own property.

1992   The new constitution of Vietnam grants increased freedom of religion, but religious activity is still largely controlled by the government.

1993   Because of critics who fear the growth of "foreign" religions in Russia, the 1990 Law on Freedom of Conscience is amended to control the activities of Pentecostal and other religious organizations. The government also abolishes the Council for Religious Affairs, which regulated religion in the Soviet Union; in some republics, it is replaced by other agencies or offices that continue to administer religious matters.

1993   The constitution of Chile is revised to guarantee cultural and religious freedom to Native Americans. The new law also protects ancient religious sites.

1993   The U.S. Supreme Court finds unconstitutional laws that ban animal sacrifice for religious purposes. The Court rules that such laws discriminate against the free exercise of religion, a decision especially relevant for the Santeria religion, which requires sacrifices of animals such as chickens and goats, which are eaten after their ritual use.

1993   The U.S. Religious Freedom Restoration Act requiring government agencies to provide a compelling reason to restrict any form of religious practice is passed by Congress in reaction to the 1990 *Employment Division v. Smith* Supreme Court ruling that dealt with peyote use. In June 1997 the Supreme Court rules that the act is unconstitutional.

1993   Albania enacts a Charter of Rights granting religious freedom. The charter ends Albania's status as the only officially atheistic state in the world.

1993   The European Court of Human Rights rules in the Kokkinakis case that Greece's prosecution of a Jehovah's Witness for proselytizing is not in accord with the freedom of religion guaranteed by the European Convention on Human Rights. The court, however, does not rule on the legitimacy of Greek laws banning proselytizing in general.

1993   The Committee for the Salvation of Youth is formed by parents in the Russian Federation who are concerned about the influence of the Japanese Aum Shrinrikyo (Supreme Truth) cult on their children; founded in Japan in 1989 by Shoko Asahara, the cult preaches that it will take over the world. The committee later turns its attention to other religious groups such as the Baptists and Jehovah's Witnesses.

1994   In China, the government issues a new policy on religion. Registration is required for the establishment of a venue for religious activities, giving the government control over all religious activity.

1994   Taslima Nasrin, a feminist writer, is charged by a court in Bangladesh with offending the Muslim faith and is threatened with death by Islamic militants. Nasrin goes into exile in Sweden but returns to Bangladesh in 1999 to care for her sick mother.

1995   The Welfare Party is the first Islamic political party to win a general election in modern Turkey when it wins the general election for seats in the legislature. The party is considered by many to represent the interests of Islamic fundamentalism, but it also advocates reforms to assist poor people; after forming a coalition government with a small secular party, it is prevented from taking power by the existing secular government, backed by the military.

1995   The Religious Corporation Revision Act enacted in Japan gives the government greater power to investigate and collect information about religious groups. The act is criticized by some as interfering with the freedom of religious expression.

1995   In *Rosenberg v. Rector and Visitors of University of Virginia*, the U.S. Supreme Court supports the free speech of university students expressing religious beliefs.

1995   The Internal Revenue Service revokes the tax-exempt status of the Church of Pierce Creek in Conklin, New York, because it engaged in prohibited political activity when it placed newspaper advertisements urging people not to vote for Bill Clinton for president.

1995–1996 When the Taliban seize control of much of Afghanistan, fundamental Islamic beliefs become the law of the land. Although the Taliban enforce internal peace, they place severe restrictions on women, make Islamic worship compulsory, and severely punish crimes.

1996 The Roman Catholic Church in Argentina asks for forgiveness for its role in the "dirty war" of 1976–83, when the military dictatorship repressed, tortured, and killed political opponents, at times with the assistance or acquiescence of the Church.

1996 The Bharatiya Janata Party, a Hindu nationalist party, wins more seats than the secular Congress Party or any other party in the parliamentary election in India.

1996 Representatives of the Islamic community in the United States are invited to the White House to mark the end of Ramadan, the Muslim holy month.

1996 A controversy erupts over how the Swiss government and Swiss banks handled money and other assets seized from Jews and deposited there by Nazi Germany during World War II; Jewish organizations and others also question the handling of money deposited in Swiss banks by Jews who died in the Holocaust. The issue is largely resolved in 1998 when several Swiss banks agree to pay $1.2 billion to survivors of the Holocaust or their descendants as compensation for money kept in Swiss bank accounts during and after World War II.

1996 The new constitution of South Africa deletes the language of earlier constitutions that implied that the country was a Christian nation.

1997 In a landmark case, a Japanese court rejects the argument of the defendants, former Ehime prefecture officials, that donations to Shinto shrines provide moral support to bereaved families and are a form of social courtesy rather than government support of religion. The ruling makes government donations to Shinto shrines illegal under the constitutional separation of church and state.

1998 In India, Hindus attack Christians (Roman Catholics and Protestants), destroying churches and raping nuns. Christians in Jakarta, Indonesia, are attacked by mobs of Javanese Muslims who destroy churches, kill 18 people, and injure dozens of others; other such attacks take place in 1999.

1998 An official report commissioned by the parliament of Germany concludes that Scientology is not a religion but a political movement with profit-making motives. The report allows the government to continue monitoring the organization, which government officials have previously accused of being totalitarian and of brainwashing its members.

1998	The first religious organization in San Francisco to refuse to provide benefits to same-sex couples, the Salvation Army gives up city funding, cuts its staff, and refuses to cooperate with a new law requiring publicly funded organizations to provide benefits to same-sex couples or unmarried partners. Salvation Army officials view the law as inconsistent with their religious beliefs, which stress the sanctity of the nuclear family.
1998	The Wisconsin Supreme Court rules that using school vouchers, which are supported by tax monies, to pay tuition in religious schools is constitutional and does not represent a violation of the separation-of-church-and-state principle. The U.S. Supreme Court refuses to hear the case on appeal, and other states are thereby encouraged to enact similar legislation.
1998	After complex negotiations involving several countries and with George Mitchell, a former U.S. senator, aiding the discussions, Roman Catholics and Protestants reach a peace agreement to end the fighting in Northern Ireland. Signed by the Republic of Ireland, Great Britain, and the political parties of Northern Ireland, and endorsed in a referendum by voters throughout Ireland, the agreement affords Northern Ireland much independence, with internal government, administrative links to Ireland, and continuing ties to Great Britain. One aspect of the long-standing conflict sprang from disagreements between Roman Catholics, most of whom had sought independence from Great Britain and unification with Ireland, and Protestants, most of whom wanted to remain part of Great Britain.
1998	A law passed in the United States calls for withholding aid and support from nations that persecute religious minorities; the bill is aimed at nations such as China, Pakistan, Sudan, and Indonesia and is in reaction to complaints about persecution of Christians in these nations. Opponents claim that the bill would not end religious persecution and instead would cause harm to the peoples of these and other nations; the law is supported by the Christian Coalition and some other religious organizations and opposed by many human rights organizations.
1998	An Islamic school funded by the government opens in Great Britain, in addition to 7,000 Christian and 24 Jewish government-funded schools. All are required to teach the national curriculum but are also allowed to teach their own religions.
1998	The Campus Freethought Alliance sets forth a Bill of Rights for Unbelievers in the United States, which states that unbelievers should have the right to express their thoughts freely, not to be discriminated against, and to abstain from oath taking.
1998	In France, the government establishes the Mission interministérielle de contre lutte les sectes (Interministerial commission to make war on the sects) to monitor religious sects.
2000	The American Center for Law and Justice appeals to the Minnesota Court of Appeals in Minneapolis in the case of a state court's dismissing a suit on behalf of a high school biology teacher

barred from teaching biology because he criticized Darwin's theory of evolution. The American Center, a public-interest law firm, states that the teacher wanted students to make up their own minds about evolution, but the school board disagreed with his approach and censored him.

2000   The U.S. Commission on International Religious Freedom, a federally constituted panel, asks the United States not to give China expanded trade privileges because of the government's persecution of religious groups. According to the commission, the rate of religious persecutions in China rose in 1999, when Catholics, Protestants, Tibetan Buddhists, and members of the Falun Gong movement were targets of government discrimination.

2000   The Uganda Human Rights Commission reports that some 500 people are burned to death in southern Uganda, by an apocalyptic cult called the Movement for the Restoration of the 10 Commandments of God. Many other violations have been attributed to the cult, which claims to be preparing people to go to heaven.

2000   In Sweden, the government and the Lutheran Church of Sweden sever most of their legal ties.

2001   The pope publicly recognizes the errors committed by the Roman Catholic Church in China. It is expected that this public acknowledgment will improve the relationship between the Vatican and China.

2002   The U.S. Supreme Court finds, in *Zelman et al. v. Simmons-Harris*, that an Ohio school-voucher program that includes an option for religious schooling conforms to First Amendment requirements. The decision reverses a federal appeals-court ruling that invalidated Cleveland's voucher program; Justice David Souter criticizes the Supreme Court decision as a "dramatic departure from basic establishment clause principle."

2002   The U.S. Ninth Circuit Court of Appeals rules that the phrase "under God" in the Pledge of Allegiance, along with the daily recitation of the pledge in school, violates the First Amendment clause prohibiting the establishment of a state religion.

2002   The U.S. Ninth Circuit Court of Appeals rules that the state of Washington is guilty of religious discrimination when it withheld a scholarship from a college student who was pursuing a theology degree. Although a Washington State law bars scholarships to students pursuing theology degrees and the Washington Higher Education Coordinating Board agreed, Judge Rymer of the circuit court finds that the law discriminates against religious ideas because it is viewpoint-based and the viewpoint is based on religion.

2002   The Equal Employment Opportunity Commission warns the National Education Association that it must stop violating the rights of teachers who object to paying union dues on religious grounds. Under Title VII of the 1964 Civil Rights Act, union members may donate their dues to charity if for religious reasons they object to their union's position or choice of charities.

2002   The U.S. Ninth Circuit Court of Appeals dismisses the case of *Warren v. Commissioner of Internal Revenue*, after previously announcing that it would consider whether the housing exemption for clergy, who can deduct from federal taxes a part of their income used for housing, is constitutional. To prevent the court's challenge, the U.S. Congress passes a bill protecting the housing allowance by amending the Internal Revenue Code to state that the housing exemption cannot exceed the "fair rental value" of a house, including furnishings.

2002   A U.S. federal judge rules that the Ten Commandments may remain on display in three Kentucky counties. The American Civil Liberties Union sued the counties, whose case was supported by Christian-based civil-liberties groups.

2002   In central Sulawesi, Indonesia, five people are killed and houses are looted and burned when attackers, said to be Islamic-extremist Laskar Jihad fighters armed with automatic weapons, storm three Christian villages. The Indonesian government has not attempted to disarm the attackers, who are thought to be trying to destroy all Christians in central Sulawesi.

2002   A Colorado family asks the American Civil Liberties Union of Colorado to help end religious exercises in a Kiowa County, Colorado, public school, including a school-sponsored prayer at the school's graduation ceremony.

2002   About 800 people, largely Muslims, are killed in rioting in India in Gujarat state. After a Muslim mob set fire to a train of Hindus, the Hindus attack and kill Muslims and destroy their homes and businesses in one of the worst religious riots in recent times.

2002   The Supreme Court of India decides not to allow Hindu nationalists to hold a religious ceremony in Ayodhya, where Hindu nationalists destroyed a Muslim mosque in 1992.

2002   A lesbian counselor and a Jewish psychotherapist, who were denied the right to work in the United Methodist Children's Home in Decatur, Georgia, for religious reasons, along with other taxpayers in Georgia, sue the United Methodist Home, charging it with discrimination and imposing religious beliefs on young people. The home obtains 40 percent of its funding from the state of Georgia but hires only Christians to work there.

2002   Members of the American Catholic movement Voice of the Faithful are prohibited from holding meetings in Church facilities. The group, founded in Boston in reaction to revelations of the sexual abuse of children by priests, is composed of lay Catholics who seek an increased role in the church, as well as reform among the clergy and the church hierarchy, which they say knowingly covered up priests' transgressions and allowed offenders to continue serving the Church. The organization, which claims to be centrist, is accused of undermining Church authority.

CHAPTER FOUR

WOMEN'S RIGHTS

2640 B.C.E.	The wife of the emperor of China pioneers the development of silk manufacture.
c. 2300 B.C.E.	Writing her verses in cuneiform on clay tablets, the first known woman poet is Enheduanna, daughter of King Sargon. As high priestess of the temple of the moon god at Ur in southern Mesopotamia (modern Iraq), she addresses her poems to the gods.
1850 B.C.E.	The earliest known mention of ways of averting pregnancy occurs in the Petrie Papyrus in Egypt. In addition to describing a tampon-like device made of shredded linen and powder from crushed branches of acacia, the Petrie Papyrus mentions coitus interruptus, coitus obstructus (by applying pressure on the base of the uterus, semen is forced into the bladder), and inserting into the vagina a mix of crocodile dung and honey before intercourse.
c. 1792–1750 B.C.E.	Babylonian women enjoy protection under the Law Code instituted by King Hammurabi of Babylon in Mesopotamia (modern Iraq). Men who wish to divorce their wives must provide them with financial compensation, generally but not always repaying the wealth the woman had brought to the marriage, and the wives of prisoners of war are granted the right to take a lover if there is "not sufficient to live on in his house." On the other hand, mother-son incest is punished by burning both to death.
1500s–1100s B.C.E.	A law requiring a woman to wear a veil unless she is a prostitute is promulgated in the Middle Assyrian period in Assyria (modern northern Iraq). During this repressive time, Assyrian women are subject first to their fathers, then to their husbands and fathers-in-law, and then to their sons; a woman who oversteps her rights can be expelled naked from the house by her sons.
c. 612 B.C.E.	Sappho is born on the Aegean island of Lesbos. Although women are second-class citizens in ancient Greece, she will achieve recognition and lasting fame as a lyric poet.
c. 550 B.C.E.	The first known occasion of a woman practicing law occurs in Babylonia when a woman successfully argues a case.
400s B.C.E.	A medical treatise in the Hippocratic Collection traditionally associated with the Greek physician Hippocrates (though he was probably the author of only a few of these treatises) includes a pledge not to cause an abortion by giving a woman a pessary (vaginal suppository).

c. 400 B.C.E.	The first woman known to administer an academy of natural philosophy, Arete of Cyrene in North Africa, assumes leadership of the academy on the death of her father, Aristippus, and teaches philosophy to more than 100 students.
c. 400 B.C.E.	The law of *epikleroi*, granting women legal control of their property, is established in Athens, Greece. This right is given to women at the age of 14 years, the age at which many girls marry.
18 B.C.E.	The Roman emperor Augustus introduces marriage laws, including the *Lex Julia de adulteriis* (Law restraining adultery), which establishes that a wife's adultery is both a public and private crime. Convicted wives may be subject to banishment or even killing (under the law, Augustus is forced to banish his own daughter, Julia), but women cannot prosecute an adulterous husband.
60 C.E.	King Prasutagus of Iceni in ancient Britain dies and wills his wife Boudica (or Boadicea) and their two daughters half of his kingdom, leaving the other half to the Roman Empire. Since women cannot inherit under Roman law, the Roman administrator ignores the will and takes over the entire kingdom. According to the Roman historian Tacitus, after Boudica is flogged and her daughters raped during the plundering of the kingdom that followed, Boudica leads a rebellion against the empire. Despite early victories, Boudica's Iceni tribe, which joined forces with the Trinobantes tribe, is defeated in 62 c.e., at which time she and her daughters poison themselves to escape capture by the Romans.
c. 62	The apostle Paul writes (1 Cor. 11.8–10, New English Bible): "For man did not originally spring from woman, but woman was made out of man; and man was not created for woman's sake, but woman for the sake of man."
102	A Greek biographer working in Rome, Plutarch describes German barbarian women fighting alongside their men against the Roman legions. The barbarian women fight with swords and axes as fiercely as the men and fall "upon their opponents uttering a hideous outcry."
200	Roman marriage and family law is reformed with the acceptance of descent through the female line. Additionally, marriage with *manus*, the transfer of a woman directly from the control of the father to the husband, shifts to marriage without *manus*, where the woman gains more control over her affairs as she becomes a mother and grows older.
300–309	Eighty-one canons promulgated at the Council of Elvira of the Synod of the Roman Catholic Church, held near Grenada in Spain, include 22 canons that focus on women and deal with adultery, fornication, divorce, abortion, prostitution, and premarital sex. The canons take a markedly punitive approach to female sexual behavior.
c. 370–415	Hypatia, daughter of Theon, a Greek mathematician and astronomer, lectures on science and philosophy in Alexandria, Egypt.

Inventor of the astrolabe, an instrument used to calculate the positions of the heavenly bodies, Hypatia is murdered by a Christian mob that accuses her of being a pagan.

c. 500 The *Lex Burgundionum* or *Lex Gundobada*, the law code instituted by Gundobad, king of the Germanic Burgundians in Europe, gives the husband the property of a woman whom he marries but establishes that a mother's claim to guardianship of her children takes precedence over other claims. At about the same time, the legal code of the Visigoths, another Germanic tribe in Europe, grants widows guardianship of their sons.

507–511 The *Lex Salica* (Salic law), the penal and civil code of the Salic Franks who conquered Gaul in the fifth century, states that women cannot inherit land. The law is later extended to stop women from acceding to the throne, and in 1337 it is used to deny the French crown to King Edward III of England, whose mother is a daughter of the French king Philip IV; the Hundred Years War ensues as a result.

533 Having at first played an important role in administration and in performing both liturgical and catechetic functions in the early Christian Church, women are now excluded from the Church hierarchy by the Germanic kingdoms of medieval Europe. Only with the establishment of the first nunnery in the eastern section of the Carolingian Empire in 733–37 do women once again participate in active service in the Church.

600 An Anglo-Saxon law setting prices on women is instituted in Great Britain: 50 shillings for sex with a woman under the king's charge; 12 shillings if the woman comes from the lower classes. Marriage laws call for specific payments to purchase a maiden, and there are financial penalties for kidnapping or raping women.

c. 650 The Qur'an, the sacred text of Islam, states that men are superior to women. Men may keep as many as four wives and may divorce a wife by appearing before a judge and stating three times: "I divorce thee."

720 Introduced in the Byzantine Empire (eastern Roman Empire) by Emperor Leo III, the *Ecloga* (law code, written in Greek) states that marriage requires the consent of both husband and wife and that a widow must be granted custody of the children and receive her dowry and prenuptial gifts.

733–735 The Roman *Lex Julia* is reformed, and some of the penalties directed against celibates and women without children are removed, but divorce is almost impossible.

743 The Council of Leptines, called by the Roman Catholic Church and held in Leptines (now Lessines, near Ath in modern Belgium), repudiates the notion that women are controlled by infernal nocturnal powers. The council also condemns the superstition popular during the early Middle Ages in Europe that the menstrual cycle is evidence that women are agents of cosmic spirits bent on capturing the hearts of men; nevertheless, women

	are blamed for many of the evils of medieval life.

780　In Great Britain, Saxon law requires that after a husband's death his minor children be raised by his male relatives, not the children's mother.

785　The notion that women can voluntarily assume magical powers and join the legions of the Devil is repudiated at the Roman Catholic Synod of Paderborn in Germany. The synod also establishes the death penalty for burning a woman on the grounds that she is a witch.

c. 800　The *jus primae noctis* (law of the first night), granting lords the right to rape the brides of their retainers and serfs, is promulgated by the Scottish ruler Ewen III. According to this custom (also known as *droit du seigneur*, or the lord's right), a man who has sex with his wife before the lord does so is subject to penalty.

841　Judith of Bavaria, wife of Louis the Pious, king of France and Germany and emperor of the West, is the first woman to assume leadership of a medieval European army during the years of the Germanic kingdoms. Although female members of Germanic royal families often exert tremendous power, ordinary women are not so favored; adultery is punished by death, and marriage can occur by capture, purchase, or mutual consent.

1003–1035　The Anglo-Saxon Code of Canute of Denmark, king of England and Denmark, states that a woman found guilty of adultery must have her nose and ears cut off.

c. 1010　Shibuku Murasaki, a lady of the imperial Japanese court, writes *Genji Monogatari* (The tale of Genji), considered the world's first full novel. It focuses on the handsome, aristocratic Prince Genji and the various women in his life and provides a richly detailed picture of the court as well as glimpses of town and countryside. The daughter of a scholar, Murasaki also writes poetry and keeps an important diary.

1193　Licensed prostitution is established in Japan.

1206　A religious movement, the Beguine, arises in the Netherlands, Switzerland, the Rhineland, and northern France. Philanthropic organizations of laywomen agree to practice celibacy, remain poor, engage in manual labor, and worship together in self-governing communities.

1215　The Magna Carta, a charter of freedoms that English barons force King John to agree to at Runnymede in Great Britain, gives widows the right to inherit and remarry, or not to remarry if they choose.

1234　As the Albigensian Crusade (against heretics in southern France) spreads, women take up arms in France to help resist the arrest of female heretics. Calling for men to aid them as the Catholic Inquisition attempts to enforce its decision forbidding laypersons to read the Bible, the women are finally defeated in 1243 when some 200 male and female resisters are burned to death.

1240	Raziya, the daughter of the Delhi sultan Iltutmish in India, is named head of the Muslim state when she succeeds her father.
1242	Il statuto Veneto, or Il statuto Giacomo Tiepolo (Statute of the Veneto, a district in Italy, or Statute of Giacomo Tiepelo), stipulates that a wife maintains control of the capital of her dowry unless she is unfaithful and that her husband must provide an account of how he uses any of the funds. A widow retains her husband's patrimony until she remarries or dies.
1347	Jane I, the countess of Provence, a region in southern France, allows a brothel to be licensed in the city of Avignon. The countess orders the women to be examined weekly; those who have contracted a sexual disease may no longer work for fear of making the customers sick.
c. 1387–1400	In *The Canterbury Tales*, the English poet Geoffrey Chaucer creates the Wife of Bath, a character who argues with memorable vehemence against the medieval doctrines of virginity and wifely subservience.
1405	*The Book of the City of the Ladies*, defending women's rights and abilities, is written by Christine de Pisan, a French poet and writer. Christine writes that, because women have more understanding than men, women's intelligence should be developed by educating them in the same areas of arts and science that men study.
1429	Hearing voices telling her that France can be saved by a virgin, Jeanne d'Arc (Joan of Arc), a 17-year-old shepherd, leads a French army against the British. Dressed as a male warrior, she liberates Orléans, is then captured and tried in an ecclesiastical court, is found guilty of heresy and witchcraft, and is burned at the stake in 1431; in 1456, however, the results of the trial are overthrown, and she is canonized a saint in 1920.
1484	*Summis Desiderantes Affectibus*, the papal bull of Pope Innocent VIII, declares that harsh measures will be taken against German "witches." Witches were often merely midwives who threatened the domain of male physicians, but the papal bull fuels hysteria about witchcraft.
c. 1486	In the wake of his bull condemning the spread of witchcraft in Germany, Pope Innocent VIII authorizes two Dominican scholars, Heinrich Krämer and Johann Sprenger, the latter an inquisitor in the Tirol region of Austria, to eradicate the unholy practices. The two men publish *Malleus maleficarum* (Witches' hammer), describing the vile nature and acts of witches and the legal procedures for trying them; translated into many languages, the *Malleus* becomes one of the most popular and widely read books in Europe.
1529	*On the Nobility and Excellence of Women* is published by Cornelius Heinrich Agrippa von Nettesheim, a German physician and philosopher. Agrippa argues that women have the same soul, spirit, and sense of reason as men and that a difference in sex does not justify different treatment.

1554	An officer of the Inquisition states that at least 30,000 "witches" had been burned in Europe during the past 150 years.
1589	On a single day in this year, more than 130 "witches" are burned in the town of Quedlenburg, Germany.
1603	Kabuki theater is established in Kyoto, Japan, with women playing all the roles, male and female. In 1629, however, Iemitsu, the Tokugawa shogun, declares it immoral for women to dance in public, and henceforth all roles in Kabuki are performed by men, as in the Elizabethan theater in Great Britain.
1609	The Englishwoman Mary Ward founds a religious community for women in France and later establishes similar communities in Prague, Rome, Naples, Vienna, and Cologne. The communities include schools for English boarding students as well as local girls.
1617	A local lord in Edo, Japan (Tokyo), is permitted to establish supervised brothels, the Yoshiwara brothels, if he agrees to maintain order. A census taken in 1689 counts 2,800 prostitutes at work in Edo's brothels.
1632	A manual of women's legal rights published in Great Britain states that a husband may beat his wife and that she has no redress. A woman's personal belongings—her money, furniture, and linens—become her husband's property on marriage, and he need not pass them on to her heirs.
1637	Anne Hutchinson is banished from the Massachusetts Bay Colony for promoting her personal theological opinions during prayer meetings held at her home. Although women are permitted to hold such gatherings in order to discuss Sabbath sermons, Puritan doctrine dictates that they may not express opinions independent of their husbands, as per I Timothy 2:12. For this reason, and because the Puritan magistrates deem many of Hutchinson's teachings heretical, she is banished in November after a trial of several months and is officially excommunicated in March of the following year.
1641	A wife-abuse law passed in the Massachusetts Bay Colony in America denies a husband the right to beat his wife except in self-defense.
1649	In Japan, the Tokugawa shogun promulgates a proclamation on women's rights, which declares that a farmer may divorce his wife if she does not get up early in the morning, collect hay to feed the livestock, work in the rice fields during the day, and make rope from rice straw in the evening. She must take good care of her husband and cannot drink too much tea or enjoy too much leisure time.
1650	The amendment of the existing law of the Massachusetts Bay Colony restricts the penalties for adultery. No longer a capital offense, adultery is now punished by whipping and by making the offender wear the scarlet letter *A* for life.
1650	The first published poet of America is Anne Dudley Bradstreet,

whose work The *Tenth Muse Lately Sprung Up in America* is published in London. Bradstreet's poetry conveys her belief that women have a right to education and self-expression.

c. 1655   The earliest known modern mention of a contraceptive device, a linen sheath employed to keep semen from the uterus, appears in *L'École des filles* (School for young ladies), a French book that scholars consider an early example of pornography. Michel Millot and Jean L'Ange, said to be the authors, serve short terms in prison for writing the book, which is sometimes attributed to the powerful Madame de Maintenon, Louis XIV's mistress and secret second wife.

1655   A law passed by Parliament in Great Britain gives magistrates the power to grant a divorce on the grounds of desertion, impotence, or adultery.

1660   Mary Dyer is hanged in the Massachusetts Bay Colony in America after being sentenced to death by Governor John Endicott for her religious views. An early supporter of Anne Hutchinson, who opposed the strict dogma of the Puritans, Mary Dyer become a Quaker and refused to submit to banishment laws.

1663   A law is passed in Maryland prohibiting British women from marrying slaves.

1670   *The Forc'd Marriage*, a play by Aphra Behn, is performed in London, and Behn becomes the first woman in Great Britain to support herself as a writer. Behn also writes novels, most famously *Oroonoko* (1688), in which she introduces the notion of the noble savage later elaborated by Jean-Jacques Rousseau.

1675   *Essay to Revive the Ancient Education of Gentlewomen in Religion, Manners, Arts, and Tongues: With an Answer to the Objections against This Way of Education* is published in Great Britain. The author is Basua Makin, the daughter of a Sussex rector, who served as tutor to the children of King Charles I.

1678   Daughter of a noble family in Venice, Italy, Elena Lucrezia Cornaro Piscopia is the first woman known to receive a university degree when she earns a doctorate in philosophy from the University of Padua. While the university rector was prepared to grant her a degree in theology, the subject she was most interested in, the Church intercedes and she is granted her degree in philosophy instead.

1686   A convent school for girls is founded in York, Great Britain.

1686   The Maison Royale de Saint-Louis (Royal House of Saint Louis), known as Saint-Cyr, is founded in Saint-Cyr, France, by Françoise d'Aubigné, Madame de Maintenon, the second, secret wife of King Louis XIV, as a school for young noblewomen from impecunious families. The king personally selects its 250 students based on their ancestry, lack of funds, and good health, and the girls study subjects that prepare them to be good wives and mothers.

1691   A law passed in Virginia declares that the children of a union between a white woman and a black man are illegitimate.

1692 At the very time that the belief in witchcraft is dying out in Europe, dozens of witchcraft trials take place in Salem, Massachusetts Bay Colony. By the end of the Salem witchcraft hysteria, 19 people accused of being witches have been hanged, and one has been crushed to death; the estates of the guilty women are seized by their accusers, and one judge, Samuel Sewall, later publicly confesses that his decisions were wrong.

Early 1700s *Onna Daigaku* (Great learning for women), a neo-Confucian guide for women written by the Japanese philosopher Ekiken Kaibara, establishes the ideal image of women in Japan as obedient, selfless, obsequious, and maternal. Kaibara writes that until marriage women must obey their fathers; after marriage, they must obey their husbands, and if her husband dies a woman must obey her eldest son.

1704 The Petticoat Rebellion, sometimes called the refusal of the cassette girls, occurs when a shipload of young French women arrive in Mobile, the Louisiana colonies, with their small trunks, or cassettes, and with dowries from the French king Louis XIV. After discovering the miserable circumstances of life in the Louisiana colonies, 25 women refuse to marry their intended husbands.

1704 Sarah Campbell Knight, a 38-year-old housewife and shopkeeper, travels alone on horseback from Boston to New York to settle the estate of a relative in New York. Her journal of the trip is published in 1865.

1715 *The Rudiments of Grammar*, a guide to English grammar, by Elizabeth Elstob, is published in Great Britain. Half of the 250 published copies are sold to women, even though most women at the time are unable to read.

1750 A group of wealthy British women, led by Elizabeth Montagu, introduce assemblies devoted to intellectual rather than frivolous social pursuits. Attendees, including men such as Samuel Johnson, Horace Walpole, and Sir Joshua Reynolds along with the women, dress simply; Mrs. Montagu and her women friends are said to wear blue stockings rather than the usual black silk, and thereafter the term *Bluestocking* refers to a literary woman, sometimes in a derogatory sense.

1753 The Hardwicke Marriage Act, passed by Parliament in Great Britain, requires parental consent for marriages and forbids marriages to be performed without proper licenses or the publication of the banns. It also bans common-law marriage, a legal form of marriage under Roman law.

1764 In the case of *Davey v. Turner*, the Pennsylvania Supreme Court rules that a wife must consent to her husband's sale of her property. Under the law, a wife, questioned by a justice of the peace, formally agrees to relinquish her dower rights to any sold or transferred property.

1765–1769 *The Commentaries on the Laws of England* by William Blackstone, a professor of law and a jurist, are published and become one of the cornerstones of British and American legal practice. In his chapter "Of Husband and Wife," Blackstone writes: "By marriage, the husband and wife are one person in law; that is, the very being or legal existence of the woman is suspended during the marriage . . . even the disabilities . . . the wife lies under are . . . intended for her protection and benefit. So great a favourite is the female sex of the laws of England."

1766 Written by the British clergyman James Fordyce, the *Sermons to Young Women* is published and becomes so popular that it goes through 14 editions during the next 50 years. Fordyce writes: "Men of the best sense have been usually adverse to the thought of marrying a witty female."

1774 Female Freemason lodges in France, each affiliated with a male lodge of the fraternal order of Freemasons, are officially recognized by the Grand Orient of France, and at the start of the French Revolution in 1789 they exist in every French city and most small towns. During the revolution, female Masons are persecuted along with their male counterparts, and membership in lodges ends until the Napoleonic years from 1795 on.

1776 The constitution of New Jersey grants women who hold property worth $250 the right to vote.

1776 During the American Revolution, the "Cult of True Womanhood," or the "cult of domesticity," is created to protect family values by claiming that women are best suited for homemaking and that four characteristics central to women's identity are piety, purity, domesticity, and submissiveness. The organization spreads to most industrializing nations in the 1820s and peaks in the 1890s.

1777 The constitution of New York removes voting rights from women, even those with property.

1779 Massachusetts adopts a constitution depriving women of their right to vote.

1780 The Ladies Association of Philadelphia is founded in Philadelphia, Pennsylvania, by Esther DeBerdt Reed, to organize women to help in the American Revolution. The women collect $300,000 and deliver linen shirts to soldiers.

1784 The state of New Hampshire adopts a constitution depriving women of their right to vote.

1787 The Philadelphia Young Ladies Association is founded in Philadelphia, Pennsylvania, to promote educational instruction for girls and young women.

1790 *Letters on Education*, by Catherine Macaulay, an English reformer, is published. The author argues that equal opportunity for education would bring intellectual equality for women.

1790 The Bluestocking Society is formed by a group of women in Great Britain to advocate publishing women's writings and to work for women's education.

1791	*Les droits de la femme* (The rights of women) is written in France by Olympe de Gouges. Urging that the rights introduced during the French Revolution be extended to apply to women, de Gouges demands equal treatment for women under the law: "Woman has the right to mount the scaffold; she must equally have the right to mount the rostrum."
1792	Published in London, *Vindication of the Rights of Women* by Mary Wollstonecraft gains fame as an attack on the conventions that oppress women. Her daughter, Mary, who marries the poet Percy Bysshe Shelley, writes *Frankenstein, or The Modern Prometheus* at the age of 21.
1793	The Société des Républicaines révolutionnaires (Society of revolutionary republicans) is established in France to advocate radical social reform, including political equality and the right of both men and women to play major roles in education and the family. While women members are at first supported by their male colleagues, the Jacobins (a radical political group created during the French Revolution), the national convention six months later refuses women the right to organize separately.
1793	Lucinda Foote is denied admission to Yale University in New Haven, Connecticut, on the basis of gender. Foote is informed that she is otherwise qualified.
1795	The Female Society of Philadelphia for the Relief and Employment of the Poor is established in Philadelphia, Pennsylvania, by Ann Parrish, a Quaker.
1797	The Society for the Relief of Poor Widows with Small Children is founded in New York City by Isabella Marshall Graham and other women, including Elizabeth Seton, who later becomes the first American-born saint in the Roman Catholic Church.
1801	The Female Association for the Relief of Women and Children in Reduced Circumstances is established in Philadelphia, Pennsylvania, by Rebecca Gratz, the 20-year-old daughter of a successful Philadelphia fur trader.
1802	Established by the Moravians (a Protestant denomination originating in Moravia and Bohemia), the Female Academy at Salem, North Carolina, has a curriculum including spelling, geography, arithmetic, writing, and music and admits students from many states. The academy does not receive an official charter until 1866.
1803	Parliament in Great Britain passes a statute making abortion before "quickening" a criminal act. "Quickening" refers to the time, approximated in the statute at four and a half months, when the pregnant woman first feels the fetus moving in her womb.
1804	The first-known woman jockey is Alicia Meynell, an English rider who enters a four-mile race against Captain William Flint in York, Great Britain.
1809	The first woman to receive a U.S. patent is Mary Kies, for her

improved method of weaving straw with silk or thread.

1810   A law criminalizing abortion is passed in France. An 1814 law permits abortion only when necessary to save the mother's life.

1816   A law banning divorce is passed in France.

1818   The first woman firefighter in the United States is Molly Williams, an African-American slave owned by a New York City fire station.

1818   The Colored Female Religious and Moral Reform Society is established in Salem, Massachusetts, as the first African-American women's rights organization in the state.

1821   Emma Willard, a Connecticut educator, founds the Troy Female Seminary (now the Emma Willard School), a school for girls in Troy, New York. The school offers rigorous courses in mathematics and philosophy, a syllabus at least equivalent to that of the best high schools for boys.

1821   The Daughters of Africa, a mutual-aid society, is founded when 200 working-class women meet in Philadelphia, Pennsylvania.

1821   In the first U.S. antiabortion legislation, the Connecticut State Legislature passes a law banning abortion by poisoning after "quickening," the time the pregnant woman first feels the fetus moving in her womb. In 1830, the U.S. Congress makes abortion a crime, and in 1860 the Connecticut state legislature bans abortion before "quickening."

1824   American women and men laborers strike in Pawtucket, Rhode Island, when textile weavers stop work to protest against harsh working conditions.

1824   A boarding school for African-American girls is established in Washington, D.C.

1828   A labor strike by women workers takes place in Dover, New Hampshire, when cotton-mill owners enact harsh regulations about promptness. Several hundred women strike but come back a few days later.

1829   A law banning suttee (Sanskrit, *sati*), the burning alive of wives on their husbands' funeral pyres, is enacted in India by British authorities. During the medieval period in India, particularly in Hindu areas of south India and the northwest, suttee became established and is practiced sometimes voluntarily and sometimes by force, even to the present day.

1832   The Female Anti-Slavery Society of Salem, Massachusetts, is organized by free African-American women.

1832   The Africa-American Female Intelligence Society is established in Boston, Massachusetts, to provide education for free black women.

1832   The Massachusetts physician Charles Knowlton publishes *The Fruits of Philosophy*, advocating contraception and the use of vaginal douching for birth control. Knowlton is prosecuted, convicted of obscenity, and jailed for three months.

1833   Prudence Crandall's boarding school for girls in Canterbury, Connecticut, is the first school in the state to accept black students, when Crandall decides to accept Sarah Harris. The school orders Crandall to dismiss Harris or the white students would be dismissed; Crandall refuses and begins a school for black girls instead, but state legislators pass legislation making it difficult for out-of-state black children to attend Connecticut's schools. Crandall is arrested, convicted by the Connecticut Supreme Court, and imprisoned, but later freed on appeal on a technicality.

1833   The American Female Anti-Slavery Society is founded in Philadelphia, Pennsylvania, by Lucretia Mott after she learns that the American Anti-Slavery Society, newly founded by her abolitionist husband, James Mott, does not allow women members.

1834   A major strike of women mill workers takes place in Lowell, Massachusetts, when more than 800 women refuse to accept a 15 percent cut in their wages.

1834   An adult-education program for both women and men is established in Baden, Germany.

1834   A French woman obstetrician, Marie Durocher, is licensed to practice medicine in Rio de Janeiro, Brazil. Using modern medical practices, Dr. Durocher helps significantly reduce child-mortality rates among her patients.

1834   The Factory Girls Association is created in Lowell, Massachusetts, when women in the cotton mills organize to protest against low wages. The organization lasts only three years, dissolving during an economic crisis in 1837.

1835   Harriot K. Hunt practices medicine without a license in Boston, Massachusetts, treating women and children.

1835   An education program for girls is established in Panama.

1836   The first U.S. college chartered to grant degrees to women is the Georgia Female College in Macon, Georgia.

1836   Sarah Bagley begins work in a cotton mill in Lowell, Massachusetts, and goes on to become a labor organizer. During the 1840s, she is one of the founders of the Lowell Female Labor Reform Association and is famous for her writing and speaking.

1837   The Infant Custody Bill, which allows judges to consider the rights of mothers in cases of separation, divorce, and custody, is proposed before the British Parliament and carried in 1839. The legislation is spurred by the actions of the poet and novelist Caroline Sheridan Norton, who leaves her abusive husband and is unable to see her children unless accompanied by a lawyer.

1837   The first coeducational college in the United States is Oberlin College in Oberlin, Ohio, which admits women four years after opening. Oberlin's women students, however, must wait on the men students and cannot work in the fields with other students or recite their lessons in public.

1837   One of the first women's colleges in the United States is Mount Holyoke Female Seminary (later Mount Holyoke College), established by Mary Lyon in South Hadley, Massachusetts. Tuition is $64 a year, and the curriculum includes courses in composition, geography, chemistry, and history.

1838   *Letters on the Equality of the Sexes and the Condition of Women*, by Sarah Moore Grimké, analyzes the conditions of women in the United States and around the world. Grimké, the daughter of a Charleston, South Carolina, slaveholder, writes about legal discrimination, the lack of educational and employment opportunities for women, and the subjugation of wives by their husbands; she also argues for new biblical interpretations supporting the equal rights of women as moral beings.

1839   A married women's property law is passed in Mississippi, allowing wives to hold and own property in their own names. The law also gives wives the right to the income from their own employment.

1840   Over the objection of several men members, but with the support of William Lloyd Garrison, Abby Kelly joins the business committee of the American Anti-Slavery Society, and Lucretia Mott and Lydia Child join the executive committee. Later that same year, Lucretia Mott is one of seven women in the U.S. delegation to the World Anti-Slavery Convention in London. Despite British refusal to accept the women's credentials, the women meet at the other end of the convention hall, again with the support of Garrison.

1840s   The Daughters of Temperance is founded as an adjunct to the Sons of Temperance, but the men insist that the women merely listen and remain silent. Under the leadership of Mary Vaughn, the women break away to form their own group, which becomes the largest organization of women in America. The better-known Woman's Christian Temperance Union is founded in Cleveland, Ohio, in 1874 by Annie Wittenmyer.

1842   The British Mines Act, passed in Great Britain, prohibits the employment of girls and boys under the age of 10 years in the mines. An investigation begun in 1840 revealed that children as young as 5 years of age were working underground and that girls and women were harnessed like mules to pull coal trucks.

1843   The Lowell Female Labor Reform Association in Lowell, Massachusetts, is the first labor union organized and led by women workers in the United States. The association petitions the Massachusetts State Legislature for a 10-hour workday in Massachusetts.

1844   Margaret Fuller, the first woman staff member of a major U.S. newspaper and an internationally known social reformer, works as a foreign correspondent and literary critic for Horace Greeley's *New York Tribune*. A friend of the essayist Ralph Waldo Emerson, she taught at Bronson Alcott's innovative Temple School in Boston, Massachusetts, and was the author of several books, including *Summer on the Lakes* (1844) and *Woman in the Nineteenth Century* (1845).

1845   A law granting women the same inheritance rights as men is passed in Sweden.

1847   Legislation passed by Parliament limits women's and children's working hours in Great Britain. Children aged 13 to 18 and women are limited to 10 hours of work each day.

1847   Maria Mitchell, an American astronomer working alone, discovers a new comet and receives a gold medal from the king of Denmark. She is the first woman elected to the American Academy of Arts and Sciences; a second woman is not elected until almost 100 years later.

1848   Organized by Lucretia Mott and Elizabeth Cady Stanton, the Woman's Rights Convention is held in Seneca Falls, New York. The 300 delegates pledge to fight for women's suffrage, rights to property and guardianship of children, rights to education and employment, and elimination of the double moral standard.

1849   A law prohibiting women from voting is passed in Upper and Lower Canada.

1849   The first woman granted a doctor of medicine degree in the United States is Elizabeth Blackwell; born in England, Blackwell graduates after having been ostracized by the other students at the Geneva Medical College in Syracuse, New York. Although in 1859 she becomes the first woman to be accepted by the British Medical Register, Blackwell returns to the United States to discover that American hospitals refuse to hire her, and she establishes a private practice in New York City.

1849   The *Lily*, the first U.S. newspaper owned and controlled by a woman, is established in Seneca Falls, New York, by Amelia Bloomer. Though its first concerns are temperance issues, the *Lily* quickly becomes an advocate for women's right to vote, equal opportunities in education, and reform of marriage laws; Bloomer, with other women, also promotes dress reform.

1850   The first woman admitted to Harvard Medical School is Harriot K. Hunt, who has been treating women and children in Boston without a license since 1835. Though the dean, Oliver Wendell Holmes, admits her, Harvard's male students rebel, and Hunt is forced to leave.

1850   With support from Lucretia Mott, the Female (later Woman's) Medical College of Pennsylvania is founded in Philadelphia and is staffed by Quaker physicians. A police guard is needed to escort the first women graduates to protect them from threats made against them.

1850   In France, the Falloux Law provides that towns with more than 800 inhabitants must have schools for girls.

1851	The Combination Law in the German Empire prohibits women from participating in political organizations and meetings.
1852	The first U.S. college to grant equality to female students is Antioch College in Yellow Springs, Ohio, founded by the educator Horace Mann. Mann pledges that Antioch will be "the first American college of high rank to grant absolutely equal opportunities to women and men."
1852	An act of the British Parliament denies husbands the right to use habeas corpus provisions to force their wives to cohabit with them. Before this act, a husband could invoke a writ of habeas corpus (issued to bring a person to court) against anyone offering shelter to a wife who lives away from her husband.
1852	Catherine Beecher, sister of the author Harriet Beecher Stowe and the abolitionist Henry Ward Beecher, founds the American Women's Education Association. The organization provides funding for women's colleges, helps women continue their education, and promotes the idea of college-level study in the field of domestic economy.
1853	Women are admitted into the teaching profession in Sweden, and teacher-training colleges for women are established in that country.
1853	The first woman in the United States to be ordained as a minister in a Protestant church is Antoinette Brown Blackwell, who serves two Congregational congregations in New York City. The author of several books, including *Studies in General Science*, *The Sexes Throughout Nature*, and *The Philosophy of Individuality*, Blackwell lives long enough to cast a vote in 1920.
1854	A law giving women the same inheritance rights as men is passed in Norway.
1855	The first hospital in the world established by women for women is Women's Hospital in New York City. The hospital treats women's diseases and offers obstetric care.
1855	Harriet Goodhue Hosmer, an American sculptor born in Watertown, Massachusetts, receives her first commission. Working in London and Rome most of her life, Hosmer becomes internationally known; her many sculptures include *Puck* (1856), *Beatrice Cenci* (1857), and *Zenobia in Chains* (1859).
1855	To protest unequal rights married women's, the American suffragist Lucy Stone keeps her maiden name after marriage. Thereafter, women in the United States who keep their names after marriage are called Lucy Stoners.
1855	The first state college in the United States to admit women is the University of Iowa. In 1858, the board of managers fails in an attempt to exclude women.
1855	The Elmira Female College, the first college in the United States to grant academic degrees to women, is founded in Elmira, New York.

1856	The Widow Remarriage Act for Hindu widows is passed in India, although women who remarry lose custody of their children and suffer financial penalties; Hindu beliefs stress that a wife is married to the same husband during her many lives. Muslim Indian women may remarry more easily, but they still lose their children, so that younger widows without children take most advantage of this act.
1857	A law granting women the right to equal accessibility to jobs is passed in Denmark. Jobs in trades, crafts, and other professions previously confined to men are now open to women.
1857	The Matrimonial Causes Act is passed by the British Parliament, allowing women to divorce because of the husband's adultery, bigamy, rape, sodomy, bestiality, or desertion. The law establishes divorce courts, gives divorced women the right to their earnings, determines that husbands must provide for their wives after divorce, and creates the world's first system of alimony.
1857	A law granting women the same inheritance rights as men is passed in Denmark.
1857	Women seamstresses in New York City demonstrate for improved wages and better working conditions.
1857	Parliament in Great Britain passes legislation limiting the advertising of contraceptives.
1858	High schools for girls are established in Russia.
1858	A law grants women in Denmark the right to legal majority even if they are unmarried.
1858	Lucy Stone, the American women's voting-rights activist, refuses to pay her New Jersey property taxes as long as she cannot vote. Her household goods are sold by the tax collector, but a woman neighbor buys them and returns them to Stone.
1859	The National Woman's Suffrage Association (NWSA) is founded as the first women's suffrage organization in the United States. The NWSA is established with $50,000 donated by Elizabeth Cady Stanton, one of the organizers of the first convention for women's suffrage, the Seneca Falls Convention, held in Stanton's hometown in upstate New York in 1848.
1859	The first medical organization in the United States to condemn abortion is the American Medical Association.
1860	A law giving property rights to women is passed in New York State largely through the efforts of the reformer Susan B. Anthony. The law gives women the right to own property apart from their husbands, carry on trade, and enter into contracts; it also grants them joint custody of their children.
1860	A printing shop whose compositors are all women is established in London, England, by the feminist Emily Faithfull. In 1863, Faithfull publishes *Victoria Magazine* and promotes equal opportunity for women.

1861	A law making abortion a criminal offense is passed in Ireland by the British-led government.
1862	The first African-American woman in the United States to receive a full baccalaureate degree is Mary Jane Patterson, from Oberlin College in Oberlin, Ohio.
1862	The schoolteacher Julie-Victoire Daubié is the first French woman to receive a baccalaureate degree, which she is awarded by the University of Lyon, after the University of Paris refuses to allow her to take her examinations.
1863	The first woman in the United States to be ordained a minister with complete denominational authority is Olympia Brown, who becomes a Universalist minister. In 1867, Brown is an active participant, with Susan B. Anthony, Lucy Stone, and Elizabeth Cady Stanton, in the Kansas campaign to pass a referendum for women's suffrage.
1863	The Women's Loyal National League, founded by Elizabeth Cady Stanton and Susan B. Anthony, is the first women's suffrage organization in the United States to oppose slavery. The organizers collect the signatures of thousands calling for the end of slavery.
1863	A law granting women the right to legal majority even if they are unmarried is passed in Norway.
1863	Harriet Tubman, an escaped slave and abolitionist, becomes the first woman to lead troops in battle in the United States when she heads a raid to free 750 slaves during the Civil War. In 1850, Tubman began leading slaves from Southern plantations northward to freedom on the Underground Railroad.
1863	Women win the right to the communal vote in rural areas in Finland.
1864	A law granting women the right to equal accessibility to jobs is passed in Sweden. Professions previously confined to men are now open to women.
1865	The first woman sculptor to receive a commission from the U.S. government is Vinnie Ream Hoxie, who at the age of 18 wins a $10,000 award to create a statue of the recently assassinated Abraham Lincoln. She is immediately attacked as too young and inexperienced, but completes the statue for the Capitol rotunda in Washington, D.C., in 1871.
1865	Vassar Female College opens in Poughkeepsie, New York, with 22 female teachers and 8 male teachers. The founder is Matthew Brewer, who intends to give women all the educational advantages previously monopolized by men.
1865	The first university to admit women in Switzerland is the University of Zurich.
1865	The civil code of the unified Italy, also called the Pisanelli Code, gives single women much the same rights as men, although marriage brings women under the power of their husbands. No

woman can vote, and not until 1945 are Italian women allowed to vote in all elections.

1866   The 14th Amendment to the U.S. Constitution, which defines citizens and voters as "male," is passed by the U.S. Congress. The amendment is ratified by the states in 1868.

1866   The American Equal Rights Association is organized in New York by Elizabeth Cady Stanton and Susan B. Anthony; Lucretia Mott is president. The association works to secure equal rights, particularly the right to vote, for women and blacks; in 1869 it splinters into the National Woman Suffrage Association and the American Woman Suffrage Association, which in 1890 merge to become the National American Woman Suffrage Association.

1866   A law granting women the right to equal accessibility to jobs is passed in Norway. Professions previously confined to men are now open to women.

1867   The Cigar-Makers' Union is the first national labor union in the United States to accept women members. The union also accepts black members.

1867   Women taxpayers are granted local voting rights in New Zealand.

1867   A law instituted in Austria bans women from forming or participating in political organizations.

1867   The Scottish Women's Suffrage Society, which advocates women's right to vote, is established in Scotland.

1867   A law passed by Parliament in Great Britain extends the 1803 statute on abortion to make it clear that criminal charges will be brought against a woman if she acts to bring about her own miscarriage.

1868   Hester Vaughn, an Englishwoman who came to the United States to meet her fiancé, is convicted in Philadelphia for the murder of her illegitimate child. Vaughn discovers that her fiancé is already married, loses her job, and is discovered nearly starving, her infant dead. An all-male jury sentences her to death, but a campaign led by the suffragettes Elizabeth Cady Stanton and Susan B. Anthony results in Vaughn's pardon by the governor of Pennsylvania.

1868   The National Society for Woman Suffrage, advocating women's right to vote, is established in Great Britain. The organization fails to secure the right to vote in parliamentary elections but does make women's suffrage a public issue.

1868   The Working Women's Protective Union is the first union for women in the United States. Founded in New York City by middle- and upper-class women, the union's mandate is to provide legal services to women workers, make women aware of employment opportunities, and lobby for laws to protect women workers. Branches of the union are founded in other cities.

1869   The new Territory of Wyoming in the United States grants women the right to vote and to hold office.

1869	Higher-education classes and public lectures for women are established in Russia.
1869	Women are admitted into the teaching profession in Norway.
1869	Women are permitted to be primary school teachers in Austria.
1869	The Daughters of Saint Crispin, a U.S. national women's labor organization, is founded in Lynn, Massachusetts, as the result of an 1860 strike by 800 women shoe-factory workers seeking higher pay. The organization survives for only seven years.
1869	The Contagious Disease Act passed by Parliament in Great Britain allows police to arrest female prostitutes while ignoring the actions of their male customers.
1869	Pope Pius IX amends the canon dealing with abortion in the Code of Canon Law to state that anyone who obtains an abortion of any kind is automatically excommunicated.
1870	The Female Normal and High School in New York City is the first college in the United States to offer free education for women. Its name is soon changed to the Normal College of the City of New York, and it is charged with providing trained teachers for the city.
1870	The Married Women's Property Laws are passed in Great Britain, and passed again in 1882, despite the disapproval of Queen Victoria. The laws give married women possession of their earnings; before passage of the laws, the common-law concept of coverture dictated that a married woman's legal status be absorbed into her husband's, and she could not hold property in her own name, enter into contracts, or make a will unless joined by her husband.
1870	A law setting the parameters of marriage is passed in Japan. A man may have as many mistresses as he can manage, and the law establishes the same status for mistresses as for wives; men and women may marry only if all living parents agree.
1870	Women gain the right to vote in the Utah Territory and the right to serve on juries in the Wyoming Territory.
1870	Iowa is the first state in the United States to admit a woman to the bar, when Arabella Mansfield is granted the right to practice law.
1870	The first woman to endow a college for women is Sophia Smith, who leaves her fortune to found and endow Smith College, in Northampton, Massachusetts, which is chartered in 1871 and opens in 1875.
1870	The Spanish penal code, enacted in the Philippines, includes a law banning abortion.
1871	A law revising the criminal code in the German Empire criminalizes abortion and makes it punishable with a five-year jail term.

1871	The British Education Act allows elementary education for girls in Great Britain.
1871	A law passed in Japan allows marriages across social-class boundaries. The new legislation permits any woman to marry a samurai (warrior aristocrat), although, as with any marriage, the wife surrenders all she brings to the marriage to her husband, and, should she die, their children remain under the control of the father's family.
1871	The supreme court of Alabama rules that a man cannot choke or kick his wife or beat her with a stick.
1871	The Woman's Centenary Association is founded as the first organization of churchwomen in the United States to promote the education of women ministers.
1872	Women are permitted to attend the full range of classes at the University of Wisconsin, but only if there are not enough male students to fill up the class. Women may use the university library on the days that male students do not.
1872	A law mandating compulsory education for all children is passed in Japan, although monthly tuition fees and traditional beliefs about the female role in Japanese society mean that most Japanese girls remain at home or work as maids.
1872	Largely because of successful pressure applied by Belva Ann Lockwood, a lawyer and women's rights advocate, the U.S. Congress passes a law guaranteeing women equal pay for equal jobs.
1872	A law passed in Japan forbids parents to sell their daughters as prostitutes, because, just as horses and cows do not have to pay debts, prostitutes can leave their brothels without having to pay their debts. Since the law maintains the custom that women have no legal rights as human beings, families argue that in bad times they have no option but to sell their daughters.
1872	Nine women suffragettes, including Susan B. Anthony, are jailed in Rochester, New York, for attempting to vote. During her trial, Anthony urges women to recognize the old Revolutionary maxim that resistance to tyranny is obedience to God, and in 1873 she refuses to pay the fine imposed by the court.
1872	The U.S. Comstock Law, named for Anthony Comstock, a postal inspector, makes it a criminal offense to import, mail, or transport by interstate commerce any medical article preventing contraception or causing abortion. The law also criminalizes the mailing or transport of any information about contraception or abortion; in 1874, postal agents seize more than 60,000 condoms and 3,000 boxes of pills.
1872	Victoria Claflin Woodhull becomes the first woman candidate for president of the United States. She is nominated by the National Woman's Suffrage Association.
1873	Women with property are given the right to vote in British Columbia, Canada.

1873	The first prison with a female superintendent and female prisoners in the United States, the Indiana Women's Prison, opens with prisoners transferred from the state reformatory at Jeffersonville, Indiana, following the shocking testimony of Quaker women who saw the women prisoners forced to stand naked before male guards and who heard that the guards often raped their prisoners.
1873	A law passed by the British Parliament gives divorced women the right to custody of their children.
1873	In *Bradwell v. Illinois*, the U.S. Supreme Court rules to deny a woman the right to practice law. The Court decides that even though Myra Bradwell passed the Illinois bar examination, the state could prohibit her from practicing law because she was a woman, and family harmony requires a woman not to have a career distinct from that of her husband.
1873	The Women's Protection and Provident League is founded in Great Britain by upper- and middle-class women concerned about the health and welfare of working-class women. In 1890, it is renamed the Women's Trade Union League.
1873	The first kindergarten in the United States is created in Saint Louis, Missouri, by Susan Elizabeth Blow, an advocate of German educator Friedrich Fröbel, who believes that young children learn through free play. Blow creates a cheery, bright schoolroom where children are encouraged to learn through guided play and the next year introduces a training school for kindergarten teachers, but, as the kindergarten model spreads and is adopted by school systems, its focus shifts to caring for the children of the working poor and preparing children for elementary school.
1874	The first college to admit women in Canada is Mount Allison College in Sackville, New Brunswick, which allows women to attend all courses and to attain all degrees available to male students.
1874	The London School of Medicine for Women is established by Elizabeth Blackwell, the first female doctor to graduate from the Geneva Medical College in New York, and a Scottish medical student, Sophia Jex-Blake.
1874	A court in North Carolina concludes that a man cannot physically punish his wife, but, unless the wife suffers permanent injury, a "curtain rule" remains in effect, allowing the parties to resolve their differences in the privacy of home and marriage.
1874	The London school board agrees to grant degrees to women, after pressure from women like Emily Davies, who in 1873 had led the movement to establish Gorton College at Cambridge University. Davies was also responsible for compelling the University College in London to admit women to classes in 1870.
1875	Women in Great Britain receive the opportunity to attend the Royal College of Surgeons.
1875	Emma Patterson of London is the first woman to attend the British Trades Union Congress national meeting as a full and equal

delegate. Patterson helps organize unions for women workers in the upholstery, bookbinding, millinery, and printing trades and works to establish the Women's Committee of the Trades Union Congress.

1876   Sarah Stevenson is the first woman admitted to membership in the American Medical Association.

1876   Women physicians are permitted to register in Great Britain and begin to practice in 1877.

1876   Women begin to practice as physicians in Germany when the first German female physicians, Emilie Lehmus and Franziska Tiburntius, open a clinic in Berlin.

1876   The Toronto Women's Literary Club is established in Toronto to press for women's suffrage in Canada.

1876   Suffrage des Femmes (Women's suffrage), an organization devoted to women's rights, is founded in France by Hubertine Auclert, who leads women to demand suffrage by using boycotts, court cases, and demonstrations.

1877   Annie Wood Besant and Charles Bradlaugh are acquitted by a British court for publishing a pamphlet advocating contraception. The British suffragette movement decides not to support Besant and Bradlaugh for fear of alienating supporters; Besant loses custody of her daughter when a judge decides Besant's ideas about contraception might affect the girl.

1877   The U.S. Supreme Court denies a woman the right to register to vote in *Minor v. Happersett*. Virginia Louise Minor claimed that the provisions of the 14th Amendment to the Constitution granted her the right to vote, but Chief Justice Morrison R. Waite writes that the Constitution does not confer the right of suffrage on anyone.

1877   The International Federation of Friends of Girls is established in Geneva, Switzerland, as a worldwide organization promoting the interests of young women. The federation offers assistance, shelter, and protection to young girls around the world.

1877   The first woman to receive a doctorate from a university in the United States, Helen Magill White, accepts a Ph.D. in Greek from Boston University in Massachusetts.

1878   Lady Margaret Hall, the first college for women at Oxford University, is founded, though women are not given full membership in Oxford or the right to receive degrees there until 1920. In 1878, Oxford University also establishes the Association for the Education of Women.

1878   The first academic degrees granted to women in Great Britain are awarded by the University of London.

1878   Aletta Jacobs, a Dutch suffragette, becomes the first woman to be granted a license to practice medicine in the Netherlands.

1878   Women medical students in Scotland are permitted to obtain instruction at the Royal Free Hospital in Edinburgh.

1878	Kita Kasuse, a Japanese widow, unsuccessfully tries to vote in a local election in Japan. Informed that only men can vote because they serve in the army, she refuses to pay her local taxes and receives national publicity as "the civil rights grandmother."
1879	An amendment to the U.S. Constitution giving women the right to vote is proposed. A similar amendment is introduced every year until 1920, when women's right to vote becomes law.
1879	Belva Ann Lockwood, a lawyer and women's rights advocate, writes a law allowing women to practice before the U.S. Supreme Court. Congress passes the law this same year, and Lockwood becomes the first woman lawyer to practice before the Court.
1879	Women are permitted to attend university in Brazil.
1879	The first secretarial school in the United States, the Union School of Stenography and Typewriting, is founded by Mary Foot Seymour, who trains women to be copyists, bookkeepers, and clerks.
1880	The Japanese law about marriage is amended when the government removes the provision granting mistresses the same status as wives. Many men, however, continue to keep mistresses.
1880	A law passed in Denmark grants married women economic independence.
1880	In France, the Camille Sée Law permits girls to attend the lycée (secondary school). The law is named after Camille Sée, a French lawyer concerned with the education of women.
1880	Girls are allowed to attend secondary schools in Great Britain.
1880	Louise Blanchard Bethune begins to practice as an architect in Buffalo, New York. In 1889, she becomes the first female Fellow of the American Institute of Architects.
1881	The University of Melbourne is the first university in Australia to admit women. At this time, Australian women do not enjoy equality in education with men, and elementary education for women in all states is not compulsory until 1895.
1881	The League to Promote Female Interests is founded in Milan as the first women's rights organization in Italy. A key issue of interest to the league is the many women working in the textile trades who earn only half the salary of male workers.
1881	The Householders in Scotland Act giving women local voting rights is passed in Scotland.
1882	The Association of Collegiate Alumnae is founded in Boston, Massachusetts, as the first organization in support of women in higher education in the United States. In 1889, it merges with the Western Association of Collegiate Alumnae, formed in Chicago in 1883.
1882	The repeal of Connecticut's divorce law signals the beginning of a

period when U.S. divorce laws are tightened to discourage the growing number of divorces that resulted from the liberalized laws of 1850 to 1870. North Carolina prohibits divorce; New York grants divorce only when adultery can be proved, and New Jersey permits divorce only for adultery or desertion.

1882	Hubertine Auclert is believed to be the first person to use the term *feminist*, in an issue of the weekly newspaper *La Citoyenne* (Citizeness), published in France by the Suffrage des Femmes (Women's suffrage).
1882	Girls are given the opportunity to attend secondary schools in Japan. The schools teach primarily housekeeping, sewing, and manners, training women to become proper wives and decent daughters-in-law.
1882	The University of Mississippi permits women to attend classes.
1882	The first birth-control clinic in the world is established in Amsterdam, Netherlands, by Aletta Jacobs, the first woman granted a license to practice medicine in the country.
1883	The first woman granted a medical degree in Canada is Augusta Stowe-Gullen.
1883	After being unable to get a position elsewhere in Europe despite having been granted a Ph.D. from the University of Göttingen in Germany, Sofia Vasilevna Korvin-Kruvovskaia Kovalevskaia is the first woman to be appointed lecturer in mathematics at the University of Stockholm in Sweden. Even here she is criticized; the Swedish playwright August Strindberg thinks that a female professor is a monstrosity. In 1888, Kovalevskaia wins the Prix Bordin of the French Academy of Science for her paper "On the Rotation of a Solid Body about a Fixed Point," one of 10 major papers on mathematics Kovalevskaia publishes during her career.
1883	The Toronto Women's Literary Club is expanded to become the Canadian Woman Suffrage Association, which campaigns for women's right to vote.
1883	The first Ladies' Day in professional baseball in the United States occurs when the New York Gothams allow women into the ballpark at reduced ticket prices. Before this, spectators have been male, although in 1867 the New York Knickerbockers baseball team allowed free admission one day each month to the wives, daughters, and girlfriends of the players.
1884	With the reform of the civil law code in Germany, a law is passed granting women the right to legal majority in that country.
1884	The Norwegian Association for the Promotion of Women's Interests is founded as the first women's rights organization in Norway.
1884	The Finnish Women's Association, the first women's rights organization in Finland, is established by Baroness Alexandra Gripenberg. The association advocates equal opportunities for women

in education and employment, including equal pay for equal work.

1884 After the midwife Mitsuko Takahashi holds a successful sit-in for three days and three nights outside the gates of Tokyo's male-only Saiseigakusha Medical School, women gain the opportunity to attend medical school in Japan.

1885 Ginko Ogino is the first woman licensed to practice as a physician in Japan.

1885 The Woman's Teachers Association is founded in Toronto, and soon afterward women teachers organize in other Canadian cities.

1885 Local voting rights are granted to women in New Zealand.

1886 The Guardianship of Infants Act is passed in the British Parliament, recognizing the mother's role in the care of children.

1886 The Virginia Supreme Court, reviewing *Bailey v. Commonwealth*, upholds a rape conviction even though the victim did not physically resist. The 14-year-old stepdaughter of the rapist felt she had no ability to resist his attack, and the court rules that the lack of resistance does not signal consent.

1887 Matilda Montoya is the first woman licensed to practice medicine in Mexico.

1887 The Massachusetts legislature passes a law limiting women's working day to 10 hours.

1888 The Fadette Ladies' Orchestra of Boston, Massachusetts, organized by Caroline Nichols, becomes the first professional all-woman orchestra in the United States.

1888 The first international women's organization, the International Council of Women (ICW), is founded in Washington, D.C., by British and American women, including Susan B. Anthony, Frances Willard, and May Wright Sewall. In its early years, the ICW promotes equal access to school and training programs, equal pay for equal work, and state-supported maternity leave and benefits. In 1963, the headquarters moves to Paris.

1888 The Normal College of the City of New York offers college-level instruction and becomes the first free college to offer degrees to women in the United States. It is accredited as a college in 1905.

1889 A new constitution adopted in Japan bans women from becoming emperor.

1889 Connecticut becomes the first U.S. state to issue a druggist license to a woman.

1889 Laura Martinez de Carvajales y Camino is the first woman granted a medical degree in Cuba, and Cecilia Grierson becomes Argentina's first female physician. In the same year in Scotland, Elsie Inglis is awarded a medical degree, the first woman in that country to receive one.

1890	Dr. Ida Gray becomes the first African-American woman to practice dentistry in the United States when she receives her D.D.S. from the University of Michigan Dental School in Ann Arbor.
1890	The first teacher-training college in Egypt is founded; not until 1928 are women allowed to enter the National University.
1890	The first woman to cover a boxing match for a newspaper in the United States, Winifred Sweet Black, works as a reporter for the *San Francisco Examiner*.
1890	Founded in Germany by Helene Lang, a middle-class schoolteacher, the German Woman Teachers' Association works to allow German women access to a high school education, and Lang introduces a course of secondary education for women in a Berlin school.
1890	The Daughters of the American Revolution (DAR) is established as a women's organization to promote patriotism in the United States and to preserve American culture and its heritage and landmarks. DAR members are restricted to direct descendants of men and women who were active in the American Revolution.
1890	The General Federation of Women's Clubs in the United States, founded in New York City, unites women's clubs, literary societies, and discussion groups to work for social reform in women's causes.
1890	The National Woman's Liberal Union is founded in the United States by Matilda J. Gage, the chief architect of the National Woman Suffrage Association's 1878 campaign to liberate women from the bondage of the church. In 1893, Gage publishes *Woman, Church, and State*, a critique of religion's role in the subjugation of women.
1891	Mary Emma Woolley becomes the first woman to attend Brown University in Providence, Rhode Island. Before separate classes for women are established, Woolley attends men's classes as a guest.
1891	A law passed in the British Parliament withdraws from husbands the right to kidnap and imprison their wives.
1891	The Australian Woman Suffrage League, promoting women's right to vote, is founded by Rose Scott. The league also fights for social issues like shorter working hours for women shop assistants and raising the age of consent for women.
1891	Anne Baxter serves as a county clerk in Carthage, Jasper County, Missouri.
1891	Pope Leo XIII issues the papal encyclical *Rerum Novarum* (Of new things), discouraging the use of all artificial means of contraception. The pope states that no human law can change the principal purpose of marriage, to increase and multiply.
1892	The law of marriage is amended in Italy to raise the minimum age of marriage for women to 12 years.

1892	Founded in Washington, D.C., as the first national organization for African-American women, the Colored Women's League promotes educational opportunities for black Americans.
1892	Women are given the opportunity to attend universities in Scotland on the same terms as men.
1892	A course in women's studies, The Status of Women in the United States, is offered at the University of Kansas in the sociology department.
1893	Johns Hopkins Medical School in Baltimore, Maryland, admits women.
1893	The New York City Woman Teachers' Association petitions the New York State legislature to grant equal wages to female teachers. Women teachers have been paid $1,700 a year, while men receive $3,000.
1893	The National Council of Women of Canada is formed to unify women's organizations across Canada.
1893	The Lucy Stone League is founded in the United States to support women who decide, like Stone, to retain their maiden names rather than take the surnames of their husbands upon marriage.
1893	Colorado is the first U.S. state to grant women's voting rights by popular election, when Davis H. Waite is elected governor on a platform of unions for miners, free silver, and women's suffrage.
1893	New Zealand grants women full voting rights in federal elections, after one-third of all the women in New Zealand (31,872) have signed a petition urging the House of Representatives to grant suffrage.
1894	The first women's singles tennis match at the Wimbledon tournament held at the All-England Lawn Tennis and Croquet Club in Great Britain occurs seven years after the male players' tournaments begin. Maud Wilson of Britain is the winner.
1894	Mary Emma Woolley and Anne Tillinghast Weeden receive the first A.B. degrees awarded to women at Brown University.
1894	The Bund Deutscher Frauenvereine (Federation of German's women's associations) is founded in Germany as an organization of middle-class women's groups concerned with education and employment.
1894	The World Young Women's Christian Association (WYWCA) is organized in Geneva, Switzerland, by four national Young Men's Christian Association groups: those of Great Britain, Norway, Sweden, and the United States. The WYWCA promotes women's leadership in such causes as world justice, peace, health, and freedom.
1895	The *Woman's Bible* is prepared and published by the reformer Elizabeth Cady Stanton, who revises biblical passages degrading women. Although criticized for the revision, she publishes a second volume in 1898.

1895	Women are given the opportunity to attend university in Hungary.
1896	In France, Alice Guy-Blaché makes the film *La Fée aux choux* (Cabbage fairy), a fantasy, while working in Paris as a secretary for Leon Gaumont, who established a successful film-production company. Guy-Blaché continues to make films for Gaumont in France until 1907; subsequently, she opens her own production company, Solax, in the United States.
1896	The National Association of Colored Women (NACW) is founded in the United States when the National Federation of Afro-American Women in Boston joins the Colored Women's League of Washington, D.C., to answer the charges of James W. Jack, president of the Missouri Press Association, that "the Negroes of this country are wholly devoid of morality, the women are prostitutes and are natural thieves and liars." The NACW creates black nurseries and kindergartens and homes for girls, older people, and sick people.
1897	The Associazione Nationale per le Donne (National association for women) is founded in Rome, Italy, to advance women's rights.
1898	In Ireland, women are allowed to be seated on local district councils.
1898	Lucy Terry Prince, a former slave, becomes the first woman to address the U.S. Supreme Court, when she argues successfully before the Court on a land claim.
1898	*Women and Economics*, by the American feminist and author Charlotte Gilman, is published in the United States. The book argues that women must challenge the expectations that they should be dependent and submissive and urges women to achieve self-sufficiency and autonomy through economic independence.
1899	The Unione Femminile Nationale (National feminine union) is organized in Milan, Italy.
1899	The Married Women's Property Act is passed in Iceland.
1899	Florence Kelley, a social reformer, and other women associated with Hull House in Chicago create the National Consumers League (NCL) to improve the conditions of working-class women; with Kelley as the first head, the NCL investigates women's working conditions and publicizes abuses in retail stores. Kelley introduces the NCL White Label, displayed by employers who treat their workers fairly; the NCL pressures consumers to boycott products that do not earn this award.
c. 1900	The first women's social club in the United States, the Colony Club, is established in New York City. The Colony Club's members, from wealthy New York families, appoint a small group to investigate working conditions in New York's factories, and in 1909 club members contribute $1,000 to support the striking women shirtwaist workers.
1900	The International Ladies Garment Workers' Union (ILGWU) is

founded in New York City, with seven local chapters representing more than 2,000 workers in such cities as New York, Philadelphia, and Boston; by 1913, it is one of the largest branches of the American Federation of Labor (AFL). The ILGWU helps pave the way for shorter workweeks and better working conditions for immigrant women workers in the garment industry.

1900   The Tokyo Women's Medical School is founded by Yaie Yashioka, a woman physician who graduated from Saiseigakusha Medical School, which subsequently returned to an all-male enrollment.

1900   The Elsie Inglis Hospital, a maternity center, is established in Scotland by Dr. Elsie Inglis.

1900   Article 5 of the Security Police Law passed in Japan to regulate political activities prohibits women, as well as military men, police, clergy, and public and private schoolteachers, from joining political organizations. This prohibition remains in effect until 1945.

1900   The first U.S. women's intercollegiate basketball game takes place in California, when women from Stanford University compete against women from the University of California.

1900   Women first participate in the modern Olympic movement when the International Olympic Committee (IOC) allows women to take part in the golf and tennis competitions. During the Paris games, only 16 women compete, as compared with 1,489 men.

1901   The Women's Club of Prague is founded in Czechoslovakia as the first organization devoted to women's issues in the country.

1901   The U.S. Congress passes the Army Reorganization Act, establishing the United States Army Nurse Corps. Before 1899, enlisted males provided care for patients in army hospitals, but under the new law female nurses serve in the army for three-year renewable contracts.

1902   The Law for the Protection of the Labor of Women and Children is passed in Italy when the Italian parliament enacts legislation limiting the workday to 12 hours for women, including 2 hours for meals and rest; requiring one month's maternity leave; and recognizing the right of mothers to breast-feed at work. Limited numbers of inspectors, however, prevent full compliance.

1902   The Landsfüreningen für Kyinnans Politiska Rösträtt (Swedish women's suffrage association) is founded in Sweden.

1902   The Gesellschaft Schweizerischer Malerinnen, Bildhauerinnen, und Kunstgewerblerinnen (Society of Swiss women painters, sculptors, and arts and crafts workers) is the first organization of women artists in Switzerland. The Gesellschaft seeks equal rights for women artists, which the entrenched Swiss arts organizations refuse them.

1902   Federal voting rights are granted to women in Australia. In 1908, women achieve full voting rights in state elections.

1902   The Deutscher Verband für Frauenstimmrecht (German Union for Women's Suffrage) is organized by Anita Augsberg and Lida Heymann in Hamburg, a city where the ban against women's participation in politics is not in effect as it is elsewhere in Germany.

1903   Marie Curie becomes the first woman to win the Nobel Prize for Physics for her study of radioactivity, shared with her husband, Pierre Curie, and with A. H. Becquerel. In 1911, she wins another Nobel Prize, this time for chemistry, honoring her discovery of the elements polonium and radium.

1903   Maggie Lena Walker, the daughter of former slaves, becomes president of the Saint Luke Penny Savings Bank in Baltimore, Maryland.

1903   The Oregon state legislature passes a law prohibiting women from working more than 10 hours a day in factories and laundries. In 1908, the U.S. Supreme Court in *Muller v. State of Oregon* rules in favor of the state's law.

1903   The National Women's Trade Union League (NWTUL) is formed in the United States as the first coalition of labor officials, settlement-house workers, and working-class women dedicated to promoting unions for women. Lobbying for labor reforms and improved working conditions, NWTUL introduces such innovative programs as the Bryn Mawr Summer School for Working Women, which trains rank-and-file women workers in labor-organizing skills.

1904   The National Council of Women is organized in Hungary to fight against alcohol abuse, pornography, and white slavery.

1904   Mary McLeod Bethune founds the Daytona Normal and Industrial School for Negro Girls in Daytona Beach, Florida, and later organizes a hospital to train black nurses. In 1925, the School merges with a men's college to become Bethune-Cookman College.

1905   High schools for girls are established in Iceland.

1905   An Austrian pacifist and novelist, the Baroness Bertha von Suttner becomes the first woman to win the Nobel Prize for Peace. She is well known for her novel of 1889, *Die Waffen nieder!* (Lay down your arms!), and a journal of the same title; she is said to have influenced the Swedish industrialist Bernhard Nobel to create a peace prize.

1906   Finland gives women the right to vote in parliamentary elections.

1907   The Icelandic Women's Association is founded by Briet Bjarnhédinsdóttir.

1907   The Married Women's Property Act is passed in France, partly through the efforts of Jeanne Schmahl, one of the founders of the Union Française pour le Suffrage des Femmes (French union for women's suffrage), the major women's suffrage organization in France.

1907	Kate Barnard is the first woman elected to a major statewide political office in the United States, when she becomes commissioner of Charities and Corrections in Oklahoma.
1907	A law granting married women the right to spend their own wages is passed in France.
1907	Official policy in Australia mandating that women's wages be lower than men's is introduced and remains in effect until 1967.
1908	Madge Syers (Florence Madeleine Cave Syers), the British figure skater, wins the first Olympic gold medal in women's figure skating, as well as bronze medals for pair skating with her husband and coach, Edgar Syers, at the Olympics held in London, the first modern-day Olympic Games open to women since the Games' revival in 1896. In 1902, Syers was the first woman to enter the world championships in skating, where she finished second to Ulrich Salchow, though women are banned thereafter from this competition for a time.
1908	In a massive demonstration supporting women's suffrage, 100,000 suffragettes storm Parliament in Great Britain. Two dozen women are arrested, and the British radical reformer Emmeline Pankhurst and her daughter Christabel receive jail terms, although two cabinet ministers testify on their behalf.
1908	Women win federal voting rights in Australia.
1908	Iceland awards women municipal voting rights.
1908	The American mountaineer Annie Smith Peck, at the age of 57, becomes the first person to reach the summit of Mount Huascarán (6,768 meters), the highest mountain in Peru. In 1898, she climbed the Matterhorn (4,478 meters) in the Swiss Alps on the border between Switzerland and Italy.
1908	Women in Prussia in north-central Germany are given the opportunity to attend universities on the same terms as men.
1909	Selma Lagerlöf, a Swedish novelist, is the first woman awarded the Nobel Prize for Literature.
1909	The Uprising of the 20,000, a widespread strike of women garment workers, takes place in New York City when women members of the ILGWU and the National Women's Trade Union League leave work, walk the picket line, and face cold, hunger, and police brutality. The strike gains support from wealthy women suffragettes such as Anne Morgan, the daughter of J. P. Morgan, and spreads to other cities, but it is ultimately broken.
1909	A law grants women the right to run for municipal office in Sweden.
1909	The National Conservation Congress is formed in the United States to represent the concerns of about 30,000 women members interested in protecting the environment. The congress works to educate the public about the need for conservation and helps preserve Niagara Falls from overdevelopment by the utility industry.

1909	A believer in Booker T. Washington's teachings, Nannie Helen Burroughs, a black educator, opens a school providing vocational and missionary training for girls in Washington, D.C. In addition to the three Rs, Burroughs teaches the three Bs—Bible, bath, and broom; each student takes a course in black history.
1910	The Women's Political Union organizes a massive voting-rights parade in New York City.
1910	International Women's Day is founded when Clara Zetkin, the German delegate to the International Socialist Women's Congress at Copenhagen, Denmark, suggests that March 8 be women's equivalent of May Day. In 1911, parades and demonstrations are held in Europe and Asia, but not in the United States.
1910	The U.S. Mann Act prevents the interstate transportation of women for immoral purposes. It is enacted to deal with the issue of white slavery, the Progressive Era's term for the entrapment, transportation, and supplying of women for the purposes of prostitution; more than 1,000 slavers are prosecuted under provisions of the Mann Act.
1910	The Camp Fire Girls are founded in the United States as a girls' organization similar to the Boy Scouts, promoting outdoor skills and voluntary service.
1910	Twenty-eight percent of factory workers in Finland are women.
1911	Clothilde Luisi of Uruguay is the first woman to enter the diplomatic corps of any nation.
1911	Women gain the right to vote in Portugal.
1911	The fire at the Triangle Shirtwaist Company sweatshop in New York City causes the deaths of 146 women workers and reveals the miserable working conditions for women in the garment industry. Doors are blocked, fire hoses inaccessible, and women trapped and unable to escape from the 9th and 10th floors.
1911	Dr. Christine Bonnevie is the first woman admitted to the Norwegian Academy of Science.
1911	The Bluestocking Society is established in Japan by Raicho Hiratsuka, a young writer. The Bluestocking Society's rejection of male leadership is a key development in the modern women's movement in Japan.
1911	The state of Missouri provides financial assistance to mothers of dependent children. By 1913, 18 states will have enacted similar provisions, but strict eligibility standards and the reality that only a small percentage of those who are eligible apply mean that only a few women receive aid.
1912	Fanny Harwood is the first woman licensed in Great Britain to perform dental surgery.
1912	Isabella Goodwin, a sergeant on the police force in New York City, is appointed the first female police detective in the depart-

ment.

1912   A 40-year-old Philadelphia sportswoman and experienced moun-
taineer, Dora Keen, is the first person to climb to the top of
Mount Blackburn (4,996 meters) in Alaska after a grueling 33-
day ascent. The previous year, Keen had attempted to conquer
the peak with a troop of three gold prospectors and a dog team,
but fierce weather forced them to turn back.

1912   Massachusetts becomes the first U.S. state to pass a minimum-
wage law for women and children.

1913   The Congressional Union for Woman Suffrage is established in
the United States to advocate women's suffrage; the union
pledges to work against the political party in power if it does not
enact legislation to advance women's rights. In 1916, the union
becomes the National Woman's Party, led by Alice Paul and Lucy
Burns.

1913   Women win federal voting rights in Norway.

1914   The Women's Peace Party (WPP) is founded in Washington, D.C.,
after European advocates of women's voting rights seek support
from American women to respond to the growing violence of
World War I. The WPP becomes a national organization in 1915
when its leaders, Madeline Doty and Crystal Eastman of New
York, are joined by Jane Addams, who founded the Hull House
settlement in Chicago in 1889 and in 1920 helps establish the
American Civil Liberties Union.

1914   The Normal College of the City of New York is renamed Hunter
College of the City of New York in honor of its first president,
Thomas Hunter, who established the school in 1870 to train
women as teachers. It now offers a broad liberal arts curriculum
but does not become completely coeducational until 1964, though
graduate instruction for men and women is introduced in 1921.

1915   The Danish king signs the grant of voting rights to women in Iceland.

1915   Women win federal voting rights in Denmark.

1915   The Hague Women's Peace Conference, held at the Hague, Netherlands, meets to condemn the war in Europe and to affirm that
women can use their special skills to work for international
peace. One thousand women from neutral nations and nations
involved in the war attend.

1915   A U.S. Court of Appeals rules that night work is illegal for
women.

1915   Margaret Sanger and Mary Ware Dennert found the National
Birth Control League, the first U.S. organization promulgating
birth control. In 1918, Dennert founds the Voluntary Parenthood
League and later opposes Sanger's position that only physicians
can distribute birth control, arguing that all citizens should have
access.

1916   Margaret Sanger and her sister Ethel Byrne open the first birth-control clinic in the United States, in Brooklyn, New York. Sanger, the first person to use the term *birth control*, in a 1914 article in her journal The *Woman Rebel*, has already had a run-in with federal prosecutors over a brochure she distributed showing working-class families the benefits of condoms and douching. The birth-control clinic is raided, and after Sanger serves 30 days in jail she establishes the New York Birth Control League.

1916 In Japan, a law forbids employment of girls and boys under the age of 12 years unless the employer provides education. The law also limits working hours and regulates night work for children, but employers successfully oppose implementation of this law.

1916 The Women's National Bowling Association is formed in Saint Louis, Missouri, by 40 women bowlers. The association evolves into the Women's International Bowling Congress, the world's largest organization in women's sports.

1916 Jeannette Rankin of Montana (Republican), the first woman elected to the U.S. House of Representatives, wins after campaigning across the state on horseback, four years before women receive the right to vote in the United States. Rankin is the only member of the House to vote against U.S. participation in both world wars (1917, 1941) and later protests U.S. involvement in Vietnam.

1916 Women are granted voting rights in the Canadian provinces of Manitoba, Saskatchewan, and Alberta.

1917 Women are granted voting rights in the Canadian provinces of British Columbia and Ontario. The Military Voters Act of the same year gives the vote to women who are in active service.

1917 Miriam Amanda Ferguson is appointed governor of Texas after her husband is impeached and removed from that office.

1917 The American Women's Hospital Service (AWHS) is founded to allow women physicians to help in World War I despite their inability to join the armed forces. AWHS organizes a corps of women doctors, nurses, and ambulance drivers and sets up dispensaries in civilian areas in France.

1917 Indian women demanding improved health care, maternity services, and the same political rights as men organize the Women's Indian Association. By 1926, all the provincial legislatures in India have opened their doors to women.

1917 A march of 20,000 women in New York City helps prompt the adoption by the New York State Legislature of a constitutional amendment guaranteeing equal voting rights to women.

1917 Women are granted voting rights in Russia in the wake of the Russian Revolution.

1917 In Washington, D.C., 168 National Woman's Party members are arrested and convicted for peacefully picketing the White House on behalf of women's suffrage. In prison, they continue to protest by engaging in hunger strikes and are force-fed until public support leads to their release.

1917 Mary Florence Lathrop is the first woman admitted to membership in the American Bar Association.

1918 Anusuyaben Sarabhai, a female activist, organizes India's first major labor strike.

1918 The first province in Canada to enact a law guaranteeing women a fair wage is British Columbia.

1918 U.S. president Woodrow Wilson establishes the War Labor Board (WLB) to deal with the problems of increasing production during World War I and of properly managing troop mobilization. The WLB addresses issues such as health and safety, working hours, and the capacity of women to perform jobs they are unfamiliar with; during its year-and-a-half tenure, the WLB enforces the principle that the many women now working in industry deserve wages equal to men working at the same job.

1918 Women win general voting rights in the Canadian province of Nova Scotia, and the city of Ottawa, Ontario, grants women full suffrage for federal elections.

1918 Constance Markiewicz, an Irish Nationalist, is elected to the Dail Eireann (Irish national legislative body) although she is in jail. Representing the Saint Patrick's League of Dublin, she refuses to acknowledge allegiance to the British crown and does not take her seat.

1918 For the first time, women vote in a national election in England, Scotland, and Wales.

1918 The New Women's Association and the Women's Suffrage League of Japan are founded by Fusae Ichikawa.

1918 The Sierra Leone Women's Movement is founded by Constance Horton Cummings.

1918 Women win federal voting rights in Germany when the Socialists come to power.

1918 Women gain voting rights in Austria and Poland.

1918 The first African-American woman millionaire, Madame C. J. Walker, commissions a magnificent house in Irvington-on-the-Hudson, New York, to show what blacks can accomplish. The first African-American architect registered in New York, Vertner Woodson Tandy, designs the house, which is considered his finest work; Madame Walker's fortune came from cosmetics.

1919 Women are granted general voting rights in the Czech lands (Bohemia and Moravia) soon after the establishment of the new Czechoslovakia. Even though Czech women play an important role in the national movement and are active in women's, partisan, and charitable organizations, they are seldom elected to political office.

1919 Atarashi Onna (New women) is established in Japan when

Raicho Hiratsuka, who founded the Bluestocking Society in 1911, and the women's advocate Fusae Ichikawa join to amend the law that prohibits women from listening and responding to political speeches. *Atarashi Onna* becomes a term of contempt conservative men use to harass women activists.

1919   In the wake of World War I, more than 10 percent of the delegates to the National Assembly in Weimar, Germany, are women.

1919   Women are permitted to serve in the New Zealand Parliament.

1919   The women's section (Zhenotdel) of the secretariat of the central committee of the Russian Communist Party (after 1925, the Communist Party of the Soviet Union) is founded in Moscow to mobilize women in support of the Bolshevik revolution and to promote women's rights. Zhenotdel organizes women factory workers and peasants, sponsors literacy programs, and protests the violence directed against Muslim women of central Asia who abandon wearing the veil.

1919   The French chamber of deputies adopts a suffrage bill, but the French senate defeats it in 1922.

1919   Dr. Alice Hamilton is named assistant professor of industrial medicine at the Medical School of Harvard University. A toxicologist, she writes and lectures about hygiene and industrial diseases.

1919   Established as part of the League of Nations, the International Labour Organization (ILO) develops international standards for maternity leave, proposing leave of up to six weeks before the birth of a baby and six weeks afterward, with benefits to provide for the family during that time. The ILO becomes part of the United Nations in 1946.

1919   Nancy Witcher Langhorne Astor (later Lady Astor) becomes the first woman to sit in the British House of Commons when she is elected as a Conservative to fill her husband's seat, after he ascends to the House of Lords as the second viscount Astor. Born in the United States, Astor is one of the richest women in Great Britain and also, in the 1930s, hostess to the influential figures of the Cliveden set, named after the Astor country seat of Cliveden.

1919   Women gain voting rights in the Netherlands and Luxembourg.

1919   The Canadian province of New Brunswick grants women general voting rights.

1919   The U.S. House of Representatives passes the 19th Amendment to the Constitution, giving women the right to vote, by 304 to 89, and the Senate passes it by 56 to 25. The amendment then goes to the states for ratification.

1919–1932   One hundred twelve German women are elected to the Reichstag, the national legislature of Germany. This number amounts to between 7 and 10 percent of women in Germany, a higher percentage than the number of women elected to the U.S. Congress.

1920 Women gain federal voting rights in the United States when the Tennessee legislature ratifies the 19th Amendment to the Constitution. At the signing ceremony, neither the press nor suffragists are present, as neither group is invited.

1920 The League of Women Voters is founded in Chicago, Illinois, in the wake of the passage of the 19th Amendment. The league's mission is to give women impartial information on candidates and political issues, to inform women about their right to vote, and to promote social, economic, and political reform.

1920 The Women's Bureau of the U.S. Department of Labor is established to formulate policies improving the welfare of working women.

1920 Women professors are granted status equal to that of men at Oxford University in Great Britain.

1920 The Alaska Native Sisterhood is formed when a group of Tlingit women in Alaska organize to protect the traditional identity and culture of the Tlingits and to lobby for statehood for Alaska.

1920 Japanese feminists form a new organization, Shinfujin Kyokai (Coalition of new women), which includes the Bluestockings, teachers, and housewives. They publish a newspaper and petition the Japanese Diet (national legislature) for the right to vote.

1920 A law permits abortion in the Russian Soviet Federated Socialist Republic, and abortions are free in the Soviet Union until 1936. Although physicians are encouraged to persuade women to give birth, they cannot refuse to perform an abortion in the first 14 weeks of pregnancy.

1920 A law creating severe penalties for performing and receiving abortions is passed in France. Ostensibly meant to deal with the many deaths in World War I, the law is largely ignored, and approximately 500,000 illegal abortions are performed each year, often at great risk to the woman.

1920 A legal ruling in France equates contraception with abortion and makes birth control illegal.

1920 Women gain voting rights in Czechoslovakia.

Early 1920s The largest organization devoted to peace in its time, the National Committee on the Cause and Cure of War is formed in the United States as a coalition of the American Association of University Women, the Women's Christian Temperance Union, the General Federation of Women's Clubs, and the League of Women Voters. The committee works to support the proposed Treaty for the Renunciation of War, known as the Kellogg-Briand Pact, which is finally signed by 16 nations in Paris in 1928.

1921 The Mothers' Clinic for Constructive Birth Control is founded in North London by Marie Stopes, who in 1918 wrote *Wise Motherhood*, a book providing diagrams of the reproductive system and explaining various methods of contraception. The clinic offers advice and provides sponges and cervical caps.

1921   A law granting equal accessibility for women to government jobs is instituted in Denmark, though the law excludes jobs and appointments in the military and clergy. After World War II, women can become pastors, and in 1971 military training is opened to women in Denmark.

1921   The first black pilot in the world, Bessie Coleman, an American, receives her pilot's license in France. Coleman becomes a barnstorming (stunt) pilot in the United States in hopes of earning enough to open a school to train black pilots but dies in a crash in 1926.

1921   Women are granted voting rights in Belgium and Sweden.

1921   Voters elect the first woman to serve in Parliament in Australia.

1921   The U.S. Congress passes the Sheppard-Towner Maternity and Infancy Protection Act, establishing a health and welfare program for mothers and children in the United States, with child-health and maternity-consultation centers, mobile health clinics to provide education and care for pregnant women, and funding for midwives.

1921   The American Association of University Women (AAUW) is formed in Washington, D.C., following a merger of the Association of Collegiate Alumnae and the Southern Association of College Women. The AAUW promotes political action on issues of higher education for women and provides financial aid and fellowships for women.

1922   The Federação Brasileira pelo Progresso Feminino (Brazilian federation for the advancement of women) is founded in Brazil by the biologist Bertha Lutz. It draws many professional women as members and 10 years later is instrumental in gaining women the right to vote.

1922   The word *obey* is removed from the marriage vows of the Episcopal Church in the United States.

1922   Provincial voting rights are given to women in the Canadian province of Prince Edward's Island.

1922   Ivy Williams is admitted to the bar in Great Britain but chooses to teach at Oxford University instead, and Helen Nordmanton becomes the first woman to practice law in Britain. In the same year, Monica Cobb is the first woman actually to plead a case before a court in Britain.

1922   Elise Richter is the first woman professor in Austria.

1923   In *Adkins v. Children's Hospital*, the U.S. Supreme Court rules that a minimum-wage law for women in the District of Columbia is unconstitutional because it deprives women of the right to bargain. Based on the concept that women are equal to men since they now have the right to vote, the Court's ruling leads to the termination of all existing state minimum-wage laws.

| 1923 | Motivated by the Fascists' desire to limit female competition in the job market, the Gentile Educational Reform is enacted in Italy. The reform bans women from teaching certain subjects and from working in predominantly male schools. |

1923   Margaret Sanger organizes the first U.S. conference on birth control, and in 1925 she organizes the first worldwide conference on birth control.

1924   Nina Bang is elected a cabinet minister in Denmark.

1924   The League for Women's Suffrage is the first organization for women's suffrage in Japan. The league's 2,000 members publish a journal and campaign for male candidates who favor women's rights.

1924   Native American women in the United States are granted voting rights.

1924   Nellie Tayloe Ross, elected governor of Wyoming to complete her deceased husband's term, becomes one of the first two women to be elected governor of a U.S. state. The other is Miriam Amanda Ferguson, known as "Ma" Ferguson, whose husband was impeached as governor after serving from 1915–17; she is elected governor of Texas in the same year as Ross but is inaugurated 16 days after her.

1924   The Women's Division of the U.S. National Amateur Athletic Federation is formed to encourage sports events for women in high school and college.

1925   A law banning the requirement that women wear veils is passed in Turkey.

1925   The first woman elected to the U.S. National Academy of Science is the physician Florence Sabin.

1926   The first woman appointed sheriff in Great Britain is Lucia Welch.

1926   Violette Anderson is the first African-American woman who, as a practicing attorney, appears before the U.S. Supreme Court.

1926   The first modern prison for women prisoners in the United States, the Federal Industrial Institution for Women, is built in West Virginia. Dr. Mary Harris is appointed superintendent; the prison has no guards.

1926   Women in India gain the opportunity to run for political office when British authorities grant them the right to vote, but only in provincial elections.

1926   Bertha Knight Landes becomes the first woman elected mayor of a major city in the United States when she wins the mayoral election in Seattle.

1926   Miina Sillanpaa becomes the first female cabinet member in Finland.

1926   The first woman to swim across the English Channel is Gertrude

Ederle, an American competitive swimmer who already won gold and bronze medals in swimming at the Paris Summer Olympics in 1924. Swimming the channel, Ederle sets a new record for the 56-kilometer span from Cap Gris-Nez, France, to Dover, England: 14 hours and 31 minutes, two hours less than the previous record, which was set by a man.

1926	Women are admitted to the legal profession in Turkey.
1927	Anna Goldfarb is appointed to the position of censor in the Soviet Union.
1928	The World Association of Girl Guides and Girl Scouts is organized in London to support international recreational activities and outdoor skills for girls.
1928	The Union Française pour le Suffrage des Femmes (French union for women's suffrage) has more than 100,000 members but does not win women the right to vote until 1944.
1928	Women gain general voting rights in Ecuador and Guyana.
1928	Women in Great Britain are granted general voting rights, and the following year voters elect 13 women to Parliament.
1928	General voting rights are given to women in Puerto Rico.
1928	Women in Portugal are granted federal voting rights, although only women with a high school degree are permitted to vote.
1929	The Women's War in Nigeria, also known as the Aba Riots, occurs when women of southeastern Nigeria fight the British attempt to tax the wealth of local women. Tens of thousands of women attack the local representatives of Great Britain, and more than 50 women die.
1929	Margaret Bondfield becomes the first female cabinet minister in Great Britain. She is appointed by the Socialist prime minister Ramsay MacDonald to serve as labor minister.
1929	Pope Pius XI's encyclical *Divini Iillius Magistri* (Of that divine master) on Christian education declares that coeducation is false in theory and harmful to Christian training.
1930	A law criminalizing abortion in Italy is invoked by Benito Mussolini's government, when the Fascist leader declares abortion a crime against the health of the race. Nevertheless, illegal abortions continue to be performed, averaging about 500,000 a year.
1930	In the encyclical *Casti Connubii* (Of pious marriage), Pope Pius XI prohibits taking the life of an unborn child to save the mother's life. The Church's ruling contradicts the then customary medical practice of performing caesarean sections to remove dead fetuses; the encyclical also makes it a grave sin to practice birth control.
1930	White women are given the right to vote in South Africa, although blacks of both sexes are prohibited from voting.
1930	The Anticolonialist Women's Association, an organization of

Vietnamese women fighting for independence, is established.

1930   The Associated Country Women of the World, an organization to provide aid and support to women farmers around the world, is created in London.

1930   The Association of Southern Women for the Prevention of Lynching (ASWPL) is founded in the United States by Jesse Daniels Ames, director of the Women's Committee of the Commission on Interracial Cooperation in Atlanta, Georgia. ASWPL confronts the epidemic of lynchings of black men by the Ku Klux Klan and examines the mythologies of the pure white Southern woman and the predatory black male at the heart of bigotry in the South, which led to the justification of lynching.

1931   Women win voting rights in Spain, although only women over 23 years of age are permitted to vote.

1931   Jane Addams, the American social reformer, becomes the first U.S. woman to win the Nobel Prize for Peace, shared with the educator Nicholas Murray Butler. In addition to her work with poor people, Addams is concerned with reforming laws governing women's and children's labor, and in 1920 she helped found the American Civil Liberties Union (ACLU).

1932   Federal voting rights are granted to women in Brazil, although only women who are literate are permitted to vote. Women's right to vote is ratified in the 1934 constitution.

1932   Women are given voting rights in Uruguay, the Maldives, and Thailand.

1932   Hattie Ophelia Caraway of Arkansas becomes the first woman elected to the U.S. Senate. In November 1931 she inherited the seat of her late husband, but she wins the seat outright in a special election in January 1932 and then is reelected two more times, serving until 1944.

1932   Spurred by the Depression and a campaign to blame working wives for the country's unemployment, the U.S. Congress passes the Federal Economy Act; Section 213 prohibits married women and their spouses from obtaining federal jobs. At the same time, city school systems and the majority of the nation's banks, insurance companies, and public utilities place restrictions on the ability of married women to work.

1932   The American aviator Amelia Earhart becomes the first woman to complete a solo transatlantic airplane flight, when she flies from Newfoundland to Ireland in 14 hours and 56 minutes. In 1937, Earhart disappears in the South Pacific trying to fly westbound around the world.

1932   A performance by an orchestra composed entirely of women musicians takes place in Vienna, Austria, the first such performance in Europe.

1933   A Nazi concentration camp for women is opened at Ravensbrück, north of Berlin, in Germany; the camp commandant, guards, and administrative staff are all men, assisted by 150 SS *Aufse-herinen*, female supervisors. The first prisoners consist of 999 German women from Ravensbrück and an equal number of Jewish women from Poprad, Slovakia; fewer than one-third of the 132,000 women sent to Ravensbrück survive.

1933   Women in the United States have the opportunity to become postmistresses and to serve as public-health nurses.

1933   Nellie Tayloe Ross, former governor of Wyoming and the first woman to be elected a governor, becomes the first woman director of the U.S. Mint when President Franklin D. Roosevelt appoints her to the post, and she remains in office until the next Republican administration in 1952. Ross introduces automation in making coins and runs the Mint so efficiently that in 1950 she stuns the Congressional Appropriations Committee by trying to return about $1 million of unused appropriations. During her tenure, the Roosevelt dime and Jefferson nickel are created.

1933   Voting rights are granted to women in Turkey.

1933   Women are given federal voting rights in the Philippines, and in 1937 they win the right to vote on the same basis as men.

1933   Frances Perkins becomes the first woman cabinet minister in the United States when President Franklin D. Roosevelt names her secretary of labor. Perkins served as New York State industrial commissioner when Roosevelt was governor; she remains in the cabinet through Roosevelt's entire presidency and plays a major role in passing legislation regulating working conditions, old-age insurance, and unemployment compensation.

1933   A regulation limits a woman's right to compete in state employment examinations in Italy, and a 1938 decree sets a limit of 10 percent on the jobs that can be held by women in both state and private enterprises.

1933   Adolf Hitler, Germany's chancellor, orders that abortionists be executed; it is unlawful to dispense information about contraception, and "Aryan" Germans who marry and have children are offered cash bonuses. In this year, 56,000 people who have been deemed "unfit" are sterilized.

1934   Adolf Hitler declares that the idea of women's emancipation is a Jewish contamination and that a German woman's world is her husband, children, and home.

1934   Voting rights are given to women in Cuba.

1934   A law banning the binding of women's feet is enacted in China.

1934   Florence Ellinwood Allen, a justice of the Ohio Supreme Court, becomes the first woman to be appointed a U.S. federal judge, when President Franklin D. Roosevelt names her to the U.S. Sixth Circuit Court of Appeals. Many criticize the appointment as tokenism, but the U.S. attorney general Homer Cummings comments: "All we did was see that she was not rejected because she was a woman."

1935	The National Council of Negro Women (NCNW) is founded by Mary McLeod Bethune as a national coalition of U.S. black women's organizations, with chapters also in southern and western Africa. The NCNW fights racism and discrimination against women.
1935	The first all-women's orchestra in the United States is the New York Women's Symphony Orchestra, established by Antonia Brico, a noted American conductor. Brico is the first woman to conduct the Berlin Symphony Orchestra (1930) and the New York Philharmonic (1938).
1935	The Aid to Dependent Children, a provision of the U.S. Social Security Act, is passed. For the first time, poor single mothers with children are offered federal financial assistance to enable them to keep their children at home; today this federal program is known as Aid for Dependent Children.
1935	The Nuremberg Laws are passed at the annual convention of the National Socialist German Workers Party (Nazis) in Nuremberg, Germany. The Nuremberg laws deprive Jews of citizenship (anyone with a Jewish grandparent is considered a Jew), forbid German citizens from marrying Jews, and prohibit sexual intercourse between "Aryans" and Jews.
1935	The Frente Unica pro Derechos de la Mujer (United Front for the Rights of Woman), the first organization devoted to women's right to vote in Mexico, is established.
1936	A law discouraging divorce is passed in the Soviet Union. The law adds new fees for divorce and tightens qualifications for divorce and requirements for alimony payments; it expands welfare provisions for mothers and provides financial aid and child care for working women.
1936	Mary McLeod Bethune becomes the first African-American woman appointed to a major U.S. federal post when she is named director of Negro Affairs in the National Youth Administration. Bethune had been a founder of Bethune-Cookman College in 1923 and had organized the National Council of Negro Women in 1935.
1936	Beryl Markham, a British bush pilot and racehorse breeder in East Africa, is the first woman to fly a plane across the Atlantic Ocean solo and nonstop from London to Nova Scotia. Markham's flight time is 23 hours and 45 minutes.
1936	The U.S. Supreme Court rules in *Morehead v. New York ex rel. Tipaldo* that a minimum-wage law for women is unconstitutional. The decision is reversed in 1937 in *West Coast Hotel v. Parrish*.
1936	A law in Ireland makes it a criminal offense to import, sell, or advertise any contraceptive device or method.
1936	Stalin revokes the decree legalizing abortion in the Soviet Union, citing the need for more manpower. The new decree permits abortion only in cases where the mother's life is endangered or

the child is certain to inherit a grave disease; education about birth control is discontinued and access to contraception denied.

1936 In a case brought by Hannah Stone, an advocate of birth control, a judge of the U.S. Court of Appeals for the Second Circuit rules that the purpose of the Comstock Law of 1872 (which made it a criminal offense to mail anything of a contraceptive nature) is not to prevent the mail, sale, or importation of materials that competent physicians might use to save a life or promote a patient's welfare.

1937 The Women's Emergency Brigade is formed during a sit-down strike in Flint, Michigan, when women defy police lines to bring food and medical supplies to striking autoworkers.

1937 The Irish constitution bans divorce and denounces the idea of mothers working.

1937 A court in Waldenburg, Germany, rules that the state can take a child from parents who refuse to teach the child Nazi ideology.

1937 Women are given some voting rights in Mexico, and their right to vote is expanded in 1946, but not until 1953 are full federal voting rights granted to women in that country.

1937 A law banning the requirement that women wear a veil is passed in Albania.

1937 The first woman to serve as foreperson for a U.S. federal grand jury is Julia Sims.

1937 A mass rape and murder of more than 10,000 women by Japanese troops takes place in Nanjing (Nanking), China. From 1937 on, the Japanese imperial army kidnaps and imprisons thousands of Chinese and Korean girls and women to provide sex for their combat troops.

1937 The U.S. Federal Economy Act prohibiting married women and their spouses from getting government jobs is repealed.

1937 A law passed in Denmark permits abortion for therapeutic reasons, although the number of illegal abortions remains high. The movement for abortion on demand begins in Denmark in the 1960s and achieves success in 1973; unrestricted abortion during the first 12 weeks of pregnancy is legal and covered by national insurance.

1937 The first state contraceptive clinic in the United States opens in Raleigh, North Carolina. The state board of health creates a program to educate poor married women about contraception as part of its maternity and children's health clinic.

1937 A *fatwa*, or religious ruling, handed down by Islam's grand mufti (an Islamic legal authority) permits contraception if the man and woman both agree.

1937 A report by the Birkett Committee on Abortion issued in Great Britain concludes that women seem not to understand that self-induced abortion is illegal. Working-class women take pills not to induce abortion but to bring on their periods.

1938 The U.S. Fair Labor Standards Act guarantees a minimum wage of 25 cents an hour, rising in seven years to 45 cents an hour, and no wage difference for male and female workers. The act covers about 57 percent of working women in the country, excluding domestic service, agriculture, and small retail establishments.

1938 In *His Majesty the King v. Bourne*, a British judge rules that under some circumstances a doctor has not only the right but the duty to perform an abortion. In the case cited, a gynecologist, Alec Bourne, performed an abortion on a 14-year-old girl who had been raped by four soldiers.

1939 Dr. Freda Wünderlich becomes the dean of the Graduate School of Political and Social Sciences at the New School for Social Research in New York City, the first woman to head a graduate school in the United States.

1940 Provincial voting rights are given to women in the Canadian province of Quebec.

1941 Women gain general voting rights in Panama.

1941 The Canadian Women's Army Corps is established, giving women in Canada the opportunity to serve in the army.

1941 Church Women United is established in the United States when a coalition of religious women's groups organizes to deal with issues of war and peace, human rights, and women's poverty.

1942 The U.S. Women's Army Auxiliary Corps (WAACs; later, the Women's Army Corps) is authorized by Congress to allow women to perform noncombat jobs in the army and to free men for combat during World War II. Congress also authorizes the Women Accepted for Voluntary Emergency Service (WAVES) to allow women to serve in the navy and the Women's Auxiliary Ferrying Squadron to allow female civilians to fly aircraft to bases in noncombat zones (soon afterward absorbed into the Women's Airforce Service Pilots or WASPs).

1942 The SPARs (Semper Paratus—Always Ready), a women's auxiliary to the U.S. Coast Guard, is established to free men for sea duty during World War II.

1943 The Gruppa di Difesa della Donna e per L'Assistenza ai Combattenti per la Libertà (Women's defense groups for aid to fighters for liberty) is founded by Italian women in Lombardy and the Piedmont to resist the Nazis. On March 8 of this year, the 33rd International Women's Day, Italian women demonstrate against Mussolini's Fascist government.

1943 The first woman is elected to the federal Parliament in Australia.

1943 The All-Professional Baseball League, a professional baseball league for women, is created by the owner of the Chicago Cubs team to ensure the continuation of baseball in the United States during the years of World War II, when many male players serve in the military. As in professional male baseball, the league is segregated, and no black women can participate; the women players must wear impractical skirts and makeup and are chaperoned.

1943   Non-Jewish wives of Jews demonstrate in Berlin and block their husbands' deportation to death camps. When Nazi soldiers try again to deport the Jews a week later, a crowd mobilizes and refuses to move until Joseph Goebbels, Hitler's minister of propaganda, relents, and 1,500 Jewish men, already tattooed with concentration-camp numbers, are released.

1944   The Unione delle Donne Italiane (Union of Italian women) is formed in Italy to unite women opposed to the Fascist regime.

1944   The All-Arab Federation of Women is founded in Egypt by Huda Shaarawi, an Egyptian feminist. Returning to Egypt from a European women's conference in 1923, Shaarawi sparked the first public rebellion against Islamic traditions by removing her veil; the crowd of women who came to meet her were inspired to do the same.

1944   Federal voting rights are awarded to women in France, and the French constitutions of 1946 and 1958 include the principle of equal rights for men and women.

1944   The Japanese Girls' Volunteer Corps is organized in Japan to create a pool of factory workers and to free men for military service. Some 430,000 unmarried girls and women from the ages of 12 to 40 are put to work 15 hours a day, many on the night shift; anyone who refuses to work is subject to one year in jail and a large fine.

1945   Voting rights on the same basis as men are granted to women in Greece, Hungary, Yugoslavia, and Senegal.

1945   Women are given federal voting rights in Japan after pressure from the Allied occupation forces.

1945   Women gain federal voting rights in Italy; the previous year, with the defeat of the Fascists, the Italian government repealed the laws banning women from holding positions in secondary schools.

1945   General voting rights are granted to women in Guatemala and Argentina.

1945   The Association of Air Line Stewardesses is the first organization of female flight attendants in the United States. With many airlines insisting that women retire at the age of 35, imposing weight limitations, and prohibiting married women from working, flight attendants organize to end discriminatory actions.

1945   Kathleen Lonsdale becomes the first woman elected a fellow of the British Royal Society. Lonsdale, an Irish crystallographer, used X-ray diffraction analysis in 1929 to discover the structure of hexamethylbenzene.

1945–1946   Ilse Koch, once a doctor at the Auschwitz concentration camp in Poland, is the only woman to be tried at the war-crimes trials at

Nuremberg, Germany. Koch, known as the Bitch of Buchenwald, ordered lampshades to be made from human skin, yet seven trials are needed to convict her, for her legal status is merely that of the wife of Karl Otto Loch, the commandant at Buchenwald concentration camp in Germany.

1946   Eighty-three women run for election to the Diet (national legislature) in Japan, and 39 are successful.

1946   Felisa Rincón de Gautier is elected mayor of San Juan, Puerto Rico, after spending almost two decades trying to involve women in politics.

1946   Women are given voting rights on the same basis as men in Palestine, Kenya, Liberia, and Vietnam.

1946   The Commission on the Status of Women is created by the United Nations as a subsidiary of the Economic and Social Council and plays an important research and advisory role in women's issues.

1946   A rule overturning the requirement that women spectators at the Canadian Parliament wear hats is passed.

1946   The first U.S. Women's Open Golf Tournament takes place in Spokane, Washington.

1946   Japanese women are permitted to attend Tokyo Imperial University on the same terms as men.

1947   The passage of the U.S. Army-Navy Nurse Act provides members of the U.S. Army Nurse Corps with commissioned-officer status. The highest rank they can achieve is lieutenant colonel.

1947   The passage of a labor law in Japan allows women six weeks of maternity leave. The law also requires that employers grant menstruating women two days off a month, establishes a minimum wage and limited working hours, and requires equal pay for equal work, although this provision is largely unenforced.

1947   Spurred by administrators in the U.S. occupation forces, the Equal Rights Amendment is passed in Japan, making it illegal to discriminate against women for political, social, or economic reasons and enabling women to bring lawsuits against offenders. A department of women's and children's affairs is also established, with Kikue Yamakawa the first female director.

1947   Germaine Peyrolles becomes the first woman to preside over the National Assembly in France.

1947   Women gain general voting rights in Bolivia.

1947   Women are granted voting rights on the same basis as men in Bulgaria, China, Nepal, Pakistan, and Venezuela.

1947   The constitution of the new Republic of Italy establishes principles of equal pay for equal work, equality between spouses, equal political rights, and equal access for women in the workplace. Nevertheless, not until 1963 would a law be passed giving women access to all careers and public offices and giving them the right to serve as jurors.

1947   A civil law allowing women to marry at the age of 18 years is enacted in Japan. The law also enables women to be heads of families, gives female children equal inheritance rights, and denies husbands the rights over the property of their wives.

1948   Women gain voting rights on the same basis as men in Israel, Iraq, the Republic of Korea, and Suriname.

1948   Margaret Chase Smith of Maine (Republican) becomes the first woman elected to the U.S. Senate in her own right, rather than to fill another senator's unexpired term, and serves in the Senate until 1973. In 1960, Smith wins the first all-women's contest for the U.S. Senate when she defeats Lucia Marie Cormier, and in 1964 she becomes the first woman to seek the presidential nomination of one of the two major political parties.

1948   The World Association of Mothers for Peace is established in New York City to advocate the education of mothers throughout the world, the elimination of war, and the opportunity to raise children in peace.

1948   The Mouvement Mondial des Mères (International movement of mothers) is created as an international nongovernmental organization by the action of the Union Féminine Civique et Sociale (Women's civic and social union), a French women's group, during a UNESCO congress, to promote appreciation for women's work and family unity.

1948   An equal rights law passed in Germany undoes several crucial rights men had enjoyed in the family, such as the exclusive right to decision making. The law establishes joint ownership in the family and recognizes the right of each partner to dispose of his or her own individual wealth.

1948   Pauline Frederick is the first woman to be employed as a radio-network correspondent in the United States, when the American Broadcasting Company hires her. For many years, industry leaders claimed that a woman's voice lacks the authority of the male voice.

1948   In *Goessart v. Cleary*, the U.S. Supreme Court upholds a Michigan law denying a woman the right to work as a bartender unless she is the wife or daughter of the bar's owner. In the Court's view, unless a male is present to protect her, a female bartender may cause social or moral problems.

1948   A law permitting abortion in occupied Japan is passed as a "eugenic protection" measure.

1949   Margaret Sanger, the moving force behind the U.S. birth-control movement, founds the International Planned Parenthood Federation.

1949   The first woman to be appointed an ambassador from the United States is Eugenie Anderson of Minnesota, who is named ambassador to Denmark by President Harry S. Truman. Soon after in the same year, Perle Mesta, a Washington, D.C., hostess famed for her parties, is appointed the first U.S. ambassador to Luxembourg.

1949	Shelton Burnita Matthews, an advocate for women's rights, is the first woman to become a U.S. federal district court judge. Matthews serves for more than 30 years.
1949	Granting of voting rights to women on the same basis as men takes place in Indonesia and Costa Rica.
1949	Women gain general voting rights in Chile but must vote separately from men.
1949	General voting rights are given to women in Syria, and in 1971 they gain the right to hold political office.
1949	Arab women in Israel are granted general voting rights.
1949	*Le deuxième sexe* (The second sex) by the existentialist Simone de Beauvoir is published in France. A controversial analysis of the ways in which "womanhood" is a social construct—and a damaging one, both to women and to society—the book is widely read and discussed; an English translation is published in the United States in 1953.
1950	Women gain general voting rights in El Salvador.
1950	Women are granted voting rights on the same basis as men in Mongolia.
1950	A law banning forced marriages, child betrothals, and female infanticide is passed in the People's Republic of China. Women may also keep their own names, inherit property, and participate in work and social activities, and divorced and widowed women are free to remarry.
1950	Forty-five percent of married women work outside the home in Finland, yet women on average receive only 78 percent of men's earnings.
1950	Women are allowed to attend Harvard Law School in Cambridge, Massachusetts.
1950s	The Indian Parliament passes a law banning polygyny among Hindus in India. The law also gives girls the right to paternal property, in contradiction to the patrilineal kinship system in India, which required that inheritance, concentration of private property, and continuance of the lineage be carried through a male heir.
1951	A native of San Diego, California, Florence Chadwick becomes the first woman to swim across the English Channel from England to France, against the tide and in fogs, making the trip in 16 hours and 22 minutes. In 1953, she swims the Straits of Gibraltar and the Dardanelles and in 1955 breaks her own English Channel record by crossing in 13 hours and 33 minutes.

1952	Women are given the right to vote on the same basis as men in Argentina.
1952	Voting rights are granted to women on the same basis as men in Greece.
1952	The British Parliament passes legislation giving women civil servants the same compensation as men in similar positions.
1952	Ontario becomes the first Canadian province to pass legislation requiring equal pay for equal and comparable work, for men and women.
1953	Jacqueline Cochran, founder and director of a successful cosmetics company, is the first woman to fly faster than the speed of sound in her Canadian F-86 Sabrejet, after setting a new world speed record of 1,052.2 kilometers per hour in the same aircraft, at Edwards Air Force Base, California. In 1943, Cochran returned from flying for the British in World War II to head the Women's Airforce Service Pilots (WASPs) in the United States. In 1962, Cochran becomes the first woman to fly a jet across the Atlantic Ocean, and in 1964 she sets another women's world record of 2,300 kilometers per hour in an F-104G Super Star jet; at her death, Cochran holds more aviation records than any other pilot in history.
1953	The Women's Martí Centennial Civic Front and Society of Friends of the Republic organize a political demonstration of women in Cuba. The police beat and arrest many women who are opposing the dictatorship of Fulgencio Batista.
1953	Women are granted voting rights on the same basis as men in Sudan.
1953	The first woman to be elected president of the United Nations General Assembly is Vijaya Lakshmi Pandit of India.
1953	The first woman to win the Grand Slam of tennis is the American Maureen Connolly, who wins at Wimbledon, the French Open, the U.S. Open, and the Australian Open.
1955	Women are granted general voting rights and the right to hold political office in Honduras.
1955	Betty Robbins is the first woman to be named cantor of a Reform Jewish temple, in Massapequa, New York.
1955	The first woman to fly over and around the North Pole is Louise Boyd, a photographer who organized seven expeditions to Greenland between 1926 and 1941 and authored two important works on the region: *The Fiord Region of East Greenland* and *The Coast Region of Northeast Greenland*. She was 68 years old when she made the historic flight.
1955	Legalized abortion, subject to certain safeguards, resumes in the Soviet Union, although the government officially discourages birth control and abortion.
1956	The ministry of public health in China requires local health

agencies to promote birth control, and the government begins a widespread public-information campaign to limit family size. In 1957, the Ministry of Public Health relaxes restrictions on abortion and sterilization, and birth-control clinics establish "guidance committees."

1956	The first woman to head a firm that is a member of the New York Stock Exchange is Josephine Holt Bay, who becomes president and chairman of the board of the New York brokerage firm A. M. Kidder & Company.
1956	Cecilia Payne-Gaposhkin, a professor and head of the astronomy department, is the first woman to become a tenured professor at Harvard University in Cambridge, Massachusetts.
1956	A law outlawing brothels and licensed prostitutes is passed in Japan, though individual prostitutes can continue in business if they do not solicit in public.
1956	General voting rights are gained by women in Peru.
1956	Women are granted voting rights on the same basis as men in Egypt.
1956	General voting rights are won by women in Nicaragua.
1956	Women are granted federal voting rights in Greece.
1956	Granting of voting rights to women on the same basis as men occurs in Tunisia, Comoros, and Mauritius.
1957	Women receive the right to vote on the same basis as men in Colombia and Malaysia.
1958	Women are granted general voting rights in Algeria. Before this year, Algerian women were without legal, social, and political rights.
1958	Full political rights are granted to women in Iran, but the government suspends women's suffrage in 1962 because of religious demonstrations.
1958	A law granting women the right to choose their husbands is passed in Morocco. The law also restricts polygyny (a man's right to have several wives).
1958	Following a campaign by the Japanese feminist Fusae Ichikawa, Tokyo's prostitute district, Yoshiwara, is closed after 341 years.
1959	The Street Offenses Act is passed by Parliament in Great Britain, making it illegal for a prostitute to solicit in public or private. The law also allows constables to arrest anyone in a public place suspected of committing such an offense.
1959	Women gain voting rights on the same basis as men in Madagascar and Tanzania.
1960	Native American woman are granted voting rights in Canada.
1960	Sirimavo Bandaranaike of Ceylon is the first woman to become the head of a nation in modern times. Bandaranaike wins an

election after her husband is assassinated; she serves until her defeat in 1965, then wins again in 1970 and 1975, when Ceylon changes its name to Sri Lanka.

1960   Women are granted voting rights on the same basis as men in Gabon and Zaire.

1960   Women gain the right to vote in municipal elections in Switzerland.

1960   The Federation of Cuban Women (FMC) is founded by Vilma Espin, the wife of Raul Castro (brother of Fidel), to communicate government policies and programs to women and to bring women's needs and concerns to the government's attention. The FMC is the first mass women's political organization in Cuba after the 1959 revolution bringing Fidel Castro to power.

1960   The Canadian Bill of Rights is amended to prohibit sexual discrimination. The law guarantees women equal treatment if they are in situations identical to men, but courts seldom rule that their situations are equal.

1960   The Food and Drug Administration approves birth-control pills in the United States. In 1961, the pills are allowed to be sold.

1961   The Presidential Commission on the Status of Women in the United States is appointed. Its 1963 report notes pervasive discrimination against women, and, largely as a result, individual state commissions on women play an important part in the development of the women's movement.

1961   A ruling of the U.S. Supreme Court exempts women from jury duty unless they volunteer. Convicted by an all-male jury in Florida of murdering her husband, Gwendolynn Hoyt appealed to the Supreme Court, which rules that the right to an impartially selected jury does not entitle an accused to a jury "tailored to the circumstances of the particular case."

1961   Women Strike for Peace (WSP) is founded in the United States when women organize to oppose the nuclear-arms race and later the Vietnam War. WSP plays a leading role in advocating the nuclear test-ban treaty between the United States and the Soviet Union.

1961   Women are granted full political rights in Cameroon.

1961   Women receive general voting rights and the right to hold political office in the Bahamas.

1961   Women are granted the right to vote on the same basis as men in Rwanda.

1961   Women receive general voting rights under the new constitution of Monaco. At the same time, they receive the right to hold political office.

1961   The Dowry Prohibition Act is passed in India, making it illegal to ask for dowry and to either receive or give money or goods in consideration of the marriage. The law does allow "presents" given at the time of marriage and results in dowry murders—so-called accidental deaths by fire, occasioned by insufficient gift giving on behalf of wives.

1962 Jordanian women are granted general voting rights by Hussein I, king of Jordan.

1962 Elizabeth Lane is the first woman to serve as a high-court judge in Great Britain.

1962 *Sex and the Single Girl* by Helen Gurley Brown is published in the United States. It urges single "career women" to enjoy sexual freedom and contends that this strategy will lead to wiser and happier marriages. On the strength of the book's success, its author is offered the editorship of the failing women's magazine *Cosmopolitan*; circulation rises as she redirects the magazine's content toward a less traditional audience. She will continue as editor for 32 years.

1963 The Equal Pay Act, amending the Fair Labor Standards Act, is passed in the U.S. Congress after a 20-year struggle. The Act mandates equal pay for equal work in instances when men and women hold the same jobs, but its limited scope means that the act affects only a minority of women workers, and almost 30 years later women would still earn only 70 cents for every dollar men earn.

1963 Nancy Lotsey, an eight-year old girl in the New Jersey Small-Fry League, is the first girl to play for a previously all-boy baseball team in the United States.

1963 Women in the Congo and Morocco receive the right to vote on the same basis as men.

1963 *The Feminine Mystique* by Betty Friedan is published and helps launch the modern feminist movement in the United States. Quickly becoming a best-seller, the book sells 5 million copies by 1970.

1963 Valentina Tereshkova, a Soviet cosmonaut, becomes the first woman to fly in outer space when she orbits Earth 48 times in the *Vostok 6* flight.

1964 General voting rights are given to women in Libya.

1964 Women are granted general voting rights in San Marino.

1964 Patsy Mink of Hawaii becomes the first Asian-American woman to be elected to the U.S. Congress.

1964 An equal-rights bill granting women the right to be legal guardians of their children is passed in the Canadian province of Quebec; other provinces granted this right to women before 1923. The bill also gives women the right to sign leases and business contracts without their husbands' permission.

1964 Geraldine Mock of Germany is the first woman to fly solo around the world. Mock flies 22,859 miles in a single-engine plane, making 21 stops en route.

1964	Title VII of the U.S. Civil Rights Act prohibits job discrimination but is designed primarily to prohibit racial discrimination. The Equal Employment Opportunity Commission, created to implement Title VII, at first enforces only the provisions concerned with racial discrimination.
1964	Honored by the U.S. Congress and the New York State Senate, Shirley Muldowney is the first American woman to set a National Hot Rod Association (NHRA) record for driving a dragster. The first woman licensed to drive a dragster, Muldowney is also the first woman to drive a top-fuel dragster in an NHRA event and the first driver, male or female, to win three NHRA world championships.
1965	Women receive general voting rights under the new constitution in Afghanistan.
1965	In *Weeks v. Southern Bell*, the U.S. Supreme Court decides to curtail restrictive labor laws and company regulations affecting the hours and conditions of women's work. The decision opens previously male-only jobs to women.
1965	The U.S. Supreme Court, in *Griswold v. Connecticut*, strikes down an 1879 Connecticut state law and affirms the constitutional right of married couples to gain access to contraceptives. Justice William O. Douglas states that the state law invades the privacy guaranteed by the Bill of Rights, and by 1965, more than 700 public birth-control clinics are operating in the United States.
1966	Princess Elizabeth Bagaya of Uganda is the first African woman to practice law in an African nation.
1966	Women receive the opportunity to serve voluntarily in the military in Portugal.
1966	Married women are given general voting rights in Spain.
1966	Women receive general voting rights under the new constitution in Barbados.
1966	Indira Gandhi, daughter of the first prime minister of independent India, Jawaharlal Nehru, becomes prime minister of India and serves from 1966 to 1977 and again from 1980 to 1984.
1966	The National Organization for Women (NOW) is organized by Betty Friedan and others dissatisfied with the U.S. Equal Employment Opportunity Commission's unwillingness to treat sex discrimination in the workplace as rigorously as race discrimination. In 1970, NOW organizes a huge march to celebrate the 50th anniversary of the passage of the 19th Amendment to the U.S. Constitution, which gave women the right to vote.
1966	The Committee for the Defense of Vietnamese Woman's Human Dignity and Rights is founded to protect Vietnamese women from U.S. soldiers, in response to the operation of a brothel by the U.S. Army's First Cavalry Division at An Khe, Vietnam. The organization condemns the brothel and the rape of Vietnamese refugee

women in the military camp.

1966   At a meeting with the Revolutionary Council in Algeria, Algerian women protest against the French leadership. The women are informed that they already have all the rights they require, and that there is no further need for struggle; the women then walk out.

1966   A law outlawing abortions is enacted in Romania after a study shows that there are four abortions for every birth in the country. Regardless of the law, women still find ways to have abortions.

1966–1976   The Women's Federation is disbanded during China's Cultural Revolution, and its publication, *Women of China*, is shut down. Although women intellectuals, like their male counterparts, are branded class enemies during this period, women from working-class and peasant backgrounds make some gains in the areas of children's day care and rural women's health care.

1967   California enacts a law permitting abortions when the life or health of the pregnant woman is threatened or when the pregnancy is the result of rape or incest. The law becomes the model for other states, and similar laws are adopted in 16 states by 1972.

1967   The National Organization for Women (NOW) adds abortion to its Women's Bill of Rights, and the National Association for the Repeal of Abortion (later renamed the National Abortion Rights Action League) is founded. Abortion now becomes a major political issue in the United States.

1967   The National Health Service Family Planning Act provides free family-planning information in Great Britain. The act requires medical staff to provide advice and contraceptive devices.

1967   The Neuwirth Law permitting the sale of contraceptives is passed in France. Nevertheless, diaphragms, intrauterine devices, and spermicides are still difficult to purchase.

1967   The Fund for Population Activities of the United Nations is established to advance family planning.

1967   The Colorado state legislature passes a law liberalizing abortion policy. The new law allows therapeutic abortion if three physicians at accredited hospitals agree that the pregnancy would result in the mother's death or permanent injury to her physical or mental health, or if the child is likely to be born with severe physical or mental problems, or if the pregnancy resulted from rape or incest, and if the surgery is performed within the first 16 weeks of pregnancy.

1967   *Loving v. Virginia*, a decision by the U.S. Supreme Court, overturns the conviction of Mildred Loving, a black Native American, and her husband Richard, who is white. The decision thus reverses state laws banning marriage between men and women of different races.

1967	The National Association for the Repeal of Abortion Laws (NARAL) is formed in the United States to fight for a woman's right to choose to have an abortion. In 1970, the State of New York passes a bill permitting abortions without restrictions, and women from all over the country come to New York to obtain a safe, legal abortion.
1967	The terms *liberation* and *consciousness raising* come into use in reference to women's rights. *Liberation* is first used when the Chicago Women's Liberation Group is organized, and *consciousness raising* is introduced by the New York Radical Women, a group that encourages women to share their stories.
1967	The Royal Commission on the Status of Women is established in Canada to investigate the problems confronting Canadian women and to recommend national programs to deal with them.
1967	Although the principle of equal pay for equal work is applied in Australia, women's work is still defined as of less value than men's. Not until a law governing the definition of equal work in 1972 and a 1979 law guaranteeing the minimum wage for women are passed does their economic status begin to improve.
1967	U.S. president Lyndon B. Johnson issues Executive Order 11375, which extends the "affirmative-actions" provisions of Title VII of the Civil Rights Act of 1964 to include discrimination against women working for employers with contracts to do business with the U.S. government. The Department of Labor is granted authority to administer affirmative action and begins a program asking contractors to demonstrate what steps they are taking to comply with its provisions.
1967	Muriel Siebert pays $445,000 for a seat on the New York Stock Exchange, becoming the first woman to own a seat there. In 1992. Siebert is one of 13 women in the world named Veuve Clicquot Business Woman of the Year.
1968	In *Pennsylvania v. Daniel*, the Pennsylvania Supreme Court repudiates a state law requiring longer prison sentences for women than for men who commit the same crime. The ruling overturns the Muncy Law.
1968	Women are granted general voting rights in Ireland under a United Nations treaty. At the same time, women receive the right to hold office.
1968	In *Rosenfeld v. Southern Pacific Company*, a landmark decision in the struggle for equal rights, a U.S. federal district court rules that Title VII of the Civil Rights Act of 1964 supersedes California laws restricting women's actions on the job. The court rules that California regulations limiting women's ability to work overtime and lift weights above the restricted limit are discriminatory.
1968	The Jeannette Rankin Brigade is formed when 88-year-old Rankin, the first woman to serve in the U.S. Congress, leads 5,000 women on an anti–Vietnam War demonstration to the U.S.

Capitol. Forbidden to enter the Capitol grounds, the group sues, challenging the 1882 prohibition against peaceful Capitol demonstrations.

1968	The Toronto Women's Liberation Movement is organized in Canada by University of Toronto students.
1968	A law gives women the same political rights as men in Portugal, although still only the head of the family (generally a man) is allowed to vote in local elections.
1968	Shirley Chisholm of New York is the first African-American woman elected to the House of Representatives.
1968	Cathy Kusner is the first woman to become a licensed jockey in U.S. horse racing.
1968	Canadian women's military services are integrated with men's in the newly organized Canadian Armed Forces.
1968	The British Abortion Act permits abortion in Great Britain when two physicians determine that the pregnancy involves risks to the physical or mental health of the pregnant woman. The new law repeals the 1861 statute that criminalized all abortion.
1968	Pope Paul VI issues the papal encyclical *Humanae Vitae* (Of human life), forbidding all artificial means of contraception for members of the Roman Catholic Church.
1969	Women are introduced into the U.S. Air Force's Reserve Officers' Training Corps (ROTC).
1969	Golda Meir, at the age of 71, is the first woman to be elected prime minister of Israel.
1969	Tina Anselmi is the first woman to serve in the Italian cabinet.
1969	A. Espinoza is the first woman to serve in the Bolivian cabinet, when she becomes minister of labor.
1969	The Fifth Circuit U.S. Court of Appeals, in *Weeks v. Southern Bell*, rules that 30-pound weight-lifting restrictions for women violate Title VII. In the *Colgate-Palmolive* case, the appeals court rules that any weight-lifting test must be given to both men and women.
1969	The Boston Women's Health Collective is created in Boston, Massachusetts, to encourage women to become more aware of their bodies and to be better advocates for informed health care. In 1971, they publish *Our Bodies, Ourselves*.
1969	Aura Celina Casanova is the first woman appointed to a ministerial post in Venezuela, when she becomes minister of development.
1969	A law permitting abortion is passed in Canada as part of an all-inclusive crime bill. The statute provides for a three-physician committee to review decisions about abortion and to rule on whether continuing a pregnancy would endanger the health or life of the mother.

1969–1970	A women's studies program is introduced at San Diego State University in California. Women's studies programs are developed across the nation to correct the typical omission in college curricula of material on, about, or by women.
1970	The Family Planning and Population Research Act (Title X of the Public Health Service Act of 1970) provides funding for programs on birth control and education on reproduction, determining family size, and prenatal and postnatal care in the United States.
1970	Maria Theresa Carcomo Lobo becomes the first woman to serve as minister in the government of Portugal.
1970	A report by the Canadian Royal Commission on the Status of Women notes the need for employers to correct discrimination against women in hiring and recommends that the Canadian government institute "special steps" to employ women in jobs traditionally reserved for men.
1970	Although women are granted full voting rights in Andorra, the country is socially conservative, and women continue to be generally absent from participation in politics.
1970	Féministes Révolutionaires (Revolutionary feminists) is established in France to end male privilege and power. Members hold demonstrations and disrupt public events to bring attention to their cause.
1970	The Comisión Femenil Mexicana Nacional (National commission of Mexican women) is created as a national organization for women's rights.
1970	The Marriage Act, no-fault divorce legislation enacted in Scandinavia (Denmark, Norway, Sweden), fundamentally changes divorce law. If both parties agree, they are entitled to divorce after a one-year separation; as a result, some 90,000 more legal marriages are ended than are begun in Denmark alone from 1971 to 1982.
1970	No-fault divorce legislation enacted in California provides for the "dissolution of marriage" rather than "divorce" and establishes a standard of irreconcilable difference to replace the previous standard of adultery and cruelty.
1970	The first law granting mothers equal parental authority with fathers is passed in France. The law also mandates that a wife retains the property she owned before marriage or inherits during marriage.
1970	The North American Indian Women's Association is founded to represent Native American women in North America. It draws members from 43 tribes in both the United States and Canada.
1970	The National Organization for Women's Legal Defense and Education Fund (NOW LDEF) is established to provide educational programs promoting gender equity and to provide legal assistance in cases of sex discrimination. NOW LDEF also creates and distributes educational materials on sexual harassment, lesbian

rights, dissolution of marriages, and equal rights to employment and education.

1970   Women's Equality Day is organized to celebrate the 50th anniversary of women's right to vote in the United States.

1970   A bill prohibiting sexual discrimination in public places in New York City is signed by Mayor John Lindsay. The bill enables women to drink in McSorley's Tavern in downtown New York, and women also "liberate" the Men's Bar at the Biltmore Hotel.

1970   Cathy Rigby becomes the first U.S. woman gymnast to win an international medal, when she is awarded the silver medal at the world championships in Ljubljana, Yugoslavia, for her performance on the balance beam. Rigby also represented the United States in the 1968 and 1972 Olympics.

1970   The Women's Liberation Conference on women's rights in Great Britain is held at Ruskin College, Oxford University, and continues to be held yearly through 1978, when the movement is divided between radical and socialist feminists.

1970   The First U.S. Circuit Court of Appeals affirms the constitutional right of unmarried adults to gain access to contraceptives. The ruling strikes down a restrictive Massachusetts law.

1971   The Native Women's Association of Canada is formed.

1971   Jeanne Holm is promoted to general in the U.S. Air Force.

1971   The Women in the Arts Foundation is established in New York City and works to increase opportunities for female artists in galleries and museums and to arrange exhibitions and arts competitions.

1971   The male electorate defeats a measure granting voting rights to women in Liechtenstein.

1971   Women are granted full voting rights in Switzerland.

1971   The National Women's Political Caucus is founded in the United States by the congresswomen Bella Abzug and Shirley Chisholm and the feminist leaders Gloria Steinem and Betty Friedan. The caucus supports women candidates for political office and encourages women in both major political parties to get involved in their local and state political caucuses.

1971   Girls are given the opportunity to serve as pages in the U.S. Senate.

1971   The feminist magazine *Ms.* first appears as an insert in *New York* magazine. In July 1972, *Ms.* will begin independent publication with a cover advocating "Wonder Woman for President" and featuring articles by Germaine Greer, Letty Pogrebin, and Erica Jong, among others. Gloria Steinem is the editor. *Ms.* will achieve a circulation of 350,000 within a year.

1971   In an attempt to control population size, a policy limiting families to two children is instituted in China.

1971	*Reed v. Reed*, a decision by the U.S. Supreme Court, allows some sex-based discrimination if it is related to a legitimate state interest. The case involves the separated parents of a child who had died, with each parent seeking to be named administrator of the child's estate; a district court rules that a 1971 statute granting preference to males violates equal-protection provisions of the 14th Amendment, but the Supreme Court decides that the equal-protection clause does not preclude states from treating different classes of people in different ways, so long as that treatment is not arbitrary and is deemed to be reasonable.
1971	Las Hermanas (The sisters) is created as an organization of Roman Catholic women of Latina descent in the United States.
1971	The Association for Intercollegiate Athletics for Women (AIAW) is founded in the United States, in the wake of rules changes in women's basketball, which transformed the game. The AIAW supports a national basketball tournament for women, which is televised in 1978; the AIAW disbands in 1982, by which date women's basketball has come into its own.
1971	The National Black Women's Political Leadership Caucus is founded in the United States to spur the involvement of black women in the political process on the local and national levels.
1971	The Feminist Woman's Health Center is established in Los Angeles, California, by women's grassroots organizations and focuses on empowering women to take control of their own health. Women are taught to perform self-examinations.
1971	The Center for the American Woman and Politics is created at the Eagleton Institute of Politics at Rutgers University in New Brunswick, New Jersey. The center charts the status of women in American politics and maintains a database on women who hold public office.
1971	A battered-women's shelter is opened in Urbana, Illinois, by Cheryl Frank and Jacqueline Flenner.
1972	An emergency rape-crisis hot line is created in Washington, D.C.
1972	Marie-Claire Chevalier, a French teenager who got pregnant at the age of 16 years, decides, with the support of her mother, Michèle, to have an abortion, and both women are charged under French law. Giselle Halami, a lawyer and founder of *Choisir*, an abortion-rights magazine, argues that the law is selectively enforced against poor women; prominent women in the arts, including Simone de Beauvoir, testify that they have had abortions and have not been prosecuted. Michèle Chevalier pays a small fine, and soon thereafter doctors perform free abortions in France's major cities.
1972	Sally Priesand is ordained as a Reform Jewish rabbi in the United States.
1972	Title IX of the Educational Amendments, banning financial aid to educational institutions that discriminate on the basis of sex, is passed by Congress. After Title IX goes into effect in 1976,

women's participation in sports programs and professional schools greatly increases.

1972   The National Association of Female Executives (NAFE), an organization of women executives in the United States, is formed in New York City. NAFE chapters throughout the country help women with career planning and employment opportunities.

1972   A shelter for battered women is established in Great Britain by Erin Pizzey. By the end of the decade, more than 200 women's shelters and crisis hot lines have been set up across Great Britain, and the Women's Aid Federation has been organized to represent their interests.

1972   The Clearinghouse on Women's Issues is created to help U.S. women's organizations better communicate and disseminate educational material, particularly in the area of public policy. The clearinghouse advocates women's economic equality, legal rights, and equal opportunities in education and health.

1972   The National Association of Cuban-American Women is founded in Cuba.

1972   The National Action Committee on the Status of Women is founded in Canada.

1972   Jeanne Martin Cissé of Guinea becomes the first woman to be elected president of the Security Council of the United Nations.

1972   The Center for Women Policy Studies is established in Washington, D.C., to encourage research on issues of equality, women's health, law, and equal opportunity in education.

1972   The Pink Panthers are organized in Japan by Misako Enoki, a pharmacist, who inspires women to fight for abortion, access to birth control, equal employment rights, and equitable property settlements and alimony. The women wear white military uniforms and pink helmets.

1973   The *Roe v. Wade* decision of the U.S. Supreme Court affirms that women are entitled to have an abortion on the grounds of rights to privacy guaranteed in the Constitution, after Jane Roe, pseudonym for a Texas woman who never had an abortion, becomes a plaintiff in what eventually became the case of *Roe v. Wade*. The Court rules that in the first trimester of pregnancy the decision to abort is left to the woman and her physician. The Court's decision is written by Justice Harry Blackmun, whom President Richard M. Nixon appointed to the Court in 1970 after the nominations of G. Harold Carswell and Clement Haynsworth were successfully opposed by women's and civil rights groups.

1973   Women are given voting rights on the same basis as men in Jordan.

1973   The National Black Feminist Organization is established in New York City to represent the interests of black women, rich and poor, in the United States, particularly on issues of sexism and racism in employment. Founding members include employees of

Ms. magazine and members of radical lesbian groups, the Socialist Workers Party, and the National Organization for Women.

1973   The National Right to Life Committee is founded in the United States to block and repeal national and local laws making abortion more readily available.

1973   *Standards for the Urban Police Function*, published by the American Bar Association in New York City, advocates that cases involving a police response to domestic violence be handled "without reliance on criminal assault or disorderly conduct."

1973   Call Off Your Old Tired Ethics (COYOTE) is organized in San Francisco, California, by Margo St. James. COYOTE fights to decriminalize prostitution, improve the economic position of prostitutes, and help end violence against them.

1973   The Three Marias, a group of women in Portugal, are imprisoned for writing a feminist book. Demonstrations throughout the United States and in major European cities at Portuguese embassies lead the Portuguese government to postpone the trial, and in 1974 (after the April coup d'état and removal of the Portuguese dictatorship) the women are acquitted when a judge pronounces the book a work of literary merit.

1973   The U.S. Civil Service Commission issues rules ending physical requirements in hiring. The new rules eliminate height and weight requirements that prevented women from obtaining employment as police officers, park-service workers, and firefighters.

1973   An organization of women clerical workers called 9 to 5 is formed in Boston, Massachusetts, calling for equal pay, more promotions for women, maternity benefits, and the right not to perform non-business personal jobs for their employers. In 1978, 9 to 5 merges with a New York City organization, Women Office Workers, to form 9 to 5, National Association of Working Women, and by the 1980s the organization affiliates with the Service Employers International Union.

1973   A French physician is arrested for performing an abortion, and 10,000 people march to repeal France's abortion law. Legislation repealing the law is introduced in the French Parliament.

1974   The U.S. Women's Sport Foundation (WSF) is founded by the tennis star Billie Jean King and the Olympic gold-medal swimmer Donna de Varona as a national organization to promote the development of women's sports. WSF advocates equal opportunities for women and girls in sports and provides financial aid for female athletes.

1974   The Mexican American Women's National Association (MAWNA) is founded in California to promote economic development and educational opportunities for Hispanic and Mexican-American women. By the 1990s, MAWNA has members in 36 states and offers education in fighting teen pregnancy as well as the Hermanitas (little sisters) program.

1974	The Alliance of Displaced Homemakers is created in the United States by Tish Sommers and Laurie Shields to address issues of divorced and widowed homemakers seeking employment.
1974	Women receive full voting rights in the People's Republic of China.
1974	Ella Grasso is elected governor of Connecticut, the first woman to hold the governorship of a U.S. state in her own right (all previous women governors had been wives of former governors).
1974	Dr. Pauline Jewett becomes the first woman president of a college in Canada, when she is appointed president of Simon Fraser College.
1974	Women gain the opportunity to attend the U.S. Marine Academy. In 1975, Congress passes a bill requiring all academies of the U.S. Armed Forces to accept qualified women.
1974	The Equal Credit Opportunity Act banning discrimination against women by financial institutions becomes law. Previously, women were routinely discriminated against when they attempted to gain credit; often women had to have a man's signature on a loan application, and newly divorced and widowed women found that they had no independent credit history.
1974	The National Association of Women Business Owners is organized in the United States by women entrepreneurs to provide services to female-owned businesses.
1974	A law permitting abortion during the first three months of pregnancy is passed in Germany, but in 1976 the federal constitutional court modifies the legislation to allow abortion only in instances when the mother's health is endangered or the child would be physically handicapped, in cases of rape, or when the mother cannot adequately raise the child.
1974	The Canadian Association for Repeal of the Abortion Law is formed to fight for women's right to abortion. In 1980 it becomes the Canadian Abortion Rights Action League.
1975	The U.S. Supreme Court rules that states cannot require a girl under the age of 18 to obtain parental approval for an abortion.
1975	President Gerald R. Ford signs legislation requiring U.S. military-service academies to admit women.
1975	Joellen Drag becomes the first woman helicopter pilot in the U.S. Navy. Later she successfully sues the navy to win the right for women pilots to land at sea.
1975	The Sex Discrimination Act passed by Parliament in Great Britain, along with the 1972 Equal Pay Act, requires women to receive the same wages men receive for similar work, though many employers reclassify relevant jobs to avoid compliance.
1975	In *Taylor v. Louisiana*, the U.S. Supreme Court removes a ban on women serving on juries when it votes (8 to 1) to strike down a Louisiana statute automatically excluding women from jury

duty.

1975	A U.S. Supreme Court decision reverses a Utah law requiring child support for sons to the age of 21 and daughters to the age of 18. Justice Harry Blackmun writes that women are no longer meant only to stay at home and raise families.
1975	International Women's Year (later that year expanded into Women's Decade) and the first world conference for the Decade for Women, held in Mexico City, mark the most serious consideration of women's rights on a worldwide basis up to that time. The United Nations, along with private organizations, created the International Women's Year; each state has its own coordinating committee to raise funds and to serve as a contact point for the community.
1975	Women are given voting rights on the same basis as men in Angola.
1975	The Family Code, legislation addressing inequality in the home, is passed in Cuba. This legislation requires men and women to share household chores.
1975	No-fault divorce legislation, allowing for divorce by mutual consent, is passed in France. By 1991, the divorce rate in France reaches 33 percent; though custody of children may be awarded to either parent, it is most often given to the mother.
1975	A new constitution created in Portugal after the death of the dictator Antonio Salazar and the successful revolution of 1974 is voted on by every citizen over 18 years of age.
1975	Female federal employees in the United States gain the right to sue on the grounds of sex discrimination.
1975	The policy of automatic dismissal of pregnant women from the U.S. armed forces, practiced by the U.S. Department of Defense, is reversed.
1975	The first woman to climb to the top of Mount Everest is Junko Tahei of Japan.
1975	A law permitting birth-control education and access to birth control is passed in Italy. Abortion within the first 90 days of pregnancy is legalized in 1978 after a three-year political struggle; Pope Paul VI and Italian bishops declare they will use excommunication to counteract the new law.
1975	A law permitting abortion in France is passed provisionally and made permanent in 1979, following a large demonstration in Paris and the publication of the 1971 *Manifeste des 343* by 343 French women who had illegal abortions. The government agrees to reimburse the costs only in 1982; while contraception was legalized in 1967, not until 1974 were the costs of contraception reimbursable by national health insurance.
1976	In *Planned Parenthood of Central Missouri v. Danforth*, the U.S. Supreme Court denies states the right to require a woman to get permission from her husband to have an abortion, striking down

a Missouri law. Justice Harry Blackmun writes that, because women are more affected by pregnancy, they should be able to choose abortion.

1976 A law of the European Economic Community (EEC) granting equal pay for equal work is adopted. Although more women in the EEC enter higher-paying fields of science and engineering during the 1970s and 1980s, most women are still in lower-paying teaching, clerical, and service occupations.

1976 In *General Electric Company v. Gilbert*, the U.S. Supreme Court decides that employers are not guilty of discrimination if their insurance plan fails to provide disability benefits for pregnancy-related problems. Justice William Rehnquist's decision notes that General Electric's plan covers some risks and not others, and that there is no evidence that it is discriminatory.

1976 The Asian Women United is established in San Francisco, California, to promote Asian women's rights.

1976 The International Women's Tribune Centre is created in New York to unite organizations from around the world that seek to expand economic opportunities for women in developing nations.

1976 A law allowing no-fault divorce is passed in Australia. The new law makes it easier for women to obtain a divorce and leads to a large number of divorces.

1976 A law allowing divorce among Hindus by mutual consent, after a year's legal separation, is passed in India; Islamic law in India allows a husband to divorce his wife unilaterally, but a wife has only limited grounds for divorce. Divorced women are frowned on in India, and few Indian women opt for divorce.

1976 Voting rights are granted to women on the same basis as men in Portugal.

1976 The United Nations Tribunal on Crimes against Women is held in Brussels, Belgium. Also known as the International Tribunal on Crimes against Women, this is the first conference of the United Nations to focus on issues such as rape, battering, forced marriage, clitoridectomy, and oppression of Third World women.

1976 A Take Back the Night march is organized after a meeting of the International Tribunal on Crimes against Women in Brussels, Belgium. The march spotlights violence against women; similar marches are now held throughout the world.

1976 The first U.S. state to make marital rape a crime is Nebraska.

1977 A novel by Marilyn French, *The Women's Room*, about the meaning of women's liberation for a diverse group of contemporaries, becomes a runaway success in the United States. More than 4 million copies are sold.

1977 The U.S. Supreme Court rules in *Beal v. Doe* and *Maher v. Roe* that neither federal law nor the Constitution requires states to provide abortions, and states are not required to use federal Medicaid monies to fund elective abortions.

1977	Women receive full voting rights in Liechtenstein.
1977	A law legalizing divorce is passed in Brazil.
1977	The first American woman ordained as a priest in the Episcopal Church of the United States is Jacqueline Means, a 40-year-old nurse and prison chaplain.
1977	Janet Guthrie becomes the first American woman to qualify for the Indianapolis 500, the premier automobile race in the United States and one of the oldest auto races in the world. Thirty-three drivers compete for the world's largest purse in auto racing at the Indianapolis Motor Speedway in Indianapolis, Indiana, on the Sunday of the Memorial Day weekend.
1977	Beverly Messenger Harris is the first American woman to serve as a rector in the Episcopal Church of the United States.
1977	In *Nashville Gas v. Satty*, the U.S. Supreme Court decides that employers who deny seniority benefits to women returning to work after childbirth violate federal laws. The Court rules that the employer in the suit had discriminated by granting seniority to employees who had taken other disability leave but not to women workers who gave birth.
1977	The U.S. National Women's History Project begins in Windsor, California. The organization sponsors National Women's History Month and operates the Women's History Network.
1977	The Revolutionary Association of the Women of Afghanistan (RAWA) is established in Kabul, Afghanistan, as an independent political organization of Afghan women. RAWA fights for human rights and social justice in Afghanistan.
1977	The Congressional Caucus for Women's Issues is created in Washington, D.C., to provide bipartisan cooperation for women members of the House of Representatives on issues of women's education, employment, and health care. The first cochairs of the caucus are the Democrat Elizabeth Holtzman and the Republican Margaret Heckler.
1977	The International Center for Research for Women (ICRW) is established in Washington, D.C. The ICRW concentrates on improving opportunities for women in developing nations and focuses on small-scale economic development and farming projects for women.
1977	The Lesbian Rights Project is organized in San Francisco, California. In 1991, its name changes to the National Center for Lesbian Rights, which provides aid in areas such as family law, health, and counseling.
1977	A law criminalizing rape in marriage is passed by the Parliament of South Australia.
1977	A British court decides that a man's mistress enjoys the same protection against abuse as does his wife.
1977	The International Women's Year Conference is held in Houston,

Texas. Two thousand delegates and 20,000 others meet to discuss and adopt a U.S. National Plan of Action, including a call for action on child care, the Equal Rights Amendment, rape, reproductive freedom, and employment.

1977 — Women are permitted to serve as members of permanent aboardship crews of the U.S. Navy.

1977 — The Hyde Amendment is passed by the U.S. House of Representatives by a vote of 210 to 155, prohibiting the expenditure of federal monies for Medicaid abortions and making it difficult for lower-income women to have abortions. The same day, the Senate votes 56 to 42 to forbid public funding for elective abortions unless the woman's life is endangered.

1978 — The first attack on an abortion clinic in the United States occurs when an arsonist sets fire to the operating room of the Concerned Women's Clinic in Cleveland, Ohio, while an abortion is being performed. The clinic shuts down and sustains $30,000 in damages.

1978 — Maria Elaine Pitchford is acquitted for performing a self-induced abortion.

1978 — A vote legalizing abortion during the first 90 days of pregnancy takes place in Italy. The law requires girls under 18 years to get parental approval; many women, worrying that state-run clinics might violate their privacy, continue to seek out back-alley abortions.

1978 — The first woman to achieve the rank of brigadier general in the U.S. Marine Corps is Margaret A. Brewer.

1978 — The U.S. Pregnancy Discrimination Act, forbidding employers to discriminate against pregnant workers, is passed in response to a ruling by the Equal Employment Opportunity Commission that denying benefits to pregnant employees comparable to those provided to male and nonpregnant employees does not constitute discrimination. The act determines that discrimination based on pregnancy or conditions resulting from childbirth is indeed gender discrimination, though conditions resulting from abortion are exempted unless the life of the woman is at risk.

1978 — The U.S. Women's Educational Equity Act is established to promote curricula that encourage opportunities for girls and women and to provide funding for women's programs in mathematics and the sciences. In 1981, President Ronald Reagan cuts the funding for this act.

1978 — In *Los Angeles Department of Water and Power v. Manhart*, the U.S. Supreme Court decides that women workers are entitled to the same retirement benefits as male workers.

1978 — A decision by the Louisiana Supreme Court reaffirms the state's head and master law, which allows a husband to make all the decisions about common property shared with his wife. Three months later, the Louisiana State Senate votes the law out of existence.

1978	The U.S. National Coalition against Domestic Violence is formed in Denver, Colorado, as a group of battered-women's organizations and shelters. It works to end violence against women and in 1987 establishes the first national telephone hot line for women victims of domestic violence.
1978	The Y-Me National Breast Cancer Organization is founded in Illinois.
1978	The Women of All Red Nations (WARN) is created in the United States by Lorelei Means and Madonna (Thunder Hawk) Gilbert. WARN assists Native American women in ending forced sterilization and preventing the loss of their native land and the disappearance of their traditional culture.
1978	Federal Judge Constance Baker Motley rules that the New York Yankees had unfairly barred the *Sports Illustrated* reporter Melissa Lincoln from the locker room. Thereafter, female sportswriters, along with their male counterparts, can interview major-league baseball players in their locker rooms.
1978	The U.S. Department of Health, Education, and Welfare (HEW) issues an administrative ruling that the government will pay for abortions for poor women who are the victims of rape or incest. Joseph Califano, the secretary of HEW, rules that if the incidents are reported to the authorities within 60 days, government financing for abortion is available.
1979	The U.S. Supreme Court decides in *Colautti v. Franklin* that a 1974 Pennsylvania law requiring physicians to do whatever they can to save the life of a fetus is unconstitutional.
1979	The U.S. National Committee on Pay Equity is formed when individuals and organizations concerned with equal pay for equal work issues establish a clearinghouse.
1979	A U.S. Court of Appeals rules that employers may not require female employees to wear uniforms that their male counterparts are not required to wear.
1979	The U.S. National Displaced Homemakers Network is founded in Washington, D.C., to help women make the difficult transition from the home to the workplace.
1979	Ten thousand Iranian women march to protest the revocation of the 1975 Family Protection Law.
1979	In *Bellotti v. Baird*, the U.S. Supreme Court decides that requiring parental consent for abortions is unconstitutional. The Court rules against a Massachusetts law requiring unmarried underage girls to get permission from their parents or a judge to have an abortion.
1979	The World Health Organization (WHO), at the WHO Seminar in Khartoum, Sudan, on Traditional Practices Affecting the Health of Women and Children, identifies female genital mutilation (FGM) as a major public-health problem. The nine African and Middle Eastern countries that participate in the conference set

forth recommendations for abolishing FGM, including health-education and health-training programs.

1979 The overthrow of the shah of Iran and the assumption of power by the Ayatollah Khomeini mark major turning points for women in Iran. Khomeini institutes Islamic law, abolishes coeducational schools, and insists that women, even non-Muslim visitors from other countries, wear the chador in public.

1979 The Church of Jesus Christ of Latter-day Saints (Mormons) in the United States excommunicates Sonia Johnson for supporting the Equal Rights Amendment.

1979 The U.S. Defense Department recognizes the military service of the Women's Airforce Service Pilots almost 35 years after they served in World War II. Although the women flew more than 60 million miles during World War II and 38 died during their service to the country, they were considered civilians and denied military retirement or educational benefits.

1979 A law passed in Greece permits a spouse to receive a divorce even if the other party opposes it, as long as the couple has been separated for six years.

1979 A family law superseding traditional Islamic law is passed in Egypt. The law allows women the right to divorce, the right to gain child custody, and the ability to retain the family household.

1979 China institutes a policy establishing a limit of one child per family; the deputy premier Deng Xiaoping orders all couples to practice family planning and imposes penalties on families with two or more children. Because Chinese custom provides that girls who marry are taken into the husband's family, families fear that if their one permitted child is female they will be left to fend for themselves in old age; thus female infanticide and abortion increase with the use of ultrasound technology to determine the sex of unborn babies.

1979 Margaret Thatcher, leader of the Conservative Party, is the first woman to be elected prime minister of Great Britain. She remains in office until choosing not to run for reelection in 1990.

1979 Simone Veil, the French minister of health, is the first woman to be named president of the Parliament of the European Community.

1980 Vigdis Finnbogadottir is the first woman to be elected president of Iceland; she wins reelection to this post in 1984 and 1988. Finnbogadottir is divorced and the single mother of an adopted daughter.

1980 Women are granted voting rights on the same basis as men in Iran.

1980 The Older Women's League (OWL) is established in Washington, D.C. Also known as the Older Women's League Education Fund, OWL deals with age- and gender-discrimination issues, including obtaining health insurance and retirement benefits.

1980	The percentage of women to men in government service in the Philippines is 44.6. Though outnumbered by men, women judges serve at all levels of the Philippine judiciary system.
1980	In France, the first woman to be elected to the Académie Française since its beginning in 1635 is the French novelist Marguerite Yourcenar.
1980	The California Supreme Court decides to strike down an 1872 rape law that required the victim to attest to the level of resistance she offered in response to the attack.
1980	The United Nations World Conference of the Decade for Women is held in Copenhagen, Denmark, the second such conference. Participants draft a World Plan of Action and 48 resolutions to influence legislation and change attitudes about women.
1980	The U.S. Supreme Court upholds the Hyde Amendment of 1977, which prohibits the expenditure of federal monies for Medicaid abortions. Since passage of the amendment, the number of abortions paid for by Medicaid fell from 295,000 in 1976 to 2,100 in 1978.
1981	The U.S. Supreme Court, in *Rostker v. Goldberg*, rules that Congress can exempt women from the military draft because women are not "similarly situated" with men when it comes to combat.
1981	Sandra Day O'Connor becomes the first woman appointed a justice in the U.S. Supreme Court. In 1993, she is joined by Ruth Bader Ginsburg.
1981	National Women's History Week in the United States is proclaimed by President Jimmy Carter in response to requests by women's organizations.
1981	The National Museum of Women in the Arts is founded in Washington, D.C. The museum has a collection of more than 1,500 works by women artists from the Renaissance to the present, as well as an extensive arts library.
1981	In *County of Washington v. Gunther*, the U.S. Supreme Court decides that women alleging wage discrimination based on gender must demonstrate that a male holding the same job receives higher wages. The Court rules that women can seek remedy under the Title VII provisions of the 1964 Civil Rights Act.
1981	The National Institute for Women of Color is founded in Washington, D.C., to promote women of color in decision-making positions in public and private institutions.
1981	Legislation giving women the right to divorce is passed in Spain, but the Catholic Church in Spain forbids Catholic Spaniards to obtain a divorce under the new law.
1982	The Canadian Charter of Rights and Freedoms is adopted when Canada gains independence from Great Britain. The charter provides for affirmative programs to eliminate racial, age, and gender "disadvantages," and Section 28 grants women the same rights as men.

1983	A total of 123 incidents of violence against abortion clinics occurs; in the first 10 weeks of 1984, there are 59 incidents of harassment or violence.
1983	Women are admitted to Columbia College in New York City, the last all-male school in the Ivy League. Women were unable to attend Columbia College for 229 years.
1983	The astronaut Sally Kristin Ride becomes the first U.S. woman to go into space when she flies on a six-day mission aboard the space shuttle *Challenger*.
1983	The State Commission on the Status of Women is established in São Paulo, Brazil, to deal with issues of violence against women. A national commission established two years later involves women in drafting a new constitution for Brazil.
1983	The Seneca Women's Peace Encampment is established when more than 2,000 women surround the U.S. Army Depot in upstate New York, a storage site for missile parts, in opposition to the deployment of cruise nuclear missiles by the North Atlantic Treaty Organization (NATO).
1983	The Greek parliament passes a law allowing women an equal voice in all matters of family life. Nevertheless, in practice wives still cannot work outside the home without their husbands' permission, and daughters cannot get passports without their fathers' permission.
1983	The Equal Pay Act is amended in Great Britain to increase women's pay significantly, though British wages for women remain appreciably less than those of men, compared with other European nations.
1983	A constitutional amendment makes it mandatory for all citizens to vote in Argentina.
1983	The U.S. Supreme Court, in *Arizona Governing Committee v. Norris*, rules than an employer's decision to offer employees a choice of pension plans paying lower benefits to women employees than to men violates federal law.
1983	The U.S. Department of Health and Human Services' "squeal rule" that federally funded family-planning clinics must notify parents when daughters under the age of 18 request birth-control aids goes into effect, but a federal judge prohibits the department from effecting the rule on the grounds that it would irreparably harm sexually active adolescents by deterring them from using family-planning clinics.
1983	The U.S. Supreme Court affirms its decision in *Roe v. Wade* and strikes down several state laws restricting abortion rights. In *City of Akron v. Akron Center for Reproductive Health*, the Court rules against provisions requiring informed consent, and in *Planned Parenthood of Kansas City, Mo. v. Ashcroft*, the Court strikes down a requirement that abortions after the first trimester be performed in hospitals, not clinics.

1984	The Romanian president Nicolae Ceausescu declares that women have a patriotic duty to bear children. Under this policy, Romanian married women must take monthly pregnancy tests and must have a medical reason for not getting pregnant; police are empowered to prevent abortions; and women who do not have children may lose their jobs.
1984	Canadian women form Real, Equal, Active, for Life, an organization opposing abortion.
1984	In *Grove City College v. Bell*, the U.S. Supreme Court restricts the enforcement of Title IX violations and rules instead that federal funds designated only for the particular program in which discrimination took place would be withheld, rather than withholding all federal funds from educational institutions that discriminate by race or gender. Many investigations of compliance violations are suspended following the decision.
1984	The Soviet cosmonaut Svetlana Savitskaia becomes the first woman to walk in space. The first U.S. woman to walk in space is Kathryn D. Sullivan, in the same year.
1984	A Connecticut court decides that a city must pay damages for not adequately protecting a woman from domestic violence. In *Thurman et al. v. City of Torrington*, the court rules that the city is liable for $2.3 million damages because a police officer failed to intervene while watching the woman's estranged husband kick her as she lay bleeding from the man's knife wounds.
1984	Jeanne Sauvé is the first woman to be named governor general of Canada, following her term as speaker of the Canadian House of Commons from 1980 to 1984.
1984	Geraldine Ferraro, a U.S. congresswoman from New York City, becomes the first woman vice-presidential candidate in the United States. Ferraro runs unsuccessfully with Walter Mondale on the Democratic Party ticket.
1984	The Inter-African Committee on Traditional Practices Affecting the Health of Women and Children is organized and expanded to include affiliates in 24 African nations. At a conference in Dakar, Senegal, the committee agrees to support and sponsor programs to eradicate female genital mutilation.
1984	The U.S. Supreme Court rules in *Hishon v. King Spaulding* that a law firm cannot deny partnership participation based on gender.
1984	The U.S. Retirement Equity Act is passed to correct some of the shortcomings of the Employee Retirement Income Security Act of 1974 (ERISA), which discriminated against women workers. The Retirement Equity Act of 1984 enables women to qualify for pension programs after 10 years of employment, without maternity leave being considered an interruption in their service; allows women with less than 5 years' employment to take time off to be with their children; grants women their husbands' benefits if the husband dies before reaching the age of 55; and makes pension

benefits a required part of divorce settlements.

1985   The U.S. Supreme Court, in *Thornburgh v. American Counsel of Obstetricians and Gynecologists*, rules that a state law requiring informed consent for abortion and stipulating that physicians must attempt to save the life of a fetus is unconstitutional.

1985   Wilma Mankiller becomes the first woman chief of a modern American Indian nation when she is installed as principal chief of the Cherokee in Oklahoma. Mankiller serves until 1994.

1985   In the Soviet Union, women are given the opportunity to serve as members of the armed forces when the draft law is amended.

1985   EMILY's List (Early Money Is Like Yeast) is founded by women supporters of the Democratic Party, to aid women candidates for public office in the United States. Barbara Mikulski is the first woman candidate to benefit from EMILY's List aid when she is elected to the U.S. Senate from Maryland.

1985   The Divorce and Corollary Relief Act, no-fault divorce legislation, is passed in Canada.

1985   The New York State Court of Appeals, in *People v. Mario Liberta*, rules to revoke the marital-exemption law and finds no distinction between marital and nonmarital rape. Husbands now found guilty of the rape of their wives are subject to the same penalties of two to eight years in prison as anyone else found guilty of rape.

1985   The World Conference to Review and Appraise the Achievements of the United Nations Decade for Women is held in Nairobi, Kenya. The official conference, also known as the United Nations Third World Conference on Women, produces a plan of action for the next 15 years, stressing educational, employment, and legal rights for women.

Mid-1980s   More than 80 percent of women work full- or part-time in Denmark.

1986   Corazon Aquino is elected president of the Philippines.

1986   Vilma Espit, head of the Federation of Cuban Women, is the first woman elected to the Politburo in Cuba, following the decision to incorporate women into leadership positions. Despite Cuba's stated embrace of women's emancipation, traditional cultural and behavioral patterns of machismo still hold sway, and women do not exercise full and equal political power.

1986   The U.S. Supreme Court rules to uphold affirmative-action hiring of women and minorities to redress past discriminatory employment action.

1986   The Equal Employment Opportunity Law passed in Japan guarantees women equal opportunity with men in all aspects of employment, from recruitment to retirement. Unfortunately, women, who constitute more than 50 percent of the workplace, especially part-time female workers, are often denied equal opportunity, because male-dominated corporations lag in compliance and violators often avoid penalties.

1986	The Affirmative Action (Equal Opportunity for Women) Act is passed in Australia.
1986	The Employment Equity Act, requiring equal employment opportunities and equal pay for women and minorities, is passed in Canada.
1986	In *Meritor Savings Bank v. Vinson*, the U.S. Supreme Court rules that sexual harassment on the job violates Title VII of the Civil Rights Act.
1987	The Fund for the Feminist Majority (FFM) is established in the United States by Eleanor Smeal, a former president of the National Organization for Women. Smeal founds FFM to encourage women to run for political office.
1987	The U.S. Supreme Court, in *California Federal Savings v. Guerra*, upholds the right of pregnant women workers to take pregnancy leave. The Supreme Court ruling upholds a California law requiring up to four months' leave for pregnancy.
1988	The U.S. Civil Rights Restoration Act of 1987 is passed in response to the effects of the Supreme Court ruling in *Grove City College v. Bell*, which had restricted the enforcement powers of Title IX of the Education Act. The new act reaffirms that educational institutions must comply with the antidiscrimination protections of Title IX if any of their programs or activities receives federal funding.
1988	Benazir Bhutto of Pakistan becomes the first woman to head an Islamic nation. She promises equal pay for equal work, maternity leave, a minimum wage, and an end to discrimination against women.
1988	In *New York State Club Association, Inc. v. The City of New York*, the U.S. Supreme Court unanimously upholds a law banning discrimination against women and minorities in private clubs and rules that New York City's law does not violate First Amendment rights. The decision has the effect of opening private clubs in cities across the United States.
1988	The Equal Credit Opportunity Act is extended to cover commercial credit institutions.
1988	The National Council for Research on Women is established in New York City to link more than 100 organizations conducting research on women's issues and to set up a national database on research.
1988	The Canadian province of Ontario requires that private employers reserve 1 percent of payroll to remedy inequalities in pay for male and female employees. Employers are required to study the relationship between jobs and salaries, and certain jobs are deemed comparable, such as nursing assistants and plumbers, supermarket cashiers and meat wrappers.
1988	Canada's Supreme Court rules that a law restricting abortion is unconstitutional. In *Morganthaler, Smoling, and Scott v. Attor-*

ney General of Canada, the Court holds that the 1969 statute permitting abortions based on the review of a three-physician committee unduly restricts a woman's right to abortion, one aspect of the "right to security of the person" guaranteed to women under the 1982 Canadian Charter of Rights and Freedoms.

1988 Operation Rescue is formed in the United States when Randall Terry of Binghamton, New York, organizes antiabortion demonstrators to block the entrances to abortion clinics and doctors' offices. These demonstrations are designed to frighten and intimidate both patients who seek abortions and doctors willing to perform them.

1988 France becomes the first Western nation to approve the use of the "morning-after" pill, RU-486, which will be made available at family-planning centers in France. The government estimates that use of the pill will reduce by half the surgical and suction abortions performed in France each year.

1989 In France, women hold about 6 percent of the seats in the national assembly, about 3 percent in the senate, and about 14 percent of the seats on local councils. Although women constitute 53 percent of the electorate, few women run for office.

1989 The U.S. Supreme Court rules in *Lorance v. AT&T Technologies* that an employee filing a complaint about unfair employment practices must act within 180 days of the violation.

1989 In *Wards Cove Packing Company v. Antonio*, the U.S. Supreme Court decides that the plaintiff bears the burden of proving employment discrimination under Title VII of the Civil Rights Act.

1989 After the dictator Nicolae Ceausescu is overthrown and killed, abortion rights are granted to women in Romania.

1990 The U.S. Supreme Court decides, in *Hodgson v. Minnesota*, that a state may require a pregnant girl to inform both her parents before having an abortion.

1990 The U.S. Carl D. Perkins Vocational and Applied Technology Education Act is passed to encourage the development of the academic and occupational skills of all Americans.

1990 In *University of Pennsylvania v. EEOC*, the U.S. Supreme Court rules that a university charged with sex discrimination in connection with denial of tenure cannot refuse to disclose peer-review materials.

1990 The Society for the Advancement of Women's Health Research is created in Washington, D.C., to deal with the problem of insufficient funding for research on women's health issues.

1990 Fifty veiled Muslim women in Riyadh, Saudi Arabia, dismiss their drivers and, taking the wheels of their automobiles, drive off. They are stopped by the police, and six are suspended from their teaching jobs; the Saudi regime reinforces its edict forbidding women to drive.

1990–1991 Thirty-five thousand of the 540,000 U.S. troops serving during the Persian Gulf War are women. While technically not to engage in combat, they transport food, fuel, and troops and take part in communications and intelligence operations; 2 women are taken prisoner, and 11 die.

1991 In *Rust v. Sullivan*, the U.S. Supreme Court decides to uphold guidelines prohibiting family-planning agencies from counseling on or providing information about abortion; because the services that family-planning clinics provide do not take place postconception, there is no need to discuss abortion. The case resulted from the guidelines issued by the secretary of Health and Human Services, Louis Sullivan, in 1988, under Title X of the Public Health Service Act.

1991 The law lords of the House of Lords in Great Britain reject the 250-year-old principle that rape in marriage is not a crime.

1991 The supreme court of Brazil rules that men can no longer use the "legitimate defense of honor" as a legal defense for killing a wife accused of adultery. Nevertheless, the decision is widely ignored, and violence toward women remains a serious problem in Brazil.

1991 The number of women members in the Folketing, or parliament, of Denmark rises to 26.3 percent, up from less than 10 percent in 1950.

1991 The U.S. Supreme Court rules in *Automobile Workers v. Johnson Controls* that women cannot be excluded from jobs based on the argument which is made by the largest manufacturer of automobile batteries in the United States, that women should be excluded from work that might expose a developing fetus to lead. Labor unions and women's rights groups successfully argue, and the Court unanimously rules, that the policy violates the Civil Rights Act of 1964, and that an employer may not use gender to prohibit women from specific jobs.

1991 The U.S. Civil Rights Act expands the right of women to sue for damages under Title VII of the Civil Rights Act of 1964 if they are discriminated against by their employers. Under the 1991 act, women are entitled to compensatory damages for all injuries by an employer, including physical and emotional pain; they are also entitled to a jury trial (previously such cases were heard by a judge without a jury).

1992 The National Collegiate Athletic Association (NCAA) reports on compliance with Title IX 20 years after its passage. The NCAA finds 2.24 men participating in Division I college sports for every woman participant and 2.26 men receiving college sports scholarships for every woman; for every dollar men basketball coaches earn, women coaches receive 55 cents.

1992 In *Butler v. Her Majesty the Queen*, the Canadian Supreme Court rules to uphold the provisions of the 1982 Charter of Rights and Freedoms, prohibiting distribution of violent pornography.

1992	In the elections of the Year of the Woman in the United States, women's groups help to increase the percentage of successful women candidates from 5 to 10 percent. Forty-eight women are elected to the House of Representatives; the number of women in the U.S. Senate increases from two to six; and the percentage of women in state political offices increases to 20.
1992	The Susan B. Anthony List is founded in the U.S. to support women pro-life activists and candidates who seek national legistlation to ban abortion. It is named for the American suffragette who was also an outspoken critic of abortion.
1992	Carol Moseley Braun of Illinois becomes the first African-American woman to be elected to the U.S. Senate.
1992	The U.S. Congress passes the Nontraditional Employment for Women Act, also known as the Women in Apprenticeship and Nontraditional Occupations Act, which provides that labor unions and employers be notified about the availability of technical-assistance programs to promote employment of women in occupations traditionally unavailable to them. It also establishes a grants program for community organizations to provide training and technical assistance for women, to help them become machinists, electricians, carpenters, masons, and plumbers.
1992	Demonstrators for abortion rights in the United States gather in the largest political rally ever in Washington, D.C., with 750,000 abortion-rights marchers representing the National Organization for Women and women's and social organizations and students from more than 600 American campuses. The massive rally follows the March for Life rally by 75,000 antiabortion demonstrators earlier the same year. President George Bush had sent a personal message to the antiabortion demonstration: "I'm out there with you in spirit."
1993	In *Harris v. Forklift Systems, Inc.*, the U.S. Supreme Court rules that plaintiffs in a sexual harassment suit need not prove severe psychological damage. Justice O'Connor writes that federal law against harassment applies when "the environment would reasonably be perceived, and is perceived, as hostile or abusive."
1993	Take Our Daughters to Work Day is established in the United States by the Ms. Foundation to introduce daughters to their parents' workplaces and to encourage young women to expand their sense of potential employment opportunities.
1993	Kim Campbell is the first woman to be elected prime minister of Canada. The leader of the Progressive Conservative Party, Campbell serves for a year before she and her party lose the next election.
1993	The first American woman jockey to win a U.S. Triple Crown race is Julie Krone, who wins the Belmont Stakes riding Colonial Affair, an 11-to-1 long shot.
1993	The Vietnam Women's Memorial honoring women veterans is unveiled in Washington, D.C. The bronze sculpture shows three

women tending to a wounded soldier; the monument is dedicated to the approximately 55,000 women who served as nurses or civilian participants in the Vietnam War.

1993 The U.S. Family and Medical Leave Act is passed to protect the job status of an employee who must take time off for the birth of a child or for the care of a sick relative. The legislation provides that employers with more than 50 employees must allow workers up to 12 weeks of unpaid leave to deal with illness of relatives or the birth or adoption or foster placement of a child.

1993 President Bill Clinton reverses restrictions on abortions imposed earlier by Presidents Ronald Reagan and George Bush. Clinton orders that federally financed clinics can provide abortion counseling, that military hospitals can perform abortions, and that foreign aid can be given to international family-planning programs that include abortion-related programs.

1994 "Mama Greou," of the Mali community in France, is convicted of performing female genital mutilation and receives a one-year suspended sentence for excising two girls. She is tried again in 1999 on similar charges and allegedly has mutilated the genitals of about 50 young girls; also charged are 27 parents of the victims.

1994 A U.S. Federal Court judge rules that the Citadel, an all-male military college in South Carolina, must admit women.

1994 The U.S. Violence against Women Act, also known as Title IV of the Violent Crime Control and Law Enforcement Act, states that violent acts against women are violations of federal civil rights laws, and victims may seek damages. The act provides funding for battered-women's shelters, educational programs on rape prevention, a domestic-violence national toll-free hot line, and a program to inform court personnel and judges about rape and sexual assault.

1995 Shannon Faulkner is the first woman to be admitted to the formerly all-male Citadel in South Carolina, but she resigns in a week after harassment.

1995 The United Nations Fourth World Conference on Women is held in Beijing, China. While China limits the participation of women from Tibet and Taiwan and moves the nongovernmental forum of 30,000 women 30 miles from the official conference in Beijing, the conference organizers claim success and pass a platform for action stressing economic development for women, an end to violence, and improvment in the status of girls.

1995 The Federal Prohibition of Female Genital Mutilation Act, introduced by U.S. Representative Patricia Schroeder, bans female genital mutilation in the United States and provides for prison sentences of up to five years for anyone performing such mutilation on a person under the age of 18 years. The procedure is outlawed in Britain, Canada, France, Sweden, Switzerland, and the United States.

1996	Nineteen-year-old Fauziya Kasinga, a woman who fled Togo to escape female genital mutilation, is the first woman granted asylum in the United States on the basis of a threat of genital mutilation. Granted by the U.S. Board of Immigration Appeals, Kasinga's asylum is the first U.S. case that recognizes the threat of female genital mutilation as legitimate grounds; in 1993, Canada granted asylum to Khadra Hassan Farah, a Somali woman, and her 10-year-old daughter, because the woman feared that her child would otherwise undergo mutilation.
1999	Malicounda Bambara, a small village located about 40 miles from Dakar, the capital city of Senegal, is the first village in that country to ban female genital mutilation (FGM), and 13 villages surrounding Malicounda then also ban the practice. Women make this decision after taking classes offered by the government, religious groups, United Nations agencies, and nongovernmental organizations as part of an anti-FGM awareness campaign.
1999	Voting rights in municipal elections are granted to women in Qatar.
1999	Tori Murden from Louisville, Kentucky, is the first woman and the first American to row solo across the Atlantic Ocean, from Tenerife in the Canary Islands to the French island of Guadeloupe in the Caribbean, a distance of 4,786 kilometers.
1999	The first U.S. woman astronaut appointed shuttle commander is Lieutenant Colonel Eileen Collins, aboard the *Columbia*.
2000	RU-486, the morning-after pill, is approved for use in the United States, although the U.S. antiabortion movement puts enormous pressure on the French manufacturer, Groupe Roussel Uclaf, until it agrees to delay producing the drug. The French minister of health orders the company to resume manufacturing the drug.
2000	The governor of Khartoum (state of Sudan in Africa) imposes a ban on women working in public places, on the grounds that Islamic law prohibits it. After worldwide outrage at the ban, however, the constitutional court of Sudan suspends it, awaiting the review of an appeal filed by women's rights groups.
2000	The United Nations Population Fund announces that one in three women worldwide has been physically assaulted or abused, usually by a person known to her.
2000	Pakistan's Human Rights Commission reports that at least two women are burned daily in acts of domestic violence in the country.
2000	In Jordan, the lower house of parliament refuses to pass legislation revoking an article in the penal code that sentences males who kill female family members to minimal punishment if they show that their motive is upholding family honor; a large majority votes to defeat the bill, justifying the veto by stating that they are protecting Islamic values from Western influence. The upper house, however, votes in favor of reform; a final decision awaits a

joint session of parliament.

2000   Human Rights Watch reports that, despite a California law increasing criminal penalties for sexual misconduct against women in custody, the state has not ensured that women can report violations without fearing retaliation. Women prisoners tell Human Rights Watch that punitive actions by prison guards, such as seizing their personal possessions, holding them in custody while the accusations are investigated, and increased surveillance while they shower or undress, often result from prisoners' reporting abuse.

2000   Michigan passes a law excluding prisoners from the protections afforded by the state civil rights act prohibiting discrimination based on race and gender, thereby denying women prisoners the possibility of suing the corrections department for sexual abuse undergone in prison.

2001   Condoleezza Rice becomes the first woman to be appointed national security adviser to the president of the United States, when President George W. Bush appoints her in late 2000. Rice's experience in political science was gained at Stanford University, Stanford, California, where she is a professor, and at the Hoover Institution, where she is a senior fellow currently on leave.

2002   When asked to comment on the fact that women are excluded from the Augusta National golf club, 26-year-old Tiger Woods answers that the tournament organizers are allowed to "set up their own rules the way they want them." Though the Professional Golfers' Association (PGA) has banned holding tournaments at clubs that exclude blacks, there is no such ban on clubs that exclude women. A controversy develops when a coalition of women's groups asks the club to admit women as members and the club refuses.

2002   Halle Berry wins an Oscar for best actress at the Academy Awards for her role in *Monster's Ball*, the first black woman to win the best-actress award in the 74 years of the ceremony's history.

2002   Seven black women graduate from the Citadel in Charleston, South Carolina, the first black women to march as graduating cadets on the grounds of the military institution. In 1995, Shannon Faulkner became a Citadel cadet after a long battle in federal court and a judge's order; stress and isolation forced Faulkner to drop out in less than a week, but the Citadel reluctantly opened its doors to women in 1996, after a U.S. Supreme Court decision forced the Virginia Military Institute to accept female cadets; Nancy Mace became the first female graduate in 1999.

2002   Daw Aung San Suu Kyi, leader of the movement to restore democracy in Myanmar (Burma), is released from house arrest; she was confined on and off since 1989 for organizing protests against the military government. The daughter of U Aung San, who played a prominent part in establishing modern Myanmar,

Suu Kyi was awarded the Nobel Prize for Peace in 1991.

2002   The Senate Foreign Relations Committee approves the Convention on the Elimination of All Forms of Discrimination against Women. Some 170 nations have already ratified it. It is opposed by conservative Republicans, and the Bush administration asked for a delay on the approval.

2002   Twenty-year-old Serena Williams wins the women's singles tennis title at Wimbledon in England, beating her older sister Venus and capturing the first-place World Tennis Association ranking previously held by Venus. The match between the two sisters is the first ever played at Wimbledon between two black women.

2002   Golfer Suzy Whaley becomes the first woman to qualify for a tournament on the Professional Golfers' Association (PGA) tour. She does so by winning the PGA's Connecticut Section Championship, the first time any section championship is won by a woman.

CHAPTER FIVE

INDIGENOUS RIGHTS

1492   After his long voyage to the New World, Christopher Columbus lands on what he names San Salvador, the island that the indigenous people call Guanahani; encountering the Arawak, he names them Indios. The European discovery of the Americas leads to massive colonization and settlement, before long engendering the denial of rights to the indigenous peoples.

1494   Spain and Portugal sign the Treaty of Tordesillas, moving the demarcation line between the two countries' New World lands farther west—370 leagues west of the Cape Verde Islands in the Atlantic Ocean, to 48° W—than the division confirmed by Pope Alexander VI in his 1493 bull *Inter Caetera* (Among other works); this had fixed the division between Spanish and Portuguese territories 100 leagues west of the Cape Verde Islands. Under the treaty, Portugal now claims eastern Brazil.

1520–1524   Killing an estimated 75 percent of the native peoples, a smallpox epidemic rages through North America as a result of contact between the Florida Indians and the Spanish explorers led by Ponce de León. The Spanish also bring measles, typhoid, cholera, scarlet fever, bubonic plague, mumps, diphtheria, and venereal diseases to the Native Americans, who had been free of such maladies and therefore had no resistance to them.

1521   Hernán Cortés, the Spanish conqueror of Mexico, destroys the Aztec city of Tenochtitlán, the center of the Aztec (or Mexica, as they call themselves) Empire in central Mexico since the 13th century. It is thought that when Cortés and the Spanish arrived in 1519, the Aztec leader Montezuma mistook Cortés for the returning god Quetzalcoatl and so admitted him into the city; returning two years later with allies from other Indian tribes anxious to end Aztec rule because of the constant warfare in search of the 20,000 captives used yearly in Aztec sacrifices, Cortés destroys the city, which today lies under Mexico City.

1530s   A conquistador writes to the Spanish king about Francisco Pizarro's confrontation with the Incas in the Peruvian Andes, describing idyllic Inca kingdoms without thieves, idlers, or vice of any sort. He states that the Inca manage the land so that all people have their own holdings, which they oversee in peace.

1540–1542   Seeking gold and silver, Spanish forces invade the Zuni Pueblo in what is now New Mexico.

1550	At a council of legal scholars held by Charles V to discuss Spain's rights in the New World, Gines de Sepulveda speaks in support of defeating the Aztecs because they are "stupid, inept, uncivilized, cruel, idolatrous, and immoral . . . natural slaves." Spain brings two concepts to its dealings with native peoples: the encomienda, a land grant where the grant holder agrees to provide for the natives who work and live on the land; and the *repartimiento*, whereby Spanish colonial administrators assign native workers to a settler for a certain time; both deny the fact that the native peoples hold the land and are equal and autonomous parties, and both systems result in virtual slavery.
1552	Desperate to convert the Maya of Central America to Roman Catholicism, Bishop Diego de Landa destroys the Mayan hieroglyphic records, which he regards as pagan accounts of Mayan history and religion. He also has stone "idols" destroyed, in effect obliterating much of Mayan history, culture, and religion.
1564	Jacques Le Moyne, a French artist, makes drawings of American Indians at the French Huguenot settlement at the Saint Johns River in Florida.
1568	Jesuit missionaries found a school in Havana, Florida, for American Indians, with the intent of bringing them the benefits of European culture and hastening their assimilation.
c. 1570	Dedicated to peaceful coexistence, the Haudenasaunee (people of the longhouse, Iroquois Confederacy), is founded by 50 American Indian chiefs and led by the Huron Deganawida (peacemaker) and by Hiawatha, an Onondaga chief. A fundamental element of the Haudenasaunee is the Great Law of Peace, with its three principles: *skenno*, which concerns the health of the body and mind; *gaiiwiyo*, righteous conduct, thinking, and action; and *gashedenza*, knowledge of the spiritual powers underlying governance and defense.
1599	As the Spanish-appointed governor and captain of New Mexico, Don Juan de Oñate travels throughout the Rio Grande valley with soldiers, priests, and prospective settlers, declaring that he will protect the Indians in return for their allegiance to Spain and the Roman Catholic Church. After some Spanish troops demand food and provisions at the Acoma Pueblo, which the Indians cannot spare, the Indians resist and kill the leader and some of his men; Don Juan de Oñate and his priests attack the people of the pueblo, destroying it and capturing 500 Indians. Men of 12 to 25 years have a foot cut off, and women over 12 years serve as slaves for 20 years.
1600s	Samuel Purchas, British advocate of the colonization of the Virginia Territory, remarks about Native Americans that they are "more brutish than the beasts they hunt, more wild and unmanly than that unmanned country, which they range rather than inhabit; capitulated also to Satan's tyranny in mad pieties . . . wicked idleness, busy and bloody wickedness."
1609	Henry Hudson, an English explorer surveying the northeast

coast of North America for the Dutch East India Company, attacks a village of the Penobscot Indians of the eastern Abenaki, who inhabit the areas now known as Maine in the United States and New Brunswick in Canada.

1609
When the French explorer and trader Samuel de Champlain and a war band of Huron and Algonquin meet a Mohawk war party at what is now known as Lake Champlain, Champlain kills three Mohawk with his musket and frightens the rest into fleeing. Never forgetting their first encounter with the French, the Mohawk buy guns from the Dutch and British five years later.

1617
King James I of England asks the Anglican clergy to contribute funds for "churches and schools for the education of the children of these Barbarians in Virginia."

1620
Roman Catholic missionaries in North America ban the spiritual and religious use of peyote by Native Americans.

1624
The Dutch establish a trading post called New Amsterdam on the southern end of Manhattan (Algonquian: island of hills) island. Sailing for the Dutch East India Company, the Englishman Henry Hudson explored the area of Manhattan Island in 1609, which the Dutch then claimed.

1626
Peter Minuit, Dutch colonial governor of New Netherland (present-day New York and New Jersey), the colony's first director general and a representative of the United New Netherland Company, realizes that owning the land would secure the Dutch claim to the area. He purchases the island of Manhattan from one of the Algonquian-speaking tribes of Native Americans in the area for trinkets worth 60 guilders, later estimated to be around $24, although it is revealed that the Manhattan Indians claim to hold only hunting rights to the island. Minuit also makes New Amsterdam (present-day New York) the capital of New Netherland.

1631
In Roxbury, Massachusetts, the Reverend John Eliot creates "Indian prayer towns" to educate Indians in ethics and Christian values and requires the Native Americans to renounce tribal customs. He also demands that Indian men cut their long hair.

1632
The Zuni Indians in what is now New Mexico revolt against the *encomienda* and *repartimiento* systems that the Spanish forced on them; under these systems, the Zuni must pay taxes to colonial officials and work for them as well, rather than providing for the tribe. In 1639–40, the Taos Pueblo also rebels.

1637
Only 17 years after the first "Thanksgiving" when the Pequot Indians fed the Puritan colonists at Plymouth in the Massachusetts Bay Colony, the Puritans massacre the Pequot. Surrounding the Pequot village at Mystic River before dawn, the Puritans set wigwams on fire and shoot the Indians as they try to run to safety; almost 800 Native Americans, mostly women and children, are shot, burned, and hacked to death, but the colonists have only two casualties.

1641	The Treaty of Quillan between Spain and the Mapuche people of present-day Chile sets aside a territory of 25 million acres for the Mapuche south of the river Bio-Bio. The Indians fiercely resist encroachment on their lands until the 1880s, when the state of Chile defeats them and establishes a series of reserves where they are split apart; most of their best lands are given to white settlers.
1643	In the Bayonne–Jersey City area, Dutch settlers slaughter more than 100 Native Americans and imprison 30.
1655–1664	Desirous of controlling the fur trade and expanding their settlements, the Dutch had begun a campaign in 1639 to defeat the Esophus and Lenni Lenape tribes of the Hudson River Valley in present-day New York. The Peach War, so-called after an incident in which a Native American woman is killed for picking a peach in the orchard of a Dutch farmer, breaks out between the Dutch and the Native Americans; Peter Stuyvesant, colonial governor of New Netherland, leads a militia against the Esophus and begins to take hostages as bargaining chips; when the Esophus continue to resist, they are sold into slavery. The war ends when British invaders capture the Dutch territory, but by then the local tribes have been decimated.
1675–1676	King Philip's War marks the defeat of the Wampanoag people in what is now New England. Metacom (King Philip) had resisted the attempts of the British colonists at Plymouth Colony, Rhode Island, and Massachusetts Bay Colony to purchase native lands from individual tribe members in violation of a treaty; when violence erupts, the Nipmuck and Narraganset join Metacom; as he attempts to craft an alliance in the Hudson River Valley, his men are attacked by Mohawk Indians allied with the British. Further attacks by colonial forces, hunger, and disease decimate the Indian ranks; Metacom is killed, and his wife and son captured and sold as slaves in the West Indies.
1675–1676	Bacon's Rebellion is instigated by Nathaniel Bacon, an English settler who with an army of militia and indentured servants systematically destroys Indian villages in the Virginia Colony, whether they are hostile or not; he slaughters the Ocanecchi who are allied with the British against the Susquehannock and then attacks the Pamunkey. Sir William Berkeley, governor of Virginia, designates Bacon as a rebel, but Bacon continues to attack Indians until his death several months later.
1680	In a mass rebellion of the Pueblo Indians, in what is now New Mexico, against the Spanish colonial government, the Native American Popé galvanizes and unifies the 17,000 Pueblo; the Indians kill 40 of the 2,500 Spanish settlers, driving the rest to El Paso. The leaders of the Pueblo reject Christianity and ask their people to refrain from using the Spanish language.
1695–1698	The Spanish force the Chamorro Indians to relocate from the Mariana Islands in the Pacific to the island of Guam, and their numbers are reduced from about 100,000 to about 1,600 by 1756.

1700s	The Wabanaki Confederacy brings together the northern Indian nations who deal primarily with the French colonists: the Micmac, Passamaquoddy, Malecite, Penobscot, and Abenaki. Because the British want to occupy the indigenous lands, relations between the confederacy and the British are tense, but in 1725 the British sign treaties with the Micmac, Penobscot, and Abenaki.
1703	The English lead a force of more than 100 whites and 1,000 members of other tribes to attack and kill 200 Apalachee men in North Carolina, destroying all their towns and fields; 1,400 members of the tribe are enslaved.
1712–1737	The French-Fox War breaks out over French policy toward fur trading and French attempts to control the fur trade; when the French begin trading with the Dakota and Ojibwa, traditional enemies of the Fox, the Fox tribe imposes a tariff on French traders using their territory. The French declare war and provide arms to the enemies of the Fox; outnumbered, the Fox continue fighting until a truce is signed in 1737.
1713	The Treaty of Utrecht, signed in the Netherlands, follows a series of disputes and military action as the English contest other European nations for supremacy in America. Britain's empire is increased by the treaty settlement as well as by annexation.
1730	The Articles of Agreement, a treaty between the British and the Cherokee, stipulates that the Cherokee and English will live and trade in peace, with both allowed to live where they choose, although the English are forbidden to live in Cherokee towns. In return for 20 guns, the Cherokee agree to fight the native or white enemies of the British; since only some of the many Cherokee chiefs concur with the agreement, it is not widely recognized and remains in force for only a few years.
1741	Vitus Bering, a Danish navigator employed by Czar Peter III to discover whether Asia and North America are connected, explores the coast of Alaska and discovers the Aleutian Islands; in 1728, he sailed through the Bering Strait. When the Russians realize how much sea-otter fur is available here, traders flock to the Aleutian Islands; by 1766, mistreatment of the natives is common, and the Russians make the Aleuts Russian citizens.
1744	Benjamin Franklin reports that, when the governor of Virginia proposes to send six young Iroquois to the Anglican College of William and Mary, the Iroquois answer that other young Iroquois educated in Northern colleges knew all the sciences but when they returned were bad runners, "ignorant of every means of living in the Woods; unable to bear either Cold or Hunger, knew neither how to build a Cabin, take a Deer, or kill an Enemy, spoke our Language imperfectly, were therefore neither fit for Hunters, Warriors, or Counselors; they were totally good for nothing." Politely rejecting the governor's offer, the Iroquois counter with the suggestion that if a dozen young Virginians are sent to the Iroquois, they would "take great Care of their Education, instruct them in all we know, and make Men of them."

1751   A treaty between Sweden-Finland and Norway-Denmark divides the borders of their territory, and a codicil on the Lapps (indigenous Saami) divides the lands inhabited by these indigenous people. Today Sami rights to land and water are in dispute, and their reindeer herds are endangered by large-scale logging.

1752   Micmac leaders and the governor of Nova Scotia negotiate a treaty between the Micmac and the British, granting the Indians free hunting, fishing, and trading rights. Other indigenous nations who are members of the Abenaki Confederacy sign the treaty in 1753 and 1754.

1763   The Treaty of Paris between Great Britain, France, and Spain ends the Seven Years War in Europe and cedes all French possessions east of the Mississippi River and the Spanish possessions bordering the Gulf of Mexico and eastern Florida to the British. The indigenous peoples of those lands, who are never consulted while the European powers redistribute their colonial holdings, go to war with the British to protest the provisions of the treaty, which particularly affect the Cherokee, who successfully maintained productive relations with both the French and British.

1763   During the British campaign against the Ottawa in the region of today's border between Canada and the United States around Detroit, the former British commander in chief and governor general of British America Sir Jeffrey Amherst, now returned to England, suggests to Henry Bousquet, a British officer, that he introduce smallpox to the Indians; Bousquet writes that he will use blankets to pass on the disease to the Indians, and Amherst replies: "You will Do well to Innoculate [infect] the Indians by means of Blanketts, as well as to try every other method that can serve to Extirpate this Execrable Race." Smallpox spreads along the Ohio River Valley, destroying the Indian political alliance forged by the Ottawa chief Pontiac in the 1750s and killing as many as 100,000 people.

1763   During the Paxton Riots, settlers on the Pennsylvania frontier attack the peaceful Conestoga, convinced that they are spying for the Indian chief Pontiac in his campaign against the British, even though the Conestoga had refused to join Pontiac. A band of armed settlers kill three men, two women, and a child; those escaping are put into protective custody in the jail at Lancaster, until settlers storm the jail and murder the Indians.

1763   The Royal Proclamation of King George III of Great Britain redefines Indian policy and territory and affects the boundary lines of Cherokee territory. It is also the basis for 20th-century Algonquian claims of land rights in the province of Quebec in Canada as Quebec attempts to secede from Canada.

1770s–1780s   The Spanish colonial official José de Galvéz institutes a policy of supplying the Apache with alcohol and poorly manufactured weapons, in hopes of making them dependent. Traveling in small bands between New Mexico and Texas, the Apache had long resisted the Spanish colonial system.

1774	Lord Dunmore's War breaks out along the Ohio River Valley when John Murray, earl of Dunmore, the royal governor of Virginia, declares that western Pennsylvania is part of Virginia in violation of the Proclamation of 1763. Settlers and private land developers enter the lands of the Wyandot (Huron), Mingo (Iroquois), Ottawa, and Shawnee, and Dunmore declares war after attacks by and on settlers. The settlers are victorious, and the Shawnee agree to give up their hunting grounds in Kentucky.
1776	U.S. general Griffith Rutherford leads a military campaign against the Cherokee, who, resisting continual incursions into their lands, begin to raid white settlements. Congress, convinced that the British had provided weapons to the Cherokee, orders Rutherford to attack, and his troops destroy 36 villages and burn crops and the Indians' stored food supplies.
1777	Authorized by George Washington, U.S. general John Sullivan leads a military campaign against the Iroquois, who, after making a political alliance with the British, launch a series of attacks in the Mohawk Valley. Sullivan destroys 28 Iroquois villages, burns their crops, and drives the surviving people into Canada.
1778	When Europeans first come in contact with the Nootka of the northwest coast of Canada, the Indians number about 9,500. Disease, war, and contact with the commercial economy cause a significant decrease in population; they are integrated into Canada's Indian reserve system in 1871, and by 1900 about 60 percent have converted to Christianity.
1778	The English explorer Captain James Cook visits Hawaii, where he is killed. At the time there are 800,000 native Hawaiians; several decades later 770,000 had died from epidemics brought by the white man: flu, pox, and venereal disease.
1778	The Treaty of Fort Pitt is negotiated between the United States and the Delaware people, who allow U.S. troops to pass through their territory; agree to sell them food, horses, and supplies; and permit members of their nation to enlist in the continuing conflict between the 13 original colonies and the British near Detroit. The 1778 treaty recognizes the statehood of the confederation of indigenous tribes headed by the Delaware.
1787	A treaty between the Spanish and the Chickasaw and Choctaw peoples is viewed by Spain as a way of consolidating alliances with the Native Americans in the hope of enlisting them in the fight against the other colonial powers, England and France. The Chickasaw and Choctaw are two of the so-called five civilized tribes, along with the Creek, Cherokee, and Seminole, who collectively inhabit the territory now known as Alabama, Louisiana, Mississippi, and Georgia.
1787	The Northwest Ordinance passed by the U.S. Congress has the effect of denying the Indians title to their land northwest of the Ohio River and east of the Mississippi River, later called the Ohio Territory (Ohio, Indiana, Illinois, Michigan, Wisconsin), and of opening the territory to white settlers, providing for the

preservation of civil rights and the exclusion of slavery from the territory. While the ordinance recognizes the jurisdiction of the indigenous people, the indigenous nations deny that they agreed to give up their lands; the same year, the Ohio Land Company purchases large amounts of acreage in the territory from the U.S. Congress to establish a "legal" colony, and the indigenous peoples attack the settlers.

1788 Great Britain negotiates a treaty with the leaders of the indigenous peoples of Sierra Leone in Africa.

1789 The U.S. Constitution states in Article 1: "The Congress shall have power . . . to regulate commerce with foreign nations, and among the several states, and with the Indian tribes."

1790 The U.S. Indian Trade and Non-Intercourse Act mandates Congress's approval of land transfers from Native Americans. New England authorities enacted treaties and purchased land from individual Native Americans and, as a result, transferred enormous amounts of land from the Penobscot and Passamaquoddy Indians; not until 1980 are their ancestors able to get back a small portion of their native lands.

1790–1791 U.S. president George Washington sends the military to intervene in the Ohio Territory, but the U.S. forces are defeated, and the United States is forced to negotiate a settlement with the Indians. The Indians demand recognition that the Ohio River marks the border of their territory, a claim supported by Lord Dorchester, the British governor general of Canada; during negotiations, the Shawnee, led by Tecumseh, make a political alliance with southern tribes.

1791 The East India Company of Great Britain and the Maratha (Mahratta) people of south-central India make an agreement, but by constantly interfering in the succession of Maratha rulers and favoring whoever supports Great Britain's policies, the British manage to thwart Maratha expansion.

1795 Settling wars begun in 1794, including the Battle of Fallen Timbers between the U.S. military and a confederation of 12 Native American tribes, the Treaty of Fort Greenville is negotiated between the United States and the defeated Native Americans of the Northwest Ordinance (Ohio Territory). Chiefs of the Shawnee, Wyandot, Miami, and Delaware sign the treaty, according to which the 12 tribes are forced to surrender their ancestral lands, including the six square miles of what soon after becomes the major port of Chicago; Tecumseh, chief of the Shawnee, opposes the treaty.

1799 At Three Saints Bay on Kodiak Island in Alaska, the Russian traders Grigory Shelekhov and Ivan Golikov establish a European settlement that becomes a major force for assimilation of the native peoples. The indigenous inhabitants work for the Russians hunting sea otter and marry Russians; the children of these marriages are given Russian citizenship beginning in 1821.

1799 The Tlingit people of the northwest coast of America attack a

Russian fort in southern Alaska and hold it for two years, until the Russians reconquer it with the aid of the Aleut.

1800s   The Cherokee, in present-day Tennessee and North Carolina, develop a legal code using English, and they introduce a bicameral legislature. Sequoya (Sikwayi), an American Indian silversmith, painter, scholar, and warrior who gave his name to the giant Sequoia redwoods, creates a Cherokee syllabary that helps the Indians learn to read and write and publishes religious works and a newspaper; cognizant of the changing reality that necessitates the treaties of 1817 and 1819, the Cherokee express "their anxious desire to engage in the pursuits of agriculture and civilized life."

1801   The U.S. Congress votes to appropriate $15,000 a year "to promote civilization among the aborigines."

1802   William Henry Harrison, later president of the United States, leads a campaign to drive Indians from their lands in Indiana Territory. Indian resistance is organized by the chief Tecumseh, who sets forth the novel idea that the land belongs jointly to all indigenous peoples, and no one tribe or chief has the right to cede title; the American forces are victorious in the "the War of the Red Sticks," and in 1816 Indiana is admitted to the Union as a state.

1805   The Treaty of Mount Dexter between the United States and the Choctaw of southeastern Mississippi forces the Indians to grant 4 million acres of their land to the U.S. government, in return for debts the Choctaw accumulated at government trading posts.

1809   The Treaty of Fort Wayne, between Governor William Henry Harrison of the Indiana Territory and the Delaware, Potawatomi, and Miami Indians, gives the Indians $7,000 in goods and an annual payment of $1,750 in return for 2.5 million acres southeast of the Wabash River. Soon after, Governor Harrison negotiates a treaty with the Kickapoo and Wea for half a million acres.

1810   The U.S. Supreme Court decides, in *Fletcher v. Peck*, that the United States owns the land west of the demarcation, which the English king George III once claimed. Justice Marshall describes the land held by Native Americans there as "vacant" and makes no provision for the fact that the Indians had never ceded native lands west of the Allegheny and Appalachian Mountains to the states.

1811   Native resistance to the terms of such treaties as the one that Governor William Henry Harrison negotiated crystallizes when the brothers Tenskwatawa and Tecumseh of the Shawnee create a pan-Indian alliance and establish towns on lands ceded by the treaties. Harrison and his forces launch an attack at Tippecanoe (modern Indiana), forcing Chief Tecumseh's withdrawal, but Indian resistance continues, and Tecumseh joins the British during the War of 1812 between Great Britain and the United States.

1812	After Donald McKenzie of the Pacific Fur Company enters the territory of the Kalapuya people on the Willamette River in Oregon, contact with fur traders and settlers brings diseases, including malaria, to the Native Americans. By 1855, treaties with the whites have placed the Kalapuya on the Grande Ronde Reservation.
1814	The Treaty of Fort Jackson, sometimes called the Treaty of Horseshoe Bend, between the Creek and the United States forces the Creek Indians to cede 22 million acres of their ancestral lands, in what is now Alabama and Georgia, to the United States. The Creek, one of the five civilized tribes, had managed to maintain their independence by successfully dealing with the French, Spanish, and English until 1813, when the war with Tecumseh (in what is now Indiana) spreads south and U.S. troops defeat the Creek.
1817, 1819	Treaties between the Cherokee and the United States allow the Indians only as much land as they have under cultivation at the time. The U.S. government policy is aimed at giving the indigenous nations a choice of removal westward or accepting land under conditions that break down tribal governance and the traditional collective holding of land.
1818	The East India Company of Great Britain negotiates a commercial alliance with Selangor, a state of Malaysia.
1819	Under the Adams-Onis Treaty, Spain cedes Florida to the United States, a move that affects the status of the Seminole Indians.
1819	The U.S. Congress passes the Civilization Fund Act, appropriating to missionary groups an annual amount of $10,000 to train Indians in the "habits and arts of civilization." The missionaries are to instruct Native Americans "in the mode of agriculture suited to their situation, and . . . [teach] their children in reading, writing, and arithmetic and performing such other duties as may be enjoined."
1820	The Treaty of Doak's Stand between the Choctaw Indians and the United States continues the trend of the 1805 Treaty of Mount Dexter and the gradual removal of the Choctaw from their lands. Five million acres of Choctaw land in southeastern Mississippi are exchanged for 13 million acres of land in Arkansas and the Indian territory in Oklahoma, but much of this land is already inhabited by whites.
1820s	The Pawnee, who live in what is now Kansas and Nebraska, abandon the use of human sacrifice in the Morning Star Ceremony. Before this time, the Pawnee would capture a young girl from another tribe, treat her well for a year, and then sacrifice her by tying her to a wooden scaffold and shooting an arrow into her heart as the morning star, Mars or Venus, rose; the ceremony was thought to bring a successful corn crop and an abundance of buffalo.
1823	The U.S. Supreme Court, in *Johnson v. McIntosh*, decides the United States holds preeminent sovereignty over claimed terri-

tory. Justice Marshall declares that by virtue of the "Doctrine of Discovery" with its "Rights of Conquest," the United States has a right to acquire territory from the Native Americans, the rightful owners; the "Rights of Conquest" principle is invoked when Native Americans resist their "discoverers" and refuse to trade with them or to allow missionaries to travel in their territories.

1824   The U.S. Bureau of Indian Affairs is established by the Department of War, with responsibilities for carrying out government policies for Native Americans and Inuit (Eskimos). In 1849, the bureau becomes part of the Department of the Interior.

1828   The *Cherokee Phoenix*, a weekly Native American tribal newspaper, is published in both English and Cherokee. It is edited by Elias Boudinot, a member of the Cherokee, who states that "there must exist a vehicle of Indian intelligence, altogether different from those which have heretofore been employed . . . to remove prejudice and to give profitable information."

1829   When the Choctaw refuse to relocate westward, the state of Mississippi disbands the governing body of the Choctaw and in 1830 enacts the Treaty of Dancing Rabbit Creek, which gives Mississippi sovereignty over Choctaw land. Soon after, most of the Choctaw leave for Indian territory, many suffering and dying along the way; only 6,000 Choctaw of the 23,000 original inhabitants remain in Mississippi by 1832.

1829   William Apes, a Pequot Indian, writes the first Native American autobiography, his *A Son of the Forest: The Experience of William Apes, a Native of the Forest, Comprising a Notice of the Pequot Tribe of Indians.*

1830   The U.S. Congress passes the Indian Removal Act, allowing President Andrew Jackson to force the Cherokee, Creek, Chickasaw, Choctaw, and Seminole Indians to move from their ancestral lands east of the Mississippi to the Indian territory of Oklahoma; supposedly voluntary, the removal is forced on Native Americans when the government wants their land for white settlers. In the 1830s, the Potawatomi are removed from Indiana, and the Winnebago, Sauk, and Fox are forced to leave Wisconsin; these treaties do not keep white settlers from intruding on, or buying and selling, indigenous land. Because of fraud and mismanagement, many Indians lose their land; Georgia passes state laws dispossessing the Indians and violates the rights granted the Cherokee under the treaty.

1831   The U.S. Supreme Court decides, in *Cherokee Nation v. Georgia*, to limit American Indian rights, in a case in which the governor of Georgia had signed legislation to distribute Cherokee land, and the Cherokee protested, claiming these acts violated treaties they had negotiated with the United States. Chief Justice Marshall describes Native American tribes as "domestic dependent nations," who, although they possess certain lands are "in a state of pupilage"; he dismisses the case on the grounds that the Cherokee Nation cannot be considered a "foreign nation" as set forth by the Constitution.

1831–1832	The Kol tribal people in India revolt as a result of the appropriation of their land by nontribal people and the government. The Kol suffer further from the introduction of private property, moneylending, and service as contract labor.
1832	In *Worcester v. Georgia*, the U.S. Supreme Court decides to honor American Indian treaties, in a case involving the conviction and sentencing of an Indian man to four years' hard labor for residing in Cherokee lands without a permit from the governor of Georgia. Justice Marshall rules the Georgia statutes unlawful; although Chief Justice Marshall in his previous decision, *Cherokee Nation v. Georgia*, considered Native American tribes as "domestic dependent nations," he acknowledges in *Worcester v. Georgia* that "the Indian nations possessed a full right to the lands they occupied, until that right should be extinguished by the United States, with their consent."
1832	Previously victimized by an 1804 treaty granting them 50 million acres, the Sauk Indians in Illinois resist the decision of the U.S. General Land Office to put their land up for sale; when settlers had moved onto remaining Sauk lands in 1827, the Black Hawk War began, and in 1831 troops attacked and destroyed an Indian town. In 1832, at the Battle of Bad Axe, the Sauk are slaughtered; the survivors sign a treaty granting them up to 6 million acres of land.
1837	Colonel Richard Johnson establishes the Choctaw Academy, a manual-labor school for young Native Americans in Kentucky. The school requires that students perform six hours a day of work on a farm or in the shop and attend six hours a day of classroom study of religion and academic subjects; by 1840, there are six such manual-labor schools for Indians in the country.
1838	The United States orders the forced march of 17,000 members of the Cherokee Nation from their lands—in what is now Tennessee, Georgia, North Carolina, and Alabama—1,500 miles west to Indian territory in Oklahoma. On the "Trail of Tears," close to 50 percent, or 8,000, of the Cherokee are thought to have perished.
1840	The Treaty of Waitangi is negotiated between the British and the Maori in New Zealand, where Maori are thought to have arrived from Polynesia more than a thousand years earlier. By the 1760s, Europeans had come there for timber and to fish for seals and whales; claiming complete sovereignty, the British use this claim in dealing with other colonial powers.
1842	The Bagot Commission is established in Canada to review the work of the Office of Indian Affairs. The commission recommends that an agriculture program be established for the Indians, that schools be created to assimilate Indians into Canadian life, and that Indians be given instruction in Christianity, also to encourage assimilation.
1846	The Treaty of Washington, between the United States and British interests in North America, sets the boundary between the two powers at the 49th parallel. Europeans who settle to the

north are primarily interested in trading for furs with the indigenous peoples who hunt and trap, while territory to the south is reserved for the Americans, who are moving into the Oregon Territory.

1848   The Treaty of Guadeloupe Hidalgo, between the United States and Mexico, sets the terms to end the Mexican War. Guided by the philosophical underpinnings of the doctrine of Manifest Destiny and the quest for ever more land, the United States insists, as a condition to ending military action, on annexing what is now the southwestern United States from Mexico; while the treaty enumerates rights for the native peoples, their property rights are violated.

1849   The British proclaim the colony of Vancouver Island and grant the Hudson Bay Company (HBC) the right to settle and colonize the island for 10 years. James Douglas, head of the HBC's fur-trading operations on the island and across the mainland in New Caledonia (in British Columbia, western Canada), and the second governor of the island, concludes several "purchases" of tribal lands for white settlers to use; the HBC gains title to lands the indigenous people cultivate or had built houses on in exchange for blankets, minimal financial compensation, the freedom to hunt and fish, and the grant of small portions of land.

1850   In Colombia, when Indians resist the expropriation of their communal Indian land, the Spanish authorities set aside *resguardos* (reserves of land) for them. Nevertheless, land becomes increasingly concentrated in the hands of large landowners, and Indians become dependent sharecroppers.

1851   An unexpectedly large contingent of 10,000 Native Americans and 270 soldiers gather at Horse Creek (present-day Wyoming) to sign the Fort Laramie Treaty between the United States and the Cheyenne, Arapaho, Sioux, and Crow tribes, although before long the pressure of western expansion, the gold rush, and the Civil War lead to multiple violations of the peace. The U.S. government offers $50,000 a year for 50 years to each Indian nation in return for free and safe passage through the territories, clearly defined for each tribe, a peace treaty among the tribes, and the right to build military posts.

1854   In the Gadsden Purchase, the United States purchases land in southern Arizona and New Mexico, although neither Mexico nor the United States consults with the Chiricahua Apache or Tohono O'odham (Papago) who live in those regions.

1855   Entering into a treaty with the Blackfeet Confederacy, the United States grants the Blackfeet of the Northern Plains $20,000 worth of goods with an annual grant of $15,000 and a promise of schools, training in farming, and a guarantee of peace, in return for the rights to land for a railroad. Despite the treaty, white cattle ranchers begin enclosing Blackfeet land; in 1874, President Ulysses S. Grant issues an executive order that moves the boundaries of the 1855 treaty without any compensation to the Blackfeet for their loss of land.

1855	The Walla Walla Council is held when the Indian nations in the Northwest (Nez Percé, Cayuse, Umatilla, Walla Walla, and observers from the Yakima) meet with the superintendent of Indian Affairs for the Western Territory to discuss a treaty. After much dispute among the tribes, they agree to cede about 30,000 square miles in Oregon and Washington to the government to use for a northern route of the railroad and for settlement in return for guaranteed control of their remaining lands and a payment of up to $200,000 for each tribe; the whites, however, disregard the treaty, and by 1856, the tribes turn to violent resistance against white incursions into their remaining lands.
1856	In New Zealand, Maori chiefs form an alliance to protect themselves from British colonists, agreeing to end the sale of indigenous land to colonists and proposing a Maori government; the colonists then wage war on the Maori. Although Maori rights were guaranteed by the 1840 Treaty of Waitangi, in 1848 the British Crown demanded 30 million acres in New Zealand, half of their ancestral land.
1860	The Treaty of Managua, negotiated between Nicaragua and Great Britain, establishes that the indigenous people, the Miskito, have a right to political autonomy and to a Miskito Reserve. In 1894, however, the Nicaraguan government abolishes the reserve, and the Miskito region is reincorporated into Nicaragua as the department of Zelaya.
1862	Protesting the abuses of the reservation system, the Santee Sioux rebel in Minnesota; when the Sioux had exchanged their lands for reservation life and annuities, they became dependent on their yearly grant of food and supplies. Concerned that he will lose his financial kickback, the Indian agent refuses to issue food supplies until the tribe's cash annuities arrive; as hunger increases, some younger tribe members murder some settlers, and the Sioux invade the Indian Agency, killing 20 people. The Santee are defeated at the Battle of Wood Lake, and 38 Sioux are found guilty of murder and rape and are hanged.
1862–1869	During the building of the Transcontinental Railroad in the United States, trained marksmen kill entire herds of buffalo, the mainstay of the Native American population of the Great Plains. The Sioux and Cheyenne have been attacking workers along the line because they claim that the building of the railroad violates their treaties with the U.S. government and poses a threat to their culture. Partly to eliminate these natives and partly for sport, men hired by the Union Pacific Railroad slaughter the buffalo.
1863	Colonel Patrick Connor and members of his volunteer militia who are policing Utah attack the Shoshone and Bannock in the Bear River Campaign.
1863	The Treaty of Ruby Valley, between the United States and the Shoshone Indians, is signed but not ratified until 1869; altogether, three treaties are signed with the eastern, northwestern, and western nations of the Shoshone, establishing peace and

guaranteeing the safety of whites traveling through Shoshone territory. The Shoshone never give up the title to their ancestral lands, though the western Shoshone later agree to allow the U.S. president to set aside a reservation for them.

1864   Some 700 U.S. troops kill 105 women and children and 28 men of the Cheyenne and Arapaho at Sand Creek, Colorado. Two months earlier, one of the chiefs of the Cheyenne, Black Kettle, declared to the American soldiers that the Cheyenne were at peace with the whites, and, believing his people would be protected, he flew an American flag that had been given to him by President Abraham Lincoln; a year later, the Arapaho and the Cheyenne are expelled from the Colorado Territory.

1864–1868   On the Long Walk in the Southwest United States, nearly 10,000 Apache and Navajo peoples are forced to march 250 miles, many dying en route from dysentery, kidnappings, and the cold; some 3,500 Navajo die at their relocated home at Bosque Redondo, southeast of Santa Fe, New Mexico. In the U.S. campaign to defeat the Mescalero Apache and Navajo and to relocate them away from lands in Arizona thought to hold gold and mineral reserves, Kit Carson destroyed the agricultural resources and livestock of the Navajo, and the Navajo surrendered at Fort Defiance, Arizona; in 1868, the remaining Navajo are allowed to take the Long Walk back to Arizona.

1865   Great Britain enacts the Maori Land Court and Native Lands Act to make it easier for British settlers in New Zealand to acquire land owned by the Maori and to break down the Maori collective land holding tradition. The act requires individual Maori to record titles to their land.

1866–1868   In the Bozeman Trail Wars, the United States fights the Arapaho, Sioux, and Cheyenne Indians in the territory of today's South Dakota. The Indians oppose the construction of forts in their territory.

1867   A U.S. Peace Commission begins to negotiate a new Treaty of Fort Laramie for U.S. travel rights through Sioux territory; although the U.S. government declares that altogether nine treaties are signed with the Sioux, none of the war chiefs of the tribes are signatories. In the 1880s, the U.S. government seizes Sioux land and offers it to whites for settlement, setting aside land for Sioux reservations.

1867   The United States purchases Alaska from Russia for $7.2 million, and, regarded as Indian territory, Alaska is placed under the authority of the U.S. Department of War. The treaty with Russia requires the signatories to gain the consent of the indigenous peoples for appropriations of land, but, according to the indigenous people of Alaska, the Russians cannot transfer what they never owned (the land), only the trading rights they had negotiated with the indigenous people.

1868   The Sioux and the United States sign the Treaty of Fort Laramie, ending hostilities in the Black Hills of southwestern

South Dakota, the home of the Sioux Great Spirit, Wakan Tanka; the treaty establishes a Sioux reservation, which includes the Black Hills, and grants the Sioux hunting rights in return for their pledge not to obstruct the railroad or attack settlers. As the Sioux understand it, the treaty reserves to them in perpetuity the use and possession and legal jurisdiction of their ancestral lands—the greater Sioux territory, the lands west of the Missouri River; only the Sioux have the authority to enforce legal action against anyone violating the treaty in these lands.

1868   The Canadian Indian Act and the Enfranchisement Act establish the categories of "uncivilized Indians" and "civilized whites" in Canada. An Indian can voluntarily terminate his or her status as an Indian and thereby gain the same rights that whites enjoy.

1869   After the United States purchases Alaska from Russia, fur trappers, gold miners, and traders arrive and disrupt the traditional ways of life of the indigenous peoples of the interior. The Alaskan economy is transformed from a subsistence basis to a dependence on American and European trade.

1870s   The Basters, of Dutch descent, establish a state in what is now known as Namibia in West Africa, between the Cape Colony's northwestern frontier and the lower course of the Orange River. Missionary organizations help codify in writing the traditional political customs of the Basters, including the offices of chief and subchief and an annual tribal convocation; all community members are entitled to equal treatment, and all are liable for taxes.

1870s   In present-day Bangladesh, the British colonial authorities ban *jhuming* (traditional indigenous shifting cultivation of food crops and cotton, with a seven-year fallow period to replenish the soil) among the Chakma, Marma, and Tripura, the 3 largest of the 13 tribes of the region, in the Chittagong Hill Tracts. The British seek to increase productivity, but instead the tribal lands are overfarmed, and soil quality declines.

1870s   During the Spanish colonization in Guatemala, indigenous communal lands are transferred to wealthy landowners, and Indians are forced to work on coffee plantations.

1871   As part of the Indian Appropriations Act, the United States suspends making treaties with the Indians.

1876   During the Second Carlist War in Spain, the Basque people are caught in the middle as France and Spain attempt to firm up their national boundaries. The Basque *fueros* legal system is banned, and Basque autonomy is further threatened by mining and the growth of industry in the region as people from elsewhere in Spain move into Basque country; Euskera, the Basque language, is forbidden to be taught in the schools.

1876   Although officially described as an effort to protect native peoples and help them assimilate into white Canadian society, the Indian Act of Canada contains many provisions that disrupt traditional ways of life and encourage or force reliance on whites; Indian lands become government-controlled reservations with white management of Indian councils and food and supply rations; on some reservations, people are unable to leave without a pass. The government decides who is or is not an Indian; Indians are pressured to give up their Indian identity for Canadian citizenship and sell or trade their land to whites; women who marry nonindigenous men lose their indigenous status, as do their children.

1877   The *Reglamento de Jornaleros* (Ruling for laborers), instituted in Guatemala, forces rural workers to carry a book listing all their debts incurred working on the estates of colonial planters. Vagrancy laws enacted in 1884 force unemployed Indians to work 40 days a year on government projects.

1877   The Manypenny Agreement, passed by the U.S. Congress, allows the seizure of Sioux Indian land because the Sioux refused to sell or lease the lands of the Black Hills of South Dakota granted to them by the 1868 Treaty of Fort Laramie. Under the Manypenny Agreement, Sioux lands are seized without paying any compensation.

1877   The Nez Percé Wars begin when the U.S. government fails to keep its promise to maintain the sanctity of Nez Percé land in the Wallowa Valley of Washington; the United States already broke several treaties with the Nez Percé, including the 1855 Walla Walla agreement and the Treaty of Fort Lapwai. In 1877, the lands revert to the public domain, and the Nez Percé are ordered to the Lapwai Reservation in Idaho; the Nez Percé resist but finally surrender at Snake Creek in Montana; they are relocated to a series of reservations in Kansas, the Indian Territory, and then back to Washington.

1878   The Carlisle American Indian Industrial School is founded by Lieutenant Richard Henry Pratt in Carlisle, Pennsylvania, on the grounds of a former military camp. A boarding school, it is established to remove young Native Americans from the strong influences of family and tribe with the aim of inculcating American values; Pratt introduces a policy known as "outing," requiring young Native Americans to work as servants in white homes and forbidding them to return home on vacation.

1881–1882 In El Salvador, Mayan Indian land is appropriated to consolidate the expansion of the coffee trade. Indian land is auctioned, and the Maya are forced to become laborers on the plantations.

1882   The U.S. government decides to use abandoned forts and stockades for Indian schools, with military officers as instructors. Three years later, there are schools for Native Americans all over the country, with inadequately trained teachers and overcrowded facilities; students are required to dress in military uniforms, to march, and to attend Christian services, and they may not use their native languages.

1883   In *Ex parte Crow Dog*, the U.S. Supreme Court decides that the government has no jurisdiction to prosecute a Native American for the murder of another Native American on a reservation, a ruling that somewhat limits the federal government's jurisdiction over Native Americans.

1885   The U.S. Congress passes the Major Crimes Act, extending federal judicial authority limited by the 1883 Supreme Court decision and declaring that the government holds jurisdiction over Native American territories; previously, individual tribes exercised jurisdiction within their territories, and they believed that this was understood by the United States as an expression of their sovereignty. The act specifies that federal courts have jurisdiction in cases of major crimes committed on Indian land and that these crimes committed by Indians are subject to the same laws and penalties as those of all other U.S. residents.

1885   The Berlin Africa Conference is held to consider the rights of indigenous peoples in Africa, specifically to "civilize" the indigenous peoples. The second Africa Conference, held in Brussels in 1889–90, declares that Europe has a "duty" to "raise [them] to civilization and bring about the extinction of barbarous customs, such as cannibalism and human sacrifices."

1885   In today's Namibia, the Basters conclude a treaty with the German colonial administration in which the German emperor recognizes the rights of the Basters, but the Germans fail to abide by the agreement.

1886   The U.S. commissioner of Indian Affairs orders that all instruction in boarding schools for Indian children be given only in English, not in indigenous languages. As a result, many Indian languages disappear in the following decades; in 1887, the rule is extended to apply to all schools on Indian reservations, whether run by the U.S. government or by religious organizations.

1886   The U.S. Supreme Court rules, in *United States v. Kagama*, to uphold the sovereignty of the federal branch of government over the Native American tribes, deciding that Congress can make legislation regarding Indian affairs and that these laws are not subject to constitutional review. The Court upholds the Major Crimes Act and rejects the principle of Native American national sovereignty.

1887   The speech of Chief Seattle, the bold and aggressive hereditary leader of the Suquamish tribe around Puget Sound in Washington State, was recited at 1854 treaty negotiations when the Indians were persuaded to sell 2 million acres of land to the whites for $150,000; some 30 years later, Henry Smith, who made notes of the speech, publishes his version in the *Seattle Sunday Star*. Seattle declares that the entire country is sacred to Native Americans and "every hillside, every valley, every plain and grove has been hallowed by some fond memory or some sad experience of my tribe. Even the rocks, which seem to lie dumb as they swelter in the sun along the silent shore in solemn grandeur, thrill with memories of past events connected with the fate of my people."

1887   J. D. C. Atkins, the U.S. commissioner of Indian Affairs, writes on the subject of education that "the first step to be taken toward civilization, toward teaching the Indians the mischief and folly of continuing in their barbarous practices, is to teach them the English language."

1887   The General Allotment Act, or Dawes Act, passed by the U.S. Congress divides Indian communally owned reservations into individual plots of 160 acres and sells off the remaining land to white speculators. Supposedly, the act is intended to help Native Americans become assimilated into American society, but many Indians, now among the poorest people in the United States, lose their allotment and refuse to be assimilated; much allotment land also goes to whites through illegal land purchases or trades, and during the next 50 years about 100 million acres, or about two-thirds of the lands reserved for Native Americans in the United States, are taken from them and given to the government or private individuals.

1888   The Fort Belknap Agreement between the United States and the Atsina and Assiniboin Indians is signed by President Grover Cleveland, marking the cession of a large part of reservation lands. The Atsina, known also as the Gros Ventre, originally occupied lands in what is now Minnesota but by the mid-18th century had moved west; in 1873, along with the Assiniboin and Blackfeet, U.S. president Ulysses S. Grant awards them a large reservation in Montana, which the Fort Belknap Agreement reduces to 600,000 acres.

1889   The U.S. commissioner for Indian Affairs, Thomas Morgan, explains current educational policy toward Native Americans in his annual report, stating that "education should seek the disintegration of the tribes, and not their segregation. . . . In short, the public school should do for them what it is so successfully doing for all the other races in this country, assimilate them."

1895   The Basque Nationalist Party (PNV) is founded in Spain. Since then, the PNV has advocated the creation of an independent Basque state, Euskadi.

1897   The annual report of the U.S. superintendent of Indian Schools reveals that Native American students, despite the extraordinary efforts made by the school system to inculcate new American values, "return to their respective reservations merely to relapse into so-called Indian savagism, in most cases, even an aggravated form."

1897   Louis Sockalexis, a Penobscot Indian playing for the Cleveland Spiders of the National League, is the first American Indian to play major league baseball.

1898   The Newlands Joint Resolution annexing Hawaii to the United States is signed by President William McKinley; in 1893, the United States invaded Hawaii, notwithstanding its 70-year-long recognition of the island's sovereignty. Queen Liliuokalani abdicates, stating that, though she is yielding her authority to U.S. armed might, she does not give up her authority as constitutional sovereign of the Hawaiian Islands.

1900   The British colonial authorities in present-day Bangladesh pass the Chittagong Hill Tracts Regulation, affirming some aspects of tribal autonomy, including policing, tax collection, and administration of civil law by tribal authorities. The regulation also creates strict rules for entry and residence requirements for nontribals.

1903   In *Lone Wolf v. Hitchcock*, the U.S. Supreme Court rules that congressional legislation may abrogate treaties negotiated by the government and Native American tribes. Lone Wolf, a Kiowa chief, sought an injunction against congressional approval of a 1900 agreement involving the loss of 2 million acres of land held by the Kiowa, Comanche, and Apache, claiming that the agreement to hand over the land was reached without the consent of tribal members; 300 tribal members urge Congress not to ratify the agreement because it violates the 1867 Treaty of Medicine Lodge stipulating that lands cannot be ceded without the consent of "three-fourths of all adult male Indians." Justice White declares that the 1900 agreement abrogates the 1867 treaty, and that Congress has always exercised plenary power over the tribes; in effect, the Court rules that certain sections of treaties can be legally violated without the consent of Native Americans, and the many treaties setting out Native American sovereignty and political and land rights are no longer enforceable.

1905   In *United States v. Winans*, the U.S. Supreme Court decides that a tribe may have some reserved rights not specified by treaty, when it declares that the Yakima retain their rights to hunt for game.

1906   The Germans and British begin mining for phosphate on the island of Naura in Oceania without permission of the Naurans; some years later, control of the mining shifts to the British Phosphate Commission, a venture of England, Australia, and New Zealand. While the League of Nations and then the United Nations mandate that Australia must guarantee the rights of the Naurans, the islanders press for reparations, claiming their land was destroyed and they were paid only a miniscule portion of the profits.

1908   In *Winters v. United States* the U.S. Supreme Court rules that the Atsina and Assiniboin of the Fort Belknap Reservation in Montana retain their Milk River water rights, even though those rights were not included in an 1877 treaty in which the tribes gave up land and agreed that the Milk River would be the northernmost boundary of their reservation. Although Supreme Court decisions protect the native nations from actions by states and individuals, they also reaffirm the preeminence of Congress, which continues to make the practical decisions limiting Indian life.

1908   Anthropologist John Reed Swanton locates the last Ofo speaker, Rosa Pierrette of Marksville, Louisiana, who was taught the language of her ancestors by her grandmother. The Ofo or Ofogoula, known to whites as the Dog People, had moved in 1673 from land along the Ohio River to land in Mississippi along the Yazoo River and sided with the French against the British, suffering great casualties; there is no recorded mention of the Ofo after 1784. Rosa Pierrette is instrumental in the Smithsonian Institution's publication of a dictionary of the language in 1912.

1909	Louis Tewanima is the first Native American to hold the world record for the 10-mile run in track. As a member of the U.S. Olympic team in 1908 and 1912, Tewanima, a Hopi, wins silver medals in both the 5,000-meter and 10,000-meter runs.
1911	The U.S. Department of the Interior prohibits hunting of sea lions by the Aleut of the Aleutian Islands of Alaska, although seal hunting contributes a major portion of Aleut livelihood. In 1913, the Aleutian Islands are declared a National Wildlife Refuge, and the Department of the Interior bans additional hunting; many Aleut abandon their traditional ways to find work in the canneries.
1911	Ishi, "the last wild Indian," the last surviving member of the Yahi people, appears in Oroville in northern California. The Yahi had been marginalized and slaughtered, and Ishi and the few remaining Yahi managed to hide for several years; when Ishi emerges, the anthropologists Alfred Kroeber and Thomas Waterman house him in the Museum of Anthropology at the University of California, and Ishi performs public demonstrations of Yahi skills, making fires and tools of stone.
1911	The first Native American professional baseball player to be named best pitcher of the year is Charles Bender, a Chippewa. In 1953, Bender is named to the Baseball Hall of Fame.
1912	The first Native American athlete to win an Olympic gold medal is Jim Thorpe, of the Sac and Fox-Potawatomi in Oklahoma; Thorpe wins the decathlon and pentathlon events at the Olympics, but subsequently his medals are taken away because the International Olympic Committee rules he received money while an amateur athlete—$2 a day for expenses while playing baseball in the minor leagues. From 1913 to 1919, he plays baseball for the New York Giants, and from 1920 to 1929 he plays football for the New York Giants; he is voted the greatest athlete of the first half of the 20th century by the Associated Press, and in 1973 his amateur status is reinstated.
1912	The Alaska Native Brotherhood is founded in Sitka, Alaska, by Tlingit and Tsimshian people to advocate for native rights and citizenship.
1913	The Alaska Native Sisterhood is formed in Juneau, Alaska.
1914–1918	Late in World War I, the United States employs 14 Choctaw code talkers, who use the Choctaw language to send and receive important messages in various field headquarters. Even though the German Army intercepts many of these messages, the Germans cannot break the code.
1916	The Basters, of Dutch descent, participate with other peoples in

a rebellion against the Germans occupying the area of West Africa known today as Namibia. After the Germans are defeated, Great Britain begins a military occupation of Southwest Africa, introducing a long period of colonial encroachment on the Basters' right to self-determination.

1916 The United States and Great Britain on behalf of Canada enact the Migratory Birds Convention, and in 1917, the Canadian Parliament passes the Migratory Birds Convention Act, setting regulations regarding migratory birds and creating open and closed seasons for hunting. While the convention allows in some cases for the Inuit and other indigenous peoples to take birds for food and clothing, it has the effect of limiting complete access, particularly for the northernmost hunters, to migratory game birds; when the indigenous peoples challenge this convention, the Canadian government states that the relationship between the convention and existing treaties and land claims "is unclear" and pledges to make an effort to amend it.

1917 The Imashaghen (Tuareg) unsuccessfully wage war against the French, who seize their traditional grazing lands; the Tuareg inhabit the territory in northwestern Africa of today's southern Algeria, northeastern Mali, and northern Niger. Without adequate pasture for their livestock, they are forced into dependence.

1917 The U.S. Army occupies the Nisqually Reservation on the northwest coast in the state of Washington; the Nisqually were penalized by the 1850 Donation Act of Oregon, which allowed settlers to move onto and build on Nisqually territory, although their reservation were established by the Treaties of Medicine Creek (1854), Point No Point (1855), and Point Elliot (1855). During World War I, the army expropriates two-thirds of their lands, forcing them to move to other reservations.

1917 The All-Pueblo Council, founded in Santo Domingo, New Mexico, is the first organization to represent the Pueblo Indians of the American Southwest; it is established to counter proposed U.S. legislation, the Bursum Bill, which would confirm the legal titles of all non-Pueblo Indian claimants of Pueblo land, as well as transfer control of Pueblo water to the state courts of New Mexico. John Collier, a visitor to New Mexico in 1917 and later the first commissioner of Indian Affairs, learns about the pending Bursum Bill and travels around the state informing the Pueblo Indians of the bill's implications.

1921 In an agreement with the Canadian government, the Hare or Kawchittine, facing hunger and epidemics, grant their lands to Canada in return for medicine and education. The 700 Hare had lived on more than 45,000 square miles of sub-Arctic land until the late 19th century, when they encountered whites and became involved in the fur trade; with the decline in fur trading, they are pressured into forsaking their traditional life for jobs in oil refineries.

1922 Canada and the Inuit of the Northwest Territories negotiate the

Nunavut Agreement.

1922 Natives of Alaska are granted U.S. voting rights.

1922 The American Indian Defense Association (AIDA) is created as the first white organization formed to advocate for Native American rights. From 1923 to 1933, the executive secretary is John Collier, who is later appointed by President Franklin D. Roosevelt as commissioner of Indian Affairs; AIDA merges with the National Association of Indian Affairs in 1936 and becomes the Association of American Indian Affairs.

1924 The U.S. Congress gives the Native Americans U.S. citizenship and the right to vote. Nevertheless, tribes like the Onondaga and Hopi refuse to acknowledge the validity of the act and declare their sovereignty, issuing passports, for example.

1924 The first Native American named captain of the U.S. Olympic hockey team is Clarence "Taffy" Abel, a Sault Sainte Marie Chippewa. Abel plays professional hockey with the New York Rangers from 1926 to 1929 and with the Chicago Black Hawks from 1929 to 1934, winning the Stanley Cup in 1934; he is named to the U.S. Hockey Hall of Fame in 1973.

1924 The U.S. Pueblo Land Act, passed after the defeat of the Bursum Bill, accepts the land rights of the Pueblo as established by Spain and allows the eviction of white squatters from Pueblo Indian lands.

1926 In an international adjudication of the Cayuga Indians' claim to constitute a nation (*Canada v. United States*), the tribunal rules that the Cayuga do not constitute a nation and that a tribe is not a "legal unit of international law." Indian tribes are said to exist as legal entities only by virtue of the laws of the power in whose territories the tribes live.

1928 In an international adjudication of the islands of Palmas (Miangas in Malaysia; *United States v. Netherlands*), the arbitrator implies that "discovery" accompanied by occupation and possession can be invoked to presume title and that treaties between the East India Company and indigenous leaders are not treaties in the sense of international law.

1928 *The Problem of Indian Administration*, by Lewis Meriam, published in the United States, reports on the great poverty among the Native American peoples and reveals the failures of the 1887 Dawes Act allotment system, which divided tribal lands into individual family plots. Land controlled by the indigenous peoples dwindles from 138 million acres in 1887 to 52 million acres by 1934.

1928 James Mooney's *The Aboriginal Population of America North of Mexico* buttresses the traditional notions that European settlers found only small, scattered, and mostly undeveloped numbers of native peoples and states that only about 1,152,590 people inhabited North America before European colonization. Recent anthropological work and studies of agricultural techniques have arrived at estimates ranging from 90 to 112 million people on the continent, with 12.5 million living north of the Rio Grande; the debate over the estimated numbers is related to whether European colonial powers encountered, in John Locke's terms, "waste land" subject to the Doctrine of Discovery and the Rights of Conquest and wilderness that required cultivation and civilization, or whether they found autonomous and independent civilizations that deserved respect.

1931   As a result of Joseph Stalin's desire to subordinate the Autonomous Republic of the Abkhazians, Abkhazia is absorbed into the Republic of Georgia in the Soviet Union. One of the first peoples to have inhabited the lands bordering the Black Sea, the Abkhazians suffer under Stalin's banning of their language and disbanding of their institutions; as a result of deportation, violence, and the resettlement of Georgians on their lands, the Abkhazian population sharply decreases.

1932   The Army of El Salvador slaughters 30,000 farmers and indigenous people, in response to the efforts of Augustin Farabundo Martí to organize the Indians to take back the lands expropriated by large coffee plantations. The indigenous peoples of El Salvador, including the Pipile and Lenca, have fought for many years for land reform and have supported the Democratic Revolutionary Front in its struggle against the Salvadoran government.

1932   The Tofa, nomadic hunters living in the Sayan Mountains of the western Irkutsk region of Siberia, are mandated by Soviet policy to live in settlements, allowing the Soviets to claim the territory of the Tofa clans and to harvest the forests. Intermarriage and collectivization take their toll on a people accustomed to riding reindeer to hunt and trap, until today only a few elders still speak the Tofa language.

1933   The U.S. Indian Emergency Conservation Work (IECW) program is established as part of President Franklin D. Roosevelt's Civilian Conservation Corps. Managed by the Bureau of Indian Affairs, the IECW employs 85,000 Native Americans in conservation and environmental-management projects.

1934   The U.S. Indian Reorganization Act ends the allotment of lands, attempts to reacquire tribal lands for the Indians, and encourages Native Americans to organize their own governments, with the approval of the Department of the Interior. President Franklin D. Roosevelt appoints John Collier, an idealistic advocate of reform, the commissioner of Indian Affairs, and Collier promotes a change of policy that supports the maintenance of traditional Indian values, although Congress does not accept his most sweeping proposals.

1935   The U.S. Indian Arts and Crafts Board is created as an agency in the U.S. Department of the Interior to promote Native American arts and crafts by providing information and funds and by helping to create tribally owned marketing cooperatives for crafts, as well as attempting to prevent the sale of fraudulent "Indian" crafts. The board establishes a trademark system for Navajo wool and rugs, Hopi and Pueblo silver products, and so on; in the 1960s, the board begins to manage the Southern Plains Museum in Oklahoma, the Museum of the Plains Indian in Montana, and the Sioux Indian Museum in South Dakota.

1936 The Scheduled Tribes Act passed in India grants rights to indigenous peoples. The act is superseded in later years.

1936 With the onset of the Spanish Civil War, Spain grants the Basques an autonomy statute. After years of political struggle, amid the war the Basques create a government, establish embassies, levy taxes, and distribute currency, but the defeat of the Spanish resistance and the victory of Francisco Franco and the Spanish Nationalists in 1939 mark the end of this brief attempt at Basque autonomy.

1938 The Navajo Tribal Council is established in response to the need to make decisions about the discovery of oil, gas, and uranium on reservation lands in northern New Mexico and Arizona.

1939 When Francisco Franco becomes dictator in Spain, he mounts a relentless campaign against the Basques, imprisoning and executing members of the Basque political organizations and the Basque army, the Eusko Gudarostea. Euskera, the Basque language, and Ikurriña, the flag, are banned.

1939–1956 During World War II, the Nazis slaughter the Roma people (Gypsies), the only other people besides the Jews doomed to death by virtue of their race. Roma have been persecuted since their appearance in Europe before the 12th century, and Adolf Hitler is thought to have killed a half million; 5 to 6 million Roma are estimated to remain in Europe, mostly in eastern Europe.

1940 The Inter-American Indigenous Congress is established in Patzcuaro, Mexico, when 19 indigenous delegations sign a treaty and pledge to hold a conference every four years. The congress, while accepting the de facto policies of integration of the indigenous people, nevertheless advocates for a heightened recognition of their cultures.

1941–1945 During World War II, the U.S. Army employs Comanche and Navajo code talkers to send messages that the Nazis and Japanese cannot understand. The Comanche use the term *posah-tai-vo* ("crazy white man") for *Adolf Hitler*, and the Navajos use *besh-lo* ("iron fish") for *submarine*.

1942 Uranium mining begins on Navajo reservation lands in the United States, with more than 13 million tons taken, leaving some 1,000 highly contaminated underground and open-pit mines abandoned and unreclaimed; there are high rates of cancer and leukemia on the reservation. Contracts with Kerr McKee Corporation for uranium mining and Peabody Coal had been signed by tribal councils, with pressure from the Bureau of Indian Affairs, without the informed knowledge and consent of tribal members.

338 *The Wilson Chronology of Human Rights*

1944	The National Congress of American Indians (NCAI) is created by members of 50 tribes as a coalition of sovereign nations recognized by treaty or executive agreement by the United States. NCAI works to safeguard Native American rights, promotes increased educational opportunities, and opposes the U.S. policies of termination and relocation.
1944–1989	The Communist government of Bulgaria institutes a Bulgarization campaign against the Pomak peoples, who converted to Islam centuries earlier. Pomak are forced to change their names and are banned from practicing their religion and culture under penalty of prison or death.
1946	The United Nations Trusteeship of Southwest Africa is established.
1946	The U.S. Indian Claims Commission Act establishes the Claims Commission and requires it to assign monetary compensation to Native Americans whose lands were illegally expropriated on the basis of the price the land was worth at the time it was taken. The commission does not return any land; it merely sets an unfairly low price for its worth if it determines the land had been illegally seized.
1947	After independence from Great Britain, India enacts Article 46 of its constitution, recognizing a widespread colonial pattern of appropriation of tribal land and exploitation of tribal peoples. The article attempts to both protect tribal identity and stimulate assimilation.
1948	During the first Arab-Israeli war, when armies from Egypt, Jordan, Syria, Lebanon, and Iraq invade Israel to join Palestinian guerrillas in trying to stop the establishment of the Israeli state, around 770,000 Palestinians flee, and 400 villages are destroyed. During the 1968 Arab-Israeli war, 200,000 Palestinians of the West Bank flee to Jordan.
1948	The first Native American named captain of the U.S. Olympic basketball team is Jessie Renick, a Choctaw, who was an All-American basketball player at Oklahoma A&M in 1939 and 1940. The 1948 U.S. Olympic basketball team wins the gold medal.
1949	The United States objects to a United Nations General Assembly study of the problems of indigenous peoples, and as a result the United Nations Sub-committee on Minorities is temporarily suspended.
1949	The People's Republic of China iterates its position on the status of national minorities with the issuance of the Common Program, which states that all nationalities in China are equal. There are now five autonomous regions—Inner Mongolia, Tibet, Ningxia Hui, Guangxi Zhuang, and Xinjiang Uygur—and representatives are granted 150 seats in the National People's Congress, twice the number they would hold on a proportional basis; yet independence and autonomy have been sacrificed to the project of creating a vast and powerful centralized state.

1949	After the Chinese Revolution, the People's Republic of China initiates a massive program to assimilate the Turkic people of the Xinjiang area, inhabiting what they regard as Turkistan, on lands in the Soviet Union and China. Though Communist policy recognizes the right to self-determination, China bans the use of their language, destroys hundreds of thousands of books in Arabic, closes their mosques, and outlaws the Koran.
1950	Claiming that Tibet belongs to China, the People's Republic of China invades Tibet and replaces the Tibetan Buddhist government with its own choice of leaders. The spiritual and political ruler of Tibet, the Dalai Lama, goes into exile in 1959, and the government-in-exile claims that more than a million Tibetans died as result of the struggle against Chinese tyranny between 1950 and 1980.
1950	The U.S. Congress passes the Navajo-Hopi Long Range Rehabilitation Act after the revelation of miserable living conditions on the Navajo and Hopi reservations, with schools holding only 25 percent of the students, deteriorated roads, and high infant-mortality rates. President Harry S. Truman vetoed a 1949 aid package because it contained a provision increasing the jurisdiction of the state on reservation lands, but the 1950 version excludes that; it provides funds for schools, roads, pastures, and irrigation, as well as relocating and resettling programs for Indians who choose to leave the reservations.
1950s	The United States tests nuclear weapons on the Pacific islands of Johnston Atoll, Bikini and Enewetak, and Christmas Island in Micronesia. The islanders suffer health problems, including cancer, leukemia, miscarriages, and birth defects.
1950s	The North American Indian Brotherhood (NAIB), founded by Andrew Paull, brings together Indians in Canada and the United States. NAIB sends its representatives to the United Nations to press for indigenous rights.
1951	On the withdrawal of the Dutch colonial authorities, the Republic of South Moluccas (Spice Islands) declares its independence, and the Indonesian Army invades the South Moluccas, whose indigenous people are Melanesian; the Moluccas are some 1,500 miles from Jakarta, Indonesia. In the following years, half a million settlers from Indonesia join the million South Moluccans and take large parts of their ancestral land; predominantly Christian, the South Moluccans have been forced to adopt the customs of Islam.
1951	The U.S. government appropriates Western Shoshone and Pauite land in Nevada for the testing of nuclear weapons, and it is estimated that some 800 explosions have taken place since.
1951	Undertaking the first review of the Indian Act of 1876, the Parliament of Canada passes a new Indian Act granting power over Indian life to the Department of Indian Affairs and Northern Development, including review of the actions of local councils and authority over the development of natural resources and

land. The act continues the Canadian policy of denying legal status as an indigenous person to women who marry nonindigenous men, but it does repeal certain harsh provisions of the previous legislation, allowing the performance of religious ceremonies, permitting alcohol drinking on reserved lands, permitting fundraising for political purposes, and granting the right to vote.

1952–1963 Great Britain conducts above ground nuclear tests on the Pacific islands of Emu, Monte Bello, and Maralinga, disturbing the lives of 11 indigenous peoples of Oceania. According to an investigation in 1991, there is still widespread contamination with prohibitively high levels of radiation.

1953 A law granting political authority over Kuna affairs and lands to the Kuna General Council is enacted in Panama, where the Kuna occupy lands in the San Blas area and the nearby islands on the north coast of Panama. The islands host a growing tourist trade, which has begun to threaten Kuna autonomy; after a North American hotel developer refuses to stop a project that violates Kuna General Council policy, which mandates council control over land sales and rentals, some young Kunas attack the resort, and the Panamanians close it.

1953 The U.S. Termination Act ends government recognition of some American Indian nations, and a House Concurrent Resolution unilaterally suspends federal services, with the intent of treating Native Americans like all other citizens and of working toward terminating federal responsibility for Indian affairs. The Menominee, Klamath, and tribes of western Oregon are terminated in 1954; altogether 109 Native American nations have been terminated, with a few reinstated in the 1970s.

1954 U.S. Public Law 280 places a number of "unterminated" Native American nations under state jurisdiction in Alaska, Washington, Oregon, California, Minnesota, and Nebraska.

1955 The U.S. Supreme Court, in *Tee-Hit-Ton v. United States*, rules that a tribe that has used land "since time immemorial" cannot establish title. Justice Reed rules against the Tee-Hit-Ton people of the Tlingit Alaskan nation, stating that they are not entitled to 350,000 acres because there is no evidence of a treaty with Congress recognizing title, although they have occupied and used the land since "time immemorial"; this decision effectively and completely obliterates the presumptive notion in the 1823 *Johnson v. McIntosh* case, which found that the Native Americans were rightful owners.

1956 The U.S. Relocation Act encourages Native Americans to leave reservations for urban areas, providing funding for relocation and for "job-training programs" in the cities while economic-development programs on reservations are curtailed. To become eligible for relocation and job training, Native Americans are asked to sign agreements that they will not return to their reservations; by 1980, 50 percent of the 1.5 million Native Americans are living in U.S. cities.

1956
The indigenous Saami people of northern Sweden, Norway, Finland, and the Soviet Union join together and form the Nordic Sami Council to fight for self-determination. Their traditional life of hunting, fishing, and reindeer farming has been threatened by years of development.

1956–1958
In the People's Republic of China, the government introduces the Great Leap Forward, beginning the process of regulating the lives and customs of its native peoples. Women in Tibet are forbidden to wear headdresses; the Naxi of Yunnan Province, a matrilineal culture where women play the major role in managing work and agriculture and are the village leaders, are profoundly affected by the change to wage labor, traditional monogamy, and the Chinese tradition of men controlling income.

1957
The International Labour Organization's policy toward indigenous peoples is established in Convention 107, issued in Geneva, Switzerland. Because a major focus of Convention 107 is integrating indigenous peoples into the mainstream of their nations rather than promoting their autonomy and right to self-determination, indigenous organizations view it as paternalistic.

1957
As construction on the Dalles Dam is completed in Oregon, a sacred site of worship on the Columbia River at Celilo Falls is flooded. Used for fishing as well, the site is important to the Umatilla, Yakima, Nez Percé, and Warm Springs peoples.

1957
The Australian government grants permission to Comalco, Ltd., a subsidiary of the U.S. Kaiser Corporation, and Rio Tinto Zinc of England to mine bauxite on a vast tract of Aboriginal lands. The companies pay only a small percentage of the usual mineral lease rates, and the Aboriginal inhabitants are relocated to a small government compound.

1958
The Nootka people on Vancouver Island off the northwest coast of Canada establish the West Coast Allied Tribes. After many years during which they were converted to Christianity and became assimilated into white society, a movement develops among the Nootka to reestablish their tribal identity and to fight for the recognition of their land claims; the organization's name changes first to the West Coast District Council and then to the Nuu-chah-nulth Tribal Council.

1959
The Federal Council for the Advancement of Aboriginals and Torres Strait Islanders, an Aboriginal-rights organization, is founded to fight for the land claims of the Aboriginal peoples of Australia. With unemployment rates six times higher than those of other Australians, a life span 20 years shorter, and the likelihood of being incarcerated 45 times higher, the Aborigines fight to regain the land that was taken from them and to reestablish their culture.

1959
In *Hitchcock v. Lee*, the U.S. Supreme Court rules that a Native American tribe has the right to try a case in tribal court, in a case involving the attempts of a non-Indian who operates a store on Navajo lands to collect a debt from a married Navajo couple. Jus-

tice Hugo L. Black declares that exclusive jurisdiction of a case involving a non-Indian whose transaction occurs on reservation lands lies with the Navajo court.

1960–1965 France conducts aboveground nuclear-weapons testing in the Sahara Desert, spreading radiation and endangering the indigenous peoples of northern Africa.

1960s Thailand constructs roads into the ancestral northern hills of the Karen people, 200,000 of whose 3 million members live in Thailand, while the rest live in Myanmar (Burma). The influx of Thai farmers and loggers which preceeded the roads' construction has already destroyed the traditional life of the Karen, who according to Thai law do not hold legal title to their ancestral land; Karen men have been forced to work in the mines and on tea plantations; many Karen women have been forced into prostitution in Thailand's thriving sex trade; and Karen have become addicted to opium at five times the rate of other Thai. The new roads exacerbate this situation.

1961 The First Annual World Eskimo-Indian Olympics, four days of athletic events, is held in Fairbanks, Alaska. Events include traditional sports, including the Alaskan high lick, greased-pole walk, and Indian-stick pull, accompanied by dance team events and fish-cutting and seal-skinning competitions.

1961 Ten Native American college students meeting in Gallup, New Mexico, organize the National Indian Youth Council (NIYC). NIYC begins to publish a newspaper, *Americans before Columbus*, and participates in the political "fish-in" campaign in Washington State; it also creates the Clyde Warrior Institute in American Indian Studies and forms a Native American film company, Circle Film.

1961 The first Native American to win the world archery championship is Joe Trindle Thornton, a Cherokee, who is a member of the 1967 and 1971 U.S. archery teams that win world championships. At the age of 54, Thornton wins the U.S. national archery championship.

1962 The U.S. Institute of American Indian Art, founded in Santa Fe, New Mexico, is a project of the Bureau of Indian Affairs, providing training for talented Native American artists. Now known as the Institute of American Indian and Alaska Native Culture and Arts Development, the institute becomes independent of the Bureau of Indian Affairs in 1988 and is a program of the U.S. Congress.

1962 The Moviemiento Indio Tupas Katari (MITKA), a Bolivian Indian-rights organization founded by Constantino Lima, has faced prosecution from its inception and has been functioning as a clandestine force. MITKA is active in union organizing and national politics.

1962 The New York Agreement between the Dutch and Indonesia, brokered by the United States, concerns the fate of West Papua, New Guinea; it establishes a period of United Nations stewardship, followed by administration by Indonesia, and then the Act of Free Choice, which allows for a referendum on independence to be held in six years. West Papua greeted the Dutch attempt to continue its administration after the war with an organized movement for independence, but the Indonesians dissolve the Papuan Parliament and ban all political activity.

1963   During construction of the Glen Canyon Dam on the Colorado River, a sacred site of worship at the Rainbow Natural Bridge is destroyed in Utah. The Navajo, Pueblo, and Pauite performed spiritual ceremonies at the sandstone arch.

1964   Young Native Americans of the National Indian Youth Council insist on their right to fish in waters in Washington State, where state and local authorities had prohibited fishing to protect commercial interests. With support from the actor Marlon Brando and the comedian Dick Gregory, the council gains publicity for asserting that fishing rights were granted to Native Americans by treaty.

1964–1970s   Bougainville, the largest of the Solomon Islands in the Pacific Ocean and formerly under Australia's colonial control, is the site of prospecting by Bougainville Copper, Ltd., a transnational group of Australian-based companies, which began prospecting in 1963 in the foothills and mountains that are home to 14,000 indigenous Torau peoples. In Rorovana, women, the traditional landowners, defend their land with nonviolent protests, and the Australians respond with riot troops.

1965   The Free Papua Movement begins a guerrilla war against Indonesia's occupation of West Papua, New Guinea. When it is time to implement the Act of Free Choice, under which people can vote for independence, instead of holding an election in which everyone of age can vote, Indonesia appoints 1,025 representatives to express the will of the Papuan people; under duress, they vote unanimously to remain under the control of Indonesia.

1966   The Rough Rock Demonstration School, the first Indian-controlled elementary school, is founded by the Navajo Nation after an all-Navajo nonprofit organization lobbies for $3 million from the Bureau of Indian Affairs. With a Native American school board, a curriculum designed with input from the community, and classes in both English and Navajo, the school teaches children about the Navajo way of life.

1966   The first Native American professional football player named to the Hall of Fame is Joseph Guyon, a White Earth Chippewa, who had been named an All-American in 1917–18 while playing for Georgia Tech University. Guyon goes on to play professional football with the New York Giants from 1920 to 1927.

1966–1969   The Cultural Revolution in the People's Republic of China has significant impact on indigenous minorities. In their misplaced zeal to reinvigorate the socialist revolution, Red Guard cadres attack the political leadership of Inner Mongolia, oppose the Muslim religion, and attack temples and Buddhist traditions in

Tibet.

1966–1974 France conducts nuclear-weapons testing in the atmosphere above the Pacific islands of Tahiti, Moruroa, Fangataufa, and Hao, detonating 44 nuclear bombs. From 1975 to 1991, France detonates 131 explosions underground in the atolls of Moruroa and Fangataufa.

1967 Established when the Ethiopian government, ruled by the minority Amhara people, outlaws an Oromo organization in an effort to maintain political control, the Oromo Liberation Front (OLF) campaigns to organize the 15 million Oromo people, the largest of Ethiopia's more than 70 indigenous peoples. After the government institutes a forced resettlement program and places other peoples on Oromo land, the OLF begins organizing farmers and students; in 1978, student demonstrations to preserve the teaching of their language are met with military force, and 250 students are killed.

1967 The American Indian Law Center is established in New Mexico to help Native American tribes press their legal claims and to educate judges and administrators in matters of tribal law.

1967 When the Indonesian Army clears indigenous land in West Papua, New Guinea, for the U.S.-based Freeport Indonesia Inc. (FII) mining conglomerate, the Amungme people of the region are forcibly dislocated. FII creates Tembagapura, the world's largest and highest copper mine, on lands the Amungme used for local gardens and hunting; working 24 hours a day, the mine produces an estimated 90,000 tons per day and uses the Ajikwa River to dispose of its tailings.

1968 Asserting their treaty rights to cross the border freely, the Mohawk blockade the Cornwall Bridge at Cornwall, Ontario, between Canada and the United States. The Mohawk are arrested, and a court subsequently rules that the treaty is beyond its jurisdiction.

1968 The American Indian Movement (AIM) a pan-Indian movement, emerges in Minneapolis, Minnesota, as an offshoot of the U.S. civil rights movement. AIM opposes the disproportionate arrest of Native Americans in the Minneapolis area, advocates a wide range of programs focused on reclaiming native rights, and leads several major protests: the 1969–71 takeover of Alcatraz Island in San Francisco Bay; the 1972 occupation of the Washington, D.C., office of the Bureau of Indian Affairs; and the 1973 occupation of Wounded Knee, South Dakota, which lasts 71 days.

1968 The Euskadi ta Askatasuna (Basque country and freedom), or ETA, the armed wing of the indigenous Basque (inhabitants of the western Pyrenees in Spain) separatists, is created as a military response to the continuing repression during Franco's dictatorship in Spain. After Franco's death in 1975, ETA's methods become more controversial, and moderate Basques think there are less violent ways to press for their cause than those adopted by ETA; ETA's attacks on the Spanish military, the Guardia

Civil (Civil guard), have injured more than 700 soldiers and civilians over the years.

1968 The International Work Group for Indigenous Affairs (IWGIA) is created in Denmark to work for the rights of indigenous peoples. IWGIA has produced numerous articles about, and collected documents on, the affairs of indigenous people and has advocated against their forced assimilation.

1968 The Indian Civil Rights Act, contained in special sections of the 1964 U.S. Civil Rights Act, reforms government policy on Indian civil rights by recognizing the inherent sovereign rights of tribal government. The legislation offers a selective list of rights extended to Native Americans, such as authorizing a writ of habeas corpus for anyone detained by a tribe and guaranteeing free exercise of religion; the states no longer have jurisdiction in civil and criminal matters on Indian reservations.

1968 An extended drought forces the Imashaghen (Tuareg) to migrate from their tribal lands in parts of Algeria, Mali, and Mauritania to the cities of Niger and Mali, where they live in refugee camps; others move to Libya and Algeria. Tough life in camps caused their anger to turn to violence; their allegiance lies with fellow Tuaregs rather than with the countries in which they live.

1968 The Navajo Community College, established by the Navajo Nation, is the first tribally controlled college in the United States. The first fully accredited four-year tribally controlled college is the Sinte Glista College of the Rosebud Sioux Reservation.

1969 The U.S. Senate issues the report *Indian Education: A National Tragedy—A National Challenge*. The report declares that the federal policies for educating Indians are a major failure; the average educational level for Indians is five school years, with dropout rates twice the national average; only 3 percent of Indians enrolled in college graduate.

1969 The United Nations approves of the Papuan decision to remain under Indonesian control, despite a United Nations observer who states that the rights provided for in the New York Agreement are not implemented and that Indonesia maintains strict control over the population.

1969–1971 Wanting to establish a Center for Native American Studies in the unused buildings, Native Americans occupy Alcatraz Island, which the U.S. government closed in 1962. Recalling the precedent of the transfer of unused federal property in Roswell, New Mexico, and the Nevada Stead Air Force Base, the Indians, organized as the Indians of All Tribes, are arrested by federal marshals.

1969–1972 On the island of Bougainville in the Solomon Islands in the West Pacific, Australia grants Bougainville Copper, Ltd., leases for mining, roads, and dump sites for tailings, without an environmental impact study; as a result, the Panguna mine has become one of the world's largest open-cut mines, and waste rock, silt, and chemical residues are discharged into the Karewong and

Jaba Rivers with disastrous results for the ecosystem. Thousands of indigenous people oppose not only the copper company but impending control by Papua New Guinea; when the Bougainville Revolutionary Army is formed, the struggle turns violent.

1970   The Brazilian Plan for National Integration is developed to open up the interior of the country, the Amazon region, for development. The plan calls for roads through dense forests and the creation of settlements along the way, incurring the relocation of 5 million peasants and the destruction of indigenous cultures.

1970   The U.S. government had made Blue Lake, New Mexico, part of the Carson National Forest in 1960. Ten years later, it is returned to the Taos Pueblo Indians, who use it as a sacred site of worship.

1970   Some 150 members of the Achumawi (Pit River Indians) demonstrate to assert their land claims by occupying Lassen National Park and Pacific Gas and Electric lands in northern California. The Achumawi, about 3,000 strong in 1828 when the first settlers came to northern California, were concentrated on a reservation of 8,700 acres in 1938.

1970   Efforts to forestall the encroachment on Guayamí lands in Panama in Central America begin after the government and its state mining corporation, CODEMIN, give a Canadian mining company rights to explore for minerals in Cerro Colorado. One billion tons of copper ore are found on the lands of the Guayamí, a people of 80,000.

1970   Dartmouth College in Dartmouth, New Hampshire, is the first college in the United States to drop the use of a Native American name for a school mascot or sports team, when the Dartmouth Indians are renamed the "Big Green."

1970   The Americans for Indian Opportunity is established in Washington, D.C., by LaDonna Harris, a political activist of Comanche heritage, to promote Native American self-sufficiency.

1970   The Native American Rights Fund (NARF) is created in Boulder, Colorado, to help protect tribal life and the environment. As a nonprofit legal fund, NARF represents tribal clients in legal cases in state and federal courts, including a successful case by the Penobscot and Passamaquoddy tribes against the State of Maine in 1980; NARF creates a National Indian Law Library in 1972.

1970   The U.S. government's policy toward Native Americans shifts toward having Indians themselves administer federal programs in health, education, welfare, and housing for Native Americans.

1970s   The U.S. Alaska Native Claims Settlement Act dissolves the preexisting Alaskan native nations; indigenous peoples complain that the act is not accepted on the village level, that they were not consulted about it, and that their social structure has been endangered. Alaskan natives also complain about overfishing, negative impact from a growing tourist trade, and environmental abuse of Alaskan lands and seas by the U.S. military; one of the largest problems is the increased pressure for oil and gas production, including drilling at the Porcupine Wildlife Refuge, which could endanger the caribou herd critical to the survival of the 7,000 members of the Gwich'in.

1970s   Napidokae Navitu, an organization of inhabitants of the island of Bougainville in the Solomon Islands in the West Pacific, is created to fight for indigenous identity and autonomy and to crystallize opposition to the mining company Bougainville Copper, Ltd. (BCL). By 1972, the group has 8,000 followers who oppose not only BCL but the forthcoming political control by Papua New Guinea.

1971   When great amounts of crude oil are discovered on the North Slope of Alaska, prompting the U.S. government and the oil companies to resolve a dispute over title to the land, Congress passes the U.S. Alaska Native Claims Settlement Act to settle native Alaskan land claims. The Inuit and Aleut peoples own the surface rights to 44 million acres and are offered financial compensation of almost $1 billion for the remainder of their land claims and a grant of 140 million acres of land; Indian corporations are set up to administer the land and money, and 1988 amendments to the act make it difficult for non-Indians to gain control.

1971   Chief Dan George is the first Native American nominated for an Academy Award for best supporting actor in a motion picture. Nominated for his role in the 1970 film *Little Big Man*, George does not win the Oscar, but does win the New York Critics Award and the National Society of Film Critics Award for his performance.

1971   The Regional Indian Council of the Cauca (CRIC) is created in Colombia when the 500,000 indigenous peoples of Colombia organize to fight against the occupation of their lands. In 1850, Colombia abolished the Incan tradition of communal ownership, but the Indians continue to fight to preserve the boundaries of the *resguardos*, the reserves set aside for them by the Spanish authorities.

1971   The World Romani Congress, held near London, England, results in the establishment of the International Romani Union, an organization of 70 groups representing the Roma (Gypsies) in 28 countries. Congress members vote to call themselves Roma, adopt a flag, and make *Opre Roma!* (Roma, arise!) their call to action; the World Council of Churches and the government of India partly fund the congress.

1971   After the creation of Bangladesh, new government policy reverses the Chittagong Hill Tracts Regulation of 1900 and transfers revenue collection and development rights to a government deputy-commissioner, thereby depriving the indigenous people of the Tracts of their autonomy. In 1979, President Ziaur Rahman pushes a development program allowing 100,000 people to move to the indigenous lands.

1972	The American Indian Movement meets at Cass Lake, Minnesota, and blocks roads, with some members of the Chippewa Indians carrying arms. Resort owners agree to restore to the Chippewa their right to police the fishing areas in their tribal lands.
1972	Made part of the Gifford Pinchot National Forest early in the 20th century, Mount Adams in Washington State is returned to the Yakima Indians, who consider it a sacred site of worship.
1972	The tribal community in the Chamoli district of Uttar Pradesh, India, successfully resists the government sale of their ash trees. When the Indian government diverts their tribal allocation of lumber, used for building and tool making, to manufacturing cricket bats and tennis rackets, the villagers surround the trees, and the government relents; this nonviolent movement to save tribal forests spreads across the Himalayan Mountains.
1972	President Ferdinand Marcos of the Philippines launches a war against the indigenous Bangsa Moro people; more than 2 million Bangsa Moro make their home south of Mindanao and on the islands of Sulu, Basilan, and Palawan. Marcos declares their communal lands public domain; military action results in the loss of about 90,000 lives and the destruction of a quarter-million homes.
1972	The National Indian Brotherhood of Canada holds an assembly at which delegates decide to have an international conference of indigenous peoples. As a result, three years later the World Council of Indigenous Peoples is founded.
1972	Native American activists travel across the United States to protest the legacy of treaties that had been violated and to call attention to the poor treatment of Indians. Organized by Dennis Means and Hank Adams, the Trail of Broken Treaties arrives in Washington, D.C., days before the presidential election and gathers in the headquarters of the Bureau of Indian Affairs until negotiations grant them immunity for damage to the building and transportation costs home.
1972	The American Indian Athletic Hall of Fame is created on the campus of Haskell Indian Junior College in Lawrence, Kansas, to honor Native American athletes and to preserve a record of their accomplishments.
1972	The American Indian Higher Education Consortium (AIHEC) is founded when leaders from six Native American tribal colleges organize to advocate for the interests of tribally controlled higher education. AIHEC fights to maintain control by Native Americans, lobbies for more funding, designs training programs for Native American teachers and administrators, and encourages the preservation of native traditions and languages.
1973	The U.S. Supreme Court rules, in *United States v. Washington*, that a tribe has a right to an equal share of the salmon harvest in the Northwest.
1973	Indians into Medicine is founded in Grand Forks, North Dakota,

to provide assistance to Native Americans interested in careers in health.

1973   The Saami Parliament, representing Saami (indigenous inhabitants of the region) political interests in Finland, is established. In 1987, a Saami Parliament is established in Norway.

1973   The U.S. Supreme Court rules, in *McClanahan v. Arizona Tax Commission*, that Indian sovereignty is a legal fiction, but states that the notion of sovereignty can serve as a "backdrop" for interpreting the meaning and status of treaties and agreements.

1973   Canada establishes a federal policy for settling aboriginal claims. According to the Department of Indian Affairs and Northern Development: "The federal policy stipulates that land claims may be negotiated with Aboriginal groups in areas where claims to Aboriginal title have not been addressed by treaty or through other legal means."

1973   Sioux activists and the American Indian Movement, protesting the lenient treatment of a white man charged with stabbing Wesley Bad Heart Bull, a Lakotan, to death, take over Wounded Knee in South Dakota. Confrontations between police and the Indians in Custer, South Dakota, led to the arrest of Indians for rioting and injuries to police, and Bad Heart Bull's mother faced 40 years in jail, while her son's murderer faced only 10 years; U.S. marshals and Federal Bureau of Investigation agents surround the protesters, who occupy Wounded Knee for 71 days; two activists are killed.

1973   The Supreme Court of Canada upholds the right of the Canadian government to deny Indian status to women who marry non-Indians. The Court rules against Jeanette Lavell, an Ojibwa, and upholds the provisions of the Canadian Indian Act of 1951.

1973–1980   According to the estimates of Amnesty International, 48 organizers of the Regional Indian Council of the Cauca of Colombia have been assassinated during this period.

1974   The National Indian Brotherhood of Canada is granted status as a nongovernmental organization by the Economic and Social Council of the United Nations.

1974   Bontoc women in the Philippines barricade their land to protest gold mining by the Benquet Consolidated Mining Corporation. In 1975, President Ferdinand Marcos grants a request from mining companies and bans gold panning by the indigenous peoples.

1974   The American Indian Parliament meets, with representatives from indigenous peoples from Bolivia, Argentina, Paraguay, Brazil, and Venezuela in attendance.

1974   A law passed in Peru protects the Huitoto and Bora Indians living along the Ampiyacu River by granting them legal recognition and title to land. In the 1980s, 13 communities organize the Federación de Communidades Nativas del Rio Ampiyacu (Federation of native communities of the Ampiyacu River), or FECONA, to fight against corrupt traders and exploitation of their land by logging companies and hunters and to advocate for more land.

1974   The U.S. Congress passes the Navajo-Hopi Land Settlement Act to settle land disputes arising between the two tribes because of the vague language of the executive order, signed by President Chester A. Arthur in 1882, that created an executive-order reservation

1974   The International Indian Treaty Council is organized in San Francisco, California, by Lakota elders to create links with indigenous peoples throughout the world and to bring the issues of these peoples to international forums and organizations. In 1977, the organization brings representatives from 89 indigenous nations together in Geneva, Switzerland; the same year, it receives the status of a nongovernmental organization at the United Nations and plays an important part in the establishment of the Working Group on Indigenous Populations.

1974   The Determined Residents United for Mohawk Sovereignty (DRUMS) is created at the Akwesasne Mohawk Reservation in New York State and Canada, in response to smuggling operations and illegal bars and casinos operating on reservation land. In 1989, the Federal Bureau of Investigation and New York State police raid the reservation, and an armed confrontation results in the death of two Mohawk.

1975   The U.S. Congress passes a law allowing Native Americans to take over some government programs for Indians, including posts in the Bureau of Indian Affairs.

1975   The World Council of Indigenous Peoples, established in Ottawa, Ontario, meets as a result of a resolution to hold an international conference, made at the 1972 Assembly of the National Indian Brotherhood of Canada. The council aims to promote unity among the indigenous peoples of the world, to combat racism and ethnocide, and to ensure that indigenous peoples are treated justly.

1975   The American Indian Film Institute is founded in Culver City, California, to highlight the work of Native American filmmakers and actors. It sponsors the American Indian Film Festival held each year in San Francisco.

1975   The U.S. Indian Self-Determination and Educational Assistance Act is passed to assure maximum participation in directing educational and other federal services to Indian communities so as to make the programs more responsive to the wishes of the communities. The act provides for preferential hiring of Native Americans for federal contracts with tribes and encourages the development of tribal schools, but the Bureau of Indian Affairs still has the authority to accept or deny tribal contracts.

1975   The International Work Group for Indigenous Affairs issues a report by Jürgen Riester on the status of Chiquitano slaves in eastern Bolivia. These slaves work for rubber extractors and are always paid in merchandise worth less than the rubber they extract; if they manage to escape, they are pursued and sometimes shot.

1975   The National Council of Indigenous Peoples is created in Mexico as a coalition of representatives of 56 different indigenous peoples in the country. Displeased with the official governmental organization, the National Indigenest Institute, and its *politica indigenista* (centralized policy), the council fights for political power and the right to make the decisions that affect indigenous people.

1975   The U.S. Council of Energy Resource Tribes is created when representatives from 25 Native American tribes that hold energy reserves form a coalition to gain more control over their resources.

1975   The James Bay and Northern Quebec Agreement, between the Canadian government and the Cree of Quebec and the Inuit of Quebec and Port Burwell, is the first comprehensive claim to be settled by the government of Canada with the indigenous peoples of Canada; it is followed by the 1978 Northeastern Quebec Agreement. The agreements come as a result of the opposition of the indigenous peoples to a massive hydroelectric project on lands they claim, which Canada designates without their consent; the government grants the 19,000 Cree, and Inuit, and Naskapi ownership of 1.3 percent of their ancestral lands, exclusive hunting and trapping rights in other lands, and a cash payment.

1975   The U.S. Congress establishes the American Indian Policy Review Commission to review federal policy toward Native Americans, with recommendations "by Indians for Indians." The 11-member commission urges that the role of the U.S. Bureau of Indian Affairs be shifted to an independent Indian agency.

1975   The International Conference of Indigenous Peoples is held in Port Alberni, British Columbia, hosted by the Sheshaht Band of Nootka Indians. The conference decides to prepare a study of discrimination against indigenous peoples for submission to the United Nations, develops a charter for the World Council of Indigenous Peoples, and decides to accept the nongovernmental-organization status that the Assembly of the National Indian Brotherhood of Canada holds at the United Nations.

1975   After the Democratic Republic of East Timor declares independence following the collapse of the Portuguese dictatorship in 1974 and the withdrawal of Portuguese colonial authorities, the Indonesian Army invades East Timor. The resulting war brings death to hundreds of thousands of people.

1976   After the Spanish cede control of the western Sahara to Morocco, the Sahrawis, an indigenous people, fight for independence and establish a council of ministers of the Saharan Arab Democratic Republic, which is granted diplomatic recognition by many African nations. Its army, Frente Polisario, has been waging war against Morocco, which in 1985 states that all indigenous populations in Morocco have the same rights and are subject to the same obligations.

1976	The Integrated Project in Arid Lands is established in the Marabit district of Kenya, West Africa, as part of the United Nations Environment Program to deal with increasing desertification. One of the aspects of the program is to aid in efforts to settle the Rendille, desert dwellers whose land area has decreased sharply because of British colonial policy, increased population pressure from Somalia, Ethiopia, and Sudan, and drought and hunger forcing more and more Rendille into settlements and dependence on aid programs.
1976	In *Fisher v. District Court*, the U.S. Supreme Court decides that a state cannot interfere in a tribal adoption.
1976	The Aceh Merdeka or Aceh/Sumatra National Liberation Front is created in Indonesia in response to the government's policy of using force against those who refuse to submit to its authority. The Acehnese, who live in northern Sumatra in Indonesia, have fought for independence for years; in 1873, they began a 30-year war against the Dutch; they fought for Indonesia's independence in 1945–49; and since the 1950s, they have fought for their own autonomy.
1977	The *ley indigena* (indigenous law), a major land-law in Costa Rica, sets aside about 250,000 acres for indigenous peoples and prohibits access by non-Indians. There are 20,000 Indians in Costa Rica from six ethnic groups; one group has lost 90 percent of its lands, while commercial logging, oil exploration, and hydroelectric projects on indigenous land, as well as sugar and coffee plantations, all violate the rights of Indian communities.
1977	The Regional Coordinator for Indigenous Peoples is founded in Panama to support and advocate for the interests of indigenous peoples of Central America.
1977	The National Alliance of Associations of Bilingual Indian Professionals is established in Mexico to represent the interests of the Indian people of Mexico. The alliance supports the rights of Indian teachers to participate more fully in the national education system and opposes a governmental policy that discourages the use of Indian languages; the alliance estimates that there are 10 million Indians speaking more than 56 Indian languages and millions more who no longer speak an Indian language but maintain the customs and traditions of their indigenous nation.
1977	The Mualvatumauri, or National Council of Chiefs, a coordinating body of 22 chiefs elected by the indigenous people of Vanuatu, is founded on the island of Vanuatu in Oceania. The council works to protect and reestablish traditional meeting places and to reemphasize traditional customs.
1977	The Inuit Circumpolar Conference brings together those peoples whose home lies below the Arctic Circle in Alaska, Canada, Greenland, and the Soviet Union. The conference's main offices are in Nuuk, Greenland.
1977	At a regional conference of indigenous peoples in Panama, the organization of Central American Indigenous Peoples is formed.

1977	The Accelerated Mahweli Development Scheme of Sri Lanka (Ceylon) forces the relocation of several villages of the Wanniy-alaeto (or Vedda) forest-dwelling indigenous people. Ironically, they are moved to make way for the 200-square-mile Maduru Oya National Park, a protected reserve for endangered animals like elephants and leopards.
1977	Agro-Gabon, a French-Belgian company, expropriates 18,500 acres of Kélé farmland in Gabon, West Africa, to create a palm-tree plantation and factory for palm oil. The Kélé, formerly a seminomadic people who were settled in a village in the 1930s, are now forced to travel long distances to find land to farm; palm oil from the factory pollutes the Ogooué River, destroying the tribe's ability to fish. This causes the Kélé to turn to alcohol and violence.
1977	In India, the Bihar Forest Development Corporation campaigns to replace native sal trees with commercial teak, despite strong resistance from the tribal peoples of the region who rely on the sal tree. Having received an inadequate response to their petitions, the indigenous peoples begin to destroy teak saplings; government police intervene, and in 1980, 13 tribespeople are shot and 200 arrested.
1977	The International Nongovernmental Organization Conference on Discrimination against Indigenous Peoples in the Americas is held in Geneva, Switzerland, as a follow-up to the creation of the United Nations Decade against Racism in 1973. The conference delegates urge that the International Labour Organization Convention statement on indigenous peoples be revised.
1977	The U.S. Supreme Court decides that congressional legislation about Native American tribes is subject to constitutional review, in *Delaware v. Weeks*. This decision challenges the doctrine of congressional "plenary power" over Native American tribes, which the Court solidified with its ruling in *United States v Kagama* in 1886.
1977	The American Indian Science and Engineering Society is established in Boulder, Colorado, to provide teacher training, curriculum development, and scholarships to promote opportunities for Native American students to study science and engineering.
1977	The Asociación Indigena de Costa Rica (Indigenous people's organization) is established to guarantee the rights of the minority indigenous population of Costa Rica and to enforce the provisions of the 1977 law guaranteeing their inalienable rights to indigenous land reserves. In a 1983 report, the association notes that 25,000 acres of indigenous forest are being threatened by a North American logging firm; the president of the group, Daniel Rojas Maroto, comments that current theories and practices of "development" threaten indigenous peoples.
1978	The report of the Anti-Slavery Society on Enslavement of Indians in Paraguay is issued to the United Nations Commission on Human Rights. The report describes Aché Indians who are

bought and sold for $5 or $56 by landowners to clear their lands and are considered part of the landowners' property.

1978   The U.S. Congress passes the American Indian Religious Freedom Act, stating that the United States must protect the right of freedom of belief and expression for Native Americans, after years of government regulations prohibiting the exercise of traditional spiritual ceremonies like the Lakota Sun Dance. The act does not guarantee the rights of Native Americans to conduct ceremonies at sacred places on now public land.

1978   The *New York Times* publishes a report on the working conditions of Guatemalan Indians on plantations. The article describes the crowded sleeping conditions of Indian cane cutters and their families, the lack of plumbing facilities, the close contact with heavy doses of pesticides, and the many tropical diseases contracted by the workers.

1978   The World Conference to Combat Racism, held in Geneva, Switzerland, endorses the economic and cultural rights of indigenous peoples.

1978   Members of several Native American tribes walk from San Francisco, California, to Washington, D.C., in an effort to create public pressure on the U.S. government to recognize the sovereignty and rights of the Indian people. Recalling the Long Walk of the Apache and Navajo in 1868, 200 Native Americans begin their journey at Alcatraz Island, the site of the former occupation by members of the American Indian Movement.

1978   The island of Dominica in the Caribbean establishes a reserve for the indigenous Carib under Carib Reserve Act 22. Believing strongly in communal control of the land, the Carib have resisted attempts to divide their territory into privately held individual plots; their reserved territory is governed by a Carib Council and chief elected every five years.

1978   The U.S. Supreme Court rules that Native American tribes hold no criminal or civil jurisdiction over non-Indians living on their reservation, in *Oliphant v. Suquamish Indian Tribe*. The case involves the attempt of the Suquamish Indians in Washington to enforce a 1973 code extending criminal jurisdiction to both whites and Indians on Port Madison tribal lands; Chief Justice William Rehnquist rules that Congress placed limitations on tribal authority and that, unless Congress expressly delegated the power of criminal jurisdiction to the Suquamish, they do not hold it.

1978   The Indian Law Resource Center is founded in Helena, Montana, to promote the validity of international claims by indigenous peoples.

1978   In *Santa Clara Pueblo et al. v. Martinez et al.*, the U.S. Supreme Court rules that a tribal court is an appropriate forum for adjudication of personal and property matters. The case involves a suit challenging a tribal ordinance that denies membership to children of female members who marry outside the tribe, while offering citizenship to children of male members who marry outside the tribe; Justice Thurgood Marshall writes that Indian tribes are "distinct, independent political communities, retaining their original natural rights."

1978 With the passage of the U.S. Indian Child Welfare Act, prompted by the finding of a Senate committee that up to 25 percent of Indian children have been removed from their families, the government establishes policies for the adoption and foster care of native children after years of a federal system that transferred the care of native children to white-run boarding schools. The act is designed to restrict the placement of Indian children in non-Indian homes and to prevent the disintegration of Native American families; tribal courts are given jurisdiction in matters of adoption and child welfare, rather than the state courts.

1978 The Committee for Peasant Unity in Guatemala fights for the common interests of poor farmworkers and highland Indians. In 1980, the two groups launch a strike of 100,000 plantation workers that results in large wage increases, but José Ríos Montt seizes power in 1982, and in the first six months of his regime, Amnesty International estimates, 10,000 Indians and peasants are murdered by the military.

1978 The Indian Law Resource Center, established in the United States, brings legal actions on behalf of Native Americans in the U.S. courts and represents their interests before international organizations like the United Nations Commission on Human Rights.

1979 The Inter-Ethnic Association for the Development of the Peruvian Selva is founded when several indigenous organizations, representing the more than 300 groups of lowland Indians in the Amazon basin in Peru, decide to work together to preserve their territory and safeguard the natural resources from outside exploitation. The association also tries to prevent poor farmers from moving into the territory, but, though the regime of General Juan Velasco Alvarado (in power 1968–75) guarantees their territory through the Law of Native Communities, he is overthrown by a coup; the new regime suspends the law and begins granting land and rights to develop the forests to private companies.

1979 In *Washington v. Fishing Vessel Association*, the U.S. Supreme Court modifies an earlier decision that an Indian tribe has equal rights to fish, with the statement that Native Americans are entitled to a "moderate" livelihood from fishing.

1979 The Danish parliament passes the Home Rule Act granting home rule to Greenland after more than 200 years as a colony of Denmark. About 95 percent of the 55,000 inhabitants of the largest island in the world are indigenous; in 1990, the Greenland parliament, the Landsting, abolishes the "birthplace criteria," which allow native Greenlanders to receive lower wages than those born in Denmark.

1979 The indigenous Tinggian of northern Luzon Island in the Philippines issue a declaration opposing the logging of their lands, which disrupts the lives of the Tinggian, Isneg, Kalinga, Kankanai, and Bontoc and their mountain environment.

1979 The Kwaio Cultural Center is built when the indigenous mountain Kwaio people of Malaita in the Solomon Islands organize schools and a program to preserve their culture. Close to half of the Kwaio still practice their ancestral religion, and they have experienced pressure from the logging industry and from the spread of Christianity.

1979 In Chile, the passage of Decree Law 2568, "Indians, Indian Lands, the Division of the Reserves, and the Liquidation of the Indian Communities," permits any resident of Mapuche land, whether of Mapuche descent or not, to claim a piece of traditional communal lands, and once divided these lands are no longer considered indigenous. The decline in territory and communities leads the Mapuche people to resist, which prompts a violent response by the Chilean army; Mapuche leaders are jailed, murdered, and forced into exile.

1979 The ADMAPU, the national organization of the Mapuche people of Chile, is founded to fight for their right to maintain some of their ancestral lands, in the wake of the 1973 coup by the Chilean armed forces and the murder of President Allende, which reverses the government efforts at agrarian reform.

1979 The constitution of the island of Palau in Oceania, approved by 92 percent of the voters, bans the storage, disposal, or testing of nuclear material on the island. Governed under the trust-territory system established after World War II, the island has attempted to pass a compact of free association with the United States, but attempts have stalled with the insistence that 75 percent of voters are required to waive the nuclear weapons and waste provisions, which the United States opposes.

1979 The western Shoshone (Newe) people of eastern Nevada refuse to accept U.S. government moneys for lands whose title they believe is guaranteed by the Treaty of Ruby Valley signed in 1863. Under the provisions of the Indian Claims Commission Act of 1946, the Shoshone believe that if they accept the money they will relinquish their claims to the land; the money remains in a trust account.

1979 The People's Union for Civil Liberties and Democratic Rights in India investigates the deaths and beatings of tribal protesters in the Singhbhum district of Bihar State. Innocent people are arrested, the police fire without reason, and charges are concocted after the event.

1979 The Saami people in Norway protest the Alta River Dam project, one of the large-scale hydroelectric projects in Norway responsible for destroying large amounts of the traditional, collectively owned land of the Saami and forcing most Saami to abandon their traditional livelihood of fishing, hunting, and reindeer farming.

1979–1981	The Report of the Commissioner for Scheduled Castes and Scheduled Tribes in India states that most tribal communities live below the poverty level; fewer *adivasis* (tribespeople) attend school, are literate, and have access to health care than any other segment of the population. The report comments on the effects of development, stating that opening up tribal lands to nontribals is still prevalent.
1980	Aboriginals in Noonkanbah, Australia, stage a successful protest against oil exploration on their land.
1980	The Bertrand Russell Tribunal on the Rights of the Indians of the Americas, held in Rotterdam, Netherlands, is a follow-up to the 1977 Conference on Discrimination against Indigenous Peoples in the Americas. The Russell Tribunal brings together an international jury of legal scholars and lawyers to hear cases involving abuse of the rights of indigenous peoples.
1980	In connection with the Sioux claim to the Black Hills of South Dakota, the U.S. Supreme Court states that the United States dishonorably confiscated the land and that the Sioux were pressured, by the threat of starvation, into selling the Black Hills. The Court agrees to a 1979 Court of Claims ruling that the Sioux are entitled to compensation of $106 million for the 1877 Manypenny Agreement seizure of their lands, but the Sioux continue to fight for the return of their land.
1980	When Bangladesh troops and Bengali settlers attack Kaokhali Bazar in Bangladesh, 300 indigenous peoples of the country are murdered. An estimated 30,000 troops are stationed in the Chittagong Hill Tracts to counter the efforts of Shanti Bahini, the indigenous guerrilla force fighting for autonomy of the region and the return of tribal lands seized by the government, developers, and settlers; it is estimated that by 1981 40,000 indigenous people have fled the area to avoid persecution, becoming refugees in India.
1980	Under the Maine Indian Claims Settlement Act, the state of Maine awards money to the Penobscot and Passamaquoddy to settle their suit claiming their land had been seized and ceded in violation of the Indian Trade and Non-Intercourse Act of 1790. The tribes purchase land, improve housing and educational opportunities, and set up a casino.
1980	In *Budoni v. Higginson*, also known as the Rainbow Bridge Case, the U.S. Supreme Court rules that a Navajo and Hopi joint effort to preserve a site of spiritual importance is superseded by U.S. interests. The Court lets stand a lower-court decision that effectively limits the scope of the 1978 American Indian Religious Freedom Act, under which the Navajo and Hopi sued, hoping to prevent the flooding of this important area for the Glen Canyon Dam.
1980	The New Forest Bill passed in India empowers government forest officials to punish *adivasis* (tribespeople) with up to six years in prison for collecting wood for fuel for their families, while

large-scale commercial exploitation of the forests continues.

1980   The Sandinista government in Nicaragua issues a policy statement about indigenous peoples and establishes MISURASATA, an organization of Miskito, Sumu, and Rama peoples; the policy states that indigenous people should legitimately own their lands and should be taught their own language in schools. By 1981, relations between the Sandinistas and the Miskitos have deteriorated; the government believes the Miskitos are collaborating with the Contra forces trying to overthrow the Sandinista revolution. Nicaragua guarantees that the indigenous people can own their land as communities or cooperatives but also emphasizes that Nicaragua is one country whose official language is Spanish.

1980   The Union of Indian Nations in Brazil is formed when leaders of nine tribes come together to fight to preserve indigenous land and their cultural heritage in Brazil.

1980   The U.S. Congress settles with three Native American tribes in Maine, giving them a cash settlement and 300,000 acres of land. Congress also establishes regulations so that tribes not recognized as Indian can acquire Indian status.

1980   The South American Indian Council is founded in Ollantaytambo near Cuzco, Peru, at the first Congreso de los Movimentos Indios de Sud America (Congress of Indian movements of South America). The council affirms the principles of autonomy and self-determination and rejects the notion that Indians are beneficiaries of the state; it also affirms the Indian tradition of communalism rather than Western political and social models.

1980   The Brazilian Society of Indigenists is formed when 80 members of the government's National Indian Foundation express their dissatisfaction with the agency's failure to protect indigenous people and their land. The Brazilian Society of Indigenists offers support to the growing movement for Indian rights in Brazil.

1980   The National Council for the Coordination of the Indigenous Nations of Ecuador affirms its support of the struggle to regain communal-land rights for indigenous peoples rather than individual holdings. With respect to the question of integration of Indians into Ecuadorian society, a council statement reads: "We see that in mestizo society there are sectors which are aware of indigenous peoples and respect us. But the great majority of mestizo society considers us as animals."

1980   Rio Tinto Zinc of London, England, takes over copper-mining operations in Cerro Colorado, Panama, estimating that the project involves relocating 15 Guayamí communities of 10,000 people. The Guayamí challenge the project, insisting the land is theirs, while the government claims that it has the right to develop natural resources for the benefit of the entire society.

1980s   The Bushmen Development Program in Botswana in Africa is organized to encourage self-reliance and economic development among the Bushmen, or San, indigenous inhabitants of most of southern Africa; the Central Kalahari Game Reserve is established to provide land and an environment for the San, but neighboring farms endanger their way of life, and cattle compete for the wild food the San rely on.

1980s The government of Iraq institutes a coordinated campaign to destroy Kurdish villages in the north. The 20 million Kurds have historically lived in an area that transcends political geography and includes the mountainous areas of Armenia, Azerbaijan, Iran, Iraq, Syria, and Turkey; speaking a language related to Persian, the Kurds, often Sunni Muslims, have seen their desires for autonomy met with relocation and violence.

1980s The government of Alberta, Canada, decides to issue 20-year logging leases for one-third of the province. Daishowa, a large Japanese paper and pulp company, receives a lease to cut on the land of the Lubicon Cree and begins cutting in 1990; as part of its operation, the company uses a toxic bleaching process.

1980s The government of Sri Lanka (Ceylon) relocates the Veddha people from their hunting grounds so that their lands can be developed for logging and commercial hunting.

1981 The United Nations Educational, Scientific, and Cultural Organization Conference on Ethnic Development and Ethnocide in Latin America adopts the Declaration of San José, Costa Rica, stating that ethnocide is a violation of international law.

1981 The United Nations rules that the 1951 Canadian Indian Act provision denying a woman's status as an Indian because she marries a non-Indian violates human rights.

1981 In *Montana v. United States*, the U.S. Supreme Court rules that non-Indians are not subject to tribal jurisdiction over hunting and fishing on the Crow Reservation. Even though the Crow Nation offered a 1868 treaty permanently reserving some of its territory for "absolute and undisturbed use and occupancy," the Court rules that non-Indians who purchase land on the reservation have unrestricted use of these restricted areas; Justice Potter Stewart writes that previous treaties did not create tribal jurisdiction over non-Indian fishing or hunting on lands held by fee by non-Indians, that they did not enter into any such agreement with the tribe, and that tribal control extends only to lands where the tribe has "absolute and undisturbed use and occupation."

1981 A follow-up to the International Nongovernmental Organization Conference on Discrimination against Indigenous Peoples, held in Geneva, Switzerland, establishes four commissions to continue work on the issues of land rights, indigenous philosophy, the effect of transnational corporations on indigenous peoples, and the impact of nuclear arms. The conference urges that the United Nations Commission on Human Rights establish a working group on indigenous peoples and that other United Nations bodies include representatives of indigenous peoples.

1981 Capemi, a Brazilian arms company, and Agromax of Japan use a version of Dow Chemical's Agent Orange to clear land for a hydroelectric plant in Brazil, exposing large numbers of indigenous people to the chemical. According to a report in a British newspaper, as many as 7,000 people may have died from illnesses related to Agent Orange exposure.

1981 The World Bank approves a loan of $300 million to the Polonoroeste Project in Brazil, for road building, agricultural development, and settlement of 160,000 square miles in western Brazil, affecting 25 indigenous groups. The World Bank states that this region of Brazil can become an important agricultural and timber region and that migrants from other areas can settle here, although the project involves some invasion of Indian lands.

1981 The Greater Carajás development project in Brazil, with an investment of over $30 billion, involves large-scale mining operations for nickel, bauxite, iron ore, gold, and manganese and large-scale agricultural development in the states of Pará and Maranhão, dislocating 100,000 people, including 10,000 Indians, and destroying the last forests in Maranhão.

1982 *Kompas*, a newspaper in Jakarta, Indonesia, reporting on the working conditions of the Ashmat tribal people in West Papua, describes the Asmat people's work cutting timber for the export trade. Since the 1970s, the government and logging companies have used violence and the threat of prosecution to force the Asmat to gather logs on the lands they own, paying them with a few packs of tobacco or an ax head, and terrorizing them if they complain about their exploitation.

1982 At the Conference on Native Resource Control and the Multinational Challenge, held in Washington, D.C., indigenous representatives and experts in development meet to talk about the effects of development on indigenous peoples and their environment.

1982 The Anti-Slavery Society's report, *Bonded Labour in India*, analyzes how government forest policy and the loss of native land have pushed the indigenous people into a system of debt bondage, where unscrupulous landowners and moneylenders lend money in return for the guarantee of labor. Charging interest of up to 200 percent a year, the landowners manipulate as many as 20 million native peoples into virtual slavery.

1982 A resolution introduced in the Hawaii House of Representatives in the effort to end practice bombing at Kaho'olawe Island states that the island has about 544 archaeological sites representing a thousand years of occupation by Hawaiian peoples. The island belongs to Hawaii, not to the U.S. Navy, which uses it for bombing practice; since 1971, the United States has invited New Zealand, Canada, and Australia to participate as well.

1982 The U.S. Indian Mineral Development Act is passed with the aim of reducing the costs of federal programs to Native Americans by encouraging the exploitation and development of mining on Indian land; while Indian land contains approximately 50 percent of the U.S. uranium deposits, 30 percent of strip-mine low-sulfur coal, and 5 percent of oil and gas, tribes have received only a small proportion of the profits. The act gives tribal governments the authority to enter into joint ventures and lease agreements with energy companies to develop oil, coal, gas, and uranium reserves; to promote economic self-sufficiency, environmental protection regulations are waived, and participation of capital-intensive corporations are encouraged.

1982 The U.S. Supreme Court rules that Native American tribes can levy severance taxes for minerals extracted from their lands, in *Merrion v. Jicarilla Apache Tribe*; this decision is the judicial counterpart to the 1982 U.S. Indian Mineral Development Act. While acknowledging native rights, the decision nevertheless ties the levying of taxes to defraying costs for "tribal self-government . . . and other programs."

1982 The government of Taiwan dumps low-level radioactive waste on Lanyu Island in the Pacific Ocean, endangering the lives and lands of about 3,000 indigenous Yami people who live two miles away.

1982 The United Nations Working Group on Indigenous Populations is created as a subsidiary of the Commission on Human Rights. The Working Group undertakes a draft of a United Nations Declaration on the Rights of Indigenous Peoples and establishes several studies, including a study of treaties and agreements between states and indigenous peoples.

1982 The Mikwobait Cultural Center is established in 1982 in Odanak, Quebec, when members of the Abenaki people organize to preserve and protect their culture. Before the French and British colonists settled the region and drove native peoples out, the natives' territory stretched from Maine's coast to Lake Champlain and from Quebec to Massachusetts.

1983 The New Zealand government amends the Fisheries Act to protect Maori fishing rights, which were guaranteed to them as part of the Treaty of Waitangi negotiated between the British and the Maori in 1840. In 1988, the government and the Maori sign an agreement returning half of the country's offshore fishing resources to Maori control for 20 years in return for a halt in Maori land claims.

1983 The U.S. Commission on Civil Rights issues a statement on the religious rights of Native Americans, stating that the government has failed to protect Indian religion and to treat it as significant. Rather, the government policy for three centuries has been to repress and erase Indian religion.

1983 The provincial government of Quebec, issues 15 principles, as part of its long-standing struggle to achieve political autonomy from Canada. Quebec recognizes indigenous claims of self-determination for economic development, culture, language, education, and acknowledges that the indigenous peoples are entitled to land, which would be negotiated later.

1983 The Project for the Study of the Management of Wildlife Areas in Kuna Yala is established in Panama, when the Kuna people declare a forest area a buffer between their autonomous reserve and settlers and ranchers who increasingly encroach on tribal lands. The Kuna are one of six groups of indigenous people in Panama, and, while their rights to autonomous areas have been recognized since 1938, pressure for land for settlers, loggers, and cattle ranchers has meant a loss of forest land.

1983   Francisca Alavarez of Guatemala makes a statement to the United Nations Working Group on Indigenous Populations in Geneva, Switzerland, describing the tortures and massacres of Indians in Guatemala, the burning of their crops, and the permanent violation of human rights. Alavarez states that the Guatemalan Army defends the interests of the wealthy against those of the Indians and poor Ladinos.

1983   Militias from the north attack Nuer villages in Sudan in Africa; 1 million Nuer inhabiting the marsh and savannah along the central-southern tributaries of the White Nile are caught up in conflict when the government of Sudan, dominated by northerners, imposes its will on the south. Sudan contracts to build a canal system through the marshlands of the Upper Nile, denies southern rights to oil, and imposes Islamic law; some of the largest oil deposits lie beneath Nuer lands, and government-sponsored raids have destroyed villages, selling captured women and children into slavery.

1983–1988   The government of Sudan begins an aerial bombing campaign of the Nuer people to the south, and many Nuer become refugees in Ethiopia.

1984   Delegates at the Conference of the World Council of Indigenous Peoples, held in Panama, tackle the difficult issue of how to achieve autonomy and equal rights.

1984   South American Indians from Peru, Bolivia, Colombia, Brazil, and Ecuador testify before the United Nations Working Group on Indigenous Peoples.

1984   The Txukurramãe, an indigenous group in Brazil, seize a ferry that provides a link to the trans-Amazonian highway in protest against the continued excursion onto their lands in Xingu Park, to which they were relocated in the 1960s. A major road was built through their land in 1970, and they were asked to leave; only half agreed to leave, and the others found themselves in conflict with settlers.

1984   The British Nuclear Test Royal Commission holds hearings on the Australian nuclear tests of the 1950s and 1960s. According to a report in the *Observer* newspaper, soldiers were threatened with disciplinary action, even the firing squad, if they revealed that they knew of any Aboriginal family who was on the test site; Aboriginals were exposed to significant levels of radiation during the tests, and some were relocated to camps, while others wandered about the unfenced test areas, exposing themselves to dangerous fallout.

1984   The Inuvialuit Final Agreement is negotiated between Canada and the Inuvialuit, providing the 2,500 Inuvialuit in the western Arctic land guaranteed hunting and trapping rights; equal participation in the management of wildlife, conservation, and the environment; a cash payment; an economic-enhancement fund; and a social-development fund.

1984   Hokkaido Utari, the Ainu-rights organization, is founded in Japan when members of the Ainu, the indigenous people of the island of Hokkaido in northern Japan, organize to press for land rights. Conquered in the ninth century by the Japanese, the Ainu have been discriminated against and have a lower standard of living than most Japanese; Hokkaido Utari advocates local control and the teaching of the native language in an effort to save the traditional Ainu culture.

1984   The Cordillera People's Alliance for the Defense of the Ancestral Domain is created in Bontoc, Luzon, the Philippines, in response to the government's 1979 decision to launch a 10-year energy plan and to build 31 dams on territory belonging to the indigenous people, destroying their agriculture and dislocating 1.5 million people. In the Chico River basin in northern Luzon, Kalinga and Bontoc residents use civil disobedience to protest these plans and are met by force from the Philippine Army; in response to repeated government attempts to enforce development against the will of the indigenous people, the protesters form an alliance with the New People's Army, the armed wing of the Philippine Communist Party, and press for the formation of an Autonomous Cordillera Region.

1985   The Intertribal Sinkyone Wilderness Council is founded when 10 Indian nations of northern California join together to protect the ancient redwood forest from being logged by the Georgia-Pacific Company. As a result of pressure from a coalition of Native Americans and environmentalists and a successful court action against the State of California, Georgia-Pacific sells 3,800 acres for $1.2 million to the Trust for Public Land; The council presses to establish the Inter Tribal Sinkyone Wilderness Park, the first U.S. park to return ancestral land to indigenous control; the park would be open to the public but managed by Native Americans.

1985   The International Convention against Apartheid in Sports, following the International Declaration against Apartheid in Sports eight years earlier, begins eliminating and punishing any and all forms of apartheid in sports. States may refuse financial or other assistance for sporting events from countries that practice apartheid and also from teams, individual sportspeople, or both, selected on the basis of apartheid.

1985   The U.S. Full Employment Action Council reports that Native American unemployment on some reservations is as high as 87 percent.

1985   After a suit by the Native Americans of the Sinkyone Wilderness area in California, the International Indian Treaty Council, the Sierra Club, and the Environmental Protection Information Center (EPIC), the California Court of Appeals prohibits the logging of ancient redwoods in that area, in *EPIC v. Johnson*. The court rules on the side of Indians and environmentalists that the California Department of Forestry violated state law by granting Georgia-Pacific the right to harvest redwoods along the coast and states that the department's response to addressing the damage to Native American archaeological sites is "inadequate."

1985   The Commonwealth Government of Australia issues the Preferred National Land Rights Model, detailing the limits granted the Aboriginal peoples of Australia on the land the government is returning to them. According to the model, Aborigines cannot veto mining on Aboriginal land; the government must make all decisions about mining and exploration; although Aborigines are entitled to payment for damages and disturbances to their land, the payment is not to reflect the value of minerals to be discovered.

1985   In *United States v. Dann*, the U.S. Supreme Court decides that payment of federal moneys into a U.S. Treasury account over which Native Americans have no control constitutes compensation for lost land. This case highlights the catch-22 status of Native Americans who never receive, and have no control of, moneys intended to compensate them; a practical result is the eviction of indigent Native Americans from their family lands even though they have not received payment for their property.

1985   The Parliament of Canada enacts a limited revision of the 1951 Indian Act, repealing the provision that an indigenous woman who marries a nonindigenous man loses her status as an Indian, and her children are not considered Indians. The United Nations had ruled in 1981 that such provisions violate international human rights covenants.

1985   The Anti-Slavery Society on Human Rights Violations in Burma reports that the Burmese Army treats indigenous villagers as virtual slaves. Local army commanders are said to conscript any villagers they can find; the conscripts are badly treated, often being sent ahead into mined areas; this treatment is typical not only of areas of active insurgency but also of peaceful areas where there is no expectation of rebel attack.

1985   The Kenyah and Kayan indigenous people of Malaysia form the Residents' Action Committee to protest the Bakun Dam project, which would flood their land and force the relocation of 5,000 tribal people. The people declare that their land is necessary for their survival and that no money payment can compensate them for the loss of their land.

1986   The Confederation of Indigenous Nationalities of Ecuador (CONAIE) is founded when two regional indigenous organizations, CONACNIE and CONFENIAE, decide to put aside their differences in language to unite and press for resolutions of land issues and unify the Quicha language. CONAIE signs an agreement with the Ministry of Education and Culture in Ecuador for a program in bilingual education.

1986, 1990	In *Simon v. The Queen* and *The Queen v. Sioui*, courts in Canada affirm that the Canadian government has jurisdiction over Indian lands, based on the interpretation of the Constitution Act of 1867; provinces have jurisdiction over property and civil rights and local undertakings.
1987	The Indigenous Tawahka Federation of Honduras is formed to fight for control of ancestral lands in the rain forest bordering the Patuca River in Honduras. The 1,000 surviving Tawahka advocate the creation of a protected reserve to halt the increased exploitation of their lands for lumber and cattle grazing.
1987	The Coalition for Indian Education is established in Albuquerque, New Mexico, to promote and provide quality education for Native Americans.
1987	The Intertribal Agriculture Council is founded when members of Native American nations in the United States organize a coordinating committee to promote the productive use of tribal lands for agriculture and land conservation. The council represents Indian nations that control over 43 million of the 54 million acres of land held by Native Americans.
1987	At the first Constitutional Convention at Keaukaha, Hawaii, the Ka Lahui Hawaii is established after eight years of discussion among native Hawaiians committed to developing a sovereign government. Some 250 delegates debate and ratify a constitution that provides for autonomy in the preexisting U.S. federal structure.
1987	The Penan and Dayak peoples of Sarawak in Malaysia blockade logging roads and shut down logging operations in the Tutoh River basin to protest deforestation. After years of appeal to the Sarawak government to halt the destruction of the native forests, the Dayaks state that the government must stop destroying the forest or they will be forced to protect it; the state government votes to add to the forest ordinance an amendment making it a crime punishable by up to two years in prison and a $2,000 fine for anyone to obstruct a logging road.
1987	The government of Chile issues a decree allowing the logging of the araucaria tree, which was given the status of a national monument in 1976. Perhaps the oldest living tree species on earth, the araucaria grows on the land of the Pewenche in the Quinquen Valley in southern Chile; the Pewenche have managed to protect it, though logging has increased since the 1987 decree.
1987	At a meeting of experts convened in Geneva, Switzerland, to revise Convention 107 of 1957, the International Labour Organization revises its policy toward indigenous peoples. The revisions include allowing indigenous people to control their lands and social and economic development and granting them the right to interact with the rest of society through their indigenous institutions.
1987	The United Nations grants consultative status to several indigenous organizations, including the Grand Council of the Cree, the

South American Indian Council, the National Aboriginal and Islander Legal Services Secretariat, the Inuit Circumpolar Conference, the Indian Law Resource Center, the Four Directions Council, the National Indian Youth Council, and the Indigenous World Association.

1987   In the kingdom of Bhutan in the Himalayan Mountains, the One Nation, One People component of the sixth five-year plan is a legal effort to create cultural conformity. The plan requires that all residents of Bhutan conform to *driglam namzha*, the customs of the Ngalung people who live primarily in the north and rule the nation; this requirement discriminates against the cultural rights of the people in the south who are mainly Hindu (Ngalung are Buddhists) and whose freedom to worship is restricted.

1987   The U.S. Federal Energy Regulatory Commission denies a license for hydroelectric power on the Kootenai River, where seven electric-power cooperatives in the states of Idaho and Montana sought to build a dam and power plant on a site at Kootenai Falls, Montana. This site is sacred to the Kootenai Indians, who hold lands in both states and in British Columbia, Canada.

1988   The U.S. Supreme Court, in *Lyng, Secretary of Agriculture, et al. v. Northwest Cemetery Protective Association et al.*, permits the U.S. Forest Service to disturb sacred sites of Native Americans. The Court rules that the Forest Service has the right to pave six miles of road in the Six Rivers National Forest of California to open the lands for commercial foresting, even though this would disrupt sites central to religious worship of the Tolowa, Karok, and Yurok; the Court states that the free-exercise clause of the Constitution does not keep the government from using its lands as it wishes.

1988   Members of the Blackfeet retrieve Native American bones from the collection of the Smithsonian Institution in Washington, D.C., and return to the reservation with the remains of 15 ancestors.

1988   The U.S. Congress passes the Indian Gaming Regulatory Act, allowing Native American tribes to generate income through gambling.

1988   The U.S. White Earth Land Recovery Project is instituted to counter the extraordinary loss of the Minnesota reservation land of the Anishinabe (Ojibway), who since the middle of the nineteenth century have lost control of 90 percent of their lands to timber companies, speculators, and Indian agents. The Anishinabe form the project to purchase back approximately 750 acres of their land each year.

1988   The Association of Khakass People is formed to represent the interests of the indigenous people of the Sayan Mountains of southern Siberia. With the weakening of centralized government in the Soviet Union in the late 1980s, many indigenous peoples begin to organize to press for land and for cultural, political, and other rights that have been ignored during the years of Communist rule.

1988   The International Centre for Human Rights and Democratic Development (ICHRDD) is established when the Parliament of Canada votes to fund an organization devoted to promoting human rights around the world. The center supports indigenous peoples' rights in the Americas and aids programs in El Salvador, Guatemala, Haiti, Mexico, and Peru.

1988   The Caribbean Organization of Indigenous Peoples is organized when representatives of the Carib people of Dominica, the Carib of Sandy Bay of Saint Vincent and the Grenadines, and the Garifuna of Belize meet with the Arawak and the Carib of Guyana. All these groups are partly descended from the Carib and Arawak who inhabited the Caribbean islands when Columbus arrived in 1492.

1989   An agreement between the federal minister of Indian Affairs in Canada and the Federation of Saskatchewan Indian Nations is negotiated.

1989   The U.S. Supreme Court rules, in *Brendale v. Confederated Tribes and Bands of the Yakima Nation*, that a Native American tribe cannot restrict the land use of nonwhites on the reservation. The Court denies the right of the Yakima Tribal Government to enact zoning ordinances that limit the use of land by nonwhites living on the reservation, further eroding any notion of inherent sovereignty.

1989   The State Museum in Albany, New York, returns 12 wampum belts to the Onandaga Nation.

1989   The International Labour Organization adopts a revised policy toward indigenous peoples at a meeting in Geneva, Switzerland. The revisions change the assimilationist orientation of earlier standards, promote respect toward indigenous traditions and practices, and promote indigenous human rights without discrimination. Indigenous peoples have the right to participate in government to the extent of the rest of the population and the right to use their land in accordance with cultural traditions.

1989   The revised Indian Act passed in Canada gives, for the first time, local band councils the right to assign possession of some reserved land to individuals. The act includes provisions mandating the government to recognize the security of band reserves and establishing a shared responsibility for distributing financial royalties due to the bands; the government guarantees educational opportunities on an equal basis and requires school attendance.

1989   The National Museum of the American Indian is founded when the U.S. Congress transfers the collection of the American Indian/Heye Foundation to the Smithsonian Institution. Located in New York City, the museum preserves and exhibits the life, history, languages, and arts of Native American peoples.

1989   Kansas enacts new legislation about skeletal remains of Native

Americans, and members of Caddoan tribes rebury the bones of 146 members that were on public display at a tourist attraction.

1989   The American Museum of Natural History in New York City refuses to return a sacred bundle of the Cree Indians, after a Canadian Cree man ran 2,700 miles on the unsuccessful mission to retrieve the 150-year-old tribal artifact for his people.

1989   Stanford University agrees to return its collection of Indian bones to the Ohlone'Costonoan people, who rebury the skeletal remains.

1989   The National Museum of the American Indian Act becomes law when President George Bush signs legislation requiring the Smithsonian Institution in Washington, D.C., to return parts of its collection of 18,000 skeletal remains and much of its collection of funerary objects to Native American tribes that can prove proper ownership.

1990   The U.S. Supreme Court rules, in *Employment Division, Department of Human Resources of Oregon v. Smith*, that the use of peyote by the Native American Church is not protected by the First Amendment of the Constitution. Though a controlled substance under the Federal Comprehensive Drug Abuse Prevention and Control Act, peyote has long been used by Native Americans to induce a hallucinogenic spiritual state, but Justice Antonin Scalia rules that such use does not fall under the free-exercise clause of the First Amendment, stating that the clause "does not relieve an individual of the obligation to comply with a law that incidentally forbids (or requires) the performance of an act that his religious belief requires (or forbids) if the law is not specifically directed to religious practice and is otherwise constitutional as applied to those who engage in the specified act for nonreligious reasons."

1990   The U.S. Congress passes the Native American Grave Protection and Repatriation Act, recognizing Native American concern for the desecration of ancestral graves and the collection and display of Native American bones. The legislation provides for the protection of grave sites and for the return of sacred objects, funerary objects, and identifiable skeletal remains.

1990   The U.S. Indian Nations at Risk Task Force is created to study the state of education for Native Americans. It recommends that Native Americans develop educational structures that satisfy their needs, because the existing education has not effectively worked to educate the Indians.

1990   In *Delgamuuk et al. v. The Queen*, the decision of the Supreme Court of British Columbia, Canada, displays a bias against indigenous people. Chief Justice Allan McEachern writes that the plaintiffs' ancestors could not write, had no horses or wheeled vehicles, and frequently warred with neighbors; quoting the English philosopher Thomas Hobbes, he finds aboriginal life at best "nasty, brutish, and short."

1990   The U.S. Indian Arts and Crafts Act makes it illegal to sell falsely any good as an Indian-produced product; a person must be a member of a federally or state recognized tribe or certified as an Indian artist by a tribe to be legally considered an Indian artist or craftsperson. Recognized artists are required to present official tribal documents to verify their status.

1990   The Meech Lake Accord is defeated in Canada when leaders of Canadian indigenous peoples successfully block passage of a provision to grant French-speaking Quebec special status as one of the founding nations of Canada while denying the same status to native peoples. Additionally, the Meech Lake Accord proposes that to establish a new province of Quebec requires the unanimous consent of all 10 existing provinces; since the existing provinces covet land held by the indigenous peoples, this proposal limits the chance for native peoples to gain provincial status for their own territories. The sole indigenous member of the Manitoba Legislative Assembly, Elijah Harper, thwarts the unanimous-consent provision of that body regarding public hearings on the matter, and Prime Minister Brian Mulroney's deadline for passage of Meech Lake is not met.

1990   The Ogoni Bill of Rights set forth by the minority Ogoni tribal people of Nigeria, while maintaining loyalty to the nation, calls for political control over their own affairs, control of Ogoni economic resources, and the right to protect their environment, ecology, and culture from further destruction.

1990   Seven hundred Mojo, Chimane, Siriono, and Trinitario Indians in Bolivia protest the deeding of 750,000 acres of their land to lumber companies. Organized by the Central de Pueblos Indigenas de Beni (Organization of the Indigenous Peoples of the Beni Region), they march 400 miles from Trinidad to the Bolivian capital of La Paz to gather support and argue that they had not been consulted about the loss of their homeland; as a result, an executive degree grants them 11,500 square miles, but three years later members of the Chimane still are unable to prevent the illegal cutting of mahogany, and the Siriono are fighting cattle ranchers who have taken a third of their lands.

1990   The U.S. Native American Languages Act declares the need to "preserve, protect, and promote the rights and freedom of Native Americans to use, practice, and develop Native American languages."

1990   The Rehoboth People's Motion in the Wake of Namibian Independence is issued following the end of rule by South Africa and the successful establishment of the government of Namibia, which the Basters, a partly Dutch group, see as a threat to their independence. The requirement that English be the official language of the nation means the Rehoboth people must dismantle their administrative and educational system based on Afrikaans; they claim, as well, that their communal land is being seized as public land in violation of the United Nations Declaration on the Rights of Indigenous Peoples.

1990   The Association of Numerically-Small Peoples of Chukotka and

Kolyma is established to help the indigenous Asiatic Eskimo and Chukchi peoples in far eastern Siberia cope with the drastic changes that the Soviet economy brought to their traditional land, including collectivized farming, resettlement, destruction of the tundra environment, exploitation of coal, oil, and gas, and new diseases. All these imposed changes transformed the traditional lives of people who had previously subsisted by hunting seal and walrus and breeding reindeer.

1990 The Amazon Coalition is established at a meeting in Iquitos, Peru, when representatives of U.S. environmental organizations join with representatives of the Coordinating Body of Indigenous Peoples' Organizations of the Amazon Basin to work together. The group declares that the best way to defend the Amazon is to support indigenous claims to territory, and it urges environmentalists to develop policies and strategies that value the Amazon as a biosphere of flora, fauna, and human life.

1990 The Tofa join the Association of Small-Numbered Peoples of Siberia and demand better treatment and more control over natural resources.

1990 The Movement for the Survival of the Ogoni People is created in Nigeria, with Ken Saro-Wiwa as its leader. The movement is a prime force in developing the Ogoni bill of rights, asserting the demand for autonomy and self-determination; the movement leads demonstrations against Shell Oil's presence and policies in Nigeria.

1990 The Mouvement populaire de l'Azaouad (Popular Movement of the Azaouad) and the Front Islamique arabe de l'Azaouad (Islamic Arab Front of the Azaouad) are created in Mali, Africa, when the frustration of the approximately 3 million Imashaghen (or Tuareg) indigenous people over President Moussa Traoré's dictatorial rule turns to armed resistance; the Imashaghen of the areas now part of Algeria, Mali, and Niger had been dispossessed of their lands and nomadic way of life when their land was developed for its mineral deposits. Uranium represents 90 percent of export earnings (France gets 24 percent of its uranium from Niger), and not only do the Imashaghen not benefit from this lucrative trade, but young members of their people work in the uranium pits in unsafe conditions.

1990s The government of Zambia in central Africa grants the Nkoya people control of their traditional lands, which were transformed by the British colonial authorities into the Kafue National Park, where the Nkoya were forced to pay for the right to hunt. The government cedes the land to the Nkoya to develop a privately owned wildlife reserve that will promote ecotourism, create economic-development opportunities for the Nkoya, and spur new initiatives to preserve their culture.

1990s The Udege people of southeast Siberia protest the deforestation of their land where for centuries they have fished for salmon, hunted and trapped sable, and gathered ginseng. Hyundai, a South Korean firm, signed a joint-venture agreement to log

650,000 yards of timber a year by the Bikin River; the fewer than 2,000 remaining Udege and local environmentalists mount legal and political protests to block the agreement, reminding people that the area is home to some of the last remaining Siberian tigers in the world.

1990s The Lumad, 18 ethnic groups of non-Muslim indigenous peoples of Mindanao Island in the Philippines, protest the loss of their ancestral territory. One group, the Bagobo, is fighting to protect its home, the largest volcano in the Philippines, Mount Apo, from geothermal development by the Philippine National Oil Company; in the process, large stretches of forest have been destroyed, and the Philippine Army has intervened to block protests. While theoretically the constitution guarantees rights to indigenous peoples, these do not include agriculture leasing, logging, and mining; loggers have employed several paramilitary organizations to harass and threaten their critics.

1991 The Front de liberation de l'Aïr et de l'Azawagh (Liberation Front of Air and Azawagh) is founded in Niger, partly in response to the 1990 government arrest, torture, and execution of a thousand Tuareg. Amnesty International reports that the Tuareg are "striped naked, beaten, and subjected to electric shock torture in custody"; the Front reacts by attacking a prison and military facility at Tchin Tabaradan.

1991 In Australia, the Royal Commission Report on the status of the Aboriginal people details human rights abuses, including the more frequent arrest and detention of Aboriginals, poorer health, shorter life expectancy, and higher child-mortality rates than the white population. The report leads the government to develop new programs to address these issues.

1991 Graham Greene, an Oneida, is nominated for an Academy Award for best supporting actor in a motion picture for his performance in *Dances with Wolves*.

1991 After the collapse of the Soviet Union, Georgia seeks to incorporate Abkhazians and other minorities living in the Caucasus into the Georgian state. With the minority peoples refusing incorporation, the Georgian army occupies Abkhazian territory and destroys cultural institutions.

1991 Ten thousand indigenous people from Napo, Ecuador, including Huataraco, Sardinas, Maderos, Guayusa, Yuca, Guanayacu, San Pablo, Pompeya, and Itaya peoples, seize installations owned by ORIX (U.S.) and Petroecuador (Ecuadoran-U.S.) to protest ecological devastation caused by the oil industry. After more than a month, the indigenous people withdraw, their demands for a thorough ecological study and passage of the Law of Indigenous Nations unmet.

1991 After the dissolution of Yugoslavia, the republic of Macedonia is established, though many nations hesitate to accord it official status. Both Greece and Bulgaria deny that there is a separate entity of Macedonia, the Greeks claiming that they alone are

Macedonians, not the Slavs; both nations have laws restricting the use of the South Slavic Macedonian language and regard Macedonian cultural activities as threats to their states.

1991   The Havasupai people, who live in the Grand Canyon, vote to ban uranium mining, milling, and transportation on reservation land.

1991   The Supreme Court of India outlaws mining in the Sariska Tiger Reserve in Rajasthan, a decision prompted by the action of members of the Meena tribe who formed the Save Sariska Movement and marched and blocked roads to protest illegal dolomite mining on the 200,000-acre reserve. Despite the court decision, corrupt local forestry officials allow mining to continue.

1991   President Carlos Andrés Pérez of Venezuela designates 30,000 acres for protection to establish a biosphere reserve by the Orinoco and Casiquiare Rivers. While this decree ensures that the indigenous people can use their ancestral land, they are not granted title because the government claims it.

1991   At a World Series baseball game between the Atlanta Braves and the Minnesota Twins, Native Americans protest the derogatory use of an Indian name and logo.

1991   The Appeal to the International Community from the Movement for the Survival of the Ogoni People of Nigeria is issued after a year of inaction on the Ogoni bill of rights and continuing environmental damage to Ogoni lands. The appeal urges the international community to prevail on the Nigerian government to stop buying Nigerian oil and to honor the rights of the Ogoni people, and to prevail on European and American countries to grant political-refugee status to Ogoni people fleeing from genocide and persecution; it also asks Chevron and Shell for compensation for damages to the environment and people's health.

1991   The U.S. Bureau of Labor Standards publishes *Local Estimates of Resident Indian Population and Labor Force Estimates*, focusing on the status of Native Americans living on reservations and in neighboring communities. Only 25 percent of Native Americans 16 years and older, excluding students and those who have to take care of children full-time, earn more than $7,000 a year; while the average U.S. unemployment rate is about 8 percent, according to this study the rate for Native Americans is 45 percent.

1991   The U.S. Forest Service proposes to develop a site in Medicine Wheel, Wyoming, in the Bighorn Mountains, which is sacred to members of the Arapaho, Crow, Cheyenne, Lakota, Blackfeet, and Shoshone. The Forest Service entertains using the land for a tourist center and for logging.

1992   The International Alliance of Indigenous-Tribal Peoples of the Tropical Forests is established at a conference in Penang, Malaysia, bringing together Indians from Amazonia, central America, South America; tribal peoples from West and Central Africa, India, Thailand, the Philippines, Indonesia; Orang Asli and

Dayak from Peninsular Malaysia and Borneo; and Melanesian peoples from New Guinea. The alliance insists that the rights and concerns of indigenous peoples be taken into account when it comes to setting global and local policy on the rain forests.

1992   Maya Trekkers in Belize is founded by 12 Mopan Mayan men in the village of San José of the Toldeo district in Belize, Central America, in an attempt to gain from and shape the tourist industry in Mayan territory and to protect Mayan forest land from increased settlement. Maya Trekkers serves the ecotourist trade, encouraging a tourism that respects rather than endangers fragile ecosystems.

1992   The International Alliance of Indigenous-Tribal Peoples of the Tropical Forests issues its policies on economic rights, stating that development should not occur without consulting with indigenous peoples and studying the environmental and social impact. Mining concessions negotiated without consulting indigenous peoples should be canceled and renegotiated to ensure that the environment is protected, and financing should be made available for indigenous people to develop their own economies.

1992   The International Alliance of Indigenous-Tribal Peoples of the Tropical Forests issues its policies on educational rights, stating that there must be bilingual and intercultural education whose content is controlled by the indigenous peoples. Education should provide training to help indigenous peoples' economic development.

1992   The International Alliance of Indigenous-Tribal Peoples of the Tropical Forests issues its policies on intellectual-property rights, stating that because indigenous peoples' biotechnologies contribute to humanity they must have guaranteed rights to their intellectual property and control over its development.

1992   In Kari-Oco, Brazil, the World Conference of Indigenous Peoples on Territory, Environment, and Development sets forth its policy on intellectual-property rights, stating that traditional knowledge of herbs and plants must be protected and transmitted and that indigenous peoples must maintain the rights to their genetic resources, gene banks, and biotechnology. The conference plans to list the museums and other institutions that have misused indigenous peoples' cultural heritage and property.

1992   Abdel Karim al Husseini, governor of Kordofan in Sudan, declares *jihad*, or holy war, against the more than 1 million "African" Nuba who have lived as farmers and herders in the Nuba Mountains of Sudan for over a thousand years. From the onset of the fundamentalist Islamic regime of General Omar al-Bashir in 1989, the Nuba have been dispossessed of their lands and subject to what Amnesty International has called a war of ethnic cleansing.

1992   The World Bank issues guidelines on tribal peoples and economic development, providing guidance to ensure that indigenous people benefit from development projects funded by the bank and mitigating possible adverse effects of projects on indigenous people, especially those who are restricted from asserting their rights.

1992   In response to a protest by the Uighur people in the Xinjiang Uygur Autonomous Province in northwestern China, Chinese troops fire on 10,000 protesters, killing 100. Under Communist rule, the Uighur have been the subject of persecution, as the government fears that the Uighur seek independence for the region and are alligned with their Muslim coreligionists in central Asia. The government has encouraged the settlement of millions of Han Chinese in the region, making the Uighur a minority in their homeland.

1992   The Organization of Indigenous Peoples of Pastaza Province in Ecuador organizes a march from the Amazon rain forests over the Andes Mountains to the Ecuadoran capital of Quito after three unsuccessful years of negotiating to gain recognition of their land rights. In response to the protest, President Rodrigo Borja confers a grant to about 59 percent of the land in the province that the people claimed; their demand that the Ecuadorian constitution be revised to guarantee cultural diversity is referred to Congress, and the government reserves 30 percent of indigenous land for the military as a security zone.

1992   The Adygea Republic, in the northern Caucasus, demands autonomy from Russia; although it became an autonomous republic after the collapse of the Soviet Union in 1991, it actually has the status of an autonomous region in the Krasnodar district of Russia. The ethnic Adygei, who are Islamic, make up about 22 percent of the population; the remaining 78 percent are ethnic Russians and other peoples; the national language is Adyge, one of some 40 languages spoken in the Caucasus and written in Cyrillic.

1992   The World Conference of Indigenous Peoples on Territory, Environment, and Development is held in Kari-Oco, Brazil. The Indigenous Peoples Earth Charter adopted at the conference states that indigenous peoples have the right to self-determination and to their cultural identity, despite centuries of assimilation and genocide.

1992   The United Nations Conference on Environment and Development adopts a document titled *Recognizing and Strengthening the Role of Indigenous People and Their Communities*, which urges establishing a process to empower indigenous people by recognizing that their communities must be protected from environmentally unsound or culturally inappropriate activities. The document also urges recognizing indigenous cultural values so as to promote sound development.

1992   In Papua New Guinea, the April-Salumei timber-rights purchase takes place just before the country adopts a new, strict forest policy. Local landowners are pressured to sell up to 1 million acres of rain forest, threatening the existence of the Bitara and Bahinemo indigenous people.

1992	In a case brought by the Nasion Chamoru organization against the government of Guam, the court orders the government to enforce the 1974 Chamoru Land Trust Act, which provides for the use of public land by the Chamoru people. Nasion Chamoru, an organization devoted to the environment and indigenous education, has also been pressing for the right of the Chamoru to self-determination.
1992	The *Study on Treaties, Agreements, and Other Constructive Arrangements between States and Indigenous Populations* is submitted by Miguel Alfonso Martinez to the United Nations Commission on Human Rights. Martinez acknowledges that it is difficult for nonindigenous observers to have a thorough understanding of indigenous cultures and societies, especially of their political and judicial institutions.
1992	The Solemn Declaration of the Establishment of Authority is issued by the Kanak, indigenous people of New Caledonia in the Pacific Ocean, who possess 40 percent of the nickel deposits on earth, with industry central to France's military and nuclear-energy program. In the statement, the Kanak declare their independence and equality and affirm that they are the sole legitimate owners of Kanak land and its resources.
1992	In *Mabo v. Queensland*, an Australian court recognizes the existence of indigenous peoples' land titles. Ruling on a claim to lands on an island of the Torres Strait, the court contradicts the notion of *terra nullius* (empty land, or no man's land) underpinning the claim that settlers from Great Britain had inhabited uninhabited land and thus had no need to compensate the Aboriginals, but the decision does not completely resolve the questions of which territory came under native title and which indigenous people hold these rights.
1992	In Honduras in Central America, President Rafael Callejas delegates 3,500 square miles for two national parks and the homeland for the Tawahka people but does not confer title for these lands to the Tawahka. The Tawahka have created the Indigenous Tawahka Federation of Honduras to marshal political pressure to win recognition of their claims for title to the land.
1992	The First People of the Kalahari, the Nharo people of the Ghanzi district of western Botswana and eastern Namibia, issue a letter to the government of Botswana in Africa, stating that the Ghanzi no longer can support subsistence living, and the Nharo depend on the government for food. The letter calls for restoration of the land taken from the Nharo in the last century and government programs to "meet the special needs" of the Nharo.
1992	The Taino nation is reestablished when descendants of the Taino people from Puerto Rico, Santo Domingo, and Cuba meet and hold a ceremony of restoration. A Council of Nitaynos publishes a newsletter, holds cultural events, and organizes conferences of Taino.
1992	Grand Chief Jean-Maurice Matchewan delivers a statement of

the Algonquian People to the Committee to Examine Matters Relating to the Accession of Quebec to Sovereignty, stating that self-determination belongs to peoples, not to territories, and that if Quebec has a right to self-determination, then the Algonquian have a prior right.

1992   The International Alliance of Indigenous-Tribal Peoples of the Tropical Forests establishes policies on political decision-making rights. The alliance's charter stipulates that development should be contingent on indigenous consent, that indigenous legal representatives should have the right to make decisions, and that the indigenous people should choose their own leaders and choose and revoke government representatives.

1992   In an agreement negotiated between Canada and the Gwich'in Indians, the Indians are granted land in the northwestern portion of the Northwest Territories, including the Yukon, and they are to receive a nontaxable payment to be paid over 15 years, a share of royalties from the resources of the Mackenzie Valley, subsurface rights, hunting rights, and a larger role in the management of wildlife, land, and the environment.

1992   Track and field athlete Cathy Freeman becomes the first Aborigine to represent Australia in the Olympics, appearing in the 1992 Games, held in Barcelona, Spain. At the 2000 Olympics, held in Sydney, Australia, Freeman gains international recognition by lighting the Olympic cauldron at the opening ceremonies amidst protest from many Australians, and winning a gold medal—the first for an Aborigine—on September 25, 2000, in the 400-meter run.

1993   The Nunavut Land Claims Agreement between the Canadian government and the Tungavik Federation of Nunavut, the largest comprehensive claim negotiated in Canada, provides the 17,500 Inuit of the eastern Arctic with land, financial compensation of $1.17 billion over 14 years, the right to royalties from resources, hunting rights, and a greater role in the management of the environment.

1993   Belgium introduces an amendment that constitutionally reorganizes the country along ethnic lines by dividing it into three administrative regions—Flanders, where the Flemish speak dialects of Dutch; Wallonia, where the Walloons speak French; and bilingual Brussels; the German-speaking region is also afforded cultural autonomy. Earlier constitutions recognized the different cultural communities but did not administratively divide the nation to protect the rights of each group as well as the German speakers.

1993   U.S. Public Law 100-150, Joint Resolution 19, of the 103d Congress contains the U.S. government's apology for overthrowing the kingdom of Hawaii in 1893. The resolution states: "Whereas, in pursuance of the conspiracy to overthrow the Government of Hawaii, the United States Minister and the naval representatives of the United States caused armed naval forces to invade the sovereign Hawaiian nation. . . . The Congress . . . apologizes to Native Hawaiians on behalf of the people of the United States for the overthrow of the Kingdom of Hawaii."

1993   Canada, the Yukon territorial government, and the Council for Yukon Indians, representing the 14 Yukon First Nations, sign the Umbrella Final Agreement setting out terms for final land-claim settlement in the territory; agreements are reached with four of the First Nations: the Vuntut Gwitchin First Nation, the Champagne and Aishihik First Nations, the Teslin Tlingit Council, and the First Nation of Na-cho Ny'a'k Dun. They will receive financial benefits of almost $80 million, a land settlement, and participation in wildlife boards; the indigenous people also negotiate self-government agreements that give them more control over land use and greater authority in matters such as language, health care, social services, and education.

1993   The Hui Na'auao (Native Hawaiian Advisory Council) is founded as a coalition of more than 50 Hawaiian organizations fighting for the autonomy of na Hawaii, the sovereign home of the indigenous people of the islands. Elizabeth Ann Ho'oipo Kalaena'auao Pa Martin ko'u inoa, president of Hui Na'auao, testifies before the United Nations Working Group on Indigenous Populations to gain support for a recognition of their water rights, which are acknowledged in the Hawaii state constitution and the 1987 water code but ignored in practice.

1993   The Ogoni people protest Shell Oil's destruction of Ogoni land in Nigeria. Protesters are concerned about oil spills from Shell's old pipelines, gas flares, and toxic waste dumps; later the same year, Shell's construction activities for a new pipeline destroy farmland, and Nigerian soldiers open fire on a peaceful protest demonstration by 10,000 Ogoni.

1993   The Second Summit Meeting of Indigenous Peoples is held in Oaxtepec, Mexico, convened by Rigoberta Menchu, the organizer of Mayan people in Guatemala who is the winner of the 1992 Nobel Prize for Peace and the United Nations Goodwill Ambassador for Indigenous Peoples. The Oaxtepec Declaration states that the indigenous people's condition has deteriorated because of the failure to enforce laws, environmental degradation, and abuse of natural resources.

1993   The International Decade of the World's Indigenous People (1995–2004) is established with the passage of Resolution 48/163 by the United Nations General Assembly. The objective of the resolution is to strengthen international cooperation in solving the problems of indigenous peoples in regard to human rights, the environment, development, education, and health.

1994   The Nigerian government mobilizes all its armed forces to "restore and maintain law and order in Ogoni-land"; laws are passed enacting the death sentence for those found guilty of fomenting communal clashes.

1994   The Pacific Northwest Treaty is established when Indian nations in the Canadian province of British Columbia and in the U.S.

states of Alaska, Washington, Oregon, Idaho, and Montana agree to work together. The treaty is signed by dozens of tribes in a ceremony hosted by the Suquamish Nation, and a follow-up Visions Conference is held in 1995 to "promote and encourage more Indigenous Nations to sign the Treaty" and to hear from representatives from Hawaii and Australia who want to participate.

1994 The Nigerian government arrests Ken Saro-Wiwa, the organizer of the Ogoni in Nigeria. Amnesty International reports that Nigerian authorities do not say where Ken Saro-Wiwa is being detained.

1994 The Conference on Cooperation and Indigenous Peoples, held in Vitoria-Gasteiz, Euzkadi, the Basque Country of Spain, is designed to give indigenous peoples the opportunity to discuss their views about how better to work with national and international aid organizations, nongovernmental organizations, and public and private institutions.

1994 The International Confederation of Autonomous Chapters of the American Indian Movement (AIM) makes a statement to the United Nations Working Group on Indigenous Peoples in Geneva, Switzerland. AIM reports that indigenous peoples in the United States still suffer from treaty violations, land theft, and violence. They have high prison rates, high teen-suicide rates, and the worst health, education, and housing systems in the country.

1994 The agreement between Canada and the Sahtu Dene and Métis calls for the Indians to receive land (some with mineral rights), a grant of $75 million over 15 years, a share of royalties from natural resources from the Mackenzie Valley, guaranteed wildlife-harvesting rights, and participation in decision-making bodies that deal with land-use planning, renewable resources, environmental impact, and water- and land-use regulations.

1994 Kanaka Maoli Nationals and Descendants of Hawaii issue the Proclamation of Restoration of the Independent and Sovereign Nation-State of Hawai'i.

1995 The Toledo Maya Cultural Council is established to represent the interests of 10,000 Mopan and Kekchí Maya in southern Belize in Central America. Faced with the prospect of large-scale logging of 200,000 rain-forest acres of the Columbia Forest Reserve by the Malaysian firm Atlantic International Company Ltd., the council fights for a clearly defined Maya homeland to protect the reserve; the government counters that these are "crown lands," and the lease payments for these lands come to about 60 cents per acre.

1996 The agreement in principle for a treaty between the Nisga'a, British Columbia, and Canada represents the conclusion of an effort begun in 1887 when Nisga'a chiefs went to Victoria to demand recognition of their tribal lands. The agreement calls for a payment of $190 million and the formation of a Nisga'a central government with authority and ownership of land and subsurface rights in the Nass River Valley; Nisga'a jurisdiction over Nisga'a citizens on Nisga'a land will be phased in over time, including the making of laws and the taxing of Nisga'a citizens.

1998   The U'wa people of Colombia issue a statement supporting work stoppages and peaceful demonstrations to oppose oil exploration and exploitation on indigenous lands. In 1983, Occidental Petroleum had found oil deposits of close to a billion barrels in the Cano Limo'n field along the Aruca River in Colombia, and the subsequent roads, bridges, and pipelines have disrupted and degraded the life and environment of the U'Wa.

1998   The U.S. Second Circuit Court of Appeals reverses the 1996 decision of a federal district court, which ruled it did not have jurisdiction over a suit by the indigenous peoples of Ecuador, claiming that Texaco had dumped crude oil into the environment. The Second Circuit Court states that the case can proceed in the United States, making this one of the first cases in which foreign citizens have sued a U.S.-based international oil company in a U.S. federal court.

1999   The Historical Clarification Commission in Guatemala issues a report acknowledging the role of the Guatemalan military, with U.S. support, in the kidnapping and death of up to 200,000 civilians, mainly Mayan indigenous peoples, during the 36-year civil war.

1999   Guerrillas of the Revolutionary Armed Forces of Colombia (FARC), supposedly acting independently of the FARC organization, murder three U.S. indigenous rights activists working in Colombia as part of a campaign to support the U'wa indigenous community. Their blindfolded and tied-up bodies are dumped over the border in Venezuela.

1999   The U.S. Supreme Court rules that the Chippewa Indians can hunt and fish on 13 million acres of public land in Minnesota, after Minnesota officials had argued that a 1837 treaty guaranteeing Chippewa tribes "the right to fish, to hunt, and to gather wild rice" on lands they ceded to the United States had expired; Justice Sandra Day O'Connor declares that the Chippewa retain the rights guaranteed in the 1837 treaty.

1999   After negotiations held by the United Nations, Indonesia announces an agreement in principle to allow the people of East Timor to vote on whether they will become independent and part of Indonesia or independent and autonomous. The 800,000 people of East Timor have been caught up in political and military conflict since Indonesia's 1975 invasion, after Portugal ended its colonial relationship with East Timor.

2000   Clashes occur in the republic of Adygea in the North Caucasus, when ethnic Adygei refugees, who fled from Kosovo to avoid the fighting, return to their homeland. The Adygei represent only 22 percent of the population of Adygea, 78 percent of whom are ethnic Russians.

2000   The Philippine Supreme Court upholds the constitutionality of the 1997 Indigenous Peoples' Rights Act, the first known occasion of an Asian national court recognizing indigenous territorial rights.

2000   The Supreme Court of India rules that the construction of a megadam on the Narmada River can proceed, despite the displacement of 200,000 people and the loss of the fertile Narmada Valley. The World Bank and German and Japanese financial institutions refused to fund the dam project because of its human and environmental effects; the government of India is funding the dam by redirecting health and education moneys.

2000   Lynette Liddle is the first Australian Aborigine to receive a training-course scholarship to the Israeli foreign ministry's center for International Cooperation, where she completes a course on women's empowerment for the management of peoples' organizations, in Kfar Saba, Israel. Liddle, an education officer at the Murrumbidgee College of Agriculture in Leeton, Australia, is the also first Aborigine woman to receive a B.S. degree in agriculture from the University of Adelaide and an M.S. in environmental management and development from the Australian National University.

2000   The United Nations Economic and Social Council issues a resolution establishing a permanent forum for indigenous peoples within the United Nations system.

2001   The senate of Mexico approves the Initiative for the Constitutional Reform on Indian Rights and Culture, guaranteeing indigenous people constitutional rights, self-determination, and autonomy. The Mexican Army is ordered to withdraw from Chiapas, release Indian prisoners, and dismantle military checkpoints, so that negotiations can begin to reach a peaceful settlement of the conflict in Chiapas.

2001   The World Conference Against Racism, Racial Discrimination, Xenophobia, and Related Intolerances is held in Geneva, Switzerland.

2002   The first session of the Permanent Forum on Indigenous Issues is held at United Nations headquarters in New York City. The forum gives indigenous peoples a voice in the United Nations at local, national, and international levels.

2002   The Minority Rights Group International voices its concern that the World Summit on Sustainable Development, held in Johannesburg, South Africa, may block discussion of indigenous issues because of pressure from governments that wish to avoid discussing development projects on tribal lands, environmental degradation, and self-determination for indigenous peoples.

2002   Rural Litigation and Entitlement Kendra, a tribal rights nongovernmental organization in India that is working with indigenous peoples of the Himalayan foothills, supports the statement of a large group of scientists endorsing indigenous agricultural and medical practices. The statement is presented to the United Nations World Summit on Sustainable Development, held in

Johannesburg, South Africa.

2002   The Washington, D.C., Office on Latin America reports that U.S.-trained and financed security forces acting to stamp out coca growing in the Chapara region of Bolivia have caused social havoc and human rights violations. The security forces have killed some 10 coca growers and beaten and detained 350 others who were protesting the eradication campaign.

2002   In Nairobi, Kenya, a lawsuit in which the Ogiek indigenous people are asking the government to preserve their ancestral lands is again postponed. The government decided to end protection of Ogiek lands and to open the area to settlement by other tribes, and the Ogiek suit was instituted in 1997; the Kenyan high court issued an injunction preventing any government allocation of Ogiek lands until the case comes to court.

2002   In Nigeria, a commission orders the federal government to compensate the Ogoni people for exploitation of their tribal lands because of excess oil production.

2002   Environmental activists lobby the U.S. Export-Import Bank and the Inter-American Development Bank in Washington, D.C., to block loans for a controversial gas and pipeline project in Peru. The project threatens isolated indigenous peoples in the Amazon territory.

2002   Japan deprives its indigenous peoples of whaling quotas, retaliating against the antiwhaling countries that refused to grant Japan quotas for its coastal waters. International conservation and wildlife organizations protest Japan's action.

2002   Despite political opposition, the Supreme Court of India issues an order for the closure of the Andaman Trunk Road and for the removal of settlers from indigenous lands, thus allowing the Jarawa people of the Andaman Islands to continue to exist.

2002   The energy plan proposed by U.S. president George W. Bush, which emphasizes increasing the global sources of oil and gas in West Africa, central Asia, the Caucasus, South America, and southeast Asia, may aggravate the ongoing ethnic conflicts in these countries. Although Bush's proposal calls for heightened efforts to produce more oil and gas in these areas, it does not state its position on the conflicts in these regions and overlooks the impact on indigenous peoples who oppose large-scale energy projects, the adverse reactions of peoples on whose lands energy sources are found, or the likelihood that new gas and oil projects will benefit the rich, not the poorest people.

2002   After several years of protests about the negative impact of its oil studies on the forest environment of Colombia, Occidental Petroleum decides not to pursue oil exploration in the forest area that is home to the U'wa people.

2002   The decision of a judge in Botswana, Africa, to throw out a landmark case against the government for encroaching on the land rights of a small indigenous group from the Kalahari region is labeled a "mockery of justice" by an indigenous rights group in the country.

2002   In Sarawak, Malaysia, barricades are erected and protests staged on access roads to prevent logging and plantation companies' vehicles from moving and to focus the attention of government authorities on the exploitation of the forests. Indigenous inhabitants of Sarawak have used such blockades since 2000 as a means of protest, although the government has yet to respond satisfactorily to their demands.

2002   Several indigenous organizations in India demand an amendment to the Wildlife (Protection) Act of 1972 to allow tribal people to exercise their traditional rights over the forests. Arguing that tribal people should not be forced to leave the Kudremukh National Park, the organizations state that the government should permit not only wildlife but also indigenous people to inhabit their traditional forest homes.

CHAPTER SIX

CHILDREN'S RIGHTS

1200s   The Gulatingsloven and Magnus Lagaboters Rettergangsbot, the penal code of Norway, mandates that children are not to be punished as harshly as adults and provides that illegitimate children be taken care of by the mother until the age of three years and by the father until the age of seven.

1513   In Spain, the law of Burgos is set up by a royal committee of legal experts and theologians to resolve disputes between the *encomenderos*, Spanish conquistadors in the New World who hold slaves under the *encomienda* lease system, and the Dominican friars who believe that the indigenous Taino people of Hispaniola (present-day Haiti) should be treated like the other vassals of the Spanish crown. At the urging of the friars, several amendments are added to the law, including the provision that children are to be assigned tasks "proper to children such as weeding the fields and the like," but these laws are difficult to enforce, and abuse is widespread.

1605   Legislation creating children's houses for orphans and for children whose families are financially unable to provide employment for their children is passed in Norway and Denmark and amended in 1609 and 1620. While working hours in these houses are long and discipline is enforced, the children are trained as spinners, weavers, or dyers; before the institutions cease operation, 400 boys are trained.

1630   Legislation establishing public guardians to ensure that children go to school is passed in Norway and Denmark. Schooling is not compulsory, but these guardians, appointed by the towns, are empowered to make sure children are either schooled or employed; vagrant children are sent to institutions that combine aspects of prison and employment training.

1641   The Massachusetts Bay Colony adopts the Body of Liberties, sometimes called the stubborn-child law. Its tough provisions include the following: "If any child, or children, above sixteen years old, and of sufficient understanding, shall curse or smite their natural father, or mother, he or she shall be putt to death, unless it can be sufficiently testifyed that the Parents have been very unchristianly negligent in the education of such children: so provoked them by extreme and cruel correction, that they have been forced thereunto, to preserve themselves from death or maiming."

1646   In the Virginia Colony, a statute allows parents to place their children in other households to work, in a situation called binding out. The statute declares: "Whereas sundry laws and statutes by act of parliament established, have with great wisdom ordained for the better educating of youth in honest and profitable trades and manufactures, as also to avoyd sloath and idlenesse wherewith such young children are easily corrupted . . . the justices of the peace should at their discretion, bind out children to tradesmen or husbandmen to be brought up in some good and lawfull calling."

1646   The Body of Liberties is amended to allow rebellious children to be brought before a court. The Massachusetts General Court rules: "If a man have a stubborn or rebellious son, of sufficient years and understanding (viz.) sixteen years of age, which will not obey the voice of his Father, or the voice of his Mother, and that when they have chastened him will not hearken unto them: then shall his Father and Mother being his natural parents, lay hold on him, and bring him to the Magistrates assembled in Court and testify unto them, that their son is stubborn and rebellious and will not obey their voice and chastisement, but lives in sundry notorious crimes, such a son shall be put to death."

1648   In the Massachusetts Bay Colony, the Laws and Liberties of Massachusetts mention a rationale for establishing schools: common schools are required to thwart the "one chief project of that old deluder, Satan, to keep men from the knowledge of the Scriptures."

1670   A law passed in the Virginia Colony establishes that young slave children transported to Virginia by land must serve as slaves until they are 30 years old.

1673   The Suffolk County Court in the Massachusetts Bay colony upholds the whipping of children. In the case of two children who had behaved badly, the court orders them to be beaten with up to 15 stripes each.

1681   A law passed in the Maryland colony establishes special juries to consider the property rights of orphans and to check on their well-being.

1729   A home for orphans is founded at the Ursuline Convent in New Orleans, Louisiana (at this time the Mississippi River basin area), which is under the control of France.

1737   The Board of Selectmen (governing council) of Watertown, Massachusetts, passes a resolution about poor families and children. The resolution states that families: "under very needy & suffering circumstances" who had shown "negligence and indulgence" and raised their children in "idleness, ignorance, and ereligion" should "take care to put out and dispose of their children to such families where they may be taken good care of."

1739   The Public School Act providing for the religious and moral education of children is enacted in Norway and Denmark.

1740	The evangelist George Whitfield, who founded an orphanage in Georgia, describes orphans who were worked at hard labor before coming to his orphanage. Treatment at the orphanage, however, is often no better; Colonel William Stephens relates in his journal for 1741 that the body of a boy who had run away from the orphanage was covered with "Scars and Wounds not yet healed" from beatings.
1783	Schools in Poland decide to end corporal punishment.
1800s	In Great Britain, children of poor families and orphans work in cotton mills, sometimes receiving only room and board and working 13 or more hours a day. Children are also exploited in factories in the United States, where they constitute as much as one-third of the labor force.
1802	The Health and Morals of Apprentices Act is enacted in Great Britain to improve working conditions for apprentices. The act abolishes night work and limits the working hours of apprentices in cotton mills to 12 hours a day.
1813	In Connecticut, a law is passed requiring children working in factories to receive some education.
1819	Sir Robert Peel, a member of Parliament in Great Britain, sponsors a law prohibiting the employment of children under the age of nine years in the cotton mills, and Parliament passes it. Because there is no independent inspection system, however, mill owners often ignore the law.
1825	The New York House of Refuge is the first institution established in the United States to deal with juvenile delinquents. Created by the efforts of the Society for the Reformation of Juvenile Delinquents, the house offers "such employments as will tend to encourage industry," and education in "reading, writing, and arithmetic," with an emphasis on "the nature of their moral and religious obligations."
1828	The House of Reformation is founded in Boston, Massachusetts, and admits children convicted of a crime, beggars, and "other idle, disorderly, and lewd persons." Local authorities like mayors and aldermen can recommend for sentencing "all children who live an idle or dissolute life, whose parents are dead, or if living, from drunkeness, or other vices, neglect to provide any suitable employment, or exercise any salutary control over said children . . . [to] be kept governed and disposed of, as hereinafter provided, the males till they are of the age of twenty-one years, and the females of eighteen years."
1831	In *Commonwealth v. M'Keagy*, the Court of Common Pleas in Philadelphia, Pennsylvania, orders the release of a juvenile held in a juvenile reformatory, where his father committed him because the boy was idle and disorderly. Questioning the charter's vague understanding of idleness and vagrancy, the court declares: "It is when the law is attempted to be applied to subjects who are not vagrants in the just and legal acceptation of the term: preservation becomes mixed with a punitory character,

that doubts are started and difficulties arise, which often involve the most solemn questions of individual and constitutional rights."

1833   The Factory Act is passed in Great Britain, correcting some of the weaknesses of the 1819 legislation; the act not only outlaws employment of children under the age of nine years in all textile factories but mandates the appointment of four "independent factory inspectors." These four inspectors must deal with 3,000 manufacturers, and, unfortunately, because there is no comprehensive birth registry until the 1830s, the act is easily contravened.

1839   The Pennsylvania Supreme Court, in *Ex parte Crouse*, decides that institutions for juvenile delinquents are legal. The decision also upholds the ability of courts to commit children over the objections of their parents.

1842   The Mines Act protecting children working in mines is passed in Great Britain, after a commission investigates employment in the mines in 1840; the act prohibits the employment in mines of children under 10 years of age and sets restrictions on the kinds of work children over 10 can perform. Working in mines is more arduous than in factories: small children sit for 13 or 14 hours at a time in the dark, operating ventilating traps; they also work as "hurriers," bending over and pushing loads of coal with their heads.

1849   George W. Matsell, chief of police for New York City, issues a report claiming that approximately 3,000 street children in the city are "vagrant, idle, and vicious." "From this corrupt and festering fountain," Matsell said, "flows a ceaseless stream to our lowest brothels, to the Penitentiary and the State Prison."

1852   In Massachusetts, a law making school attendance compulsory is passed.

1853   Spurred by the efforts of the New York Association for Improving the Condition of the Poor, a truancy law is passed in New York City, providing that children considered to be orphans or "habitual wanderers" found on the street can be taken from their families by state action. Aid to families is tied to school attendance.

1853   The New York Children's Aid Society is established in New York City by Charles Loring Brace, in part because of concern about the growing numbers of vagrant children on the streets and because of a perceived increase in juvenile crime.

1870   The Elementary Education Act passed in Great Britain makes school attendance compulsory for children under the age of 10 years.

1875   U.S. president Ulysses S. Grant speaks on the separation of religion and public school education in Des Moines, Iowa. He tells the audience: "Encourage free schools and resolve that not one dollar appropriated for their support shall be appropriated for the support of any sectarian schools. . . . Keep the church and state forever separated."

1875 The Society for the Prevention of Cruelty to Children (SPCC) is established in New York City after a volunteer social worker and the wife of a wealthy businessman try to help an abused 10-year-old girl; her case is brought to the court's attention by the Society for the Prevention to Cruelty to Animals (SPCA), the only existing agency that intervenes. After the judge places the girl in the custody of the SPCA and the SPCA arranges for a foster home, SPCC is founded with support from some of New York's wealthiest residents and with the guidance of the SPCA's lawyer, Elbridge Thomas Gerry.

1878 The Factory and Workshops Act passed in Great Britain expands the Factory Act of 1833 to industries other than textiles, raises the entry age of children into the workplace to 10 years, and limits the workday of children to half that of adults.

1884 The Brooklyn Society for the Prevention of Cruelty to Children issues guidelines about the nature of "cruelty." Cruelty is considered any treatment that needlessly causes physical pain; is dangerous to life and limb; neglects to provide food, clothing, shelter, and care; exposes children to bad weather for long periods; is degrading or unlawful; overtaxes the powers of children or makes them work unreasonably long hours; and employs children as beggars.

1886 The Factory Act passed in New York prohibits the employment of children under the age of 13 years in factories and mandates that children must present proof of their age. Enforcement is provided by only two inspectors for the more than 42,000 factories in the state, however.

1889 The American Pediatric Society is founded.

1892 Kate Douglas Wiggan, author of *Rebecca of Sunnybrook Farm*, publishes *Children's Rights*, in which she urges a less authoritarian system of discipline for children.

1892 Writing to Friedrich Engels, the German socialist who helped Karl Marx spread communist thought, Florence Kelley, the first Illinois state factory inspector, describes the cruel conditions of child labor in Chicago.

1894 *If Christ Came to Chicago*, by William T. Stead, is published. The book helps efforts to create a juvenile-court system in the United States.

1896 The educator John Dewey establishes the Laboratory School at the University of Chicago in Chicago, Illinois. Dewey's school focuses on the study of child development and encourages children to learn an activity by doing it.

1896 The Child Protection Act passed in Norway establishes the principle that the state is responsible for caring for neglected children. Children who do not attend school, commit crimes, or are neglected by their parents are removed from their homes and provided with an education in orphanages or reform schools.

1897	The National Congress of Parents and Teachers in the United States is created by members of the National Congress of Mothers, to improve the education of children and to involve parents in the educational process.
1899	The National Consumers League is established in the United States under the direction of Florence Kelley, a former factory inspector in Illinois. The group organizes a campaign to expose and end child labor.
1899	The Illinois Juvenile Court Act establishes the first juvenile-court system in the United States, to protect the best interests of young people under the age of 16 years; children may request a trial by jury. The act provides that "any respectable person" with knowledge of any child who "appears to be either neglected, dependent, or delinquent" can notify the court.
1899	The *School and Society*, by John Dewey, is published. The foremost advocate of "progressive" education for children in the United States, Dewey believes that children learn a skill by doing it.
1900	Ellen Key publishes *The Century of the Child*, advocating the idea that children are basically good and urging more humane treatment of young people.
1901	The Illinois Juvenile Court Act of 1899 is amended to define a delinquent as a child under 16 years, "who is incorrigible; or who knowingly associates with thieves, vicious or immoral persons; or who is growing up in idleness or crime; or who frequents a house of ill-fame; or who knowingly patronizes any policy shop or place where any gaming device is, or shall be operated."
1902	The New York Child Labor Committee is created in New York by a group of people including Florence Kelley, Robert Hunter of University Settlement, and Lillian Wald of the Henry Street Settlement to address the issues of child labor. Although the committee hires a press person, conducts visits to factories, drafts successful legislation, and attracts support from prominent New Yorkers, it is difficult to enforce legislative reforms.
1903	Mary Harris Jones, a labor organizer, leads a march from Kensington, Pennsylvania, to President Theodore Roosevelt's home in Oyster Bay, New York, to ask for changes in existing laws regarding child labor. President Roosevelt does not meet with them, but dispatches a representative who rejects their demands.
1904	The National Child Labor Committee is founded as an outgrowth of the New York committee to work for improvements in working conditions for children in the United States.
1904	*Adolescence* is published by G. Stanley Hall.
1905	The Pennsylvania Supreme Court, in *Commonwealth v. Fisher*, decides that juvenile courts are legal.
1905	In the United States, the National Child Labor Committee, in a study of child labor in the Pennsylvania coal mines, reports that

boys sit for 10 or 11 hours a day over coal chutes, picking out the waste from the coal passing through the chutes.

1905 In the United States, the National Child Labor Committee begins to investigate child-labor conditions in the cotton mills of the South. In 1900–01, a British reformer, Irene Ashby, found children six and seven years old working 12 hours a day in mills in Alabama. The committee drafts legislation to raise the minimum age for girls and illiterates working in factories to 14 years and to prohibit night work for children under 14, but the congressional delegation from North Carolina kills the bill in committee.

1906 In the United States, a law prohibiting the employment of children under the age of 12 years (unless they have dependent parents) in factories and textile mills is passed in Georgia with the help of the National Child Labor Committee.

1906 The Playground and Recreation Association of America is created to work for safe areas for children to play in.

1907 Maria Montessori, an Italian educator and physician, introduces a method of teaching young children that will spread throughout the world. By encouraging children to work independently on their individual interests within a strictly disciplined setting, the Montessori method fosters the development of initiative and self-reliance.

1908 The Children Act passed by Parliament in Great Britain establishes juvenile courts.

1909 Under President William Howard Taft, the Conference of the Care of Dependent Children is held at the White House. The conference urges that a U.S. children's bureau be established and declares that children should not be removed from their families solely because of poverty.

1909 Largely because of the efforts of the National Child Labor Committee, a law is passed in Pennsylvania regulating child labor in anthracite coal mines.

1910 The Boy Scouts of America is established in Washington, D.C.

1910 The Camp Fire Girls is founded in Lake Sebago, Maine.

1911 In a fire at the Triangle Shirtwaist Company in New York City, workers trapped on the top three floors cannot gain access to the one fire escape that is not blocked; 140 workers, including young girls and boys, are killed; some jump from windows with their clothing and hair on fire. The *New York World* newspaper account graphically describes the tragedy: "Screaming men and women and boys and girls crowded out on the many window ledges and threw themselves into the streets far below. They jumped with their clothes ablaze. The hair of some of the girls streamed up aflame as they leaped."

1912 The Girl Scouts of America is organized in Savannah, Georgia, by Juliette Gordon Low.

1912 A Children's Bureau is established in the U.S. Department of

Commerce and Labor to investigate and report on "all matters pertaining to the welfare of children and child life among all classes of our people, and shall especially investigate the questions of infant mortality, the birth rate, orphanage, juvenile courts, desertion, dangerous occupations, accidents and diseases of children, employment, legislation affecting children in the several States and Territories."

1916   The Keating-Owens Act regulating child labor is passed by the U.S. Congress and signed by President Woodrow Wilson. For products in interstate and foreign commerce, the act limits the ages of children working, depending on the nature of the concern, to 14 or 16 years, and limits the number of hours they can work.

1918   In *Hammer v. Dagenhart*, the U.S. Supreme Court decides that the Keating-Owens Act is unconstitutional and exceeds the commerce power of Congress. Justice William R. Day writes that regulating "the hours of labor of children in factories and mines within the States [is] a purely state authority."

1919   The U.S. Child Labor Tax Law is enacted, taxing businesses that employ children under the age of 14 years or children between the ages of 14 and 16 years who work more than eight hours a day or more than six days a week or during the night. The tax rate is 10 percent of profits.

1919   The General Conference of the International Labour Organization, meeting in Washington, D.C., adopts a minimum-age convention for ratification by member states. According to the convention, children under the age of 14 years shall not work in any public or private industry (such as mining, manufacturing, construction, demolition, or transport), unless only members of the same family are employed in the undertaking.

1920   The Employment of Women, Young Persons, and Children Act, passed in Great Britain, raises the minimum age for full-time employment in factories to 14 years. The act also restricts children under 14 years from working aboard ships except for family vessels or training ships.

1921   At the Convention Concerning the Age for Admission of Children to Employment in Agriculture, delegates of the International Labour Organisation adopt the proposal that children under the age of 14 years not be employed in agriculture except when they are not attending school. If school hours are arranged to permit children to carry out light work connected with the harvest, the school year must not be less than eight months long.

1921   The U.S. Congress passes the Sheppard-Towner Act, which creates a federally financed state program to reduce infant mortality by funding public-health nurses to help parents care for children and clinics where children can be examined and parents can learn about nutrition. The act stresses preventive care, especially prenatal care for pregnant women; the American Medical Association and other critics oppose the act, claiming that its aims are too radical and socialistic.

| 1921 | The Child Welfare League of America is founded in New York City as a coalition of U.S. organizations devoted to helping children at risk. Still active today in Washington, D.C., the league is an association of almost 1,000 organizations working to prevent and treat child abuse and neglect; its programs address family foster care, adoption services, residential youth care, child care, and pregnant and parenting teenagers. |

1922
The Children's Charter issued by the International Council of Women is developed by women's groups in both Italy and the United States concerned about the need for a special charter of the rights of children around the world. Provisions in the charter concern the care of mothers and prenatal care, the care of children up to the age of elementary school, children of school age, children at work, delinquent children, national departments for children, and international coordination and conferences on children.

1922
The U.S. Supreme Court, in *Bailey v. Drexel Furniture Company*, decides that the Child Labor Tax Law is unconstitutional. Chief Justice Taft explains that the law seeks to impose federal control over an area rightly controlled by the states.

1922
The Young Workers International and the International Union of Socialist Youth Organizations issue the Declaration of the Rights of the Adolescent, recommending economic rights of children, including limits on the workday, restrictions on employment for preschool and school-age children, pre-work medical exams for children, and an improved apprenticeship system.

1923
The U.S. Supreme Court reverses a Nebraska law restricting the teaching of a foreign language to children who have passed the eighth grade. Justice James C. McReynolds notes that restricting the age at which one can learn a language is arbitrary and that foreign languages are best learned at an early age.

1923
The American Child Health Organization is established.

1924
The International Social Service (ISS) is created in Geneva, Switzerland. ISS has branches in countries around the world and works to combat the illegal transfer and abduction of children, intrafamilial abduction, and trafficking and sale of children.

1924
The Save the Children International Union issues the Declaration on the Rights of the Child and presents it to the regional government of Geneva, Switzerland, after two years of deliberations. The declaration is ultimately adopted by the League of Nations, the first occasion that an international body ratifies basic rights for children.

1925
In *Pierce v. Society of Sisters*, the U.S. Supreme Court reverses an Oregon law requiring all children between the ages of 8 and 16 years to attend public schools. The Society of Sisters, an Oregon corporation formed in 1880 to establish schools and orphanages and offer secular and religious instruction and moral training according to the tenets of the Roman Catholic Church, argues that the Oregon law conflicts with the rights of parents to

choose schools and with the rights of their school to engage in a useful business and is therefore unconstitutional; Justice James C. McReynolds states that the Oregon law "unreasonably interferes with the liberty of parents and guardians to direct the upbringing and education of children under their control."

1926   When the Sheppard-Towner Act comes up for renewal, opponents claim that the act's female administrators are socialists. Conservative senators repeal the act in 1928; between then and 1932, 14 attempts to reverse the repeal are defeated.

1927   In *Farrington v. T. Tokushige*, the U.S. Supreme Court affirms that Hawaiian laws regulating foreign-language schools violate constitutional rights as well as Acts 30 of 1920, 171 of 1923, and A152 of 1925 of the Hawaiian legislature, which mandate that applicants to teach in foreign-language schools must be completely knowledgeable about the English language and must understand the ideals of democracy and have the knowledge of American history to promote Americanism in the students. Justice James C. McReynolds writes that "the School Act and the measures adopted thereunder go far beyond mere regulation of privately supported schools, where children obtain instruction deemed valuable by their parents and which is not obviously in conflict with any public interests."

1930   The U.S. Supreme Court, in *Cochran v. Louisiana State Board of Education*, decides that a Louisiana law using state funds to provide free textbooks for children, including pupils of church and sectarian schools, is not unconstitutional. Although appellants contend that under the 14th Amendment taxation for the purchase of school books constitutes a taking of private property for a private purpose, to aid private, religious, sectarian schools not embraced by the public-education system, Chief Justice Charles Evans Hughes quotes the opinion of the state supreme court that the law does not violate the Constitution.

1930   The General Convention of the International Labour Organization, meeting in Geneva, Switzerland, adopts a forced-labor convention. All member states ratifying the convention are asked to suppress the use of forced or compulsory labor, including child labor, except for compulsory military service or work that is part of a citizen's normal obligations.

1933   The U.S. National Recovery Act, part of President Franklin D. Roosevelt's New Deal program, includes a law prohibiting children under the age of 16 years from working.

1933   The Children and Young Persons Act, passed in Great Britain, prohibits children under the age of 16 years from working more than two hours on a school day, beginning work before 7 A.M., or continuing beyond 7 P.M. The act also prohibits street trading by children under the age of 17 years and creates penalties for employers who violate provisions of the act.

1934   The staff of the U.S. Children's Bureau produces the study *Security for Children*, which helps to create the mandate for the

Social Security Act and highlights the reality that of 8 million people on relief, 40 percent are children under 16 years.

1935 The Aid to Families with Dependent Children program of the Social Security Act is created. The act includes provisions on child health, maternal health, aid to handicapped children, and a program for child-welfare services; it also creates grants to the states for programs for neglected and abused children, though many states do not take advantage of the program.

1935 Under the aegis of President Franklin D. Roosevelt, the U.S. National Youth Administration is founded to create programs for young people. From 1935 through 1943, 2.5 million young people (including a million and a half high school–aged youth) 16 years and older are involved in work projects.

1936 The New York Society for the Prevention of Cruelty to Children is investigated to examine how it uses its broad powers charging adults with neglect and abuse of children. The study reveals that many of the society's agents have no special training and are often appointed through political connections; Judge Justine Potter of the Domestic Relations Court points out that, because the society is private, its shelters for children are not visited or inspected by New York's Board of Social Welfare.

1936 The U.S. Walsh-Healy Act prohibits companies accepting federal contracts from using child labor.

1936 The U.S. Children's Bureau study on child labor, *Young Workers and Their Jobs*, compiled by Helen Wood, states that, of the 2,000 children interviewed, all have left school for employment. Some of the interviewees are under 16 years of age.

1938 The U.S. Fair Labor Standards Act, signed by President Franklin D. Roosevelt, includes a provision prohibiting the transportation by interstate commerce of goods made by firms employing children under the age of 16 years and by companies that employ young people under 18 years in hazardous jobs.

1940 In *Minersville School District v. Board of Education*, the U.S. Supreme Court decides that laws requiring children to salute the flag and recite the pledge of allegiance do not violate their constitutional rights. The case involves two children expelled from a public school for refusing to salute the American flag and recite the pledge of allegiance because the ceremony conflicts with their religious beliefs as Jehovah's Witnesses; Justice Felix Frankfurter states that an individual's scruples do not exempt him or her from obeying a general law "not aimed at the promotion or restriction of religious rights."

1940 The White House Conference on Children in a Democracy is held in Washington, D.C., to investigate conditions for children. The final report declares: "Recent years have brought considerable understanding of the reasons that make particular children delinquent and of ways of treatment that give promise of improvement in individual cases and may help to prevent delinquency in others. . . . This recent knowledge has penetrated only in a meager way the procedures of many courts and institutions dealing with delinquent children."

1941   The U.S. Children's Bureau sponsors a conference in Washington, D.C., about children deprived of maternal care because of increased employment of women in the war effort. The conference is held to coordinate efforts among various agencies: the Works Progress Administration, the Office of Education of the Federal Security Agency, and the Children's Bureau.

1942   The U.S. Lanham Act embraces day care for children.

1942   The Declaration of Opportunities for Children is issued during the eighth Pan American Child Conference in Washington, D.C. The declaration addresses how to guarantee that the needs of children in peacetime as well as war will be met, how to establish guidelines to ensure child welfare after the end of World War II, and how to coordinate programs among participating countries.

1942   The U.S. Community Facilities Act of 1940 is amended to provide day care, because of a growing concern that mothers working in war industries need care for their children. Communities are required to provide a 50 percent match of the operating funds received from the government, and many withdraw from the program, but by 1944, there are 3,102 day care centers with 129,357 children attending.

1943   The U.S. Congress funds the Emergency Maternal and Infant Care program to provide maternity care for wives of enlisted men. When the program ends in 1949, a million and a half mothers and children have benefited.

1943   Child-labor laws in the United States are relaxed to permit teenagers to find factory employment during World War II. One year later, 2.9 million American teenagers are working.

1943   In *West Virginia State Board of Education v. Barnette*, the U.S. Supreme Court reverses a previous decision and asserts that First Amendment rights are violated by compulsory saluting of the flag in schools. Justice Howell E. Jackson writes: "It is now a commonplace that censorship or suppression of expression of opinion is tolerated by our Constitution only when the expression presents a clear and present danger of action of a kind the State is empowered to prevent and punish."

1944   The Children's Bureau creates and funds the Experimental Emergency Maternal and Infant Care program in the state of Washington. The program is severely criticized by the American Academy of Pediatrics: "In the development of this program the physicians of the country were given no voice in the formation of plans and policies . . . [and] the function and purpose of the Children's Bureau have been abruptly changed so that it is now an active factor in the practice of medicine throughout the United States, dictatorially regulating fees and conditions of practice on a federal basis."

1944   The U.S. Supreme Court affirms, in *Prince v. Commonwealth of*

Massachusetts, a Massachusetts law restricting boys under 12 years and girls under 18 years from selling papers or merchandise in the street or public places. The case involves two children selling literature of the Jehovah's Witnesses under the orders of an older woman; Justice Rutledge writes: "Acting to safeguard the general interests in youth's well being, the state as parens patriae may restrict the parent's control by requiring school attendance, regulating or prohibiting the child's labor, and in many other ways."

1945   The Children's Bureau publishes *Care of Infants Whose Mothers Are Employed: Policies Recommended by the Children's Bureau;* the Children's Bureau recommends that children under two years and hose mothers are working be placed in a foster-family setting rather than in group day care.

1946   The U.S. Supreme Court rules, in *Haley v. Ohio*, that holding a minor incommunicado and without counsel violates his or her constitutional rights. The case involves the arrest of a 15-year-old black youth in a shooting and robbery in Canton, Ohio; the boy, who allegedly served as the lookout for two older boys, is beaten in jail and denied the right to see his mother or a lawyer and, even after he signs a confession, is denied counsel.

1946   The United Nations International Children's Emergency Fund (UNICEF) is established one year after the founding of the United Nations. UNICEF deals with the enormous suffering and dislocation of children around the world as a result of the violence of World War II.

1946   A bill to provide national maternal and child care, proposed by Senator Claude Pepper, is defeated. Pepper's bill also includes provisions to provide aid to crippled children and to create a national child-welfare program.

1946   A radiologist finds that subdural hematomas (blood clots on the brain) and fractures of long bones in children are associated with cases of physical abuse, a finding that signals the importance of X rays in demonstrating the existence of child abuse.

1946   The U.S. National School Lunch Act provides subsidies for school lunches for public-school students.

1946   The International Labour Organization's Convention Concerning Medical Examination for Fitness for Employment in Industry of Children and Young Persons is adopted. The convention provides that children under 18 years (21 years for dangerous occupations) may not be employed unless they are found fit by a medical examination.

1947   The U.S. Supreme Court, in *Everson v. Board of Education of the Township of Ewing*, affirms the right of New Jersey to reimburse parents for the cost of transporting children to parochial schools. In a suit by a taxpayer, the New Jersey Supreme Court had ruled that the state legislature did not have the power to authorize reimbursement to parents of bus fares paid for the transportation of their children to schools other than public schools; the court of appeals reversed that decision, and the Supreme Court agrees.

1948 The Bureau International Catholique de l'enfance (International Catholic Child Bureau) is established in Geneva, Switzerland, with offices in Austria, Belgium, France, Germany, Italy, the Ivory Coast, Philippines, Uruguay, and the United States. The bureau hosts a program in eight countries to strengthen local resources to deal with sexual abuse and exploitation of children.

1948 The Quaker United Nations Office is founded in Geneva, Switzerland, and is active in Bangladesh, El Salvador, Ethiopia, Eritrea, Guatemala, Guinea Bissau, Kenya, Nicaragua, Pakistan, Peru, South Africa, Sudan, Vietnam, and Yemen. Its projects are concerned with children in armed conflicts, child soldiers, and displaced children.

1948 In *McCollum v. Board of Education*, the U.S. Supreme Court decides that voluntary religious instruction during school hours violates the 1st and 14th Amendments. In a suit brought by a parent in Illinois to force the Champaign Board of Education "to adopt and enforce rules and regulations prohibiting all instruction in and teaching of all religious education," Justice Hugo L. Black writes that using tax-supported public schools to help religious groups denies the separation between church and state.

1948 The International Labour Organization's Convention concerning the Night Work of Young Persons Employed in Industry (Revised) is adopted. Young people under the age of 18 years cannot be employed for work at night except for purposes of training, and even then they must be given 13 hours' rest between work periods.

1949 The Convention for the Protection of Civilian Persons in Time of War is held in Geneva, Switzerland.

1950 At the Mid-Century Conference on Children and Youth, the Pledge to Children is adopted. The pledge promises to promote education, improve workplace conditions for young people, strengthen family life, work for equal rights and nondiscrimination, and promote opportunities for young people.

1951 The U.S. Federal Youth Correction Act advocates rehabilitation and parole for youthful offenders.

1951 Japan adopts the Children's Charter, which is part of the effort to create a new constitution for postwar Japan. The charter details the government's responsibilities in safeguarding the rights of children, including respect for children and the necessity of providing a healthy environment for them.

1953 The U.S. Senate Subcommittee to Investigate Juvenile Delinquency is created. In 1955, it holds public televised hearings in Washington, D.C., under the chairmanship of Senator Estes Kefauver, and concentrates on the role of the media in promoting juvenile delinquency.

1954 Frederick Wertham, a psychiatrist, claims in his *Seduction of the*

Innocent that crime comic books are a cause of juvenile delinquency; publishers of these comics adopt a voluntary policy and code to reduce vulgarity, obscenity, and excessive violence. Wertham testifies before a Senate subcommittee that comic books, especially those that highlight crime, are partially responsible for increased delinquency.

1956   The United Nations Supplementary Convention on the Abolition of Slavery, the Slave Trade, and Institutions and Practices Similar to Slavery proclaims the following concerning children and young people: "Each of the States Parties to this Convention shall take all practicable and necessary legislative and other measures to bring about progressively and as soon as possible the complete abolition or abandonment of the following institutions and practices, where they still exist. . . . Any institution or practice whereby a child or young person under the age of 18 years is delivered by either or both of his natural parents or by his guardian to another person, whether for reward or not, with a view to the exploitation of the child or young person or of his labour."

1956   The International Labour Organization adopts its own Supplementary Convention on the Abolition of Slavery, the Slave Trade, and Institutions and Practices Similar to Slavery. All the parties to the convention must take measures to end such practices and institutions, including practices in which a person under the age of 18 years is exploited for his or her labor.

1959   The United Nations adopts the Declaration on the Rights of the Child, which expands the work of the 1924 Declaration of Geneva.

1960   A pilot project of the Legal Aid Society that provides lawyers for children facing legal action is organized in New York City; the project is initiated by the New York Citizens' Committee for Children and the New York City Bar Association. Workers in the project discover many instances where children are denied procedural rights and treated unfairly.

1960–1961   The "suitable home" test for Aid to Dependent Children recipients takes place in Arkansas, Texas, Virginia, Georgia, Michigan, and Mississippi. The U.S. Congress eliminates the test in 1961.

1961   C. Henry Kempe, a pediatrician at the University of Colorado, introduces the term *battered child syndrome* at a meeting of the American Academy of Pediatrics.

1962   The Conference on Child Abuse in Washington, D.C., sponsored by the Children's Bureau, helps to promote the passage of legislation that requires the reporting of incidences of child abuse.

1962   In *Engel v. Vitale*, the U.S. Supreme Court decides that a New York State Board of Regents–approved prayer to be recited by schoolchildren violates the 1st and 14th Amendments to the Constitution. After parents in New Hyde Park, New York, challenge the constitutionality of the prayer approved by the New York

Board of Regents, the New York Court of Appeals rules that the prayer can be used so long as no pupil is compelled to join in the prayer; Justice Hugo L. Black states that the prayer is a religious activity limited by the Constitution.

1962 The Family Court Act, passed in New York, requires that lawyers represent children in formal proceedings before the family courts in New York.

1962 C. Henry Kempe publishes "Battered Child Syndrome," an article in the *Journal of the American Medical Association*. Kempe writes, "The *battered child syndrome* is a term used by us to characterize a clinical condition in young children who have received serious physical abuse, generally from a parent or foster parent. . . . A marked discrepancy between clinical findings and historical data as supplied by the parents is a major diagnostic feature of the battered child syndrome."

1962 In *Gallegos v. Colorado*, the U.S. Supreme Court decides that a confession by a 14 year old, made without counsel or the ability to see a parent, violates the person's constitutional rights. The case involves a 14-year-old boy who, with another juvenile, assaulted and robbed an old man who died several weeks later; the boy is charged with first-degree murder, and the jury finds him guilty following the introduction into evidence of a confession the boy signed after having being held for five days without the opportunity to see a lawyer or parent. Justice William O. Douglas writes: "The youth of the petitioner, the long detention, the failure to send for his parents, the failure immediately to bring him to the judge of the Juvenile Court, the failure to see to it that he had the advice of lawyer or a friend—all these combine to make us conclude that the formal confession on which this conviction may have rested . . . was obtained in violation of due process."

1963 The U.S. Supreme Court rules that a state's requirement that passages from the Bible or the Lord's Prayer be recited at the start of school days violates the 1st and 14th Amendments to the Constitution. In *Abingdon School District v. Schempp*, Justice Clark writes that this requirement violates "the command of the First Amendment that the Government maintain strict neutrality, neither aiding nor opposing religion."

1964 Title IV of the U.S. Civil Rights Act delineates the federal government's policy on school desegregation and creates a mechanism for the attorney general to institute suits to force the integration of schools, colleges, and universities that receive federal aid.

1965 The U.S. Elementary and Secondary Education Act is passed as part of a comprehensive assistance package for public education.

1965 The U.S. Economic Opportunity Amendments establish the Head Start program to assist children of low-income families by creating a preschool program so that children can make an effective transition into kindergarten or first-grade classes.

| 1965 | The International Labour Organization's Convention Concerning the Minimum Age for Admission to Employment Underground in Mines specifies that persons under the age of 16 years cannot be employed or work underground in mines. |

1966   The U.S. Child Nutrition Act creates an expanded school breakfast program for children.

1966   The United Nations International Covenant on Economic, Social, and Cultural Rights is adopted. The covenant specifies measures to protect children from economic and social exploitation; it mandates subscribing states to set minimun age requirements for the employment of young people and stresses the importance of establishing free primary, secondary, and higher systems of education.

1966   In *Kent v. United States*, the U.S. Supreme Court declares that juvenile-court authorities must follow required procedures and must act in the best interests of the child rather than try to fix criminal responsibility and guilt. When a 16-year-old is arrested in Washington, D.C., for housebreaking, robbery, and rape, the police do not inform his mother, and the boy confesses without consulting an attorney; the judge waives jurisdiction and does not rule on any of the motions that the boy's attorney had submitted.

1966   The United Nations adopts the International Covenant on Civil and Political Rights. Concerning children and young people, the covenant states that death sentences should not be imposed on people under the age of 18 years; accused juveniles should be separated from adults; the penitentiary system should aim for rehabilitation; children should be given names and have the right to a nationality.

1966   The International Federation terre des hommes is established in Geneva, Switzerland, with offices in France, Germany, Luxembourg, and the Netherlands. It works with organizations throughout the world on projects concerned with children and armed conflict and has been active in the campaign to ban land mines.

1967   The *Task Force Report: Juvenile Delinquency and Youth Crime* is issued in Washington, D.C., by the President's Commission on Law Enforcement and Administration of Justice. The report states that half of juvenile-court judges do not have college degrees and a fifth have no college education; a fifth are not members of the bar. The report finds that the juvenile courts do not work in the best interests of the child, but nevertheless the aim of providing rehabilitation for young offenders should not be abandoned and alternatives to adult systems of punishment should continue to be sought.

1967   The U.S. Supreme Court decides, in *In re Gault*, that detaining a juvenile in a juvenile-detention center without due-process rights violates the juvenile's constitutional rights. Justice Abe Fortas writes: "We conclude that the Due Process Clause of the Fourteenth Amendment requires that, in respect of proceedings to determine delinquency which may result in commitment to an institution in which the juvenile's freedom is curtailed, the child and his parents must be notified of the child's right to be represented by counsel retained by them, or, if they are unable to afford counsel, that counsel will be appointed to represent the child. . . . It would indeed be surprising if the privilege against self-incrimination were available to hardened criminals, but not to children."

1967   Ghana passes the Labor Decree, which prohibits the employment of children under the age of 15 years, although it does exempt "light" work from this prohibition.

1968   In *Board of Education v. Allen*, the U.S. Supreme Court decides that a New York State law requiring local public-school authorities to lend textbooks free to all students, including those in private schools, is constitutional.

1968   The U.S. Supreme Court, in *Epperson v. Arkansas*, rules that a state's right to prescribe public school curricula does not include the right to prohibit the teaching of evolution. Justice Abe Fortas writes, "Government in our democracy, state and national, must be neutral in matters of religious theory, doctrine, and practice. It may not be hostile to any religion or to the advocacy of no-religion; and it may not aid, foster, or promote one religious theory against another or even against the militant opposite."

1968   In *Levy v. Louisiana*, the U.S. Supreme Court rules that denying illegitimate children (those born out of wedlock) a right of recovery contravenes the equal-protection provisions of the 14th Amendment.

1968   The U.S. Congress passes the Juvenile Delinquency Prevention and Control Act, providing aid to courts, schools, community agencies, and correctional facilities.

1968   In the Soviet Union, the Fundamental Principles of Law and Marriage and the Family are promulgated. Article 18 establishes that parents are required to raise children "in the spirit of devotion to the motherland, to inculcate a communist attitude towards labour and train children to actively contribute to building a communist society."

1969   The U.S. Supreme Court rules, in *Tinker v. Des Moines School Dist.*, that the suspension of public school students for wearing black armbands in protest against the Vietnam War violates the students' constitutional freedoms.

1969   In Great Britain, the Committee on the Rights of Children, established by the National Council for Civil Liberties, suggests the appointment of an ombudsman to initiate legislation promoting the welfare of children. The ombudsman would also monitor compliance with existing legislation concerning child protection, arbitrate disputes between children and adult authorities, and represent children in court.

| 1969 | The American Convention on Human Rights is adopted in San José, Costa Rica. The convention includes the following provision regarding children: "Article 19. Rights of the Child. Every minor child has the right to the measures of protection required by his condition as a minor on the part of his family, society, and the state." |

1970   In *In re Winship*, the U.S. Supreme Court decides that juveniles must be held to the standard of guilt beyond a reasonable doubt in the adjudicatory stage of juvenile proceedings. In the case of a 12-year-old boy brought before the New York Family Court and charged with the theft of $112 from a woman's pocketbook, the judge admits that the proof might not establish guilt beyond a reasonable doubt and rejects the contention of the appellant that such proof is required by the 14th Amendment; Justice William J. Brennan, however, states that "the constitutional safeguard of proof beyond a reasonable doubt is . . . required during the adjudicatory stage of a delinquency proceeding . . . —notice of charges, right to counsel, the rights of confrontation and examination, and the privilege against self-incrimination."

1970   The Conference on Children, held at the White House in Washington, D.C., adopts the Children's Bill of Rights. The Bill of Rights highlights the rights considered "central to a child's well-being," such as the right to be born healthy and wanted through childhood; the right to growth and development; the right to be nurtured by affectionate parents; the right to make choices and have a voice in one's community; the right to be educated up to one's potential; and the right to have societal protection and enforcement of those rights.

1970   David Gils in *Violence against Children: Physical Child Abuse in the United States* notes that it is difficult to know the actual number of cases of child abuse. He writes: "The basic question seems to be not which measure to select for combating child abuse but whether American society is indeed committed to the well being of all its children and to the eradication of all violence toward them, be it violence perpetrated by individual caretakers, or violence perpetuated collectively by society."

1970   Lois G. Forer, an attorney representing young people before the juvenile court in Philadelphia, Pennsylvania, publishes *No One Will Listen: How Our Legal System Brutalizes the Youthful Poor*. Forer writes of her young clients: "None of them expected that innocence would result in acquittal in a court of law, or that the law would provide redress for the wrongs they had suffered."

1970   The National Center for Youth Law is created in San Francisco, California.

1971   The Declaration of the Rights of Youth is adopted by the White House Conference on Youth Issues, held in Washington, D.C. The conference emphasizes the issues facing young people in the United States between the ages of 14 and 24; it focuses on the right of young people to adequate food, clothing, and a decent home; the right of adolescents to express their individuality so long as their behavior does not interfere with the rights of others; the right of individuals to preserve and cultivate their cultural and ethnic heritage; and the right to expect the protection and enforcement of these rights.

1971   In *McKeiver v. Pennsylvania*, the U.S. Supreme Court decides that, despite shortcomings in the juvenile-justice system, a jury trial is not required.

1972   In *Weber v. Aetna Casualty & Surety Co.*, the U.S. Supreme Court rules that dependent unacknowledged illegitimate children are entitled to recover the same workmen's compensation benefits as are legitimate children.

1972   In *Wisconsin v. Yoder*, the U.S. Supreme Court rules that a Wisconsin law mandating compulsory school attendance violates the First Amendment rights of the Amish, who believe that education past the eighth grade is harmful to Amish children. After several young members of the Amish religion challenge the Wisconsin school-attendance law, Chief Justice Warren E. Burger states that enforcement of the law would "gravely endanger if not destroy the free exercise of respondents' religious beliefs."

1972   In *Pennsylvania Association for Retarded Children (PARC) v. Commonwealth of Pennsylvania*, a federal district court decides that excluding mentally handicapped children from public schools in Pennsylvania violates the Constitution. Settled by a consent decree, the court rules that the state cannot deny an education to mentally handicapped children without a hearing, and that the practice of offering an education to some children while denying it to others can be a violation of the equal-protection clause of the 14th Amendment.

1972   Great Britain's Department of Health and Social Security commissions a research project by Emrys Davies, *Work out of School*.

1972   Random samples of students in 40 secondary schools in England and Wales show that 23 percent of girls and 42 percent of boys have part-time jobs covered by local bylaws; children also work in jobs that are not covered, and when both categories are combined, nearly half of all children in school between the ages of 13 and 16 years are working.

1973   The Employment of Children Act is passed in Great Britain, largely in response to the aftereffects of the Department of Health and Social Security study *Work out of School*. The act sets forth standard regulations to ensure that all local authorities enforce the same policies regarding child labor.

1973   Meeting in Geneva, Switzerland, the International Labour Organization's General Conference adopts a series of articles, including requiring member states to abolish child labor and to set a minimum age for admission to work, and setting the minimum age for the completion of compulsory schooling at no less than 15 years. The conference also specifies 18 years as the minimum age for employment that might be hazardous to young people.

1973   The U.S. Rehabilitation Act is passed by Congress. The act establishes entitlement programs for handicapped children.

1973   Robert Mnookin's article "Foster Care—In Whose Best Interest?" appears in the *Harvard Educational Review*. Mnookin, a law professor at Stanford University in Stanford, California, criticizes the U.S. child-welfare system and writes that the regulations "are vague and open-ended, they require highly subjective determinations, and they permit intervention not only when the child has been demonstrably harmed or is physically endangered but also when parental habits or attitudes are adverse to the inculcation of proper moral values."

1973   In *Beyond the Best Interests of the Child*, the authors Joseph Goldstein, Anna Freud, and Albert Solnit suggest the following priorities for foster-care placement: it should safeguard the child's need for continuity; it should reflect the child's sense of time, not the adult's; it must take into account that the law cannot supervise interpersonal relationships; it should be the least detrimental alternative for the child.

1973   The Children's Defense Fund (CDF) is established in the United States and works to "leave no child behind and to ensure every child a healthy start, a head start, a fair start, a safe start, and a moral start in life and successful passage to adulthood with the help of caring families and communities." Led by Marian Wright Edelman and Justine Wise Polier, the CDF is especially concerned with minority and poor children, offering extensive education programs and organizing for stronger support for children's programs; it receives financial support from individuals, foundations, and corporations but does not take government funding.

1974   The U.S. Child Abuse Prevention and Treatment Act (amended in subsequent years) provides funding to states to finance prevention, investigation, prosecution, and treatment of child abuse; identifies the federal role in various research activities; and calls for states to appoint guardians whose job it is to represent children in civil-court proceedings involving neglect and abuse. The act creates programs for abused children, but it is criticized as intrusive into family rights by some and for not going far enough by others.

1974   John Holt, a proponent of the emerging movement of child liberation, writes in *Escape from Childhood*: "I have come to feel that the fact of being a 'child,' of being wholly subservient and dependent, of being seen by older people as a mixture of expensive nuisance, slave, and super pet, does most young people more harm than good." Holt urges that children be given the right to vote, to be legally responsible for themselves, to be financially independent, to direct their own education, to select their own guardians, and the "right to do, in general, what any adult may legally do."

1974   Richard Farson's *Birthrights* describes children as oppressed and powerless and stresses the need for children's liberation.

1974   The U.S. Family Educational Rights and Privacy Act reauthorizes federal educational programs and allows parents to gain access to student records.

1975   The U.S. Supreme Court rules, in *Goss v. Lopez*, that students facing temporary suspension from a public school qualify for protection under the due-process clause of the 14th Amendment. Justice Byron White declares that a student must "be given oral or written notice of the charges against him and, if he denies them, an explanation of the evidence the authorities have and an opportunity to present his side of the story."

1975   The U.S. Supreme Court decides, in *Breed v Jones*, that prosecuting someone as an adult after an adjudicatory finding in juvenile court violates the double-jeopardy clause of the 5th and 14th Amendments.

1975   The Children's Express is founded as a voice for the concerns of children and teens. Publishing a newspaper written by and for young people, Children's Express covers local, national, and international politics and sends reporters around the world to cover such events as the International Conference on Child Labor in Oslo, Norway.

1976   In *The History of Childhood*, edited by Lloyd deMause, deMause reports that the infanticide of legitimate as well as "illegitimate" children "was a regular practice of antiquity, that the killing of legitimate children was only slowly reduced during the Middle Ages (hence the grossly unequal ratios of men to women in many societies), and that illegitimate children continued to be regularly killed right up into the 19th century."

1976   In *Planned Parenthood of Missouri v. Danforth*, the U.S. Supreme Court declares unconstitutional a Missouri law requiring minors under the age of 18 years to obtain parental consent for an abortion: "Any independent interest the parents may have in the termination of the minor daughter's pregnancy is no more weighty than the right of privacy of the competent minor mature enough to have become pregnant. We emphasize that our holding that 3(4) is invalid does not suggest that every minor, regardless of age or maturity, may give effective consent for termination of her pregnancy. See *Bellotti v. Baird*, post, p. 132. The fault with 3(4) is that it imposes a special-consent provision, exercisable by a person other than the woman and her physician, as a prerequisite to a minor's termination of her pregnancy and does so without a sufficient justification for the restriction. It violates the strictures of *Roe* and *Doe*."

1976   In Great Britain, the Inner London Education Authority issues regulations on child labor. Children are prohibited from working in the morning before school, except for milk or newspaper deliveries, and Sunday employment is limited to two hours between 7:00 A.M. and 10:00 A.M.

1977   The International Society for the Prevention of Child Abuse and Neglect is created in Chicago, Illinois, and works to prevent child abuse, neglect, and cruelty to children. The society publishes research results and an international newsletter and organizes conferences and workshops to increase international collaboration.

1977   A program for court-appointed special advocates for children begins in Seattle, Washington.

1977   The Children's Rights Commission is created in Sweden.

1977   The U.S. Supreme Court decides, in *Ingraham v. Wright*, that corporal punishment of a student by a teacher does not violate constitutional protections against cruel and unusual punishment or due process.

1979   The *Children's Rights Journal* is published.

1979   The International Year of the Child is proclaimed by the General Assembly of the United Nations in New York City to promote the well-being of children, study their needs, and encourage national action on behalf of child workers and children who are underprivileged.

1979   The General Conference of the International Labour Organization adopts a resolution calling for member states to "strengthen their efforts for the elimination of child labor and for the protection of children." The resolution asks member states to recognize that any labor undertaken by children who have not completed their compulsory education must not affect their education or development; states must identify children's special needs and work to improve families' economic and social well-being.

1979   Sweden becomes the first country to ban physical punishment of children, when the Swedish Parenthood and Guardianship Code is amended.

1979   The Children's Rights Project is established by the American Civil Liberties Union to strengthen the rights of children. The project uses litigation and court action to ensure that state, federal, and local laws protecting children are adequately enforced in the United States

1979   The Children's Legal Centre is created in Great Britain to campaign for children's legal rights and to provide legal advice for children.

1979   Defence for Children International (DCI) is established in Geneva, Switzerland, during the International Year of the Child. With sections and members in 60 countries, DCI, an independent nongovernmental organization, publishes a newsletter, takes on specific cases of the violation of children's rights, monitors the implementation of children's rights, and works for improved international standards for children's rights.

1979   The Foundation for Child Development Center is established in Bangkok, Thailand, as a nongovernmental organization concerned with the problems of children in Thailand. It sponsors projects that focus on child labor, hunger, and family development.

1980	The Fundación para la Protección de la Infancia Dañada por los Estados de Emergencia is founded in Santiago, Chile, to provide psychosocial assistance to children at risk. It also publishes a bulletin on children's rights and broadcasts a radio program, *Children's Rights: Dreams and Realities*.
1980	The U.S. Adoption Assistance and Child Welfare Act is passed. The act limits the use of foster care.
1981	Casa Alianza/Covenant House Latin America has legal-aid offices in Costa Rica, Guatemala, Honduras, and Mexico to help defend child victims of human rights abuses.
1981	The Children's Interests Bureau is established in Australia under the Community Welfare Amendment Act to advocate on behalf of children and to promote their welfare and interests; in 1995, the bureau is amalgamated into the Office for Families and Children. The bureau sponsors research; comments on current and proposed laws, policy matters, and practice; and hears complaints about governmental and nongovernmental actions regarding Australia's responsibilities under the Convention on the Rights of the Child.
1981	Peter S. Prescott's *The Child Savers: Juvenile Justice Observed*, a study of the Legal Aid Society's pilot project, states: "The nature of the hearings and the purpose of the judgments were rarely explained to the children, who sometimes realized the seriousness of their situation only when they were placed in detention, and who had no way of knowing whether the testimony offered against them was legal."
1981	The Ombudsman Office for Children is created in Norway after passage of legislation in Norway's parliament, the Storting. Norway recognizes the need to strengthen child advocacy, "promote the interests of children vis-à-vis public and private authorities, and . . . follow the development of conditions under which children grow up."
1982	In *Santosky v. Kramer*, the U.S. Supreme Court decides that clear and convincing evidence is required before parental rights can be severed by the state.
1982	The children's ombudsman's office of Finland is created as part of the Mannerheim League for Child Welfare; it has no official status and is funded by private grants and government money. The office provides independent legal information and counsel to children, seeks to influence legislation, and offers information to professionals who work with children and young people.
1982	The European Human Rights Commission affirms Sweden's 1979 law prohibiting physical punishment of children. The commission rejects an appeal by Swedish parents that the ban on parental punishment violates their right to respect for family life.
1982	The U.S. Supreme Court decides that New York State may constitutionally prohibit dissemination of pornographic depictions of

children, in *New York v. Ferber*.

1983   The report *Youth and Policy*, issued in Great Britain, reports that in 1977, 280,000 children lived in poverty, and between 1979 and 1981, the number of children living below the poverty line doubled. By 1981, there were 879,000 children in families receiving supplementary financial aid, and 660,000 children living in single-parent families receiving supplementary aid.

1983   The Child Custody and Right of Access Act is passed in Finland. The law stresses some general principles: "A child should be brought up in a secure and stimulating environment and should receive an education that corresponds to his wishes, inclinations, and talents. A child shall be brought up in a spirit of understanding, security, and love."

1984   The Police and Criminal Evidence Act is passed by Parliament in Great Britain. The act sets out rules for questioning of suspects, and in the case of juveniles, makes it a practical necessity to shift the traditional practice of questioning them in their homes to questioning them at the police station; the act also requires that if a parent cannot be contacted or found, those under the age of 16 years must be questioned in the presence of a social worker or of an adult not employed by the police.

1984   In Scotland, the Citizens' Rights Office publishes *Basic Rights: Information for Young People in Scotland*. The report describes the rights of young people at various ages.

1984   The Inter-African Committee is established in Addis Ababa, Ethiopia, and in Geneva, Switzerland, with the mission of combating harmful practices like genital mutilation and early marriage. Active in 25 countries, the committee encourages family planning and breast-feeding and provides educational materials.

1985   Child Workers in Asia is founded in Bangkok, Thailand, as a regional network of nongovernmental organizations and individuals involved in the issues of child labor in Asia. The organization's objectives include: "To promote the rights of working children at local, national, and regional levels within the context of the United Nations' Convention on Rights of the Child. . . . To provide a channel of communication and sharing of experiences, information, ideas among organizations and individuals involved in action against child labor."

1985   The Brazilian Movement for Street Children is created in Brazil, and the first national meeting of street children is held in Brasília. About 400 street children between the ages of 8 and 16 years meet to discuss issues of violence, health, work, education, and political organizing.

1985   In *New Jersey v. T. L. O.*, the U.S. Supreme Court rules that school officials need not obtain a search warrant to conduct a reasonable search of a student. When students are caught smoking in the lavatory in violation of school rules and one student's purse is searched, a pack of cigarettes, cigarette rolling papers, a small amount of marijuana, a pipe, a list of students on an index card, a substantial amount of dollar bills, and two letters implicating the student in dealing marijuana are discovered; the student moves to suppress this evidence on the basis that it is tainted by the allegedly unlawful search, but Justice Byron White declares that "the legality of a search of a student should depend simply on the reasonableness, under all circumstances of the search."

1985   In Great Britain, more than 200,000 young people participate in a national strike from school to protest government compulsory employment-training programs. Participants demand training programs at trade-union rates of pay, a guaranteed job once they finish the program, and a policy preventing government-sponsored youth training-program participants from replacing workers working for union wages.

1986   In China, a law is passed requiring nine years of compulsory education for children.

1986   The U.S. Supreme Court rules that schools may discipline students for lewd and indecent speech, in *Bethel School District No. 403 v. Fraser*. In 1983, a student delivering a nominating speech during an assembly referred to the candidate in a graphic and explicit sexual metaphor, causing students to hoot and yell and make graphic gestures; Chief Justice Warren E. Burger declares: "The undoubted freedom to advocate unpopular and controversial views in schools and classrooms must be balanced against the society's countervailing interest in teaching students the boundaries of socially appropriate behavior."

1986   A court in Great Britain decides, in *Gillick v. West Norfolk and Wisbech Area Health Authority*, that a girl under 16 years, sufficiently mature to understand her decision, is entitled to contraception without parental consent. The court decides the girl is sufficiently mature to understand the implications of the decision and thus is legally capable of making a valid decision.

1987   Plan International is established in Surrey, England, to work for the rights of street children. Regional program offices are located in eastern and southern Africa, the Caribbean and Central America, South Asia, South America, Southeast Asia, and West Africa.

1987   The Deputy Ombudsman for Children and Youth in British Columbia, Canada, is founded within the existing Office of Ombudsman; British Columbia is the only Canadian province to establish such an entity. Independent of government, the ombudsman has a mandate to protect and promote children's rights, to investigate complaints, and to ensure that children's rights are considered in decisions that affect them.

1987   Defensor de la Infancia (Ombudsman for Children) is organized in Costa Rica. It is mandated to protect and promote children's rights by investigating complaints of abuse and discrimination and by encouraging awareness of children's rights and the Convention on the Rights of the Child.

1987   The Kinder Kommision (Commission for children's concerns) is established in Germany to represent children's interests in a wide variety of issues, monitor the effects of legislation on children, and when necessary suggest amendments. The commission offers advice to the committees on women and youth, family affairs, and senior citizens in the Bundestag (Germany's parliament); funded by public money, the commission promotes the implementation of the Convention on the Rights of the Child.

1988   The UNICEF International Child Development Centre, also called the Innocenti Centre, is created in Florence, Italy, as an international forum on children's issues. The Center is located in the Spedale degli innocenti, a hospital established in 1445 to treat abandoned and poor children.

1988   In *Hazelwood School District v. Kuhlmeier*, the U.S. Supreme Court decides that school officials may exercise editorial control over the contents of school newspapers. After two former high school students sued the school district and school officials alleging their First Amendment rights were violated by the deletion of articles in a school newspaper, Justice Byron White finds that a school newspaper is not a forum for public expression and that the principal correctly concluded that certain articles were unsuitable for publication.

1988   A children's rights officer is appointed by the Leicestershire County Council in Great Britain to process complaints from children in the care of the local authority and to arbitrate disputes between children and social workers and child care authorities. The officer is mandated to help "all children in care by developing and promoting an awareness, sensitivity, and respect of, and for, their rights and interests."

1989   A study by the Massachusetts Bar Association of the legal needs of children is published in the *Child Advocacy and Protection Newsletter*. The recommendations include: "1. clear standards for intervening in families; 2. the appointment of counsel in cases where parental rights were to be terminated; 3. standards for termination; 4. a special children's service division within the program that provided public defenders; 5. a statute defining the role of the guardian ad litem; and 6. providing counsel for children in custody cases."

1989   Austria's Family Law and Youth Welfare Act is amended so that in dealing with children "using violence and inflicting physical or mental suffering is unlawful."

1989   The United Nations Convention on the Rights of the Child agrees that the best interests of the child shall be the main consideration in all actions about children; states are to take all measures to implement the rights in the convention; children's views are to be respected; and children must be protected from physical and mental abuse, neglect, and exploitation.

1989   The Children Act passed in Great Britain declares that the courts should, when deciding on issues affecting child welfare, ascertain the "wishes and feelings of the child concerned (considered in the light of his age and understanding)." Section 17 (10) states: "It shall be the duty of every local authority (a) to safeguard and promote the welfare of children within their area who are in need; and (b) so far as is consistent with that duty, to promote the upbringing of such children by their families, by providing a range and level of services appropriate to those children's needs."

1989   Lawyers for Human Rights and Legal Aid is established in Karachi, Pakistan, to provide free legal services in cases of child abuse, rape, torture, divorce, inheritance, illegal detention, and child custody. The organization also conducts training for paralegals and lobbies for reform of discriminatory legislation.

1989   The Office of the Commissioner for Children in New Zealand is created under the Children, Young Persons, and Family Act; though funded by public money, it operates independently of government. The office is charged with the welfare of children and young people and is required to conduct research studies, to monitor and report on legislation and practice, and to raise public awareness of child-related matters.

1989   The Association François-Xavier Bagnoud (AFXB) is created in Asia and offers programs for abandoned children in Goa (India), AFXB houses for abandoned children in Chiang Mai (Thailand) who are HIV-positive, and reintegration programs for former young sex workers in Myanmar (Burma).

1989   WOMANKIND Worldwide is established in London, England. It sponsors a program to combat female genital mutilation in Ghana and establishes programs to educate girls in several countries around the world.

1990   The American Civil Liberties Union (ACLU) begins litigation on behalf of child victims of child welfare services. This court action is a result of the ACLU's children's rights projects.

1990   Penal codes with provisions for children are passed in Laos. Section 92 penalizes the abduction and trading of children for ransom or sale; Sections 119–120m protect children against sexual abuse.

1990   EPOCH Worldwide (End Physical Punishment of Children) is founded in London, England, as a network of more than 70 organizations to lobby against the physical punishment of children.

1990   WAO Afrique is organized in Lomé, Togo, and works in Benin, Cameroon, Ivory Coast, Niger, Senegal, and Togo. The organization has conducted studies on child domestics, children in bondage, and trafficking in children and provides vocational training and literacy programs for child victims.

1990   The Open Line for Students of the Ministry of Education, Culture, and Sport in Israel addresses the concerns of pupils in schools and increases awareness of children's rights among education workers, parents, and pupils. The Open Line provides individual advocacy in cases of discrimination and injustice and makes recommendations regarding legislation and policy.

1990 The ombudsman for children and youth of the National Council for the Child in Israel is created to safeguard children's rights, to investigate and resolve complaints, and through the Centre for the Child and the Law to advocate in cases that require legal action. Privately funded and run by nongovernmental organizations, it serves all Israeli children, including members of the Ethiopian and Russian immigrant communities as well as Arab children.

1990 Defensoria de los Derechos de la Niñez de la Procuraduria de los Derechos Humanos (Office for the defense of children's rights of the procurator of human rights) in Guatemala is charged with promoting and protecting children's rights. It investigates individual cases of reported violations of the rights of children and monitors public institutions that provide services for children; it also holds educational and training programs for professionals and teachers.

1991 End Child Prostitution, Child Pornography, and the Trafficking of Children for Sexual Purposes (ECPAT) is established in Bangkok, Thailand, to work with nongovernmental organizations, UNICEF, and the International Labour Organization to monitor the activities of child traffickers and sex abusers and to find solutions to commercial sex abuse and child pornography. In 1996, ECPAT initiates the World Congress against the Commercial Sexual Exploitation of Children, held in Stockholm, Sweden.

1991 In his article "Bully/Victim Problems among Schoolchildren: Basic Facts and Effects of a School-Based Intervention Program" (published in D. Peeler and K. Rubin, eds., *The Development and Treatment of Childhood Aggression*), Dan Olwens discusses the results of his study of bullying among schoolchildren in Norway. With the use of a national questionnaire, Olwens finds that about 15 percent of pupils are involved in bully/victim problems; a program introduced in Norway to combat the problem reduces bullying incidents by 50 percent.

1991 A law criminalizing the abduction and sale of children is passed in China by the Standing Committee of the National People's Congress. The law makes illegal the "abduction for sale of women and children; kidnap of women and children, kidnap for purposes of blackmail; purchase of abducted and kidnapped women and children; abuse of office to hinder the rescue of abducted and kidnapped women and children."

1991 The Protection of Minors Act is passed in China, requiring parents to prohibit their children from engaging in prostitution.

1991 The Adoption Act is passed in China, prohibiting the sale of children for adoptions.

1991 In China, a law prohibiting the use of child laborers under the age of 16 years is passed.

1991   A population census in Nepal reveals that about 532,000 children between the ages of 10 and 14 years are working, 22 percent of the population of this age group, less than the 57 percent of children aged 10 to 14 who were working in 1981. Nevertheless, it appears that the actual number of working children is higher than these figures reveal because children below the age of 10 years are working.

1992   The International Labour Organization establishes the International Programme on the Elimination of Child Labour, to develop and implement a comprehensive, global program dealing with child labor and protecting working children. As of 1997, the following nations had signed a Memorandum of Understanding mandating the creation of a National Steering Committee of representatives from government, trade unions, and employers: Argentina, Bangladesh, Bolivia, Brazil, Chile, Costa Rica, Egypt, El Salvador, Guatemala, Honduras, India, Indonesia, Kenya, Nepal, Nicaragua, Pakistan, Panama, Philippines, Sri Lanka, Tanzania, Thailand, Turkey, Venezuela.

1992   The Supreme Court of Namibia rules that corporal punishment in schools and the prison system is unconstitutional.

1992   A national publicity campaign against the exploitation of child domestic workers is launched in Sri Lanka. The Department of Probation and Child Care creates a national telephone hot line and encourages concerned observers and affected children to report cases of abuse; the program ends in 1993, but while the hot line is active, hundreds of calls are logged and investigated.

1992   In *Lee et al. v. Weisman*, the U.S. Supreme Court decides that including clergy who offer prayers as part of an official public-school graduation violates the establishment clause of the Constitution. Justice Anthony Kennedy writes that "though the First Amendment does not allow the government to stifle prayers, . . . neither does it permit the government to undertake that task for itself."

1992   Brazil establishes a child workers' program of the National Confederation of Workers in Agriculture, uniting 24 state federations and 3,200 trade unions representing 9 million farm workers. The child workers' program has created an action program that includes distribution of a pamphlet on the rights of rural working children, a training course for union organizers and leaders on the issue of child labor, and efforts to involve parents in improving living conditions of children in rural areas.

1992   In Great Britain, the Children's Rights Development Unit is created to ensure that the implementation of the United Nations Convention on the Rights of the Child applies equally to all children of the Great Britain, that the work of the unit is informed by the views and experiences of children and young people, and that the unit's work enjoys the widest possible consultation and collaboration with experts in the field. The unit raises awareness of the convention and its possible implementation in law, social policy, and practice and monitors the progress toward implementation.

1992   The Children's Defense Fund issues *America's Children Falling Behind: The USA and the Convention on the Rights of the Child.* The report reveals that 14 million American children live in poverty; an estimated 10,000 children die each year as a direct result of that poverty; in 1991, there were 2.7 million cases of child abuse, three times as many as in 1980; criminal penalties in 24 states allow for the death penalty for children under the age of 18; 500,000 juveniles are imprisoned; 7 million children are working, including 2 million working illegally; and many children rarely have a say in judicial decisions determining their status in foster care, custody, or adoption cases.

1992   In *South Glamorgan County Council v. W. and B.*, the High Court in Great Britain decides that a 15-year-old girl can be removed from her home to a psychiatric unit although she had clearly refused assessment.

1992   In Zimbabwe, a law is passed overruling the 1989 decision of the Supreme Court to outlaw judicial whipping of juveniles.

1992   At the Children's Summit of South Africa, a representative group of young people adopts a charter of rights, including Article 5, which states: "All children have the right to be protected from all types of violence."

1992   In Thailand, the Development and Education Programme for Daughters and Communities is created to prevent child prostitution and child labor. The program provides alternative education to girls at high risk of exploitation: children from families in extreme poverty, children of tribal communities, children from broken homes, and children of drug-addicted parents.

1992   The U.S. National Institute of Justice Study of the Department of Justice issues *The Cycle of Violence*, by C. Spatz Widom. According to the study, being abused as a child or being a victim of child neglect increases by 53 percent the likelihood of being arrested as a juvenile; being arrested as an adult by 38 percent; and being arrested for a violent crime by 38 percent.

1992   The Consortium for Street Children UK is organized in London, England, and aids a variety of organizations working with street children in the developing world and in Europe.

1992   Kind en Gezin, an ombudsman service for children, is established in Belgium to look out for the interests of children under three years of age. Complaints on behalf of children are brought by adults to the Kind en Gezin, and the agency attempts to safeguard and improve the way children are treated by child care agencies and institutions.

1992   The Defensoria Municipal del Niño y Adolescente is founded in Peru as part of the Child and Adolescent Code under law decree 26102. The agency offers individual casework but not legal advocacy and is charged with encouraging family ties and the recognition of paternity; it intervenes or mediates to defend the rights of children in cases where the courts are not involved.

1992   The Centre for Children Working on the Streets of Ankara is organized in Turkey by the municipality of Greater Ankara, with support from the International Labour Organization's International Programme on the Elimination of Child Labour. The center is created to improve the working conditions of children in the short run and to work to prevent child labor in the long run; in 1994–97, the center encourages 1,200 children of the 5,000 it reachs to return to school.

1992   The Campaign Against Child Labour is active in 12 states of India, with 700 members, including trade unions, women's organizations, children's organizations, academic institutions, and concerned citizens. Its objectives are "to create awareness on child labour; highlight violations inflicted upon child labourers; promote justice through fact-finding and litigation; review policies and legislation on child labour; and to put forth successful strategies and alternatives for the rehabilitation of working children."

1993   The Primary Education Act comes into effect in Bangladesh. The act establishes compulsory primary education for children six years and older; by 1995, enrollment of children aged 6 to 10 years old is 82 percent, and 44 percent have reached the fifth grade.

1993   In Sweden, the office of the children's ombudsman is created through an act of Parliament passed after the Convention on the Rights of the Child is ratified. Funded by public money, the ombudsman is charged with safeguarding the rights, needs, and interest of children and young persons and providing children with a voice.

1993   Fe y Alegría (Faith and Joy Integral Popular Education Movement Association) in Peru is a church-affiliated network of education programs associated with the International Labour Organization's International Programme on the Elimination of Child Labour; it provides education for children 5 to 16 years old who are in danger of dropping out and emphasizes practical and work skills.

1993   The American Bar Association publishes *America's Children at Risk*, which states that poverty influences every aspect of a young person's life, including health and how well he or she does in school; citing figures showing that 24 percent of U.S. preschool children live in impoverished families, the study finds poverty extending throughout the country, in rural as well as urban areas. The report recommends that lawyers work to improve the condition of American children, not only by offering legal representation in child-law cases involving education, abuse, foster care, juvenile justice, and health care, but also by supporting legislative and administrative reform.

1993   The New Zealand Commissioner for Children publishes *Think about It: Is Hitting Your Child a Good Idea?*, launching a campaign to remove the statutory right of parents to use physical punishment with their children.

1993 The Summary Report of the American Psychological Association Commission on Violence and Youth, *Violence and Youth: Psychology's Response*, declares that "youth at risk of becoming extremely aggressive and violent tend to share common experiences that appear to place them on a 'trajectory towards violence.' These youth tend to have experienced weak bonding to caretakers in infancy and ineffective parenting techniques, including lack of supervision, inconsistent discipline, highly punitive or abusive treatment, and failure to reinforce positive, pro-social behavior."

1993 In *Re S*, a court in Great Britain rules that an 11-year-old boy cannot invoke Section 8 of the 1989 Children Act to involve himself in decisions about family breakup. Although children's wishes are to be considered and respected, the law must protect the interests of children who are vulnerable and lacking insight.

1993 In Great Britain a court decides in *Re H* that a youth 15.5 years old can, under Section 8 of the Children Act, be involved, with his solicitor, in court proceedings. Mrs. Justice Booth notes that the boy was closely involved with the proceedings and had sufficient understanding of the process and was therefore able to keep his own solicitor and legal representation; nevertheless, she rules that the official solicitor should continue to be involved, serve as a special adviser to the court, and bring any evidence that might not have been put before it.

1993 In *Re C*, a court in Great Britain decides that a 13-year-old girl cannot attend High Court appeals. A girl in care by the local authority wants to return to live with her ill, 64-year-old divorced father; she was present throughout the proceedings in the family court after the guardian ad litem, according to court rules, decided that attending court proceedings would be in the best interests of the child. Yet when she goes to the High Court, Mr. Justice Waite objects, stating: "young children should be discouraged from attending High Court appeals from justices in family proceedings." Declaring that a child should not have to listen to lawyers debating her future and that she is too young to carry the weight of responsibility for a parent who might play on her feelings, Justice Waite rules against her desire to live with her father.

1993 In *Re F*, a court in Great Britain decides that boys 12 and 9 years old can refuse to see their transsexual father even though professionals and the mother recommend the visits. *Re F*, according to Cristina Lyon and Nigel Parton, in "Children's Rights and the Children Act 1989," in *The Handbook of Children's Rights,* is an example "where[, if] the children's views are considered by the judges to be 'right' ones, then the judges are happy to go along with those views."

1993 After James Bulger, a 2-year-old boy, is abducted and murdered in Liverpool, England, by two 10-year-old boys, the boys are held in separate units for six months before trial without any form of treatment, to prevent prejudicing the prosecution. Tried in adult court, the boys are sentenced by the judge to be detained "at her Majesty's pleasure" (an indeterminate sentence); the judge declares their actions "an act of unparalleled evil and barbarity," reveals their identities, and recommends that they be imprisoned for a minimum of 8 years, which is increased to 10 years by the lord chief justice and then to 15 years by the home secretary. In 1997, the House of Lords judges the method of sentencing employed by the home secretary to have been unlawful.

1994   The results of a national survey of children in the United States ages 10 to 16 years, published in *Pediatrics* by D. Finkelhor and J. Dziuba-Leatherman, show that young people are reporting that they have been victims of violence at rates far exceeding official U.S. government statistics. The incidence of rape is five times higher than official statistics; 25 percent of those surveyed report they have been the victim of violence other than corporal punishment during the last year; more than 33 percent report they were victims of attempted or completed violence.

1994   In India, the Rugmark Foundation, an independent body offering a voluntary program of certification for the carpet industry, is created to ensure and certify that carpet makers are not employing child laborers. The foundation carries out spot checks to ensure compliance; 300,000 children are estimated to be working in the carpet belt of Uttar Pradesh.

1994   The Children's Rights Project of Human Rights Watch is organized in New York to monitor children's rights issues around the world. The project has been active in Brazil, Bulgaria, China, Great Britain, Guatemala, India, Jamaica, Kenya, Liberia, Mexico, Myanmar, Nepal, Pakistan, Romania, Sudan, Turkey, and the United States; it publishes reports on children's rights, violence to street children, and illegal detention of children.

1994   In Brazil, the National Forum for the Prevention and Eradication of Child Labour is coordinated by the ministry of labor and is concerned with child labor issues and charged with eliminating the worst forms of child labor. In 1997, an estimated 2,100 children leave work in charcoal and maté production in Mato Gross do Sul, and 8,000 child workers leave sisal and quarry work in Bahia to return to school.

1994   A labor-force survey conducted in Turkey reveals that of 11.9 million children aged 6 to 14 years, nearly 4 million work, and 13 percent of children in this age group are not attending school.

1995   *Hazardous Child Labour in Bangladesh*, a study by the Bangladesh Ministry of Labour and Manpower and UNICEF, identifies 27 hazardous economic activities involving Bangladeshi children, including battery-recharging–shop work; brick and stone crushing, car and metal-furniture painting, spray painting, child prostitution, and rickshaw pulling.

1995   The Philippine National Statistics Office and the International

Labour Organization's International Programme on the Elimination of Child Labour undertake a national survey of child labor in the Philippines, designed to develop a dependable database for policy formation and to craft a national program on child labor.

1995   In the Netherlands, the Nike Fair Play campaign is undertaken to educate young people who buy Nike sports products about the working conditions faced by Nike employees in the developing world, especially the many young women workers. Nike Fair Play demands that Nike pay more than the prevailing minimum wages in these countries, abide by international health and safety precautions, and implement monitoring of working conditions by an independent body.

1995   The Bunyad Literacy Community Council program, with support from the International Labour Organization's International Programme on the Elimination of Child Labour, begins a literacy program in rural carpet-weaving communities in Pakistan, which reveals that some carpet-weaving children work with families at home, while others go off to work in loom sheds. It is estimated that 80 percent of the total production of hand-knotted carpets are made in remote villages of Punjab; the program initiates local family education committees and selects local personnel, establishes teacher training and classes for girls and boys, and has now been enlarged to involve more than 5,000 children working primarily in soccer-ball stitching in the Sialkot district.

1995   The U.S. Supreme Court, in *Vernonia's School District 47J v. Acton*, decides that school districts have the right to institute random urinalysis drug testing of student athletes. Justice Scalia declares: "Taking into account . . .—the decreased expectation of privacy, the relative unobtrusiveness of the search, and the severity of the need met by the search—we conclude Vernonia's Policy is reasonable and hence constitutional."

1995   The African Network for the Prevention and Protection against Child Abuse and Neglect is founded in Nairobi, Kenya. Active in many African countries, the network attacks child abuse and neglect issues, including physical and sexual trauma, armed conflict, and child labor.

1995   Free the Children is established by a 12-year-old Canadian boy, Craig Kielburger, to organize opposition to the evils of child labor in the world. After reading about the murder of a Pakistani boy forced to work in a rug factory, Kielburger raises money from the Ontario Federation of Labour and begins to organize chapters in North America; Free the Children relies mostly on the labor and contributions of young people; it has 5,000 members and chapters in 20 countries.

1995   The National Council for Children's Rights is created in Denmark in the ministry of social affairs. The council is mandated to establish contact with children of representative social and age groups and to facilitate communication between children and the government.

1995   An ombudsman is created for children in Iceland by an act of parliament; appointed by the president, the ombudsman reports to the prime minister, but operates independently of the government and is mandated to safeguard the interests, needs, and rights of children. The ombudsman provides proposals for policy and compliance with international law, particularly the Convention on the Rights of the Child.

1995   Care & Fair—Carpet Trade against Child Labour is organized by European businesses involved in the carpet trade. Members certify that their suppliers and producers do not use child labor, and Care & Fair supports projects in India, Nepal, and Pakistan to build schools and provide free medical care to young people.

1995   A report of the Commission on Children and Violence, convened by the Gulbenkian Foundation in London, notes the following incidences of violence to children in Great Britain: homicide, 0.007 per 1,000 children; child abduction, 0.026 per 1,000 children; sexual assault, 0.26 per 1,000 children; emotional abuse, 0.3 per 1,000 children; sexual abuse, 0.7 per 1,000 children; physical abuse, 1 per 1,000 children; assault outside the home, 330 per 1,000 children; bullying at school, 580 per 1,000 children; physical punishment, 770 per 1,000 children.

1995   Human Rights Watch Children's Rights Project issues a report titled *Generation under Fire: Children and Violence in Colombia*. According to the organization: "Street children and other youths in Colombia face an extraordinary level of danger from both uniformed members of the security forces and police-tolerated private vigilantes. . . . Of the 2,190 murders of children in 1993, only twelve cases have resulted in trials."

1995   Human Rights Watch issues a report titled *U.S.: A World Leader in Executing Juveniles*. According to the organization, "More juvenile offenders sit on death row in the United States than in any other country in the world. . . . Nine juvenile offenders whose crimes were committed when they were under the age of eighteen have been executed in the United States since the U.S. Supreme Court reinstated the death penalty in 1976."

1995   G. Boswell's *Violent Victims: The Prevalence of Abuse and Loss in the Lives of Section 53 Offenders* is issued by The Prince's Trust in London. The study finds that 72 percent of the young people who committed murder or other grave crimes had been the victim of abuse; 57 percent had experienced the death or loss of someone significant; 35 percent had experienced both abuse and loss; and a total of 91 percent had experienced either one or the other.

1995   *Resource Guidelines: Improving Court Practice in Child Abuse and Neglect Cases* is issued by David E. Grossman and the Victims of Child Abuse Project of the National Council of Juvenile and Family Court Judges. According to the study: "These guidelines recognize the need to assure safe and permanent homes for abused or neglected children and the prominent role of the judiciary in the process."

1995	Human Rights Watch issues the report *Children in Sudan: Slaves, Street Children, and Child Soldiers*. According to the organization, "the Khartoum government turns a blind eye to Sudanese army and militia forces who capture southern and Nuba children and subject them to forced labor or slavery. . . . Many alleged street children are not street children at all, but were living with their families, and were captured while they were running errands such as going to market."
1995	*United States: Children in Confinement in Louisiana* is issued by the Human Rights Watch Children's Rights Program. According to the organization, "substantial numbers of the children confined by the State of Louisiana in its four post-adjudication correctional facilities are regularly physically abused by guards, are improperly kept in isolation for long periods of time, and are improperly restrained by handcuffs."
1995	The Bangladesh Garment Manufacturers and Exporters Association, UNICEF, and the International Labour Organization sign a memorandum of understanding agreeing that Bangladesh will phase out child workers under the age of 14 years and will discontinue hiring underage children; will place the children removed from garment factories in educational programs with a monthly stipend; and will offer the children's jobs to qualified adult family members.
1995	Twenty-eight monitors are trained to make regular inspections of factory sites in Dhaka and Chittagong, Bangladesh, for child laborers and to monitor the school attendance of children. In coordination with the memorandum signed by the Bangladesh Garment Manufacturers Association, UNICEF, and the International Labour Organization, more than 8,000 children are withdrawn from factories and placed in schools; in 1997, a surprise monitoring program finds that only 12 percent of factories are employing children, compared with 43 percent in 1995.
1996	A pilot project to eliminate child labor in the shoe-production center of Rio Grande do Sul, Brazil, is undertaken by a Brazilian nongovernmental organization, with support from the International Labour Organization. The program is designed to promote labor inspections, withdrawal of children from shoe production and participation in formal schools and education centers, negotiation with the shoe industry to eliminate child labor, and initial withdrawal in the municipalities of Novo Hamburgo and Dois Irmãos of 120 children from work in the shoe industry.
1996	In Italy, the supreme court prohibits the use of violence for educational purposes in schools and in families.
1996	The International Federation of Football Associations (FIFA), the International Textile, Garment, and Leather Workers Federation, and the International Federation of Commercial, Clerical, Professional, and Technical Employees agree on a code of conduct regarding child labor. The code stipulates that companies licensed to produce sports equipment for FIFA will implement and respect the following: no use of forced or bonded labor, equal-

opportunities policies, no child labor, only workers over 15 years, freedom of association and collective bargaining to be respected, payment of legal minimum wage or industry standards, reasonable hours of work, and little use of temporary or casual labor.

1996   A national child-labor survey conducted in Pakistan discovers that 8.3 percent (3.3 million) of the 40 million children aged 5 to 14 years are working full-time. A large proportion of child workers are employed more than 56 hours a week, and 7.0 percent of working children suffer from illness or are injured.

1996   A ministerial notice to screen Chinese children being adopted abroad is passed in China.

1996   The U.S. Department of Health and Human Services issues *Child Maltreatment, 1996: Reports from the States to the National Child Abuse and Neglect Data System*, a report documenting more than 2 million reports of alleged child mistreatment involving more than 3 million American children in 1996. The report notes that the national rate of children who are reported is 44 per 1,000 children in the population; a greater proportion of neglect and medical-neglect victims are children younger than eight years, while a greater proportion of physical-, sexual-, and emotional-abuse victims are older than eight years. The report profiles the perpetrators of child maltreatment and notes that 77 percent of perpetrators are parents and that 11 percent are other relatives of the victim.

1996   *The Executive Summary of the Third National Incidence Study of Child Abuse and Neglect (NIS)*, by Andrea J. Sedlak and Diane D. Broadhurst, reports the findings from the Third NIS conducted for the U.S. Department of Health and Human Services. The summary finds that "a child's risk of experiencing harm-causing abuse or neglect in 1993 was one and one-half times the child's risk in 1986. . . . Physical abuse nearly doubled, sexual abuse more than doubled, and emotional abuse, physical neglect, and emotional neglect were all more than two and one-half times their NIS-2 levels."

1996   Human Rights Watch issues the report *Children of Bulgaria: Police Violence and Arbitrary Confinement*. According to the organization, "Human Rights Watch interviewed street children in five cities in Bulgaria (Sofia, Plovdiv, Varna, Pleven, and Sliven) and has concluded that street children, who are predominantly of Roma (Gypsy) origin, are frequently subjected to harassment and physical abuse by police, both on the street and in detention. . . . Roma street children are also frequently the victims of racially motivated violent attacks by skinhead and other youth gangs."

1996   The Child Abuse Prevention and Treatment Act Amendments (Public Law 104-235) are enacted by the U.S. Congress to establish the National Clearinghouse on Child Abuse and Neglect Information.

1996   The Department of Health and Social Affairs in Sweden reports, concerning the incidents of physical punishment of children, that as of 1994 only 11 percent of the Swedish population still endorses the physical punishment of children, compared with 65 percent who approved of it 20 years before. Only 1 percent of the large numbers of 15-year-olds who participated in the study report ever having been hit by an adult, compared with up to 25 percent of children in some age groups in Great Britain (and other countries) who report having been physically punished.

1996 The United Nations General Assembly issues a report titled *Impact of Armed Conflict on Children*. Graça Machel of Mozambique writes: "In the past decade, 2 million children have been killed in armed conflict. Three times as many have been seriously injured or permanently disabled. Millions of others have been forced to witness or even take part in horrifying acts of violence."

1996 A status report on the efforts of Morocco to enforce the Convention on the Rights of the Child is published in the newsletter of Defence for Children International. According to Victoria Bateg, "It drew attention to the differences in treatment of children in urban and rural areas, and between legitimate and illegitimate children . . . [and] no legislation exists for the protection of child victims of family violence, conforming to Article 19 of the Convention, although the judge may take specific protection measures at his own discretion."

1996 A status report on the efforts of Hong Kong to enforce the Convention on the Rights of the Child is published in the newsletter of Defence for Children International. According to Stéphanie Schwarz, "The Committee noted that the extremely low age of seven for criminal responsibility is in contradiction with the spirit of the Convention . . . [and] strongly recommended that this aspect of penal law should be reviewed."

1996 A status report on the efforts of Uruguay to enforce the Convention on the Rights of the Child is published in the newsletter of Defence for Children International. According to Alex Lorite, "The Committee expressed its concern about the possibility, on the basis of a decree of July 1995, of young people in conflict with the law being jailed in prisons for adults. . . . Finally, the particular question of children 'disappeared' during the dictatorship period was raised."

1997 An agreement on child labor and the sporting goods industry is issued in Sialkot, Pakistan. According to Christian Aid's *A Sporting Chance: Tackling Child Labour in India's Sports Goods Industry*, three-quarters of the world's hand-stitched footballs are made in the northeastern Pakistani city of Sialkot and its neighboring villages; the agreement stipulates that subcontractors will be subject to inspections to ensure that they are not hiring underage workers, and measures will be taken to ensure that the elimination of child labor does not cause other serious problems in the communities.

1997 The findings of the jury at the second National Convention of

Child Labourers in India, *Testimonies of Abuse, Dreams of Happiness*, include recommendations that no child under the age of 14 years be employed and that free education be provided to all children.

1997   The child-labor inspection program begins in Turkey, with 108 labor inspectors trained in courses designed in conjunction with the International Labour Organization. The program's strategy emphasizes persuasion and collaboration rather than punitive action.

1997   The International Labour Organization establishes the Statistical Information and Monitoring Programme on Child Labour, created to collect data on child labor in 12 countries, including South Africa, the West Bank and Gaza, Ukraine, Trinidad and Tobago, and the Republic of Georgia.

1997   The Jagaran Group is established in Kathmandu, Nepal, by a group of former street children involved in street theater. Organized as a scrap-collection center employing street children and acting as a focus for nonformal education, the group aims to prevent children from becoming street children, to build self-respect among street children through constructive action, and to inform governmental and nongovernmental organizations about the real lives of street children.

1997   A status report on the efforts of Myanmar (Burma) to enforce the Convention on the Rights of the Child is published in the newsletter of Defence for Children International. According to Safir Syed, "The Committee questioned the delegation about the large number of girls raped by soldiers; the recruitment of young boys into the army; the use of child porters for infrastructure projects; and the traumatic impact of forced relocation on children. . . . In other areas, the Committee recommended urgent measures to combat sexual abuse and child labour."

1997   The Defence for Children International (DCI) Network on Juvenile Justice is founded in Geneva, Switzerland, following a seminar in Dakar, Senegal, on children in conflict with the law. The DCI Network facilitates the exchange of information on juvenile-justice issues and coordinates activities related to juvenile justice; it helps participating states meet the requirements of the United Nations Convention on the Rights of the Child when designing or modifying juvenile-justice systems.

1997   The Ministry of Women, Children, and Social Welfare of Nepal, with the support of UNICEF and the International Labour Organization, establishes the National Task Force on Trafficking to deal with the trafficking and sale of girls. The task force begins a dialogue with India to strengthen prevention and control cross-border trafficking in children.

1997   The Forum on Children and Violence is organized in London, England, by the Commission on Children and Violence to work for an end to violence involving children.

1997   A status report on Syria's efforts to enforce the Convention on the Rights of the Child is published in the newsletter of Defence for Children International. According to Martine Wierenga, "A particular group of children in Syria that received the Committee's attention was the stateless Syrian-born Kurdish children. Those children are either considered as foreigners or as maktoumeen (unregistered). . . . Another issue of concern was the low age of criminal responsibility, which stands at 7."

1997   A status report on New Zealand's efforts to enforce the Convention on the Rights of the Child is published in the newsletter of Defence for Children International. According to Martine Wierenga, "The Committee expressed a number of specific concerns, such as the phenomenon of teenage suicide. New Zealand has the highest female teenage suicide rate in the world. . . . The Committee noted the absence of an overall strategy for children, affirming that children did not seem to be a high priority."

1997   A status report on the efforts of Mauritius to enforce the Convention on the Rights of the Child is published in the newsletter of Defence for Children International. According to Victoria Bateg, "Although the principle of non-discrimination is enshrined in the Constitution of Mauritius, there was evidence of systematic disregard for this principle in relation to the status of girls, illegitimate children, children from minority groups, and disabled children."

1997   A status report on Slovenia's efforts to enforce the Convention on the Rights of the Child is published in the newsletter of Defence for Children International. According to Anne Grandjean, areas of concern are the increased unemployment and lawlessness in Slovenia, which "inevitably have an impact on children (in the form of increased child abuse, for example)."

1997   A status report on Nigeria's efforts to enforce the Convention on the Rights of the Child is published in the newsletter of Defence for Children International. According to Martine Wierenga, "Among these [areas of concern] was the very low age of criminal responsibility in Nigeria, which is currently age seven. . . . The Committee was also deeply concerned about the application of capital punishment to children below the age of eighteen. . . . Another area of concern raised by the Committee was the fact that certain traditional practices like early marriage, female genital mutilation, and widowhood practices still exist in Nigeria, though in small numbers."

1997   A status report on Azerbaijan's efforts to enforce the Convention on the Rights of the Child is published in the newsletter of Defence for Children International. According to Arianna Saulim, "The Committee expressed concern that there was a lack of family planning and the continued use of abortion for birth control. Crime among juveniles and drug abuse has been increasing, and the Committee recommended that reforms be carried out to guarantee adequate provisions for juvenile justice."

1997   A status report on Ghana's efforts to enforce the Convention on the Rights of the Child is published in the newsletter of Defence for Children International. According to Marian Fynn, "The incidence of street children in Ghana caused a lot of concern. Street children of all ages seems to be growing in number. . . . The Delegation mentioned that different forms of domestic abuse and poverty have brought these children to the streets."

1997   A status report on Paraguay's efforts to enforce the Convention on the Rights of the Child is published in the newsletter of Defence for Children International. According to Gaelle Haeny, "The Committee regretted that the age of sexual consent is low and not standardised (14 for girls, 16 for boys) and deplored the fact that no modification is being envisaged by the State Party."

1997   A status report on Bulgaria's efforts to enforce the Convention on the Rights of the Child is published in the newsletter of Defence for Children International. According to Safir Syed, "The brutality of police and state officials against children during interrogation, in police detention, and in labour schools, chronicled in the Human Rights Watch report, was simply unacceptable and warranted swift action on behalf of the state. . . . The prohibition of corporal punishment and sexual abuse needed to be clearly delineated in the law, and the punishment of those responsible had to be meted out in a manner that would restore children's faith in the system."

1997   A status report on Ethiopia's efforts to enforce the Convention on the Rights of the Child is published in the newsletter of Defence for Children International. According to Martine Wierenga, "Among the more specific concerns discussed by the Committee were harmful traditional practices in Ethiopia, early marriage in particular."

1997   A status report on Panama's efforts to enforce the Convention on the Rights of the Child is published in the newsletter of Defence for Children International. According to Alex Lorite, "The Committee pointed to the fact that 68% of children below   sixteen years of age were 'poor.' . . . On juvenile justice, the Committee stressed that the age limit for imprisonment was too low, noting that there was no lower age for criminal responsibility."

1997   A status report on the efforts of Bangladesh to enforce the Convention on the Rights of the Child is published in the newsletter of Defence for Children International. According to Samantha Schasberger, "The Chittagong Hill Tracts Children . . . are part of a minority group which has come into conflict with the Bangladeshi army. . . . Various NGOs raised the issue of the violation of the rights of these children in their reports to the Committee."

1997   A status report on Cuba's efforts to enforce the Convention on the Rights of the Child is published in the newsletter of Defence for Children International. According to Judith Le Large, "The Committee expressed its concern about the fact that, in many cases, young people in conflict with the law are being jailed in prisons for adults because of lack of space in youth institutions. . . . The Committee expressed concern about the young age at which girls could marry, 14, as opposed to 16 for boys."

1997   A joint statement by the participants in the Nepal-India Cooper-ation Meeting against Trafficking and Prevention is issued. The statement declares: "We are fully aware that trafficking and sell-ing in girls from Nepal to India has been increasing with every passing year and in order to prevent and control such crime, we seriously realise that the administrative cooperation across the border has to be strengthened to work together in all different points: points of origin, point of border, and point of destination."

1997   A story bringing attention to the trafficking of children is pub-lished in the newsletter of Child Workers in Asia. Harka Maya, a Nepali, the youngest daughter of a *kami* (untouchable) caste family, has a father, four sisters, and a brother; she is finally res-cued from a brothel by Child Workers in Nepal. "I tried to run away more than three times from the brothel, but I failed. I even tried to kill myself to be free of such slavery, but I was strictly watched by brothel security guards who put an end to my attempts."

1997   A report on the trafficking of women and children in Pakistan, issued by the Lawyers for Human Rights and Legal Aid and pub-lished in the newsletter of Child Workers in Asia, states that in poor Bangladeshi families fathers may allow their children and wives to work abroad in hopes of having a better life; agents charge from $145 to $453 to take them to Pakistan; some women and children are abducted from outside their homes; crying chil-dren are left behind to die; the children and women are forced to walk long distances from Bangladesh to Pakistan and once in Karachi are kept crowded together in small rooms in the slums. A fake marriage takes place, and the buyer marries the woman he has bought, thus legalizing the transaction; the buyer either sells the woman or child for profit or keeps her in a brothel.

1997   A report on the trafficking of Laotian children, "The Trafficking in Women and Children in the Mekong Sub-region," by Vitit Muntarbhorn, is published in the 1997 newsletter of Child Work-ers in Asia. According to Muntarbhorn, many of the more than 15,000 young people who seek work in Thailand leave Laos ille-gally. Because they have few skills and limited employment opportunities, girls are easily lured into prostitution, working as hostesses in bars.

1997   A United Nations report condemning violent images and toys is published in the UNICEF International Child Centre's "Children and Violence" issue of *Innocenti Digest*. The report states that violent images in the media are thought to increase levels of interpersonal violence; Sweden has banned such toys, and Spain and Germany forbid their advertisement; countries should seek to replace such toys with more constructive playthings.

1997   The International Children's Parliament is held at the Common-wealth Children's Summit in Edinburgh, Scotland. Children from England, South Africa, Antigua, Scotland, Wales, the Baha-mas, Canada, and India meet and craft a Children's Bill of Rights, whose provisions include the following: "Children should

have the right to claim our own identity, name and nationality. .
. . Children have the right to be loved, to be cared for, to feel safe
and secure, and to feel that they belong to a family or a
community. . . . Children should have freedom from war and not
be forced to fight for their country."

1997   The Adoption and Safe Families Act is passed by the U.S. Congress. The act amends Section 471(a)(15) of the Social Security
Act to provide that the child's health and safety should be the
primary concern; efforts should be made to preserve family structure, to eliminate the need to put children in foster care, and to
return children to their home from the foster family.

1998   A status report on Ireland's efforts to enforce the Convention on
the Rights of the Child is published in the newsletter of Defence
for Children International. According to Shanaz Sajadi, the Irish
delegation reported that one of every three students from working-class families drops out of school before obtaining a certificate; the age of criminal responsibility is seven; nearly 6,000
cases of sexual abuse of children have been brought a year.

1998   A status report on the efforts of Micronesia to enforce the Convention on the Rights of the Child is published in the newsletter
of Defence for Children International. According to Caroline
Bourquin, Micronesia accepts two forms of adoption—traditional
and legal; traditional adoption is common, and children remain
in contact with their biological families.

1998   A status report on the efforts of Libya to enforce the Convention
on the Rights of the Child is published in the newsletter of
Defence for Children International. According to Christine
Caputo, minors under 15 cannot be employed; children under 14
are generally not considered to be criminally responsible. The
Committee expressed concern for the status of children born outside marriage because Islamic tradition does not permit their
existence, and the Libyan delegation explained that there are
institutions for these children, and that "illegitimate" children
enjoy full rights.

1998   A status report on Algeria's efforts to enforce the Convention on
the Rights of the Child is published in the newsletter of Defence
for Children International. The committee expressed concern
that children between 16 and 18 years, suspected of terrorist
activities, are tried by criminal courts as adults; though it is illegal to employ children, there was concern that the law may not
be enforced in rural areas and in the informal sector of the economy.

1998   A national plan of action against trafficking in children is developed in Nepal following a meeting of 60 representatives of government and nongovernmental organizations, employers, unions,
United Nations agencies, and law enforcement in Kathmandu.

1998   The Kamaiya Liberation Forum is created in Nepal to assert the
rights of the Kamaiyas, indigenous peoples of the Terai region in
southern Nepal, half of whom work for landlords. Children as

young as five years work as cowherds and perform other labor for the landlords.

1998 *Trafficking in Children for Labour Exploitation in the Mekong Sub-region: A Framework for Action* is published following an International Labour Organization conference in Bangkok, Thailand. The report estimates that of the foreign prostitutes in Thailand, 30 percent are younger than 18 years, and 75 percent started to work as prostitutes when they were younger than 18; the young women trafficked to Thailand for prostitution come from Myanmar, Yunnan Province (in China), Laos, and South Vietnam, and 15 percent are under 15 years of age.

1998 Child Workers in Asia sponsors a conference on migrant children in the Mekong region of Southeast Asia, with representatives from Thailand, Cambodia, and Laos. A summary of the conference reports that foreign child beggars are organized by gangsters and suffer extreme abuse; the most vulnerable children are those who cross into Thailand from Laos to work illegally.

1998 Benetton, the Italian textile company, suspends contracts with six Turkish companies when it learns that the companies employ children under the age of 14 years in the manufacture of garments. Benetton announces that it is sending investigators to Turkey following charges by Turkish trade unions of child-labor violations by the Turkish company Bermuda Tekstil.

1999 A resolution on Thai child workers is issued at the fifth Regional Consultation of Child Workers in Asia, held in Bangkok, Thailand. The resolution states that laws protecting children and labor laws should be strictly enforced, and the health and welfare of children in the workplace should be protected; employers must give children a choice of employment appropriate to their ages and arrange for breaks, medical checkups, and good food.

2000 Human Rights Watch reports that schoolgirls in South Africa, of every race and economic group, are harassed and subjected to sexual violence on a daily basis. Girls describe being raped in bathrooms and empty classrooms, being verbally degraded, and being subjected to sexual advances by teachers and other students.

2000 Human Rights Watch has documented numerous instances of abuse by rebel forces in Sierra Leone, Africa, including rapes of girls as young as 11 years old.

2000 The United Nations estimates that 92 percent of children orphaned because of acquired immunodeficiency syndrome (AIDS) are in sub-Saharan Africa. In Africa, extended families usually care for orphans and children needing special attention; with so many deaths from AIDS, often no family remains to look after the orphans. The United Nations estimates that about 11 million children under the age of 15 in sub-Saharan Africa have lost their mothers or both parents to AIDS.

2000 Human Rights Watch reports that children born in the Dominican Republic to Haitian parents are routinely denied identity documents even though the constitution grants citizenship to everyone born in the country. Children without documents are denied high school diplomas and are often not permitted to take mandatory examinations necessary to enter secondary school.

2000   A United Nations report estimates that between 15 and 30 percent of newly recruited soldiers in the Democratic Republic of Congo are children under 18 years of age, with many under the age of 12.

2001   In Northern Ireland, parents and politicians say that police fail to protect Catholic-minority schoolchildren from attacks by Loyalist protesters. Protesters try to keep children from reaching a Catholic school in a Protestant-dominated enclave in Belfast; they spit, curse, and throw stones at the children and their parents.

2001   The United Nations Children's Fund (UNICEF) supervises the demobilization of more than 2,500 children soldiers between the ages of 8 and 18 years from the Sudan People's Liberation Army in southern Sudan. Demobilizations will continue until all of the estimated 10,000 child soldiers in Sudan are demobilized.

2001   The Democratic Republic of Congo agrees not to put to death four child soldiers and imprisons them instead.

2001   In Iran, the death sentence of a 13-year-old boy is commuted to life in prison, but Amnesty International states that even life imprisonment violates international standards, which specify no capital punishment or life imprisonment without the possibility of release for offenses committed by a person under 18 years.

2001   Human Rights Watch reports that children fleeing the fighting in northern Liberia are forcibly recruited and trained by government forces to fight the rebels. Children as young as nine years old are taken off buses at military checkpoints or are taken from displaced persons' camps.

2002   In Trenton, New Jersey, a federal-court judge directs the state child-welfare system to open its records and allow plaintiffs in the case of *Charlie and Nadine H. v. McGreevey* access to 500 children's case files so that the plaintiffs can collect information on the harm to children in the state's custody. Lawyers for the plaintiffs expect to find evidence that New Jersey's child-welfare system violates children's rights.

2002   Human Rights Watch charges that Moroccan migrant children in Spain are frequently beaten and abused by police, staff, and other children and are kept in crowded and dirty shelters. Spain also expels these children, some as young as 11 years of age, to Morocco, where they are badly treated by the police and then left abandoned on the streets.

2002   The Children's Rights organization asks the Target Foundation to reconsider its donation of $40 million to support Mary Jo Copeland's proposed home for children. Children's Rights states that research has shown that Copeland's proposed orphanage will work against family building and community strengthening and will deny children a stable environment in families who love them.

2002   In Tehran, Iran, runaway and delinquent children are detained; girls may be sent back home or to a refuge if the family refuses to accept them; if the girl has run away with a boy, the girl is subjected to a virginity test and the two are forced to marry if they have had sex. If the boy belongs to a gang that takes runaways to be sold as prostitutes, he may be imprisoned.

2002   In Honduras, 18 children and youth are murdered during the month of February, after the new president, Ricardo Maduro, announces his policy of zero tolerance. In January, the total number of child murders was 50.

2002   Russian president Vladimir Putin criticizes the deputy prime minister in charge of social issues for the government's failure to deal with homeless and runaway children. Putin orders Prime Minister Mikhail Kasianov to draw up plans for a solution to the problems of homeless children and criminalization of teenagers, which have reached alarming proportions in Russia.

2002   The U.S. Supreme Court, in *Ashcroft v. Free Speech Coalition*, expands the federal prohibition on child pornography in the 1996 Child Pornography Prevention Act to include "any visual depiction" of a minor engaged in "sexually explicit conduct."

2002   The U.S. Supreme Court, in *Board of Education of Independent School Dist. No. 92 v. Earls*, rules that the Fourth Amendment does not prevent school districts from conducting drug testing of students involved in competitive sports. The Court finds testing a reasonable way to further the school district's interest in preventing drug use.

CHAPTER SEVEN

GAY RIGHTS

1250s	The earliest known legislation against male sodomy in Scandinavia is Norway's Law of the Gulathing, which makes a permanent fugitive of any man caught having sex with a person of his own gender.
1608	The Appendix of the (secular) Law Book of Sweden mentions homosexual acts, with punishment justified by reference to the biblical book of Leviticus.
1610	The first sodomy law in the British colonies in America is enacted in the Virginia colony.
1636–1647	In the Massachusetts Bay colony, the law code lists sodomy and buggery, along with such offenses as murder and witchcraft, as crimes for which the penalty is death.
1656	Citing verses from the New Testament Epistle to the Romans, the law code of the New Haven colony in America criminalizes same-sex behavior between women.
1778	The first American soldier to be discharged from the military on the basis of a charge of attempted sodomy is Lieutenant Frederick Gotthold Enslin, at Valley Forge, Pennsylvania.
1810	The Code Napoleon, enacted in France and widely imitated in western Europe and Latin America, includes a legal reform affecting the status of homosexuals. A collection of 28 separate legal codes covering all the changes enacted since the Revolution of 1789, the code incorporates the 1791 decision of the Constituent Assembly to omit sodomy from the list of sexual offenses.
1832	The imperial Russian government passes a law banning men from having anal sex. Those convicted of such an offense are sentenced to four to five years of exile in Siberia.
1852	In Austria, a law making sex between women illegal is passed, although penalties for sex between men are reduced at this time.
1864	The first person in Germany known to identify himself openly as being attracted to those of his own gender is the activist lawyer Karl Heinrich Ulrichs. His attempt to address the question of repealing legislation prohibiting same-sex activities at the Congress of German Jurists in Munich, Germany, is met first with an outcry from the floor and then with permission to continue only if he speaks in Latin.

1864	Karl Heinrich Ulrichs publishes the first pamphlet in a series of 12, containing social and legal studies on same-sex behavior. The set is later printed in book form under the title *Research into the Riddle of Love between Men*.
1873	A law against same-gender sexual behavior, passed in Japan as part of a campaign of modernization, carries a penalty of 90 days' imprisonment.
1889	The penal code of Finland criminalizes homosexual acts between men and also extends this prohibition to similar acts between women.
1895	In a pamphlet titled *Homogenic Love and Its Place in a Free Society*, published in Great Britain, Edward Carpenter, an advocate of socialism and democracy, argues that men and women engaged in such relationships make a positive contribution to their civilizations.
1895–1897	The Irish wit and playwright Oscar Wilde, convicted of homosexual practices, serves two years at hard labor in Reading Goal, England.
1896–1931	Under the leadership of the editor Adolf Brand, *Der Eigene* (One's own, or The special ones), an early periodical published in Germany by and for homosexuals, comes to espouse a slightly more radical definition of homosexual identity than that of the medically based Scientific Humanitarian Committee led by Dr. Magnus Hirschfeld. Brand believes that same-sex love, especially between men and boys, is the highest expression of masculinity.
1897	A petition presented to the Reichstag, the German parliament, asks that Paragraph 175, the section of law defining homosexuality as a crime, be abolished. Following this initial effort, the petition is repeatedly presented in Germany until the collapse of the Weimar Republic in 1933, with increasing numbers of endorsements, but without success.
1906	In Austria, an organization advocating civil emancipation and equality for homosexuals is formed in Vienna as a branch of Dr. Magnus Hirschfeld's Scientific Humanitarian Committee, founded in 1897 to fight persecution of those whom Hirschfeld, a German physician, calls "sexual intermediates." Hirschfeld's committee works to change the German law code, especially Paragraph 175, which prohibits sex between men, but the law remains in effect.
1907	The first public address on homosexuality delivered in the United States is given in New York City by Dr. Otto Spengler, representing Magnus Hirschfeld's Scientific Humanitarian Committee.
1913	Colonel Alfred Redl, a member of the General Staff of the Imperial Austro-Hungarian Army, commits suicide after having been a spy for the czarist Russian intelligence service for several years. His defection has been cited as a reason that homosexuals should be excluded from serving in the armed forces on the

grounds that they pose security risks, although this is the only documented case.

1917   Scrapping the czarist criminal code, the new revolutionary government in Russia replaces it with revolutionary justice giving gay men and lesbians a period of legal freedom. This ends in 1934, with the purge of homosexuals that Stalin orders to be initiated in major cities; those arrested are deported to prison camps.

1919   At the Naval Training Station in Newport, Rhode Island, Acting Secretary of the Navy Franklin D. Roosevelt establishes a vice squad to investigate reports of immoral conditions at the station (then processing 15,000–20,000 men in preparation for service in World War I); using members of the navy as decoys for entrapment, the agents then identify the persons making sexual overtures and remove them from the service. After review by a navy court of inquiry, the action becomes a public scandal in 1921, when the Senate Naval Affairs Committee releases a report severely criticizing Roosevelt.

1923   National Socialist Party (Nazi) members disrupt a public rally of Germany's homophile movement in Vienna.

1924   The first gay rights organization formally created in the United States is the Society for Friendship and Freedom, formed in Chicago, Illinois, by Henry Gerber, a German immigrant who was exposed to the diversity of German organizations working for the betterment of the legal and social conditions of homosexuals while serving in the army in his homeland after World War I. The society's purpose is "to promote and protect the interest of people who by reasons of mental or physical abnormalities are abused and hindered in the pursuit of happiness which is guaranteed them by the Declaration of Independence"; the Chicago police suppress it in 1925.

1924–1925   The periodical *Friendship and Freedom*, published in Chicago, Illinois, by the Society for Friendship and Freedom, is the first newspaper in the United States aimed at inspiring the homosexual community to press for improvement of its civil rights.

1928   Radclyffe Hall, an English novelist, publishes *The Well of Loneliness*, a semiautobiographical account of a lesbian's unhappy life. A London magistrate bans the book and orders all copies destroyed on the grounds that it constitutes an unjustified appeal for sympathy.

1933   Article 121 of the Soviet penal code criminalizes sexual relations between adult homosexual men, imposing five years of hard labor for voluntary acts and eight years for situations with a minor or where force is used. The law is made compulsory for all member republics of the Soviet Union in 1934, on the first anniversary of the Nazi Party's seizure of power in Germany.

1935   The Nazi government of Germany broadens the existing legal provisions prohibiting sex between two men (Paragraph 175 of the law code) to cover any act that the courts determine to be "criminally indecent."

1939 Levensrecht, a group working to promote greater openness for homosexuals, is founded in the Netherlands and later suppressed when the Nazis occupy the country.

1942 In Nazi Germany, legislation making same-sex acts a capital crime is enacted.

1942 The Vichy (collaborationist) government in France enacts a law making homosexual acts with an individual under 21 years of age a crime. The first change in French laws dealing with homosexuality since 1810, the law remains on the books until its repeal by a new socialist government in 1981.

1945 The Religious Society of Friends is founded in New York City as a social-welfare agency to assist people arrested for same-sex offenses.

1946 Founded in Netherlands to work for homosexual civil rights, the Cultuur-en Ontspannings Centrum becomes one of the most successful such groups both in the country and worldwide,

1947–1948 *Vice Versa*, a lesbian periodical, is published in Los Angeles, California. Edited by the movie-studio secretary Edith Eyde under the pseudonym Lisa Ben (an anagram of *lesbian*), the periodical presages the more widely distributed publication of the Daughters of Bilitis, the *Ladder*.

1948 The League is founded in Denmark to serve a function similar to American homophile groups such as the Mattachine Society. By the 1980s, it is the only such organization left in the country and changes its name to the more open Danish Association of Gays and Lesbians.

1950 The homophile activist Harry Hay calls a meeting in Los Angeles, California, that leads to the birth of the Mattachine Society, the first post–World War II U.S. organization working to change public and legal perceptions of homosexuals.

1950 A gay and lesbian organization is founded in Sweden; in 1952, its name is changed to the National Federation for Sexual Equality.

1950 The Knights of the Clock, founded by a group of black and white men and women in Los Angeles, California, serves as a support group for interracial heterosexual, lesbian, and gay couples.

1950s In Boston, Massachusetts, the local community leader Prescott Townsend founds the Demophile Group, an organization for homosexuals. The first acknowledged homosexual to address the state legislature of Massachusetts, Townsend lives to see the beginnings of the gay liberation movement and to attend the first Christopher Street Liberation Day parade in New York City; he dies at home in 1973 at the age of 78.

1951 In the case of *Stoumen v. Reilly*, the California Supreme Court rules that suspending the license of the Black Cat Restaurant in Los Angeles because it caters to homosexuals is arbitrary and therefore a violation of the state constitution. The California board of equalization suspended the license on the grounds of a provision of the state Alcohol Beverage Control Act, which prohibits the running of a disorderly house.

1952 After Senator Joseph McCarthy, notorious for his witch-hunts of Communists in government, names Roy Cohn principal counsel of his Government Committee on Operations of the Senate, McCarthy opponents leak rumors that Cohn and McCarthy are homosexual, in an effort to discredit the senator. In 1954, McCarthy is censured by the Senate, and Cohn is forced to resign, but he continues to oppose homosexual civil rights efforts despite his personal life as a gay man.

1952 *ONE*, a periodical published for and marketed to the homosexual community first appears; it later makes journalistic history with its successful legal challenge of federal postal regulations limiting the mailing of gay and lesbian materials. A 1957 lower-court judgment that the contents of the publication are obscene is appealed to the U.S. Supreme Court, which reverses the ruling in 1958, extending the protection of freedom of speech to the gay and lesbian press.

1952 Alan Turing, the brilliant British mathematician who developed proto-computers and helped break German codes during World War II, is tried for the offense of homosexuality on March 31, 1952, convicted, and given a choice between prison and hormonal treatments (he chooses the latter). Now considered a security risk, he is kept from new decoding work. He poisons himself in June 1954.

1953 U.S. president D. Dwight Eisenhower issues Executive Order 10450, which calls for the immediate dismissal of all federal government workers found guilty of "sexual perversion." In the following 18 months, more than 600 people lose their jobs.

1956 A public meeting of the Mattachine Society of New York is held at the Diplomat Hotel in New York City.

1956 Four people affiliated with the magazine *ONE*, including Jim Kepner and Dorr Legg, give classes known as U.S. homophile studies classes, a field that would later be called gay and lesbian studies. They provide a forum for consciousness raising about the civil status of homosexuals at this time.

1956–1960 The San Francisco activist Phyllis Lyon, editor of the American lesbian journal the *Ladder*, bravely begins using her real name after the fourth issue.

1956–1972 The monthly journal the *Ladder* is the first publication for a lesbian audience to be circulated nationally in the United States. It continues to serve as a forum for discussion of gay women's issues until the final issue.

1957 In Great Britain, the executive committee of the Church of England votes to remove the stigma from homosexual acts between consenting adults, under the influence of the recently published Wolfenden Report to Parliament and the suggested liberalization of British law on sexuality. Similarly, a vote by the Methodist Church of England in 1958 calls for the legalization of homosexual acts in private.

1958　　The Homosexual Law Reform Society is formed in Great Britain by a group of chiefly heterosexual men and women who support the implementation of the sex-law reforms proposed in the 1957 Wolfenden Commission Report to Parliament, among them that private sex acts between men over 21 years of age be decriminalized. In 1960, the society calls a public meeting attended by more than 1,000 people.

1960　　Operation P, the Cuban government's persecution campaign against those it considers sexual deviants, begins. Aimed at prostitutes, pimps, and "pederasts," it results in the arrest and detention of numerous men and women suspected of being homosexual.

1960　　The Daughters of Bilitis sponsors a national convention for lesbians in San Francisco, California.

1960　　An entrapment campaign against homosexuals carried out by plainclothes campus police at the University of Michigan in Ann Arbor results in the eventual arrest of 34 people, only 9 of whom plead guilty. The enraged judge tells the accused not to waste his time by demanding a trial by jury; 1 person commits suicide while his case is being appealed. This case, which attracts substantial media attention, is only one of three such efforts initiated in Ann Arbor between 1958 and 1962.

1960　　In the United States, the Reverend Robert Wood's *Christ and the Homosexual* is the first book that summarizes and questions the historical condemnation of homosexuals by Christian denominations. One section notes the social problems facing homosexuals at the time, such as employment discrimination, undesirable discharges from the military, and blackmail.

1960s　　The Albany Trust, a homophile society, is formed in Great Britain.

1961　　The first openly gay man to run for public office in the United States is the entertainer Jose Sarria, who campaigns for election to San Francisco's board of supervisors. Although unsuccessful, Sarria receives 6,000 votes, demonstrating the possibility of gay political clout.

1961　　During the British colonial administration of India, Section 377, which is added to the Indian penal code, outlaws unnatural carnal intercourse. Its repeal is the subject of discussion at all gay activist conferences held in the subcontinent in the 20th century.

1962　　Randy Wicker of the Homosexual League of New York is the first acknowledged homosexual to speak on American radio and the first openly gay person to appear on national television, on *The Les Crane Show*.

1962　　The Tavern Guild, an association of gay bar owners and employees, is formed in San Francisco, California.

1962	A reform of the law code of Illinois goes into effect. Included in the reform is a measure making consensual same-sex acts legal between consenting adults, the first such measure enacted by a state.
1963	The East Coast Homophile Organization (ECHO) is the first U.S. alliance of activist groups concerned with homosexual civil rights to be formed in the Atlantic-coast states. Founding members are the New York chapter of the Daughters of Bilitis, the Mattachine Society chapters in New York City and Washington, D.C., and the Janus Society of Philadelphia, Pennsylvania.
1963	In Great Britain, the Quakers are the first major religious group to issue a statement opposing discrimination against lesbians and gay men.
1964	*TWO* magazine, first issued by Kamp Publishing in Toronto, Canada, is a voice for the homophile movement in that country. Its name is inspired by the American gay periodical *ONE*.
1964	"Homosexuality in America," an article in *Life*, the widely read American weekly magazine, challenges the dominant stereotype of male effeminacy and offers information on the emerging gay and lesbian subculture.
1964	The Association for Social Knowledge, a Canadian gay rights organization, is founded in Vancouver, British Columbia.
1964	At a retreat near San Francisco, California, held as a dialogue between Protestant churches and homophile organizations, the vagueness of sex laws and legislation used against lesbians and gay men are among the issues discussed. The meeting concludes with the formation of the Council on Religion and the Homosexual, which becomes an influential lobby for change in organized religion's approach to sexual law reform, public education, and civil rights.
1964–1971	*Arena Three*, a lesbian magazine, is published in London, England, by the Minorities Research Group.
1965	Ten members of the East Coast Homophile Organization demonstrate in front of the White House in Washington, D.C., protesting U.S. government discrimination against gays and lesbians.
1965	The U.S. Court of Appeals for the District of Columbia states in a majority opinion that the vague general stigma of immoral conduct is insufficient grounds for termination of employment. The court requires the U.S. Civil Service Commission to state explicitly the types of objectionable conduct for which employees can be fired and to relate these to fitness for work.
1965	A demonstration against the discriminatory hiring practices of the U.S. government in regard to homosexuals is held at the Civil Service Commission building in Washington, D.C. Agency officials respond by arranging a meeting between representatives of the commissioners and members of the Mattachine Society of Washington, at which a 17-page statement entitled "Federal Employment of Homosexual Citizens" is distributed, the first

instance in which the commission offers a written rationale for its discriminatory hiring policies.

1965   A protest by homosexuals at Independence Hall in Philadelphia, Pennsylvania, held on Independence Day, becomes a yearly protest event highlighting the legal oppressions faced by American homosexuals. Known among homophile activists as The Annual Reminder, it consists of a public picket line of conservatively dressed men and women carrying placards calling for law reforms; the demonstration is discontinued after the eclipse of the homophile philosophy by the more radical and confrontational gay liberation movement in 1969.

1965   The first organization concerned with homosexual rights to appear in Chicago, Illinois, since the demise of Henry Gerber's short-lived Society for Friendship and Freedom is Mattachine Midwest. Mattachine holds an open meeting in Chicago, featuring an address by veteran civil rights lawyer Pearl Hart, who urges her audience to assert the equal rights they possess under law.

1966   The activist group Society for Individual Rights opens a gay community center in San Francisco, California.

1967   The New Jersey Supreme Court rules that the state's Liquor Commission is no longer justified in forbidding bars to serve gay men and lesbians. A similar ruling using this decision as precedent follows shortly in New York State.

1967   Great Britain decriminalizes private consensual acts between adults, including same-sex sodomy. Sodomy had been made punishable by death in England when Henry VIII issued the Statute of 1533, and it remained a capital offense until 1828, except for a brief hiatus in the 1500s; after 1828, it is punishable by imprisonment.

1968   At a meeting in a private home in Los Angeles, California, the Reverend Troy Perry creates the Metropolitan Community Church, a religious denomination affirming the value of gay men and lesbians and the morality of their relationships. The new congregation grows rapidly, while Perry becomes one of the most consistently outspoken leaders of the American gay community on matters of civil rights; his two autobiographies discuss the role of religion in the gay rights struggle, *The Lord Is My Shepherd and He Knows I'm Gay* (1972) and *Don't Be Afraid Anymore* (1990).

1968   The play *The Boys in the Band*, by Mart Crowley, premiers off-Broadway and is lauded for its uniquely candid portrayal of homosexual life. It runs until 1970, when it is adapted for the big screen, becoming the first Hollywood feature film to look closely at gay culture. The movie receives mixed reviews and is a modest commercial success.

1969   The American Sociological Association, a professional society of sociologists, issues an official statement of support for the American gay rights movement and condemns "oppressive actions against any persons for reasons of sexual preference."

1969   The founding of the Gay Activists Alliance of New York marks the birth of a new radical approach to opposing the accepted social perceptions and restrictive legal treatment of homosexuals.

1969   On the night of June 27–28, a routine police raid on the Stonewall Inn, an unlicensed gay social club in New York's Greenwich Village, escalates into a melee and then a riot as patrons and bystanders resist arrest and fight police officers. Skirmishes continue for three days. The Stonewall Riots, as they come to be called, mark the beginning of a new assertiveness in the gay community. Several activist organizations, including the Gay Liberation Front (GLF), derive from this event.

1969   *Come Out!*, the first newspaper by and for the gay community to appear in New York City, is published by a collective of Gay Liberation Front members.

1969   A national planning conference of homophile organizations is held in Kansas City, Missouri.

1969   At the Eastern Regional Conference of Homophile Organizations in Philadelphia, Pennsylvania, the New York City Gay Liberation Front and three Student Homophile League chapters create an atmosphere in which radical viewpoints receive sympathetic hearing. One decision taken at this conference marks the end of the homophile era and the beginning of what would be known as gay liberation: the abandonment of the symbolic annual protest for gay civil rights (held at Independence Hall in Philadelphia and sponsored by the conference since 1965) in favor of a Christopher Street Liberation Day, to be held in New York City on the last Saturday of June every year. This marks the origin of the idea of the gay pride parades and celebrations, which become a familiar feature across the United States within several years.

1969   In the case of *Norton v. Macy*, the chief justice of the District Court for the District of Columbia rules that the U.S. Civil Service Commission failed to provide proof of its claims that off-duty homosexual activities by employees is sufficient grounds for termination.

1970   United Nations secretary-general U Thant receives a document from the American Homophile Youth Movement containing four recommendations for desired actions, one of which addresses the issue of legal rights for homosexuals, stating that every nation's laws should ensure basic civil rights protection for gay and lesbian persons, and that the United Nations should assist homophile movements around the world in their struggles for social justice. The recommendations are forwarded to the Subcommission on Prevention of Discrimination and Protection of Minorities without comment.

1970   The first gay pride parade in the United States is held in New York City.

1970	A branch of the Daughters of Bilitis, a homophile organization, is created in Melbourne, Australia.
1970	*Mattachine Forum*, on KQED-FM, the city's independent educational radio station, airs in San Francisco, California, for the gay community.
1970	At a meeting of the Western Homophile Conference in Los Angeles, California, 84 delegates representing 22 groups of homosexual activists acknowledge that the struggle for homosexual rights is "undeniably part of a general struggle for human rights and dignity." Resolutions to offer gay rights planks to the conventions of the Republican, Democratic, and Peace and Freedom Parties are adopted.
1970	During the Second Congress to Unite Women in New York City, 17 women wearing T-shirts bearing the legend "Lavender Menace" come to the stage, while others rise in the audience. As a result of the debate this action triggers, the National Organization for Women acknowledges in 1971 that "oppression of lesbians" is "a legitimate concern of feminism."
1970	At a special session of the American Psychiatric Association in New York City, protesters attack an Australian doctor's paper on the use of electroshock aversion therapy as a method of eliminating homosexual desires. The demonstrators tell the stunned audience "You don't own us."
1970	A group of people interested in creating a gay liberation group meet at the Grace Church on Wisconsin Avenue in Washington, D.C.
1970	Great Britain's Gay Liberation Front meets at the London School of Economics; the meeting is hosted by Bob Mellors and Aubrey Walter.
1970	Carl Wittman's "Refugees from Amerika: A Gay Manifesto" appears in the *San Francisco Free Press*. Widely reprinted across the United States during the following year, it becomes the bible of the gay liberation movement.
1970	The student homophile group Fight Repression of Erotic Expression (FREE) at the University of Minnesota hosts a regional gay convention in Minneapolis. Originally the convention is meant for the 10-state region near Minnesota but is expanded to allow all interested gay people to attend.
1970	The first application by two men for a marriage license in the state of Minnesota is filed by librarian James M. McConnell and law student Jack Baker. The vagueness of the existing language in the state statute is used to justify this action, which reaches the Minnesota Supreme Court in 1971.
1970s	The poet Gennady Trifonov, the first Russian writer to use homoerotic themes in his work since Mikhail Kuzmin in the early 20th century, is persecuted by the Soviet secret police (the KGB), imprisoned in a labor camp, and repeatedly threatened with violence on the basis of his homosexuality following his release.

1971   During Gay Pride Week, a multigroup conference of gay liberation groups is held in a private home in Portland, Oregon. Communities represented include Seattle and Eugene, Oregon, as well as Portland.

1971   The founder of the Mattachine Society of Washington, D.C., Dr. Frank Kameny, is the first openly gay American to stand for election to the U.S. Congress. Kameny comes in fourth among six candidates, winning just 1.6 percent of the vote.

1971   A new labor code issued in Cuba bars homosexuals from working in the fields of medicine, education, and sports.

1971   The first gay activist group in Cleveland, Ohio, is a short-lived chapter of the Gay Activists Alliance. It lasts only a few years, to be superseded by the GEAR Foundation in 1975.

1971   Legislation decriminalizing same-sex relations is passed in Austria.

1971   The penal code of Finland is amended to provide sentences of from six months to four years for persons encouraging "unchastity between persons of the same sex." A Finnish national gay rights body, Sexuaalinen Tasavertaisuus, is established in 1981, with the repeal of the 1971 amendment as one of its objectives.

1971   *Gay Perspectives*, sponsored by the Milwaukee Gay Liberation, is the first gay radio program broadcast in the American Midwest.

1971   Denied a marriage license by the auditor of King County in the state of Washington, John Singer and Paul Barwick sue on the grounds that the law as written does not prohibit same-sex unions; attacking the opposition's presumptive use of the belief that "same-sex marriages are destructive to society," they cite the Equal Rights Amendment to the Washington State Constitution and the 8th, 9th, and 14th Amendments to the U.S. Constitution.

1972   The first openly gay person to address a major national political convention is Jim Foster of San Francisco, California, who delivers a 10-minute speech at the Democratic National Convention.

1972   Presbyterians for Lesbian and Gay Concerns, founded in Chicago, Illinois, by the Reverend David Sindt, is a caucus formed in the Presbyterian Church to work for more equitable treatment of gay members of the congregation. The group is recognized by the church only in 1979 and in 1999 merges with the More Light movement to become More Light Presbyterians, while retaining the same goals of opposing homophobia and antigay discrimination.

1972   San Francisco's Alice B. Toklas Memorial Club (named after the partner of the poet and author Gertrude Stein) is the first all-gay Democratic club formed in California. The club is organized in response to a suggestion by a staff member of the McGovern presidential campaign that organized gay representation at the party's nominating caucuses is desirable.

1972   In a lawsuit brought against the University of Minnesota Board of Regents over employment discrimination based on sexual orientation, James M. McConnell claims he was refused appointment as a librarian because of his very public gay identity; the board of regents appeals a court order in McConnell's favor. The Eighth Circuit Court of Appeals in St. Louis, Missouri, finds for the Regents in an appeal ruling, citing McConnell's wish to pursue the implementation of his "unconventional ideas" about homosexual social status. The U.S. Supreme Court refuses to hear the case.

1972   John Lindsay, mayor of New York City, issues an executive order stating that a person's sexual orientation is not to be considered relevant in city housing decisions. This order follows the pattern of a similar 1969 ruling from the city's civil service commission, stating that homosexuality is no longer acceptable as grounds for firing an employee.

1972   The city council of East Lansing, Michigan, enacts an amendment barring discrimination in hiring on the grounds of homosexuality.

1972   A local board of education in Washington, D.C., passes a resolution banning employment discrimination based on sexual orientation.

1972   At the Democratic National Convention in Miami Beach, Florida, the journalists Guy Charles and David Aitken representing the gay newspaper the *Advocate* receive clearance from the Secret Service.

1972   *Coming Out! A Documentary Play about Gay Life and Liberation in the United States*, written by the activist Jonathan Katz and first performed in New York City at The Firehouse, is the first theatrical work meant both to entertain and to reinforce the struggle for gay liberation. The play is a public interweaving of personal histories recounting the joys and perils of acknowledging a homosexual identity.

1972   The Stonewall Republicans, a gay organization, is founded in New York City to support Republican candidates for public office.

1972   State teaching certification in the fields of earth and space science of Joseph Acanfora, an education major at Pennsylvania State University, is held up because of his involvement with a campus gay activist organization. Following graduation, he obtains employment at a junior high school in Montgomery County, Maryland, only to be removed from the classroom and assigned to nonteaching duties when the story of his university dispute appears in the *New York Times*. Acanfora files suit in Federal District Court in Baltimore seeking an injunction against the school district and reinstatement, but in 1973 Judge Joseph Young denies his suit, ruling that his interviews and media appearances to publicize the case have exceeded the bounds of reasonable self-defense; the U.S. Supreme Court refuses to hear the appeal, while allowing to stand a decision by the Fourth Circuit Court of Appeals in Richmond, Virginia, that homosexuality is not a sufficient reason for denial of employment.

1972 Removed from her teaching position on the basis of a rumor that she is homosexual, the Salem, Oregon, instructor Peggy Burton retains counsel, citing state law that removed all criminal sanctions against homosexuality except in cases of rape. In 1973, Judge Robert Belloni rules that the statute used by the Cascade School District to fire Burton is unconstitutionally vague and orders her outstanding salary and court costs to be paid, but does not reinstate her; a Federal Appeals Court in San Francisco, California, affirms this ruling in 1974, and in 1975 the U.S. Supreme Court refuses to hear her appeal for reinstatement.

1972 The New Jersey Superior Court issues a temporary injunction against the School Board of Paramus, when John Gish is ordered to submit to a psychiatric examination to prove his fitness to teach after he makes a statement supporting gay rights. In 1975, New Jersey's education commissioner rules that Gish should be reinstated but required to take the psychiatric examination; in 1976, a New Jersey state appeals court rules that Gish must submit to the test; after the U.S. Supreme Court refuses to hear his case, Gish is promoted to an administrative post by the Paramus district, effectively removing him from teaching.

1972 The United Church of Christ in San Carlos, California, officially receives William Johnson, an open homosexual, as a member of its clergy.

1972–1973 Serving as the voice of a small protest movement, *Aghois*, a Spanish publication, fights against the Franco government's restriction on homosexuals in Spain.

1973 The first same-sex wedding celebrated in Boston, Massachusetts, is performed at the Old West Church by the Methodist clergyman Reverend William Alberts, in defiance of a letter of instruction from the regional bishop specifically forbidding the ceremony. Alberts is subsequently placed on disability leave and charged with suffering from mental illness; he announces his intention to sue the bishop over his forced retirement.

1973 At a conference in Kansas City, Missouri, 25 delegates from the major Protestant denominations create the National Task Force on Gay People in the Church, a lobby for gay issues, and plan to press the National Council of Churches to rethink its position on gay Christians.

1973 The Frente de Liberacíon Homosexual is founded in Argentina as a gay activist organization; the Nuevo Mundo, a gay rights group, had been created earlier.

1973 The Lambda Legal Defense and Education Fund is incorporated in New York State as a legal and political advocate group for gays and lesbians. Its agenda includes litigation of test cases on specific gay rights issues (including homosexuals' right to serve in the military and the challenging of state sodomy laws) and a variety of education programs.

1973   The *Gay Community News*, a newspaper aimed at the Boston-area homosexual community, first appears as a mimeographed news sheet at the Gay Pride celebrations in Boston, Massachusetts. It swiftly acquires a reputation as a radical voice in the gay movement and suffers an arson attack on its offices in 1982.

1973   The All-Ohio Gay Conference convenes in Columbus, Ohio, to discuss the conditions facing gay people in small towns and gay students in the state university system.

1974   The Union of American Hebrew Congregations admits Beth Chayim Chadashim Synagogue of Los Angeles, California, whose members are openly gay and lesbian, thereby becoming the first Jewish religious organization to accept such a synagogue as a member.

1974   An agreement between the police of Denver, Colorado, and the city's gay community halting harassment of gays by police officers is signed. The document is an outgrowth of a complaint based on past actions filed by the Gay Coalition of Denver.

1974   The quarterly *Journal of Homosexuality* marks the beginning of a group of periodicals in the social sciences that lays the groundwork for the creation of gay and lesbian studies as a distinct academic focus.

1974   The first U.S. state legislator to reveal a homosexual identity while still in office is state senator Allen Spear of Minnesota, in an article in the *Minneapolis Star*.

1974   The first public gay advertising campaign in the history of Boston, Massachusetts, features a lavender rhino to fight the invisibility of the city's gay population.

1974   The Massachusetts state representative Elaine Noble is the first prominent lesbian to stand for election to a state legislature and to win election; she is reelected in 1976. Her success serves as a model for other American lesbians to seek public office without hiding their sexual orientation.

1974   Kathy Kozachenko, who wins a seat on the Ann Arbor City Council, is the first openly gay candidate elected to public office in Michigan.

1974   *The Latecomer* by Sarah Aldridge is published by the lesbian publishing house Naiad Press, which has continued to serve as a central source for lesbian writings of all genres, including political theory and social criticism.

1974   The Dorian Group, later the major statewide gay and lesbian organization of Washington State, establishes a program emphasizing public education and civil rights and creating a public forum blending gay community concerns with mainstream politics.

1974   Lesbian Mothers National Defense Fund, formed in Eatonville, Washington, by 12 "founding mothers," is the first U.S. organization to champion the rights of lesbian mothers in various jurisdictions. Its headquarters later moves to Seattle.

1974   The anniversary of the founding of the National Gay and Lesbian Task Force is celebrated by a discussion at the New York University Medical Center in New York City. Themes are the goals of gay liberation for the next five years, with issues such as the contemporary state of relevant civil rights legislation, the lack of a feminist-oriented approach in the liberation philosophy of the time, and the need for more community services and fund-raising dominating the meeting.

1974   Formal demands by Gay Alternatives Pittsburgh, a local organization advocating homosexual rights, are presented to the city council of Pittsburgh, Pennsylvania; the request is held over until the next public session and subsequently referred to the mayor's Human Rights Committee. The demands address three areas where change is felt to be necessary: elimination of legal codes dealing with immoral solicitation; addition of sexual orientation to all human relations statutes; and social-education programs on sexual minorities for the police force.

1974   Warren Bennis, president of the University of Cincinnati, issues an executive order removing homosexuality as a reason for discrimination in any university activity, including employment. This is a clear break from the institution's past positions on this issue; for instance, a panel was created in 1964 for the purpose of "ferreting out homosexual faculty and staff."

1974   International Business Machines (IBM) offers protection from employment discrimination to gays and lesbians.

1975   Bishop Paul Moore in New York City ordains Ellen Marie Barrett, an open lesbian, as a deacon in the Episcopal Church. Moore summarizes the ensuing controversy (both within and outside the Episcopal community) in his 1979 book *Take a Bishop Like Me*.

1975   The first-known U.S. jury trial involving the custody rights of a homosexual parent begins in Dallas, Texas, when Mary Jo Risher seeks to retain custody of her nine-year-old son, while his father tries to remove the child from what he views as an unhealthy environment. The Dallas Domestic Relations Court awards the father custody, and a challenge to this ruling in the Fifth Civil Court of Appeals is dismissed for want of jurisdiction; Risher and her partner subsequently set out the story of the trial in a book titled *By Her Own Admission* (1977).

1975   Gay American Indians is created in San Francisco, California, to address the cultural and legal issues of gay and lesbian Native Americans.

1975   Ensign Vernon E. Berg becomes the first U.S. Navy officer to challenge the navy's policy of immediate termination for homosexuals. He initiates two years of ultimately unsuccessful legal proceedings, which later appear in *Get off My Ship*, the only account of a case of military discrimination written by the victim.

1975	*High GEAR*, a community newspaper created in Cleveland, Ohio, serves as a forum for gay and lesbian issues. The title is based on the name of its sponsoring body, the Gay Educational Awareness and Resources Foundation.
1975	At the organizational meeting of the Cleveland Gay Federation, the statement of purpose stresses the group's focus on gay rights. The federation later changes its name to the Cleveland Gay Political Union and centers its attention on achieving enactment of civil rights legislation for lesbians and gays in the communities of Cuyahoga County, Ohio.
1975	When Sergeant Leonard Matlovich hands his superior officer at Langley Air Force Base in Virginia a letter stating his sexual preference, he triggers a five-year series of hearings and court cases, which ultimately result in a ruling that the air force policy about the antihomosexual regulations in the Uniform Code of Military Justice is too ambiguous and unfair. Matlovich accepts a $160,000 settlement of the case in 1980 on the advice of his lawyers; subsequently he works as an AIDS activist before his death in 1988.
1975	Radio Free Lambda, a half-hour radio program broadcast from Station WRUW at Case Western Reserve University, Cleveland, Ohio, with graduate student John Vogel as moderator, is a forum for sharing information with the widely scattered members of the Cleveland homosexual community.
1975	A major piece of gay civil rights legislation introduced on the floor of the U.S. Congress is the Civil Rights Amendments of 1975, formally filed by Representative Bella Abzug of New York and 23 cosponsors, including Patricia Schroeder, Shirley Chisholm, and Gerry Studds. The measure seeks to amend the Civil Rights Act of 1964 and related acts to prohibit discrimination on the basis of affectional or sexual preference.
1975	Milton Shapp, governor of Pennsylvania, issues an executive order committing the state to end antigay discrimination, the first state to do so. State legislators respond by introducing five antigay bills.
1975	The Society for the Protection of Personal Rights, a gay organization, is founded in Israel.
1975	The U.S. Civil Service Commission issues a news release stating that it is changing its policy of excluding homosexuals from government employment.
1975	Oliver ("Billy") Sipple, a Marine Corps veteran of Vietnam, thwarts Sara Jane Moore's attempt to assassinate President Gerald R. Ford in San Francisco on September 22. In follow-up stories, several newspapers identify Sipple as a member of San Francisco's gay community. This exposure of his private life, which he has kept secret from his parents, causes Sipple untold distress; he sues the *San Francisco Chronicle* and six other papers for damages, but the suit is ultimately dismissed. The entire affair provokes questions about the ethics of "outing," the

ethics of journalists, and the right to privacy.

1975   Retired NFL football player David Kopay becomes the first professional athlete in the three major American sports to reveal he
is gay. Kopay, a nine-year veteran who retired in 1972, admits
his homosexuality in reaction to a story on gay athletes that
appeared in the *Washington Star* in December 1975. After giving
an exclusive interview to the *Star* two days later, Kopay writes a
book, *The David Kopay Story*, that makes the *New York Times*
best-seller list the following year.

1976   Father John J. McNeill's *The Church and the Homosexual* examines life conditions facing gays and lesbians in areas the Catholic
Church might assist in, among them civil rights law reforms and
antigay violence. As a result of this book, the order of silence
imposed on him in 1973 is reinstated in 1977; he is forbidden to
speak publicly on sexual ethics or homosexuality, and the Vatican formally withdraws approval from all future editions of his
book.

1976   Judge Harry Glassman of the Maine Superior Court awards
Carol Whitehead unconditional custody of her two children, in a
case considering the rights of a homosexual parent.

1976   A meeting of the Gertrude Stein Democratic Club is held in
Washington, D.C., to "to assure gay people a role in the greater
Washington area's political process."

1976   The *Washington Blade* is published in Washington, D.C. It
becomes the principal forum for lesbian and gay journalism in
America's capital.

1976   The Southeastern Conference for Lesbians and Gay Men,
founded at the University of North Carolina, Chapel Hill, is a
local regional organization for homosexual men and women in
the southern United States.

1976   Station WHPK-FM at the University of Chicago begins airing a
new series of radio programs called *Chicago Gay Forum*. Produced by the campus gay liberation front, the series addresses
such issues as employment rights and the legal status of homosexuality and profiles the city's gay and lesbian organizations.

1976   At the meeting of the board of the Gay Rights National Lobby,
members agree that the first priority of the new organization is
to seek federal legislation eliminating discrimination in employment. The lobby becomes increasingly financially handicapped
until it is absorbed by the Human Rights Campaign Fund in
1985.

1976   The first course to be offered in any U.S. law school on the rights
of homosexuals is given at the University of Southern California
by the attorney Don Knutson. The course is The Civil Liberties of
Gay People.

1976   The first-known openly gay person in the United States to be
hired as a law-enforcement officer is the deputy sheriff Rudi Cox
of San Francisco, California.

1976	Delivering an address at the second annual convention of Integrity in San Francisco, California, the activist author and Episcopal priest Malcolm Boyd acknowledges the value of recognizing varying degrees of individual liberation but warns against a new conformity requiring everyone who is lesbian or gay to "come out."
1977	The Illinois State House of Representatives votes on a gay rights measure, House Bill 575, intended to ban employment discrimination on the basis of sexual orientation at public colleges and universities.
1977	Despite the climate of social tolerance in the Netherlands, not until this late date does a gay pride celebration occur in the country.
1977	The first public-service employment bill barring discrimination on the basis of sexual orientation to be passed in the United States clears the Massachusetts State Senate.
1977	The first openly gay candidate elected to office in New York City is the political-science professor Kevin Sherrill, who wins a seat on the city's Democratic Committee.
1977	At a meeting held at Bowling Green State University, in Ohio, a statewide coalition of gay rights organizations in Ohio is formed. Initially known as the Ohio Gay Rights Efforts, the multicity network alters its name later that year to the Ohio Gay Rights Coalition.
1977	After more than 12 years of requests for a meeting of presidential staff and leaders of lesbian and gay organizations, the White House responds during the administration of President Jimmy Carter. A delegation including Jean O'Leary and Bruce Voeller of the National Gay Task Force; Dr. Frank Kameny from the D.C. Mattachine Society; Ray Hartmann of the Gay Rights National Lobby; Charlotte Spitzer, founder of Parents of Gays of Los Angeles; State Representative Elaine Noble of Massachusetts; and Charlotte Bunch, editor of the lesbian feminist periodical *Quest*, are received at the White House by Marilyn Haft, associate director of the White House Office of Public Liaison, presidential aide Midge Costanza, and Annie Gutierrez of the Domestic Policy staff.
1977	In the first successful blasphemy trial in Britain in 55 years, Denis Lemon, editor of the London newspaper *Gay News*, is convicted in the Old Bailey, fined 500 pounds, and given a nine-month suspended sentence. Charged by the conservative activist Mary Whitehouse with having committed blasphemy through the publication of "The Love That Dares to Speak Its Name," by James Kirkup, a religious poem on the Crucifixion that has sexual overtones, Lemon ceases publication of *Gay News* in 1983.
1977	After the state attorney general issues an opinion that a gay rights ordinance is not in violation of state sodomy laws as then written, the city of Wichita, Kansas, passes such an ordinance. Local conservative organizations immediately begin a petition

drive calling for repeal, and the ordinance is rescinded in 1978, the third (after Miami and Saint Paul) in a series of successful legal challenges to local gay and lesbian civil rights legislation mounted in the late 1970s.

1977   The police raid the offices of the *Body Politic*, a gay paper, in Toronto, Canada, and seize 12 cartons of newspaper property, using a warrant so broad as to be illegal under Canadian law. The paper is taken to court no fewer than three times in an effort by the provincial attorney general to obtain a conviction, before being finally cleared in 1983.

1977   *Word Is Out*, a documentary film on gay life that receives widespread screening in the United States, offers lengthy interviews with 26 lesbians and gay men, among them the San Francisco activist Sally Gearhart, the writer Else Gidlow, and the veteran homosexual rights leader Harry Hay. The film is produced by the Mariposa Film Group.

1977   The Save the Children campaign, led by the former Miss Oklahoma Anita Bryant, a devout Southern Baptist, a Miami resident, a spokesperson for the Florida citrus industry, and a singer who has entertained 14 times at the White House for President Lyndon B. Johnson, aims at rescinding an ordinance passed in Dade County, Florida (including the city of Miami), that prohibits antigay discrimination. Literature distributed by the campaign charges that, if homosexuals are free from discrimination, they would attempt to increase their numbers by preying on children, and a referendum repeals the ordinance. The victory sparks numerous other attempts at the city and county levels across the United States in the late 1970s and early 1980s to eliminate legislation protecting the civil rights of gay and lesbian people.

1977   The sitcom *Soap* premieres on ABC and features the first openly gay character in the history of American television—Jodie Dallas, played by Billy Crystal. Jodie is originally written very effeminate, but after homosexual groups protest that the character is stereotypical and offensive, Crystal and the writers tone down the portrayal and win praise from the National Gay Task Force. Despite objections from a number of church and family-oriented groups, *Soap* attracts a loyal following and remains on the air until 1981.

1978   *O Lampão*, a publication aimed at creating a sense of identity among the gay population of Brazil, is founded.

1978   The International Gay Association, founded to share information on the legal status and social condition of gays and lesbians worldwide, holds a conference in Coventry, Great Britain, attended by representatives of 17 organizations from 14 European countries. In 1986, the body changes its name to the International Gay and Lesbian Association to reflect the increased involvement of women's groups.

1978   The rainbow flag, later adopted as a symbol of the gay and lesbian movement, first appears at San Francisco's Gay Freedom Day Parade. It is designed by the local artist Gilbert Baker.

1978   The More Light declaration, issued by the West Park Presbyterian Church in New York City, initiates a movement that seeks support for gay civil rights and opposition to homophobia in the Presbyterian denomination. The name is based on a 1620 quote by the Reverend John Robinson that man should not limit the scope of divine will by human understanding, there being more light yet to be revealed.

1978   The first gay official in the United States to be murdered while in office is San Francisco supervisor Harvey Milk, shot in his chambers in city hall by ex–city supervisor Dan White; White also slays Mayor George Moscone that same day. News that White is found guilty of voluntary manslaughter rather than first-degree murder in 1979 triggers a massive angry protest and clashes with police by the city's gay community, later termed "the White Night Riots."

1978   Malcolm Boyd's *Take Off the Masks*, the autobiography of an openly gay American religious leader, is published.

1978   Proposition 6, or the Briggs Initiative, named for its sponsor, California state senator John Briggs, targets homosexuals in secondary schools, granting local school boards the power to fire or refuse employment to teachers who encourage or promote homosexuality as a viable lifestyle. The measure is strongly opposed by a broadly based coalition of mainstream groups including unions and educational and religious organizations, as well as gay groups across the state, and is eventually defeated by a popular vote of 58 to 42 percent.

1979   Robert McQueen, then editor of the widely read gay periodical the *Advocate*, is excommunicated from the Church of Jesus Christ of Latter-day Saints (Mormons). McQueen wrote a detailed article on Mormonism's stance on and treatment of homosexuality and homosexuals, citing the high suicide rate in those counseled to change.

1979   The gay rights organization Somos (We are) is created in São Paulo, Brazil.

1979   The Lesbian and Gay Asian Collective, organized during the first National Third World Lesbian and Gay Conference in Washington, D.C., is formed to address the marginal status of the lesbian and gay rights movement in the Asian American community.

1979   Senators Paul Tsongas, Lowell Weicker, and Daniel Patrick Moynihan introduce the first gay civil rights bill ever to be filed in the U.S. Senate.

1979   Gathering at the Friends Meeting House in Philadelphia, Pennsylvania, the Walt Whitman Democratic Club hosts a meeting that eventuates in the first large gay and lesbian march on Washington, D.C. The original concept of the march begins in Minnesota in 1978, following the repeal of a gay civil rights ordinance by referendum in the city of Saint Paul.

1979   In a complaint to the United Nations Human Rights Commission, the Finnish Organization for Sexual Equality charges that a provision of Finland's penal code (which forbids the public discussion of homosexuality in any but a negative tone) was used against the Finnish Broadcasting Company to restrict homosexuals' right to free speech; the source of the issue was a news item stating that homosexuality had been removed from the list of mental illnesses recognized by the American Psychiatric Association. The complaint is accepted by the commission.

1979   The judiciary committee of the state of Arizona passes an amendment to existing adoption procedures, prohibiting homosexuals and bisexuals from adopting children. Its sponsor admits she knows of no such requests ever having been filed anywhere in the state, but files the measure "so there will be no potential for this to happen."

1979   *Gai Pied*, a periodical of the French gay rights movement, is published in France.

1979   The supreme court of the state of Michigan reverses a lower-court decision denying custody to a gay parent and restores Jillian Miller to her mother, Margaret.

1980   The first openly gay candidate for the office of vice president in the history of the United States, Melvin Boozer of the District of Columbia, addresses the Democratic National Convention in New York City.

1980   The activist Joni Crone, whose media appearance substantially raises public awareness of the presence and status of lesbians in Ireland, is the first acknowledged lesbian to receive coverage on Irish television.

1980   Bay Area Lawyers for Individual Freedom, founded in San Francisco, California, as a professional group in the legal profession, works for the appointment of open gays and lesbians to the bench and public commissions in the San Francisco region.

1980   Lesbian Unidas, a Latina lesbian organization, is formed in Los Angeles, California. A larger national body, National Latino/a Lesbian and Gay Association, is created in 1987.

1980   The first Spanish gay or lesbian organization to receive government recognition is the Gay Liberation Front of Catalonia, Spain.

1980   The first openly gay person to have won a delegate spot to the Republican National Convention, Tim Drake of Illinois, is barred from speaking by the Temporary Committee on Resolutions on the grounds of "scheduling difficulties." A delegate representing religious interests is granted floor time instead.

1980   The first political campaign mounted in Canada by an openly gay person seeking public office is that of George Hislop, who unsuccessfully stands for election from ward 6 of Toronto.

1980   The Human Rights Campaign Fund, founded in Washington,

D.C., is the first gay political-action committee whose scope of activity is the entire United States. The fund aims to support federal-level candidates through campaigning and contributions.

1980–1985 The publication *No Bad News* serves and informs the Saint Louis, Missouri, homosexual community, providing an alternative voice on lesbian and gay issues for the state of Missouri and laying the groundwork for the later creation of the *Gay News-Telegraph*.

1980s The Colectiva Ayuquelen, a lesbian organization, is founded in Santiago, Chile.

1980s E.O.K., a gay organization, is recognized by the government in Greece.

1981 A conference of gay men held in Hyderabad, India, is attended by more than 40 delegates from India's largest cities who discuss working for the repeal of antigay laws, organizing legal help for gay people being subjected to blackmail, and social and domestic concerns associated with being homosexual in Indian society. At this time, Section 377 of the Indian penal code sets imprisonment of 10 years or life as the punishment for those convicted of committing "unnatural offenses."

1981 Norway is the first country in the world to ban discrimination based on sexual orientation.

1981 The Gay Press Association, formed in New York City at a meeting of 80 delegates chaired by Joseph di Sabato of Rivendell Publishing, is a professional alliance of gay and lesbian members of the journalistic community.

1981 Edward Koch, mayor of New York City, states at a meeting of the Greater Gotham Business Council, a gay organization, that he will not attempt to influence opponents in the city council to pass pending gay civil rights legislation. Koch regards such decisions as "a matter of conscience."

1981 The newly formed Gay Press Association holds a national conference in Denver, Colorado, to create and extend a network of effective journalism to ensure accurate reporting of news for the American gay community.

1981 A self-identified gay and lesbian contingent participates in the mass antiwar demonstration at the Pentagon in Washington, D.C., to protest increased military spending by the Reagan administration.

1981 *Gaydreams*, a news and entertainment radio program for the gay community of greater Cincinnati, Ohio, airs on station WAIF, with journalist John Zeh as host. The show quickly becomes controversial through such actions as Zeh's readings of the works of Allen Ginsberg, and obscenity charges are filed by the Hamilton County prosecutor; although initially dismissed, the charges are upheld by the Ohio First District Court of Appeals in 1982.

1982 In January 1982, after a sudden rise in the death rate among gay men in the United States and rumors of a mysterious new "gay cancer," six men in New York organize Gay Men's Health Crisis (GMHC) to care for the sick and raise money for biomedical research. Nine months later, the "gay cancer" is officially named acquired immunodeficiency syndrome (AIDS) by the Federal Centers for Disease Control and Prevention. As scientists learn more about the disease, GMHC widens its mission to include education of the public and campaigns for patients' and partners' rights.

1982   *The Mayor of Castro Street*, by Randy Shilts, is a biography of the murdered San Francisco gay activist and city supervisor Harvey Milk. In addition to covering Milk's career, the work provides a useful history of the evolution of gay political clout in San Francisco.

1982   *Zami: A New Spelling of My Name*, the "biomythography" of Audre Lorde, a black lesbian poet, is published.

1982   The first legislative body in North America to grant domestic-partner benefits for same-sex couples is the Parliament of Quebec, Canada.

1982   The West German government agrees that compensation be granted to gay survivors of Nazi concentration camps, some thirty years after reparations had been made to other persecuted groups.

1982   The annual convention of the International Gay Alliance (later known as the International Gay and Lesbian Alliance) meets in Washington, D.C., which is chosen as the convention site partly because of restrictive U.S. rules on the immigration of openly homosexual people.

1982   Wisconsin is the first state to pass a comprehensive measure adding the term *sexual orientation* to all laws covering classes protected from discrimination in housing, employment, public accommodations, and contractual matters, when the state senate gives the bill final approval. The law is widely viewed as a model for other states to emulate.

1982   The first Washington, D.C., police officer to serve as an openly gay man is Robert Almstead. The city police force accepts his presence with an unusual degree of equanimity.

1982   *Out!*, a statewide newspaper serving the Wisconsin homosexual community, appears. In 1987, it is succeeded by the *Wisconsin Light*.

1983   A meeting of the Governor's Council on Lesbian and Gay Issues, formed by an executive order, is held in Madison, Wisconsin.

1983   The Wisconsin state legislature passes AB 250, known as the consenting-adults bill. The bill was introduced at two-year intervals since 1975; its chief sponsor is the openly gay state representative David Clarenbach.

1983   Representative Gerry Studds of Massachusetts acknowledges his homosexuality in a public statement on the floor of the U.S. House of Representatives and despite some controversy goes on to serve a total of 12 terms for his district before retiring in 1995. In the 1970s, Studds was censured by the House on charges of sexual misconduct with a congressional page.

1983	Boston Project, an attempt by the city of Boston to assess the needs of its gay and lesbian citizens, results in an 80-page report containing some 200 recommendations.
1983	Governor Richard Celeste of Ohio issues an order protecting gays and lesbians against discrimination in state employment. This action makes Ohio the fifth state to extend such rights to its state civil-service workers.
1983	The Midwest Regional Conference of the Gay Press Association is held in Saint Louis, Missouri. A major topic of discussion is finding effective means of supporting the numerous small publications constituting the region's lesbian and gay journalistic cadre.
1983–1985	Lesbians in Love and Compromising Situations, a lesbian organization, is active in Cape Town, South Africa.
1984	The National Gay and Lesbian Task Force releases a survey examining the incidence of hate crimes against gays and lesbians in the United States. Data show that 94 percent of respondents have experienced some form of verbal, physical, or property abuse, and that 83 percent fear enduring it in the future.
1984	In response to a lawsuit filed by the Los Angeles activist Dan Siminowski, some 7,500 pages of memoranda and files released under the Freedom of Information Act reveal decades of government monitoring of gay rights organizations. The documents verify infiltration and observation beginning in the 1950s and escalating during the next two decades; the rationale of the Federal Bureau of Investigation appears to be that lesbians and gays represent threats to national security.
1985	A parade celebrating gay and lesbian rights is held in Cincinnati, Ohio.
1985	The Gay and Lesbian Alliance against Defamation is formed by a group of writers in New York City to respond to the misrepresentation of homosexuality in various types of journalism.
1985	The Annual Conference for Black Lesbians and Gays, held in St. Louis, Missouri, calls for more public involvement by this community in the broader civil rights work of the African-American community.
1985	Tony Anaya, governor of New Mexico, issues an official executive instruction protecting the employment of openly gay and lesbian people in the state civil service.
1985	Hearings in the matter of *Her Majesty's Government v. Gay's the Word* begin in London, England; the prosecution seeks to convict a large gay and lesbian bookstore in London, raided by officers of Customs and Excise, on charges of conspiracy to import obscene

literature under an 1876 customs law. After protests in Great Britain and the United States, most of the books are returned and the charges dropped; Member of Parliament Chris Smith announces the introduction of a bill to scrap the provisions of the 19th-century statute used as a basis for the raid.

1985 The popular movie and television actor Rock Hudson dies of complications from AIDS after admitting to his homosexuality. His search for a cure and subsequent death bring worldwide attention to the AIDS crisis.

1986 In *Bowers v. Hardwick*, the U.S. Supreme Court rules that a Georgia law assigning criminal penalties to persons found guilty of sodomy does not infringe on the due-process clause "right of privacy," though one justice later describes his aye vote as a mistake. In 1999, the Georgia Supreme Court strikes down the statute challenged in *Bowers* as a violation of the Georgia Constitution.

1986 *In the Life*, edited by the Philadelphia author Joseph Beam, is a collection of writings aimed at reclaiming a positive image for African-American gay men. A common thread in all the contributed essays is the need to challenge homophobia within the black community on both personal and institutional levels.

1986 The first hearing of the U.S. Congress oever n the topic of anti-gay violence takes place when the Criminal Justice Subcommittee of the House Judiciary Committee hears public testimony on the rising incidence of violent acts against lesbian and gay people or persons presumed to be so. Those testifying are four victims and directors of the local violence-monitoring projects of the National Gay and Lesbian Task Force from New York and San Francisco, the latter documenting a sharp rise in the rate of assaults.

1986 In the city of Arad in Romania, more than 100 gay men are arrested, tortured, and forced to name other gay men, who are then arrested, during the Ceausescu regime's campaign against gays.

1987 The first court case involving the sodomy laws of Ireland to come before the European Court of Human Rights is initiated by the activist David Norris, who had won election to the Upper House of the Dail (Irish parliament). In 1988, the court rules Ireland's laws to be in violation of the European Charter of Human Rights; in 1993, same-sex relations for consenting adults are decriminalized in Ireland, and a universal age of consent is set.

1987 *And the Band Played On*, written by the investigative journalist Randy Shilts and made into a film, is the first major popular history chronicling the lives of gay men living in New York and the effects on their lives of the rapidly evolving AIDS pandemic in the United States.

1987 The AIDS Coalition to Unleash Power (ACT UP), a gay direct-action group, organizes a mass protest in New York City, when some 600 demonstrators block all traffic on Wall Street. At issue are the failure of the Reagan administration to make experimental AIDS drugs available and its unwillingness to confront the emerging crisis of the pandemic.

1987   Governor Rudy Perpich of Minnesota issues an executive order prohibiting discrimination in state employment on grounds of sexual orientation.

1987   An attempt to hold a gay pride parade in Dubuque, Iowa, is met with thrown rocks and eggs, obscenities, and hurled bottles, while local police response to protect the marchers is virtually nil. This event sparks national outrage in the gay community and an outpouring of support, reflected in the appearance of 600 people for the 1988 parade.

1987   John Sununu, governor of New Hampshire, signs legislation prohibiting gay people from becoming adoptive or foster parents, making New Hampshire the first state to do so. A similar bill passed in neighboring Massachusetts by the House of Delegates at this time is sent to the state senate for review.

1987   In Turkey, 14 people participate in hunger strikes in Ankara and Istanbul, held to protest police brutality and raids on gay bars. Although homosexuality is not considered illegal under Turkish civil and martial law, activists report that police beat of gay bars patrons, completely shave their heads, and force them to undergo compulsory testing for venereal diseases.

1987   Guidelines issued by the Irish Congress of Trade Unions, covering a workplace environment where lesbian and gay workers are free from harassment and have equal opportunity, is adopted.

1987   The Canadian province of Manitoba passes a Human Rights Code banning discrimination based on political belief, pregnancy, or sexual orientation. The culmination of two years of lobbying work by an alliance including labor and teachers' groups as well as gays and lesbians, the code is passed with the adoption of an added amendment stating that nothing in the code condemns or condones the activities or lifestyles of the people protected by the measure.

1987   The March on Washington, a national gay and lesbian civil rights protest action, is held in Washington, D.C. Seven specific demands are stated: legal recognition of lesbian and gay relationships, repeal of all sodomy laws, a presidential order banning antigay discrimination by the federal government, passage of the gay civil rights bill then being considered by Congress, reproductive freedom, cessation of discrimination against people with AIDS or related disease complexes, and an end to racism and apartheid.

1987   As part of the March on Washington, the NAMES Quilt, initially created as the gay community's way to memorialize and highlight the massive numbers of deaths from AIDS, is displayed on the Mall in Washington, D.C.

1987   The Tennessee Gay and Lesbian Task Force, the first statewide gay political action committee formed in Tennessee, is created to work for repeal of the state's "crimes against nature" law and to assess and document the extent of local antigay discrimination.

1987 The Latin American and Caribbean Lesbian/Feminist Conference is held in Mexico City, Mexico.

1987 *Gaya Nusantara*, a newspaper published by the Working Group of Indonesian Lesbians and Gay Men, appears.

1987 *The Celluloid Closet: Homosexuality in the Movies* by Vito Russo is published by Harper and Row. The book addresses the manner in which Hollywood has ignored, disguised, and ridiculed homosexuality in films during the 20th century.

1988 The mayor of São Paulo (and former president of Brazil), Janio da Silva Quadros, forbids homosexuals to attend the prestigious São Paulo Ballet School, and the school is threatened with closure if the staff does not follow this instruction. An international protest campaign is mounted over this issue.

1988 *Homosexualists*, the magazine of the Front d'Alliberament Gai de Catalunya, appears in Barcelona, Spain.

1988 Svend Robinson, a nine-year veteran of the House of Commons of the Canadian Parliament, is the first Canadian member of Parliament to admit being gay.

1988 The Grupo Gay Da Bahia, a gay organization in the state of Bahia in northeastern Brazil, is granted the status of *grupo da utilidad public* (public-utility corporation) by the municipality of Salvador. Such legal recognition makes the group's bargaining position stronger with both the police and government agencies.

1988 The Grupo Somos is founded to work for improved civil rights conditions for gay people during the military dictatorship in Uruguay.

1988 A conference entitled The Basket and the Bow, held at the American Indian Center in Minneapolis, Minnesota, is the first gathering of Indian gays and lesbians in the United States. Topics discussed by the 60 participants include the search for wholeness among Native American gay people.

1988 The Gay and Lesbian Arabic Society, a support network for gays and lesbians of Arab descent, is formed in the United States.

1988 The first Eastern European country to extend recognition to a gay and lesbian organization is Hungary, which gives Homeros Lambda official status.

1988 The Gay and Lesbian Organization of the Witwatersrand is founded in South Africa by the activist Simon Nkoli as a multiracial group.

1988 The county commissioner of Fulton County, addressing the annual fund-raising dinner of the Greater Atlanta Political Awareness Coalition in Atlanta, Georgia, urges his lesbian and gay constituents to "never allow anyone to exercise unjust power over you."

1988   The Chicago City Council passes the Human Rights Ordinance, legislation adding sexual-orientation protections to various city laws already in force. This act ends 15 years of lobbying efforts by Chicago activists.

1988   Measure 8, a legislative proposal offered for public debate in Oregon, calls for the repeal of an executive order issued by former governor Neil Goldschmidt, barring state agencies from using sexual preference as a discriminatory category; although approved by the voters, it never goes into effect, as the Oregon Court of Appeals rules it to be unconstitutional. In response, the Oregon Citizens Alliance in 1992 places on the ballot Measure 9, a more strongly worded proposal, which prohibits using sexual orientation as a basis for civil rights law and legislation and requires local governments, school districts, and the state government itself to discourage homosexuality; the proposition is defeated by a margin of 57 to 42 percent.

1988   The Cleveland gay community demonstrates against federal AIDS policy in its first public protest action since the 1970s.

1988   The Comunidad Triangulo Rosa, a gay organization, is founded in Guadalajara, Mexico. *Triangulo rosa* means "pink triangle" and refers to the patch that homsexuals were forced to wear in Nazi Germany.

1988   The North American Gay and Lesbian Asian Conference is held in Toronto, Canada.

1988   Apple Computer announces in an internal employee newsletter a new policy of nondiscrimination on the basis of sexual orientation.

1988   The first organization representing gay and lesbian rights to testify before a platform committee of the Republican Party is the Human Rights Campaign Fund, whose representative John Thomas meets with that body in Kansas City, Missouri. Thomas urges the party to work for the elimination of exclusionary policies against gays and lesbians in immigration law and the armed forces, the recognition of same-gender marriage, and support for antidiscrimination legislation.

1988   A global conference to end homophobia, held in Chevy Chase, Maryland, draws a hundred clergy, educators, health and sexuality specialists, and mass media professionals.

1988   Clause 28 in the Local Government Act passed in Great Britain originates in complaints by the London tabloids that a children's book, *Jenny Lives with Eric and Martin* (depicting a girl being raised by her father and his partner) by Susanne Bosche, proselytizes for a gay lifestyle in the schools. Clause 28 bans open discussion or presentation of homosexuality, whether in print, electronic media, dance, theater, music, or book form, but is later repealed by the Thatcher government.

1988   A documentary film dealing with homosexuality is produced in the Soviet Union by Andrei Nikichine. Titled *Risk Group*, it debuts at the Eighth International Film Festival in Amiens, France.

1988   Club Lambda, an organization for gays and lesbians, is founded in Liberia, West Africa.

1988   After trying and failing to obtain a marriage license in Illinois on the grounds of the recently passed Chicago Human Rights Ordinance, the journalists Paul Varnell and Rex Wockner appeal to the Illinois Human Rights Commission but are refused. The commission acknowledges that although the Chicago measure outlaws discrimination based on gender, it is not intended to supersede the state marriage statute, which defines marriage partners as of opposite sexes.

1989   Pride 89 is the first gay pride parade held in Cleveland, Ohio, after a hiatus of well over a decade.

1989   Gays and Lesbians of Zimbabwe is founded in Zimbabwe to provide a forum for communication for the country's male and female homosexuals. Following a period centered on hosting social events, the group expands its concerns and eventually comes to public notice; its major focus is the integration of gay rights with other basic civil liberties in the local political process.

1989   *Tongues Untied*, a documentary film addressing homophobia in the African-American community from a black point of view, is produced by filmmaker Marlon Riggs, who dies in 1994 of an AIDS-related condition.

1989   The *San Francisco Examiner*, a mass-circulation newspaper, runs a 16-day series titled "Gay in America." The presentation examines the 20 years since the Stonewall Riots in 1969 (when gays protested police harassment in New York City), including consideration of the public image of gay rights, problems of gay people of color, and bias in sports.

1989   The Prohibition of Incitement to Hatred Act, passed by the Dail, the Irish parliament, includes bans on hate speech against homosexuals.

1989   A public rally to mark the creation in Saskatchewan, Canada, of a chapter of Equality for Gays and Lesbians Everywhere is held in Regina, capital of the province. Equality is the Canadian equivalent of America's National Gay and Lesbian Task Force, and the new chapter pledges to work toward adding sexual-orientation protections to Saskatchewan's human rights code.

1989   Ned McWhirter, governor of Tennessee, signs into law a reform of Tennessee state law covering "crimes against nature." The new measure replaces the older archaic language with text specifically banning homosexual acts.

1989   C'aslen (a native term for *life*), a gay organization, is founded in Guatemala City, Guatemala.

1989   Eleven male couples are joined in marriage at the Copenhagen city hall in Denmark on the first day that new Danish legislation recognizing lesbian and gay marriages is in force.

1989   Lambda, a gay organization founded in Poland by Warsaw's Dr. Ryszard Ziobro and activists from across the country, is concerned with establishing a working relationship with the Solidarity Party.

1990   Graziella Bertozzo, the first woman elected national secretary of Arci Gay, Italy's predominantly male national gay and lesbian task force, accepts the position at the group's convention in Bologna. The event is promptly denounced by the Italian Lesbian League.

1990   A conference on homosexuality called Sexual Minorities: Changing Attitudes towards Homosexuality in 20th Century Europe is held in Estonia, in the Academy of Sciences in Tallinn. An address by Raul Karu, Estonia's minister of social affairs, opens the conference.

1990   Terry Branstad, governor of Iowa, enacts a hate-crimes law protecting gays and lesbians. The measure increases penalties for bias- or hate-based crimes, allows victims to bring civil lawsuits, and mandates collection of statistics on hate crimes in the state; passage is obtained through negotiation of language stating that the law does not grant civil rights protections to lesbians and gays.

1990   Lambda Union, Czechoslovakia's first officially registered homosexual organization, hosts a national gay conference in Prague.

1990   The eighth state to increase legal penalties for crimes motivated by another person's real or perceived sexual orientation, Connecticut signs into law a hate-crimes bill. Those convicted face a $5,000 fine and up to five years in prison.

1990   The Hague, Netherlands, recruits lesbians and gay men for its police force by advertising in the country's leading gay paper, *De Gay Krant*. City officials view the move as a way of increasing tolerance in police ranks.

1990   The first gay pride parade held anywhere on the African continent occurs in South Africa when a mixed-race crowd of more than 800 people march through the Johannesburg neighborhoods of Hillbrow and Braamfontein. Sponsoring the march, which draws participants from as far off as Durban and Cape Town, is the Gay and Lesbian Organization of the Witwatersrand, whose founder, Simon Nkoli, addresses the event.

1990   The first Eastern European exhibition of panels of the NAMES Project AIDS Memorial Quilt is held in Prague's Saint Nicholas Church. More than 90 panels are on display.

1990   In a ruling on a test case brought by five activists and the Texas Human Rights Fund challenging Section 21.06 of the state penal code, a district court judge in Austin, Texas, decides that the law as written is unconstitutional, as it deprives lesbian and gay people of the constitutional rights of privacy, due process, and equal protection under the law. State officials appealed the judgment, which was amended in 1993.

1990 Allan Berube's *Coming Out Under Fire*, a research study of the history of homosexual men and women in the U.S. armed forces during World War II, is published.

1990 *Outwaves*, a half-hour gay radio show, airs in Ireland, serving County Wicklow and the greater Dublin region.

1990 The activist group Your Family, Friends, and Neighbors hosts a gay pride parade in Boise, Idaho.

1990 Homan, a civil rights group formed to work for full legal protection for Iranian gay and lesbian individuals, is founded in exile in Stockholm, Sweden. Its primary mission is to call attention to the dire conditions facing homosexuals in Iran under the Islamic fundamentalist government, where sodomy and lesbianism carry the death penalty.

1990 An Asian lesbian conference is held in Bangkok, Thailand.

1990 In a campaign against homosexuals by the fundamentalist government of Iran, three gay men are publicly beheaded in the city of Nehavend, while two accused lesbians are stoned to death in Langrood. The Iranian chief justice Morteza Moghtadai tells the press that homosexuality is punished by death, including being buried alive, being thrown from a mountain or tall building, or having a wall deliberately collapsed on the guilty person, as well as stoning and beheading.

1990 The Freedom from Violence Act, signed into law by Governor James Thompson, is the first pro-gay law to be enacted statewide in Illinois. Its provisions amend a current state law covering penalties for crimes based on race, religion, or ethnic background by expanding the list of protected classes, adding ancestry, mental and physical disability, and sexual orientation. The measure becomes effective in 1991.

1990 The first city political campaign with two admitted lesbians as candidates for the same office is the election for the Board of Supervisors in San Francisco, California, where the civil rights attorney Roberta Achtenberg and the city Democratic Party chair Carole Migden are on the ballot.

1990 The first U.S. university to extend spousal benefits to the domestic partners of its students, including gay and lesbian couples, is Stanford University in California.

1990 Drill sergeant Miriam Ben-Shalom forms the Gay, Lesbian, and Bisexual Veterans Association to acknowledge the contributions of homosexual women and men in the armed forces of the United States.

1990 Amnesty International Members for Lesbian and Gay Concerns, a focus group in Amnesty International, promotes policies and international law designed to protect gay, lesbian, bisexual, and transgendered people and their advocates from human rights violations. In 1991, their efforts result in an expansion of the definition of "prisoner of conscience" to include those imprisoned because of their homosexuality.

1990	Queer Nation, whose initial chapter is organized in New York City, is a direct-action group formed to fight homophobia and hate crimes against gay people. By the mid-1990s, it has established chapters in cities nationwide (some of which dissolve through internal disputes) but has not articulated a coherent agenda.
1990	The Hate Crimes Statistics Act, signed into law by President George Bush, is the first piece of U.S. legislation calling for the collection of statistics on the incidence of crimes based on various types of prejudice. Sexual orientation is included as one of the grounds for prejudice.
1991	The first public company to offer health-insurance coverage to same-sex partners is the software manufacturer Lotus Development Corporation (acquired by IBM in 1995). IBM, Hewlett-Packard, Microsoft, Intel, and Apple Computer do the same shortly afterward.
1991	While campaigning for president, Bill Clinton, at a news conference at Harvard University in Cambridge, Massachusetts, responds to a question about lifting the ban on gays in the military by saying that, if elected, he would overturn the ban, on the grounds that gay people should be given the opportunity to serve their nation. Following his election in 1992, massive public opposition to the idea of such a move emerges, led by conservative elements including General Colin L. Powell, chairman of the Joint Chiefs of Staff, and Senator Sam Nunn, chair of the Senate Armed Services Committee.
1991	Lambda Prague, a gay organization formed by a high school teacher, Jan Lany, is founded in Czechoslovakia after the collapse of Communism.
1991	The first Oregon state legislator to acknowledge her homosexuality is Gail Shibley of Portland, who comes out at a press conference moments after being sworn in.
1991	The first openly gay candidate to stand for election to an at-large seat on the Kansas City, Missouri, city council is Jon Barnett, who is sponsored by the area's Green Party.
1991	In San Francisco, California, Tom Rielly and Karen Wickre form Digital Queers, a group of computer professionals dedicated to helping lesbian and gay organizations make effective use of cyberspace. The group also solicits computer-industry philanthropy for gay and lesbian causes.
1991	The first officially registered gay organization to appear in Russia is Kryl'ia (Wings), a gay and lesbian center in Saint Petersburg, named for the early-20th-century novel of the same title by the homosexual writer Mikhail Kuzmin. Kryl'ia works for protection of gay and lesbian rights, increased gay awareness, and

legalization of same-sex relationships.

1991   The International Gay and Lesbian Human Rights Commission, created in San Francisco, California, works primarily at monitoring and documenting worldwide human rights abuses against homosexual, bisexual, and transgendered people as well as persons with human immunodeficiency virus (HIV) or AIDS, and the mobilization of responses to such actions.

1991   The Stanley Kubrick film *Spartacus* (1960) is rereleased with a previously deleted bathing scene involving Tony Curtis and Sir Laurence Olivier. The studio, Universal Pictures, originally deemed the scene too risqué and suggestive of homosexuality and ordered it cut from the film.

1991   Part 1 of the two-part drama *Angels in America* by Tony Kushner premieres at the Eureka Theater Company in San Francisco, California. Entitled *Millennium Approaches*, the play and its sequel, *Perestroika*, deal openly with AIDS and the homosexuality of its four main characters, one of whom is a fictional representation of the McCarthy-era right-wing lawyer Roy Cohn, who died of AIDS in 1986. *Millennium Approaches* is widely praised and is a huge success. After its Broadway premiere in 1992, it goes on to win the 1993 Pulitzer Prize for drama and four Tony Awards.

1992   After a group of homosexual and bisexual men and women belonging to the Irish-American community petition the association sponsoring Boston's Saint Patrick's Day Parade for permission to march and are refused, they initiate a lawsuit. The U.S. Supreme Court finally determines that the celebration is a private rather than public event, and as such the organizers cannot be forced to violate their First Amendment rights of association and expression.

1992   In Sasebo, Japan, radioman Allen Schindler is murdered by another member of the U.S. Navy on the grounds that Schindler is gay. Schindler's brutal death does little to shift opposition to homosexuals in the military, although his killer is eventually sentenced to life imprisonment.

1992   The first public meeting of the Lesbian Avengers, a direct-action group whose stated purpose is "to fight for lesbian survival and visibility," takes place at the New York City Lesbian and Gay Community Services Center. By 1996, there are 35 chapters in North America and Europe.

1992   The European Deaf Lesbian and Gay Conference, an international meeting devoted to the concerns of hearing-impaired and deaf homosexual men and women, is held in Paris, France.

1992   In Nicaragua, same-sex relations and promotion of homosexuality are criminalized.

1992   A public celebration of gay and lesbian pride is held in Buenos Aires, Argentina.

1992   The Queer Resources Directory, an online electronic research library "dedicated to sexual minorities," becomes active and serves as a forum for both civil rights organizations and discussions of specific issues.

1992   In India, a public demonstration representing gay people as individuals with rights that should be respected, is held outside the police headquarters in Delhi. At issue is an entrapment campaign against homosexuals under way in the city's central park.

1992   Colorado passes a provision in its constitution, Amendment 2, which attempts to bar permanently the enactment of civil rights laws for gays and lesbians by prohibiting the enactment of any laws giving preferred or protected status to homosexuals; the amendment repeals antidiscrimination laws in Boulder, Aspen, and Denver. In *Romer v. Evans*, the U.S. Supreme Court rules in 1996 that the amendment has no rational basis and violates the equal protection rights of homosexuals; the Supreme Court also affirms the similar judgment rendered by the Supreme Court of Colorado.

1993   The European Court of Human Rights rules that, in the case of *Modinos v. Cyprus*, Sections 171 and 173 of the Cypriot criminal code, which prohibit "carnal knowledge against the laws of nature" (punishable with up to five years' imprisonment), are in violation of an individual's right to privacy as guaranteed under Article 8 of the European Convention on Human Rights. The government of Cyprus is ordered to repeal these laws but as of 1997 had not done so.

1993   In *Baehr v. Miike*, a case in which three same-gender couples apply for marriage licenses and are denied, the Hawaii Supreme Court rules that the existing state ban on marriage between persons of the same gender constitutes discrimination by sex and is therefore a violation of the Hawaii constitution. As the court also rules that discrimination is justified only if the state can show a compelling interest, the case is sent back to the circuit court, where in 1996 Judge Kevin Chang rules that the state representatives were not able to justify the ban on same-sex marriages and that marriage licenses could not be denied simply on the basis of gender. Opponents of this ruling then work to pass an amendment to the state constitution defining marriage as between one man and one woman; such an amendment is passed by the Hawaii legislature in 1998. As a result, several mainland states' legislatures pass measures either redefining marriage as between man and woman or stating that same-sex marriages certified in other states would not be recognized in their local jurisdictions.

1993   Homosexuality is decriminalized in the newly independent Lithuania.

1993   President Bill Clinton offers a compromise, popularly known as "Don't Ask, Don't Tell," in the controversy over gays in the military. A version of this measure, revised so as to strengthen military services' positions with regard to identifying and separating homosexuals, is enacted into law.

1993	In Denmark, a television advertisement for a newspaper, *Politiken*, features two men kissing, thought to be the first such ad.
1994	More than 1,200 people attend the first gay pride celebration to be held in Japan, which occurs in the streets of Tokyo.
1994	The Equal Treatment Act, outlawing any discrimination based on sexuality, is signed into law in the Netherlands.
1994	The public-interest court case filed by the activist group AIDS Bhedbhav Virodhi Andolan in the Delhi High Court in India is based on the refusal by authorities of Delhi's Tihar Jail to allow the distribution of condoms to prisoners, on the grounds that this would be abetting a crime. The suit calls for the repeal of Section 377 of the penal code as a violation of the basic rights of life and liberty contained in the Indian constitution and also cites India's signing of the United Nations Declaration of Human Rights.
1994	Utah is the first state in the United States to pass legislation barring the extension of legal recognition to same-sex marriages licensed in other states. By 1997, 16 U.S. states prohibit such status.
1994	With the passage of the Criminal Law Amendment Act in the German Federal Parliament, new provisions eliminating those sections of the criminal code discriminating against gay people are adopted. The action marks the final repeal of the notorious Paragraph 175, the legal text originally a part of the Prussian law code, which had been used for 124 years as grounds for the arrest and conviction of thousands of gay men.
1994	*Rights of Gay Men and Lesbians in the Russian Federation*, issued by the International Gay Lesbian Human Rights Commission, describes the human rights situations facing homosexual men and women in the aftermath of the collapse of the Soviet Union.
1994	The European Parliament adopts a resolution calling on member nations of the European Community to repeal all antihomosexual provisions of their law codes and to end discrimination based on sexual orientation in all sections of society.
1994	In Tasmania, a state of Australia, the case of *Nicholas Toonen v. Australia* results in a change in the laws of same-sex relations, after the United Nations Human Rights Committee calls on Australia to eliminate legislation prohibiting sexual contact between consenting adult males. Toonen filed a complaint with the committee charging that Australia had violated its obligations under Articles 2 (nondiscrimination), 17 (right to privacy), and 26 (equal protection under the law) of the International Covenant on Civil and Political Rights; the committee finds Australia in violation of Articles 2 and 17, but the Tasmanian law is not repealed until 1997.
1994	The first organization for homosexuals to appear in Albania after the Communist government falls is announced through letters sent to newspapers in the capital city, Tirana. Declaring that

Albania is no longer the only country in Europe without a formal gay presence, the Gay Albanian Society pledges to work for equality and to challenge popular prejudices about homosexuality and AIDS.

1994   The Felipa da Souza Awards are presented by the International Gay and Lesbian Human Rights Commission during the Stonewall 25 celebrations in New York City; the awards are named for a Brazilian woman who was tortured by the Inquisition in 1591 for having lesbian sex. Recipients are the Belgrade lesbian Lepa Mladjenovic (cofounder of Serbia's first gay rights group); the Bogota, Colombia, civil rights lawyer Juan Pablo Ordonez; and the Cape Town, South Africa, organization ABIGALE.

1994   The first gay rights court decision in modern Japan comes when Tokyo District Court Judge Toshiaki Harada rules that the city of Tokyo has discriminated against members of OCCUR, the nation's leading gay activist organization, when it barred them from staying at a city lodge and recreation center for fear they would have sex and upset straight guests. Damages of $2,600 are awarded.

1994   In Great Britain, the House of Lords votes to make male rape a crime, in response to several gang rapes by antigay heterosexuals the previous year.

1994   Challenging the equality rights section of Canada's Charter of Rights and Freedoms, James Egan and Jack Nesbit, a gay couple, appeal to the Canadian Supreme Court for access to the federal allowance for spouses of low-income pensioners after being together for 46 years.

1994   Attended by 70 men from Bangladesh, India, Sri Lanka, Pakistan, and Nepal, a conference for gay men in South Asia, organized by the activist and publisher Ashok Row Kavi, is held near Mumbai (Bombay), India. The meeting calls for the repeal of India's law against same-gender sex, which mandates a punishment of up to 10 years in jail.

1994   Tom Hanks receives an Oscar for his performance in *Philadelphia*, the first mainstream American movie to portray a character with AIDS. Hanks plays a homosexual corporate lawyer who is dismissed from his job on a pretext when he shows signs of illness; he brings charges of AIDS discrimination against the firm. The film is based in part on the real-life suit brought by Clarence Cain, a young black attorney, against the Hyatt Legal Services chain, where he had been employed as a regional director. Cain won the case two months before he died.

1995   Organizations formed in Romania to work for the improvement of social and legal conditions facing homosexuals collapse in this year, and deeply conservative attitudes toward homosexuality as a foreign influence pose significant obstacles for change. Total Relations, founded in 1993, and Group 200, created in 1994, are unable to sustain any interest from the highly fearful Romanian gay population.

1995   The parliament of Albania acts to legalize gay sex by repealing the penal code Section 137, which calls for up to 10 years in prison for persons convicted of simply being homosexual. Lobbying by activists from Shoqata Gay Albania (Gay Albanian Society) helped create awareness that such persecution is not compatible with the idea of a modern democratic society.

1995   U.S. president Bill Clinton announces that federal employers are no longer allowed to deny their employees security clearance on the grounds of sexual orientation.

1995   Denmark, Norway, and Sweden create a common Nordic commission on marriage and agree to recognize same-sex partnerships registered in other countries.

1995   The draft of a new constitution for Poland, being prepared by a parliamentary commission, is expanded to ban discrimination based on sexual orientation. Approval by both houses of parliament and a popular referendum are required before the new document can become law, but the representative of President Lech Walesa opposes the 16-to-6 vote in favor of the ban, stating that it might lead to gay marriages or adoptions.

1995   At the services held to mark the 50th anniversary of the liberation of the Sachsenhausen concentration camp in Germany, the historian Gunter Grau, a representative of German gay organizations, calls on the German government to compensate gay victims of the Third Reich. Grau notes that previous commemorations excluded homosexuals because organizers believed they would dishonor the other prisoners.

1995   Orguyo (Pride) is the first gay organization to appear on the Caribbean island of Curaçao.

1995   A Costa Rican gay group seeking formal recognition from the Office of Registration of Organizations is initially denied legal status on the grounds that its purposes would be morally offensive. The group, based in the city of San José, later changes its name to Triangulo Rosa (Pink Triangle, referring to the patch that homosexuals were forced to wear in Nazi Germany) and succeeds in obtaining registration.

1995   A national conference of violence against gays and lesbians is held at the University of Sydney in Australia. Among the topics discussed are gay-oriented hate crimes and school-based violence.

1995   The Sisters of Venus, a lesbian organization, is founded in Turkey.

1995   The Constitutional court of Hungary rules that same-sex common-law marriages should be recognized and orders parliament to make all necessary changes to implement gay common-law marriage by 1996. Under Hungarian law, common-law couples receive all benefits granted to formal civil marriages; the suit occasioning this ruling is initiated by the gay activist group Homeros Lambda.

1995	Separated from the Royal Air Force in 1994 for being a lesbian, nurse Jeannette Smith files suit before a London High Court judge, alleging her dismissal to have been unlawful. The court rules the next year that her suit can proceed, as the air force policy may be in violation of the European Union's antidiscrimination laws.
1995	At the International Tribunal on Human Rights Violations against Sexual Minorities, held in New York City, representatives from the Philippines, Zimbabwe, Romania, India, El Salvador, Turkey, the United States, and Argentina address persecutions and rights violations based both on HIV status and sexual orientation. Judges for the tribunal are drawn from the Robert F. Kennedy Human Rights Center and Human Rights Watch, the Parliament of Brazil, and the South African delegation to the Beijing World Conference on Women.
1995	*Queer in America*, written by the New York City radical journalist Michelangelo Signorile, is the first nonfiction work to support the practice of publicly revealing a person's gay or lesbian nature (known as "outing") as a revolutionary tactic. Developing ideas first aired in columns for the defunct magazine *Outweek*, Signorile reflects both personal anger and the confrontational activist philosophies of ACT UP (AIDS Coalition to Unleash Power).
1995	Claudia Roth, German Green Party member of the European Parliament, is awarded the ÉGALITÉ Prize, given annually to an individual who has advanced the rights of Europe's lesbian and gay citizens. Roth is a principal author of the report *Equal Rights for Homosexuals and Lesbians in the EC*.
1995	The first day that a new law recognizing same-sex weddings goes into effect in Sweden, Hans Jonsson and Sven-Olov Janssen are joined at the City Hall of Ostersund by the former member of Parliament Jorn Svenson, who advocated for same-gender marriage in Sweden as early as 1973.
1995	George Chauncey's *Gay New York: Gender, Urban Culture, and the Making of the Gay World, 1890–1940* traces a pattern of anti-gay discrimination during several decades before World War II.
1996	The Defense of Marriage Act, signed into law by President Bill Clinton, grants states the right to refuse to recognize same-gender marriages in the United States.
1996	South Africa is the first country in the world to incorporate into its constitution a prohibition of discrimination on the basis of sexual orientation, in Clause 9.3, which includes sexual orientation, as well as race, gender, sex, color, and belief, among forbidden grounds of discrimination. A similar provision had been included in the Interim Constitution of 1993; in 1996, every political party except for the minority African Christian Democratic Party states its support of the constitutional protection of gays and lesbians.
1996	As a challenge to the effectiveness of the human rights ordinance of Pittsburgh, Pennsylvania, Deborah Henson, an instructor at

the University of Pittsburgh, files a suit against the university on the issue of its refusal to grant her same-gender partner domestic-partner benefits, because Pennsylvania law does not prohibit discrimination based on sexual orientation.

1996 Published by the International Gay and Lesbian Human Rights Commission, *Epidemic of Hate* is a report on the conditions of life for homosexuals in Brazil.

1996 The Althing, the parliament of Iceland, passes a law granting legal recognition to same-sex couples. By the end of the year, 17 couples have formally registered their partnerships.

1997 Toni McNaron's *Poisoned Ivy: Lesbian and Gay Academics Confronting Homophobia* documents the employment problems and harassment faced by homosexual men and women employed in the U.S. higher education system.

1997 In the principality of San Marino, Article 274 (originally adopted in 1975) of the criminal code, which had punished homosexual contacts with imprisonment for up to one year and the loss of all political rights for a period ranging from nine months to two years, is repealed.

1997 Ecuador's Constitutional Tribunal, asked to review the constitutional status of the first part of Section 516 of the penal code making same-sex relations punishable with between four and eight years in prison, rules that this law is unconstitutional. Activists had been attempting to remove the law for more than 10 years, charging that it violates the American Convention on Human Rights; the ruling leaves only three Latin American nations with laws declaring homosexuality to be a crime: Puerto Rico, Chile, and Nicaragua.

1997 In an episode on April 30, the character Ellen Morgan on the TV show *Ellen* admits she is a lesbian and becomes the first lead character in a television series to be homosexual. The character is played by actress/comedienne Ellen DeGeneres, who has come out in real life two weeks earlier. An estimated 42 million viewers tune in to watch the hour-long episode.

1998 OUTFRONT, a program launched by Amnesty International, addresses the issue of human rights violations based on sexual identity and marks the formal adoption of this issue as part of the organization's general world agenda.

1998 Marina Cetiner of Romania is pardoned by Emil Constantinescu, president of Romania, after serving two years of a three-year sentence for attempting to seduce another woman. Although the International Gay and Lesbian Rights Commission states that the president had promised to pardon all prisoners jailed for gay and lesbian charges, the law making homosexuality a crime punishable by prison sentences is still in effect in Romania.

1998 In the new constitution passed by Fiji, an article in the bill of rights includes sexual minorities in the classes of persons protected from discrimination. In 1999, conservative opponents introduce a bill in the Fijian parliament to maintain the prohibitions against same-gender marriage and the legal punishments against unnatural acts already in force under the Marriage Act and the existing penal code; this bill is challenged by the Coalition on the Right to Sexual Orientation as a violation of the sanctity of the constitution.

1998   Commissioners of Dade County, Florida, pass a nondiscrimination ordinance banning discrimination on the basis of sexual orientation in employment and housing, effectively negating Anita Bryant's efforts which began in 1977.

1998   In October Matthew Shephard, a 21-year-old college student, is abducted from a bar in Laramie, Wyoming, by two young men, beaten into a coma, and left for dead because he is homosexual. He dies a few days later in the hospital. The story prompts national outrage and inspires the play *The Laramie Project*, written by Moisés Kaufman and the members of Tectonic Theater Project in New York City. The play premieres in 2000 at the Union Square Theater in New York and is adapted for television by HBO (broadcast in March 2002).

1999   A meeting organized by the homosexual activist Mel White and the Reverend Jerry Falwell, a conservative Evangelical social activist, of the Christian Right is held in Virginia.

1999   The Equality Begins at Home campaign, a one-week effort coordinated by the National Gay and Lesbian Task Force, focuses attention on gay and lesbian civil rights issues at the state and local levels in the United States. Demonstrations and rallies are planned for all 50 state capitals as well as the District of Columbia and Puerto Rico.

1999   The Supreme Court of Canada rules that when common-law relationships fail, whether homosexual or heterosexual, the poorer spouse is eligible for spousal-support payments under the Family Law Act of Ontario Province. The court also rules that restricting such payments to heterosexual couples violates the Canadian Charter of Rights and Freedoms.

1999   Martin Mawyer, president of the Christian Action Network, asks the chair of the Federal Communications Commission to have an "HC" label placed on television programs that portray homosexual acts.

1999   *Queer As Folk*, a television drama depicting Manchester gay club life, debuts in Great Britain. An American version premiers in the U.S. in 2000.

2000   The Millennium March on Washington for Equality is the first massive public rally in support of gay and lesbian civil rights to occur in Washington, D.C., in the 21st century.

2002   A public controversy develops over lesbian support for the WNBA (Women's National Basketball Association) when lesbians argue that they constitute a substantial percentage of the fan base but are ignored by the teams and advertisers, who instead promote traditional families and lifestyles and heterosexual players.

2002   In a groundbreaking legal settlement, a gay student who sued his high school in Reno, Nevada, for permitting antigay harassment signs an agreement that protects gay and lesbian students. According to the agreement, which is the first in the country to recognize the constitutional right of gay and lesbian young people to be open about their sexual orientation in school, the high school agrees to protect gay and lesbian students from discrimination and to train staff to deal with sexual harassment, a decision that affects gay and lesbian students nationwide.

2002   In Virginia, Linda Kaufman, a lesbian Episcopal priest, reaches a settlement with the state, permitting her to adopt a child from the District of Columbia. Virginia child-welfare officials will now stop forbidding adoptions on the basis of the parents' sexual orientation. The adoption was approved by both a Virginia adoption agency and Washington officials before Virginia refused to approve it because Kaufman is a lesbian.

2002   In *Lawrence and Garner v. Texas*, Lambda Legal, representing two Houston men, asks the U.S. Supreme Court to review the constitutionality of the Texas Homosexual Conduct Law, which forbids intimate relations between consenting adults of the same sex; the Texas law does not pertain to heterosexual couples. The two men were arrested and convicted for having sex in the privacy of one man's home; Lambda Legal also asks the Court to reconsider the 1986 case of *Bowers v. Hardwick*, which upheld Georgia's sodomy law.

2002   The Arkansas Supreme Court rules in *Jegley v. Picado* that Arkansas's state sodomy law violates the state's protection of constitutional rights to privacy and equal protection, in a case in which seven gay and lesbian residents challenged the law. The court rules that Arkansas's ban on intimate relations between consenting adults of the same sex violates the right to privacy under the state constitution, the first time that an Arkansas court acknowledged this right.

2002   The International Gay and Lesbian Human Rights Commission condemns the detention and trial of 50 defendants in Cairo, Egypt, charged with debauchery because of their alleged sexual orientation, although the Egyptian government states that consensual sexual conduct between men is not a crime. Two men have already been sentenced to hard labor after being convicted of "contempt of religion."

2002   In Austria, a law equalizing the age of consent for both heterosexual and homosexual relations comes into effect. Article 209 of the Austrian Penal Code, which stipulated 18 years as the age of consent for homosexual relations, in contrast to 14 years for heterosexual relations, is deleted from the code.

2002   The Movimiento Homosexual de Lima (Homosexual Movement of Lima) announces that the Pride Parade and other activities to be held in Lima, Peru, have been authorized by the Cercado de

Lima district after being refused by the Miraflores district in Lima. A parade, rally, and speeches by human rights representatives will be part of the celebration.

2002   Marta Alvarez, a Colombian lesbian imprisoned in the Armenia Women's Jail for murder, is denied the right to conjugal visits. Alvarez has been fighting since 1994 for the right to have conjugal visits, which are allowed for other prisoners but not for lesbians or gays; the Interamerican Human Rights Commission acknowledged that the denial of visits to Alvarez was discrimination based on sexual orientation and mediated between Alvarez and the Colombian government, which recently allowed conjugal visits for another lesbian prisoner but not for Alvarez.

2002   In Bangalore, India, police stop human rights activists from entering Sangama, a local center that allows *hijras* (transgendered people and people with intersex conditions) to meet there. Police had notified Sangama that *hijras* can meet only outside the city.

2002   In Miami, Florida, the head of Concerned Women for America, Sandy Rice, states her concern about the arrest of Anthony Verdugo, a pro-family man leading a drive to repeal a local gay rights law. Accusing them of ignoring the civil rights of anyone opposed to them, Rice warns that homosexual activists "will stop at nothing to win"; Verdugo is charged with falsely certifying a petition, though he had certified thousands of the 51,000 petitions approved by election officials.

2002   The *New York Times* announces that it will begin listing marriage announcements for same-sex partners.

2002   *Take Me Out*, a play by Richard Greenberg about an All-Star major league baseball player who admits to his homosexuality during the season, premieres at the Donmar Warehouse in London, England. The play details the fallout from the player's announcement as news spreads through the team, the media, and the United States.

CHAPTER EIGHT

DISABLED RIGHTS

c. 3500 B.C.E.	The first recorded mention of a prosthesis appears in the *Rig-Veda*, an ancient Asian Indian epic written in Sanskrit. A warrior, Queen Vishpla, loses her leg in battle, is fitted with an iron prosthesis, and then returns to battle.
c. 380s B.C.E.	Although many ancient cultures look on mental illness as possession by evil spirits and often consider epilepsy as god-given, the Greek physician Hippocrates considers it to be a physical disorder of the brain. Hippocrates describes mania, melancholia or depression, and phrenitis or brain fever as mental illnesses that should be treated humanely.
c. 355 B.C.E.	Deafness is equated with stupidity for the first time in Western thought by the Greek philosopher Aristotle, who says that those "born deaf become senseless and incapable of reason."
700s C.E.	In Baghdad and later in other Islamic cities, asylums are established to offer people with mental illnesses humane treatment, in comfortable settings, with music and special foods. In Islamic belief, Allah loves people who are insane, and thus they deserve special care, in contrast to harsh methods, like chaining an afflicted person, used in the West.
c. 1500	The Italian Girolamo Cardano is the first physician to argue that deaf people can think like people with speech.
1616	*Of the Art of Signs*, by G. Bonifacio, is the first book to discuss sign language for deaf and mute people. Bonifacio's sign language uses most parts of the body for conversing.
1696	The first modern prosthesis is invented by the Dutch surgeon Pieter Andriannszoon Verduyn. It is the first nonlocking, below-knee prosthesis, and modern jointed devices are similar to it.
1755	The first speaking school for deaf people is established in Germany by Samuel Heinicke, who believes that deaf children should be taught lipreading and speech. In the same year, the first free school for the deaf is established by Charles Michel, abbé de l'Épée, in Paris, France; he advocates signing and finger spelling as the best method of educating deaf children. These two contrasting methods of teaching deaf people are still used today.
1760	Thomas Braidwood founds the first school for deaf people in Britain.
1775	The Spanish lawyer Lasso is the first Western legal scholar to

advocate rights for deaf people. He argues that deaf people who learn to speak are no longer dumb and should have rights to inherit property.

1784   The first school for the deaf in Italy is opened by Abba Silvestri in Rome.

1784–1786 The first book in raised letters (script letters slightly raised above the page) is published by Valentin Haüy in Paris, France. Haüy also founds the first school for deaf people in Paris, the Institution Nationale, still functioning today.

1790   In France, a prohibition is placed on the use of restraints for mentally ill people.

1801   Dr. Jean-Marc-Gaspard Itard begins attempting to train the Savage of Aveyron, a boy of 12 or so found running wild in the French countryside and brought to Paris, where the eminent French psychologist Philippe Pinel judged him "feebleminded." After five years of efforts, Itard is unable to teach the boy (whom he calls Victor) to speak, read, or become sufficiently socialized to make his wants known; nevertheless, Itard's experiences with Victor help him develop methods of teaching deaf people.

1812   *Medical Inquiries and Observations upon the Diseases of the Mind* by the American physician Benjamin Rush is the first book to attempt to explain mental illness in the modern world; although Rush's treatment methods are sometimes controversial, he advocates humane treatment of mentally ill people and is sometimes considered the founder of American psychiatry. Rush's career outside medicine is also distinguished; he was a signer of the Declaration of Independence and served as treasurer of the U.S. Mint from 1797 to his death in 1813.

1817   The Connecticut Asylum for the Education and Instruction of Deaf and Dumb Persons is founded in Hartford as the first school for the deaf in the United States.

1829   The first school for blind people in the United States, founded in Boston, Massachusetts, by Dr. John Dix Fisher, is incorporated. Later known as Perkins Institute for the Blind, the school moves to Watertown, Massachusetts, in 1913; Helen Keller's teacher, Anne Sullivan, is trained at the Perkins Institute.

1829   The raised-point-alphabet (later called Braille) reading system for blind people is invented in France by Louis Braille, who lost his sight in an accident at the age of 3 years. Braille was sent to the Paris Blind School when he was 10 years old.

1837   Samuel Gridley Howe, director of the Perkins Institute for the Blind in Boston, Massachusetts, undertakes the education of a blind-deaf child, publicizes the case, and establishes that such children can be educated and brought into society.

1846   The *American Annals of the Deaf* begins publication at the American School for the Deaf in Hartford, Connecticut, as the first periodical on deafness.

1860	The Braille system is brought to the United States and is used at the Saint Louis School for the Blind in Saint Louis, Missouri.

1872   A school for teachers of deaf people is opened in Boston, Massachusetts, by Alexander Graham Bell. In addition to later inventing the telephone and experimenting with other such devices, Bell teaches the visible-speech system invented by his father, Alexander Melville Bell, in which the positions of the vocal organs are visually presented for each sound.

1887   Women are admitted for the first time to the National Deaf-Mute College (now Gallaudet University) in Washington, D.C.

1904   On October 28 gymnast George Eyser of the United States wins three gold medals, two silver, and one bronze at the Olympic Games in St. Louis, Missouri, despite having a wooden left leg.

1918   British Braille is recognized as the English-language standard for blind people. Although both New York Point (in which the number of points is governed by the relative frequency of sounds or letters) and American Braille had been used in the United States, British Braille is ultimately selected because of the wealth of code already available in Great Britain, but even today the British and American Braille codes are not identical.

1921   The American Foundation for the Blind is founded with the help of Helen Keller, the noted author and lecturer, as the first organization for blind people in the United States. Keller devotes much of her life to raising funds for the foundation.

1924   The Comité Internationale des Sports des Sourds (International committee of sports for deaf people) is founded in France as the first sports organization for disabled athletes. In the same year, the first international sports competition for disabled athletes, the World Games for the Deaf, is held in Paris.

1929   The Seeing Eye, in Morristown, New Jersey, is founded to supply trained guide dogs to blind people. Nowadays, it is but one of numerous programs that supply dogs and other animals to people in need: Canine Companions for Independence trains dogs to help people with physical disabilities, assist deaf and hearing-impaired people, and provide pet-facilitated therapy for people with developmental disabilities; other dogs are trained in seizure detection for people with epilepsy; therapy dogs and handlers visit sick people in hospitals and elderly residents of various institutions.

1935   The League for the Physically Handicapped is established in New York City as the first disabled rights organization in the United States. Formed by people disabled by polio and cerebral palsy, the league combats employment discrimination and protests against discrimination by the Works Progress Administration; eventually the league's efforts generate several thousand jobs nationwide.

1939   In Germany, Adolf Hitler orders the killing of sick and disabled people, which he describes as "mercy killing." Code-named

Aktion T4, the program is meant to eliminate "life unworthy of life"; although officially ended in August 1941, after nearly 100,000 people have been killed by gassing, it continues, with people now killed by drugs or starvation.

1944

The National Spine Injuries Centre is founded as the first facility for the treatment of spinal injuries in Great Britain. The first wheelchair sports program, the Stoke Mandeville Games, is introduced here in 1948, as the result of the hospital's experience in rehabilitating World War II veterans with spinal injuries.

1949

The National Wheelchair Basketball Association is founded in the United States and serves as the governing body for wheelchair basketball.

1952

The first international sports competition for athletes with spinal-cord injuries is held at the Stoke Mandeville Hospital in Aylesbury, England, with competitors from Great Britain and the Netherlands. Ludwig Guttman, a Jewish refugee and neurologist from Germany, originates the games as part of the rehabilitation process.

1958

The National Wheelchair Games are held in the United States. The games lead to the formation of the National Wheelchair Association (now Wheelchair Sports, USA), the governing body for all wheelchair sports except basketball.

1960

The first International Games for the Disabled are held in Rome, Italy. As the first international sports festival for disabled athletes, the games are modeled on the Olympics; in 1980, the name is changed to the Paralympics.

1968

The Special Olympics is founded by Eunice Kennedy Shriver in Maryland as the first organized sports competition for mentally challenged people.

1969

The North American Riding for the Handicapped Association is founded to promote therapeutic horseback riding in the United States and Canada for people with physical, emotional, and learning disabilities; similar organizations are also created throughout Europe. Therapeutic riding helps disabled people develop balance, coordination, motor skills, and emotional well-being.

1970s

The independent-living movement for disabled people develops in Berkeley, California, led by Ed Roberts, who had polio in 1953, and other disabled people. Roberts is instrumental in founding the Rolling Quads at the University of California at Berkeley Health Center in 1970 and then the Disabled Students' Program; he and others establish the first Center for Independent Living in Berkeley in 1971.

1973

The U.S. Rehabilitation Act passed by Congress calls for businesses that have government contracts to practice affirmative action by hiring disabled workers and providing accommodations for them.

1974

The Disabled Women's Coalition is founded at the University of

California at Berkeley by Susan Sygall, Deborah Kaplan, and others. The organization runs support groups, holds disabled women's retreats, writes for feminist publications, and lectures on women and disability.

1975 The U.S. Education for All Handicapped Children Act is the first law to require equal educational opportunities for disabled children in the United States. The act guarantees that eligible children and youth with disabilities will have available to them a free appropriate public education designed to meet their unique educational needs.

1975 The Declaration on the Rights of Disabled Persons is proclaimed by the United Nations General Assembly.

1976 In the United States, the Federal Communications Commission authorizes reserving Line 21 on television sets for closed captions for the hearing impaired.

1977 In Great Britain, Anne Begg is the first person in a wheelchair who is elected a member of Parliament.

1977 The first demonstration by disabled people against federal policy in the United States lasts for a month. A group of disabled people take over the San Francisco offices of the Department of Health, Education, and Welfare to protest the department's failure to issue strong regulations concerning the disabled; the takeover is successful, and the regulations are finally signed and issued.

1980 The Olympics for the Disabled in Arnhem, Netherlands, are the first international sports festival to involve people with all types of disabilities. The last groups of disabled to be included are the ambulatory athletes with cerebral palsy.

1980–1983 The National Disabled Women's Educational Equity Project conducts the first national study of disability and gender in the United States. The organization publishes *No More Stares* and develops training programs for young disabled women.

1981 The United Nations declares the first International Year for Disabled Persons.

1983 ADAPT, a project of the Atlantis Community in Denver, Colorado, begins a national campaign for lifts on buses and access to public transit for people with disabilities. The first organization in the United States to advocate disability services in the community, ADAPT blocks buses in cities across the United States for seven years to demonstrate the need for disabled access to public transit, and in 1990, laws are enacted making public transportation accessible to the disabled.

1984 Events for disabled people are included in the Olympics for the first time at the Los Angeles Olympics, when the demonstration 800-meter race for women and 1,500-meter race for men are contested.

1988 Dr. I. King Jordan is appointed the first deaf president of Gallaudet University in Washington, D.C.; his appointment follows the

"Deaf President Now" protest at the school. Gallaudet remains the only liberal arts college for deaf students in the United States.

1990   The Americans with Disabilities Act is passed in the United States as the first comprehensive law concerning the rights of disabled people. The purpose of the law is stated as follows: "(1) to provide a clear and comprehensive national mandate for the elimination of discrimination against individuals with disabilities; (2) to provide clear, strong, consistent, enforceable standards addressing discrimination against individuals with disabilities; (3) to ensure that the Federal Government plays a central role in enforcing the standards established in this Act on behalf of individuals with disabilities; and (4) to invoke the sweep of congressional authority, including the power to enforce the fourteenth amendment and to regulate commerce, in order to address the major areas of discrimination faced day-to-day by people with disabilities."

1993   The United Nations develops the Standard Rules for Equalization of Opportunities for Disabled Persons, with the help of Disabled Peoples' International, a global organization working to promote the cause of the disabled.

1993   Pope John Paul II declares that disabled people have inalienable rights.

1995   The first disabled persons are elected to parliaments in southern African nations when Maria Rantho is elected in South Africa and Ronah Moyo is elected in Zimbabwe. The elections are hailed as an important step for disabled rights in Africa.

1995   The International Symposium on Issues of Women with Disabilities is held in Beijing, China, in conjunction with the Fourth World Conference.

1996   The World Association of Persons with Disabilities is formally incorporated in Texas, with the goal of breaking down economic and social barriers for disabled people worldwide.

1997   The Individuals with Disabilities Education Act Amendments make significant changes to the Education for All Handicapped Children Act of 1975 in assessment-testing programs, parent participation in eligibility and placement decisions, program development and review, transition planning, and discipline of children with disabilities.

1998   Tom Whittaker, who lost his left foot in a head-on collision with a drunk driver, becomes the first amputee to climb to the summit of Mount Everest.

1998   Actor Michael J. Fox reveals that he has Parkinson's disease. Fox's announcement and subsequent advocacy efforts raise public awareness of how people with the condition can continue to lead full and productive lives.

1999   The U.S. Supreme Court, in *Sutton v. United Air Lines*, decides that two nearsighted sisters who fail to meet United's vision standards were not discriminated against when the airline refused to hire them as pilots. As long as their vision can be corrected with eyeglasses or contact lenses, the sisters are not disabled under the 1990 Americans with Disabilities Act, which bans discrimination against a "qualified individual with a disability."

1999   In *Murphy v. United Parcel Service*, the U.S. Supreme Court rules that United Parcel Service did not discriminate by firing a mechanic whose high blood pressure violated Department of Transportation safety standards. The mechanic's job required him to drive, but because his high blood pressure was correctable and he could do other work, he was not considered disabled.

1999   The U.S. Supreme Court, in *Albertsons, Inc. v. Kirkingburg*, decides that a supermarket chain did not discriminate by firing a truck driver who was nearly blind in one eye and could not meet federal vision standards for commercial drivers.

1999   In *Olmstead v. L. C.*, the U.S. Supreme Court rules that states must move people with certain mental disabilities from hospitals to community homes, to comply with the Americans with Disabilities Act.

2000   The Disability Rights Commission (DRC) is established in the United Kingdom as an independent agency to investigate cases of alleged inequality in the workplace and if necessary to take legal action.

2001   A statue of Franklin D. Roosevelt seated in a wheelchair is displayed in Washington, D.C., the first statue showing him in a wheelchair. During his presidency from 1932 to 1945, Roosevelt concealed the fact that he could not walk unaided as a result of polio he contracted in 1921.

2001   Representative Jim Langevin (Democrat) from Rhode Island is the first quadriplegic to serve in the U.S. Congress. He has a battery-powered wheelchair and voice-recognition software to dictate material on his computer.

2001   The Educational Testing Service announces that it will stop flagging the reports of individuals who take some of its standardized tests; the flagging indicates that individuals with physical or mental disabilities were given special accommodation, such as more time, in taking the test. The announcement is part of the settlement of a lawsuit filed in 1999 by a man in California who claims discrimination when his test report was flagged and he was not accepted to business school; in 2002, the College Board announces that in 2003 it will also stop flagging the Scholastic Aptitude Test (SAT).

2001   The National Disabled Students Union (NDSU) is founded in the United States. It is a reaction by students to the U.S. Supreme Court decision in *Board of Trustees of the University of Alabama et al. v. Garrett et al.*, limiting the enforcement of Title I of the 1990 Americans with Disabilities Act.

2002   The U.S. Supreme Court, in *Atkins v. Virginia,* rules that execut-
            ing mentally retarded convicts violates the Eighth Amendment's
            constitutional protection against cruel and unusual punishment.
            The decision reverses a 1998 Supreme Court decision.

2002   In *Toyota v. Williams*, the U.S. Supreme Court rules that a
            worker whose carpal-tunnel syndrome prevents her from work-
            ing at a factory job is not necessarily disabled under the 1990
            Americans with Disabilities Act. The Court decides that workers
            are not disabled as long as their condition can be "mitigated"
            through medication or other means.

2002   In *US Airways v. Barnett*, the U.S. Supreme Court rules that the
            Americans with Disabilities Act does not entitle disabled workers
            to expect workplace-seniority systems to be bypassed in search of
            suitable jobs for a worker who is handicapped.

2002   In *Chevron v. Echazabal*, the U.S. Supreme Court rules that the
            Americans with Disabilities Act does not force a company to give
            a disabled worker a job that the company believes jeopardizes
            the worker's health or safety.

CHAPTER NINE

REFUGEE RIGHTS

c. 1000 B.C.E.	According to Roman mythology, after the Greeks capture Troy, a city-state in Asia Minor, only a few Trojans escape the destruction; one is Aeneas, a Trojan prince, who flees with his son and his parents to seek refuge elsewhere, perhaps the earliest mentioned refugees. After years of wandering filled with dramatic adventures, Aeneas reaches Italy and eventually becomes king of Latium, thus fathering the Roman people; Virgil tells the story in his *Aeneid*.
1889 C.E.	The Montevideo Treaty on International Criminal Law Instrument is the first treaty governing asylum in Latin America. In 1954, it is extended by the Caracas Convention on Territorial Asylum.
1914–1919	A major displacement of people in Europe takes place during and following World War I.
1921	To deal with the European refugee and displaced-person crisis, the League of Nations appoints Fridtjof Nansen of Norway as the first High Commissioner for Refugees.
1933	The League of Nations establishes the office of High Commissioner for Refugees from Germany, to deal with Jews and others fleeing Nazi Germany. Because Germany is a member of the League of Nations, the office operates outside the league, although it comes under league supervision after Germany resigns.
1933	The Convention Relating to the International Status of Refugees, the first international convention on refugees, deals with refugees from Russia, Armenia, Turkey, and parts of the Middle East.
1938	A conference about Jewish refugees in Europe, convened by U.S. president Franklin D. Roosevelt at Évian-les-Bains in France, results in the formation of the Intergovernmental Committee on Refugees, whose mission is to negotiate with Germany about Jewish refugees. The director of the committee discusses with Nazi Germany a plan to fund the exit of Jews with the proceeds of Jewish property in Germany, but these efforts are fruitless.
1938	The Convention Concerning the Status of Refugees Coming from Germany is established but offers only limited protection.
1939	A single High Commissioner for Refugees under the control of

the League of Nations is established. It combines the offices of the High Commissioner founded in Norway in 1921 and the High Commissioner for Refugees from Germany established in 1933.

1943   The United Nations establishes the United Nations Relief and Rehabilitation Administration, which provides relief and repatriation services to war victims and displaced persons in post–World War II Europe.

1943   The American Council for Voluntary Agencies in Foreign Service is founded as the first central refugee-relief organization in the United States to coordinate the activities of organizations providing assistance to refugees and displaced people in Europe.

1946   The United Nations establishes the International Refugee Organization. It takes over the tasks of the United Nations Relief and Rehabilitation Administration, with the temporary authority to register, protect, resettle, and repatriate refugees.

1948   The United Nations Relief and Works Agency for Palestine Refugees is established to assist Palestinians displaced by the formation of the nation of Israel.

1950   The United Nations Korean Reconstruction Agency is established to assist the millions of people displaced by the Korean War.

1950   The office of the United Nations High Commissioner for Refugees is authorized and begins operations in 1951 to lead and coordinate action for the worldwide protection of refugees. The first high commissioner, Gerrit J. van Heuven Goedhart of the Netherlands, serves until 1956.

1951   In Geneva, Switzerland, the United Nations Conference of Plenipotentiaries on the Status of Refugees and Stateless Persons adopts the Convention Relating to the Status of Refugees, which becomes the basic document about refugee rights around the world. The convention affirms that because all human beings enjoy basic freedoms without discrimination, all states concerned with the problems of refugees must agree to work together to solve these problems, including the granting of asylum; for the states to reach agreement, however, the convention must cover only events occurring before 1951, primarily in Europe.

1951   The Intergovernmental Commission for European Migration, a European organization for refugees and displaced people, deals with resettlement and migrant issues on a worldwide basis. It is later renamed the International Organization for Migration.

1954   The first refugee organization to win the Nobel Prize for Peace is the office of the United Nations High Commissioner for Refugees. It is awarded the prize again in 1981.

1954   The first United Nations document pertaining to stateless persons is the Convention Relating to the Status of Stateless Persons. The convention defines a stateless person as one not considered a national by any state under the operation of its law; it also sets forth the standards of treatment to be accorded to stateless persons.

1959 The Council of Europe adopts the European Agreement on the Abolition of Visas for Refugees. The council subsequently adopts other instruments including Resolution 14 (1967) on Asylum to Persons in Danger of Persecution; the European Agreement on Transfer of Responsibility for Refugees (1980); Recommendation on the Harmonization of National Procedures Relating to Asylum (1981); Recommendation on the Protection of Persons Satisfying the Criteria in the Geneva Convention Who Are Not Formally Refugees (1984); and the Dublin Convention (1990), which sets forth criteria for determining which member state is responsible for examining an asylum request when an applicant files an application for asylum with one or more member states of the community.

1959 World Refugee Year is proclaimed.

1960 West Germany establishes an indemnification fund for victims of Nazism. The fund is administered by the office of the United Nations High Commissioner for Refugees.

1961 The Convention on the Reduction of Statelessness provides protections for stateless persons in addition to those provided by the 1954 United Nations Convention Relating to the Status of Stateless Persons. A state that is party to this convention agrees to grant nationality to a person born in that state who would otherwise be stateless; states also agree not to deprive people of their nationality if doing so would make them stateless.

1962 The International Council of Voluntary Agencies is founded to coordinate the efforts of international refugee agencies.

1967 The Protocol Relating to the Status of Refugees revises the 1951 Convention Relating to the Status of Refugees by extending coverage to people who become refugees after 1951 in all parts of the world; since then, the two documents have been the basis of international refugee law. Refugees are guaranteed the right to work, the right to education, the right to social security, and access to courts.

1967 The United Nations Declaration on Territorial Asylum establishes basic principles of asylum, including the fact that the granting of territorial asylum by one state cannot be considered an unfriendly act by another state. The declaration also broadly defines *nonrefoulement*, the principle that a nation may neither expel nor prevent entry of a person whose life is in danger in another nation; though *nonrefoulement* is a principle of international law, states often ignore it and attempt to return refugees to countries where they are at risk or close their borders and refuse to let refugees enter.

1969 The Organization of African Unity Convention, concerning refugee rights, territorial asylum, voluntary repatriation, and the prohibition of subversive activities by refugees, is issued to deal with the growing number of refugees in Africa. The convention provides a broader definition of a refugee than does the United

Nations 1951 Convention: *refugee* here refers to people who must leave their place of residence to seek refuge elsewhere because of external aggression or other events disturbing the public order in their country.

1980 The U.S. Refugee Act is enacted to establish comprehensive legislation dealing with the admission of refugees.

1984 The Cartagena Declaration on International Protection of Refugees in Central America, Mexico, and Panama is issued by nations hosting large refugee populations from other nations. The declaration sets forth the legal foundations for the treatment of Central American refugees, including the principle of *nonrefoulement* and the importance of integrating refugees and undertaking efforts to eradicate the causes of the refugee problem; although not binding on the nations, the declaration has been followed by several nations and also incorporated into domestic legislation.

1985 The Schengen Agreement, involving Belgium, the Netherlands, Luxembourg, West Germany, and France, moves to open common borders to refugees in Western Europe.

1989 In the wake of the fall of Saigon that ended the war in Vietnam and the flood of refugees fleeing by boat to other countries, the Comprehensive Plan of Action for Indochinese Refugees, signed by Western and Asian countries, gives the Asian countries with Vietnamese refugee camps the right to decide who qualifies as a refugee. Those who are designated refugees are settled in Western countries, the United States alone accepting more than 30,000 Vietnamese by 1994; those who do not qualify are sent back to Vietnam.

1991 The office of the United Nations High Commissioner for Refugees provides food and medicine to refugees in the former Yugoslavia after the outbreak of war in that region. With other agencies, the office establishes safe zones for civilians.

1992 The United Nations Department of Humanitarian Affairs is established to mobilize the international community to provide humanitarian aid to people in emergencies or disasters. The department also works to help those people move from relief to rehabilitation.

1992–1994 The office of the United Nations High Commissioner for Refugees assists people suffering from starvation in Somalia.

1993 Germany passes a restrictive asylum law, altering the country's previously liberal policy by severely restricting the ability of those seeking asylum to remain in Germany.

1994 The office of the United Nations High Commissioner for Refugees is one of several organizations working during ethnic conflicts in Rwanda to set up refugee camps on the border of Rwanda and Zaire to prevent Zaire from being overrun by people fleeing from the war.

1998 The Department of Humanitarian Affairs becomes the United

Nations Office for the Coordination of Humanitarian Affairs, with expanded responsibilities for dealing with complex emergency situations.

2001   Human Rights Watch condemns the decision of countries in a preparatory meeting of the United Nations World Conference Against Racism, Racial Discrimination, Xenophobia, and Related Intolerances not to refer to the 1951 refugee convention on the conference's program. Rachael Reilly, refugee policy director of Human Rights Watch, states that refugees and asylum seekers often flee their countries to escape intolerance and then undergo the same treatment in their countries of refuge.

2001   The U.S. Patriot Act is passed by Congress and signed into law by President George W. Bush the following day, supplementing 1996 laws limiting immigrants' access to courts and allowing for the retroactive removal of immigrants for minor offenses. The new act increases the Border Patrol's and the U.S. government's power to deport or deny admission to anyone suspected of terrorism; the act also limits immigrants' ability to challenge the government's decision in court and allows for imprisonment of noncitizens suspected of terrorism; finally, by defining terrorism broadly, the act permits domestic surveillance with few restrictions, as well as similar activities previously practiced only in foreign undercover work.

2002   Attorney General John Ashcroft announces new rules for the Justice Department's adjudication at the U.S. Immigration Appeals Board, drastically speeding up the review process and, according to critics, gutting due process for refugees seeking asylum. Hoping to shorten the two-year period customary for appeals to the board, Ashcroft wants to eliminate de novo review, increase summary decisions, and require judges to clear the current backlog of 55,000 cases in 15 days, forcing each judge to decide one case every 15 minutes.

2002   The United States and Canada draft an agreement requiring asylum seekers to apply where they first arrive, even if they are traveling through one country to the other, and making it difficult to apply for asylum at the border between the two countries. This agreement would shift much of the Canadian caseload to the United States, as Canadian officials state that in 2001 about 35 percent of asylum seekers in Canada had come from the United States; the agreement would also prevent many refugees from joining family or friends while they undergo the immigration process.

2002   On October 29 roughly 200 Haitian refugees leap from a freighter into shallow water on the shore of Miami, Florida, and attempt to evade U.S. Coast Guard and other law enforcement officials. The event is broadcast live on national television by a local news helicopter, which shows refugees scrambling into passing cars and onto the backs of pickup trucks. Others are caught and detained by police, an act that draws protests from residents of Miami's Little Haiti, as well as civil rights and immigrants' rights activists. U.S. policy dictates that only Haitians seeking political asylum may remain in America while their cases are reviewed and that all others must be returned to Haiti.

Bibliography

Abbott, Edith, Grace Firestone, and Shulamith Firestone, eds. *Ready Reference: Women's Issues*. Englewood Cliffs, N.J.: Salem Press, 1997.

Adelman, Howard, and John Sorenson, eds. *African Refugees: Development Aid and Repatriation*. Boulder: Westview Press, 1994.

Ahlstrom, Sydney E. *A Religious History of the American People*. New Haven: Yale University Press, 1972.

Aptheker, Herbert, ed. *A Documentary History of the Negro People in the United States*. New York: Carol Publishing Group, 1990.

Bainton, Roland H. *Christendom: A Short History of Christianity and Its Impact on Western Civilization*. New York: Harper, 1964.

Bokenkotter, Thomas. *A Concise History of the Catholic Church*. Revised and expanded edition. New York: Doubleday, 1990.

Boyle, Kevin, and Juliet Sheen, eds. *Freedom of Religion and Belief: A World Report*. London: Routledge, 1997.

Burger, Julian. *Report from the Frontier: The State of the World's Indigenous Peoples*. London: Zed Books, 1987.

Carabillo, Toni, Judith Meuli, and June Bundy Csida. *Feminist Chronicles 1953–1993*. Los Angeles: Women's Graphics, 1993.

Center for World Indigenous Studies. *The Fourth World Documentation Project Archives*. Web site: *http://www.halcyon.com/FWDP/fwdp.html*.

Child Rights Information Network (CRIN) c/o Save The Children. Web site: *http://www.childhub.ch/webpub/crhome*.

Child Workers in Asia. Web site: *http://cwa.tnet.com*.

Christian Aid. Web site: *http://www.christian-aid.org.uk*.

Davis, Mary B., ed. *Native Americans in the Twentieth Century: An Encyclopedia*. New York: Garland, 1994.

Defence for Children International Information Services. Web site: *http://www.childhub.ch/webpub/dcihome*.

Estell, Kenneth, ed. *The African American Almanac*. Detroit: Gale Research, 1994.

Fourth World Center. Web site: *http://www.cudenver.edu/public/fwc*.

Franklin, Bob, ed. *The Handbook of Children's Rights*. London: Routledge, 1995.

———. *The Rights of Children*. Oxford: Basil Blackwell, 1986.

Gibetz, Judah, Edward L. Greenstein, and Regina Stein. *The Timetables of Jewish History*. New York: Simon and Schuster, 1993.

Goodwin-Gill, Guy S. *The Refugee in International Law*. 2d edition. Oxford: Clarendon Press, 1996.

Gordenker, Leon. *Refugees in International Politics*. London: Croom Helm, 1987.

Gorman, Robert F., and Edward S. Mihalkanin. *Historical Dictionary of Human Rights and Humanitarian Organizations*. Lanham, Md.: Scarecrow Press, 1997.

Greenspan, Karen. *The Timetable of Women's History*. New York: Simon and Schuster, 1994.

Hamilton, Clarence H. *Buddhism in India, Ceylon, China, and Japan*. Chicago: University of Chicago Press, 1931.

Hamilton, Ira, ed. *Ready Reference: American Indians*. Englewood Cliffs, N.J.: Salem Press, 1995.

Hardacre, Helen. *Shinto and the State, 1868–1989*. Princeton: Princeton University Press, 1989.

Hirschfelder, Arlene, and Martha Kreipe de Montaño. *The Native American Almanac: A Portrait of Native America Today*. New York: Prentice Hall General Reference, 1993.

Hornsby, Alton Jr. *Chronology of African American History*. Detroit: Gale Research, 1991.

Hoxie, Frederick, ed. *Encyclopedia of North American Indians*. Boston: Houghton Mifflin, 1996.

Human Rights Watch. New York. Web site: *http://www.hrw.org*.

Hunt, Lynn, ed. and trans. *The French Revolution and Human Rights: A Brief Documentary History*. New York: St. Martin's Press, 1996.

Indigenous Peoples' Center for Documentation, Research, and Information. Web site: *http://docip.org*.

Indigenous Peoples, Forest, and Biodiversity. London: International Alliance of Indigenous-Tribal Peoples of the Tropical Forests and International Work Group for Indigenous Affairs, 1996.

International Programme on the Elimination of Child Labour (IPEC). E-mail: ipec@ilo.org.

Ishay, Micheline R., ed. *The Human Rights Reader*. New York and London: Routledge, 1997.

Joly, Daniele, with Clive Nettleton and Hugh Poulton. *Refugees: Asylum in Europe?* Boulder, Colo.: Westview Press, 1992.

Karatnycky, Adrian, et al. *Freedom in the World: The Annual Survey of Political Rights and Civil Liberties, 1996–1997*. New Brunswick, N.J.: Transaction Publishers, 1997.

Kato, Genichi. *A Historical Study of the Religious Development of Shinto*. 1973. Translated by Shoyu Hanayama. New York: Greenwood Press, 1988.

Lauren, Paul Gordon. *The Evolution of International Human Rights*. Philadelphia: University of Pennsylvania Press, 1998.

Levinson, David, ed. *The Wilson Chronology of the World's Religions*. New York: H. W. Wilson, 1999.

Loescher, Gil, and Ann Dull Loescher. *The Global Refugee Crisis: A Reference Handbook*. Santa Barbara, Calif.: ABC-Clio, 1994.

Low, W. A., and Virgil A. Clift, eds. *Encyclopedia of Black America*. New York: McGraw-Hill, 1981.

Martinez, Miguel Alfonso. *Discrimination against Indigenous Peoples: Study on Treaties, Agreements, and other Constructive Arrangements between States and Indigenous Populations*. New York: Sub-Commission on Prevention of Discrimination and Protection of Minorities, United Nations Commission on Human Rights, 1992.

Moen, Matthew C., and Lowell S. Gustafson, eds. *The Religious Challenge to the State*. Philadelphia: Temple University Press, 1992.

NativeWeb. Web site: *http://www.nativeweb.org*.

Norwood, Frederick A. *Strangers and Exiles: A History of Religious Refugees*. Vol. 1. Nashville: Abingdon Press, 1969.

Numbers, Ronald L. *The Creationists: The Evolution of Scientific Creationism*. New York: Alfred A. Knopf, 1992.

Olson, James S., ed. *An Ethnohistorical Dictionary of the Russian and Soviet Empires*. Westport, Conn.: Greenwood Press, 1994.

Riester, Jurgen. *Indians of Eastern Bolivia: Aspects of Their Present Situation*. Kobenhavn: International Work Group for Indigenous Affairs (IWGIA), 1975.

Rodriquez, Junius P., ed. *The Historical Encyclopedia of World Slavery*. Santa Barbara, Calif.: ABC-Clio, 1997.

Sacher, Howard. *A History of Jews in America*. New York: Alfred A. Knopf, 1992.

Salzman, Jack, David Lionel Smith, and Cornel West, eds. *Encyclopedia of African American Culture and History*. New York: Macmillan Library Reference USA, 1996.

Schweitzer, Frederick M. *A History of the Jews Since the First Century A.D.* New York: Macmillan, 1971.

Sherrill, C., ed. *Sports and Disabled Athletes*. Champaign, Ill.: Human Kinetics, 1984.

Simpson, George E. *Black Religions in the New World*. New York: Columbia University Press, 1978.

Tierney, Helen, ed. *Women's Studies Encyclopedia*. New York: Greenwood Press, 1991.

Trager, James. *The Women's Chronology*. New York: Henry Holt, 1994.

UNICEF International Child Development Centre (Innocenti Centre). Web site: *http://www.unicef-icdc.org*.

Utter, Glenn H., and John W. Storey. *The Religious Right: A Reference Handbook*. Santa Barbara, Calif.: ABC-Clio, 1995.

Whalen, Lucille. *Contemporary World Issues: Human Rights*. Santa Barbara, Calif.: ABC-Clio, 1989.

Wistrich, Robert S. *Antisemitism: The Longest Hatred*. New York: Pantheon Books, 1991.

Witte, John Jr., and Johan D. van der Vyver, eds., *Religious Human Rights in Global Perspective*. The Hague: Martinus Nijhoff, 1996.

Wronka, Joseph. *Human Rights and Social Policy in the 21st Century*. Lanham, Md.: University Press of America, 1998.

Zophy, Angela Howard, with Frances M. Kavenik, eds. *Handbook of American Women's History*. New York: Garland, 1990.

INDEX

Ferguson, Miriam Amanda, 264, 269
Ferraro, Geraldine, 302
Fetherston, Richard, 29
Fez, Morocco, 151
FGM. *See* female genital mutilation
Field, Stephen Johnson, 65
fight for indigenous identity, 347
Fight Repression of Erotic Expression
   (FREE), 440
Fiji, 213
   gay rights and, 469–470
Fillmore, Millard, 56
final solution (term), 204
Finch, Robert, 103
Finkelhor, D., 416
Finland
   and children's rights, 406, 407
   and gay rights, 432, 451
   and indigenous rights, 349
   and religious rights, 188
   and women's rights, 247, 254, 260,
      262, 269, 279
Finnbogadottir, Vigdis, 299
Finnish Organization for Sexual Equal-
   ity, 451
Finnish Women's Association, 254
*Firefighters Local Union No. 1784 v. Sto-
   tts*, 118–119
First Born Church of Christ, 195
First Chinese Temple (San Francisco),
   185
First Helvetic Confession, 165
First People of the Kalahari, 375
Fisher v. District Court, 352
Fisher, John Dix, 474
Fisheries Act (New Zealand, 1983), 361
fishing rights, 343
   of indigenous peoples, 348, 355, 361,
      381
   See also property rights of Native
      Americans
Fisk University, 58, 63
Five Mile Act (Great Britain, 1665), 182
Flenner, Jacqueline, 290
Fletcher v. Peck, 321
Florentine Codex, 169
Flores historiarum, 154–155
FOIA. *See* Freedom of Information Act
   (U.S., 1984)
football, 68, 72, 101, 343
Foote, Lucinda, 240
Foraker, Joseph, 69

The Forc'd Marriage (Behn), 237
forced relocations
   of indigenous peoples, 326, 353, 358,
      359
   of Native Americans, 316, 323, 324,
      327, 329, 334, 340
Ford, Gerald R., 111, 293, 446–447
Ford, Henry, 197–198
Ford, Nelson, 56
Fordyce, James, 239
Foreign and American Anti-Slavery Soci-
   ety, 53
Foreign Miners Tax Law, U.S., 56
Forer, Lois G., 401
Forest Service, U.S., 372
Forsythe, Albert, 78
Fort Belknap Agreement, 331
Fort Belknap Reservation, 332
Fort Carolusburg, West Africa, 30
Fort Defiance, Arizona, 327
Fort Laramie Treaty (1851), 325
Fortalitium fidei, 160
Fortas, Abe, 399–400
Forten, James, Jr., 43
Forten, James, Sr., 46
Forum on Children and Violence
   (England), 422
foster care, 395, 403, 406, 426
"Foster Care—In Whose Best Interest?"
   (Mnookin), 403
Foster, Jim, 441
Foundation for Child Development Cen-
   ter, 405
Four Directions Council, 365
Fourth Lateran Council, 155
Fourth World Conference on Women
   (U.N.), 308
Fox Indians, 317, 323
Fox, George, 173
Fox, Michael J., 478
Fox-Potawatomi Indians, 333
France
   and capital punishment, 35, 41, 78,
      117
   and Catholic Church, 193
   and civil rights, 31, 38, 66, 69, 82, 120
   and disabled rights, 474
   and gay rights, 431, 434, 451
   and human rights, 5, 12
   and indigenous rights, 318, 334, 342,
      344